Newbery and Caldecott Medalists and Honor Book Winners

NEWBERY
and
CALDECOTT
Medalists and Honor Book Winners

Bibliographies and Resource Material
through 1977

Jim Roginski,
Compiler

1982
LIBRARIES UNLIMITED, INC.
Littleton, Colorado

LIBRARIES UNLIMITED, INC.
P. O. Box 263
Littleton, Colorado 80160

Library of Congress Cataloging in Publication Data

Main entry under title:

Newbery and Caldecott medalists and honor book winners.

    Includes indexes.
    1. Children--Books and reading--Bibliography.
2. Children's literature--Bibliography. 3. Literary
prizes. I. Roginski, James W., 1945-
Z1037.N653 1982 [PN1009.A1]   011'.62'079   82-20362
ISBN 0-87287-296-3

Libraries Unlimited cover material meets and exceeds National Association of State Textbook
Administrators' material specifications Class A through E.

For
Gail and Wally Klemm

TABLE OF CONTENTS

ACKNOWLEDGMENTS

A book of this scope requires the work and energy of many people. To each of the authors, artists, and/or their estates or representatives listed below I offer my grateful thanks. Their contributions to this volume are inestimable; without them this work would have been incomplete.

Adrienne Adams
Helen Simmons Adams estate
Julia Davis Adams
Lloyd Alexander
Carl B. Allen
John Lonzo Anderson
Valenti Angelo
William H. Armstrong
Natalie Babbitt
Elizabeth Chesley Baity
Caroline Dale Owen Baldwin
Arnold E. Bare
Leonard Baskin
Norton Baskin
Byrd Baylor
Alice Anne Rice Bell
Pamela Bianco
Abe Birnbaum estate
Claire Huchet Bishop
Nancy Bond
H. Mark Bowman
Roderick S. Brace
Carol Ryrie Brink
Beverly Brodsky
Marcia Brown
Bernarda Bryson
Betsy Byars
Natalie Savage Carlson
Mary Jane Carr
Rebecca Caudill
Mary Louise Chrisman
Ann Nolan Clark
James Lincoln Collier
Barbara Cooney
Susan Cooper
Harold Courlander
Charles M. Daugherty

Ingri D'Aulaire
Alida D. Davis
Marguerite de Angeli
Meindert DeJong
Tomie dePaola
Janina Domanska
Carolyn W. Downey
Douglas Duchin
David Durand
Roger Duvoisin
Winifred Eaton
Alan W. Eckert
Walter D. Edmonds
Fritz Eichenberg
Ed Emberley
Sylvia Louise Engdahl
Eleanor Estes
Marie Hall Ets
Margaret B. Evans
Elinor Whitney Field
Paula Fox
Antonio Frasconi
Lydia Freeman
Ruth Chrisman Gannett
Ruth Stiles Gannett
Doris Gates
Theodore Seuss Geisel
Jean George
Jennifer Gile
M. B. Goffstein
Barbara J. Gosda
Margaret Bloy Graham
Leo Gurko
Virginia Hamilton
Walter Havighurst
Bess Lomax Hawes
Marguerite Henry

9

Patricia C. Hill
Ned Hills
Lynn Stuart Hoerner
Irene Hunt
Mabel Leigh Hunt estate
Anna Marie Imitto
Robert Janssen
Randall Jarrell estate
Susan Jeffers
Elizabeth Kalashnikoff
Francis Kalnay
Ezra Jack Keats
Harold Keith
Katherine C. Kelly
Carol S. Kendall
Juliet Kepes
E. L. Konigsburg
Joseph Krumgold
Jean Lee Latham
Helen Finger Leflar
Madeleine L'Engle
Leo Lionni
Arnold Lobel
Christopher Lofting
Helen Simmons Adams Louden
David Macaulay
Roger MacBride
Patricia Miles Martin
Sharon Bell Mathis
Robert McCloskey
Beverly B. McDermott
Eloise Jarvis McGraw
Florence Crannell Means
Frances M. Moon
Janet Gaylord Moore
Elizabeth Morton
Emily Cheney Neville
Scott O'Dell
Arielle North Olson
Robert Andrew Parker
Peter Parnall
Arthur Pell
Marjorie R. Petersham
Robert Plunkett
Leo Politi

Elizabeth Marie Pope
Cyrus Porter
Ellen Raskin
Selma Rayfield
Joan Robbins
Nina Rojankovsky
Mari Sandoz estate
Charles Schlessiger
Jack Schaefer
Jane Schofer
Georges Schreiber estate
Alice Schreyer
Charles Seeger
Maurice Sendak
Meryl Shera
Uri Shulevitz
Marc Simont
Isaac Bashevis Singer
Zilpha K. Snyder
Elizabeth George Speare
Peter Spier
Mary Q. Steele
William O. Steele
William Steig
Mary Stolz
Helen Todd Stone
George C. Thompson
George Selden Thompson
Carolyn Treffinger
Elizabeth Borton de Treviño
Tasha Tudor
Elizabeth Tunis
Henry Van Loon
Mary Hays Weik
Esther Weir
Leonard Weisgard
E. B. White
Ellen Whitney
Maia Wojciechowska
Taro Yashima
Elizabeth Yates
Laurence Yep
Ed Young
Margot Zemach

Thanks, too, must go to the staffs of libraries and museums, publishers, and producers of non-book media who spent time in helping me locate authors and artists, and in answering many questions to set the historical record straight, wherever possible.

Special thanks go to Mary Jane Anderson of the American Library Association/Association for Library Services to Children Division; Mary Bogan, Ed Kemp, Karen Nelson Hoyle, and Beth Perry, children's literature archivists extraordinaire; Heather Cameron, James H. Fraser, John Goldthwaite, Ann Hartman, and Kathy Wisch, each of whom did background work for me in very select ways; M. Jean Greenlaw, who devoted much time and energy to this volume; Kay Minnis, for her excellent composition work; and to John Donovan, Paula Quint, Christine Stawicki, and Pat Hall of the Children's Book Council, a valuable resource if ever there was one.

And, of course, to Jackie. Her patience is laudatory.

INTRODUCTION

SCOPE

This book is an inclusive listing of publications and related materials of 266 authors and illustrators who have been recipients of the Newbery, Caldecott, and Honor Book medals. Inclusive dates for the authors and illustrators are from the beginning of their publishing careers through the 1977 award year, or the 1976 publishing year. This book provides, for the first time, an accessible and readable single-volume reference work of verified bibliographic and related data pertinent to the medalists and Honor Book awardees.

METHODOLOGY

It would be good to say that measurable quantitative, qualitative, and scientific approaches to this book were employed in uncovering the material here. Alas, they were not. Instead, a simplistic method was adopted: reading and note-taking, and a great deal of cooperation from everyone involved, including the U.S. Post Office.

When beginning general lists were organized, they were sent to the awardees, the awardees' estates or representatives, media producers, librarians, and museum curators for verification of, correction of, and addition to the information listed. Publishers, private book collectors, children's literature researchers, children's literature bibliographers, and antiquarian booksellers were also called upon for specific information requests. The responses from these people were incorporated into the final lists.

Wherever possible, entries in this book have been double- and triple-verified in public printed sources (rather than relying solely on responses from correspondents) to ensure accuracy.

My queries resulted in an astonishingly high rate of return—approximately 60%. This positive response seems to indicate efforts by individuals and institutions to establish a verifiable historical record of the medalists, the Honor Book awardees, and their publications, and a continuing, lasting interest in the same.

PURPOSE AND AUDIENCE

When I was a children's literature specialist for a large urban library in the mid-1970s, the questions most commonly asked of me related to the Newbery-Caldecott medalists and their books. The questions and their answers were developed into a time-honored librarians' tool—*lists*—for quick reference response. After eight years and some restructuring, those lists formed the nucleus for this book.

The questions asked then are still being asked today:

"What other books has X done?"

"What (films/filmstrips/slides/etc.) are (or have been) made from X's books?"

"Where can I find original (art or manuscript) material by X?"

"Where can I find biographical material about X?"

"How many (Newbery, Caldecott, Medal Books, Honor Books) has X won?"

"What year did X publish (title) in?"

"How many exhibitions has X illustrator displayed in?"

. . .and so on.

This book will answer those questions, and any number of others that creative use of this work can provide. It allows for beginning in-depth studies of an individual's work, or the work of similar or dissimilar groups of individuals. It can help identify publishing, writing, and illustrating trends as exemplified by the medalists and Honor Book awardees. It highlights 266 bodies of works and related materials that have been buried in various books related or unrelated to children's literature. Curiously, this book provides a simultaneous approach to contemporary and historical children's literature, from the view of the medalists and Honor Book awardees for the first 55 years of the Newbery award and the first 39 years of the Caldecott award. Use of the book is not defined by the material herein; rather, it is defined by the user.

This book is for children's and adult public librarians, especially the beleaguered adult reference desk librarian who knows little about children's books (and doesn't necessarily need to) to answer those quick questions relating to the medalists and Honor Book awardees that often take up much valuable searching time in too many reference books, regardless of the age of the patron. It is for the academic reference librarian who works with teachers of children's literature and their students. (I have learned that the textures of the questions stay the same; only the settings differ.) It is for teachers of children's literature to use with undergraduate- and graduate-level courses, or for those college-level individuals involved with children's literature in general, or the more specialized arena of the Newbery-Caldecott medals. It is for antiquarian booksellers to use as an identification and verification tool in their work with the medalists' books. It is for the specialized researcher/bibliographer of children's literature to expand upon and work from. And it is for children, albeit in a distilled form.

CAVEAT

A book of this sort relies heavily on other public and private documents—and telephone calls, letters, memory, chance, and luck. I have discovered, too painfully and often with great consternation, from working on this project that professional indexing and documentation sources have hidden prejudices and dangers of their own. These professional pitfalls are compounded by a lack of accessibility and readability, and sometimes, credibility. The skills of indexing and documentation strike me as still very young, very human crafts subject to error, misinterpretation, and unintentional misrepresentation.

Because of this, it would be foolhardy to boldly state that this book is without error. I will not. It is not. The number of entries and the quantity of bibliographic data here, compounded by incomplete or blind entries in professional reference books and indexes, confused by correspondence with comments such as, "Did I really do *all* those books?," "I think it was 1938, not 1939, but I'm not sure. Maybe it was 1937," or "Our records indicate that X died in 1926. We have no further records on this individual," and other manner of unclear, vague, and questionable responses, allow for only a cautious statement: the rate of error has been kept to a minimum as much as was possible within the structure of the material here located.

Thus, a request to the users of this book. Any additions, corrections, or suggestions that need to be made in the event of an expansion of this book should be sent to me in care of this publisher. Be sure to enclose a citation or source for your comments.

Jim Roginski
Re: Newbery-Caldecott Medalists
c/o Libraries Unlimited, Inc.
P. O. Box 263
Littleton, CO 80160

THE MEDALS:
A Brief Summary

There is no doubt that Frederic Melcher was a shrewd man. He not only financed and developed the guidelines for the Newbery-Caldecott medals and Honor Books (called Runner-Up Books until 1971), but also found an agency to administer them, the currently named Association for Library Services to Children (ALSC) of the American Library Association (ALA). The Newbery Medal came first, and was seen to be a promotion vehicle for publishers and booksellers to encourage the publication and sale of more and better children's books. Melcher realized the possibilities of satisfyingly long-term sales of children's books, and wanted others to understand this, too. After a few sluggish years, Melcher's aim was beginning to be accomplished, primarily with the sale of books to schools and libraries. In 1938, the first Caldecott Medal was awarded in response to librarian requests for a similar award for the best-illustrated children's books. The Newbery is awarded annually for the "most distinguished" book of text of the preceding year, the Caldecott for the book with the "most distinguished" illustrations of the previous year. The Newbery-Caldecott medals and Honor Books always follow one year after publication.

The books are chosen by two committees of the ALA/ALSC membership, one for each medal and the Honor Books. Up until 1981, or the 1980 award year, one committee was delegated to select the winners. Because of various complaints by past committee members, two committees were formed for the 1981 award year (the 1980 publishing year) to allow more time for concentrated discussion of the contenders. Committee appointment varies; selection of members is done by membership vote and by appointment from the ALSC office for a specified period of time.

Announcements of the winning Medal Books and Honor Books are made annually in January at the Midwinter meeting of the ALA. International impact is generally immediate and continues throughout the year. A medal-winning book, in particular—as well as the medalist, the medalist's agent (if there is one), the publisher (most specifically, the sales, rights, and permissions departments)—feels the first impact. When the winning books are announced to the public, orders come quickly because everyone wants to read a winner. The medalist needs to prepare a speech to be read at the summer ALA meeting; the editor works on a possible new manuscript with the author or artist; the publisher reprints more copies of the book to meet the increased demand; the books are shipped as quickly as possible to meet the demand. Rights are very often sold for filmstrips, TV adaptations, feature-length movies, excerpts in school textbooks, illustration reproductions, and the like. The international community at large regards the Newbery-Caldecott awards as the most prestigious in the United States. Because of this prestige, books are often sold for foreign-language translations for overseas readers. At the end of this very long line of adults working with children's books are the readers themselves. They generally find the winning books in one of three ways: by choice (which includes the very well developed "I-liked-it-you'll-like-it" method among friends); by recommendations of school or public librarians and other adults interested in children's books who think a child will enjoy reading the book; or by the suggestion of a well-meaning adult, usually a classroom teacher, friendly neighbor, or relative, who wants children to read only the "best."

"Best," as it is used above, is the frequently misused term for the guidelines' "most distinguished." The term has never been adequately defined and creates annual consternation for all involved.

A great deal of space in the professional library and book journals has been devoted to the rules and governance of the medals. Very little has been seen in the popular press. Of the over 500 articles cited in the standard magazine indexes (*Readers' Guide*, etc.) or of the many books which include some references to the medals, a few can be recommended without reservation as necessary reading.

Of all the professional articles about the medals, only one seems to stand out. This is Zena Sutherland's "Not *Another* Article on the Newbery-Caldecott Awards?" (*Top of the News* 20 [April 1974] : 249-53). The author, an internationally recognized critic and reviewer of children's books, outlines major criticisms of the selection process, committee appointments, and governance and administration of the medals over the years, summarizes the association's actions taken to rectify the criticisms, and adds cogent insights of her own about the medals.

Irene Smith's *A History of the Newbery and Caldecott Medals* (New York: Viking, 1957; now out of print but available in many large libraries) provides an affectionate and personal view of the medals. Although not necessarily mandatory reading, it does provide insights that no other book or article on the subject does.

Acceptance speeches may be found in the ongoing series published by Horn Book, Inc., edited by Lee Kingman and Bertha Mahony Miller. These are described in the bibliography of this book, (see pages 327-28). The speeches are also printed in the *Horn Book* and *Top of the News* magazines in the year of the awarding of the medals.

Among the most overlooked areas of the medals are the Honor Books. Very fine writing and illustration can also be found in them, although in the rush of the excitement over the medal-winning books—and continuing as years go by—the Honor Book slips back to a humbler, secondary category. Only one article has been located on this subject. This is Margaret Hodges' "They Also Serve: The Newbery-Caldecott Runners-Up," (*Top of the News* 22 [January 1966] : 139-55), which provides brief synopses of the Honor Books (or, runners-up), background, and a description of that year's winners, along with some highlights from previous years. It is included here for the historical record only.

As with the Honor Books, there is a great need for study of the impact of the medals, the books, and the winners. A survey of doctoral dissertations and master's theses on the subject revealed that little of substance is being done at the university or college level, outside of reading surveys, bibliographies, and testing of various elements found in the books. None of it is valuable for the general reader; little is valuable for the researcher. There are no studies dealing with the impact that winning the award has on an author or illustrator, the publisher and editor or the international community. In addition, outside of journal articles and some university-level writing about children's likes and dislikes of the books, there seem to be no fresh discoveries of the impact, if any, of the books on reading development, habits, and attitudes of children. As will be seen in the Background Reading sections which appear at the ends of the awardee bibliographies, there is a severe paucity of *critical* and *evaluative* material on individual authors and illustrators. Most articles about these people tend to be light, airy, and of a promotional nature, adding little to the considered study of children's book creators. A few journals devote themselves to the ongoing study and criticism of children's books, often including articles on the medal-winning books or medalists. Among these are *Horn Book Magazine*, *Children's Literature in Education*, and *The Children's Literature Quarterly*. Readers of this book are directed to those magazines, and their back issues, for some readings and studies about the awardees and their books.

HOW TO READ THE ENTRIES

Each author entry is arranged in five categories; each author-illustrator or illustrator entry is arranged in six categories:

> Awards
>
> Bibliography
>
> Media
>
> Exhibitions (for author-illustrators or illustrators only)
>
> Collections
>
> Background Readings

If research on the individuals did not yield any pertinent information for any category outside of Award or Bibliography, that category is not listed in the write-up.

Name

"Name" entries are arranged alphabetically by the awardee's legal name or pseudonym used at the time of the award announcement. The sole exception to this is Nicolas Mordvinoff, who illustrated under the name of "Nicolas." Life dates, when known, follow each name listing. Pseudonyms, if any, used in book publication, in addition to the legal name listed, follow the main name entry. Name changed by marriage or by the courts, and not used for book publication, are not listed.

A designation of "author," "author-illustrator," or "illustrator" signifies the area of publishing with which each awardee is most closely associated, regardless of the award(s) bestowed.

Awards

"Awards" alphabetically lists the Newbery and/or Caldecott Medal and/or Honor Book(s) for each awardee. Book titles that appear in parentheses indicate a winning title by *another* awardee in this volume. This is included to show the full range of honors, direct and indirect, for the awardee.

Sample listing (for Maurice Sendak)

> (*Along Came a Dog*. Newbery Honor Book, 1959.)
> (*Animal Family*. Newbery Honor Book, 1966.)
> (*House of Sixty Fathers*. Newbery Honor Book, 1957.)
> (*Hurry Home, Candy*. Newbery Honor Book, 1954.)

In the Night Kitchen. Caldecott Honor Book, 1971.
Little Bear's Visit. Caldecott Honor Book, 1962.
Mr. Rabbit and the Lovely Present. Caldecott Honor Book, 1963.
Moon Jumpers. Caldecott Honor Book, 1960.
Very Special House. Caldecott Honor Book, 1954.
What Do You Say, Dear? Caldecott Honor Book, 1959.
(*Wheel on the School*. Newbery Medal Book, 1955.)
Where the Wild Things Are. Caldecott Medal Book, 1964.
(*Zlateh the Goat*. Newbery Honor Book, 1967.)

This example shows that Mr. Sendak has been awarded seven Caldecott Medals or Honor Book awards and has illustrated six books that won the Newbery Medal or Honor Book award.

Entry format:

by awardee
Short Title/Award/Year of Award

by another awardee
(Short Title/Award/Year of Award)

Bibliography

"Bibliography" is arranged alphabetically by title and incorporates all printed materials, including books, keepsakes, pamphlets, speeches, etc., published by the awardee from the beginning of a writing or illustrating career through the 1977 award year, or the 1976 publishing year. Emphasis has been placed on American trade books. Initial articles of "The," "A," and "An" have been dropped.

Each title listing was researched for the following points: title, author(s), illustrator(s), editor(s), translator(s), musician(s), publisher, and publication date, and includes information about reillustrated, revised, and/or reissued books by a publisher other than the original. Also identified are portfolios, limited and privately printed editions, original foreign-language editions, and title, illustrator, and publisher changes from American publications to British publications. With rare exception, American publications are listed first. When a foreign edition is published first, the American edition, if there is one, follows.

All publisher names are in short form, e.g., "Putnam" for G. P. Putnam's Sons. Because of mergers, corporate name changes, and disappearance of publishers, record-keeping and maintenance of full publisher or corporate names proved difficult for this volume.

Some books, it will be noted, were announced as one title and published as another. This information is included in parentheses following the particular title listing. For an example of this, see the entry for Susan Cooper's *Grey King* on page 76.

Two types of translator and editor entries appear in the bibliographies. When the abbreviation (tr.) or (ed.) appears before a title listing, this indicates that the author or author-illustrator has translated or edited the particular book. If the words "translated by" or "edited by" appear within the citation, followed by a name, the book was translated or edited by the person identified in the listing.

Unclear or questionable publishers and/or dates of publication are identified by "Putnam (?)" or "1969 (?)." If the publisher or date of publication is unknown, the abbreviations "n. p." or "n. d." appear in place. Other symbols and abbreviations used throughout this book will be found on pages 21-22. An idiosyncrasies list appears on page 22, listing other exceptions to the general guidelines used for the bibliographic entries in this book.

Entry format:

for authors

Title/Illustrator/Publisher/Publication Date

for illustrators

Title/Author/Publisher/Publication Date

for author-illustrators

Title/(Author or Illustrator)/Publisher/Publication Date*

Media

"Media" is an alphabetical title listing of publications listed in the individual bibliographies that have been converted to non-book formats, or of original material created for media release. Listings emphasize the producer or co-producers of the media formats listed. A slash between names (e.g., Columbia Broadcasting System/DePatie-Freleng Enterprises) indicates co-producers. Distributors are not listed unless they have been identified as producers or co-producers of any work listed here.

Most of the material in this section dates from *ca.*1947, except for feature-length motion pictures, radio programs, and materials for the handicapped.

Books for the blind and physically handicapped, those titles followed by BB, CB, MT, TB, and occasionally, C, do not appear with a producer or date of release if produced by a library or other publicly funded institution. These listings are elusive, the formats in some cases questionable. Many of the identified titles are no longer available, but are represented here to show the ongoing interest by American libraries, primarily, in providing books in various formats for the blind and physically handicapped. Part of that interest is reflected in the number of children's books transcribed yearly. Users of this volume who wish to locate materials for the blind and physically handicapped should contact their local library, regional library depository, or the Library of Congress for currently available materials.

In developing this section, I was fortunate enough to have discovered a handlist of books for the handicapped in the Texas State Library in Austin, Texas, which was an informal record of these productions from across the United States. It was one of the most complete lists I found to work from.

---

* When an author-illustrator listing does not clearly identify another author or illustrator for a particular listing, it may be assumed that the awardee in question wrote and illustrated the book. If an author listing does not include an illustrator listing, it may be assumed that the book is unillustrated.

Producers and dates of release for all other media formats are identified as correctly as possible. The user of this book cannot help but notice the preponderance of question-marked names and dates, due to conflicting information between the producers and reference books on the subject.

Entry format:

for materials for the handicapped
Title/(Format)

for all other media
Title/Producer(s)/Year/(Format)

Collections

"Collections" is an alphabetical listing of international academic and public libraries and museums which retain original manuscript, art, and non-book material by the awardee and under the awardee's name. It also lists those collections in which materials by the awardee appear, but which are listed under a different person's or collection's name. Emphasis has been placed upon the holdings of the deGrummond Collection (University of Southern Mississippi), the Kerlan Collection (University of Minnesota), the Library of Congress, the May Massee Collection (Emporia State College), and the University of Oregon. These are believed to be the largest collections of original children's literature material in the United States.

Entry format:
Collection or Institution Name/(Place)

Exhibitions

"Exhibitions," for author-illustrators or illustrators only, is an alphabetical listing by gallery, museum, or exhibition name of one-person, group, national, and/or international art shows. Because many illustrators are regarded also as fine artists, this listing is included for those who wish to study an individual's art beyond that of book illustration and in a larger context. Length of listings does not imply importance. Next to media producers and dates of release of the same, this section proved to be among the most elusive to trace because of many inaccuracies and little or no available information. The maximum number of entries here for any illustrator is 15.

Entry format:
Gallery, Museum, or Exhibition Name/Date/City

Background Reading

"Background Reading" is a selective listing of media and book and magazine articles relating directly to the awardee and the awardee's professional work. Listings vary in coverage and quality, due to the varied nature of the sources listed. Stress was placed on biographical information (including obituaries, which, in some cases, were the only bits of information located on an awardee), "personality" articles and interviews, and critical and/or evaluative studies. Acceptance speeches by the medalists are included.

Some awardees have received more coverage than others. Length of listings does not imply importance. Initial articles of "The," "A," and "An" have been dropped.

Background readings are entered in two methods. Periodical citations include the last name of the author of the article, the author's initial of the first name, the title, and the citation. Book citations use the author's last name and a short title. Full bibliographic information for book citations will be found in the Subject Bibliography on pages 324-30.

Entry format:

for books

Author Last Name/Short Title

for periodical articles

Author Last Name, First Initial/Title/Periodical/Date

for media formats

Title/Date/Format

Symbols and Abbreviations

Symbols and abbreviations used throughout this book are:

+	a bibliography that has *not* been verified by the awardee or the awardee's estate or representative; those bibliographies without this symbol have been read and verified, when possible, by the awardee, or the awardee's representative
*	an autobiography or a fiction book which draws from the awardee's life
?	an unclear book publisher, media producer, or date of publication; the ? appears in parentheses, e.g., 1969 (?) or Putnam (?)
adapt.	adaptor, adapted by
a.k.a.	also known as
BB	book in Braille
C	cassette tape recording
ca.	circa, about
CB	cassette book without filmstrip
comp(s).	compiler(s), compiled by
ed(s).	editor(s), edited by
F	feature-length or educational film, including original screenplays which are so identified
FS	filmstrip without sound

FSS   sound filmstrip, which may include a separate cassette tape or recording

il(ls).   illustrator(s), illustrated by

MT   magnetic (open-reel) tape recording

n. d.   no date of publication or media release located

n. p.   no publisher or media producer located

pseud(s).   pseudonym(s)

R   phonograph recording

Ra   radio production, including original radio plays which are so indicated

S   slide set(s)

TB   talking book

tr(s).   translator(s), translated by

TV   television production, including original teleplays which are so identified

Vol(s).   volume(s)

VT   videotape

Idiosyncrasies

For every rule there is an exception. The listings below provide examples of these exceptions throughout this volume.

Names. A few authors and illustrators use only their first or last names for publication. The name not used for publication appears in parentheses.

> *Examples:*   (Louis F.) Cary
>   Genia (Wennerstrom)

Publishers. When a place of publication is known, and the publisher is not, the place of publication is inserted in parentheses.

> *Example*:   *Hey, Grasshopper!* (Durant, Oklahoma)...

Two examples of American and British publishers with the same names are Oxford and Macmillan. To avoid confusion and only when necessary, the city of publication follows the publisher's name.

> *Examples*:   Oxford (London)
>   Macmillan (New York)

Dates. Most date entries in this volume appear either complete or with the symbol "n. d." Some dates appear as "197?," etc., indicating the decade of appearance but an unclear or unknown year.

Bibliography.

a.k.a. In addition to using the *a.k.a.* abbreviation for title changes, it is also used to indicate variant titles when books have been adapted to plays, motion pictures, etc.

Examples: *Polly Patchwork. . .; a.k.a. Polly Patchwork (Comedy in Three Scenes) from the Story of the Same Title. . .*

Old Yeller. . .; a.k.a. Walt Disney's Old Yeller, from the Walt Disney Motion Picture "Old Yeller" Based on the Novel of the Same Title, Told by Irwin Shapiro. . .

Also in. If a title appears in another volume by the same awardee, the words "also in" show this.

Example: *Polly Patchwork. . .also in Rachel Field Storybook,* below. (The words "below" or "above" indicate the listing which precedes or follows the particular listing in that bibliography.)

Related titles. For publications built on a character or title originally published by the awardee and subsequently written by another author, the words "related" titles precedes a separate section in the bibliography. They are included in these few instances to show publisher expansion of a successful idea or concept initially created by the author.

Example: *Doctor Dolittle and the Pirates* by Al Perkins. . .

Background Reading. All Newbery-Caldecott Medal acceptance speeches that appear in book form for the inclusive dates of this volume are included in the Background Reading sections. Four speeches, however, refer the reader to the journals which have printed these speeches, since they had not appeared in book form at the time this book was in preparation. These speeches are by Susan Cooper, Diane and Leo Dillon, and Mildred Taylor.

OTHER MATERIAL IN THIS BOOK

Appendices A and B, on pages 299-316, provide a yearly listing of the Newbery Medal and Honor Books, 1922-1977, and of the Caldecott Medal and Honor Books, 1938-1977. Due to a ruling in 1971 that from that date forward the term "Honor Book" would be used in place of "Runner-Up," I have used the term "Honor Book" throughout for consistency.

The bibliography, on pages 317-30, provides a subject approach, which follows the format of the text, indicating primary reference sources for each section.

The index on pages 331-39 is a quick reference to the medalists, the Honor Book winners, and their medal-winning and Honor Books.

BIBLIOGRAPHIES

ADRIENNE ADAMS, 1906-
author-illustrator

AWARDS

Day We Saw the Sun Come Up. Caldecott Honor Book, 1962.

Houses from the Sea. Caldecott Honor Book, 1960.

BIBLIOGRAPHY

Angela of Angel Court; by Elizabeth Rogers. Crowell, 1954.

Baby House; by Norma Simon. Lippincott, 1955.

Bag of Smoke: The Story of the First Balloon; by (John) Lonzo Anderson. Scribner, 1965.

Blue Mountain; by Beth Lewis, *pseud.* (Beth Lipkin). Knopf, 1956.

Boy Jones; by Patricia Gordon, *pseud.* (Joan Howard). Viking, 1943.

Bring a Torch, Jeanette Isabella: A Provençal Carol; by Nicholas Sabloy. Scribner, 1963

Butterfly Time; by Alice Goudey. Scribner, 1964.

Cabbage Moon; by Jan Wahl. Holt, 1965.

Candy Floss; by Rumer Godden. Viking, 1960.

Captain Ramsay's Daughter; by Elizabeth Torjesen. Lothrop, 1953.

Day We Saw the Sun Come Up; by Alice Goudey. Scribner, 1961.

Easter Bunny That Overslept; by Priscilla and Otto Friedrich. Lothrop, 1957.

Easter Egg Artists; Scribner, 1976.

Fairy Doll; by Rumer Godden. Viking, 1960.

Favorite Fairy Tales Told in Scotland; by Virginia Haviland. Little, 1963.

Going Barefoot; by Aileen Fisher. Crowell, 1960.

Great Aunt Victoria's House; by Margaret Otto. Holt, 1957.

Hansel and Gretel; by Jacob and Wilhelm Grimm. Tr. Charles Scribner, Jr. Scribner, 1975.

Houses from the Sea; by Alice Goudey. Scribner, 1959.

Impunity Jane: The Story of a Pocket Doll; by Rumer Godden. Viking, 1954.

In the Middle of the Night; by Aileen Fisher. Drowell, 1965.

Izzard; by (John) Lonzo Anderson. Scribner, 1973.

Jenny; by Mary Kennedy. Lothrop, 1954.

Jorinda and Joringel; by Jacob and Wilhelm Grimm. Tr. Elizabeth Shub. Scribner, 1968.

Laird of Cockpen; by Sorche N. Leodhas, *pseud.* (Leclaire G. Alger). Holt, 1969.

Light in the Tower; by Patricia Gordon, *pseud.* (Joan Howard). Lothrop, 1960.

Littlest Witch; by Jeanne Massey. Knopf, 1959.

Mary's Marvelous Mouse; by Mary F. Shura. Knopf, 1962.

Mr. Biddle and the Birds; by (John) Lonzo Anderson. Scribner, 1971.

Mouse House; by Rumer Godden. Viking, 1957.

Mouse Palace; by Frances Carpenter. McGraw, 1964.

Painting the Moon: A Folktale from Estonia; Retold; by Carl Withers. Dutton, 1970.

(comp.) *Poetry of Earth.* Scribner, 1972.

Ponies of Mykillengi; by (John) Lonzo Anderson. Scribner, 1966.

Pulling Strings; by Madeleine Myers. Holt, 1965.

Rachel Field Storybook; by Rachel Field. Doubleday, 1958.

River Bank: From the Wind in the Willows; by Kenneth Grahame. Scribner, 1977.

Shoemaker and the Elves; by Jacob and Wilhelm Grimm. Tr. Wayne Andrews. Scribner, 1960.

Snow White and Rose Red; by Jacob and Wilhelm Grimm. Tr. Wayne Andrews. Scribner, 1964.

Story of Holly and Ivy; by Rumer Godden. Viking, 1958.

Summer Is Magic; by Patricia Gordon, *pseud.* (Joan Howard). Lothrop, 1952.

Summer's Coming In; by Natalia Belting. Holt, 1970.

Theodore's Parents; by Janice M. Udry. Lothrop, 1958.

13th Is Magic; by Patricia Gordon, *pseud.* (Joan Howard). Lothrop, 1950.

Thumbelina; by Hans C. Andersen. Tr. Richard P. Keigwin. Scribner, 1961.

Tip and Dip; by Suzanne Gleaves and Lael T. Wertenbaker. Lippincott, 1960.

Trudy's First Day at Camp; by Paula Hendrich. Lothrop, 1959.

Twelve Dancing Princesses; by Andrew Lang. Holt, 1966.

Two Hundred Rabbits; by (John) Lonzo Anderson. Viking, 1968.

Ugly Duckling; by Hans C. Andersen. Tr. Richard P. Keigwin. Scribner, 1961.

BIBLIOGRAPHY (cont'd)

What Makes a Shadow?; by Clyde R. Bulla. Crowell, 1962.

Where Does Everyone Go?; by Aileen Fisher. Crowell, 1961.

White Rat's Tale; by Barbara Schiller. Holt, 1967.

Woggle of Witches. Scribner, 1971.

MEDIA

Houses from the Sea. Miller-Brody Productions, 1974 (FSS); *a.k.a. Casitas en el Mar*, 1974 (FSS).

Izzard. (BB).

Shoemaker and the Elves. Miller-Brody Productions, 1974 (FSS); *a.k.a. Zapatero y los Duendes*, 1974 (FSS).

Two Hundred Rabbits. Taylor Associates, 1973 (FSS); Viking Press, 1972 (FSS).

Ugly Duckling. Miller-Brody Productions, 1974 (FSS); *a.k.a. Primera Pate*, 1974 (FSS).

Woggle of Witches. Miller-Brody Productions, 1974 (FSS); *a.k.a. Noche de Brujas*, 1974 (FSS).

COLLECTIONS

deGrummond Collection, University of Southern Mississippi. (Hattiesburg, Mississippi).

Free Library of Philadelphia. (Philadelphia, Pennsylvania).

Kerlan Collection, University of Minnesota. (Minneapolis, Minnesota).

BACKGROUND READING

Bader. *American Picturebooks from Noah's Ark to The Beast Within*.

Commire. *Something about the Author*.

Contemporary Authors.

DeMontreville. *Third Book of Junior Authors*.

Hopkins. *Books Are by People*.

Kingman. *Illustrators of Children's Books, 1957-1966*.

Kingman. *Illustrators of Children's Books, 1967-1976*.

Miller. *Illustrators of Children's Books, 1946-1956*.

Sadowski, E. "Glimpses of an Artist: Adrienne Adams." *Elementary English*, October 1974.

Smaridge. *Famous Literary Teams for Young People*.

Ward. *Illustrators of Books for Young People, Second Edition*.

JULIA DAVIS ADAMS, 1900-
author
a.k.a. Julia Davis
pseudonym F. Draco

AWARDS

Mountains Are Free. Newbery Honor Book, 1931.

Vaino: A Boy of New Finland. Newbery Honor Book, 1930.

BIBLIOGRAPHY

as Julia Davis Adams:

Anvil: The Trial of John Brown, a Two-Act Drama. Harper, 1963.

*Legacy of Love. Harcourt, 1961.

Mount Up: A True Story Based on the Reminiscences of Major E. A. H. McDonald of the Confederate Cavalry. Harcourt, 1967.

Mountains Are Free. il. Theodore Nadejen. Dutton, 1930.

No Other White Men. il. Caroline Gray. Dutton, 1937.

Ride with the Eagle: The Expedition of the First Missouri in the War with Mexico, 1846. il. Jean P. Tremblay. Harcourt, 1962.

Swords of the Vikings: Stories from the Works of Saxo Grammaticus, Adapted. il. Suzanne Larsen. Dutton. 1928.

Vaino: A Boy of New Finland. il. Lempi Ostman. Dutton, 1929.

Valley and a Song: The Story of the Shenandoah River. il. Joan Berg. Holt, 1963.

as Julia Davis:

Bridle the Wind. Rinehart, 1953.

Cloud on the Land. Rinehart, 1951.

Peter Hale. il. Louis Wiesenberg. Dutton, 1939.

Remember and Forget. il. Mabel Pugh. Dutton, 1932.

Shenandoah. il. Frederic Taubes. Farrar, 1945.

Stonewall. il. Cameron Wright. Dutton, 1931.

Sun Climbs Slow. Dutton, 1942; *a.k.a. Wind and the Grass*. Hodder, 1943.

as F. Draco:

Cruise with Death. Rinehart, 1952.

Devil's Church. Rinehart, 1951.

MEDIA

Legacy of Love. (BB, TB).

Sun Climbs Slow. (BB).

COLLECTIONS

deGrummond Collection, University of Southern Mississippi. (Hattiesburg, Mississippi).

BACKGROUND READING

Burke. *American Authors and Books, 1640 to the Present Day*.

Commire. *Something about the Author*.

Contemporary Authors.

Kunitz. *Junior Book of Authors*.

Kunitz. *Junior Books of Authors, Second Edition Revised*.

LLOYD CHUDLEY ALEXANDER, 1924-
author

AWARDS

Black Cauldron. Newbery Honor Book, 1966.

High King. Newbery Medal Book, 1969.

BIBLIOGRAPHY

And Let the Credit Go. Crowell, 1955.

Black Cauldron. Holt, 1965.

Book of Three. Holt, 1964.

Border Hawk: August Bondi. il. Bernard Krigstein. Farrar, 1958.

Castle of Llyr. Holt, 1966.

Cat Who Wished to Be a Man. Dutton, 1973.

Coll and His White Pig. il. Evaline Ness. Holt, 1965.

Fifty Years in the Doghouse. Putnam, 1964; *a.k.a. Send for Ryan!* Allen, 1965.

Flagship Hope (and) Aaron Lopez. il. Bernard Krigstein. Farrar, 1960.

Foundling and Other Tales of Prydain. il. Margot Zemach. Holt, 1973.

Four Donkeys. il. Lester Abrams. Holt, 1972.

High King. Holt, 1968.

(tr.) *Intimacy, and Other Stories*; by Jean Paul Sartre. Neville, 1949.

*Janine Is French. Crowell, 1959.

King's Fountain. il. Ezra J. Keats. Dutton, 1971.

Marvelous Misadventures of Sebastian, Grand Extravaganza, Including a Performance by the Entire Cast of the Gallimaufry-Theatricus. Dutton, 1970.

My Five Tigers. il. Peggy Bacon. Crowell, 1956.

*My Love Affair with Music. il. (Mircea) Vasiliu. Crowell, 1960.

(tr.) *Nausea*; by Jean Paul Sartre. New Directions, 1949; *a.k.a. Diary of Antoine Roquentin*. Lehmann, 1949.

Park Avenue Vet; with Louis Camuti. Holt, 1962.

(tr.) *Sea Rose*; by Paul Vialar. Copp, 1952.

(tr.) *Selected Writings of Paul Éluard*; by Paul Éluard, *pseud*. (Eugene Grindel). New Directions, 1951; *a.k.a. Uninterrupted Poetry, Selected Writings*, 1975.

Taran Wanderer. Holt, 1967.

Time Cat: The Remarkable Journeys of Jason and Gareth. il. Bill Sokol. Holt, 1963; *a.k.a. Nine Lives*. Cassell, 1963.

Town Cats and Other Stories. il. Lazlo Kubinyi. Dutton, 1977.

Truthful Harp. il. Evaline Ness. Holt, 1967.

(tr.) *Wall, and Other Stories*; by Jean Paul Sartre. New Directions, 1948.

Wizard in the Tree. il. Lazlo Kubinyi. Dutton, 1975.

MEDIA

Black Cauldron. (BB, TB).

Book of Three. (BB,TB).

Castle of Llyr. (TB).

Cat Who Wished to Be a Man. (CB).

Coll and His White Pig. (BB).

Fifty Years in the Doghouse. (BB, TB).

Foundling and Other Tales of Prydain. (TB).

Four Donkeys. (TB).

High King. (TB); Miller-Brody Productions, 1974 (FSS).

Janine Is French. (TB).

King's Fountain. (BB).

Marvelous Misadventures of Sebastian. (TB).

My Five Tigers. (BB).

My Love Affair with Music. (BB, TB).

Park Avenue Vet. (TB).

Taran Wanderer. (TB).

Time Cat. (BB, TB).

BACKGROUND READING

Alexander, L. "Flat-Heeled Muse." *Horn Book*, April 1965.

Alexander, L. "High Fantasy and Heroic Romance." *Horn Book*, December 1971.

BACKGROUND READING (cont'd)

Alexander, L. "No Laughter in Heaven." *Horn Book*, February 1970.

Alexander, L. "On Responsibility and Authority." *Horn Book*, August 1974.

Alexander, L. "Truth about Fantasy." *Top of the News*, January 1968.

Alexander, L. "Wishful Thinking or Hopeful Dreaming?" *Horn Book*, August 1968.

Commire. *Something about the Author*.

Contemporary Authors.

DeMontreville. *Third Book of Junior Authors*.

Hopkins. *More Books by More People*.

Kingman. *Newbery and Caldecott Medal Books, 1966-1975*.

Kirkpatrick. *Twentieth Century Children's Writers*.

Livingston, Myra C. *Tribute to Lloyd Alexander*. Drexel Institute, 1976.

Lloyd Alexander, Evaline Ness and Anne Durrell. Profiles in Literature, 1972 (VT).

Meet the Newbery Author: Lloyd Alexander. Miller-Brody Productions, 1974 (FSS).

Ward. *Authors of Books for Young People, Second Edition*.

Wintle. *Pied Pipers*.

+MARJORIE HILL ALLEE, 1890-1945
author

AWARDS

Jane's Island. Newbery Honor Book, 1932.

BIBLIOGRAPHY

Ann's Surprising Summer. il. Maitland DeGogorza. Houghton, 1933.

Camp at Westlands. il. Erick Berry, *pseud.* (Evangel A. Best). Houghton, 1941.

Christmas Eve at the Tavern. (Yellow Springs, Ohio), 1940.

Great Tradition. il. Cyrus L. Baldridge. Houghton, 1937.

House. il. Helen Blair. Houghton, 1944.

House of Her Own. il. Manning DeV. Lee. Houghton, 1934.

Jane's Island. il. Maitland DeGogorza. Houghton, 1931.

Judith Lankester. il. Hattie L. Price. Houghton, 1930.

Jungle Island; with Warder C. Allee. Rand, 1925.

Little American Girl. il. Paul Quinn. Houghton, 1938.

Off to Philadelphia! il. David Hendrickson. Houghton, 1936.

Road to Carolina. il. Manning DeV. Lee. Houghton, 1932.

Runaway Linda. il. David Hendrickson. Houghton, 1939.

Smoke Jumper. il. Manning DeV. Lee. Houghton, 1945.

Susanna and Tristram. il. Hattie L. Price. Houghton, 1929.

Winter's Mischief. il. George Whitney. Houghton, 1942.

MEDIA

House. (BB).

Winter's Mischief. (BB).

BACKGROUND READING

Burke. *American Authors and Books, 1640 to the Present Day*.

Current Biography.

Kunitz. *Junior Book of Authors*.

Kunitz. *Junior Book of Authors, Second Edition Revised*.

Thompson. *Indiana Authors and Their Books, 1917-1966*.

Winslow, A. "Marjorie Hill Allee: June 2, 1890-April 30, 1945." *Horn Book*, May 1946.

Young Wings. *Writing Books for Boys and Girls*.

VALENTIN ANGELO, 1897-
author-illustrator
a.k.a. Valenti

AWARDS

Nino. Newbery Honor Book, 1939.

(*Roller Skates*. Newbery Medal Book, 1937.)

BIBLIOGRAPHY

Acorn Tree. Viking, 1958.

America; by Ruth Tooze. Viking, 1956.

American Taste; by Louis Mumford. Westgate, 1929.

Angelino and the Barefoot Saint. Viking, 1961.

Animals' Christmas: Poems, Carols and Stories; by Anne T. Eaton. Viking, 1944.

Auguries of Innocence; by William Blake. (Bronxville, New York), 1968.

Barefoot Saint; by Stephen V. Benét. Doubleday, 1929.

Battle in Greece; by Stephen Crane. Peter Pauper, 1936. (Limited edition).

Battle in Washington Square. Golden Cross, 1942.

Bells of Bleeker Street. Viking, 1949.

Benito; by Clyde R. Bulla. Crowell, 1961.

Bible Story for Children. n. p., 1959.

Big Little Island. Viking, 1955.

Birthday of Little Jesus; by Sterling North. Grosset, 1952.

Blood of the Martyr; by Stephen Crane. Peter Pauper(?), 1939.

Book of Esther; from the *Bible*. Grabhorn(?), 1935.

Book of Job; from the *Bible*. Grabhorn, 1926.

Book of Jonah; from the *Bible*. n. p., 1960.

Book of Proverbs from the Authorized King James Version; from the *Bible*. Limited Editions, 1963.

Book of Ruth; from the *Bible*. Grabhorn, 1926.

Book of Ruth and Boaz. Press of Valenti Angelo, 1949.

Book of the Thousand Nights and a Night: from the Arabian Nights. Limited Editions, 1934.

California As It Is & As It May Be; by Felix P. Wierzbicki. Grabhorn, 1933.

Candy Basket. Viking, 1960.

Cherry Ripe; by Alfred E. Coppard. Hawthorn, 1935.

Chinese Fairy Tales. Peter Pauper, 1938.

Chinese Love Tales; by Charles G. Soulié. Three Sirens, 1935.

Cradle Songs, The Divine Image, A Dream (and) Night; by William Blake. Press of Valenti Angelo, 1949.

Dago Red; by John Fante. Viking, 1940.

Donkey for the King; by Olive Price. McGraw, 1955.

Fables of Europe. Peter Pauper(?), 1930.

Fairy Tales; by Oscar Wilde. Peter Pauper, 1942.

Fiscal Hoboes: A Short, Short Story; by William Saroyan. Duschnes, 1949. (Limited edition).

Golden Gate. Viking, 1939.

Golden Touch: Being the Legend of King Midas; by Nathaniel Hawthorne. Grabhorn, 1927; Peter Pauper, 1939. (Limited edition).

Hey, Mr. Grasshopper!; by Flory P. Gates. (Durant, Oklahoma), 1949.

Hill of Little Miracles. Viking, 1942.

Honey Boat. Viking, 1959.

Hound of Heaven; by Frances Thompson. Peter Pauper, 1953.

House of the Seven Gables: A Romance; by Nathaniel Hawthorne. Limited Editions, 1935.

Hymns to Aphrodite; by Homer. Tr. John Edgar. Press of Valenti Angelo, 1949.

Imitation of Christ; by Thomas à Kempis. Peter Pauper, 1947.

Japanese Fairy Tales; by Lafacadio Hearn. Peter Pauper, 1936.

Joan of Arc; by Nancy Ross. Random, 1953.

Journey to Bethlehem; by Delos W. Lovelace. Crowell, 1953.

Kasidah of Haji Abdu El-Yezdi: A Lay of Higher Law; Tr. Richard Burton. Limited Editions, 1937.

Leaves of Grass: Comprising the Poems Written by Walt Whitman, Following the Arrangement of the Edition of 1891-92; by Walt Whitman. Random, 1930.

Let's Read Aloud: Stories and Poems; by Ruth Gagliardo. Lippincott, 1962.

Letters of Amerigo Vespucci; by Amerigo Vespucci. Grabhorn, 1926.

Life and Death of King John; by William Shakespeare. Limited Editions, 1940.

Light of Asia: Being the Life and Teaching of Guatema, Prince of India and Founder of Buddhism, as Told by an Indian Buddhist; by Edwin Arnold. Peter Pauper, 1946.

Little Flowers of St. Francis of Assisi; by Francis of Assisi. Tr. Thomas Okey. Peter Pauper, 1943.

Long Christmas: Old Tales Interspersed with Carols and Christmas Rhymes; by Ruth Sawyer. Viking, 1941.

Look Out Yonder. Viking, 1943.

Luck of Roaring Camp and Other Stories; by Bret Harte. Peter Pauper, 1943.

Lytell Geste of Robyn Hode and His Meiny. Westgate, 1932.

Man without a Country; by Edward E. Hale. Peter Pauper, 1938.

Marble Fountain. Viking, 1951.

Merry Marcos. Viking, 1963.

Nino. Viking, 1938.

Not So Deep as a Well: Collected Poems; by Dorothy Parker. Viking, 1936.

Paradise Valley. Viking, 1940.

Paula; by Marguerite Vance. Dodd, 1939.

Persian Fairy Tales. Peter Pauper, 1939.

BIBLIOGRAPHY (cont'd)

Philobiblion; by Richard DeBury (*a.k.a.* Richard Aungerville). Tr. Andrew Fleming. Duschnes, 1945. (Limited edition).

Pierrot of the Minute; by Ernest Dowson. Windsor, 1932.

Prelude to Man; by Charles P. Smith. Peter Pauper, 1936.

Psalms of David in the King James Version; from the *Bible*. Peter Pauper, 1936.

Quattrocentisteria: How Sandro Botticelli Saw Simonetta in the Spring; by Maurice Hewlett. Duschnes, 1937. (Limited edition).

Red Badge of Courage; by Stephen Crane. Random, 1931.

Roller Skates; by Ruth Sawyer. Viking, 1936.

Rooster Club. Viking, 1944.

Rubiyat of Omar Khayyam of Naishapur. Limited Editions, 1935.

Salome; by Oscar Wilde. Grabhorn, 1927.

Sayings of Jesus; from the *Bible*. Peter Pauper, 1940.

Scarlet Letter; by Nathaniel Hawthorne. Random, 1928.

Second Chapter of the Gospel According to St. Luke; from the *Bible*. n.p., 1956.

Sentimental Journey; by Laurence Sterne. Dodd, 1929.

Sermon on the Mount and Other Sayings of Jesus; from the *Bible*. Peter Pauper, 1949.

Sermon on the Mount: Being the Fifth, Sixth and Seventh Chapters of the Gospel According to St. Matthew, in the King James Version of the Holy Bible; from the *Bible*. Golden Cross, 1935.

Sir Frances Drake; by John W. Robinson. n. p., 1926.

Song of Hiawatha; by Henry W. Longfellow. Peter Pauper, 1942.

Song of Roland: Done into English in the Original Measure; by Charles S. Moncrieff. Limited Editions, 1938.

Song of Songs, Which Is Solomon's; from the *Bible*. Heritage, 1952.

Song of St. Francis; by Clyde R. Bulla. Crowell, 1952.

Sonnets from the Portuguese; by Elizabeth B. Browning. Heritage, 1945.

Sonnets of William Shakespeare; by William Shakespeare. Heritage, 1941.

South Wind; by Norman Douglas. Dodd, 1929.

Splendid Gift. il. with Harriet Whedon. Hawthorn, 1940.

St. Valentine's Day; by Clyde R. Bulla. Crowell, 1965.

Subtyl Histories & Fables of Esop; by Aesop. Tr. William Caxton. Grabhorn, 1930.

Tale of a Donkey. Viking, 1966.

Three Musketeers; by Alexandre Dumas. Three Sirens, 1934.

Tragedy of Hamlet; by William Shakespeare. Peter Pauper, 1950.

Twenty-Five Poems about Trees and Leaves Including Some Prints of Leaves. Hammer Creek, 1959.

Twice-Told Tales; by Nathaniel Hawthorne. Limited Editions, 1966.

Two Unpublished Manuscripts; by Charles A. Swinburne. Grabhorn, 1927.

Vathek: An Arabian Tale; by William Beckford. Tr. Herbert Grimsditch. Limited Editions, 1945.

Verses; by William Blake. Press of Valenti Angelo, 1949.

Visit from St. Nicholas; by Clement C. Moore. Hawthorne, 1937.

Voiage and Travaile of Sir John Mondeville; by John Maundeville. Grabhorn, 1928

Welcome Christmas! A Garland of Poems; by Anne T. Eaton. Viking, 1955.

Wife of Martin Guerre; by Janet Lewis. Colt, 1941.

Writing and Criticism: A Book for Margery Bianco; by Anne C. Moore and Bertha E. Mahony. Horn Book, 1951.

Zadig; by Voltaire. Doubleday, 1929; Rimington, 1929. (Limited edition).

MEDIA

Marble Fountain. (BB).

Tale of a Donkey. (BB).

EXHIBITIONS

Feragil Gallery, 1933. (New York, New York).

San Francisco Public Library, 1975. (San Francisco, California).

COLLECTIONS

Bancroft Library, University of California. (Berkeley, California).

Kerlan Collection, University of Minnesota. (Minneapolis, Minnesota).

May Massee Collection, Emporia State College. (Emporia, Kansas).

Milwaukee Public Library. (Milwaukee, Wisconsin).

Rare Book and Manuscript Library, Columbia University. (New York, New York).

San Francisco Public Library. (San Francisco, California).

Special Collections, University Research Library, University of California. (Los Angeles, California).

BACKGROUND READING

Angelo, V. "There Was a Book." *Horn Book*, March 1943.

Burke. *American Authors and Books, 1640 to the Present Day*.

Commire. *Something about the Author*.

Contemporary Authors.

Duff, A. "Valenti Angelo—Artist, Writer, Man." *Top of the News*, October 1961.

Ellis. *Book Illustration*.

Haas, I. "Bibliography of the Work of Valenti Angelo." *Print*, June 1937.

Kent, N. "Tuscan Spirit Transplanted." *American Artist*, April 1944.

Kingman. *Illustrators of Children's Books, 1957-1966*.

Kirkpatrick. *Twentieth Century Children's Writers*.

Kunitz. *Junior Book of Authors, Second Edition Revised*.

Mahony. *Illustrators of Children's Books, 1744-1945*.

Miller. *Illustrators of Children's Books, 1946-1956*.

Valenti Angelo: Author, Illustrator, Printer: A Checklist of His Work from 1926-1970. (Bronxville, New York), 1972; also issued by The Book Club of California, 1976.

Ward. *Authors of Books for Young People, Second Edition*.

Young Wings. *Writing Books for Boys and Girls*.

+LAURA ADAMS ARMER, 1874-1963
author-illustrator

AWARDS

Forest Pool. Caldecott Honor Book, 1939.

Waterless Mountain. Newbery Medal Book, 1932.

BIBLIOGRAPHY

Beautyway: A Navaho Ceremonial; with Leland C. Wyman, et al. Pantheon, 1957.

Cactus. il. Sidney Armer. Longmans, 1933.

Farthest West. il. Sidney Armer. Longmans, 1939.

Forest Pool. Longmans, 1938.

In Navajo Land. photographs by Sidney and Austin Armer. McKay, 1962.

Sand-Painting of the Navaho Indians. Exposition of Indian Tribal Arts, 1931.

Southwest. Longmans, 1935.

Trader's Children. il. Sidney Armer and photographs. Longmans, 1937.

Waterless Mountain. il. Sidney Armer. Longmans, 1931.

MEDIA

Mountain Chant. n. p., 1926 (original F).

Waterless Mountain. (BB).

BACKGROUND READING

Burke. *American Authors and Books, 1640 to the Present Day*.

Commire. *Something about the Author*.

Contemporary Authors.

Kunitz. *Authors Today and Yesterday*.

Kunitz. *Junior Book of Authors*.

Kunitz. *Junior Book of Authors, Second Edition Revised*.

Mahony. *Illustrators of Children's Books, 1744-1945*.

Miller. *Newbery Medal Books, 1922-1955*.

Obituary. *Publishers Weekly*, April 15, 1963.

Ward. *Authors of Books for Young People, Second Edition*.

Young Wings. *Writing Books for Boys and Girls*.

WILLIAM HOWARD ARMSTRONG, 1914-
author

AWARDS

Sounder. Newbery Medal Book, 1970.

BIBLIOGRAPHY

Animal Tales, Adapted; by Hana Doskočilová. il. Mirko Hanák. Doubleday, 1970.

Barefoot in the Grass: The Story of Grandma Moses. Doubleday, 1970.

Education of Abraham Lincoln. Coward, 1974.

BIBLIOGRAPHY (cont'd)

87 Ways to Help Your Child in School. Barron's, 1961.

Hadassah: Ester, the Orphan Queen. il. Barbara N. Byfield. Doubleday, 1972.

Joanna's Miracle. Broadman, 1977.

MacLeod Place. Coward, 1972.

Mills of God. il. David Armstrong. Doubleday, 1973.

My Animals. il. Mirko Hanák. Doubleday, 1974.

Peoples of the Ancient World; with Joseph Swain. Harper, 1959.

Sounder. il. James Barkley. Harper, 1969.

Sour Land. il. James Barkley. Harper, 1971.

Study Is Hard Work. Harper, 1956; second edition, 1967.

Study Tips: How to Improve Your Grades. Barron's, 1976.

Through Troubled Waters. Harper, 1957.

Tools of Thinking: A Self-Help Workbook for Students in Grades 5-9. Barron's, 1969.

Word Power in 5 Easy Lessons: A Simplified Approach to Excellence in Grammar, Punctuation, Sentence Structure, Spelling and Penmanship. Barron's, 1969.

MEDIA

My Animals. (BB).

Sounder. (C, CB, MT, TB); Miller-Brody Productions, 1970 (C, R); Radnitz-Mattel/Twentieth-Century Fox Film Corporation, 1971 (F).

Sour Land. (CB, TB).

Through Troubled Waters. (BB).

COLLECTIONS

Kerlan Collection, University of Minnesota. (Minneapolis, Minnesota).

BACKGROUND READING

Biography News.

Commire. *Something about the Author*.

Contemporary Authors.

DeMontreville. *Third Book of Junior Authors*.

Hopkins. *More Books by More People*.

Kingman. *Newbery and Caldecott Medal Books, 1966-1975*.

Kirkpatrick. *Twentieth Century Children's Writers*.

Meet the Newbery Author: William Armstrong. Miller-Brody Productions, 1977 (FSS).

Nykoruk. *Authors in the News*.

Ward. *Authors of Books for Young People, Second Edition*.

+BORIS MIKHAILOVICH ARTZYBASHEFF, 1899-1965
author-illustrator
a.k.a. Boris Artzybashev

AWARDS

(*Gay-Neck*. Newbery Medal Book, 1928.)

(*Nansen*. Newbery Honor Book, 1941.)

Seven Simeons. Caldecott Honor Book, 1938.

(*Wonder Smith and His Son*. Newbery Honor Book, 1928.)

BIBLIOGRAPHY

Aesop's Fables; by Aesop. Viking, 1933.

Apple Tree; by Margery W. Bianco. Doran, 1926.

Arabian Nights Edited to Fit the Interests and Abilities of Young Readers; edited by Edward L. Thorndike. Appleton, 1937.

As I See: Notes to Folios by the Artist. Dodd, 1954.

Axis in Agony! Presenting a Series of Caricatures from the Brush of Boris Artzybasheff. Wickwire Spencer Steel, 1944.

Behind Moroccan Walls; by Henriette Celáiré. Tr. Constance L. Morris. Macmillan, 1931.

Circus of Dr. Lao; by Charles G. Finney. Viking, 1935.

Creatures; by Padraic Colum. Macmillan, 1927.

Droll Stories: Thirty Tales; by Honoré de Balzac. Tr. Jacques LeClerq. Heritage, 1939.

Evenings with Nino: A Didactic Poem Containing a Translation of Racine's Bernice; by Louis How. Harbor, 1941.

Fairy Shoemaker, and Other Fairy Poems; by William Allingham, et al. Macmillan, 1928.

Feats on the Fiord; by Harriet Martineau. Macmillan, 1925.

Fireflies; by Rabinadranath Tagore. Macmillan, 1928.

Forge in the Forest; by Padraic Colum. Macmillan, 1925.

Funnybone Alley; by Alfred Kreymborg. Macaulay, 1927.

Gay-Neck: The Story of a Pigeon; by Dhan G. Mukerji. Dutton, 1927.

Ghond: The Hunter; by Dhan G. Mukerji. Dutton, 1928.

Henry the Navigator; by Maude B. Lynch. Nelson, 1935.

Herodotus; edited by Gordon King. Doubleday, 1929.

Jonah: Or, The Withering Vine; by Robert Nathan. Knopf, 1934.

Kirdy, the Road out of the World; by Harold Lamb. Doubleday, 1933.

Let George Do It! A Talk Delivered at the Meeting of the Trade Book Clinic in New York City, December 5, 1940. American Institute of Graphic Arts, 1941.

Little Brother Francis of Assisi; by Michael Williams. Macmillan, 1926.

Little Princess Nina; by Lidiya A. Charskaya. Holt, 1924.

Nadya Makes Her Bow; by Helen Haskell. Dutton, 1938.

Nansen; by Anna G. Hall. Viking, 1940.

Orpheus: Myths of the World; by Padraic Colum. Macmillan, 1930; *a.k.a. Myths of the World*. Grosset, 1959.

Poor Shadydullah. Macmillan, 1931.

Roses of the Winds; by Sonia Lustig. Doubleday, 1926.

Rug That Went to Mecca; by Youel B. Mirza. Stokes, 1939.

Seven Simeons: A Russian Tale Retold. Viking, 1937; new edition, 1961.

Siberian Gold; by Theodore and Winifred Harper. Doubleday, 1927.

Son of the Sword; by Youel B. Mirza. Viking, 1934.

This Casual Glory; by Hugh J. Chisholm. Ashlar, 1934.

Three and the Moon: Legendary Stories of Old Brittany, Normandy and Provence; by Jacques Dorey. Knopf, 1929.

Tree of Life: Selections from the Literature of the World's Religions; by Ruth P. Smith. Macmillan, 1942.

Undertaker's Garland; by John P. Bishop and Edmund Wilson. Knopf, 1922.

Verotchka's Tales; by Mamin-Siberiak, *pseud.* (Dmitrii N. Mamin). Tr. Ray Davidson. Dutton, 1922.

War Posters. Wickwire Spencer Steel, *ca.*1942.

What Makes the Wheels Go 'Round; by George E. Bock. Macmillan, 1931.

Wonder Smith and His Son: A Tale from the Golden Childhood of the World, Retold; by Ella Young. Longmans, 1927.

MEDIA

Aesop's Fables. (BB).

Seven Simeons. (BB).

EXHIBITIONS

Feragil Gallery, 1931. (New York, New York).

Leggett Studio Gallery, 1931. (New York, New York).

COLLECTIONS

Arents Research Library, Syracuse University. (Syracuse, New York).

Kerlan Collection, University of Minnesota. (Minneapolis, Minnesota).

May Massee Collection, Emporia State College. (Emporia, Kansas).

Rare Book and Manuscript Library, Columbia University. (New York, New York).

Special Collections, University Research Library, University of California. (Los Angeles, California).

BACKGROUND READING

"Art of Boris Artzybasheff." *American Artist*, December 1941.

Bader. *American Picturebooks from Noah's Ark to the Beast Within*.

Bechtel, L. "Boris Artzybasheff." *Horn Book*, April 1966.

Burke. *American Authors and Books, 1640 to the Present Day*.

Commire. *Something about the Author*.

Cooper. *Authors and Others*.

Current Biography.

Ellis. *Book Illustration*.

Kunitz. *Junior Book of Authors*.

Kunitz. *Junior Book of Authors, Second Edition Revised*.

Lockwood, B. "Boris Artzybasheff, Creative Artist." *Art*, January 1933.

Mahony. *Contemporary Illustrators of Children's Books*.

Mahony. *Illustrators of Children's Books, 1744-1945*.

Obituary. *Library Journal*, September 15, 1965.

Obituary. *Newsweek*, July 26, 1965.

Obituary. *New York Times*, July 18, 1965.

Obituary. *Time*, July 26, 1965.

Ward. *Authors of Books for Young People, Second Edition*.

+RICHARD TUPPER ATWATER, 1892-1948
author
> *pseudonym* Riq

and

+FLORENCE CARROLL ATWATER
author

AWARDS

Mr. Popper's Penguins. Newbery Honor Book, 1939.

BIBLIOGRAPHY

Richard and Florence Atwater:

Mr. Popper's Penguins. il. Robert Lawson. Little, 1938.

Richard Atwater:

Doris and the Trolls. il. John Gee. Rand, 1931.

(tr.) *Secret History of Procopius*; by Procopius of Caesarea. Covici-Friede, 1927.

as Riq:

Rickety Rimes of Riq. Ballou, 1925.

MEDIA

Mr. Popper's Penguins. (BB, TB); Miller-Brody Productions, 1975 (C, R); Pied Piper Productions, 197?. (FSS).

BACKGROUND READING

Burke. *American Authors and Books, 1640 to the Present Day*.

Kirkpatrick. *Twentieth Century Children's Writers*.

Montgomery. *Story behind Modern Books*.

NATALIE BABBITT, 1932-
author-illustrator

AWARDS

Knee-Knock Rise. Newbery Honor Book, 1971.

BIBLIOGRAPHY

Devil's Storybook. Farrar, 1974.

Dick Foote and the Shark. Farrar, 1967.

Eyes of the Amaryllis. Farrar, 1977.

Forty-ninth Magician; by Samuel Babbitt. Pantheon, 1966.

Goody Hall. Farrar, 1971.

Knee-Knock Rise. Farrar, 1970.

More Small Poems; by Valerie Worth. Farrar, 1976.

Phoebe's Revolt. Farrar, 1968.

Search for Delicious. Farrar, 1969.

Small Poems; by Valerie Worth. Farrar, 1972.

Something. Farrar, 1970.

Tuck Everlasting. Farrar, 1975.

MEDIA

Devil's Storybook. (TB).

Goody Hall. (TB).

Knee-Knock Rise. (BB, TB); Miller-Brody Productions, 1975 (FSS).

Phoebe's Revolt. (TB).

Search for Delicious. (TB).

Tuck Everlasting. (CB).

BACKGROUND READING

Babbitt, N. "Between Innocence and Maturity." *Horn Book*, December 1972.

Babbitt, N. "Great American Novel for Children—and Why Not." *Horn Book*, April 1974.

Babbitt, N. "Happy Endings? Of Course, and Also Joy." *New York Times Book Review*, November 8, 1970.

Babbitt, N. "How Can We Write Children's Books If We Don't Know Anything about Children?" *Publishers Weekly*, July 19, 1971.

Babbitt, N. "Learning the Language." *Language Arts*, December 1977.

Babbitt, N. "What Makes a Book Worth Reading?" *Language Arts*, October 1975.

Commire. *Something about the Author*.

Contemporary Authors.

DeMontreville. *Fourth Book of Junior Authors*.

Kingman. *Illustrators of Children's Books, 1967-1976*.

Kirkpatrick. *Twentieth Century Children's Writers*.

Mercier, J. "Natalie Babbitt." *Publishers Weekly*, July 1975.

TOM BAHTI, 1926-1972
author-illustrator

AWARDS

When Clay Sings. Caldecott Honor Book, 1973.

BIBLIOGRAPHY

Before You Came This Way; by Byrd Baylor. Dutton, 1969.

Introduction to Southwestern Indian Arts and Crafts. Photos. by K. Camille den Dooven. K. C. Publications, 1970.

Southwestern Indian Ceremonials. K. C. Publications, 1970.

Southwestern Indian Tribes. K. C. Publications, 1968.

When Clay Sings; by Byrd Baylor. Scribner, 1972.

MEDIA

Southwestern Indian Tribes. (C, MT).

BACKGROUND READING

Ward. *Illustrators of Books for Young People, Second Edition*.

CAROLYN SHERWIN BAILEY, 1876-1961
author

AWARDS

Miss Hickory. Newbery Medal Book, 1947.

BIBLIOGRAPHY

All the Year Play Games: Boys' and Girls' Book of Merry Pastimes. il. Cobb X. Shinn. Whitman, 1924.

Bailey's In and Out-Door Play Games: Boys' and Girls' Book of What to Play and Make. il. Cobb X. Shinn. Whitman, 1923; *a.k.a. Sixty Games and Pastimes for All Occasions*. il. Cobb X. Shinn and Milo Winter. Whitman, 1928.

Boys and Girls of Colonial Days. il. Uldene Shriver. Flanagan, 1917.

Boys and Girls of Discovery Days. il. Dorothy Dulin. Flanagan, 1926.

Boys and Girls of Modern Days. il. Dorothy Dulin. Flanagan, 1929.

Boys and Girls of Pioneer Days: From Washington to Lincoln. Flanagan, 1924.

Boys' Make-at-Home Things; with Marian E. Bailey. Stokes, 1912.

Broad Stripes and Bright Stars: Stories of American History. il. Power O'Malley. Bradley, 1919; *a.k.a. Boy Heroes in Making America*. il. Lee Norris and Power O'Malley. Flanagan, 1931.

Candle for Your Cake: Twenty-four Birthday Stories of Famous Men and Women. il. Margaret Ayer. Lippincott, 1952.

Children of the Handcrafts. il. Grace Paull. Viking, 1935.

Children's Book of Games and Parties. Donohue, 1913.

Christmas Party. il. Cyndy Szekeres. Pantheon, 1975.

Country-Stop. il. Grace Paull. Viking, 1942; *a.k.a. Wishing-Well House*. Muller, 1950.

Daily Program of Gift and Occupation Work; with Marian E. Bailey. Bradley, 1904.

Enchanted Bugle and Other Stories. Owen, 1920.

Enchanted Village. il. Eileen Evans. Viking, 1950.

(ed.) *Evangeline: A Romance of Acadia*; by Henry W. Longfellow. il. with scenes from the motion picture. Bradley, 1922.

Every Child's Folk Songs and Games. Bradley, 1914.

Everyday Play for Children. Donohue, 1916.

Everyday Stories. il. Frederick Knowles. Bradley, 1919.

Favorite Stories for the Children's Hour; with Clara Lewis. il. Bonnie and Bill Rutherford. Platt, 1965.

Finnegan II: His Nine Lives. il. Kate Seredy. Viking, 1953.

Firelight Stories: Folk Tales Retold for Kindergarten, School and Home. il. Diantha W. Thorne. Bradley, 1907.

Flickertail. il. Garry MacKenzie. Walck, 1962.

Flint: The Story of a Trail. il. Charles Lassell. Bradley, 1922.

Folk Stories and Fables. il. Frederick A. Nagler. Bradley, 1919.

(ed.) *For the Children's Hour*; with Clara Lewis. il. William G. Breck. Bradley, 1906; also il. Frederick A. Nagler, 1916-1917 (3 vols.); also il. Rhoda Chase, 1930.

For the Story Teller: Story Telling and Stories to Tell. Bradley, 1913.

Forest, Field and Stream Stories. il. Dorothy Dulin. Flanagan, 1928.

Friendly Tales: A Community Story Book. Bradley, 1923.

From Moccasin to Wings: Stories of Our Travel Ways. il. Margaret Ayer. Bradley, 1938.

Garden, Orchard and Meadow Stories. il. Dorothy Dulin. Flanagan, 1929.

Girls' Make-at-Home Things. Stokes, 1912.

Hero Stories. il. Frederick Knowles. Bradley, 1917.

Homespun Playdays. il. Grace Paull. Viking, 1941.

In Nature's Fairyland. Owen, ca.1919.

(ed.) *In the Animal World*. Bradley, 1924.

Jingle Primer: A First Book in Reading Based on Mother Goose Rhymes and Folk Tales; with Clara L. Brown. American Book, 1906.

BIBLIOGRAPHY (cont'd)

Legends from Many Lands. Owen, 1919.

Letting in the Gang. Tapley, 1916.

Li'l Hannibal. Platt, 1938.

Lincoln Time Stories. Whitman, 1924.

Little Gray Lamb. Vagabond, 1954.

Little Men and Women Stories. Whitman, 1924; revised, 1927; revised, 1935.

Little Rabbit Who Wanted Red Wings. il. Dorothy Grider. Platt, 1945.

Little Reader Series; with Alice Hanethorn. il. Ruth M. Hallock, et al. McLoughlin, 1934.

First Readers: *My First Little Book, My First Story Book, Little Folk Tales, My First Work Book.*

Second Readers: *Adventure Stories, Everyday Stories, My Book of Games, My Second Workbook.*

Little Red Schoolhouse. il. Dorothy B. Morse. Viking, 1957.

(ed.) *Lorna Doone: A Romance of Exmoor*. il. Harold Brett. Bradley, 1921.

Marionettes, a Toy Theatre; Presenting the Play: This Way to Animal Land; with Ditzy Baker. Saalfield, 1936.

Merry Christmas Book. il. Eunice Y. Smith. Whitman, 1948.

(comp.) *Merry Tales for Children, Best Stories of Humor for Boys and Girls*. Bradley, 1921.

Miss Hickory. il. Ruth C. Gannett. Viking, 1946.

Montessori Children. il. photographs. Holt, 1915.

Old Man Rabbit's Dinner Party. il. Robinson. Platt, 1949; edited by Nora Nestrick; il. Bonnie and Bill Rutherford, 1961.

Once Upon a Time Animal Stories. Bradley, 1918.

Our Friends at the Zoo; with Alice Hanethorn. il. Ruth M. Hallock. McLoughlin, 1934.

Outdoor Story Book. Pilgrim, 1918.

Peter Newell Mother Goose: The Old Rhymes Reproduced in Connection with Their Voracious History. il. Peter Newell. Holt, 1905.

Pioneer Art in America. il. Grace Paull. Viking, 1944.

Plays for Children's Hour: An American Childhood Presentation. Bradley, 1931.

Read Aloud Stories. il. Hildegard Lupprian. Bradley, 1929.

Reading Time Stories. Whitman, 1923.

(ed.) *Schoolroom Plans and Projects*. Bradley, 1932.

Sketches along Life's Road; with Elizabeth Harrison. Stratford, 1930.

Songs of Happiness. il. Christine Wright. Bradley, 1909; with music by Mary B. Ehrmann, 1912.

Stories and Rhymes for a Child. il. Christine Wright. Bradley, 1909.

(ed.) *Stories Children Need*. Bradley, 1916.

(ed.) *Stories Children Want*. il. Jack Perkins. Bradley, 1931.

Stories for Any Day. Pilgrim, 1917.

Stories for Every Holiday. Abingdon, 1918.

Stories for Sunday Telling. Pilgrim, 1916.

Stories from an Indian Cave: The Cherokee Cave Builder. il. Joseph E. Dash. Whitman, 1924.

Stories of Great Adventures: Adapted from the Classics. il. Clara M. Burd. Bradley, 1919.

Story Lessons in Everyday Manners. Owen, ca.1920.

Story-Telling Hour: Edited for the New York Story League. Dodd, 1934.

Surprise Stories. Whitman, 1923; revised, 1936.

Tell Me a Birthday Story. il. Margaret Ayer. Stokes, 1935.

(ed.) *Tell Me Another Story: The Book of Story Programs*. Bradley, 1918.

(ed.) *Three Musketeers: Adapted for Juvenile Readers*; by Alexandre Dumas. il. Harold Brett. Bradley, 1920.

Tops and Whistles: True Stories of Early American Toys and Children. il. Grace Paull. Viking, 1937.

Torch of Courage and Other Stories. Bradley, 1921.

Untold History Stories. il. Lillian O. Titus. Owen, 1927.

Way of the Gate; with Hershey Sneath, et al. Macmillan, 1917.

What Happened at the Zoo and Other Stories. Owen, ca.1920.

What to Do for Uncle Sam: A First Book of Citizenship. Flanagan, 1918; revised, 1926.

When Grandfather Was a Boy: Stories to Read to Children. Pilgrim, 1923.

Wonder Stories: The Best Myths for Boys and Girls. il. Clara M. Burd. Bradley, 1920.

Wonderful Days. il. Joseph E. Dash and Charles B. Falls. Whitman, 1925.

Wonderful Tree and Other Golden Day Stories. il. Joseph E. Dash. Whitman, 1925.

Wonderful Window and Other Stories. il. Katherine B. Wireman. Cokesbury, 1926.

MEDIA

Candle for Your Cake. (BB, TB).

Children of the Handcrafts. (BB).

Enchanted Village. (BB).

Finnegan II. (BB, TB).

Folk Stories and Fables. (BB).

Little Rabbit Who Wanted Red Wings. (BB).

Miss Hickory. (TB); Gloria Chandler Recordings, n. d. (R); Mercury Sound Books, 1957 (R); Viking Press, 1972 (C, R).

Once upon a Time Animal Stories. (BB).

COLLECTIONS

Buley Library, Southern Connecticut State College. (New Haven, Connecticut).

BACKGROUND READING

Commire. *Something about the Author*.

Contemporary Authors.

Current Biography.

Davis, Dorothy R. *Carolyn Sherwin Bailey, 1876-1961: Profile and Bibliography*. Eastern Press, 1967.

Davis, Dorothy R. *Carolyn Sherwin Bailey Historical Collection of Children's Books: A Catalogue*. Southern Connecticut State College, 1966.

Kirkpatrick. *Twentieth Century Children's Writers*.

Miller. *Newbery Medal Books, 1922-1955*.

Obituary. *New York Times*, December 25, 1961.

Obituary. *Publishers Weekly*, January 1962.

Ward. *Authors of Books for Young People, Second Edition*.

Young Wings. *Writing Books for Boys and Girls*.

ELIZABETH CHESLEY BAITY, 1907-
author
a.k.a. Elizabeth Chesley

AWARDS

Americans before Columbus. Newbery Honor Book, 1952.

BIBLIOGRAPHY

America before Man. il. Charles B. Falls. Viking, 1953; revised, 1964.

Americans before Columbus. il. Charles B. Falls. Viking, 1951; revised, 1960.

Building and Furnishing a Home. University of North Carolina, 1938.

Man Is a Weaver. il. Charles B. Falls and maps. Viking, 1942.

Modern Woman. University of North Carolina, 1937.

Modern Woman's Bookshelf. University of North Carolina, 1939.

Modern Woman's Unfinished Business. University of North Carolina, 1941.

(ed.) Tanganyika Literarcy Workshop Series. (Kinampanda, Tanzania), 1956. (21 vols.); *a.k.a. Tanganyika Reading Series: Selections from Village Improvement, Women's Reader and Complete Text of Song of Rejoicing*. Committee on World Literacy and Christian Literature, 1958.

Women and the Wide World. University of North Carolina, 1946.

MEDIA

America before Man. (TB).

Americans before Columbus. Educational Reading Service, 1968 (FSS).

In Search of the Firewalkers. Alan Landsberg, n. d. (original script, TV).

Malaria Eradication. Brazilian Public Health Service, 1944 (original text, FSS).

COLLECTIONS

May Massee Collection, Emporia State College. (Emporia, Kansas).

BACKGROUND READING

Burke. *American Authors and Books, 1640 to the Present Day*.

Commire. *Something about the Author*.

Contemporary Authors.

Fuller. *More Junior Authors*.

Young Wings. *Writing Books for Boys and Girls*.

ARNOLD EDWIN BARE, 1920-
author-illustrator

AWARDS

Pierre Pidgeon. Caldecott Honor Book, 1944.

BIBLIOGRAPHY

Golden Goose: Grimm's Tale Retold; by Jacob and Wilhelm Grimm. Houghton, 1947.

Ilenka; by Lee Kingman. Houghton, 1945.

BIBLIOGRAPHY (cont'd)

Maui's Summer. Houghton, 1952.

Mikko's Fortune; by Lee Kingman. Farrar, 1955.

Mooky and Tooky; by Janet F. Heath. Howell, 1946.

Peter Paints the U.S.A.; by Jean P. Colby. Houghton, 1948.

Pierre Pidgeon; by Lee Kingman. Houghton, 1943.

Play Party Book, Singing Games for Children; by Edwin Durlacher. Music by Ken Macdonald. Devin, 1945.

COLLECTIONS

Kerlan Collection, University of Minnesota. (Minneapolis, Minnesota).

BACKGROUND READING

Mahony. *Illustrators of Children's Books, 1744-1945*.

Miller. *Illustrators of Children's Books, 1946-1956*.

Ward. *Illustrators of Books for Young People, Second Edition*.

NANCY BARNES, *pseudonym*, 1897-1972
author
a.k.a. Helen Simmons Adams

AWARDS

Wonderful Year. Newbery Honor Book, 1947.

BIBLIOGRAPHY

Carlotta, American Princess. il. John Barber. Messner, 1943.

Tough Little Trollop. Hartney, 1935.

Wonderful Year. il. Kate Seredy. Messner, 1946.

+JAY HYDE BARNUM, 1888?-1962
author-illustrator

AWARDS

Boats on the River. Caldecott Honor Book, 1947.

BIBLIOGRAPHY

Abraham Lincoln; by Bella Koral. il. with John A. Maxwell. Random, 1952.

Adventures of Robin Hood, Retold; by Eleanor G. Vance. Random, 1953.

Boats on the River; by Marjorie Flack. Viking, 1946.

Buddy and the Old Pro; by John R. Tunis. Morrow, 1955.

Champion's Choice; by John R. Tunis. Harcourt, 1940.

Charley and the New Car; by Jane Thayer, *pseud.* (Catherine Woolley). Morrow, 1957.

Horse with the Easter Bonnet; by Jane Thayer, *pseud.* (Catherine Woolley). Morrow, 1953.

Kid from Tomkinsville; by John R. Tunis. Harcourt, 1940.

King Arthur and the Knights of the Round Table: Adapted from Howard Pyle's Story of King Arthur and His Knights; by Estelle Schneider. Random, 1954.

Little Giant of the North: The Boy Who Won a Fur Empire; by Alida S. Malkus. Winston, 1952.

Little Old Truck. Morrow, 1953.

Little Red Horse; by Ruth Sawyer. Viking, 1950.

Motorcycle Dog. Morrow, 1958.

Mystery at Boulder Point; by Eleanor M. Jewett. Viking, 1949.

New Fire Engine. Morrow, 1952.

Popcorn Dragon; by Jane Thayer, *pseud.* (Catherine Woolley). Morrow, 1953.

Too Many Cherries; by Carl Carmer. Viking, 1949.

Two-Bow Bill; by Gladys Brown. Morrow, 1955.

Vanilla Village; by Priscilla Carden. Pellegrini, 1952.

World Series; by John R. Tunis. Harcourt, 1941.

BACKGROUND READING

Miller. *Illustrators of Children's Books, 1946-1956*.

Obituary. *New York Times*, September 14, 1962.

Ward. *Authors of Books for Young People, Second Edition*.

LEONARD BASKIN, 1922-
author-illustrator

AWARDS

Hosie's Alphabet. Caldecott Honor Book, 1973.

BIBLIOGRAPHY

ABC with Best Wishes for 1958. Gehenna, 1958.

Ars Anatomica, a Medical Fantasia: Thirteen Drawings. Medicina Rara, 1972.

Auguries of Innocence; by William Blake. Gehenna, 1959.

Baskin: Sculpture, Drawings and Prints. Braziller, 1970.

Beowulf. Tr. Burton Raffel. University of Massachusetts, 1963.

Bird of Paradise; by Robert Graves. Doubleday, 1963.

Blake and the Youthful Ancients, Being Portraits of William Blake and His Followers. Gehenna, 1965.

Cancellersca Bastarda. Gehenna, 1965.

Caprices and Grotesques. Gehenna, 1965.

Castle Street Dogs. Gehenna, 1952; second edition, 1954; third edition, 1959.

Eat Crow; by Ted Hughes. Rainbow, 1971.

Encantadas; by Herman Melville. Gehenna, 1963.

Etchings of Ten Favorite Artists. Delphic Arts, 1963.

Fifteen Woodcuts. Boston University, 1962.

Figures of Dead Men; photographs by Hyman Edelstein. University of Massachusetts, 1968.

Five Addled Etchers. Dartmouth, 1969.

Four Drawings, and an Essay on Kollwitz. (Amherst, Massachusetts), 1968.

George Stubbs, William Morris, Albrecht Altdorfer, Jacopo de Barbari, Andrea Mantegna, and Vittore Pisanello. Porpoise, 1960.

Hippolytos; by Euripedes. Tr. Robert Bragg. Gehenna, 1969.

Homage to the Book. West Virginia Pulp and Paper, 1968.

Horned Beetles and Other Insects. Gehenna, 1958.

Hosie's Alphabet; by Hosea, Tobias and Lisa Baskin. Viking, 1972.

Iliad; by Homer. Tr. Richard Lattimore. University of Chicago, 1962.

Laus Pictorum: Portraits of Nineteenth-Century Artists Invented and Engraved. Gehenna, 1969.

Letter from Ernst Barlach; by Ernst Barlach. Gehenna, 1957.

Letter from William Blake; by William Blake. Gehenna, 1964.

Letters to and from the Ford Motor Company; by Marianne Moore and David Wallace. Pierpont Morgan, 1958.

Little Book of Natural History. Gehenna, 1951.

Modest Proposal; by Jonathan Swift. Grossman, 1969.

My Objection to Being Stepped On; by Robert Frost. Spiral, 1957.

On a Pyre of Withered Roses. Gehenna, 1942.

Passover Haggadah. Grossman, 1974.

Poem Called The Tunning of Elynour Rummynge: The Famous Ale-Wife of England; by John Skelton. Gehenna, 1953.

Politics and Poetics; by Aristotle. Stinehour, 1964.

Poppy and Other Deadly Plants; by Esther Baskin. Delacorte, 1967.

Portraits of Ten Artists. Delphic Arts, 1964.

Prometheus on His Crag; by Ted Hughes. Rainbow, 1973.

Pursuit; by Sylvia Plath. Rainbow, 1973.

Seven Deadly Sins; by Anthony Hecht. Gehenna, 1958.

Some Engravings. Gehenna, 1952.

Speech of Acceptance of Receiving the Medal of the American Institute of Art, New York, April 28, 1965. Spiral, 1965.

Struwelpeter; by Anthony Hecht. Gehenna, 1958.

Ten Woodcuts. Light, 1961.

Thee, a Poem; by Conrad Aiken. Braziller, 1967.

Thirteen Poems; by Wilfred Owen. il. with Ben Shahn. Gehenna, 1956.

Tiresias; by Alfred Tennyson. Gehenna, 1970.

Titus Andronicus; by William Shakespeare. Gehenna, 1973.

Tradition of Conscience; by Joseph Pulitzer. Pultizer, 1965.

Voyage, Six Poems; by Hart Crane. Gehenna, 1957; a.k.a. *Voyage: Six Poems from White Buildings.* Museum of Modern Art, 1957.

Wood Engravings of Leonard Baskin. Gehenna, 1961.

EXHIBITIONS

Amon Carter Museum, 1972. (Fort Worth, Texas).

Borgenicht Gallery, 1957-58, 1961, 1964-65, 1969, 1974. (New York, New York).

Chicago Art Institute, 1962. (Chicago, Illinois).

FAR Gallery, 1970. (New York, New York).

Hobson Gallery, 1978. (London, England).

Kennedy Gallery, 1971, 1973-75. (New York, New York).

Martin Gallery, 1964. (New York, New York).

Mirski Gallery, 1954-56, 1964-65. (Boston, Massachusetts).

National Museum, 1968. (Stockholm, Sweden).

Philadelphia Museum of Art, 1962. (Philadelphia, Pennsylvania).

Portland Museum of Art, 1962. (Portland, Oregon).

Smithsonian Institution, 1970. (Washington, D.C.).

Yale University, 1970. (New Haven, Connecticut).

COLLECTIONS

Amon Carter Museum. (Ft. Worth, Texas).

COLLECTIONS (cont'd)

Boston Museum of Fine Arts. (Boston, Massachusetts).

Brooklyn Institute of Arts and Sciences Museum. (Brooklyn, New York).

Chicago Art Institute. (Chicago, Illinois).

Collection of American Literature, Beinecke Library, Yale University. (New Haven, Connecticut).

Fogg Art Museum. (Cambridge, Massachusetts).

Metropolitan Museum of Art. (New York, New York).

National Gallery of Art. (Washington, D.C.).

New York Public Library. (New York, New York).

Philadelphia Museum of Art. (Philadelphia, Pennsylvania).

Prints and Photographs Division, Library of Congress. (Washington, D.C.).

Rare Books and Manuscript Library, Columbia University. (New York, New York).

Worcester Museum. (Worcester, Massachusetts).

BACKGROUND READING

"Artist and Printer." *Art in America*, Winter 1959.

Baskin, L. "Roots and Veins, a Testament." *Atlantic Monthly*, September 1964.

Current Biography.

Davis, D. "Art's Poet Laureate." *Newsweek*, June 29, 1970.

"Images of Mortality." *Life*, March 25, 1957.

Kingman. *Illustrators of Children's Books, 1967-1976*.

Klemin. *Illustrated Book: Its Art and Craft*.

"Notes on the Gehenna Press." *Printing and the Graphic Arts*, June 1959.

O'Doherty, B. "Leonard Baskin." *Art in America*, Summer 1962.

"Pleasant Pariah." *Life*, January 24, 1964.

Roylance, D. "Leonard Baskin's Gehenna Press." *Art in America*, November 1966.

Spence, R. "Leonard Baskin." *Art Journal*, Winter 1962.

Werner, A. "Leonard Baskin, Art for Life's Sake." *American Artist*, November 1964.

+LUDWIG BEMELMANS, 1898-1962
author-illustrator

AWARDS

Golden Basket. Newbery Honor Book, 1937.

Madeline. Caldecott Honor Book, 1940.

Madeline's Rescue. Caldecott Medal Book, 1954.

BIBLIOGRAPHY

Are You Hungry, Are You Cold? World, 1960.

At Your Service: The Way of Life in a Hotel. Row, 1941.

*Best of Times: An Account of Europe Revisited. Simon, 1948.

Blue Danube. Viking, 1937.

Bonne Table; edited by Donald and Eleanor Friede. Simon, 1964.

Castle Number Nine. Viking, 1937.

Dirty Eddie. Viking, 1947.

Donkey Inside. Viking, 1941.

Elephant Cutlet. (Alhambra, California), 1966.

Eye of God. Viking, 1949; *a.k.a. Snow Mountain*. Hamilton, 1950.

*Father, Dear Father. Viking, 1953.

Fifi. Simon, 1940.

Golden Basket. Viking, 1936.

Hansi. Viking, 1934.

Happy Place. Little, 1952.

High World. Harper, 1954.

(ed.) *Holiday in France*. Houghton, 1957.

Hotel Bemelmans. Viking, 1946.

Hotel Splendide. Viking, 1939.

How to Have Europe All to Yourself. European Travel Commission, 1960.

How to Travel Incognito. Little, 1952.

I Love You, I Love You, I Love You. Viking, 1942.

Italian Holiday. Houghton, 1961.

Life Class. Viking, 1938.

Literary Life and the Hell with It; by Whit Burnett. Harper, 1939.

Luchow's German Cookbook: The Story and the Favorite Dishes of America's Most Famous German Restaurant; by Leonard J. Mitchell. Doubleday, 1952.

Madeline. Viking, 1939.

Madeline and the Bad Hat. Viking, 1957.

Madeline and the Gypsies. Viking, 1959.

Madeline in London. Viking, 1961.

Madeline's Christmas in Texas. Neiman-Marcus, 1955.

Madeline's Rescue. Viking, 1953.

Marina. Harper, 1962.

*My Life in Art. Harper, 1958.

My War with the United States. Viking, 1937.

Noodle; by Munro Leaf. Stokes, 1937.

Now I Lay Me Down to Sleep. Viking, 1943.

On Board Noah's Ark. Viking, 1962.

Parsley. Harper, 1955.

Quito Express. Viking, 1938.

Rosebud. Random, 1942.

Small Bear. Putnam, 1939.

Street Where the Heart Lies. World, 1963.

Sunshine: A Story about the City of New York. Simon, 1950.

Tale of Two Glimps. Columbia Broadcasting System, 1947.

To the One I Love Best. Viking, 1955.

Welcome Home! After a Poem by Beverly Bogert. Harper, 1960.

Woman of My Life. Viking, 1957.

World of Bemelmans: An Omnibus. Viking, 1955.

MEDIA

Blue Danube. (TB).

Castle Number Nine in *Madeline and the Gypsies and Other Stories*, below.

Donkey Inside. (BB).

Father, Dear Father. (BB, TB).

Fifi. (TB); also in *Ten Stories for the Youngest* (TB).

Hansi. (BB).

Happy Place in *Madeline and Other Bemelmans*, below.

High World. (BB, TB).

Hotel Bemelmans. (TB).

Hotel Splendide. (TB).

How to Travel Incognito. (TB).

I Love You. (TB).

Madeline. (TB); United Productions of America, 1955 (F); Viking Press, 1975 (C); also in *Ten Stories for the Youngest* (TB); also in *Madeline and Other Bemelmans*, below.

Madeline and Other Bemelmans. Caedmon, 1959 (C, R). (Includes *Happy Place*, *Madeline*, *Madeline and the Bad Hat*, and *Madeline's Rescue*.)

Madeline and the Bad Hat. (TB); Rembrandt Films/Kratky Films, 1960 (F); also in *Madeline and Other Bemelmans*, above.

Madeline and the Gypsies. Rembrandt Films/Kratky Films, 1960 (F); also in *Madeline and the Gypsies and Other Stories by Ludwig Bemelmans*, below.

Madeline and the Gypsies and Other Stories by Ludwig Bemelmans. Caedmon, n. d. (R). (Includes *Castle Number Nine*, *Madeline and the Gypsies*, *Madeline in London*, and *Quito Express*.)

Madeline in London in *Madeline and the Gypsies and Other Stories by Ludwig Bemelmans*, above.

Madeline's Rescue. (TB); Rembrandt Films/Kratky Films, 196? (F); Weston Woods Studios, 1960 (FSS); also in Weston Woods Studios Set No. 8, 1965 (FSS); also in *Madeline and Other Bemelmans*, above.

Now I Lay Me Down to Sleep. (TB).

On Board Noah's Ark. (BB).

Parsley. (TB); also in *Ten Stories for the Youngest* (TB).

Quito Express in *Madeline and the Gypsies and Other Stories by Ludwig Bemelmans*, above.

Street Where the Heart Lies. (BB).

Sunshine. Macmillan Films, n. d. (F).

To the One I Love Best. (BB).

EXHIBITIONS

Feragil Gallery, 1950-53. (New York, New York).

Hammer Gallery, 1955-56, 1958-59, 1961, 1964. (New York, New York).

COLLECTIONS

Central Children's Room, Donnell Library Center, New York Public Library. (New York, New York).

Dana Library, Rutgers University. (Newark, New Jersey).

Gary Public Library. (Gary, Indiana).

May Massee Collection, Emporia State College. (Emporia, Kansas).

Milwaukee Public Library. (Milwaukee, Wisconsin).

Special Collections, University Research Library, University of California. (Los Angeles, California).

BACKGROUND READING

Bader. *American Picturebooks from Noah's Ark to The Beast Within*.

Bemelmans, L. "Birth of Madeline." *Junior Bookshelf*, December 1954.

Burke. *American Authors and Books, 1640 to the Present Day*.

Contemporary Authors.

Current Biography.

Dolbier, M. "Ludwig Bemelmans." *New York Herald Tribune Book Review*, December 15, 1957.

BACKGROUND READING (cont'd)

Doyle. *Who's Who of Children's Literature.*

Fuller. *More Junior Authors.*

Goff, P. "Children's World of Ludwig Bemelmans." *Elementary English*, October 1966.

Graham, M. "Artist's Choice." *Horn Book*, December 1955.

Hoffman. *Authors and Illustrators of Children's Books.*

Hutchens, J. "On an Author." *New York Herald Tribune Book Review*, August 23, 1952.

Kingman. *Illustrators of Children's Books, 1957-1966.*

Kirkpatrick. *Twentieth Century Children's Writers.*

Klemin. *Illustrated Book: Its Art and Craft.*

Kunitz. *Twentieth Century Authors.*

Kunitz. *Twentieth Century Authors, First Supplement.*

Mahony. *Illustrators of Children's Books, 1744-1945.*

Miller. *Caldecott Medal Books, 1938-1957.*

Miller. *Illustrators of Children's Books, 1946-1956.*

Nichols, L. "Talk with Mr. Bemelmans." *New York Times Book Review*, August 30, 1953.

Pitz, H. "Ludwig Bemelmans." *American Artist*, May 1951.

Root, S. "Ludwig Bemelmans and His Books for Children." *Elementary English*, January 1957.

Smaridge. *Famous Author-Illustrators for Young People.*

"Story of Bemelmans' Madeline." *Publishers Weekly*, November 14, 1960.

Ward. *Authors of Books for Young People, Second Edition.*

Ward. *Illustrators of Books for Young People, Second Edition.*

Warfel. *American Novelists of Today.*

Young Wings. *Writing Books for Boys and Girls.*

+JOHN BENNETT, 1865-1956
author-illustrator

AWARDS

Pigtail of Ah Lee Ben Loo. Newbery Honor Book, 1929.

BIBLIOGRAPHY

Apothecaries' Hall: A Unique Exhibit at the Charleston Museum, an Ancient Drug-Shop Whose Business Survived Plaques, Wars, Great Fires and Earthquakes for One Hundred Forty Years; Its History Including Some Remarks upon the State of Pharmacy and Medicine in Charleston, South Carolina, at the Close of the Eighteenth Century. Charleston Museum, 1923.

Barnaby Lee. il. Reginald Birch. Century, 1897; also il. C. O. Deland, 1902; also il. Henry C. Pitz, 1922.

Blue Jacket, War Chief of the Shawnees, and His Part in Ohio's History. Ross County Historical Society, 1943.

Doctor to the Dead, Grotesque Legends and Folk Tales of Old Charleston. Rinehart, 1946.

Madame Margot: A Grotesque Legend of Old Charleston. Century, 1921.

Master Skylark: A Story of Shakespere's Time. il. Reginald Birch. Century, 1897; also il. Henry C. Pitz, 1922; a.k.a. *Master Skylark: A Story of Shakespeare's Time Prepared for the Use of Elementary Schools in New York City by Anna Lütkenhaus.* Century, 1914; a.k.a. *Master Skylark: A Story of Shakespeare's Time, Adapted by Kathryn Mahoney and Laura Preble.* il. Mary Landrigan. Globe, 1953.

Pigtail of Ah Lee Ben Loo: With Seventeen Other Laughable Tales and 200 Comical Silhouettes. Longmans, 1928.

Songs Which My Youth Sung. Daggett, 1914.

Treasure of Peyre Gaillard: Being an Account of the Recovery, on a South Carolina Plantation, of a Treasure, Which Had Remained Buried and Lost in a Vast Swamp for over a Hundred Years; After the Ms. Narrative by Buck Buignard, Esq. Century, 1906.

MEDIA

Barnaby Lee. (BB).

Master Skylark. (BB).

COLLECTIONS

Charleston Library Society. (Charleston, South Carolina).

Cooper Library, University of South Carolina. (Columbia, South Carolina).

Perkins Library, Duke University. (Durham, South Carolina).

South Carolina Historical Society. (Charleston, South Carolina).

BACKGROUND READING

Bennett, M. "Youth in Pleasant Places." *Horn Book*, June 1960.

Commire. *Yesterday's Authors of Books for Children.*

Coyle. *Ohio Authors and Their Books.*

Current Biography.

Hart. *Oxford Companion to American Literature, Fourth Edition*.

Kunitz. *Junior Book of Authors*.

Kunitz. *Junior Book of Authors, Second Edition Revised*.

Mahony. *Contemporary Illustrators of Children's Books*.

Mahony. *Illustrators of Children's Books, 1744-1945*.

Smith, J. "Author for Children in the South." *Horn Book*, March 1942.

Smith, J. "John Bennett of Chillicothe." *Horn Book*, January 1943.

+ERICK BERRY, *pseudonym,* 1892-1974
author-illustrator

a.k.a. Evangel Allena Champlin Best,

and as

Ann Maxon, *pseudonym*

AWARDS

(*Apprentice of Florence*. Newbery Honor Book, 1934.)

(*Garram the Hunter*. Newbery Honor Book, 1931.)

Winged Girl of Knossos. Newbery Honor Book, 1934.

BIBLIOGRAPHY

as Erick Berry:

Apprentice of Florence; by Anne D. Kyle. Houghton, 1933.

Araminta; by Eva K. Evans. Minton, 1935.

Araminta's Goat; by Eva K. Evans. Putnam, 1938.

Beckoning Landfall. Day, 1959

Black Folk Tales: Retold from the Haussa of Northern Nigeria, West Africa. Harper, 1928.

Blueberry Muffin; by Mary Thompson. Longmans, 1942.

Border Iron; by Herbert Best. Viking, 1945.

Box of Daylight; by William Hillyer. Knopf, 1931.

Camp at Westlands; by Marjorie H. Allee. Houghton, 1941.

Careers of Cynthia. il. Ruth King. Harcourt, 1932.

Cat Had Nine Lives: Adventures and Reminiscences; by Achmed Abdullah. Farrar, 1933.

Chang of the Siamese Jungle; by Elizabeth Morse. Dutton, 1933.

Charles Proteus Steinmetz: Wizard of Electricity. il. John Martinez. Macmillan, 1966.

Circus ABC; by Dixie Willson. Stokes, 1924.

Circus Comes to Town; by Veronica Hutchinson. Minton, 1932.

Clown Town; by Dixie Willson. Doubleday, 1924.

Concertina Farm; with Herbert Best. Joseph, 1943.

Country of the Dwarfs; by Paul DuChaillu. Harper, 1928.

Cynthia Steps Out. Goldsmith, 1937.

Dragon Fly of Zuñi; by Alida S. Malkus. Harcourt, 1928.

Eating and Cooking around the World: Fingers before Forks. Day, 1963.

Etiquette, Jr.; by Margery Clark, *pseud.* (Mary E. Clark and Margery C. Quigley). Doubleday, 1926.

Father's Gone a-Whaling; by Alice C. Gardiner and Nancy C. Osborne. Doubleday, 1926.

Fiddle Away; by May Justus. Grosset, 1942.

Fifth for the King: A Story of the Conquest of Yucatan and the Discovery of the Amazon; by Alida S. Malkus. Harper, 1931.

Flag of the Desert; by Herbert Best. Viking, 1936.

Forty-seven Keys. Macmillan, 1949.

Four Londons of William Hogarth. il. William Hogarth engravings. McKay, 1964.

Garram the Chief: The Story of the Hill Tribes; by Herbert Best. Doubleday, 1932.

Garram the Hunter: A Boy of the Hill Tribes; by Herbert Best. Doubleday, 1930.

Girls in Africa. Macmillan, 1928.

Go and Find Wind. Oxford, 1939.

Green Door to the Sea. Viking, 1955.

Gunsmith's Boy; by Herbert Best. Winston, 1942.

Harvest of the Hudson. Macmillan, 1945.

Hay-Foot, Straw-Foot. Viking, 1954.

Hearthstone in the Wilderness. Macmillan, 1944.

Homespun. il. Harold von Schmidt. Lothrop, 1937.

Honey of the Nile. Oxford, 1938; revised, Viking, 1963.

Horses for the General. Macmillan, 1956.

House in No-End Hollow; by May Justus. Doubleday, 1938.

Hudson Frontier. Oxford, 1942.

Humbo the Hippo. Grosset, 1938.

Humbo the Hippo and Little-Boy Bumbo. Harper, 1932.

BIBLIOGRAPHY (cont'd)

as Erick Berry (cont'd)

Illustrations of Cynthia: A Story of Art School. il. Ruth King. Harcourt, 1931.

Jerome Anthony; by Eva K. Evans. Putnam, 1936.

Juma of the Hills: A Story of West Africa. Harcourt, 1932.

Key Corner; by Eva K. Evans. Putnam, 1938.

King's Jewel. il. Frederick T. Chapman. Viking, 1957.

Land and People of Finland. Lippincott, 1959; revised, 1972.

Land and People of Iceland. Lippincott, 1959; revised, 1972.

Leif the Lucky: Discoverer of America. il. William Plummer. Garrard, 1961.

Little Brown Baby: Poems for Young People; by Paul L. Dunbar with biographical sketch by Bertha Rodgers. Dodd, 1940.

Little Cumsee in Dixie; by Halsa A. Kyser. Longmans, 1938.

Little Farm in the Big City. Viking, 1947.

Little Henry and the Tiger; by Felicite LeFèvre, pseud. (Margaret Smith-Masters). Harper, 1931.

Little Men; by Louisa M. Alcott. Harper, 1933.

Lock Her Through. Oxford, 1940.

Long Portage: A Story of Ticonderoga and Lord Howe; by Herbert Best. Viking, 1948; *a.k.a. Road to Ticonderoga: Or, The Long Portage*. Penguin, 1954.

Lost in the Jungle; by Paul DuChaillu. Harper, 1928.

Mad Dogs and Englishmen. Joseph, 1941.

Magic Banana and Other Polynesian Tales. il. Nicholas Amorosi. Day, 1968.

Men, Moss and Reindeer: The Challenge of Lapland. il. Wes McKeown. Coward, 1955.

Men Who Changed the Map, AD 400-1914; with Herbert Best. il. Lazlo Matulay. Funk, 1968.

Mr. Arctic: An Account of Vilhajalmur Stefansson. McKay, 1966.

Mr. Jones and Mr. Finnigan; by Eva K. Evans. Oxford, 1941.

Mom du Jos: The Story of a Little Black Doll. Doubleday, 1931.

My Apingi Kingdom: With Life in the Great Sahara; by Paul DuChaillu. Harper, 1928.

My Book of Parties; by Madeline Snyder. Doubleday, 1928.

Mystery of the Flaming Hut; by Herbert Best. Harper, 1932.

Nancy Herself. Goldsmith, 1937.

Nancy Sails; by Mildred Wasson. Harper, 1936.

Not without Danger: A Story of the Colony of Jamaica in Revolutionary Days. Viking, 1951.

One-String Fiddle. Music by Lillian Webster, Winston, 1939.

Penny-Whistle. Macmillan, 1930.

Pilgrim Goose; by Keith Robertson. Viking, 1956.

Polynesian Triangle; with Herbert Best. Funk, 1968.

Potter's Wheel. Nelson, 1939.

Pretty Little Doll. Oxford, 1946.

Princess Comes to Our Town; by Rose Fyleman. Doubleday, 1928.

Ranger's Ransom: A Story of Ticonderoga; by Herbert Best. Aladdin, 1953.

Road Runs Both Ways. Macmillan, 1950.

Robert E. Peary: North Pole Conqueror. il. Frederick T. Chapman, Garrard, 1963.

Seven Beaver Skins: A Story of the Dutch in New Amsterdam. Winston, 1948.

Shipment for Susannah; by Eleanor Nolan. Nelson, 1938.

Sojo: The Story of Little Lazy-Bones. Harper, 1934.

Son of the White Man; by Herbert Best. Doubleday, 1931.

Spindle Imp and Other Tales of Maya Myth and Folklore; by Alida S. Malkus. Harcourt, 1931.

Springing of the Rice: A Story of Thailand. il. John Kaufman. Macmillan, 1966.

Stars in My Pocket: Based on Events in the Life of Maria Mitchell, America's First Woman Astronomer. Day, 1960.

Stories of the Gorilla Country; by Paul DuChaillu. Harper, 1928.

Strings to Adventure. Lothrop, 1935.

Sunhelmet Sue. Lothrop, 1936.

Sybil Ludington's Ride. Viking, 1952.

Tal of the Four Tribes; by Herbert Best. Doubleday, 1938.

There Is the Land. Oxford, 1943.

Tinmaker Man of New Amsterdam. Music by Nelson Sprackling. Winston, 1941.

Underwater Warriors: Story of the American Frogmen. McKay, 1967.

Valiant Captive: A Story of Margaret Eames, Captured in 1676 by the Indians, from the New Settlement, Which Later Became Framingham, Massachusetts. Chilton, 1962.

Valiant Little Potter, Retold. il. Nahid Haghighat. Ginn, 1973.

Watergate: A Story of the Irish and the Erie Canal;
by Herbert Best. Winston, 1951.

Wavering Flame: Connecticut, 1776. Scribner, 1953.

When Wagon Trains Rolled to Santa Fe. il. Charles
Waterhouse. Garrard, 1966.

Whistle Round the Bend. Oxford, 1941.

White Heron Feather; by Gertrude Robinson. Harper,
1930.

Wild Life under the Equator; by Paul DuChaillu.
Harper, 1928.

Winged Girl of Knossos. Appleton, 1933.

World Explorer: Fridtjof Nansen. il. William
Hutchinson. Garrard, 1969.

Writing for Children; with Herbert Best. Viking,
1947; second edition, University of Miami, 1964.

*You Have to Go Out! The Story of the U.S. Coast
Guard*. McKay, 1964.

Your Cup and Saucer. Nelson, 1938.

as Anne Maxon:

House That Jill Built. Dodd, 1934.

MEDIA

Hay-Foot, Straw-Foot. (BB).

Magic Banana and Other Polynesian Tales as *South Sea
Island Tales*. Caedmon, 1974 (R).

One-String Fiddle. RCA Victor, n. d. (R).

Penny Whistle. Young People's Records, n. d. (R).

Sybil Ludington's Ride. (BB).

Valiant Captive. (BB).

Writing for Children. (BB).

COLLECTIONS

deGrummond Collection, University of Southern
Mississippi. (Hattiesburg, Mississippi).

May Massee Collection, Emporia State College.
(Emporia, Kansas).

University of Oregon. (Eugene, Oregon).

BACKGROUND READING

Berry, E. "Collaborating with Herbert Best." *Horn
Book*, July 1938.

Commire. *Something about the Author*.

Contemporary Authors.

"Interview with a Famous Author." *Instructor*,
November 1950.

Kunitz. *Junior Book of Authors*.

Kunitz. *Junior Book of Authors, Second Edition
Revised*.

Mahony. *Contemporary Illustrators of Children's
Books*.

Mahony. *Illustrators of Children's Books, 1744-1945*.

Malkus, A. "Erick Berry and Her Books." *Horn Book*,
January 1939.

Miller. *Illustrators of Children's Books, 1946-1956*.

Ward. *Authors of Books for Young People, Second
Edition*.

Young Wings. *Writing Books for Boys and Girls*.

+ HERBERT BEST, 1894-
author
a.k.a. Oswald Herbert Best

AWARDS

Garram the Hunter. Newbery Honor Book, 1931.

BIBLIOGRAPHY

Border Iron. il. Erick Berry, *pseud*. (Evangel A. C.
Best). Viking, 1945.

Bright Hunter of the Skies. il. Bernarda Bryson.
Macmillan, 1961.

Carolina Gold. Day, 1961.

Columbus Canon. Viking, 1954.

Concertina Farm; with Erick Berry, *pseud*. (Evangel
A. C. Best). Joseph, 1943.

Desmond and Dog Friday. il. Witold T. Mars. Viking,
1968.

*Desmond and the Peppermint Ghost: The Dog Detec-
tive's Third Case*. il. Lilian Obligado. Viking, 1962.

*Desmond the Dog Detective: The Case of the Lone
Stranger*. il. Lilian Obligado. Viking, 1962.

Desmond's First Case. il. Ezra J. Keats. Viking, 1961.

Diane. Morrow, 1954.

Flag of the Desert. il. Erick Berry, *pseud*. (Evangel
A. C. Best). Viking, 1936.

Garram the Chief: The Story of the Hill Tribes. il.
Erick Berry, *pseud*. (Evangel A. C. Best). Doubleday, 1932.

Garram the Hunter: A Boy of the Hill Tribes. il. Erick
Berry, *pseud*. (Evangel A. C. Best). Doubleday,
1930.

Gunsmith's Boy. il. Erick Berry, *pseud*. (Evangel A. C.
Best). Winston, 1942.

BIBLIOGRAPHY (cont'd)

Long Portage: A Story of Ticonderoga and Lord Howe. il. Erick Berry, *pseud.* (Evangel A. C. Best). Viking, 1948; *a.k.a. Road to Ticonderoga: Or, The Long Portage.* Penguin, 1954.

Low River. Hurst, 1937.

Men Who Changed the Map, AD 400-1944; with Erick Berry, *pseud.* (Evangel A. C. Best). il. Lazlo Matualy. Funk, 1968.

Mystery of the Flaming Hut. il. Erick Berry, *pseud.* (Evangel A. C. Best). Harper, 1932.

Not without Danger: A Story of the Colony of Jamaica in Revolutionary Days. il. Erick Berry, *pseud.* (Evangel A. C. Best). Viking, 1951.

Parachute to Survival. Day, 1964.

Polynesian Triangle; with Erick Berry, *pseud.* (Evangel A. C. Best). Funk, 1968.

Ranger's Ransom: A Story of Ticonderoga. il. Erick Berry, *pseud.* (Evangel A. C. Best). Aladdin, 1953.

Rumor of Drums. McKay, 1963; *a.k.a. Rumour of Drums.* Cassell, 1962.

Sea Warriors. Macmillan, 1959.

Skull beneath the Eaves. Grayson, 1933.

Son of the White Man. il. Erick Berry, *pseud.* (Evangel A. C. Best). Doubleday, 1931.

Tal of the Four Tribes. il. Erick Berry, *pseud.* (Evangel A. C. Best). Doubleday, 1938.

Twenty-fifth Hour. Random, 1940.

Watergate: A Story of the Irish on the Erie Canal. il. Erick Berry, *pseud.* (Evangel A. C. Best). Winston, 1951.

Webfoot Warriors: The Story of the UDT, the U.S. Navy's Underwater Demolition Team. Day, 1962.

Whistle, Daughter, Whistle. Macmillan, 1947.

Winds Whisper. Hurst, 1937.

Writing for Children; with Erick Berry, *pseud.* (Evangel A. C. Best). Viking, 1947; second edition, University of Miami, 1964.

Young'un. Macmillan, 1944.

MEDIA

Columbus Canon. (BB).

Desmond the Dog Detective. (BB).

Rumor of Drums. (BB).

Whistle, Daughter, Whistle. (BB).

Writing for Children. (BB).

Young'un. (TB).

COLLECTIONS

deGrummond Collection, University of Southern Mississippi. (Hattiesburg, Mississippi).

University of Oregon. (Eugene, Oregon).

BACKGROUND READING

Berry, E. "Collaborating with Herbert Best." *Horn Book*, July 1938.

Burke. *American Authors and Books, 1640 to the Present Day.*

Commire. *Something about the Author.*

Contemporary Authors.

"Interview with a Famous Author." *Instructor*, November 1950.

Kirkpatrick. *Twentieth Century Children's Writers.*

Kunitz. *Junior Book of Authors.*

Kunitz. *Junior Book of Authors, Second Edition Revised.*

Ward. *Authors of Books for Young People, Second Edition.*

Warfel. *American Novelists of Today.*

Young Wings. *Writing Books for Boys and Girls.*

+CATHERINE BESTERMAN, 1908-
author

AWARDS

Quaint and Curious Education of Johnny Longfoot. Newbery Honor Book, 1948.

BIBLIOGRAPHY

Extraordinary Education of Johnny Longfoot in His Search for the Magic Hat. il. Warren Chappell. Bobbs, 1949.

Quaint and Curious Education of Johnny Longfoot, the Shoe King's Son. il. Warren Chappell. Bobbs, 1947.

MARGERY WILLIAMS BIANCO, 1881-1944
author
a.k.a. Margery Williams

AWARDS

Winterbound. Newbery Honor Book, 1937.

BIBLIOGRAPHY

as Margery Williams Bianco:

Adventures of Andy. il. Leon Underwood. Doran, 1927.

(tr.) *African Saga*; by Blaise Cendrars. Payson, 1927.

All about Pets. il. Grace Gilkinson. Macmillan, 1929.

Apple Tree. il. Boris Artzybasheff. Doran, 1926.

Bright Morning. il. Margaret Platt. Viking, 1942.

Candlestick. il. Ludovic Rodo. Doubleday, 1929.

Comprehension Cards. Nisbet, 1959. (24 vols.).

Five-and-a-Half Club; with Mabel O'Donnell. il. Margaret Ayer. Row, 1942.

Forward, Commandos! il. Rafaello Busoni. Viking, 1944.

(tr.) *Four Cents an Acre: The Story of Louisiana under the French*; by Georges Oudard. Brewer, 1931.

Franzi and Gigi. il. Gisella Loffler. Messner, 1941.

Good Friends. il. Grace Paull. Viking, 1934.

Green Grows the Garden. il. Grace Paull. Macmillan, 1936.

Herbert's Zoo and Other Favorite Stories. il. Julian. Simon, 1949.

House That Grew Smaller. il. Rachel Field. Macmillan, 1931.

Hurdy-Gurdy Man. il. Robert Lawson. Oxford, 1933.

(tr.) *Juniper Farm*; by Réné Bazin. il. Anne M. Peck. Macmillan, 1928.

(tr.) *Little Black Stories for Little While Children*; by Blaise Cendrars. il. Pierre Pinsard. Payson, 1929.

Little Wooden Doll. il. Pamela Bianco. Macmillan, 1925.

More about Animals. il. Helen Torrey. Macmillan, 1934.

New Five-and-a-Half Club; with Mabel O'Donnell. il. Margaret Ayer. Row, 1951.

Other People's Houses. Viking, 1939.

Out of the Night: A Mystery Comedy; with Harold Hutchinson. French, 1929.

Penny and the White Horse; with Marjory Collison. Messner, 1942.

Poor Cecco: The Wonderful Story of a Wonderful Wooden Dog Who Was the Jolliest Toy in the House until He Went Out to Explore the World. il. Arthur Rackham. Doran, 1925; also il. Anthony Maitland. Deutsch, 1973.

Rufus the Fox: Adapted from the French of Samivel. Harper, 1937.

Seven Silly Wise Men; with James C. Bowman. il. John Faulkner. Tr. Aili Kolehamainen. Whitman, 1964.

(tr.) *Sidsel Longskirt: A Girl of Norway*; with Dagny Mortensen; by Hans Aanrud. il. Edgar Parin and Ingri D'Aulaire. Winston, 1935; *a.k.a. Sidsel Longskirt and Solve Suntrap: Two Children of Norway*, 1935.

Skin Horse. il. Pamela Bianco. Doran, 1927.

(tr.) *Solve Suntrap: A Boy of Norway*; with Dagny Mortensen; by Hans Aanrud. il. Edgar Parin and Ingri D'Aulaire. Winston, 1935; *a.k.a. Sidsel Long- skirt and Solve Suntrap: Two Children of Norway*, 1935.

Street of Little Shops. il. Grace Paull. Doubleday, 1932.

Tales from a Finnish Tupa; with James C. Bowman. il. Laura Bannon. Tr. Aili Kolehamainen. Whitman, 1936.

Who Was Tricked?; with James C. Bowman. il. John Faulkner. Tr. Aili Kolehamainen. Whitman, 1964.

Winterbound. il. Kate Seredy. Viking, 1936.

as Margery Williams:

And New York. il. Allan Stewart. Macmillan, 1910.

Bar. Methuen, 1906.

Late Returning. Macmillan, 1902.

Paris: Peeps at Great Cities. il. Allan Stewart. Black, 1910.

Price of Youth. Macmillan, 1904.

Spendthrift Summer. Heineman, 1903.

Thing in the Woods. Duckworth, 1913.

Velveteen Rabbit: Or, How Toys Become Real. il. William Nicholson. Doran, 1922; also il. Marie Angel. Press of A. Colish, 1974.

MEDIA

Little Wooden Doll. (BB).

Street of Little Shops. (BB).

Tales from a Finnish Tupa. (TB).

Velveteen Rabbit. (BB, TB); LSB Productions, 1974 (F); Miller-Brody Productions, 1976 (FSS).

Who Was Tricked? Educational Enrichment Materials, 1969 (FSS).

Winterbound. (BB).

BACKGROUND READING

Bechtel, L. "Tribute to Margery Bianco." *Elementary English*, June 1935.

Burke. *American Authors and Books, 1640 to the Present Day*.

Doyle. *Who's Who of Children's Literature*.

Kirkpatrick. *Twentieth Century Children's Writers*.

Kunitz. *Junior Book of Authors*.

Kunitz. *Junior Book of Authors, Second Edition Revised*.

Kunitz. *Living Authors*.

BACKGROUND READING (cont'd)

Moore, Anne C., and Mahony, Bertha E. *Writing and Criticism: A Book for Margery Bianco*. il. Valenti Angelo. Horn Book, 1951.

Ward. *Authors of Books for Young People, Second Edition*.

Young Wings. *Writing Books for Boys and Girls*.

+MARVIN BILECK, 1920-
illustrator

AWARDS

Rain Makes Applesauce. Caldecott Honor Book, 1965.

BIBLIOGRAPHY

All about the Stars; by Anne T. White. Random, 1954.

Crissy at the Wheel; by Mildred Lawrence. Harcourt, 1952.

Nipper Shiffer's Donkey; by Fingel von Sudorf, *pseud*. (Fingel Rosenquist). Harper, 1955.

Nobody's Birthday; by Anne Colver. Knopf, 1961.

Penny; by Beatrice S. deRegniers. Viking, 1966.

Penny That Rolled Away; by Louis Malone, *pseud*. (Louis MacNiece). Putnam, 1954.

Rain Makes Applesauce; by Julian Scheer. Holiday, 1964.

Sugarplum; by Johanna Johnston. Knopf, 1955.

Timi: A Tale of a Griffin; by Barbara Freeman. Grosset, 1970.

Walker in the City; by Alfred Kazin. Harcourt, 1968.

BACKGROUND READING

Bader. *American Picturebooks from Noah's Ark to The Beast Within*.

DeMontreville. *Third Book of Junior Authors*.

Kingman. *Illustrators of Children's Books, 1957-1966*.

Miller. *Illustrators of Children's Books, 1946-1956*.

Ward. *Illustrators of Books for Young People, Second Edition*.

ABE BIRNBAUM, 1899-1966
author-illustrator

AWARDS

Green Eyes. Caldecott Honor Book, 1954.

BIBLIOGRAPHY

Did a Bear Just Walk There?; by Ann Rand. Harcourt, 1966.

Green Eyes. Capitol, 1953.

Supposing; by Alastair Reid. Atlantic, 1960.

MEDIA

Green Eyes. (CB); Bank Street College of Education, 1967 (F); Western Publishing Company, 1972 (FSS).

BACKGROUND READING

Obituary. *New York Times*, June 20, 1966.

Obituary. *New Yorker*, July 2, 1966.

Obituary. *Newsweek*, July 4, 1966.

CLAIRE HUCHET BISHOP
author
a.k.a. Claire Huchet

AWARDS

All Alone. Newbery Honor Book, 1954.

Pancakes-Paris. Newbery Honor Book, 1948.

BIBLIOGRAPHY

as Claire Huchet Bishop:

All Alone. il. Feodor Rojankovsky. Viking, 1953.

All Things Common. Harper, 1950.

Augustus. il. Grace Paull. Viking, 1945.

Bernard and His Dogs. il. Maurice Brevannes. Houghton, 1952.

Big Loop. il. Charles Fontseré. Viking, 1955; large print edition, Thorpe, 1965.

Blue Spring Farm. Viking, 1948.

Christopher, the Giant. il. Berkeley Williams, Jr. Houghton, 1950.

Ferryman. il. Kurt Wiese. Coward, 1941.

Five Chinese Brothers. il. Kurt Wiese. Coward, 1938; *a.k.a. Cinq Frères Chinois*, 1960; *a.k.a. Fiev Chienees Bruthers*. Scholastic, 1965.

France Alive. McMullen, 1947.

French Children's Books for English Speaking Children: A Unique Descriptive List of French Books Which English Speaking Boys and Girls with a Very Elementary Knowledge of French, or Even No Knowledge At All, May Enjoy: Prepared to

Assist Children, Parents, Teachers, and Librarians in Selecting Interesting Books for a Beginner's Collection. Sheridan Square, 1938.

French Roundabout. Dodd, 1960; revised, 1966.

Georgette. il. Ursula Landshoff. Coward, 1973.

(ed.) *Happy Christmas, Tales for Boys and Girls.* il. Ellen Raskin. Daye, 1956.

(ed.) *Has Anti-Semitism Roots in Christianity?*; by Jules Isaac. Tr. D. Parkes. National Conference of Christians and Jews, 19?.

Here is France. Farrar, 1969.

How Catholics Look at Jews: Inquiries into Italian, Spanish and French Teaching Materials. Paulist, 1974.

(ed.) *Jesus and Israel*; by Jules Isaac. Tr. Sally Gran. Holt, 1971.

Johann Sebastian Bach, Music Giant. il. Russell Hoover. Garrard, 1972.

King's Day. il. Doris Speigel. Coward, 1940.

Lafayette: French-American Hero. il. Maurice Brevannes. Garrard, 1960.

Man Who Lost His Head. il. Robert McCloskey. Viking, 1942.

Martin de Porrés, Hero. il. Jean Charlot. Houghton, 1954.

Mozart, Music Magician. il. Paul Frame. Garrard, 1968.

Pancakes-Paris. il. Georges Schreiber. Viking, 1947.

Present from Petros. il. Dimitri Davis. Viking, 1961.

(ed.) *Teaching of Contempt*; by Jules Isaac. Tr. Helen Weaver. Holt, *ca.*1971.

Toto's Triumph. il. Claude Ponsot. Viking, 1957.

Truffle Pig. il. Kurt Wiese. Coward, 1971.

Twenty and Ten, as Told by Janet Joly. il. William P. du Bois. Viking, 1952.

Twenty-two Bears. il. Kurt Wiese. Viking, 1964.

as Claire Huchet:

Yeshu, Called Jesus. il. Don Bolognese. Farrar, 1966.

MEDIA

All Alone. (BB).

Big Loop. (BB).

Five Chinese Brothers. (BB, TB); Weston Woods Studios, 1958 (F), 19? (FSS); also in Weston Woods Studios Set No. 5, 1965 (FSS); *a.k.a. Cinq Frères Chinos.* Weston Woods Studios, 1960 (F); *a.k.a. Cinco Hermanos Chinos.* Weston Woods Studios, 1960 (F).

Happy Christmas. (BB, TB).

Johann Sebastian Bach. (TB).

Man Who Lost His Head. (BB).

Martin de Porrés. (BB).

Mozart. (TB).

Pancakes-Paris. (BB).

Toto's Triumph. (TB).

Truffle Pig. (TB).

Twenty and Ten. (BB).

COLLECTIONS

May Massee Collection, Emporia State College. (Emporia, Kansas).

BACKGROUND READING

Commire. *Something about the Author.*

Contemporary Authors.

Hopkins. *Books Are by People.*

Kirkpatrick. *Twentieth Century Children's Writers.*

Kunitz. *Junior Book of Authors, Second Edition Revised.*

Montgomery. *Story behind Modern Books.*

Smaridge. *Famous Modern Storytellers for Young People.*

Ward. *Authors of Books for Young People, Second Edition.*

NANCY BARBARA BOND, 1945-
author

AWARDS

String in the Harp. Newbery Honor Book, 1977.

BIBLIOGRAPHY

String in the Harp. Atheneum, 1976.

BACKGROUND READING

Contemporary Authors.

+ARNA WENDELL BONTEMPS, 1902-1973
author

AWARDS

Story of the Negro. Newbery Honor Book, 1949.

BIBLIOGRAPHY

American Missionary Archives in Fisk University Library. (Nashville, Tennessee), 1947.

American Negro Heritage; with others. Century Schoolbook, 1965.

(ed.) *American Negro Poetry*. Hill, 1964; revised, 1974.

Black Thunder. Macmillan, 1936.

Book of Negro Folklore; with Langston Hughes. Dodd, 1958.

Chariot in the Sky: A Story of the Jubilee Singers. il. Cyrus L. Baldridge. Winston, 1951.

Drums at Dusk. il. Margenta. Macmillan, 1939.

Famous Negro Athletes. Dodd, 1964.

Fast Sooner Hound; with Jack Conroy. il. Virginia L. Burton. Houghton, 1942.

(ed.) *Father of the Blues: An Autobiography*; by William C. Handy. Macmillan, 1941.

(ed.) *Five Black Lives: The Autobiographies of Venture Smith, James Mars, William Grimes, G. W. Offley, James L. Smith*. Wesleyan University, 1971.

Frederick Douglass: Slave, Fighter, Freeman. il. Harper Johnson. Knopf, 1958.

Free and Easy; with Countee Cullen. n. p., 1949.

Free At Last: The Life of Frederick Douglass. Dodd, 1971.

George Washington Carver. il. Cleveland L. Woodward. Row, 1950.

God Sends Sunday. Harcourt, 1931; *a.k.a. St. Louis Woman*; with Countee Cullen. n. p., 1946.

(comp.) *Golden Slippers: An Anthology of Negro Poetry for Young Readers*. il. Henrietta B. Sharon. Harper, 1941.

(comp.) *Great Slave Narratives*. Beacon, 1969.

Harlem Renaissance Remembered, Essays: Edited, with a Memoir. Dodd, 1972.

(ed.) *Hold Fast to Dreams: Poems Old and New*. Follett, 1969.

Lonesome Boy. il. Feliks Topolski. Houghton, 1955.

Mr. Kelso's Lion. il. Len Ebert. Lippincott, 1970.

Old South, A Summer Tragedy, and Other Stories of the Thirties. Dodd, 1973.

100 Years of Negro Freedom. Dodd, 1961.

Personals. Bremen, 1963; second edition, 1973.

Poetry of the Negro, 1746-1949: An Anthology; with Langston Hughes. Doubleday, 1949; revised, 1967.

Popo and Fifina: Children of Haiti; with Langston Hughes. il. E. Simms Campbell. Macmillan, 1932.

Sad-faced Boy. il. Virginia L. Burton. Houghton, 1937.

Sam Patch: The High, Wide and Handsome Jumper; with Jack Conroy. il. Paul Brown. Houghton, 1951.

Slappy Hooper: The Wonderful Sign Painter; with Jack Conroy. il. Ursula Koering. Houghton, 1946.

Story of George Washington Carver. il. Harper Johnson. Grosset, 1954.

Story of the Negro. il. Raymond Lufkin. Knopf, 1948; second edition, 1950; third edition, 1958; fourth edition, 1964; fifth edition, 1969.

They Seek a City; with Jack Conroy. Doubleday, 1945; revised as *Anyplace but Here*. Hill, 1966.

We Have Tomorrow. il. Marian Palfi. Houghton, 1945.

You Can't Pet a Possum. il. Ilse Bischoff. Morrow, 1934.

Young Booker T. Washington's Early Days. Dodd, 1972.

MEDIA

American Negro Poetry. (C, CB, MT).

Anthology of Negro Poetry for Young People. Folkways Records, 1958 (R).

Anyplace but Here. (TB); also as *They Seek a City*, below.

Bible Stories for Children: In the Beginning. Folkways Records, 1953 (R).

Black Thunder. (C, MT).

Famous Negro Athletes. (BB).

Fast Sooner Hound. (BB).

George Washington Carver. (BB).

Golden Slippers. (BB).

Great Slave Narratives. (C, MT).

Joseph and His Brothers. Folkways Records, 1953 (R).

Lonesome Boy. (BB, TB).

Negro Poets in the U.S.A. (TB).

100 Years of Negro Freedom. (C, MT).

Sad-faced Boy. (TB).

Story of the Negro. (BB).

They Seek a City. (TB); also as *Anyplace but Here*, above.

You Can't Pet a Possum. (BB).

COLLECTIONS

Bontemps and Braithwaite Collections, Arents Research Library, Syracuse University. (Syracuse, New York).

Collection of American Literature, Beinecke Library, Yale University. (New Haven, Connecticut).

BACKGROUND READING

Arna Bontemps. Pathways to Children's Literature, 196? (C); Profiles in Literature, 1971 (VT).

Burke. *American Authors and Books, 1640 to the Present Day*.

Commire. *Something about the Author*.

Contemporary Authors.

Current Biography.

Davis. *From the Dark Tower*.

Dreer. *American Literature by American Negroes*.

Hart. *Oxford Companion to American Literature, Fourth Edition*.

Hopkins. *More Books by More People*.

Kunitz. *Junior Book of Authors, Second Edition Revised*.

New York Times Biographical Edition.

Rider, I. "Arna Bontemps: Sad-faced Author." *Horn Book*, January 1939.

Rollins. *Famous American Negro Poets*.

Rusk. *Black American Writers Past and Present*.

Ward. *Authors of Books for Young People, Second Edition*.

Warfel. *American Novelists of Today*.

+WILLIAM ALVIN BOWEN, 1877-1937
author

AWARDS

Old Tobacco Shop. Newbery Honor Book, 1922.

BIBLIOGRAPHY

Enchanted Forest. il. Maud and Miska Petersham. Macmillan, 1920.

Merrimeg. il. Emma Brock. Macmillan, 1923.

Old Tobacco Shop: A True Account of What Befell a Boy in Search of Adventure. il. Reginald Birch. Macmillan, 1921.

Philip and the Faun. Little, 1926.

Solario the Tailor: His Tales of the Magic Doublet. Macmillan, 1922.

BACKGROUND READING

Obituary. *New York Times*, September 19, 1937.

+JAMES CLOYD BOWMAN, 1880-1961
author

AWARDS

Pecos Bill. Newbery Honor Book, 1938.

BIBLIOGRAPHY

Adventures of Paul Bunyan. Century, 1927.

Composition and Selected Essays, for Normal Schools and Colleges, with J. L. Eason. Harcourt, 1923.

(ed.) *Contemporary American Criticism*. Holt, 1926.

Essays for College English; with others. Heath, 1915 (first series); 1918 (second series).

Gift of White Roses. Pilgrim, 1914.

(ed.) *Inland Voyage, and Travels with a Donkey*; by Robert L. Stevenson. Allyn, 1918.

Into the Depths: (A Story of Protecting) Sympathy, Together with Sixteen Miscellaneous Poems. University, 1905. (Identified as "Jas. C. Bowman.")

John Henry: The Rambling Black Ulysses. il. Roy LaGrone. Whitman, 1942.

Knight of the Chinese Dragon. University Herald, 1913.

Mike Fink, the Snapping Turtle of the O-hi-oo and the Snag of the Mas-sas-sip. il. Leonard E. Fisher. Little, 1957.

Mystery Mountain. il. Lucille Wallower. Whitman, 1940.

On the Des Moines. Cornhill, 1921.

(ed.) *Oregon Trail*; by Francis Parkman. Scribner, 1924.

Pecos Bill: The Greatest Cowboy of All Time. il. Laura E. Bannon. Little, 1937.

Promise of Country Life: Descriptions, Narrations without Plot. Heath, 1916.

Seven Silly Wise Men; with Margery Bianco. il. John Faulkner. Tr. Aili Kolehamainen. Whitman, 1964.

Tales from a Finnish Tupa; with Margery Bianco. il. Laura Bannon. Tr. Aili Kolehamainen. Whitman, 1936.

(ed.) *Walden: Or, a Life in the Woods; Edited for School Use*; by Henry D. Thoreau. Scott, 1922.

When I Write a Theme: A Series of Oral and Written Assignments Based on Models Selected Primarily from the Actual Work of Pupils; with Charles S. Thomas. Ginn, 1930.

Who Was Tricked?; with Margery Bianco. il. John Faulkner. Tr. Aili Kolehamainen. Whitman, 1964.

Winabajo: Master of Life. il. Armstrong Sperry. Whitman, 1941.

MEDIA

Pecos Bill. (BB, TB).

Tales from a Finnish Tupa. (TB).

Who Was Tricked? Educational Enrichment Materials, 1969 (FSS).

COLLECTIONS

Kerlan Collection, University of Minnesota. (Minneapolis, Minnesota).

BACKGROUND READING

Burke. *American Authors and Books, 1640 to the Present Day*.

Coyle. *Ohio Authors and Their Books*.

Kunitz. *Junior Book of Authors, Second Edition Revised*.

Kunitz. *Twentieth Century Authors*.

Obituary. *New York Times*, September 28, 1961.

Ward. *Authors of Books for Young People, Second Edition*.

Young Wings. *Writing Books for Boys and Girls*.

CAROL RYRIE BRINK, 1895-
author

AWARDS

Caddie Woodlawn. Newbery Medal Book, 1936.

BIBLIOGRAPHY

All over Town. il. Dorothy Bayley. Macmillan, 1939.

Andy Buckram's Tin Men. il. Witold T. Mars. Viking, 1966.

Anything Can Happen on the River! il. W. W. Berger. Macmillan, 1934.

Baby Island. il. Helen Sewell. Macmillan, 1937.

Bad Times of Irma Baumlein. il. Trina S. Hyman. *Macmillan, 1972*.

Bellini Look. Bantam, 1976

(comp.) *Best Short Stories for Boys and Girls*. Row, 1936-41.

(comp.) *Best Short Stories for Children*. Row, 1935.

Buffalo Coat. Macmillan, 1944.

Caddie Woodlawn. il. Kate Seredy. Macmillan, 1935; also il. Trina S. Hyman, 1973; also as *Caddie Woodlawn, a Play: A Dramatization of the Newbery Medal Book*, 1945.

Château Saint-Barnabé. il. Marshall Davis. Macmillan, 1963.

Cupboard Was Bare. Eldridge, 1928.

Family Grandstand. il. Jean M. Porter. Viking, 1952.

Family Sabbatical. il. Susan Foster. Viking, 1956.

*Four Girls on a Homestead. Latah County Museum, 1977.

*Harps in the Wind: The Story of the Singing Hutchinsons. Macmillan, 1947.

Headland. Macmillan, 1955.

Highly Trained Dogs of Professor Pettit. il. Robert Henneberger. Macmillan, 1953.

Lad with a Whistle. il. Robert Ball. Macmillan, 1941.

Lafayette. il. Dorothy B. Morse. Row, 1953.

Louly. il. Ingrid Fetz. Macmillan, 1974.

Mademoiselle Misfortune. il. Kate Seredy. Macmillan, 1936.

Magical Melons: More Stories about Caddie Woodlawn. Macmillan, 1944.

Narcissa Whitman: Pioneer to the Oregon Country. il. Samuel Armstrong. Row, 1950.

Pink Motel. il. Sheila Greenwald. Macmillan, 1959.

Queen of Dolls, a Pantomimed Reading. Eldridge, 1928.

Snow in the River. Macmillan, 1964.

Stopover. Macmillan, 1951.

Stranger in the Forest. Macmillan, 1959.

Twin Cities. Macmillan, 1961.

Two Are Better Than One. il. Fermin Rocker. Macmillan, 1968.

Winter Cottage. il. Fermin Rocker. Macmillan, 1968.

MEDIA

Andy Buckram's Tin Men. (BB).

Baby Island. (TB).

Bad Times of Irma Baumlein. (TB).

Caddie Woodlawn. (BB, CB, TB); Miller-Brody Productions, 1972 (FSS).

Caddie Woodlawn, a Play. (BB).

Family Grandstand. (TB).

Family Sabbatical. (BB).

Headland. (BB).

Lafayette. (BB).

Magical Melons. (TB).

Narcissa Whitman. (BB).

Snow in the River. (BB).

Stranger in the Forest. (BB, TB).

COLLECTIONS

deGrummond Collection, University of Southern Mississippi. (Hattiesburg, Mississippi).

Kerlan Collection, University of Monnesota. (Minneapolis, Minnesota).

University of Idaho Library. (Moscow, Idaho).

BACKGROUND READING

Brink, C. "Remarks on Caddie Woodlawn." *ALA Bulletin*, August 1936.

Buchheimer, N. "Magical Caddie." *Elementary English*, February 1953.

Burke. *American Authors and Books, 1640 to the Present Day*.

Commire. *Something about the Author*.

Contemporary Authors.

Current Biography.

Hadlow, R. "Caddlie Woodlawn." *Elementary English*, April 1960.

Hopkins. *More Books by More People*.

Kirkpatrick. *Twentieth Century Children's Writers*.

Kunitz. *Junior Book of Authors, Second Edition Revised*.

Meet the Newbery Author: Carol Ryrie Brink. Miller-Brody Productions, 1976 (FSS).

Miller. *Newbery Medal Books, 1922-1955*.

Montgomery. *Story behind Modern Books*.

Odland, N. "Carol Ryrie Brink and Caddie Woodlawn." *Elementary English*, April 1968.

Richards. *Minnesota Writers*.

Smaridge. *Famous Modern Storytellers for Young People*.

Ward. *Authors of Books for Young People, Second Edition*.

MARCIA JOAN BROWN, 1918-

author-illustrator

AWARDS

Cinderella. Caldecott Medal Book, 1955.

Dick Whittington and His Cat. Caldecott Honor Book, 1951.

Henry-Fisherman. Caldecott Honor Book, 1950.

Once a Mouse. Caldecott Medal Book, 1962.

Puss in Boots. Caldecott Honor Book, 1953.

Skipper John's Cook. Caldecott Honor Book, 1952.

Steadfast Tin Soldier. Caldecott Honor Book, 1954.

Stone Soup. Caldecott Honor Book, 1948.

BIBLIOGRAPHY

All Butterflies: An ABC Cut. Scribner, 1974; also issued as portfolio.

Anansi the Spider Man: Jamaican Folk Tales; by Philip M. Sherlock. Crowell, 1954.

Backbone of the King: The Story of Paka'a and His Son Ku, a Retelling from the Hawaiian of Moses Nakuina; by Dorothy M. Kahanaui. Scribner, 1966.

Blue Jackal. Scribner, 1977.

(tr.) *Cinderella: Or, The Little Glass Slipper*; by Charles Perrault. Scribner, 1954.

Dick Whittington and His Cat, Retold. Scribner, 1950.

Felice. Scribner, 1958.

Flying Carpet, Retold from Richard Burton. Scribner, 1956.

Giselle, Or The Wilis; by Theophile Gautier, adapted by Violette Verdy. McGraw, 1970; new edition, Dekker, 1977.

Henry-Fisherman: A Story of the Virgin Islands. Scribner, 1949.

How, Hippo! Scribner, 1969.

Little Carousel. Scribner, 1946.

Neighbors, Retold. Scribner, 1967.

Once a Mouse. . . , Retold from The Hitopadesa: A Fable Cut in Wood. Scribner, 1961.

Peter Piper's Alphabet. Scribner, 1959.

(tr.) *Puss in Boots*; by Charles Perrault. Scribner, 1952.

Skipper John's Cook. Scribner, 1951.

Snow Queen; by Hans C. Andersen. Tr. Richard P. Keigwin. Scribner, 1972.

Steadfast Tin Soldier; by Hans C. Andersen. Tr. Montague R. James. Scribner, 1953.

Stone Soup, an Old Tale. Scribner, 1947.

Tamarindo! Scribner, 1960.

Three Billy Goats Gruff; by Peter C. Asbjörnsen and Jörgen Moe. Harcourt, 1957.

Trail of Courage: A Story of New Amsterdam; by Virginia Watson. Coward, 1948.

Wild Swans; by Hans C. Andersen. Tr. Montague R. James. Scribner, 1963.

MEDIA

Backbone of the King. (BB, TB).

Cinderella. Miller-Brody Productions, 1974 (FSS); *a.k.a. Cencienta, Part 1 and Part 2*. Miller-Brody Productions, 1974 (FSS).

MEDIA (cont'd)

Crystal Cavern. Lyceum, 1974 (original text and illustrations, FS).

Dick Whittington and His Cat. (BB).

Felice. (BB).

How, Hippo! Miller-Brody Productions, 1974 (FSS); *a.k.a.* ¡Ay, Hipo! Miller-Brody Productions, 1974 (FSS).

Little Carousel. (BB).

Neighbors. (TB).

Once a Mouse. Miller-Brody Productions, 1977 (FSS); also in *Little Poems and Stories for Younger Readers*. (TB).

Stone Soup. (BB); Weston Woods Studios, 1955 (F), 1957 (FSS); also in Weston Woods Studios Set No. 2, 1965 (FSS).

Three Billy Goats Gruff. Weston Woods Studios, 1962 (FSS).

EXHIBITIONS

Booklyn Institute of Arts and Sciences, 1953. (Brooklyn, New York).

Carnegie Institute, *ca.*1950. (Pittsburgh, Pennsylvania).

Hacker Gallery, *ca.*1950. (New York, New York).

Library of Congress, *ca.*1950. (Washington, D.C.).

Peridot Gallery, *ca.*1950. (New York, New York).

Philadelphia Print Club, *ca.*1950. (Philadelphia, Pennsylvania).

COLLECTIONS

deGrummond Collection, University of Southern Mississippi. (Hattiesburg, Mississippi).

Free Library of Philadelphia. (Philadelphia, Pennsylvania).

Kerlan Collection, University of Minnesota. (Minneapolis, Minnesota).

Prints and Photographs Division and Children's Literature Center, Library of Congress. (Washington, D.C.).

BACKGROUND READING

Bader. *American Picturebooks from Noah's Ark to The Beast Within*.

Brown, M. "Distinction in Picture Books." *Horn Book*, June 1967.

Brown, M. "Hero Within." *Elementary English*, December 1966; also in *English Journal*, December 1966.

Brown, M. "Illustrating Books for Children." *Design*, January 1959.

Brown, M. "In and Out of Time." *Catholic Library World*, March 1977.

Brown, M. "My Goals as an Illustrator." *Horn Book*, June 1967.

Burke. *American Authors and Books, 1640 to the Present Day*.

Commire. *Something about the Author*.

Contemporary Authors.

Fuller. *More Junior Authors*.

Hopkins. *Books Are by People*.

Kent, N. "Marcia Brown, Author and Illustrator." *American Artist*, January 1963.

Kerstig, M. "Miss Marcia Brown's Day." *Elementary English*, March 1956.

Kingman. *Illustrators of Children's Books, 1957-1966*.

Kingman. *Illustrators of Children's Books, 1967-1976*.

Kingman. *Newbery and Caldecott Medal Books, 1938-1957*.

Loranger, J. "Special Vision of Marcia Brown." *Catholic Library World*, February 1977.

Miller. *Caldecott Medal Books, 1938-1957*.

Miller. *Illustrators of Children's Books, 1946-1956*.

Painter, H. "Marcia Brown, a Study in Versatility." *Elementary English*, December 1966.

Smaridge. *Famous Author-Illustrators for Young People*.

Ward. *Authors of Books for Young People, Second Edition*.

Ward. *Illustrators of Books for Young People, Second Edition*.

Young Wings. *Writing Books for Boys and Girls*.

BERNARDA BRYSON, 1903-
author-illustrator
a.k.a. Bernarda Bryson Shahn

AWARDS

Sun Is a Golden Earring. Caldecott Honor Book, 1963.

BIBLIOGRAPHY

as Bernarda Bryson:

Alphabet for Johanna; by Horace Gregory. Holt, 1963.

Bright Hunter of the Skies; by Herbert Best. Macmillan, 1961.

Calendar Moon; by Natalia M. Belting. Holt, 1964.

Gilgamesh: Man's First Story. Holt, 1967.

Grindstone of God: A Fable Retold; by Carl Withers. Holt, 1970.

Mr. Chu; by Norma Keating. Macmillan, 1965.

Pride and Prejudice; by Jane Austen. Macmillan, 1962.

Return of the Twelves; by Pauline Clarke. Coward, 1964.

River of Life; by Rutherford Platt. Simon, 1956.

Shepherd of the Sun; by Benjamin Appel. Oblensky, 1961.

Storyteller's Pack, a Frank Stockton Reader; by Frank Stockton. Scribner, 1968.

Sun Is a Golden Earring; by Natalia M. Belting. Holt, 1962.

Twenty Miracles of Saint Nicholas. Little, 1960.

White Falcon; by Charlton Ogburn. Houghton, 1955.

Wuthering Heights; by Emily Brontë. Macmillan, 1963.

Zoo of Zeus: A Handbook of Mythological Beasts and Creatures, with Comments by the Artist. Grossman, 1964.

as Bernarda Bryson Shahn:

Ben Shahn. Abrams, 1972.

MEDIA

Gilgamesh. (BB).

Twenty Miracles of Saint Nicholas. (BB).

COLLECTIONS

Archives of American Art. (Detroit, Michigan).

BACKGROUND READING

Commire. *Something about the Author.*

Contemporary Authors.

DeMontreville. *Third Book of Junior Authors.*

Kingman. *Illustrators of Children's Books, 1957-1966.*

Klemin. *Illustrated Book: Its Art and Craft.*

Lynes, R. "Bernarda Bryson, Illustrator." *Print,* September 1955.

Miller. *Illustrators of Books for Young People, 1946-1956.*

Ward. *Illustrators of Books for Young People, Second Edition.*

+CONRAD BUFF, 1886-
author-illustrator

and

MARY MARSH BUFF, 1890-1970
author-illustrator

AWARDS

Apple and the Arrow. Newbery Honor Book, 1952.

Big Tree. Newbery Honor Book, 1947.

Dash and Dart. Caldecott Honor Book, 1943.

Magic Maize. Newbery Honor Book, 1954.

BIBLIOGRAPHY

Apple and the Arrow. Houghton, 1951.

Big Tree. Viking, 1946.

Colorado: River of Mystery. Ritchie, 1968.

Dancing Cloud: The Navajo Boy. Viking, 1937; new edition, 1957.

Dash and Dart: A Story of Two Fawns. Viking, 1942.

Elf Owl. Viking, 1958.

Forest Folk. Viking, 1962.

Hah-Nee of the Cliff Dwellers. Houghton, 1956.

Hurry, Skurry and Flurry. Viking, 1954.

Kemi: An Indian Boy before the White Men Came. Ritchie, 1966.

Kobi: A Boy of Switzerland. Viking, 1939.

Magic Maize. Houghton, 1953.

Peter's Pinto: A Story of Utah. Viking, 1949.

Trix and Vix. Houghton, 1960.

MEDIA

Apple and the Arrow. (BB).

Dash and Dart. (BB).

Elf-Owl. (BB).

Forest Folk. (BB).

EXHIBITIONS (Conrad Buff)

Boston Museum of Fine Arts, n. d. (Boston, Massachusetts).

British Museum, n.d. (London, England).

Chicago Art Institute, n. d. (Chicago, Illinois).

Metropolitan Museum of Art, n. d. (New York, New York).

EXHIBITIONS (cont'd)

National Gallery of Art, n. d. (Washington, D.C.).

COLLECTIONS

British Museum. (London, England).

deGrummond Collection, University of Southern Mississippi. (Hattiesburg, Mississippi).

Kerlan Collection, University of Minnesota. (Minneapolis, Minnesota).

Los Angeles Museum. (Los Angeles, California).

May Massee Collection, Emporia State College. (Emporia, Kansas).

Metropolitan Museum of Art. (New York, New York).

Special Collections, University Research Library, University of California. (Los Angeles, California).

BACKGROUND READING

Burke. *American Authors and Books, 1640 to the Present Day*.

Kingman. *Illustrators of Children's Books, 1957-1966*.

Kirkpatrick. *Twentieth Century Children's Writers*.

Mahony. *Illustrators of Children's Books, 1744-1945*.

Miller. *Illustrators of Children's Books, 1946-1956*.

Smaridge. *Famous Literary Teams for Young People*.

Ward. *Authors of Books for Young People, Second Edition*.

Young Wings. *Writing Books for Boys and Girls*.

+NORA BURGLON
author

AWARDS

Children of the Soil. Newbery Honor Book, 1933.

BIBLIOGRAPHY

Around the Caribbean; with Thelma Glazer and Eula M. Phillips. il. Anne Eshner. Heath, 1941.

Children of the Soil: A Story of Scandinavia. il. Edgar P. D'Aulaire. Doubleday, 1932.

Cukoo Calls: A Story of Finland. il. Edgar P. and Ingri D'Aulaire. Winston, 1940.

Deep Silver: A Story of the Cod Banks. il. Peter Hurd. Houghton, 1938.

Diego Wins and Other Caribbean Stories. il. Anne Eshner and Katharine Knight. Random, 1941.

Gate Swings In. il. Richard Floethe. Little, 1937.

Ghost Ship: A Story of Norway. il. Arthur R. Nelson. Little, 1936.

Lost Island. il. James Reid. Winston, 1939.

Shark Hole: A Story of Modern Hawaii. il. Cyrus L. Baldridge. Holiday, 1943.

Slave Girl. il. Manning DeV. Lee. Stephen-Paul, 1947.

Sticks across the Chimney: A Story of Denmark. il. Fritz Eichenberg. Holiday, 1938.

BACKGROUND READING

Kunitz. *Junior Book of Authors, Second Edition Revised*.

"True Story about Nora Burglon." *St. Nicholas*, December 1932.

Young Wings. *Writing Books for Boys and Girls*.

+NANCY EKHOLM BURKERT, 1933-
illustrator

AWARDS

Snow-White and the Seven Dwarfs. Caldecott Honor Book, 1973.

BIBLIOGRAPHY

Big Goose and the Little White Duck; by Meindert DeJong. Harper, 1963.

Child's Calendar; by John Updike. Knopf, 1965.

Fir Tree; by Hans C. Andersen. Harper, 1970.

James and the Giant Peach: A Children's Story; by Roald Dahl. Knopf, 1961.

Jean-Claude's Island; by Natalie S. Carlson. Harper, 1963.

Nightingale; by Hans C. Andersen. Tr. Eva LeGallienne. Harper, 1965.

Scroobius Pip; by Edward Lear, completed by Ogden Nash. Harper, 1968.

Snow-White and the Seven Dwarfs: A Tale from the Brothers Grimm; by Jacob and Wilhelm Grimm. Tr. Randall Jarrell. Farrar, 1972.

BACKGROUND READING

DeMontreville. *Third Book of Junior Authors*.

Kingman. *Illustrators of Children's Books, 1957-1966*.

Kingman. *Illustrators of Children's Books, 1967-1976*.

Larkin, David. *Art of Nancy Ekholm Burkert*. Harper, 1977.

Ward. *Illustrators of Books for Young People, Second Edition*.

+VIRGINIA LEE BURTON, 1909-1968
author-illustrator

AWARDS

Little House. Caldecott Medal Book, 1943.

Song of Robin Hood. Caldecott Honor Book, 1948.

BIBLIOGRAPHY

Calico, the Wonder Horse; Or, The Saga of Stewy Slinker. Houghton, 1941; revised, Faber, 1958.

Choo Choo: The Story of a Little Engine Who Ran Away. Houghton, 1937.

Don Coyote; by Leigh Peck. Houghton, 1942.

Emperor's New Clothes; by Hans C. Andersen. Houghton, 1949.

Fast Sooner Hound; by Arna Bontemps and Jack Conroy. Houghton, 1942.

Katy and the Big Snow. Houghton, 1943.

Life Story: A Play in Five Acts. Houghton, 1962.

Little House. Houghton, 1942.

Manual of American Mountaineering; edited by Kenneth A. Henderson. American Alpine Club, 1941.

Maybelle, the Cable Car. Houghton, 1952.

Mike Mulligan and His Steam Shovel. Houghton, 1939; International Teaching Alphabet Edition, Faber, 1966.

Sad-faced Boy; by Arna Bontemps. Houghton, 1937.

Song of Robin Hood; edited by Anne Malcolmson. Music by Grace Castagnetta. Houghton, 1947.

MEDIA

Choo Choo. (TB).

Katy and the Big Snow. (TB); Teaching Resources Films, 1971 (FSS).

Life Story. Teaching Resources Films, 197? (FSS).

Little House. (BB); Walt Disney Productions, 1973 (FSS); Weston Woods Studios, 1973 (FSS).

Maybelle, the Cable Car. Teaching Resources Films, 197? (FSS, 2 parts).

Mike Mulligan. (BB, TB); Weston Woods Studios, 1956 (F), 1957 (FSS); also in Weston Woods Studios Set No. 1, 1968 (FSS); *a.k.a. Miguel Muligan y Su Pala de Vapor*. Weston Woods Studios, 1960 (F).

COLLECTIONS

Kerlan Collection, University of Minnesota. (Minneapolis, Minnesota).

BACKGROUND READING

Bader. *American Picturebooks from Noah's Ark to The Beast Within*.

Burke. *American Authors and Books, 1640 to the Present Day*.

Burns, P., and Hines, R. "Virginia Lee Burton." *Elementary English*, April 1967.

Burton, V. "Symphony in Comics." *Horn Book*, July 1941.

Colby, J. "Book Production Story." *Horn Book*, March 1948.

Commire. *Something about the Author*.

Contemporary Authors.

Current Biography.

Hoffman. *Authors and Illustrators of Children's Books*.

Kingman. *Illustrators of Children's Books, 1957-1966*.

Kingman. "Virginia Lee Burton, 1909-1968." *Horn Book*, February 1969.

Kingman. "Virginia Lee Burton's Dynamic Sense of Design." *Horn Book*, October 1970.

Kirkpatrick. *Twentieth Century Children's Writers*.

Kunitz. *Junior Book of Authors, Second Edition Revised*.

MacCampbell, J. "Virginia Lee Burton: Artist-Storyteller." *Elementary English*, January 1956.

Mahony. *Illustrators of Children's Books, 1744-1945*.

Miller. *Caldecott Medal Books, 1938-1957*.

Miller. *Illustrators of Children's Books, 1946-1956*.

Obituary. *New York Times*, October 16, 1968.

Obituary. *Publishers Weekly*, December 2, 1968.

Thompson, L. "Creator of Mike Mulligan." *Junior Bookshelf*, November 1943.

Thompson, L. "Versatility of Virginia Lee Burton." *Publishers Weekly*, June 19, 1943.

Ward. *Authors of Books for Young People, Second Edition*.

Ward. *Illustrators of Books for Young People, Second Edition*.

BETSY CROMER BYARS, 1928-
author-illustrator

AWARDS

Summer of the Swans. Newbery Medal Book, 1971.

BIBLIOGRAPHY

After the Goat Man. il. Ronald Himler. Viking, 1974.

Clementine. il. Charles Wilton. Houghton, 1962.

Dancing Camel. il. Harold Berson. Viking, 1965.

18th Emergency. il. Robert Grossman. Viking, 1973.

Go and Hush the Baby. il. Emily McCully. Viking, 1971.

House of Wings. il. Daniel Schwartz. Viking, 1972.

Lace Snail. Viking, 1975.

Midnight Fox. il. Ann Grifalconi. Viking, 1968; also il. Gareth Floyd. Faber, 1970.

Pinballs. Harper, 1976.

Rama, the Gypsy Cat. il. Peggy Bacon. Viking, 1966.

Summer of the Swans. il. Ted CoConis. Viking, 1970.

Trouble River. il. Rocco Negri. Viking, 1969.

TV Kid. il. Richard Cuffari. Viking, 1976.

Winged Colt of Casa Mia. il. Richard Cuffari. Viking, 1973.

MEDIA

After the Goat Man. (TB).

18th Emergency. (CB); American Broadcasting Corporation/Martin Tahse Productions, 1973 (TV).

Go and Hush the Baby. (TB).

House of Wings. (TB).

Lace Snail. Viking Press, 1976 (FSS).

Midnight Fox. (TB); Viking Press, 1973 (C, R).

Pinballs. American Broadcasting Corporation/Martin Tahse Productions, 1977 (TV).

Summer of the Swans. (TB); American Broadcasting Corporation/Martin Tahse Productions, 1974 (TV); Viking Press, 1972 (C, R).

Trouble River. (TB); American Broadcasting Corporation/Martin Tahse Productions, 1977 (TV).

TV Kid. Viking Press, 1977 (C, R).

Winged Colt of Casa Mia. American Broadcasting Corporation, 1977 (TV).

BACKGROUND READING

Byars, B. "Authoress Betsy Tells It Like It Is." *West Virginia Libraries*, Fall 1971.

Commire. *Something about the Author*.

Contemporary Authors.

DeMontreville. *Third Book of Junior Authors*.

Hopkins. *More Books by More People*.

Kingman. *Newbery and Caldecott Medal Books, 1966-1975*.

Kirkpatrick. *Twentieth Century Children's Writers*.

Ward. *Authors of Books for Young People, Second Edition*.

NATALIE SAVAGE CARLSON, 1906-
author

AWARDS

Family under the Bridge. Newbery Honor Book, 1959.

BIBLIOGRAPHY

Alphonse, That Bearded One. il. Nicolas (Mordvinoff). Harcourt, 1954.

Ann Aurelia and Dorothy. il. Dale Payson. Harper, 1968.

Befana's Gift. il. Robert Quackenbush. Harper, 1969; a.k.a. *Grandson for the Asking*. Blackie, 1970.

Brother for the Orphelines. il. Garth Williams. Harper, 1962; also il. Pearl Falconer. Blackie, 1964.

Carnival in Paris. il. Fermin Rocker. Harper, 1962; also il. Geraldine Spence. Blackie, 1964.

Chalou. il. George Loh. Harper, 1967; also il. Jillian Willett. Blackie, 1968.

Empty Schoolhouse. il. John Kaufman. Harper, 1965.

Evangeline, Pigeon of Paris. il. Nicolas (Mordvinoff). Harcourt, 1960; a.k.a. *Pigeon of Paris*. il. Quentin Blake. Blackie, 1972.

Family under the Bridge. il. Garth Williams. Harper, 1958; a.k.a. *Under the Bridge*. il. David Knight. Blackie, 1969.

Half-Sisters. il. Thomas DiGrazia. Harper, 1970; also il. Faith Jacques. Blackie, 1972.

Happy Orpheline. il. Garth Williams. Harper, 1967; also il. Pearl Falconer. Blackie, 1960.

Hortense, the Cow for a Queen. il. Nicolas (Mordvinoff). Harcourt, 1957.

Jean-Claude's Island. il. Nancy E. Burkert. Harper, 1963; also il. Pearl Falconer. Blackie, 1965.

Letter on the Tree. il. John Kaufman. Harper, 1964; also il. Jillian Willett. Blackie, 1967.

Luigi on the Streets. il. Emily A. McCully. Harper, 1967; a.k.a. *Family on the Waterfront*. Blackie, 1969.

Luvvy and the Girls. il. Thomas DiGrazia. Harper, 1971.

Marchers for the Dream. il. Alvin Smith. Harper, 1969; also il. Bernard Blatch. Blackie, 1971.

Marie Louise and Christophe. il. Jose Areugo and Ariane Dewey. Scribner, 1974.

Marie Louise's Heyday. il. Jose Areugo and Ariane Dewey. Scribner, 1975.

Orphelines in the Enchanted Castle. il. Adriana Saviozzi. Harper, 1964.

Pet for the Orphelines. il. Fermin Rocker. Harper, 1962; also il. Pearl Falconer. Blackie, 1963.

Runaway Marie Louise. il. Jose Areugo and Ariane Dewey. Scribner, 1977.

Sailor's Choice. il. George Loh. Harper, 1966.

Sashes Red and Blue. il. Rita Fava. Harper, 1956.

School Bell in the Valley. il. Gilbert Riswold. Harcourt, 1963.

Song of the Lop-eared Mule. il. Janina Domanska. Harper, 1961.

Talking Cat and Other Stories of French Canada, Retold. il. Roger Duvoisin. Harper, 1952.

Tomahawk Family. il. Stephen Cook. Harper, 1960.

Wings against the Wind. il. Mircea Vasiliu. Harper, 1955.

MEDIA

Alphonse, That Bearded One. (BB, TB).

Empty Schoolhouse. (BB, TB).

Happy Orpheline. (BB).

Letter on the Tree. (TB).

Marie Louise's Heyday. (TB).

Talking Cat. (TB).

COLLECTIONS

deGrummond Collection, University of Southern Mississippi. (Hattiesburg, Mississippi).

Kerlan Collection, University of Minnesota. (Minneapolis, Minnesota).

BACKGROUND READING

Burke. *American Authors and Books, 1640 to the Present Day*.

Carlson, J. "Family Unity in Natalie Savage Carlson's Books for Children." *Elementary English*, February 1968.

Commire. *Something about the Author*.

Contemporary Authors.

Foremost Women in Communications.

Fuller. *More Junior Authors*.

Hoffman. *Authors and Illustrators of Children's Books*.

Hopkins. *More Books by More People*.

Kirkpatrick. *Twentieth Century Children's Writers*.

Ward. *Authors of Books for Young People, Second Edition*.

MARY JANE CARR, 1899-
author

AWARDS

Young Mac of Fort Vancouver. Newbery Honor Book, 1941.

BIBLIOGRAPHY

Children of the Covered Wagon: A Story of the Old Oregon Trail. il. Esther Brann. Crowell, 1934; also il. Bob Kuhn, 1943.

Magic of May: A Fantasy for Children in Two Acts. Catholic Dramatic, 1928.

Peggy and Paul and Laddy. il. Kathleen Voute. Crowell, 1936.

Stranger on the Apple Ranch. Silver, 1946.

Top of the Morning. il. Henrietta Jones. Crowell, 1941.

Young Mac of Fort Vancouver. il. Richard Holberg. Crowell, 1940.

MEDIA

Children of the Covered Wagon. (BB); *a.k.a. Westward Ho, the Wagons*. Walt Disney Productions, 1955-56 (TV).

Peggy and Paul and Laddy. (BB).

Top of the Morning. Bowmar, n. d. (R).

Young Mac of Fort Vancouver. (BB).

COLLECTIONS

Kerlan Collection, University of Minnesota. (Minneapolis, Minnesota).

University of Oregon Library. (Eugene, Oregon).

BACKGROUND READING

Commire. *Something about the Author*.

Contemporary Authors.

Kunitz. *Junior Book of Authors, Second Edition Revised*.

Ward. *Authors of Books for Young People, Second Edition*.

Young Wings. *Writing Books for Boys and Girls*.

REBECCA CAUDILL, 1899-
author

AWARDS

(*Pocketful of Cricket*. Caldecott Honor Book, 1965.)

AWARDS (cont'd)

Tree of Freedom. Newbery Honor Book, 1950.

BIBLIOGRAPHY

Barrie and Daughter. il. Berkeley Williams, Jr. Viking, 1943.

Best-Loved Doll. il. Elliott Gilbert. Holt, 1962.

Certain Small Shepherd. il. William Pène du Bois. Holt, 1965.

Come Along! il. Ellen Raskin. Holt, 1969.

Contrary Jenkins; with James Ayars. il. Glen Rounds. Holt, 1969.

Did You Carry the Flag Today, Charley? il. Nancy Grossman. Holt, 1966.

Far-Off Land. il. Brinton Turkle. Viking, 1964.

Florence Nightingale. il. William Neebe. Row, 1950.

Happy Little Family. il. Decie Merwin. Winston, 1947.

Higgins and the Great Big Scare. il. Beth Krush. Holt, 1960.

High Cost of Writing. Southeast Community College, 1965.

House of Fifers. il. Genia (Wennerstrom). Longmans, 1954.

*My Appalachia: A Reminiscence. photographs by Edward Wallowtich. Holt, 1966.

Pocketful of Cricket. il. Evaline Ness. Holt, 1964.

Saturday Cousins. il. Nancy Woltemate. Winston, 1953.

Schoolhouse in the Parlor. il. Decie Merwin. Winston, 1959.

Schoolhouse in the Woods. il. Decie Merwin. Winston, 1949.

Somebody Go and Bang the Drum. il. Jack Hearne. Dutton, 1974.

Susan Cornish. il. E. Harper Johnson. Viking, 1955.

Time for Lissa. il. Velma Ilsley. Nelson, 1959.

Tree of Freedom. il. Dorothy B. Morse. Viking, 1949.

Up and Down the River. il. Decie Merwin. Winston, 1951.

Wind, Sand and Sky. il. Donald Carrick. Dutton, 1976.

MEDIA

Certain Small Shepherd. (BB, TB).

Contrary Jenkins. (TB).

Did You Carry the Flag Today, Charley? (BB, TB).

Far-Off Land. (TB).

Pocketful of Cricket. (BB); Miller-Brody Productions, 1976 (FSS).

Tree of Freedom. (TB).

COLLECTIONS

deGrummond Collection, University of Southern Mississippi. (Hattiesburg, Mississippi).

Kerlan Collection, University of Minnesota. (Minneapolis, Minnesota).

May Massee Collection, Emporia State College. (Emporia, Kansas).

University of Kentucky Library. (Lexington, Kentucky).

BACKGROUND READING

Burke. *American Authors and Books, 1640 to the Present Day.*

Burns, P., and Hines, R. "Rebecca Caudill." *Elementary English*, November 1963.

Caudill, R. "Appalachian Heritage." *Horn Book*, April 1969.

Caudill, R. "Serving the Needs and Interests of Youth." *Illinois Library Association Record*, March 1949.

Caudill, R. "Writing for Children." *Illinois Libraries,* June 1957.

Child of Appalachia, Rebecca Caudill. Kenneth Van Horn/University of Northern Illinois, 1977 (F).

Commire. *Something about the Author.*

Contemporary Authors.

Current Biography.

Foremost Women in Communications.

Fuller. *More Junior Authors.*

Kirkpatrick. *Twentieth Century Children's Writers.*

Toothaker, R. "Reminiscing with Rebecca Caudill," *Top of the News*, January 1972.

Ward. *Authors of Books for Young People, Second Edition.*

Young Wings. *Writing Books for Boys and Girls.*

+PLATO X. CHAN, 1931-
illustrator

AWARDS

Good-Luck Horse. Caldecott Honor Book, 1944.

BIBLIOGRAPHY

Good-Luck Horse: Adapted from an Old Chinese Legend; by Chin-Yi Chan. McGraw, 1943.

Magic Monkey: Adapted from an Old Chinese Legend; by Christina Chan. McGraw, 1944.

BACKGROUND READING

Dayot, M. "Plato X. Chan." *Art et Artist*, May 1938.

Mahony. *Illustrators of Children's Books, 1744-1945*.

Moore, A. "Three Owls." *Horn Book*, January 1944.

+JEAN PALANI CHARLOT, 1898-
author-illustrator

AWARDS

(*. . .And Now Miguel*. Newbery Medal Book, 1954.)

Child's Good Night Book. Caldecott Honor Book, 1944.

(*Corn Grows Ripe*. Newbery Honor Book, 1957.)

(*Secret of the Andes*. Newbery Medal Book, 1953.)

When Will the World Be Mine? Caldecott Honor Book, 1954.

BIBLIOGRAPHY

. . .And Now Miguel; by Joseph Krumgold. Crowell, 1953.

Anglais Devant a Loi. Colin, 1968.

Art from the Mayans to Disney. Sheed, 1939.

Artist on Art: Collected Essays. University Press of Hawaii, 1972.

Art-Making from Mexico to China. Sheed, 1950.

Boy Who Could Do Anything and Other Mexican Folk Tales; by Anita Brenner. Scott, 1942.

Carmen; by Prosper Mérimée. Tr. Lady Mary Lloyd. Limited Editions, 1941.

Charlot Murals in Georgia; photographs by Eugene Payor. University of Georgia, 1945.

Child's Good Morning; by Margaret W. Brown. Scott, 1952.

Child's Good Night Book; by Margaret W. Brown. Scott, 1943.

Choris and Kamehameha: An Artist's Study of the Various Portraits of Kamehameha I by Louis Choris. Bishop Museum, 1958.

Corn Grows Ripe; by Dorothy Rhoads. Viking, 1956.

Dance of Death: 50 Drawings and Captions. Sheed, 1951.

Digging in Yucatan; by Ann A. Morris. Doubleday, 1931.

(ed.) *Donald Angus Collection of Oil Paintings by Maude Tennent*. Contemporary Arts Center of Hawaii (?), 1968.

Dumb Juan and the Bandits; by Anita Brenner. Scott, 1957.

Fox Eyes; by Margaret W. Brown. Pantheon, 1951.

Français et de Gaulle. Plon, 1971.

Gaullisme. Colin, 1970.

Hero by Mistake; by Anita Brenner. Scott, 1953.

Hester and the Gnomes; by Marigold Hunt. McGraw, 1955.

Jean Charlot, Instructor: Life Drawing, Painting, Composition; by the Art Students League. Ajay, ca.1940.

Julio; by Loretta Tyman. Abelard, 1955.

Kittens, Cubs and Babies; by Miriam Schlein. Scott, 1959.

Livre de Christophe Colomb: Drame Lyrique en Deux Parties; by Paul Claudel. Gallimard, 1933.

Martin de Porrés, Hero; by Claire H. Bishop. Houghton, 1954.

Mayas de la Región Central de América; with others. Institución Carnegie, 1931.

Mexican Art and the Academy of San Carlos, 1785-1815. University of Texas, 1962.

Mexican Mural Rennaissance, 1920-1925. Yale University, 1963.

Mexihkanatli (Mexican Mother), 10 Chromolithographs on Stone. Estampa Mexicana, 1947. (Portfolio).

Mowentihke Chalman. n. p., 1969.

Na Lono Elua, Two Lonos, Three-Act Play. (?), ca.1967.

Our Lady of Guadelupe; by Helen R. Parish. Viking, 1955.

(comp.) *Partis Politiques*. Colin, 1971.

Phenomene Gaulliste. Fayard, 1970; *a.k.a. Gaullist Phenomenon, the Gaullist Movement in the Fifth Republic*. Tr. Monica Charlot and Marianne Neighbour. Praeger, 1971.

Picture Book, 32 Original Lithographs; text by Paul Claudel. Tr. Elise Cavanna. Becker, 1933; *a.k.a. Picture Book II, 32 Original Lithographs and Captions*. Zeitlin and VerBrugge, 1973.

Poppy Seeds; by Clyde R. Bulla. Crowell, 1955.

Posada's Dance of Death, with 4 Relief Engravings by José G. Posada; title page engraving by Fritz Eichenberg. Pratt Graphic Art Center, 1964.

BIBLIOGRAPHY (cont'd)

Preliminary Studies of the Ruins of Cóba, Quintana, Mexico; with John E. Thompson and Harry E. D. Pollack. Carnegie Institute, 1932.

Quand la Gauche Peut Gagner (Les Elections Legislatives des 4-11 Mars 1973); with Jean Stoetzel. Moreau, 1973.

Rèpetoiré des Publications des Partis Politiques Français, 1944-1967. Colin, 1970.

Secret of the Andes; by Ann N. Clark. Viking, 1952.

Seven Stories about a Cat Named Sneakers; by Margaret W. Brown. Scott, 1955.

Spoken Hawaiian; by Samuel H. Elbert. University of Hawaii, 1970.

Story of Chan Yuc; by Dorothy Rhoads. Doubleday, 1941.

Sun, the Moon and a Rabbit; by Amelia M. Del Rio. Sheed, 1935.

Tawnymore; by Monica Shannon. Doubleday, 1931.

Temple of the Warriors at Chicken Itzá, Yucatan; with Ann A. and Earl Morris. Carnegie Institute, 1931.

Three Plays of Ancient Hawaii. University of Hawaii, 1963.

Timid Ghost; by Anita Brenner. Scott, 1966.

Tito's Hats; by Melchor Ferrer. Garden City, 1940.

Two Little Trains; by Margaret W. Brown. Scott, 1949.

Two Lonos: A One-Act Play. n. p., *ca*.1965.

When Will the World Be Mine? The Story of a Snowshoe Rabbit; by Miriam Schlein. Scott, 1953.

EXHIBITIONS

American Institute of Graphic Arts, 1947. (New York, New York).

Associated American Artists Gallery, 1951. (New York, New York).

Baltimore Museum of Art, 1942. (Baltimore, Maryland).

Becker Gallery, 1931, 1933. (New York, New York).

Bonestell Gallery, 1940, 1942. (New York, New York).

California Palace of Legion of Honor, 1942. (San Francisco, California).

DeYoung Museum, 1942. (Cleveland, Ohio).

Guggenheim Museum, 1945. (New York, New York).

Honolulu Academy of Art, 1966. (Honolulu, Hawaii).

Levy Gallery, 1931, 1933, 1936. (New York, New York).

Los Angeles Center of Art, 1968. (Los Angeles, California).

Morgan Gallery, 1937. (New York, New York).

Museum Arte Moderne, 1968. (Mexico City, Mexico).

Passedoit Gallery, 1938. (New York, New York).

Smith College Museum, 1948. (Northampton, Massachusetts).

COLLECTIONS

deGrummond Collection, University of Southern Mississippi. (Hattiesburg, Mississippi).

Free Library of Philadelphia. (Philadelphia, Pennsylvania).

Honolulu Academy of Art. (Honolulu, Hawaii).

Kerlan Collection, University of Minnesota. (Minneapolis, Minnesota).

May Massee Collection, Emporia State College. (Emporia, Kansas).

Metropolitan Museum of Art. (New York, New York).

Museum Arte Moderne. (Mexico City, Mexico).

Philadelphia Museum of Art. (Philadelphia, Pennsylvania).

Rare Book and Manuscript Library, Columbia University. (New York, New York).

BACKGROUND READING

Bacin, S. "Jean Charlot." *Américas*, July 1970.

Bader. *American Picturebooks from Noah's Ark to The Beast Within*.

Claudel, Paul. *Jean Charlot*. Busson, 1933.

Commire. *Something about the Author*.

Contemporary Authors.

Current Biography.

Fuller. *More Junior Authors*.

"Jean Charlot." *American Artist*, June 1956.

Kingman. *Illustrators of Children's Books, 1957-1966*.

Kingman. *Illustrators of Children's Books, 1967-1976*.

Kirsten, L. "Jean Charlot." *Creative Art*, October 1931.

Mahony. *Illustrators of Children's Books, 1744-1945*.

Miller. *Illustrators of Children's Books, 1946-1956*.

Orozco, Jose C. *Artist in New York: Letters to Jean Charlot and Unpublished Writings, 1925-1929*. Foreword and notes by Jean Charlot. Lithographs by Ruth L. C. Sims. University of Texas, 1974.

Reed. *Mexican Muralists*.

Sendak, M. "Artist's Choice." *Horn Book*, August 1955.

Ward. *Illustrators of Books for Young People, Second Edition*.

ARTHUR BOWIE CHRISMAN, 1889-1953
author

AWARDS

Shen of the Sea. Newbery Medal Book, 1926.

BIBLIOGRAPHY

Clarke County, 1836-1936: Historical Sketch. Clarke Courier, 1936.

Shen of the Sea: A Book for Children. il. Else Hasselriis. Dutton, 1925; new edition, 1968.

Treasures Long Hidden: Old Tales and New Tales of the East. il. Weda Yap. Dutton, 1941.

Wind That Wouldn't Blow: Stories of the Merry Middle Kingdom for Children and Myself. il. Else Hasselriis. Dutton, 1927.

MEDIA

Shen of the Sea. (BB, CB, TB); Miller-Brody Productions, 1974 (FSS, R); *a.k.a. Rain King's Daughter and Other Tales from Shen of the Sea*. Miller-Brody Productions, 1974 (FSS, R); *a.k.a. Shen of the Sea, Series 1*. Miller-Brody Productions, 1974 (FSS); *a.k.a. Shen of the Sea, Series 2*. Miller-Brody Productions, 1974 (FSS).

Wind That Wouldn't Blow. (BB).

BACKGROUND READING

Burke. *American Authors and Books, 1640 to the Present Day*.

Commire. *Yesterday's Authors of Books for Children*.

Kunitz. *Junior Book of Authors*.

Kunitz. *Junior Book of Authors, Second Edition Revised*.

Kunitz. *Living Authors*.

Miller. *Newbery Medal Books, 1922-1955*.

Ward. *Authors of Books for Young People, Second Edition*.

ANN NOLAN CLARK, 1896-
author

AWARDS

(*In My Mother's House*. Caldecott Honor Book, 1942.)

Secret of the Andes. Newbery Medal Book, 1953.

BIBLIOGRAPHY

About the Grass Mountain Mouse. il. Andrew Standing Soldier. Office of Indian Affairs, 1943; *a.k.a. Grass Mountain Mouse*, 1954.

About the Hen of Wahpeton. il. Andrew Standing Soldier. Office of Indian Affairs, 1943; *a.k.a. Hen of Wahpeton*, 1954.

About the Slim Butte Raccoon. il. Andrew Standing Soldier. Office of Indian Affairs, 1942.

All This Wild Land. Viking, 1976.

Along Sandy Trails. il. Alfred A. Cohen. Viking, 1969.

Bear Cub. il. Charles Fracé. Viking, 1965.

Blue Canyon Horse. il. Alan Houser. Viking, 1954.

Brave against the Enemy: A Story of Three Generations—of the Day before Yesterday, of Yesterday, and of Tomorrow. Office of Indian Affairs, 1944.

Bringer of the Mystery Dog: A Story of a Young Boy, Who in His Quest for Bravery Brought the First Horse to His People, the Antelope Band. il. Oscar Howe. Office of Indian Affairs, 1943.

Brother André of Montreal. il. Harold Lang. Farrar, 1967.

Buey que Queriá Vivir en la Casa. Government Printing Office, 1948.

Buffalo Caller: The Story of a Young Sioux Boy of the Early 1700's, before the Coming of the Horse. il. Marian Hulziger. Row, 1942.

Cerdito que Fué al Mercado. Government Printing Office, 1942.

Child's Story of New Mexico; with Frances Carey. il. Mary Royt and George Buctel. University Publishing, 1941; second edition, 1952; third edition, 1960.

Circle of Seasons. il. Witold T. Mars. Farrar, 1970.

Desert People. il. Alan Houser. Viking, 1962.

En el Camino de la Escuela. Government Printing Office, 1949.

Father Kino: Priest to the Primas. il. H. Lawrence Hoffman. Farrar, 1963.

Gallina que Queriá Aydar. Government Printing Office, 1948.

Hoofprint on the Wind. il. Robert A. Parker. Viking, 1972.

In My Mother's House. il. Velino Herrera. Viking, 1941.

*Journey to the People. Viking, 1969.

Juan el Poblano. Government Printing Office, 1949.

Keepsake. Viking, 1963.

Linda Rita. Government Printing Office, 1948.

BIBLIOGRAPHY (cont'd)

Little Boy with Three Names: Story of the Taos Pueblo; edited by Willard W. Beatty. il. Tonita Lujan. Office of Indian Affairs, 1940.

Little Herder in Autumn. il. Hoke Denetsosie. Office of Indian Affairs, 1940; *a.k.a. Little Herder in Autumn and Little Herder in Winter*, 1950.

Little Herder in Spring. il. Hoke Denetsosie. Office of Indian Affairs, 1940; *a.k.a. Little Herder in Spring and Little Herder in Summer*, 1950.

Little Herder in Summer. il. Hoke Denetsosie. Office of Indian Affairs, 1942; *a.k.a. Little Herder in Spring and Little Herder in Summer,* 1950.

Little Herder in Winter. il. Hoke Denetsosie. Office of Indian Affairs, 1940; *a.k.a. Little Herder in Autumn and Little Herder in Winter*, 1950.

Little Indian Basket Maker. il. Harrison Begay. Melmont, 1955.

Little Indian Pottery Maker. il. Don Perceval. Melmont, 1955.

Little Navajo Bluebird. il. Paul Lantz. Viking, 1943.

Little Navajo Herder. il. Hoke Denetsosie. United States Indian Service, 1951.

Looking-for-Something: The Story of a Stray Burro of Ecuador. il. Leo Politi. Viking, 1952.

Maestro Rural en la Comunidad; et al. Department of Rural Education, 1948.

Magic Money. il. Leo Politi. Viking, 1950.

Medicine Man's Daughter. il. Don Bolognese. Farrar, 1963.

Paco's Miracle. il. Agnes Tait. Farrar, 1962.

Patos son Diferentes. Government Printing Office, 1948.

Pine Ridge Porcupine. Office of Indian Affairs, 1941.

Santiago. il. Lynd Ward. Viking, 1955.

Santo for Pasqualita. il. Mary Villarejo. Viking, 1959.

Secret of the Andes. il. Jean Charlot. Viking, 1952.

Singing Sioux Cowboy Primer. il. Andrew Standing Soldier. United States Indian Service, 1945.

Singing Sioux Cowboy Reader. il. Andrew Standing Soldier. United States Indian Service, 1947.

Summer Is for Growing. il. Agnes Tait. Farrar, 1968.

Sun Journey: A Story of the Zuñi Pueblo. il. Percy Tsisette. Office of Indian Affairs, 1945.

There Are Still Buffalo. il. Andrew Standing Soldier. Office of Indian Affairs, 1942.

These Were the Valiant: A Collection of New Mexico Profiles. Horn, 1969.

Third Monkey. il. Don Freeman. Viking, 1956.

This for That. il. Don Freeman. Golden Gate, 1965.

Tía María's Garden. il. Ezra J. Keats. Viking, 1963.

Who Wants to Be a Prairie Dog? il. Van Tishnajinnie. Office of Indian Affairs, 1940.

World Song. il. Kurt Wiese. Viking, 1960.

Year Walk. Viking, 1975.

Young Hunter of Picuris. il. Velino Herrera. Office of Indian Affairs, 1943.

MEDIA

Along Sandy Trails. Viking Press, 1971 (FSS).

Blue Canyon Horse. (TB).

Hoofprint on the Wind. (TB).

In My Mother's House. (BB, TB).

Looking-for-Something. (BB).

Paco's Miracle. (BB).

Santiago. (BB).

Secret of the Andes. (BB).

Tía María's Garden. (BB, TB).

COLLECTIONS

deGrummond Collection, University of Southern Mississippi. (Hattiesburg, Mississippi).

BACKGROUND READING

Bishop, C. "Ann Nolan Clark." *Catholic Library World*, February 1963.

Burke. *American Authors and Books, 1640 to the Present Day*.

Commire. *Something about the Author*.

Contemporary Authors.

Griese, A. "Ann Nolan Clark: Building Bridges of Cultural Understanding." *Elementary English*, May 1972.

Hoffman. *Authors and Illustrators of Children's Books*.

Hopkins. *More Books by More People*.

Kirkpatrick. *Twentieth Century Children's Writers*.

Kunitz. *Junior Book of Authors, Second Edition Revised*.

Miller. *Newbery Medal Books, 1922-1955*.

Ward. *Authors of Books for Young People, Second Edition*.

Young Wings. *Writing Books for Boys and Girls*.

+ELIZABETH JANE COATSWORTH, 1893-
author

AWARDS

Cat Who Went to Heaven. Newbery Medal Book, 1931.

BIBLIOGRAPHY

Alice-All-by-Herself. il. Marguerite de Angeli. Macmillan, 1937.

Alice and Jerry Books: Sixth Reader; with Mabel O'Donnell. Row, *ca.*1940.

All-of-a-Sudden Susan. il. Richard Cuffari. Macmillan, 1974.

American Adventures, 1620-1945. il. Robert Frankenberg. Macmillan, 1968.

Atlas and Beyond: A Book of Poems. il. Harry Cimino. Harper, 1924.

Aunt Flora. il. Manning DeV. Lee. Macmillan, 1953.

Away Goes Sally. il. Helen Sewell. Macmillan, 1934; also il. Caroline Sharpe. Blackie, 1970.

Bess and the Sphinx. il. Berniece Lowenstein. Macmillan, 1967.

Big Green Umbrella. il. Helen Sewell. Grosset, 1944.

Bob Bodden and the Good Ship Rover. il. Ted Schroeder. Garrard, 1968.

Bob Bodden and the Seagoing Farm. il. Frank Aloise. Garrard, 1970.

Boston Bells. il. Manning DeV. Lee. Macmillan, 1952.

Boy with the Parrot, a Story of Guatemala. il. Wilfred A. Bronson. Macmillan, 1930.

Captain's Daughter. il. Ralph Ray. Macmillan, 1950.

Cat and the Captain. il. Gertrude Kaye. Macmillan, 1927; also il. Berniece Lowenstein, 1974.

Cat Who Went to Heaven. il. Lynd Ward. Macmillan, 1930; new edition, 1958.

Cave. il. Allan Houser. Viking, 1958; *a.k.a. Cave of Ghosts*. Hamilton, 1971.

Cherry Ann and the Dragon Horse. il. Manning DeV. Lee. Macmillan, 1955.

Children Come Running. il. Roger Duvoisin, et al. Golden, 1960.

(ed.) *Chimney Farm Bedtime Stories*; by Henry Beston. il. Maurice Day. Holt, 1966.

Compass Rose. Coward, 1929.

Country Neighborhood. il. Hildegard Woodward. Macmillan, 1944.

Country Poems. Macmillan, 1942.

Creaking Stair. il. William A. Dwiggins. Coward, 1949.

Cricket and the Emperor's Son. il. Weda Yap. Macmillan, 1932; also il. Juliette Palmer. World's Work, 1962.

Daisy. il. Judith G. Brown. Macmillan, 1973.

Dancing Tom. il. Grace Paull. Macmillan, 1938.

Daniel Webster's Horses. il. (Louis F.) Cary. Garrard, 1971.

Desert Dan. il. Harper Johnson. Viking, 1960.

Dog from Nowhere. il. Don Sibley. Row, 1958.

Dollar for Luck. il. George and Doris Hauman. Macmillan, 1951; *a.k.a. Sailing Hatrack*. il. Gavin Rowe. Blackie, 1972.

Door to the North: A Saga of Fourteenth Century America. il. Frederick T. Chapman. Winston, 1950.

Down Half the World. il. Zena Bernstein. Macmillan, 1968.

Down Tumbledown Mountain. il. Aldren Watson. Row, 1958.

Enchanted, an Incredible Tale. il. Robert Winthrop. Pantheon, 1951; also il. Mary Frank, 1968; also il. Joan Kiddell-Monroe. Dent, 1952.

(ed.) *Especially Maine: Natural World from Cape Cod to the St. Lawrence*; by Henry Beston. Greene, 1970.

Fair American. il. Helen Sewell. Macmillan, 1940; also il. Caroline Sharpe. Blackie, 1970.

First Adventure. il. Ralph Ray. Macmillan, 1950.

Five Bushel Farm. il. Helen Sewell. Macmillan, 1939; also il. Caroline Sharpe. Blackie, 1970.

Forgotten Island. il. Grace Paull. Grosset, 1942.

Fox Footprints. Knopf, 1923.

Fox Friend. il. John Hamberger. Macmillan, 1966.

George and Red. il. Paul Giovanopoulos. Macmillan, 1969.

Giant Golden Book of Cat Stories; with Kate Barnes. il. Feodor Rojankovsky. Golden, 1953; *a.k.a. Giant Golden Book of Dogs, Cats, and Horses*, 1957.

Giant Golden Book of Dog Stories. il. Feodor Rojankovsky. Golden, 1953; *a.k.a. Giant Golden Book of Dogs, Cats, and Horses*, 1957.

Giant Golden Book of Horse Stories; with Kate Barnes. il. Feodor Rojankovsky. Golden, 1954; *a.k.a. Giant Golden Book of Dogs, Cats, and Horses*, 1957.

Golden Horseshoe. il. Robert Lawson. Macmillan, 1935; new edition, 1968; *a.k.a. Tamar's Wager*. il. Roger Payne. Blackie, 1971.

Good Night. il. Jose Areugo. Macmillan, 1972.

BIBLIOGRAPHY (cont'd)

Grandmother Cat and the Hermit. il. Irving Boker. Macmillan, 1970; *a.k.a. Grandmother Cat*. Bodley Head, 1971.

Hand of Apollo. il. Robin Jacques. Viking, 1965.

Here I Stay. il. Edwin Earle. Coward, 1938.

Hide and Seek. il. Genevieve Vaughan-Jackson. Pantheon, 1956.

House of the Swan. il. Kathleen Voute. Macmillan, 1948.

Houseboat Summer. il. Marguerite Davis. Macmillan, 1942.

(ed.) *Indian Encounters: An Anthology of Stories and Poems*. il. Frederick T. Chapman. Macmillan, 1960.

Indian Mound Farm. il. Fermin Rocker. Macmillan, 1969.

Jock's Island. il. Lilian Obligado. Viking, 1963.

Jon the Unlucky. il. Esta Nesbitt. Holt, 1964.

Kitten Stand. il. Katharine Keeler. Grosset, 1945.

Knock at the Door. il. Frances D. Bedford. Macmillan, 1931.

Last Fort: A Story of the French Voyageurs. il. Edward Shenton. Winston, 1952.

Lighthouse Island. il. Symeon Shimin. Norton, 1968.

Little Haymakers. il. Grace Paull. Macmillan, 1949.

Littlest House. il. Marguerite Davis. Macmillan, 1940.

Lonely Maria. il. Evaline Ness. Pantheon, 1960.

Lucky Ones: Five Journeys toward a Home. il. Janet Doyle. Macmillan, 1968.

*Maine Memories. Greene, 1968.

Maine Ways. il. Mildred Coughlin. Macmillan, 1947.

Marra's World. il. Krystyna Turska. Greenwillow, 1975.

Mary's Song. Nash, 1938.

Mountain Bride. Pantheon, 1954.

Mouse Chorus. il. Genevieve Vaughan-Jackson. Pantheon, 1955.

Night and the Cat. il. Foujita. Macmillan, 1950.

Noble Doll. il. Leo Politi. Viking, 1961.

Old Whirlwind: The Story of Davy Crockett. il. Manning DeV. Lee. Macmillan, 1953.

Ox-Team. il. Peter Warner. Hamilton, 1967.

Peaceable Kingdom, and Other Poems. il. Fritz Eichenberg. Pantheon, 1958.

Peddler's Cart. il. Zhenya Gay. Macmillan, 1956; also il. Margery Gill. Blackie, 1971.

*Personal Geography, Almost an Autobiography. Greene, 1976.

Pika and the Roses. il. Kurt Wiese. Pantheon, 1959.

Place. il. Marjorie Auerbach. Holt, 1966.

Plum Daffy Adventure. il. Marguerite Davis. Macmillan, 1947.

Poems. il. Vee Guthrie. Macmillan, 1957.

Princess and the Lion. il. Evaline Ness. Pantheon, 1963; also il. Tessa Jordan. Hamilton, 1971.

Pure Magic. il. Ingrid Fetz. Macmillan, 1974; *a.k.a. Werefox*. Collier, 1975; *a.k.a. Fox Boy*. Blackie, 1975.

Reading Round Table, Blue Book: Stories by Elizabeth Coatsworth; edited by George Manolakes. American Book, 1965.

Reading Round Table, Green Book. American Book, 1965.

Ronnie and the Chief's Son. il. Stefan Martin. Macmillan, 1962.

Runaway Home; with Mabel O'Donnell. il. Gustaf Tenggren. Row, 1942.

Secret. il. Don Bolognese. Macmillan, 1962.

Silky: An Incredible Tale. il. John Carroll. Pantheon, 1953.

Snow Parlor and Other Bedtime Stories. il. Charles Robinson. Grosset, 1971.

Sod House. il. Manning DeV. Lee. Macmillan, 1954.

South Shore Town. Macmillan, 1948.

Sparrow Bush, Rhymes. il. Stefan Martin. Norton, 1966.

Summer Green. il. Nora S. Unwin. Macmillan, 1948.

Sun's Diary: A Book of Days for Any Year. Macmillan, 1929.

Sword of the Wilderness. il. Harvé Stein. Macmillan, 1936.

(ed.) *Tales of the Gauchos*; by William H. Hudson. il. Henry C. Pitz. Knopf, 1946.

They Walk in the Night. il. Stefan Martin. Norton, 1969.

Thief Island. il. Jon Wonsetler. Macmillan, 1943.

Toast to the King. il. Forrest Orr. Coward, 1940.

Toñio and the Stranger: A Mexican Adventure. il. Wilfrid S. Bronson. Grosset, 1941.

Toutou in Bondage. il. Thomas Handforth. Macmillan, 1929.

Troll Weather. il. Ursula Arndt. Macmillan, 1967.

Trudy and the Tree House. il. Marguerite Davis. Macmillan, 1944.

Trunk. Macmillan, 1941.

Twelve Months Make a Year. il. Marguerite Davis. Macmillan, 1943.

Under the Green Willow. il. Janina Domanska. Macmillan, 1971.

UNICEF Christmas Book. UNICEF, 1960.

Up Hill and Down: Stories. il. James H. Davis. Knopf, 1947.

Wanderers. il. Trina S. Hyman. Four Winds, 1972.

White Horse. il. Helen Sewell. Macmillan, 1942; *a.k.a. White Horse of Morocco*. il. Caroline Sharpe. Blackie, 1972.

White Room. il. George W. Thompson. Pantheon, 1958.

Wishing Pear. il. Ralph Ray. Macmillan, 1951.

With Car and Trailer across the U.S.A.: The Harding Family Seeks a New Home. Klett (?), 1949.

Wonderful Day. il. Helen Sewell. Macmillan, 1946; also il. Caroline Sharpe. Blackie, 1973.

You Say You Saw a Camel? il. Brinton Turkle. Row, 1958.

You Shall Have a Carriage. il. Henry C. Pitz. Macmillan, 1941.

MEDIA

Away Goes Sally. (TB).

Bob Bodden and the Good Ship Rover. Taylor Associates, 1970 (FSS).

Cat Who Went to Heaven. (BB, TB); Miller-Brody Productions, 1970 (FSS); Newbery Award Records, 1969 (C, R).

Country Neighborhood. (BB).

Enchanted. (BB, TB).

Good Night. (BB).

Here I Stay. (TB).

Houseboat Summer. (BB).

Last Fort. (BB).

Lonely Maria. (TB).

Mountain Bride. (BB).

Old Whirlwind. (BB).

Personal Geography. (TB).

Poems. (BB).

Princess and the Lion. (TB).

Pure Magic. (TB).

Ronnie and the Chief's Son. (BB, TB).

Silky. (BB).

Swift Things Are Beautiful. Pied Piper Productions, 19? (FSS).

Toast to the King. (BB).

Trunk. (BB).

White Room. (BB).

Wishing Pear. (BB).

COLLECTIONS

Baker Library, Dartmouth College. (Hanover, New Hampshire).

deGrummond Collection, University of Southern Mississippi. (Hattiesburg, Mississippi).

Department of Rare Books and Manuscripts, Boston Public Library. (Boston, Massachusetts).

Kerlan Collection, University of Minnesota. (Minneapolis, Minnesota).

Lockwood Memorial Library, State University of New York. (Buffalo, New York).

Miller Library, Colby College. (Waterville, Maine).

Rare Book and Manuscript Library, Columbia University. (New York, New York).

Rare Book Room, Buffalo and Erie County Public Library. (Buffalo, New York).

Special Collections, University Research Library, University of California. (Los Angeles, California).

Vassar College Library. (Poughkeepsie, New York).

BACKGROUND READING

Abbott, B. "To Timbucktoo and Back: Elizabeth Coatsworth's Books for Children." *Horn Book*, November 1930.

Bechtel, L. "Elizabeth Coatsworth, Poet and Writer." *Horn Book*, January 1936.

Burke. *American Authors and Books, 1640 to the Present Day*.

Coatsworth, E. "Upon Writing for Children." *Horn Book*, September 1948.

Commire. *Something about the Author*.

Contemporary Authors.

Doyle. *Who's Who of Children's Literature*.

Hart. *Oxford Companion to American Literature, Fourth Edition*.

Hoffman. *Authors and Illustrators of Children's Books*.

Hopkins. *More Books by More People*.

Jacobs, L. "Elizabeth Coatsworth." *Instructor*, November 1962.

Kirkpatrick. *Twentieth Century Children's Writers*.

Kuhn, D. "Elizabeth Coatsworth, Perceptive Impressionist." *Elementary English*, December 1969.

Kunitz. *Junior Book of Authors*.

Kunitz. *Junior Book of Authors, Second Edition Revised*.

BACKGROUND READING (cont'd)

Kunitz. *Living Authors.*

Kunitz. *Twentieth Century Authors.*

Kunitz. *Twentieth Century Authors, First Supplement.*

Miller. *Newbery Medal Books, 1922-1955.*

Rice, M. "Poetic Prose of Elizabeth Coatsworth." *Elementary English*, January 1954.

Smaridge. *Famous Modern Storytellers for Young People.*

Ward. *Authors of Books for Young People, Second Edition.*

Warfel. *American Novelists of Today.*

+CATHERINE CATE COBLENTZ, 1897-1951
author

AWARDS

Blue Cat of Castle Town. Newbery Honor Book, 1950.

BIBLIOGRAPHY

Amazon. il. Peitro Lazzari. (Washington, D.C.), 1944.

Animal Pioneers. il. Kurt Wiese. Little, 1936.

Beggar's Penny. il. Hilda Van Stockum. Longmans, 1934.

Bells of Leyden Sing. il. Hilda Van Stockum. Longmans, 1944; also il. Eva Najum. Grey Walls, 1948.

Blue and Silver Necklace. il. Edwin Earle. Little, 1937.

Blue Cat of Castle Town. il. Janice Holland. Longmans, 1949; new edition, Countryman, 1977.

Falcon of Eric the Red. il. Henry C. Pitz. Longmans, 1942.

Martin and Abraham Lincoln: Based on a True Incident. il. Trientja (Engelbrecht). Children's, 1947.

Pan-American Highway. il. Dorothy Sweetzer. Pan-American Union, 1942.

Scatter, the Chipmunk. il. Bert Schwarz. Children's, 1946.

Sequoya. il. Ralph Ray. Longmans, 1946.

MEDIA

Blue Cat of Castle Town. (BB, TB).

BACKGROUND READING

Coblentz, C. "Through a Diamond Pane." *Horn Book*, September 1943.

Coblentz, C. "Wading into Yesterday." *Horn Book*, July 1944.

Kunitz. *Junior Book of Authors, Second Edition Revised.*

+CHRISTOPHER COLLIER, 1930-
author

and

JAMES LINCOLN COLLIER, 1928-
author

AWARDS

My Brother Sam Is Dead. Newbery Honor Book, 1975.

BIBLIOGRAPHY

by Christopher Collier:

Connecticut in the Continental Congress. Pequot, 1972.

Roger Sherman's Connecticut, Yankee Politics and the American Revolution. Wesleyan, 1971.

by James Lincoln Collier:

Battleground: The U.S. Army in World War II. Norton, 1965.

Danny Goes to the Hospital. photographs by Yale Joel. Norton, 1970.

Give Dad My Best. Four Winds, 1976.

Great Jazz Artists. il. Robert A. Parker. Four Winds, 1977.

Hard Life of the Teenager. Four Winds, 1972.

Hypocritical American: An Essay on Sex Attitudes in America. Bobbs, 1964.

Inside Jazz. Four Winds, 1973.

It's Murder at St. Basket's. Grosset. 1972.

Jug Bands and Handmade Music: Creative Approach to Music Theory and the Instruments. Grosset, 1973.

Making Music for Money. il. Robert Censoni. Watts, 1976.

Making of Man: The Story of Our Ancient Ancestors. Four Winds, 1974.

Practical Music Theory: How Music Is Put Together from Bach to Rock. Norton, 1970.

Rich and Famous: The Further Adventures of George Stable. Four Winds, 1975.

Rock Star. Four Winds, 1970.

(ed.) *Sex Education U.S.A.: A Community Approach.* Guidance Associates, 1968.

Teddy Bear Habit, Or How I Became a Winner. il. Lee Lorenz. Norton, 1967.

Visit to the Firehouse. photographs by Yale Joel. Norton, 1967.

Which Musical Instrument Shall I Play? photographs by Yale Joel. Norton, 1969.

Why Does Everyone Think I'm Nutty? Grosset, 1971.

by Christopher and James Lincoln Collier:

Bloody Country. Four Winds, 1976.

My Brother Sam Is Dead. Four Winds, 1974.

MEDIA

Hard Life of the Teenager. (TB).

It's Murder at St. Basket's. (TB).

My Brother Sam Is Dead. (TB); Miller-Brody Productions, 1976 (C, R).

Teddy Bear Habit. (TB).

Which Musical Instrument Shall I Play? (TB).

COLLECTIONS (Christopher Collier)

Ackerman Collection, Arents Research Library, Syracuse University. (Syracuse, New York).

BACKGROUND READING (James Lincoln Collier)

Commire. *Something about the Author.*

Contemporary Authors.

+PADRAIC COLUM, 1881-1972
author

AWARDS

Big Tree of Bunlahy. Newbery Honor Book, 1934.

Golden Fleece and the Heroes Who Lived before Achilles. Newbery Honor Book, 1922.

Voyagers. Newbery Honor Book, 1926.

BIBLIOGRAPHY

Acurain Cuilm de Bailis. Connrad na Gaedildge, 1904.

Adventures of Odysseus and the Tale of Troy. il. Willy Pogány. Macmillan, 1918; *a.k.a. Children's Homer: The Adventures of Odysseus and the Tale of Troy,* 1920.

(ed.) *Anthology of Irish Verse.* Boni, 1922; revised, Liveright, 1948.

Arthur Griffith. Browne, 1959; *a.k.a. Ourselves Alone! The Story of Arthur Griffith and the Origin of the Irish Free State.* Crown, 1960.

Balloon: A Comedy in Four Acts. Macmillan, 1929.

Betrayal: A Comedy in One Act. Mount Morris, 1920.

(ed.) *Between Friends: Letters of James Branch Cabell and Others;* by James B. Cabell; edited with Margaret F. Cabell. Harcourt, 1962.

Big Tree of Bunlahy: Stories of My Own Countryside. il. Jack B. Yeats. Macmillan, 1933.

Boy Apprenticed to an Enchanter. il. Dugald S. Walker. Macmillan, 1920; also il. Edward Leight, 1966.

Boy in Eirinn. il. Jack B. Yeats. Dutton, 1913.

Boy Who Knew What the Birds Said. il. Dugald S. Walker. Macmillan, 1918.

(ed.) *Broad-Sheet Ballads: Being a Collection of Irish Popular Songs.* il. Jack B. Yeats. Maunsel, 1913.

Castle Conquer. Macmillan, 1923.

Children of Odin: A Book of Northern Myths. il. Willy Pogány. Macmillan, 1920.

Children Who Followed the Piper. il. Dugald S. Walker. Macmillan, 1922.

Creatures. il. Boris Artzybasheff. Macmillan, 1927.

Cross-Roads in Ireland. Macmillan, 1930.

Desert: A Play in Three Acts. Newth, 1912; *a.k.a. Mogu the Wanderer: Or, The Desert, a Fantastic Comedy in Three Acts.* Little, 1917.

Destruction of the Hostel. (Dublin, Ireland), 1910.

Dramatic Legends and Other Poems. Macmillan, 1922.

Dublin Poets and Artists, No. 2. il. Jack B. Yeats. Gayfield, 1939.

Ella Young, an Appreciation. Longmans, 1931.

Fiddler's House, a Play in Three Acts. Maunsel, 1907; also in *Three Plays,* below.

Flower Pieces, New Poems. Orwell, 1938.

Flying Swans. Crown, 1957.

Forge in the Forest. il. Boris Artzybasheff. Macmillan, 1925.

Fountain of Youth: Stories to Be Told. il. Jay Van Everen. Macmillan, 1927.

Fourteen Stations of the Cross: Collotype Reproductions of Bas Reliefs by Alfeo Foggi. Seymour, ca.1928.

Frenzied Prince: Being Heroic Stories of Ancient Ireland. il. Willy Pogány. McKay, 1943.

BIBLIOGRAPHY (cont'd)

Garland Sunday. n. p., 1958.

Girl Who Sat by the Ashes. il. Dugald S. Walker. Macmillan, 1919; also il. Imero Gobbato, 1968.

Golden Fleece and the Heroes Who Lived before Achilles. il. Willy Pogány. Macmillan, 1921.

(ed.) *Gulliver's Travels*; by Jonathan Swift. il. Willy Pogány. Macmillan, 1917.

Half-Day's Ride: Or, Estates in Corsica. Macmillan, 1932.

Heather Ale: A Book of Verse. (Dublin, Ireland), 1917.

Images of Departure. Dolmen, 1969.

Irish Elegies. Dolmen, 1958; revised, 1961.

Irish Rebellion of 1916 and Its Martyrs: Erin's Tragic Easter; et al. Devin-Adair, 1916.

Island of the Mighty: Being the Hero Stories of Celtic Britain Retold from the Mabinogion. il. Wilfred Jones. Macmillan, 1924.

Jackdaw. Gayfield, 1939.

King of Ireland's Son. il. Willy Pogány. Holt, 1916.

Land: A Play in Three Acts. Maunsel, 1950; also in *Three Plays*, below.

Legend of Saint Columbia. il. Elizabeth MacKinstry. Macmillan, 1935.

Moytura: A Play for Dancers. Dolmen, 1963.

My Irish Year. Pott, 1912.

Old Pastures. Macmillan, 1930.

(ed.) *Oliver Goldsmith*. Browne, 1913.

Orpheus: Myths of the World. il. Boris Artzybasheff. Macmillan, 1930; *a.k.a. Myths of the World*. Grosset, 1959.

Our Friend James Joyce; with Mary G. Colum. Doubleday, 1958.

Peep-Show Man. il. Lois Lenski. Macmillan, 1924.

Poems. Macmillan, 1932; *a.k.a. Collected Poems*. Devin-Adair, 1953.

(ed.) *Poems of Janathan Swift*. Collier, 1962.

(ed.) *Poems of Samuel Ferguson*. Figgis, 1963.

(ed.) *Poems of the Irish Revolutionary Brotherhood*; with Edward J. H. O'Brien, et al. Small, 1916.

Poet's Circuits: Collected Poems of Ireland. Oxford, 1960.

Road Round Ireland. Macmillan, 1926.

(ed.) *Roofs of Gold: Poems to Read Aloud*. Macmillan, 1964.

Six Who Were Left in a Shoe. il. Dugald S. Walker. Volland, 1923; also il. Joseph Schindelman. McGraw, 1968.

Songs from Connacht: Nine Poems. Music by Herbert Hughes. Boosey, *ca*.1928.

Stone of Victory, and Other Tales. il. Judith G. Brown. McGraw, 1966.

Story of Lowry Maen. il. Séan O'Sullivan. Macmillan, 1937.

Storytelling New & Old. il. Jay Van Everen. Macmillan, 1961.

Studies. Maunsel, 1907.

Tales and Legends of Hawaii: At the Gateways of Day (and) The Bright Islands. il. Juliette M. Fraser. Yale University, 1924-25 (2 vols.); *a.k.a. Legends of Hawaii*. il. Don Fraser, 1937.

(ed.) *Tales of Wonder and Magnificence*. il. Eric Pape. Macmillan, 1923; also il. Lynd Ward, 1953.

Ten Poems. Dolmen, 1957.

Thomas Muskerry: A Play in Three Acts. Maunsel, 1910; also in *Three Plays*, below.

Three Men: A Tale. Mathews, 1930.

Three Plays: The Fiddler's House, The Land (and) Thomas Muskerry. Little, 1916; revised, 1925; each also issued separately, above.

(ed.) *Treasury of Irish Folklore: The Stories, the Traditions, Legends, Humor, Wisdom, Ballads and Songs of the Irish People*. Crown, 1954; revised, 1962; revised, 1967.

Vegetable Kingdom. Indiana University, 1954.

(ed.) *Vicar of Wakefield*; by Oliver Goldsmith. Collier, 1963.

Voyagers: Being Legends and Romances of Atlantic Discovery. il. Wilfred Jones, Macmillan, 1925.

Way of the Cross: Devotions on the Progress of Our Lord Jesus Christ from the Judgement Hall to Cavalry. Seymour, 1926.

Where the Winds Never Blew and the Cocks Never Crew. il. Richard Bennett. Macmillan, 1940.

White Sparrow. il. Lynd Ward. Macmillan, 1933; also il. Joseph Low. McGraw, 1972.

Wild Earth, a Book of Verse. Maunsel, 1907; *a.k.a. Wild Earth and Other Poems*, 1916; *a.k.a. Wild Earth: Poems*. Talbot, 1950.

MEDIA

Adventures of Odysseus and the Tale of Troy. (BB).

Children of Odin. (BB).

Children's Homer. (C, CB, MT).

Golden Fleece and the Heroes Who Lived before Achilles. (BB, C, CB, MT).

Legends of Hawaii. (C, MT, TB).

Our Friend James Joyce. (BB).

Story of Lowry Maen. (BB).

Tales of Wonder and Magnificence. (BB).

Twelve Labors of Hercules. Caedmon, n. d. (R).

COLLECTIONS

American Academy of Arts and Letters Library. (New York, New York).

Collection of American Literature, Beinecke Library, Yale University. (New Haven, Connecticut).

Harvard University Library. (Cambridge, Massachusetts).

Lockwood Memorial Library, State University of New York. (Buffalo, New York).

Miller Library, Colby College. (Waterville, Maine).

Modern Manuscript Collection, University of Notre Dame Library. (Notre Dame, Indiana).

New York Public Library. (New York, New York).

Princeton University Library. (Princeton, New Jersey).

Rare Book and Manuscript Library, Columbia University. (New York, New York).

University of Chicago Library. (Chicago, Illinois).

BACKGROUND READING

Bechtel, L. "Padraic Colum: A Great Story-Teller of Today." *Catholic Library World*, December 1960.

Benet. *Famous Storytellers for Young People.*

Bowen, Zack R. *Padraic Colum: A Biographical-Critical Introduction.* Southern Illinois University Press, 1970.

Burke. *American Authors and Books, 1640 to the Present Day.*

Colum, P. "Patterns for the Imagination." *Horn Book*, February 1962.

Colum, P. "Story-Teller's Story: The Power of Imagination." *Bulletin of the New York Public Library*, October 1966.

Contemporary Authors.

Dolbier, M. "Padraic Colum." *New York Herald Tribune Book Review*, June 9, 1957.

Kirkpatrick. *Twentieth Century Children's Writers.*

Kunitz. *Junior Book of Authors.*

Kunitz. *Junior Book of Authors, Second Edition Revised.*

Kunitz. *Living Authors.*

Kunitz. *Twentieth Century Authors.*

Kunitz. *Twentieth Century Authors, First Supplement.*

New York Times Biographical Edition.

Nichols, L. "Talk with Padraic Colum." *New York Times Book Review*, June 23, 1957.

Obituary. *New York Times*, January 12, 1972.

Obituary. *Newsweek*, January 24, 1972.

Obituary. *Publishers Weekly*, February 21, 1972.

Obituary. *Time*, January 21, 1972.

Ward. *Authors of Books for Young People, Second Edition.*

+OLIVIA ENSOR COOLIDGE, 1908-
author

AWARDS

Men of Athens. Newbery Honor Book, 1963.

BIBLIOGRAPHY

Apprenticeship of Abraham Lincoln. Scribner, 1974.

Caesar's Gallic War. Houghton, 1961; il. William Stobbs. Bodley Head, 1961.

Come by Here. il. Milton Johnson. Harcourt, 1970.

Cromwell's Head. il. Edward A. Wilson. Houghton, 1955.

Edith Wharton, 1862-1937. Scribner, 1964.

Egyptian Adventures. il. Joseph Low. Houghton, 1954.

Eugene O'Neill. Scribner, 1966.

Gandhi. Houghton, 1971.

George Bernard Shaw. Houghton, 1968.

Golden Days of Greece. il. Enrico Arno. Crowell, 1968.

Greek Myths. il. Edouard Sandoz. Houghton, 1949; a.k.a. *Greek Myths with Suggestions for Reading and Discussion* by George Hillocks, Jr., 1964.

King of Men. il. Ellen Raskin. Houghton, 1966.

Legends of the North. il. Edouard Sandoz. Houghton, 1951.

Lives of Famous Romans. il. Milton Johnson. Houghton, 1965.

Maid of Artemis. il. Bea Holmes. Houghton, 1969.

Makers of the Red Revolution. Houghton, 1963.

Marathon Looks on the Sea. il. Erwin Schachner. Houghton, 1967.

Men of Athens. il. Milton Johnson. Houghton, 1962.

People in Palestine. Houghton, 1965.

Roman People. il. Leo Lipinsky. Houghton, 1959.

Tales of the Crusades. il. Gustave Doré adaptations. Houghton, 1970.

BIBLIOGRAPHY (cont'd)

Three Lives of Joseph Conrad. Houghton, 1972.

Tom Paine, Revolutionary. Scribner, 1969.

Trojan War. il. Edouard Sandoz. Houghton, 1952.

Winston Churchill and the Story of Two World Wars. Houghton, 1960.

Women's Rights: The Suffrage Movement in America, 1848-1920. Dutton, 1966.

MEDIA

Apprenticeship of Abraham Lincoln. (CB).

Caesar's Gallic War. (BB)

Come by Here. (TB).

Edith Wharton. (MT).

Egyptian Adventures. (BB).

Eugene O'Neill. (BB).

Gandhi. (TB).

Golden Days of Greece. (TB).

Greek Myths. (C, MT, TB).

Legends of the North. (BB).

Lives of Famous Romans. (BB, TB).

Makers of the Red Revolution. (TB).

Men of Athens. (BB, TB).

People in Palestine. (TB).

Roman People. (BB).

Tom Paine. (BB).

Trojan War. (BB, C, MT).

Winston Churchill. (TB).

Women's Rights. (TB).

BACKGROUND READING

Commire. *Something about the Author*.

Contemporary Authors.

Coolidge, O. "Writing about Abraham Lincoln." *Horn Book*, Febrary 1975.

Fuller. *More Junior Authors*.

Kirkpatrick. *Twentieth Century Children's Writers*.

Ward. *Authors of Books for Young People, Second Edition*.

BARBARA COONEY, 1917-
author-illustrator

AWARDS

Chanticleer and the Fox. Caldecott Medal Book, 1959.

(*Kildee House*. Newbery Honor Book, 1950.)

BIBLIOGRAPHY

Åke and His World; by Carl Malmberg. Farrar, 1940.

All in a Suitcase; by Samuel F. Morse. Little, 1968.

American Folk Songs for Children in Home, School and Nursery School: A Book for Children, Parents and Teachers; by Ruth Seeger. Doubleday, 1948.

American Folk Songs for Christmas; by Ruth Seeger. Doubleday, 1953.

American Speller: An Adaptation of Noah Webster's Blue-backed Speller. Crowell, 1960.

Animal Folk Songs for Children: Traditional American Songs; by Ruth Seeger. Doubleday, 1950.

Away We Go! One-Hundred Poems for the Very Young; by Catherine S. McEwen. Crowell, 1956.

Bambi: A Life in the Woods; by Felix Salten, *pseud*. (Siegmund Salzman). Simon, 1970.

Best Christmas; by Lee Kingman. Doubleday, 1949.

Blot, Little City Cat; by Phyllis Crawford. Holt, 1946.

Brookline Trunk; by Louise Kent. Houghton, 1955.

Burton and Dudley; by Marjorie W. Sharmat. Holiday, 1975.

Captain Pottle's House. Farrar, 1943.

(adapt.) *Chanticleer and the Fox*; by Geoffrey Chaucer. Crowell, 1958.

Christmas. Crowell, 1967.

Christmas Folk; by Natalia Belting. Holt, 1969.

Christmas in the Barn; by Margaret W. Brown. Crowell, 1952.

City Springtime; by Helen Kay, *pseud*. (Helen C. Goldfrank). Hastings, 1957.

(adapt.) *Courtship, Merry Marriage, and Feast of Cock Robin and Jenny Wren: To Which Is Added the Doleful Death of Cock Robin*. Scribner, 1965.

Crows of Pearblossom; by Aldous Huxley. Random, 1967.

Demeter and Persephone: Homeric Hymn Number 2; by Homer. Tr. Penelope Proddow. Doubleday, 1972.

Dionysos and the Pirates: Homeric Hymn Number 7; by Homer. Tr. Penelope Proddow. Doubleday, 1970.

Donkey Prince; by M. Jean Craig. Doubleday, 1977.

Down to the Beach; by May Garelick. Four Winds, 1973.

Favorite Fairy Tales Told in Spain; by Virginia Haviland. Little, 1963.

Freckle Face; by Neil Anderson, *pseud*. (Jerrold Beim). Crowell, 1957.

Friends with God: Stories and Prayers of the Marshall Family; by Catherine Marshall. McGraw, 1956.

Fun for Freddy; by Jane Quigg. Oxford, 1953.

Garland of Games and Other Diversions; initial letters by Suzanne R. Morse. Holt, 1969.

Grandfather Whiskers, M.D.: A Graymouse Story; by Nellie M. Leonard. Crowell, 1953.

Graymouse Family; by Nellie M. Leonard. Crowell, 1950.

Green Wagons; by Oskar Seidlin and Senta Rypins. Houghton, 1943.

Hermes, Lord of Robbers: Homeric Hymn Number 4; by Homer. Tr. Penelope Proddow. Doubleday, 1971.

Hibouet la Poussiquette; by Edward Lear. Tr. Francis Steegmuller. Little, 1961.

Hill Ranch; by Rutherford Montgomery. Doubleday, 1951.

House Mouse; by Dorothy Morris. Warne, 1973.

Just Plain Maggie; by Lorraine Beim. Harcourt, 1950.

Katie's Magic Glasses; by Jane Goodsell. Houghton, 1965.

Kellyhorns. Farrar, 1942.

Kildee House; by Rutherford Montgomery. Doubleday, 1949.

King of Wreck Island. Farrar, 1941.

Lazy Young Duke of Dundee; by William Wise. Rand, 1970.

Little Brown Horse; by Margaret Otto. Knopf, 1959.

Little Fir Tree; by Margaret W. Brown. Crowell, 1954.

Little Juggler: Adapted from an Old French Legend. Hastings, 1961.

Little Prayer. Hastings, 1967.

Little Women: Or, Meg, Jo, Beth and Amy; by Louisa M. Alcott. Crowell, 1955.

Man Who Didn't Wash His Dishes; by Phyllis Krasilovsky. Doubleday, 1950.

Midsummer Magic: A Garland of Stories, Charms & Recipes; compiled by Ellin Greene. Lothrop, 1977.

Mother Goose in French; from Mother Goose. Tr. Hugh Latham. Crowell, 1964.

Mother Goose in Spanish; from Mother Goose. Tr. Alastair Reid and Anthony Kerrigan. Crowell, 1968.

Owl and the Pussycat; by Edward Lear. Little, 1969.

Papillot, Clignot et Dodo; by Eugene Field. Farrar, 1964.

Peacock Pie; by Walter de la Mare. Knopf, 1961.

Pepper; by Barbara Reynolds. Scribner, 1952.

Peter's Long Walk; by Lee Kingman. Doubleday, 1953.

Plant Magic; by Aileen Fisher. Bowmar, 1977.

Pony That Kept a Secret; by Elizabeth Lansing. Crowell, 1952.

Pony That Ran Away; by Elizabeth Lansing. Crowell, 1951.

Pony Worth His Salt; by Elizabeth Lansing. Drowell, 1953.

Pumpkin, Ginger, and Spice; by Margaret Otto. Holt, 1954.

Read Me Another Story; by The Child Study Association of America. Crowell, 1949.

Read Me More Stories; by The Child Study Association of America. Crowell, 1951.

Rocky Summer; by Lee Kingman. Houghton, 1948.

Sad Story of the Little Bluebird and the Hungry Cat; by Edna M. Preston. Four Winds, 1976.

Seasonal Verses Gathered by Elizabeth George Speare from the Connecticut Almanack for the Year of the Christian Era 1773; by Elizabeth G. Speare. American Library Association, 1959.

Seven Little Rabbits; by John Becker. Walker, 1973.

Shaun and the Boat: An Irish Story; by Anne Molloy. Hastings, 1965.

Shooting Star Farm; by Anne Molloy. Houghton, 1946.

Snow Birthday; by Helen Kay, *pseud.* (Helen C. Goldfrank). Farrar, 1955.

Snow-White and Rose-Red; by Jacob and Wilhelm Grimm. Delacorte, 1965.

Squawk to the Moon, Little Goose; by Edna M. Preston. Viking, 1974.

*Twenty-Five Years A-Graying: The Portrait of a College Graduate, a Pictorial Study of the Class of 1938 at Smith College, Northampton, Massachusetts, Based on Statistics Gathered in 1963 for the Occasion of Its 25th Reunion. Little, 1963.

When the Sky Is Like Lace; by Elinor Horwitz. Lippincott, 1975.

Where Have You Been?; by Margaret W. Brown. Crowell, 1952.

White Heron; by Sarah O. Jewett. Crowell, 1963.

Would You Rather Be a Tiger?; by Robyn Supraner. Houghton, 1973.

Wynken, Blynken and Nod; by Eugene Field. Houghton, 1965.

Yours, with Love Kate; by Miriam E. Mason. Houghton, 1952.

MEDIA

Burton and Dudley. (BB).

Chanticleer and the Fox. Weston Woods Studios, 1959 (FSS); also in Weston Woods Studios Set No. 7, 1965 (FSS).

Down to the Beach. (BB).

Little Juggler. (TB).

Man Who Didn't Wash His Dishes. Weston Woods Studios, 1973 (FSS).

Owl and the Pussycat. Weston Woods Studios, 1971 (F); also with *Wynken, Blynken and Nod*, Weston Woods Studios, 1967 (FSS).

Squawk to the Moon. Viking Press, 1975 (FSS).

Wynken, Blynken and Nod. Weston Woods Studios, 1971 (F); also with *Owl and the Pussycat.* Weston Woods Studios, 1967 (FSS).

COLLECTIONS

Boston Public Library. (Boston, Massachusetts).

deGrummond Collection, University of Southern Mississippi. (Hattiesburg, Mississippi).

Free Library of Philadelphia. (Philadelphia, Pennsylvania).

Gary Public Library. (Gary, Indiana).

Kerlan Collection, University of Minnesota. (Minneapolis, Minnesota).

Milwaukee Public Library. (Milwaukee, Wisconsin).

BACKGROUND READING

Burke. *American Authors and Books, 1640 to the Present Day.*

Commire. *Something about the Author.*

Contemporary Authors.

Fuller. *More Junior Authors.*

Hopkins. *Books Are by People.*

Kingman. *Illustrators of Children's Books, 1957-1966.*

Kingman. *Illustrators of Children's Books, 1967-1976.*

Kingman. *Newbery and Caldecott Medal Books, 1956-1965.*

Mahony. *Illustrators of Children's Books, 1744-1945.*

Miller. *Illustrators of Children's Books, 1946-1956.*

Ward. *Authors of Books for Young People, Second Edition.*

Ward. *Illustrators of Books for Young People, Second Edition.*

Watson, A. "Artist's Choice." *Horn Book*, October 1960.

SUSAN MARY COOPER, 1935-
author

AWARDS

Dark Is Rising. Newbery Honor Book, 1974.

Grey King. Newbery Medal Book, 1976.

BIBLIOGRAPHY

Behind the Golden Curtain: View of the U.S.A. Scribner, 1965.

Dark Is Rising. il. Alan Cober. Atheneum, 1973.

Dawn of Fear. il. Margery Gill. Harcourt, 1970.

Greenwitch. il. Michael Heslop. Atheneum, 1974.

Grey King. il. Michael Heslop. Atheneum, 1975. (Announced as *Fire on the Mountain*.)

J. B. Priestley: Essays of Five Decades. Little, 1968.

J. B. Priestley: Portrait of an Author. Heineman, 1970.

Mandrake. Cape, 1964.

Over Sea, under Stone. il. Margery Gill. Harcourt, 1966.

Silver on the Tree. il. Michael Heslop. Atheneum, 1977.

MEDIA

Dark Encounter. 1976 (original script, TV).

COLLECTIONS

Smith Collection, Toronto Public Library. (Toronto, Ontario).

BACKGROUND READING

Commire. *Something about the Author.*

Cooper, S. "Address Delivered at the Children's Round Table Breakfast: Is There Really Such a Thing as a Species Called Children's Books?" *Texas Library Journal*, May 1976.

Cooper, S. "Newbery Acceptance Speech." *Top of the News*, Fall 1976; also as "Newbery Award Acceptance: Address, July 20, 1976." *Horn Book*, August 1976.

DeMontreville. *Fourth Book of Junior Authors and Illustrators.*

Kirkpatrick. *Twentieth Century Children's Writers.*

Levin, B. "Journey through Mountain and Mist: The Grey King." *Horn Book*, August 1976.

McElderry, M. "Susan Cooper." *Horn Book*, August 1976.

Meet the Newbery Author: Susan Cooper. Miller-Brody Productions, 1977 (FSS).

HAROLD COURLANDER, 1908-
author

AWARDS

Cow-Tail Switch. Newbery Honor Book, 1948.

BIBLIOGRAPHY

African. Crown, 1967.

Big Old World of Richard Creeks. il. Bob Laurie. Chilton, 1962.

Caballero. Farrar, 1940.

Cow-Tail Switch and Other West African Stories; with George Herzog. il. Madye L. Chastain. Holt, 1947.

Drum and the Hoe: Life and Lore of the Haitian People. University of California, 1960.

Fire on the Mountain, and Other Ethiopian Stories; with Wolf Leslau. il. Robert W. Kane. Holt, 1950.

Fourth World of the Hopis. il. Enrico Arno. Crown, 1971.

Haiti Singing. University of North Carolina, 1939.

Hat-Shaking Dance and Other Tales from the Gold Coast. il. Enrico Arno. Harcourt, 1957; *a.k.a. Hat-Shaking Dance and Other Ashanti Tales from Ghana*, 19?.

Home to Langford County: A One-Act Play. Blue Ox, 1938.

Kantchil's Lime Pit, and Other Stories from Indonesia. il. Robert W. Kane. Harcourt, 1950.

King's Drum and Other African Stories. il. Enrico Arno. Harcourt, 1962.

Maurice Serle Kaplan, 1908-1951. Spiral, 1951.

Mesa of Flowers. Crown, 1977.

Negro Folk Music U.S.A. il. James and Ruth McCrea. Columbia University, 1963.

Negro Songs from Alabama. Music transcribed by John B. Brooks. Wenner-Gren Foundation, 1960; second edition, Oak, 1963.

Olode the Hunter and Other Tales from Nigeria; with Ezekiel Eshubayi. il. Enrico Arno. Harcourt, 1968; *a.k.a. Ijapa the Tortoise, and Other Nigerian Tales*. Bodley Head, 1969.

On Recognizing the Human Species. One Nation, 1960.

People of the Short Blue Corn, Tales and Legends of the Hopi Indians. il. Enrico Arno. Harcourt, 1970.

Piece of Fire, and Other Haitian Tales. il. Beth and Joe Krush. Harcourt, 1964.

Ride with the Sun: An Anthology of Folk Tales and Stories from the United Nations. il. Roger Duvoisin. McGraw, 1955.

Shaping Our Times: What the United Nations Is and Does. Oceana, 1960; revised, 1962.

Son of the Leopard. il. Rocco Negri. Crown, 1974.

Swamp Mud: A Play in Three Scenes. il. Paul McPharlin. Blue Ox, 1936.

Tales of Yoruba Gods and Heroes. il. Larry Lurin. Crown, 1973.

Terrapin's Pot of Sense. il. Elton Fax. Holt, 1957.

Tiger's Whisker and Other Tales and Legends from Asia and the Pacific. il. Enrico Arno. Harcourt, 1959.

Treasury of African Folklore: The Oral Literature, Traditions, Myths, Legends, Epics, Tales, Recollections, Wisdom, Sayings and Humor of Africa. Crown, 1975.

Uncle Bouqui of Haiti. il. Lucy H. Crockett. Morrow, 1942.

Vodoun in Haitian Culture. Institute for Cross-Cultural Research, 1966.

MEDIA

Big Old World of Richard Creeks. (BB, TB).

(comp.) *Caribbean Folk Music, Volume 1*. Folkways Records 1960 (R).

Cow-Tail Switch as *Folktales from West Africa, the Cow-Tail Switch and Other Stories*. Folkways Records, 1951 (R).

(comp.) *Drums of Haiti*. Folkways Records, 1952 (R).

Hat-Shaking Dance. (TB); also as *Ashanti Folk Tales from Ghana, the Hat-Shaking Dance and Other Tales from the Gold Coast*. Folkways Records, 1959 (R).

Kantchil's Lime Pit in *Folk Tales from Indonesia*. Folkways Records, 1951 (R).

King's Drum. (TB).

Negro Folk Music U.S.A. (C, MT).

Olode the Hunter. (BB).

Piece of Fire. (BB, TB).

Ride with the Sun. (BB); *a.k.a. Ride with the Sun: Folktales from the Philippines, China, Iceland, Egypt and Brazil*. Folkways, 1956 (R).

Shaping Our Times. (BB, TB).

Tiger's Whisker. (TB).

Uncle Bouqui. Folkways Records, 1956 (R).

(comp.) *World of Man*. Folkways Records, 1956, 1958 (2 vols. R).

COLLECTIONS

deGrummond Collection, University of Southern Mississippi. (Hattiesburg, Mississippi).

BACKGROUND READING

Commire. *Something about the Author*.

Contemporary Authors.

Fuller. *More Junior Authors*.

Thompson. *Indiana Authors and Their Books, 1917-1966*.

Ward. *Authors of Books for Young People, Second Edition*.

+PHYLLIS CRAWFORD, 1899-
author
pseudonym Josie Turner

AWARDS

"Hello, the Boat!" Newbery Honor Book, 1939.

BIBLIOGRAPHY

as Phyllis Crawford:

Blot, Little City Cat. il. Holling C. Holling. Cape, 1930; also il. Barbara Cooney. Holt, 1946.

(ed.) *Children's Catalog: Third Edition*; with Minnie E. Sears. Wilson, 1925.

(ed.) *Early Years of Childhood Education through Insight*; by Catherine Stern and Toni S. Gould. Harper, 1955.

"Hello, the Boat!" il. Edward Laning. Holt, 1938.

In England Still. Arrowsmith, 1938.

Last Semester. Holt, 1942.

Let's Go! il. Theodore Guerin. Holt, 1949.

Second Shift. il. Graham Bernbach. Holt, 1943.

Secret Brother. il. Mabel J. Woodbury. Holt, 1941.

(ed.) *Song Index*; with Minnie E. Sears. Wilson, 1926; revised, 1934.

(ed.) *Standard Catalog for Librarians*. Wilson, 1931.

(ed.) *Vertical File Service Catalog*. Wilson, 1934.

Walking on Gold. il. Russell Sherman. Messner, 1940.

as Josie Turner:

Elsie Dinsmore on the Loose. il. Eldon Kelley. Cape, 1930.

Posie Didn't Say. Howell, 1941.

COLLECTIONS

Lipscomb Library, Randolph-Macon Woman's College. (Lynchburg, Virginia).

BACKGROUND READING

Commire. *Something about the Author*.

Current Biography.

Kunitz. *Junior Book of Authors, Second Edition Revised*.

ALICE DALGLIESH, 1893-
author

AWARDS

Bears on Hemlock Mountain. Newbery Honor Book, 1953.

Courage of Sarah Noble. Newbery Honor Book, 1955.

Silver Pencil. Newbery Honor Book, 1945.

(*Thanksgiving Story*. Caldecott Honor Book, 1955.)

BIBLIOGRAPHY

Adam and the Golden Cock. il. Leonard Weisgard. Scribner, 1959.

Aids to Choosing Books for Your Children; with Annis Duff. Children's Book Council, 1957.

Along Janet's Road. il. Katherine Milhous. Scribner, 1946.

America Begins: The Story of the Finding of the New World. il. Lois Maloy. Scribner, 1938; revised, 1959.

America Builds Homes: The Story of the First Colonies. il. Lois Maloy. Scribner, 1938.

America Travels: The Story of a Hundred Years of Travel in America. il. Hildegard Woodward. Macmillan, 1933; revised, 1961.

Bears on Hemlock Mountain. il. Helen Sewell. Scribner, 1952.

Blue Teapot: Sandy Cove Stories. il. Hildegard Woodward. Macmillan, 1931.

Book for Jennifer: A Story of London Children in the Eighteenth Century and of Mr. Newbery's Juvenile Library. il. Katherine Milhous and with *Old Cuts from Old Books with an Epigram Adapted to Each Verse*. Scribner, 1940.

(ed.) *Childcraft*. Quarne, 1939 (teacher's edition); 1945 (parent's edition).

Choosing Book. il. Eloise B. Wilkin. Macmillan, 1932.

(comp.) *Christmas: A Book of Stories, Old and New*. il. Hildegard Woodward. Scribner, 1934; revised, 1950.

Columbus Story. il. Leo Politi. Scribner, 1955.

Conduct Curriculum for the Kindergarten and First Grade; with Agnes Barke, et al. Scribner, 1923.

Courage of Sarah Noble. il. Leonard Weisgard. Scribner, 1954; also il. John Lawrence. Hamilton, 1970.

Davenports and Cherry Pie. il. Flavia Gág. Scribner, 1949.

Davenports Are at Dinner. il. Flavia Gág. Scribner, 1948.

(ed.) *Enchanted Book*. il. Concetta Cacciola. Scribner, 1947.

First Experiences with Literature. Scribner, 1932.

Fourth of July Story. il. Marie Nonnast. Scribner, 1956.

(ed.) *Gay Mother Goose*; from Mother Goose. il. Françoise (Seignobosc). Scribner, 1938.

Gulliver Joins the Army. il. Ellen Segner. Scribner, 1942.

(ed.) *Happily Ever After: Fairy Tales*. il. Katherine Milhous. Scribner, 1939.

Happy School Year. il. Mary S. Brand. Rand, 1924; revised, 1933.

Hollyberries; with Cleo Bennett. il. Pru Herric. Scribner, 1939.

Horace Mann Kindergarten for Five-Year-Old Children; with Charlotte G. Garrison, et al. Teacher's College, 1937.

Little Angel: A Story of Old Rio. il. Katherine Milhous. Scribner, 1943.

Little Wooden Farmer. il. Theodora Baumeister. Macmillan, 1942; also il. Anita Lobel, 1968.

Little Wooden Farmer (and) The Story of the Jungle Pool. il. Theodora Baumeister. Macmillan, 1930.

Long Live the King! A Story Book of English Kings and Queens. il. Lois Maloy. Scribner, 1937.

(ed.) *Once on a Time*; with Katherine Milhous. Scribner, 1938.

(tr.) *Peregrin and the Goldfish: A Picture Book*; by Frau Tom Seidmann-Freud. Macmillan, 1929.

Relief's Rocker: A Story of Sandy Cove and the Sea. il. Hildegard Woodward. Macmillan, 1932.

Reuben and His Red Wheelbarrow. il. Ilse Bischoff. Grosset, 1946.

Ride on the Wind: Told from "The Spirit of St. Louis" by Charles Lindbergh. il. Georges Schreiber. Scribner, 1956.

Roundabout: Another Sandy Cove Story. il. Hildegard Woodward. Macmillan, 1934.

Sailor Sam. Scribner, 1935.

(ed.) *Saint George and the Dragon*; by Richard Johnson. il. Lois Maloy. Scribner, 1941.

(ed.) *Selected Books for Young Children (and) Selected Pictures for Young Children*; with Rita Scherman. Educational Playthings, 1934.

*Silver Pencil. il. Katherine Milhous. Scribner, 1944.

Smiths and Rusty. il. Berta and Elmer Hader. Scribner, 1936.

Thanksgiving Story. il. Helen Sewell. Scribner, 1954.

They Live in South America. il. Katherine Milhous and Frances Lichten. Scribner, 1942.

Three from Greenways: A Story of Children from England. il. Gertrude Howe. Scribner, 1941.

True Story of Fala; with Margaret L. Suckley. il. E. N. Fairchild and photographs. Scribner, 1942.

(ed.) *Tupak of the Incas*; by Philip A. Means. il. Margaret E. Price. Rand, 1926; also il. H. M. Herget. Scribner, 1942.

West Indian Play Days. il. Margaret E. Price. Rand, 1926.

Wings around South America. il. Katherine Milhous. Scribner, 1941.

(ed.) *Will James Cowboy Book*; by Will James, *pseud*. (Joseph Dufault). il. Will James, *pseud*. Scribner, 1938.

Wooden Shoes in America; with Lois Maloy. il. Lois Maloy. Scribner, 1940.

Young Aunts. il. Charlotte Becker. Scribner, 1939.

MEDIA

America Travels. (BB).

Bears on Hemlock Mountain. (BB, TB).

Columbus Story. (BB).

Courage of Sarah Noble. (BB, TB).

Fourth of July Story. (BB).

Little Wooden Farmer. il. Anita Lobel. Association Sterling/Macmillan Films, 1974 (FS).

Ride on the Wind. (BB).

They Live in South America. (BB).

COLLECTIONS

Kerlan Collection, University of Minnesota. (Minneapolis, Minnesota).

BACKGROUND READING

"Alice Dalgliesh." *Saturday Review*, July 22, 1961.

Bechtel, L. "Alice Dalgliesh and Her Books." *Horn Book*, March 1947.

Brown, M. "Alice Dalgliesh." Children's Book Council *Calendar*, January 1972.

BACKGROUND READING (cont'd)

Burke. *American Authors and Books, 1640 to the Present Day.*

Contemporary Authors.

Fuller, M. "Alice Dalgliesh of Scribner's." *Publishers Weekly*, July 30, 1949.

Kirkpatrick. *Twentieth Century Children's Writers.*

Kunitz. *Junior Book of Authors.*

Kunitz. *Junior Book of Authors, Second Edition Revised.*

Ward. *Authors of Books for Young People, Second Edition.*

"You Meet Such Interesting People." *Publishers Weekly*, March 21, 1960.

Young Wings. *Writing Books for Boys and Girls.*

JAMES HENRY DAUGHERTY, 1887-1974
author-illustrator
a.k.a. Jimmie Daugherty

AWARDS

Andy and the Lion. Caldecott Honor Book, 1939.

(*Better Known as Johnny Appleseed.* Newbery Honor Book, 1951.)

Daniel Boone. Newbery Medal Book, 1940.

Gillespie and the Guards. Caldecott Honor Book, 1957.

BIBLIOGRAPHY

Abe Lincoln Grows Up: Reprinted from Abraham Lincoln, the Prairie Years; by Carl Sandburg. Harcourt, 1928.

Abraham Lincoln. Viking, 1943.

Adventures of Johnny Appleseed; by Harry Chapin. Coward, 1930.

Adventures of Johnny T. Bear; by Margaret McElroy. Dutton, 1926.

Adventures of Tom Sawyer; by Mark Twain, *pseud.* (Samuel L. Clemens). Blue Ribbon, 1932.

All Things New; by Sonia Daugherty. Nelson, 1936.

Almanac for Americans; by Willis Thornton. Greenberg, 1941; second edition, Chilton, 1954.

American Folklore and Its Old-World Backgrounds: Following Folk Tales around the World; by Mary G. Davis. Compton, 1949.

American Life in Literature, Revised; by Jay B. Hubbell. Harper, 1949.

Andy and the Lion. Viking, 1938.

Authentic Revolution; by Erwin D. Canham. Christian Science Monitor, 1951.

Barnaby Rudge: A Tale of the Riots of '80; by Charles Dickens. Heritage, 1941.

Better Known as Johnny Appleseed; by Mabel L. Hunt. Lippincott, 1950.

Blacksmith and the Birds; by Edith Rickert. Doubleday, 1928.

Bold Dragoon and Other Ghostly Tales; by Washington Irving, edited by Anne C. Moore. Knopf, 1930.

Call of the Mountain; by Cornelia Meigs. Little, 1940.

Clue of the Faded Dress; by Maristan Chapman, *pseud.* (John and Mary Chapman). Appleton, 1938.

Comanche: The Story of America's Most Heroic Horse; by David Appel. World, 1951.

Conquest of Montezuma's Empire; by Andrew Lang. Longmans, 1928.

Courageous Companions; by Charles Finger. Longmans, 1929.

Daniel Boone. Viking, 1939.

Daniel Boone, Wilderness Scout: The Life Story and Towering Adventures of the Great Hunter, Long Knife, Who First Blazed the Wilderness Trail through the Indian's Country to Kentucky; by Stewart E. White. Doubleday, 1926.

Drake's Quest; by Cameron Rogers. Doubleday, 1927.

Early Moon; by Carl Sandburg. Harcourt, 1930.

Gillespie and the Guards; by Benjamin Elkin. Viking, 1956.

Girls of Glen Hazard; by Maristan Chapman, *pseud.* (John and Mary Chapman). Appleton, 1937.

Green Gravel; by Dora Aydelotte. Appleton, 1937.

Henry David Thoreau, a Man for Our Time. Viking, 1967.

Heroes in American Folklore; by Irwin Shapiro. il. with Donald McKay. Messner, 1962.

Hugh Gwyeth: A Roundhead Cavalier; by Beulah M. Dix. Macmillan, 1928.

In the Beginning: Being the First Chapter of Genesis from the King James Version; from the *Bible.* Oxford, 1941.

Irene of Tundra Towers; by Elizabeth Burrows. Doubleday, 1928.

Joe Magarac and His U.S.A. Citizen Papers; by Irwin Shapiro. Messner, 1948.

John Brown's Body; by Stephen V. Benét. Doubleday, 1930.

John Henry and the Double-Jointed Steam Drill; by Irwin Shapiro. Messner, 1945.

Judy of the Whale Gates: The Strange Happenings That Followed the Stranding of the Yacht Aphoon among the Volcanic Islands of Alaska; by Elizabeth Burrows. Doubleday, 1930.

King Penguin: A Legend of the South Sea Isles; by Richard H. Horne. Macmillan, 1925.

Kingdom and the Power, and the Glory: Stories of Faith and Marvel Selected from the King James Version of the Old Testament; from the *Bible*. Knopf, 1929.

Knickerbocker's History of New York; by Washington Irving, edited by Anne C. Moore. Doubleday, 1928.

Kris and Kristina; by Marie Bruce. Doubleday, 1927.

Landing of the Pilgrims. Random, 1950.

Last of the Mohicans: A Narrative of 1757; by James F. Cooper. World, 1957.

Lincoln's Gettysburg Address: A Pictorial Interpretation; by Abraham Lincoln. Whitman, 1947.

Long Way to Frisco: A Folk Adventure Novel of California and Oregon in 1852; by Alfred Powers. Little, 1951.

Lost Gospel; by Arthur Train. Scribner, 1925.

Loudest Noise in the World; by Benjamin Elkin. Viking, 1954.

Magna Charta. Random, 1956.

Marcus and Narcissa Whitman: Pioneers of Oregon. Viking, 1953.

Mashinka's Secret; by Sonia Daugherty. Stokes, 1932.

Memoirs of Benvenuto Cellini; by Benvenuto Cellini. Tr. Robert H. Cust. Duffield, 1932.

Morgan's Fourth Son; by Margaret I. Ross. Harper, 1940.

Mountain of Jade; by Violet Irwin and Vilhajalmer Stefansson. Macmillan, 1926.

Of Courage Undaunted: Across the Continent with Lewis and Clark. Viking, 1951.

Oregon Trail; by Francis Parkman. Farrar, 1931.

Outline of Government in Connecticut; edited by Philip E. Curtiss. Case, Lockwood and Brainard, 1944; revised, 1945; third edition, 1949; fourth edition, 1955; fifth edition, 1959 (?); sixth edition, 1965; seventh edition, 1968.

Over the Blue Wall; by Etta L. Mathews. University of North Carolina, 1937.

Picnic: A Frolic in 2 Colors and 3 Parts. Viking, 1958.

Plucky Allens; by Clara D. Pearson. Dutton, 1925.

Poor Richard. Viking, 1941.

Promise to Our Country: "I Pledge Allegiance...."; by James F. Calvert. McGraw, 1961.

Railroad to Freedom: A Story of the Civil War; by Hildegard H. Swift. Harcourt, 1932.

Rainbow Book of American History; by Earl S. Miers. World, 1955; revised, 1968.

Robert Goddard: Trail Blazer to the Stars; by Charles Daugherty. Macmillan, 1964.

Sign of the Buffalo Skull: The Story of Jim Bridger, Frontier Scout; by Peter O. Lamb. Stokes, 1932.

Sound of Trumpets: Selections from Ralph Waldo Emerson; by Ralph W. Emerson. Viking, 1971.

Splendid Spur: Being Memoirs of the Adventures of Mr. John Marvel, a Servant of His Majesty, King Charles I, in the Years 1642-3; by Arthur Quiller-Couch. Doubleday, 1927.

Story of Bread; by Elizabeth Watson. Harper, 1927.

Story of Milk and How It Came About; by Elizabeth Watson. Harper, 1928.

Story of Textiles; by Elizabeth Watson. Harper, 1928.

Stream of History; by Geoffrey Parsons. Scribner, 1928.

Tad Sheldon, Boy Scout: Stories of His Patrol; by John F. Wilson. Sturgis, 1913. (Identified as "James Dougherty.")

Ten Brave Men, Makers of the American Way: William Bradford, Roger Williams, Patrick Henry, Samuel Adams, Thomas Jefferson, George Washington, Benjamin Franklin, John Paul Jones, Andrew Jackson, Abraham Lincoln; by Sonia Daugherty. Lippincott, 1953.

Ten Brave Women: Anne Hutchinson, Abigail Adams, Dolly Madison, Narcissa Whitman, Julia Ward Howe, Susan B. Anthony, Dorothea Lynde Dix, Mary Lyon, Ida M. Tarbell, Eleanor Roosevelt; by Sonia Daugherty. Lippincott, 1953.

(comp.) *Their Weight in Wildcats: Tales of the Frontier*. Houghton, 1936.

Three Comedies; by William Shakespeare. Harcourt, 1929.

Three Musketeers; by Alexandre Dumas. Macmillan, 1962.

Trappers and Traders of the Far West. Random, 1952.

Treasury of Best-Loved Hymns, with Their Stories; by Daniel A. Polling. Pickwick, 1942.

Tuftoo, the Clown; by Howard R. Garis. Appleton, 1928.

Uncle Tom's Cabin; by Harriet B. Stowe; edited by Helen Black. Coward, 1929.

Vanka's Donkey; by Sonia Daugherty. Stokes, 1940.

Walt Whitman's America: Being Selections from Leaves of Grass, Democratic Vistas, Specimen Days, and Portraits of Lincoln; by Walt Whitman. World, 1964.

BIBLIOGRAPHY (cont'd)

Way of an Eagle: An Intimate Biography of Thomas Jefferson and His Fight for Democracy. Oxford, 1941; *a.k.a.* and reillustrated as *Thomas Jefferson, Fighter for Freedom and Human Rights*. Ungar, 1961.

West of Boston: Yankee Rhymes and Doggerel. Viking, 1956.

White Company; by Arthur C. Doyle. Harper, 1928.

Wild, Wild West. McKay, 1948.

William Blake. il. with Blake reproductions. Viking, 1960.

Windows on Henry Street; by Lillian D. Wald. Little, 1934.

Wings of Glory; by Sonia Daugherty. Oxford, 1940.

Wisher; by Charles Daugherty. Viking, 1960.

Wulnot the Wanderer: Story of King Alfred of England; by Herbert Inman-Escott. Longmans, 1928.

Yankee Thunder: The Legendary Life of Davy Crockett; by Irwin Shapiro. Messner, 1944.

MEDIA

Abraham Lincoln. (BB, TB).

Andy and the Lion. (BB, TB); Weston Woods Studios, 1955 (F), n. d. (FSS); also in Weston Woods Studios Set No. 4, 1968 (FSS).

Daniel Boone. (BB).

Landing of the Pilgrims. (BB); Educational Enrichment Materials, 1964 (R).

Loudest Noise in the World. Weston Woods Studios, 1967 (FSS); also in Weston Woods Studios Set No. 18, 1968 (FSS).

Magna Charta. (BB, C, MT); Educational Enrichment Materials, 1966 (R).

Marcus and Narcissa Whitman. (BB).

Of Courage Undaunted. (TB).

Picnic. (BB, TB).

Poor Richard. (BB, TB).

Trappers and Traders. Educational Enrichment Materials, 1964 (R).

EXHIBITIONS

McDowell Club, 1912. (New York, New York).

Schoelkopf Gallery, 1971, 1973. (New York, New York).

Societe Anonyme, n. d. (New York, New York).

Society of Independent Artists, n. d. (New York, New York).

COLLECTIONS

Allentown Free Public Library. (Allentown, Pennsylvania).

Kerlan Collection, University of Minnesota. (Minneapolis, Minnesota).

May Massee Collection, Emporia State College. (Emporia, Kansas).

Special Collections, University Research Library, University of California. (Los Angeles, California).

University of Oregon Library. (Eugene, Oregon).

BACKGROUND READING

Bader. *American Picturebooks from Noah's Ark to The Beast Within*.

Burke. *American Authors and Books, 1640 to the Present Day*.

Commire. *Something about the Author*.

Contemporary Authors.

Cooper. *Authors and Others*.

Current Biography.

Daugherty, J. "Illustrating Books for Children." *New York Public Library Bulletin*, November 1956.

DeSalle, A. "Pictorial Pleasantries by James Daugherty." *Print Connoisseur*, October 1929.

Ellis. *Book Illustration*.

Hopkins. *Books Are by People*.

James Daugherty. Weston Woods Studios, 1972 (F).

Kemp, E., ed. James Daugherty special issue. *Imprint: Oregon*, Fall 1975.

Kent, N. "Buckskin Illustrator." *American Artist*, March 1945.

Kingman. *Illustrators of Children's Books, 1957-1966*.

Kirkpatrick. *Twentieth Century Children's Writers*.

Kunitz. *Junior Book of Authors*.

Kunitz. *Junior Book of Authors, Second Edition Revised*.

Mahony. *Contemporary Illustrators of Children's Books*.

Mahony. *Illustrators of Children's Books, 1744-1945*.

Miller. *Illustrators of Children's Books, 1946-1956*.

Miller. *Newbery Medal Books, 1922-1955*.

Montgomery. *Story behind Modern Books*.

New York Times Biographical Service.

Ward. *Authors of Books for Young People, Second Edition*.

Young Wings. Writing Books for Boys and Girls.

INGRI MORTENSON D'AULAIRE, 1904-
author-illustrator

and

EDGAR PARIN D'AULAIRE, 1898-
author-illustrator

AWARDS

Abraham Lincoln. Caldecott Medal Book, 1940.

(*Children of the Soil*. Newbery Honor Book, 1933.)

BIBLIOGRAPHY

Edgar Parin D'Aulaire:

Blood; by Hanns H. Ewers. Heron, 1930.

Children of the Soil: A Story of Scandinavia; by Nora Burglon. Doubleday, 1932.

Coming of the Dragon Ships; by Howard Everson and Florence McClurg. Dutton, 1931.

Gao of the Ivory Coast; by Katie Seabrook. Coward, 1931.

Kari: A Story of Kari Supper from Lindeland. Norway; by Gabriel Scott. Tr. Anvor Barstad. Doubleday, 1931.

Needle in a Haystack; by John Mattheson. Morrow, 1930.

Rama, the Hero of India: Done into a Short English Version for Boys and Girls; by Dhan G. Mukerji from the *Válmiki*. Dutton, 1930.

Romance of Leonardo da Vinci; by Dmitrii Merejkowski. Tr. Herbert Trench. Putnam, 1924.

Ingri and Edgar Parin D'Aulaire:

Abraham Lincoln. Doubleday, 1939.

Animals Everywhere: First Picture Book for Youngest Children. Doubleday, 1940; new edition, 1954.

Benjamin Franklin. Doubleday, 1950.

Buffalo Bill. Doubleday, 1952.

Children of the Northlights. Viking, 1935.

Columbus. Doubleday, 1955.

Conquest of the Atlantic. Viking, 1933.

Cukoo Calls: A Story of Finland; by Nora Burglon. Winston, 1940.

D'Aulaire's Book of Greek Myths. Doubleday, 1962.

D'Aulaire's Trolls. Doubleday, 1972. (Also issued as a limited edition.)

Don't Count Your Chicks. Doubleday, 1943.

(tr.) *East of the Sun and West of the Moon: Twenty-one Norwegian Folk Tales*; by Peter C. Asbjörnsen and Jorgen Möe. Viking, 1938.

Foxie. Doubleday, 1949; a.k.a. *Foxie the Singing Dog*, 1969.

George Washington. Doubleday, 1936.

Johnny Blossom; by Dikken Zwilgmeyer. Tr. Emilie Poulsson. Pilgrim, 1948.

Leif the Lucky. Doubleday, 1941.

Lord's Prayer: Catholic Edition; from the *Bible*. Doubleday, 1934.

Lord's Prayer: Protestant Edition; from the *Bible*. Doubleday, 1934.

Magic Meadow. Doubleday, 1958.

Magic Rug. Doubleday, 1931.

Nils. Doubleday, 1948.

Norse Gods and Giants. Doubleday, 1967.

Ola. Doubleday, 1932.

Ola and Blakken and Line, Sine, Trine. Doubleday, 1933; a.k.a. *Terrible Troll Bird*. Doubleday, 1976.

Pocahontas. Doubleday, 1946.

Sidsel Longskirt: A Girl of Norway; by Hans Aanrud. Tr. Dagny Mortenson and Margery W. Bianco. Winston, 1935; a.k.a. *Sidsel Longskirt and Solve Suntrap: Two Children of Norway*, 1935.

Solve Suntrap: A Boy of Norway; by Hans Aanrud. Tr. Dagny Mortenson and Margery W. Bianco. Winston, 1935; a.k.a. *Sidsel Longskirt and Solve Suntrap: Two Children of Norway*, 1935.

Star-Spangled Banner; by Francis S. Key. Doubleday, 1942.

Too Big. Doubleday, 1945.

Two Cars. Doubleday, 1955.

Wings for Per. Doubleday, 1944.

MEDIA

Abraham Lincoln. (BB).

Benjamin Franklin. Pied Piper Productions, n. d. (FSS).

Buffalo Bill. (BB).

Children of the Northlights. (BB); Lane Morrison/ Weston Woods Studios, 1977 (F).

Don't Count Your Chicks. (BB); Weston Woods Studios, 1963 (FSS).

George Washington. (BB).

Magic Meadow. (CB).

Ola. Weston Woods Studios, 1970 (FSS).

Pocahontas. (BB). McGraw-Hill Publishing Company, 1973 (FSS).

EXHIBITIONS

Galerie Wang, 1929. (Oslo, Norway).

EXHIBITIONS (cont'd)

Sal d'Automme, 1927. (Paris, France).

COLLECTIONS

deGrummond Collection, University of Southern Mississippi. (Hattiesburg, Mississippi).

Free Library of Philadelphia. (Philadelphia, Pennsylvania).

Kerlan Collection, University of Minnesota. (Minneapolis, Minnesota).

May Massee Collection, Emporia State College. (Emporia, Kansas).

University of Oregon Library. (Eugene, Oregon).

BACKGROUND READING

Bader. *American Picturebooks from Noah's Ark to The Beast Within.*

Burke. *American Authors and Books, 1640 to the Present Day.*

Commire. *Something about the Author.*

Contemporary Authors.

Current Biography.

D'Aulaire, I. and E. "Gentle Art of Drawing Reindeer." *Horn Book*, July 1935.

Farquhar, M. "Magic Rug of Ingri and Edgar Parin D'Aulaire." *Elementary English*, April 1953.

Foster, M. "Ingri and Edgar Parin D'Aulaire." *Catholic Library World*, February 1970.

Hopkins. *Books Are by People.*

Jones, M. "Visit with Ingri and Edgar Parin D'Aulaire." *Children's Libraries Newsletter*, No. 3, 1972.

Kingman. *Illustrators of Children's Books, 1957-1966.*

Kingman. *Illustrators of Children's Books, 1967-1976.*

Kirkpatrick. *Twentieth Century Children's Writers.*

Kunitz. *Junior Book of Authors.*

Kunitz. *Junior Book of Authors, Second Edition Revised.*

Mahony. *Contemporary Illustrators of Children's Books.*

Mahony. *Illustrators of Children's Books, 1744-1945.*

Massee, M. "Ingri and Edgar Parin D'Aulaire, A Sketch." *Horn Book*, September 1935.

Miller. *Caldecott Medal Books, 1938-1952.*

Miller. *Illustrators of Children's Books, 1946-1956.*

Montgomery. *Story behind Modern Books.*

Smaridge. *Famous Literary Teams for Young People.*

Sparrow, C. "Ingri and Edgar Parin D'Aulaire." *American Scandinavian Review*, March 1942.

Ward. *Authors of Books for Young People, Second Edition.*

Ward. *Illustrators of Books for Young People, Second Edition.*

Weiderman, A. "Ola, the Bestseller." *Norseman*, No. 5, 1963.

Young Wings. Writing Books for Boys and Girls.

+MARY GOULD DAVIS, 1882-1956
author

AWARDS

Truce of the Wolf. Newbery Honor Book, 1932.

BIBLIOGRAPHY

American Folklore and Its Old-World Backgrounds: Following Folk Tales around the World. il. James Daugherty. Compton, 1949.

(ed.) *Art of the Storyteller;* by Marie Shedlock. Appleton, 1936.

Baker's Dozen: 13 Stories to Tell and to Read Aloud. il. Emma Brock. Harcourt, 1930.

(ed.) *Children's Books from 12 Countries.* American Library Association, 1930.

(ed.) *Girl's Book of Verse: A Treasury of Old and New Poems.* Stokes, 1922.

Handsome Donkey. il. Emma Brock. Harcourt, 1933.

Randolph Caldecott, 1846-1886: An Appreciation. il. Randolph Caldecott. Lippincott, 1946.

(ed.) *Reformed Pirate: Stories from The Floating Prince, Ting-A-Ling Tales and The Queen's Museum;* by Frank Stockton. il. Reginald Birch. Scribner, 1936.

Sandy's Kingdom. il. Emma Brock. Harcourt, 1935.

(ed.) *Stories: A List to Tell and to Read Aloud.* New York Public Library, 1927; second edition, 1933; third edition, 1943.

Three Golden Oranges and Other Spanish Folk Tales; with Ralph S. Boggs. il. Emma Brock. Longmans, 1936.

Truce of the Wolf and Other Tales of Old Italy. il. Jay Van Everen. Harcourt, 1931.

Wakaima and the Clay Man, and Other African Folktales; with Ernest Kalibala. il. Avery Johnson. Longmans,1946.

(ed.) *With Cap and Bells: Humorous Stories to Tell and to Read Aloud.* il. Richard Bennett. Harcourt, 1937.

MEDIA

Baker's Dozen. (BB).

Three Golden Oranges. (TB).

COLLECTIONS

New York Public Library. (New York, New York).

BACKGROUND READING

Burke. *American Authors and Books, 1640 to the Present Day.*

Davis, M. "Storyteller's Art." *Horn Book*, May 1934.

Kunitz. *Junior Book of Authors.*

Kunitz. *Junior Book of Authors, Second Edition Revised.*

"Mary Gould Davis." *Library Journal*, January 15, 1945.

Ward. *Authors of Books for Young People, Second Edition.*

MARGUERITE LOFFT DE ANGELI, 1889-
author-illustrator

AWARDS

Black Fox of Lorne. Newbery Honor Book, 1957.

Door in the Wall. Newbery Medal Book, 1950.

Marguerite de Angeli's Book of Nursery and Mother Goose Rhymes. Caldecott Honor Book, 1955.

(*Meggy MacIntosh.* Newbery Honor Book, 1931.)

Yoni Wondernose. Caldecott Honor Book, 1945.

BIBLIOGRAPHY

Alice-All-by-Herself; by Elizabeth Coatsworth. Macmillan, 1937.

Black Fox of Lorne. Doubleday, 1956.

Bright April. Doubleday, 1946.

Butter at the Old Price: The Autobiography of Marguerite de Angeli. Doubleday, 1971.

Candle in the Mist: A Story for Girls; by Florence C. Means. Houghton, 1931.

Challenge Stories of Courage and Love for Girls; by Helen Ferris. Doubleday, 1936.

Christmas Nightingale: Three Christmas Stories from Poland; by Eric Kelly. Macmillan, 1932.

Copper-Toed Boots. Doubleday, 1938.

Cousin from Clare; by Rose Sackett. Macmillan, 1932.

Covered Bridge; by Cornelia Meigs. Macmillan, 1936.

Door in the Wall. Doubleday, 1949; *a.k.a. Door in the Wall: A Play Adapted from the Novel*; with Arthur de Angeli, 1969.

Dove in the Eagle's Nest. Macmillan, 1926.

Elin's Amerika. Doubleday, 1941.

Empty Barn; with Arthur de Angeli. Westminster, 1961.

Fiddlestrings. Doubleday, 1974.

(tr.) *Goose Girl: A New Translation*; by Jacob and Wilhelm Grimm. Doubleday, 1964.

Henner's Lydia. Doubleday, 1936.

In and Out: Verses; by Tom Robinson. Viking, 1943.

It's More Fun When You Know the Rules: Etiquette Problems for Girls; by Beatrice Pierce. Farrar, 1935.

Jared's Island. Doubleday, 1947.

Joan Wanted a Kitty; by Jane Gemmill. Winston, 1937.

Just Like David. Doubleday, 1951.

Katrina Van Ost and the Silver Rose; by Elizabeth Gale. Putnam, 1934.

Lances of Lynwood; by Charlotte Yonge. Macmillan, 1929.

Lion in the Box. Doubleday, 1975.

Little Book of Prayers and Graces; by Quail Hawkins. Doubleday, 1952.

Little Duke: Richard the Fearless; by Charlotte Yonge. Macmillan, 1927.

Marguerite de Angeli's Book of Favorite Hymns. Doubleday, 1963.

Marguerite de Angeli's Book of Nursery and Mother Goose Rhymes; from Mother Goose. Doubleday, 1954.

Marguerite de Angeli's Pocket Full of Posies: A Merry Mother Goose. Doubleday, 1961.

Mario's Castle; by Helen Forbes. Macmillan, 1928.

Meggy MacIntosh; by Elizabeth J. Gray. Doubleday, 1930.

New Moon: The Story of Dick Martin's Courage, His Silver Sixpence and His Friends in the New World; by Cornelia Meigs. Macmillan, 1924.

Nina, David and Kiki. Doubleday, 1944.

Old Testament; from the *Bible*. Doubleday, 1960.

Petite Suzanne. Doubleday, 1937.

Prayers and Graces for Little Children; by Quail Hawkins. Grosset, 1941.

Prince and the Page; by Charlotte Yonge. Macmillan, 1925.

Princess and the Gypsy: A Tale of Old Spain; by Jean Rosmer, *pseud.* (Jeanne S. A. DeBrahm). Tr. Virginia Olcott. Lippincott, 1938.

BIBLIOGRAPHY (cont'd)

Red Sky over Rome; by Anne D. Kyle. Houghton, 1938.

Skippack School: Being the Story of Eli Shrawder and of One Christopher Dock, Schoolmaster, about the Year 1750. Doubleday, 1939.

Summer Day with Ted and Nina. Doubleday, 1940; also in *Ted and Nina Storybook*, below.

Ted and Nina Go to the Grocery Store. Doubleday, 1935; also in *Ted and Nina Storybook*, below.

Ted and Nina Have a Happy Rainy Day. Doubleday, 1936; also in *Ted and Nina Storybook*, below.

Ted and Nina Storybook. Doubleday, 1965. (Includes *Summer Day with Ted and Nina*, *Ted and Nina Go to the Grocery Store*, and *Ted and Nina Have a Happy Rainy Day*, each issued separately, above.)

Thee, Hannah! Doubleday, 1940.

They Loved to Laugh; by Kathryn Worth. Doubleday, 1942.

Turkey for Christmas. Westminster, 1944.

Up the Hill. Doubleday, 1942.

Whistle for the Crossing. Doubleday, 1977.

Yoni Wondernose: For Three Little Wondernoses, Nina, David and Kiki. Doubleday, 1944.

MEDIA

Black Fox of Lorne. (BB).

Bright April. (BB, TB).

Copper-Toed Boots. (BB, TB); Intercontinental Audio-Video Company, ca.1947 (R).

Door in the Wall. (BB, TB); Miller-Brody Productions, 1972 (FSS).

Elin's Amerika. (TB).

Henner's Lydia. (BB).

Jared's Island. (TB); Mercury Sound Books, 1957 (R).

Marguerite de Angeli's Book of Nursery and Mother Goose Rhymes. (BB, TB).

Thee, Hannah! (BB, TB).

Turkey for Christmas. (TB).

Yoni Wondernose. (BB).

COLLECTIONS

deGrummond Collection, University of Southern Mississippi. (Hattiesburg, Mississippi).

Free Library of Philadelphia. (Philadelphia, Pennsylvania).

Kerlan Collection, University of Minnesota. (Minneapolis, Minnesota).

May Massee Collection, Emporia State College. (Emporia, Kansas).

Special Collections, University Research Library, University of California. (Los Angeles, California).

BACKGROUND READING

Burke. *American Authors and Books, 1640 to the Present Day*.

Burns, P., and Hines, R. "Marguerite de Angeli: Faith in the Human Spirit." *Elementary English*, December 1967.

Commire. *Something about the Author*.

Contemporary Authors.

Current Biography.

Ellis. *Book Illustration*.

Hoffman. *Authors and Illustrators of Children's Books*.

Hollowell, L. "Marguerite de Angeli, Writer and Illustrator for Children." *Elementary English*, October 1952.

Hopkins. *More Books by More People*.

Hunt, Donald H. *Libraries and Reading, Their Importance in the Lives of Famous Americans: Essays by Marguerite de Angeli (et al.)*. Drexel Institute of Technology, 1964.

Kingman. *Illustrators of Children's Books, 1957-1966*.

Kingman. *Illustrators of Children's Books, 1967-1976*.

Kirkpatrick. *Twentieth Century Children's Writers*.

Kunitz. *Junior Book of Authors, Second Edition Revised*.

Lesser, M. "Marguerite de Angeli, Regina Medalist." *Catholic Library World*, December 1968.

Mahony. *Contemporary Illustrators of Children's Books*.

Mahony. *Illustrators of Children's Books, 1744-1945*.

Marguerite de Angeli. Profiles in Literature, 1976 (VT).

"Meet Marguerite de Angeli." *Instructor*, November 1952.

Miller. *Illustrators of Children's Books, 1946-1956*.

Miller. *Newbery Medal Books, 1922-1955*.

Mortenson, L. "Lapeer Michigan, Birthplace of Marguerite de Angeli: True History of Copper-Toed Boots." *Elementary English*, April 1965.

Nykoruk. *Authors in the News*.

Smaridge. *Famous Modern Storytellers for Young People*.

Ward. *Authors of Books for Young People, Second Edition*.

Young Wings. *Writing Books for Boys and Girls*.

MEiNDERT DeJONG, 1906-
author

AWARDS

Along Came a Dog. Newbery Honor Book, 1959.

House of Sixty Fathers. Newbery Honor Book, 1957.

Hurry Home, Candy. Newbery Honor Book, 1954.

Shadrach. Newbery Honor Book, 1954.

Wheel on the School. Newbery Medal Book, 1955.

BIBLIOGRAPHY

Almost All-White Rabbity Cat. il. Herman B. Vestal. Macmillan, 1972.

Along Came a Dog. il. Maurice Sendak. Harper, 1958.

Bells of the Harbor. il. Kurt Wiese. Harper, 1941.

Bible Days. il. Kreigh Collins. Fiedler, 1948.

Big Goose and the Little White Duck. il. Edna Potter. Harper, 1938; also il. Nancy E. Burkert, 1963.

Billy and the Unhappy Bull. il. Marc Simont. Harper, 1946.

Cat That Walked a Week. il. Jessie Robinson. Harper, 1943; also il. Victor Ambrus. Lutterworth, 1965.

Dirk's Dog Bello. il. Kurt Wiese. Harper, 1939.

Easter Cat. il. Lillian Hoban. Macmillan, 1971; also il. Mary Dinsdale. Lutterworth, 1972.

Far out the Long Canal. il. Nancy Grossman. Harper, 1964.

Good Luck Duck. il. Marc Simont. Harper, 1950.

Horse Came Running. il. Paul Sagsoorian. Macmillan, 1970.

House of Sixty Fathers. il. Maurice Sendak. Harper, 1956.

Hurry Home, Candy. il. Maurice Sendak. Harper, 1953.

Journey from Peppermint Street. il. Emily Arnold McCully. Harper, 1968.

Last Little Cat. il. Jim McMullan. Harper, 1961.

Little Cow and the Turtle. il. Maurice Sendak. Harper, 1955.

Little Stray Dog. il. Edward Shenton. Harper, 1943.

Mighty Ones: Great Men and Women of Early Bible Days. il. Harvey Schmidt. Harper, 1959.

Nobody Plays with a Cabbage. il. Tom Allen. Harper, 1962.

Puppy Summer. il. Anita Lobel. Harper, 1966.

Shadrach. il. Maurice Sendak. Harper, 1953.

Singing Hill. il. Maurice Sendak. Harper, 1962.

Smoke above the Lane. il. Gerard Goodenow. Harper, 1951.

Tower by the Sea. il. Barbara Comfort. Harper, 1950; also il. Susan Einzig. Lutterworth, 1964.

Wheel on the School. il. Maurice Sendak. Harper, 1954.

Wheels over the Bridge. il. Aldren Watson. Harper, 1941.

MEDIA

Along Came a Dog. (TB).

Easter Cat. (TB).

Far out the Long Canal. (TB).

House of Sixty Fathers. Miller-Brody Productions, 1974 (FSS).

Hurry Home, Candy. (BB); Miller-Brody Productions, 1976 (FSS).

Journey from Peppermint Street. (BB, TB).

Little Cow and the Turtle. (BB, TB).

Mighty Ones. (BB, TB).

Shadrach. (BB, TB).

Singing Hill. (BB).

Wheel on the School. (BB, C, MT, TB); Miller-Brody Productions, 1970 (FSS); Newbery Award Records, 1969 (C, R).

COLLECTIONS

Clarke Historical Library, Central Michigan University. (Mt. Pleasant, Michigan).

Kerlan Collection, University of Minnesota. (Minneapolis, Minnesota).

BACKGROUND READING

Burgess, E. "Meindert DeJong, Storyteller." *Elementary English,* May 1955.

Butler, C. "Meindert DeJong, Regina Medal Winner, 1972." *Catholic Library World*, February 1972.

Cianciolo, P. "Meindert DeJong." *Elementary English*, October 1968.

Commire. *Something about the Author*.

Contemporary Authors.

Current Biography.

DeJong, M. "Cry and the Creation." *Horn Book*, April 1963.

Fuller. *More Junior Authors*.

Hoffman. *Authors and Illustrators of Children's Books*.

Hopkins. *More Books by More People*.

Kirkpatrick. *Twentieth Century Children's Writers*.

Miller. *Newbery Medal Books, 1922-1955*.

BACKGROUND READING (cont'd)

Smaridge. *Famous Modern Storytellers for Young People*.

Townsend. *Sense of Story*.

Young Wings. *Writing Books for Boys and Girls*.

TOMIE DePAOLA, 1934-
author-illustrator

AWARDS

Strega Nona. Caldecott Honor Book, 1976.

BIBLIOGRAPHY

Andy, That's My Name. Prentice, 1973.

Authorized Autumn Charts of the Upper Red Canoe River Country; by Peter Z. Cohen. Atheneum, 1972.

Beat the Drum: Independence Day Has Come; edited by Lee B. Hopkins. Harcourt, 1977.

Cabinet of the President of the United States; by James A. Eichner. Watts, 1968.

Can't You Make Them Behave, King George?; by Jean Fritz. Coward, 1977.

"Charlie Needs a Cloak." Prentice, 1973.

Cloud Book. Holiday, 1975.

Danny and His Thumb; by Kathryn Ernst. Prentice, 1973.

David's Windows; by Alice Low. Putnam, 1974.

Easter People Series, Grade Two, *Belong*; by Winston, 1977.

Easter People Series, Grade Three, *Journey*; by Winston, 1977.

Fight the Night. Lippincott, 1968.

Finders Keepers, Losers Weepers; by Joan B. Lexau. Lippincott, 1967.

Four Stories for Four Seasons. Prentice, 1977.

Franklin Watts' Concise Guide to Baby-Sitting; by Rubie Saunders. Watts, 1972.

Ghost with the Halloween Hiccups; by Stephen Mooser. Watts, 1977.

Giants' Farm; by Jane Yolen. Seabury, 1977.

Good Morning to You, Valentine; by Lee B. Hopkins. Harcourt, 1975.

Helga's Dowry: A Troll Love Story. Harcourt, 1977.

Hercules: The Gentle Giant; by Nina Schneider. Hawthorn, 1969.

Hold Everything; by Samuel Epstein and Beryl Williams. Holiday, 1973.

Hot as an Ice Cube; by Phillip Balestrino. Crowell, 1971.

How to Be a Puppeteer; by Eleanor Boylan. McCall, 1970.

I Love You, Mouse; by John Graham. Harcourt, 1976.

If He's My Brother; by Barbara Williams. Harvey, 1976.

Images of Jesus; by Daniel O'Connor. Winston, 1977.

Joe and the Snow. Hawthorn, 1968.

John Fisher's Magic Book; by John Fisher. Prentice, 1971.

Journey of the Kiss. Hawthorn, 1970.

Let's Find Out about Communications; by Valerie Pitt. Watts, 1973.

Let's Find Out about Houses; by Martha and Charles Shapp. Watts, 1975.

Let's Find Out about Summer; by Martha and Charles Shapp. Watts, 1963.

Light and Sight; by Melvin L. Alexenberg. Prentice, 1969.

Look in the Mirror; by Samuel Epstein and Beryl Williams. Holiday, 1973.

Mario's Mystery Machine; by Sibyl Hancock. Putnam, 1972.

Michael Bird-Boy. Prentice, 1975.

Mixed-Up Mystery Smell; by Eleanor Coerr. Putnam, 1976.

Monsters' Ball. Hawthorn, 1970.

Monsters of the Middle Ages; by William Wise. Putnam, 1971.

Morning Glory; by Robert Bly. Kayak, 1969.

Nana Upstairs & Nana Downstairs. Putnam, 1973.

Odd Jobs; by Tony Johnston. Putnam, 1977.

Old Man Whickett's Donkey; by Mary Calhoun. Parents, 1975.

Once upon a Dinkelsbühl; by Patricia L. Gauch. Putnam, 1977.

Parker Pig, Esquire. Hawthorn, 1969.

Pick It Up; by Samuel Epstein and Beryl Williams. Holiday, 1971.

Poetry for Chuckles and Grins; by Leland B. Jacobs. Garrard, 1968.

Quicksand Book. Holiday, 1977.

Rocking-Chair Ghost; by Mary C. Jane. Lippincott, 1969.

Rutherford T. Finds 21B; by Barbara Rinkoff. Putnam, 1970.

Santa's Crash-Bang Christmas; by Steven Kroll. Holiday, 1977.

Simple Pictures Are Best; by Nancy Willard. Harcourt, 1977.

Six Impossible Things before Breakfast; by Norma Farber. il. with others. Addison, 1977.

Solomon Grundy Born on Oneday: A Finite Arithmetic Puzzle; by Malcolm Weiss. Crowell, 1977.

Sound; by Lisa Miller. Coward, 1965.

Sound Science; by Melvin L. Alexenberg. Prentice, 1968.

Star-Spangled Banana, and Other Revolutionary Riddles; by Charles Keller and Richard Baker. Prentice, 1974.

Strega Nona: An Old Tale. Prentice, 1975.

Surprise Party; by Annabelle Pragen. Pantheon, 1977.

Take This Hammer; by Samuel Epstein and Beryl Williams. Hawthorn, 1969.

Things to Make and Do for Valentine's Day. Watts, 1976.

This Is the Ambulance Leaving the Zoo; by Norma Farber. Dutton, 1975.

Tiger and the Rabbit; by Pura Belpré. Lippincott, 1965.

Tricky Peik, and Other Picture Tales; by Jeanne B. Hardendorff. Lippincott, 1967.

Tyrannosaurus Game; by Steven Kroll. Holiday, 1976.

Unicorn and the Moon. Ginn, 1973.

Watch Out for the Chicken Feet in Your Soup. Prentice, 1974.

What Is Fear?; by Jean Rosenbaum. Prentice, 1972.

Whatchamacallit Book; by Bernice K. Hunt. Putnam, 1976.

Wheels; by Lisa Miller. Coward, 1965.

When Everyone Was Fast Asleep. Holiday, 1976.

Who Needs Holes?; by Samuel Epstein and Beryl Williams. Hawthorn, 1970.

Wind and the Sun, Retold. Ginn, 1972.

Wonderful Dragon of Timlin. Bobbs, 1966.

MEDIA

Andy. Random House, 1977 (FSS).

"Charlie Needs a Cloak." (BB).

Let's Find Out about Houses. Westport Communications Group, 19? (FSS).

Let's Find Out about Summer. Westport Communications Group, 19? (FSS).

Strega Nona. (TB).

Wind and the Sun. Xerox Films/Lumin Films, 1973 (FSS).

EXHIBITIONS

Alliance Corporation, 1972. (Boston, Massachusetts).

Botolph Group, Inc., 1961, 1964, 1967, 1969, 1971-75. (Boston, Massachusetts).

Grail Festival of the Arts, 1959. (Brooklyn, New York).

Immaculate Heart College, 1969. (Los Angeles, California).

Library Arts Center, 1975. (Newport, New Hampshire).

Newton College of the Sacred Heart, 1968, 1972. (Newton, Massachusetts).

Rizzoli Gallery, 1977. (New York, New York).

San Francisco College for Women, 1969. (San Francisco, California).

South Vermont Art Center, 1958. (Manchester, Vermont).

COLLECTIONS

Kerlan Collection, University of Minnesota. (Minneapolis, Minnesota).

BACKGROUND READING

Commire. *Something about the Author*.

Contemporary Authors.

Dunning, J. "Hard Winter's Work." *New York Times Book Review*, November 13, 1977.

Kingman. *Illustrators of Children's Books, 1957-1966*.

Kingman. *Illustrators of Children's Books, 1967-1976*.

Ward. *Illustrators of Books for Young People, Second Edition*.

+DIANE DILLON, 1933-
illustrator

and

+LEO LOUIS DILLON
illustrator

AWARDS

Ashanti to Zulu. Caldecott Medal Book, 1977.

(*Hundred Penny Box*. Newbery Honor Book, 1976.)

Why Mosquitoes Buzz in People's Ears. Caldecott Medal Book, 1976.

BIBLIOGRAPHY

African Kingdoms; by Basil Davidson and the editors of Time-Life. Time-Life, 1966.

Ashanti to Zulu: African Traditions; by Margaret Musgrove. Dial, 1976.

Behind the Back of the Mountain: Black Folktales from Southern Africa, Retold; by Verna Aardema. Dial, 1973.

Burning Star; by Ethel C. Rosenberg. Houghton, 1974.

Claymore and Kilt: Tales of Scottish Kings and Castles; by Sorche N. Leodhas, *pseud.* (Leclair G. Alger). Holt, 1967.

Dark Venture; by Audrey White Beyer. Knopf, 1968.

Gassire's Lute: A West African Epic; by Alta Jablow. Dutton, 1971.

Hakon of Rogen's Saga; by Erik Haugaard. Houghton, 1963.

Horse and His Rider; by Erik Haugaard. Houghton, 1968.

Hundred Penny Box; by Sharon B. Mathis. Viking, 1975.

Ring in the Prairie: A Shawnee Legend; by John Bierhorst. Dial, 1970.

Shamrock and Spear: Tales and Legends from Ireland; by F. M. Pilkington. Holt, 1968.

Slave's Trade; by Erik Haugaard. Houghton, 1965.

Song of the Boat; by Lorenz B. Graham. Crowell, 1975.

Songs and Stories from Uganda; by W. Moses Serwadda. Crowell, 1974.

Third Gift; by Jan Carew. Little, 1974.

Untold Tale; by Erik Haugaard. Houghton, 1971.

Whirlwind Is a Ghost Dancing; by Natalia M. Belting. Dutton, 1974.

Who's in Rabbit's House: A Masai Tale; by Verna Aardema. Dial, 1977.

Why Heimdall Blew His Horn: Tale of the Norse Gods; by Frederick Liang. Silver, 1969.

Why Mosquitoes Buzz in People's Ears: A West African Tale Retold; by Verna Aardema. Dial, 1975.

MEDIA

Ashanti to Zulu. Weston Woods Studios, 1977 (FSS); also in Weston Woods Studios Set No. 44, 1977 (FSS).

Why Mosquitoes Buzz in People's Ears. Weston Woods Studios, 1976 (FSS).

BACKGROUND READING

Commire. *Something about the Author*.

Dillon, D. "Leo Dillon." *Horn Book*, August 1977.

Dillon, L. "Diane Dillon." *Horn Book*, August 1977.

Dillon, L. "Leo and Diane Dillon." *Horn Book*, August 1977.

Dillon, L. and D. "Caldecott Award Acceptance." *Horn Book*, August 1977; *Top of the News*, Summer 1977.

Dillon, L. "Caldecott Award Acceptance: Address, July 20, 1976." *Horn Book*, August 1976; also as "Caldecott Acceptance Speech." *Top of the News*, Fall 1976.

Fogleman, P. "Leo and Diane Dillon." *Horn Book*, August 1976.

Kingman. *Illustrators of Children's Books, 1967-1976*.

JANINA DOMANSKA
author-illustrator

AWARDS

If All the Seas Were One. Caldecott Honor Book, 1972.

BIBLIOGRAPHY

Best of the Bargain. Greenwillow, 1977.

Black Heart of Indri; by Dorothy Hoge. Scribner, 1966.

Clocks Tell the Time; by Alma Reck. Scribner, 1960.

(tr.) *Coconut Thieves*; adapted by Catherine Fournier. Scribner, 1964.

Din Dan Don, It's Christmas. Greenwillow, 1975.

Dragon Liked Smoked Fish; by Jerzy Laskowski. Seabury, 1967.

Gas Station Gus; by Dorothy Kunhardt. Harper, 1961.

(tr.) *Golden Seed*; by Maria Konopnicka. Scribner, 1962.

Harper Book of Princes, with Biographical Notes on Each Author; edited by Sally P. Johnson. Harper, 1964.

I Like Weather; by Aileen Fisher. Crowell, 1963.

I Saw a Ship A-Sailing. Macmillan, 1972.

If All the Seas Were One. Macmillan, 1971.

In Place of Katia; by Mara Kay. Scribner, 1963.

Light; by Bernice Kohn. Coward, 1965.

Little Red Hen. Macmillan, 1973.

Look: There Is a Turtle Flying. Macmillan, 1968.

Marilka. Macmillan, 1970.

Master of the Royal Cats; by Jerzy Laskowski. Seabury, 1965.

Mischievous Meg; by Astrid Lindgren. Tr. Gerry Bothmer. Viking, 1962.

More Tales of Faraway Folk; by Babette Deutsch and Avrahm Yarmolinsky. Harper, 1963.

Nikkos of the Pink Pelican; by Ruth Tooze. Viking, 1964.

Palmiero and the Ogre. Macmillan, 1967.

Song of the Lop-Eared Mule; by Natalie S. Carlson. Harper, 1961.

Spring Is. Greenwillow, 1976.

Steel Flea; by Nicholas Leskov, retold by Babette Deutsch and Avraham Yarmolinsky. Harper, 1964.

Trumpeter of Krakow; by Eric Kelly. Macmillan, 1966.

Turnip. Macmillan, 1969.

Under the Green Willow; by Elizabeth Coatsworth. Macmillan, 1971.

What Do You See? Macmillan, 1974.

Whizz!; by Edward Lear. Macmillan, 1973.

Why So Much Noise? Harper, 1965.

MEDIA

Look: There Is a Turtle Flying. (TB).

Turnip. Association-Sterling/Macmillan Films, 1974 (FSS).

EXHIBITIONS

All Poland Exhibition. 1946, (Warsaw, Poland).

Biennale Bratislava, 1975. (Bratislava, Czechoslovakia).

Exposition Biennale, 1951. (Genoa, Italy).

Galleria San Bernardo, 1948. (Rome, Italy).

Kottler Gallery, 1957. (New York, New York).

Polish Art Council, 1974. (Warsaw, Poland).

Roman Foundation for the Fine Arts, 1951. (Rome, Italy).

Studio 3, 1959. (Kew Gardens, New York).

Twelfth International Exhibition of Original Pictures (of children's picture books), 1977. (Tokyo, Japan).

COLLECTIONS

deGrummond Collection, University of Southern Mississippi. (Hattiesburg, Mississippi).

Fondazione Scientifica Polaccha. (Rome, Italy).

Free Library of Philadelphia. (Philadelphia, Pennsylvania).

Kerlan Collection, University of Minnesota. (Minneapolis, Minnesota).

Museum of Modern Art. (New York, New York).

BACKGROUND READING

Commire. *Something about the Author*.

Contemporary Authors.

DeMontreville. *Third Book of Junior Authors*.

Kingman. *Illustrators of Children's Books, 1957-1966*.

Kingman. *Illustrators of Children's Books, 1967-1976*.

Nykoruk. *Authors in the News*.

Ward. *Authors of Children's Books for Young People, Second Edition*.

+WILLIAM SHERMAN PÈNE DU BOIS, 1916-
author-illustrator

AWARDS

Bear Party. Caldecott Honor Book, 1952.

Lion. Caldecott Honor Book, 1957.

Twenty-one Balloons. Newbery Medal Book, 1948.

BIBLIOGRAPHY

Alligator Case. Harper, 1965.

Bear Circus. Viking, 1971.

Bear Party. Viking, 1951.

Call Me Bandicoot. Harper, 1970.

Castles and Dragons: Read-to-Yourself Fairy Tales for Boys and Girls; by The Child Study Association of America. Crowell, 1958.

Certain Small Shepherd; by Rebecca Caudill. Holt, 1965.

Digging for China: A Poem; by Richard Wilbur. Doubleday, 1956.

Elisabeth the Cow Ghost. Nelson, 1936; new edition, Viking, 1964.

Fierce John; by Edward Fenton. Doubleday, 1959.

Flying Locomotive. Viking, 1941.

Giant. Viking, 1954.

Giant Otto. Viking, 1936.

Great Geppy. Viking, 1940.

Hare and the Tortoise and the Tortoise and the Hare; with Po Lee. Doubleday, 1972.

BIBLIOGRAPHY (cont'd)

Harriett; by Charles F. McKinley. Viking, 1946.

Horse in the Camel Suit. Harper, 1967.

In France; by Marguerite Clemént. Viking, 1956.

Lazy Tommy Pumpkinhead. Harper, 1966.

Light Princess; by George MacDonald. Crowell, 1962.

Lion. Viking, 1956.

Magic Finger; by Roald Dahl. Harper, 1966.

Moon Ahead; by Leslie Greener. Viking, 1951.

Mother Goose for Christmas. Viking, 1973.

Mousewife; by Rumer Godden. Viking, 1951.

Moving Day; by Tobi Tobias. Knopf, 1976.

My Brother Bird; by Evelyn Ames. Dodd, 1954.

My Grandson Lew; by Charlotte Zolotow. Harper, 1974.

Otto and the Magic Potatoes. Viking, 1970.

Otto at Sea. Viking, 1936; revised, 1958.

Otto in Africa. Viking, 1961.

Otto in Texas: The Adventures of Otto. Viking, 1959.

Owl and the Pussycat; by Edward Lear. Doubleday, 1962.

Peter Graves. Viking, 1950.

Porko Von Popbutton. Harper, 1969.

Pretty Pretty Peggy Moffitt. Harper, 1968.

Rabbit's Umbrella; by George Plimpton. Viking, 1955.

Runaway Flying Horse; by Paul J. Bonzon. Parents, 1976.

Seal Pool; by Peter Matthiessen. Doubleday, 1972.

Squirrel Hotel. Viking, 1952.

Three Little Pigs in Verse, Author Unknown. Viking, 1962.

Three Policemen: Or, Young Bottsford of Fabre Island. Viking, 1938; new edition, 1960.

Tiger in the Teapot; by Betty Yurdin. Holt, 1968.

Topsy-Turvy Emporor of China; by Isaac B. Singer. Tr. Isaac B. Singer and Elizabeth Shub. Harper, 1971.

Twenty and Ten, as Told by Janet Joly; by Claire H. Bishop. Viking, 1952.

Twenty-one Balloons. Viking, 1947.

Unfriendly Book; by Charlotte Zolotow. Harper, 1975.

Where's Gomer?; by Norma Farber. Dutton, 1974.

William's Doll; by Charlottè Zolotow. Harper, 1972.

Witch of Scrapfaggot Green; by Patricia Gordon, *pseud*. (Joan Howard). Viking, 1948.

Young Visiters; by Daisy Ashford. Doubleday, 1951.

MEDIA

Alligator Case. (BB).

Bear Circus. (TB).

Bear Party. (BB); Taylor Associates, 1973 (FSS); Viking Press, 1970 (FSS).

Call Me Bandicoot. (BB).

Giant. (BB, TB).

Great Geppy. (TB).

Otto and the Magic Potatoes. (CB).

Otto in Texas. (BB).

Porko Von Popbutton. (TB).

Three Little Pigs. (BB).

Three Policemen. (TB).

Twenty-one Balloons. (BB, TB); Viking Press, 1970 (FSS).

William's Doll. (BB).

COLLECTIONS

May Massee Collection, Emporia State College. (Emporia, Kansas).

BACKGROUND READING

Bader. *American Picturebooks from Noah's Ark to The Beast Within*.

Burke. *American Authors and Books, 1640 to the Present Day*.

Commire. *Something about the Author*.

Contemporary Authors.

Doyle. *Who's Who in Children's Literature*.

Kingman. *Illustrators of Children's Books, 1957-1966*.

Kingman. *Illustrators of Children's Books, 1967-1976*.

Kirkpatrick. *Twentieth Century Children's Writers*.

Kunitz. *Junior Book of Authors, Second Edition Revised*.

"Lion: A Fable about the King of Beasts." *Life*, July 25, 1955.

Mahony. *Illustrators of Children's Books, 1744-1945*.

Miller. *Illustrators of Children's Books, 1946-1956*.

Miller. *Newbery Medal Books, 1922-1955*.

Ward. *Authors of Books for Young People, Second Edition*.

Young Wings. *Writing Books for Boys and Girls*.

ROGER ANTOINE DUVOISIN, 1904-
author-illustrator

AWARDS

(*Bhimsa, the Dancing Bear*. Newbery Honor Book, 1946.)

Hide and Seek Fog. Caldecott Honor Book, 1966.

White Snow, Bright Snow. Caldecott Medal Book, 1948.

BIBLIOGRAPHY

A for the Ark. Lothrop, 1952.

All Aboard! Grosset, 1935.

And There Was America. Knopf, 1938.

Angelique; by Janice (Brustlein). McGraw, 1960; *a.k.a. Duck Called Angelique*. Bodley Head, 1962.

Anna the Horse; by Louise Fatio. Aladdin, 1951.

April Umbrella; by Priscilla and Otto Friedrich. Lothrop, 1963.

Around the Corner; by Jean Showalter. Doubleday, 1966.

At Daddy's Office; by Robert J. Misch. Knopf, 1946.

At Our House; by Gale T. Parks, *pseud.* (John G. McCullough). Scott, 1943.

Autumn Harvest; by Alvin Tresselt. Lothrop, 1951.

Beaver Pond; by Alvin Tresselt. Lothrop, 1970.

Bennie, the Bear Who Grew Too Fast; by Beatrice and Ferrin L. Fraser. Lothrop, 1956.

Bhimsa, the Dancing Bear; by Christine Weston. Scribner, 1945.

Bird Book; by Richard Shaw. Warne, 1971.

Building Our America. Scribner, 1956.

Busby & Co.; by Herbert Coggins. McGraw, 1952.

Camel Who Took a Walk; by Jack Tworkov. Aladdin, 1951.

Chanticleer: The Real Story of This Famous Rooster. Grosset, 1947.

Chef's Holiday; by Idwal Jones. Longmans, 1952.

Children Come Running; by Elizabeth Coatsworth. il. with others. Simon, 1960.

Child's Garden of Verses; by Robert L. Stevenson. Limited Editions, 1944.

Christmas Book of Legends and Stories; by Alice Hazeltine and Elva S. Smith. Lothrop, 1944.

Christmas Cake in Search of Its Owner. American Artists, 1941.

Christmas Forest; by Louise Fatio. Aladdin, 1950.

Christmas on the Mayflower; by Wilma P. Hays. Coward, 1956.

Christmas Pony; by William N. Hall. Knopf, 1948.

Christmas Whale. Knopf, 1945.

Crocodile in the Tree. Knopf, 1973.

Crocus. Pantheon, 1977.

Daddies: What They Do All Day; by Helen Puner. Lothrop, 1946.

Day and Night. Knopf, 1960.

Days of Sunshine, Days of Rain; by Dean Frye. McGraw, 1965.

Does Poppy Live Here?; by Arthur S. Gregor. Lothrop, 1957.

Dog Cantbark; by Marjorie Fischer. Random, 1940.

Doll for Marie; by Louise Fatio. McGraw, 1957.

Donkey-Donkey: The Troubles of a Silly Little Donkey. Whitman, 1933; *a.k.a. Donkey, Donkey*. Grosset, 1940.

Dozens of Cousins; by Mabel Watts. McGraw, 1950.

Earth and Sky; by Mona Dayton. Harper, 1969.

Easter Treat. Knopf, 1954.

Fair, Fantastic Paris; by Harold Ettinger. Bobbs, 1944.

Farm Wanted; by Helen Hiller. Messner, 1951.

Favorite Fairy Tales Told in France: Retold from Charles Perrault and Other Old French Storytellers; by Virginia Haviland. Little, 1959.

Feast of the Lamps: A Story of India; by Charlet Root. Whitman, 1938.

Fish Is Not a Pet; by Mary N. Tabak. McGraw, 1959.

Flash of Washington Square; by Margaret Platt. Lothrop, 1954.

Follow the Road; by Alvin Tresselt. Lothrop, 1953.

Follow the Wind; by Alvin Tresselt. Lothrop, 1950.

Four Corners of the World. Knopf, 1948.

Français et la France; by Jacob Greenberg and Pierre Brodin. Merrill, 1940.

Frog in the Well; by Alvin Tresselt. Lothrop, 1958.

Gian-Carlo Menotti's Amahl and the Night Visitors: This Narrative Adaptation by Frances Frost Preserves the Exact Dialogue of the Opera; by Gian-Carlo Menotti. McGraw, 1952.

Happy Hunter. Lothrop, 1961.

Happy Lion; by Louise Fatio. McGraw, 1954; *a.k.a. Bon Lion*, 1960.

Happy Lion and the Bear; by Louise Fatio. McGraw, 1964.

Happy Lion in Africa; by Louise Fatio. McGraw, 1955.

Happy Lion Roars; by Louise Fatio. McGraw, 1957.

Happy Lion's Quest; by Louise Fatio. McGraw, 1961.

BIBLIOGRAPHY (cont'd)

Happy Lion's Rabbits; by Louise Fatio. McGraw, 1974.

Happy Lion's Treasure; by Louise Fatio. McGraw, 1971.

Happy Lion's Vacation; by Louise Fatio. McGraw, 1967; *a.k.a. Happy Lion's Holiday*. Bodley Head, 1968.

Happy Time; by Robert Fontaine. Simon, 1945. (Announced as *Name of a Blue Cow*.)

Hector and Christina; by Louise Fatio. McGraw, 1977.

Hector Penguin; by Louise Fatio. McGraw, 1973.

Heinz Hobnail and the Great Shoe Hunt; by Anne Duvoison. Abelard, 1976.

"Hi, Mister Robin!"; by Alvin Tresselt. Lothrop, 1950.

Hide and Seek Fog; by Alvin Tresselt. Lothrop, 1965.

Houn' Dog Man; by Mary Calhoun. Morrow, 1959.

House of Four Seasons. Lothrop, 1956.

Hungry Leprechaun; by Mary Calhoun. Morrow, 1962.

I Saw the Sea Come In; by Alvin Tresselt. Lothrop, 1954.

"I Won't," Said the King: Or, the Purple Flannel Underwear; by Mildred Jordan. Knopf, 1945.

In My Garden; by Charlotte Zolotow. Lothrop, 1960.

It's Time Now!; by Alvin Tresselt. Lothrop, 1969.

Jasmine. Knopf, 1973.

Johnny Maple-Leaf. Lothrop, 1948; revised, 1969.

Jo-Yo's Idea; by Kathleen M. Elliott. Knopf, 1939.

Jumpy the Kangaroo; by Janet Howard. Lothrop, 1944.

Lamb and the Child; by Dean Frye. McGraw, 1963.

Language Arts for Modern Youth; by M. V. Cassell, et al. Merrill, 1931. (3 vols.).

Life and Adventures of Robinson Crusoe; by Daniel Defoe. World, 1946; large print edition, Watts, 1966.

Lisette; by Adelaide Holl. Lothrop, 1962.

Little Boy Was Drawing. Scribner, 1932.

Little Church on the Big Rock; by Hazel Allen, *pseud.* (Hazel E. Hershberger). Scribner, 1958.

Little Red-Nose; by Miriam Schlein. Abelard, 1955.

Little Whistler; by Frances M. Frost. McGraw, 1949.

Lonely Veronica. Knopf, 1963.

Love and Dishes; by Niccolo DeQuattrociocchi. Bobbs, 1950.

Man Who Could Grow Hair: Or, Inside Andorra; by William Attwood. Knopf, 1949.

Marc and Pixie and the Walls in Mrs. Jones's Garden; with Louise Fatio. McGraw, 1975.

Military French; author unknown. n. p., *ca.*1940.

Miller, His Son and Their Donkey; by Aesop. McGraw, 1962; *a.k.a.* (tr.) *Meunier, Sons Fils, et L'Âne*, 1962.

Missing Milkman. Knopf, 1967.

Mother Goose: A Comprehensive Collection of the Rhymes Made by William R. Benét; from Mother Goose. Heritage, 1936.

Moustachio; by Douglas Rigby. Harper, 1947.

Night before Christmas; by Clement C. Moore. Garden City, 1954.

Nine Lives of Homer C. Cat; by Mary Calhoun. Morrow, 1961.

Not a Little Monkey; by Charlotte Zolotow. Lothrop, 1957.

Nubbey Bear; by William Lipkind. Harcourt, 1966.

Old Bullfrog; by Berniece Freschet. Scribner, 1968.

One Step, Two; by Charlotte Zolotow. Lothrop, 1954.

One Thousand Christmas Beards. Knopf, 1955.

Our Veronica Goes to Petunia's Farm. Knopf, 1962; *a.k.a. Veronica Goes to Petunia's Farm*. Bodley Head, 1963.

Periwinkle. Knopf, 1976.

Petits Contes Vrais; by Andre Humbert and Mary Riley. Merrill, 1940.

Petunia. Knopf, 1950.

Petunia and the Song. Knopf, 1951.

Petunia, Beware! Knopf, 1958.

Petunia, I Love You. Knopf, 1965.

Petunia Takes a Trip. Knopf, 1953.

Petunia's Christmas. Knopf, 1952.

Pied Piper of Hamelin; by Robert Browning. Grosset, 1936.

Please Pass the Grass!; by Leone Adelson. McKay, 1960.

Poems from France; by William J. Smith. Crowell, 1967.

Pointed Brush; by Patricia M. Martin. Lothrop, 1959.

Poodle Who Barked at the Wind; by Charlotte Zolotow. Lothrop, 1964.

Rain Puddle; by Adelaide Holl. Lothrop, 1965.

Red Bantam; by Louise Fatio. McGraw, 1963.

Remarkable Egg; by Adelaide Holl. Lothrop, 1968.

Rhaman: A Boy of Kashmir; by Heluiz Washburne. Whitman, 1939.

Ride with the Sun: An Anthology of Folk Tales and Stories from the United Nations; by Harold Courlander. McGraw, 1955.

Riema: Little Brown Girl of Java; by Kathleen M. Elliott. Knopf, 1937.

See What I Am. Lothrop, 1974.

Sitter Who Didn't Sit; by Helen Puner. Lothrop, 1949.

Soomoon: Boy of Bali; by Kathleen M. Elliott. Knopf, 1938.

Sophocles, the Hyena: A Fable; by James S. Moran. McGraw, 1954.

Spring Snow. Knopf, 1963.

Steam Shovel That Wouldn't Eat Dirt; by George Walters, *pseud.* (Walter Retan). Aladdin, 1948.

Successful Secretary; by Margaret Platt. Lothrop, 1946.

Sun Up; by Alvin Tresselt. Lothrop, 1949.

Sweet Patootie Doll; by Mary Calhoun. Morrow, 1957.

Talking Cat and Other Stories of French Canada, Retold; by Natalie S. Carlson. Harper, 1952.

Teddy; by Grete Janus. Lothrop, 1964.

Tell Me, Little Boy; by Doris Foster. Lothrop, 1953.

They Put Out to Sea: The Story of the Map. Knopf, 1943.

Three-Cornered Hat; by Pedro A. DeAlarcon. Limited Editions, 1959.

Three Happy Lions; by Louise Fatio. McGraw, 1959.

Three Sneezes and Other Swiss Tales. Knopf, 1941; *a.k.a. Fairy Tales from Switzerland: The Three Sneezes and Other Fairy Tales*. Muller, 1958.

Tigers Don't Bite; by Jack Tworkov. Dutton, 1956.

Timothy Robbins Climbs the Mountains; by Alvin Tresselt. Lothrop, 1960.

Travels with a Donkey; by Robert L. Stevenson. Limited Editions, 1957.

Trillium Hill; by Edith Marsh. Lothrop, 1955.

Two Lonely Ducks: A Counting Book. Knopf, 1955.

Under the Trees and through the Grass; by Alvin Tresselt. Lothrop, 1960.

Vavache: The Cow Who Painted Pictures; by Frederic Attwood. Aladdin, 1950.

Veronica. Knopf, 1961.

Veronica and the Birthday Present. Knopf, 1971.

Veronica's Smile. Knopf, 1964.

Virgin with Butterflies; by Tom Powers. Bobbs, 1945.

W. H. Hudson's Tales of the Pampas; by William H. Hudson. Knopf, 1939.

Wait till Sunday; by Susan Dorrit. Abelard, 1958.

Wake Up, City!; by Alvin Tresselt. Lothrop, 1957.

Wake Up, Farm!; by Alvin Tresselt. Lothrop, 1955.

Web in the Grass; by Berniece Freschet. Scribner, 1971.

What Did You Leave Behind?; by Alvin Tresselt. Lothrop, 1977.

What Is Right for Tulip. Knopf, 1969.

Whatever Happened to the Baxter Place?; by Pat Ross. Pantheon, 1975.

Which Is the Best Place?; by Pyotr Dudochin, adapted by Mirra Ginsburg. Macmillan, 1976.

White Snow, Bright Snow; by Alvin Tresselt. Lothrop, 1947.

Winkie's World; by William N. Hall. Doubleday, 1958.

Wishing Well in the Woods; by Priscilla and Otto Friedrich. Lothrop, 1960.

Wobble the Witch Cat; by Mary Calhoun. Morrow, 1958.

World in the Candy Egg; by Alvin Tresselt. Lothrop, 1967.

MEDIA

Camel Who Took a Walk. Weston Woods Studios, 1962 (FSS), 1956 and 1970 (F); also in Weston Woods Studios Set No. 3, 1965 (FSS).

Day and Night. Random House, 1972 (C).

Easter Treat. Random House, 1972 (C).

Happy Lion. Rembrandt Films, 1960 (F); H. M. Stone Productions, 1972 (FSS); University Films/ McGraw-Hill Publishing Company, 1971 (FSS).

Happy Lion and the Bear. University Films/McGraw-Hill Publishing Company, 1971 (FSS).

Happy Lion in Africa. University Films/McGraw-Hill Publishing Company, 1971 (FSS).

Happy Lion Roars. University Films/McGraw-Hill Publishing Company, 1971 (FSS).

Happy Lion's Quest. University Films/McGraw-Hill Publishing Company, 1971 (FSS).

Happy Lion's Treasure. University Films/McGraw-Hill Publishing Company, 1971 (FSS).

Happy Lion's Vacation. University Films/McGraw-Hill Publishing Company, 1971 (FSS).

Hide and Seek Fog. Weston Woods Studios, 1972 (FSS).

Jasmine. Spectra Films/Random House, Inc., 1974 (FSS).

Miller, His Son, and Their Donkey. Weston Woods Studios, 1962 (FSS).

Old Bullfrog. Miller-Brody Productions, 1974 (FSS).

Our Veronica Goes to Petunia's Farm. Spectra Films/ Random House, Inc., 1974 (FSS).

MEDIA (cont'd)

Petunia. (BB); Audio-Visual Aids/Weston Woods Studios, 1971 (F); Weston Woods Studios, 1963 (FSS); also in Weston Woods Studios Set No. 11, 1968 (FSS).

Petunia, Beware! in *Let's Listen*. Caedmon, 1963 (R); Random House, 1974 (C, FSS).

Petunia, I Love You. Random House, Inc., 1972 (C).

Petunia Takes a Trip. Random House, 1976 (C, FSS).

Sun Up. Weston Woods Studios, 1968 (FSS); also in Weston Woods Studios Set No. 22, 1968 (FSS).

They Put Out to Sea. (TB).

Three Happy Lions. University Films/McGraw-Hill Publishing Company, 1971 (FSS).

Three Sneezes. (TB).

Veronica. University Films/McGraw-Hill Publishing Company, 1973 (FSS).

Veronica's Smile. Random House, Inc., 1972 (C).

White Snow, Bright Snow. Weston Woods Studios, 1959 (FSS); also in Weston Woods Studios Set No. 6, 1965 (FSS).

EXHIBITIONS

American Federation of Art Traveling Exhibition, 1944. (Europe).

Museum of Modern Art, Traveling Exhibition of Children's Books in Europe, 1946-49.

Rutgers University Art Gallery, 1974. (New Brunswick, New Jersey).

United States Graphic Art Touring Exhibition, 1946. (Europe and Asia).

COLLECTIONS

Dana Library, Rutgers University. (Newark, New Jersey).

deGrummond Collection, University of Southern Mississippi. (Hattiesburg, Mississippi).

Gary Public Library. (Gary, Indiana).

Iowa City Public Library. (Iowa City, Iowa).

Kerlan Collection, University of Minnesota. (Minneapolis, Minnesota).

Milwaukee Public Library. (Milwaukee, Wisconsin).

Special Collections, University Research Library, University of California. (Los Angeles, California).

University of Oregon Library. (Eugene, Oregon).

BACKGROUND READING

Bader. *American Picturebooks from Noah's Ark to The Beast Within*.

Burke. *American Authors and Books, 1640 to the Present Day*.

Commire. *Something about the Author*.

Contemporary Authors.

Doyle. *Who's Who of Children's Literature*.

Ellis. *Book Illustration*.

Freeman, M. "Author-Illustrator Finds Subjects Near at Hand." *New York Times*, August 18, 1974.

Freeman, M. "Duvoisins." *Publishers Weekly*, February 28, 1977.

Hoffman. *Authors and Illustrators of Children's Books*.

Hopkins. *Books Are by People*.

Hutchens, J. "On an Author." *New York Herald Tribune Book Review*, November 16, 1952.

Kane, R. "Roger Duvoisin, Distinguished Creator to the World of Children's Literature." *Elementary English*, November 1956.

Kerlan, Irwin. *Roger Duvoisin Bibliography*. Bibliographical Society of the University of Virginia, 1958.

Kingman. *Illustrators of Children's Books, 1957-1966*.

Kingman. *Illustrators of Children's Books, 1966-1976*.

Kirkpatrick. *Twentieth Century Children's Writers*.

Kunitz. *Junior Book of Authors, Second Edition Revised*.

Mahony. *Illustrators of Children's Books, 1744-1945*.

Miller. *Caldecott Medal Books, 1938-1957*.

Miller. *Illustrators of Children's Books, 1946-1956*.

Pitz, H. "Roger Duvoisin." *American Artist*, December 1949.

Smaridge. *Famous Author-Illustrators for Young People*.

Unwin, N. "Artist's Choice." *Horn Book*, April 1959.

Ward. *Authors of Books for Young People, Second Edition*.

Ward. *Illustrators of Books for Young People, Second Edition*.

JEANETTE EATON, 1885-1968
author

AWARDS

Daughter of the Seine. Newbery Honor Book, 1930.

Gandhi. Newbery Honor Book, 1951.

Leader by Destiny. Newbery Honor Book, 1939.

Lone Journey. Newbery Honor Book, 1945.

BIBLIOGRAPHY

America's Own Mark Twain. il. Leonard E. Fisher. Morrow, 1958.

Behind the Show Window. Harcourt, 1935.

Betsy's Napoleon. il. Pierre Brissaud. Morrow, 1936.

Buckey O'Neill of Arizona. il. Edward Shenton. Morrow, 1949.

Commercial Work and Training for Girls; with Bertha M. Stevens. Macmillan, 1915.

Daughter of the Seine: The Life of Madame Roland. Harper, 1929; *a.k.a. Daughter of the Seine: The Life of Madame Roland, Edited by Mildred D. Williams*, 1938.

David Livingstone: Foe of Darkness. il. Ralph Ray. Morrow, 1947.

Flame: Saint Catherine of Siena. Harper, 1931.

Gandhi: Fighter without a Sword. il. Ralph Ray. Morrow, 1950.

Herdboy of Hungary: The True Story of Mosckos. il. Alexander Finta. Harper, 1932.

Heroines of the Sky; with Jean Adams and Margaret Kimball. Doubleday, 1942.

Jeanne d'Arc: The Warrior Saint. il. Harvé Stein. Harper, 1931.

Leader by Destiny: George Washington, Man and Patriot. il. Jack Rosé. Harcourt, 1938.

Leaders in Other Lands. il. Fritz Kredel. Heath, 1950.

Lee: The Gallant General. il. Harry Daugherty. Morrow, 1953.

Lone Journey: The Life of Roger Williams. il. Woodi Ishmael. Harcourt, 1944.

Narcissa Whitman: Pioneer of Oregon. il. Woodi Ishmael. Harcourt, 1941.

Roland the Warrior; with Virginia M. Collier. il. Frank E. Schoonover. Harcourt, 1934.

Story of Eleanor Roosevelt. Morrow, 1956.

Story of Light. il. Max Schwartz. Harper, 1928.

Story of Transportation. il. Maurice Day. Harper, 1927.

That Lively Man: Ben Franklin. il. Maurice Day. Harper, 1948.

Trumpeter's Tale: The Story of Young Louis Armstrong. il. Elton Fax. Morrow, 1955.

Washington: The Nation's First Hero. il. Ralph Ray. Morrow, 1951.

Young Lafayette. il. David Hendrickson. Houghton, 1932.

MEDIA

Daughter of the Seine. (BB).

David Livingstone. (BB, TB).

Flame. (BB).

Leader by Destiny. (TB).

Narcissa Whitman. (BB, TB).

Story of Eleanor Roosevelt. (BB, TB).

That Lively Man. (BB).

Trumpeter's Tale. (BB).

Young Lafayette. (BB).

COLLECTIONS

Kerlan Collection, University of Minnesota. (Minneapolis, Minnesota).

BACKGROUND READING

Burke. *American Authors and Books, 1640 to the Present Day*.

Contemporary Authors.

Coyle. *Ohio Authors and Their Books*.

Eaton, J. "Biographer's Comment." *Ohioana*, Fall 1959.

Eaton, J. "Biographer's Perilous Joy." *Horn Book*, March 1942.

Kunitz. *Junior Book of Authors*.

Kunitz. *Junior Book of Authors, Second Edition Revised*.

Obituary. *New York Times*, February 21, 1968.

Obituary. *Publishers Weekly*, March 4, 1968.

Young Wings. *Writing Books for Boys and Girls*.

ALLAN WESLEY ECKERT, 1931-
author

AWARDS

Incident at Hawk's Hill. Newbery Honor Book, 1972.

BIBLIOGRAPHY

Bayou Backwaters. il. Joseph Cellini. Doubleday, 1968.

Blue Jacket, War Chief of the Shawnees. Little, 1969.

Conquerors: A Narrative. Little, 1970.

Court-Martial of Daniel Boone. Little, 1973.

Crossbreed. il. Karl E. Karalus. Little, 1968.

Dreaming Tree. Little, 1968.

Frontiersman. Little, 1967.

Great Auk. Little, 1963.

BIBLIOGRAPHY (cont'd)

Hab Theory. Little, 1976.

In Search of a Whale. il. Joseph Cellini. Doubleday, 1970.

Incident at Hawk's Hill. il. John Schoenherr. Little, 1971; large print edition, Hall, 1974.

King Snake. il. Franz Altschuler. Little, 1968.

Owls of North America. il. Karl E. Karalus. Doubleday, 1973.

Silent Sky: The Incredible Extinction of the Passenger Pigeon. Little, 1965.

Tecumseh! A Play. Little, 1974.

Time of Terror: The Great Dayton Flood. Little, 1965; reissued, Landfall, 1973.

Wild Season. il. Karl E. Karalus. Little, 1968.

Wilderness Empire: A Narrative. Little, 1969.

MEDIA

Blue Jacket. Spiegel Productions, 1977 (F).

Crossbreed. (BB, TB); Don Meier Productions, 1976 (F).

Frontiersman. Warner Brothers/Seven Arts, Inc., 1968 (F).

Great Auk. (CB, TB).

Hab Theory. B. Rosen Productions, 1977 (F).

Incident at Hawk's Hill. Miller-Brody Productions, 1975 (C, R); Walt Disney Productions, 1975 (F).

Silent Sky. (BB, TB).

Wild Kingdom. (Original telecasts, 1968+, TV).

COLLECTIONS

Boston University Libraries. (Boston, Massachusetts).

BACKGROUND READING

Contemporary Authors.

DeMontreville. *Fourth Book of Junior Authors and Illustrators*.

WALTER DUMAUX EDMONDS, 1903-
author

AWARDS

Matchlock Gun. Newbery Medal Book, 1942.

BIBLIOGRAPHY

Beaver Valley. il. Leslie Morrill. Little, 1971.

Bert Breen's Barn. Little, 1975.

Big Barn. Little, 1930.

Boyds of Black River. Dodd, 1953.

Cadmus Henry. il. Manning DeV. Lee. Dodd, 1949.

Chad Hanna. Little, 1940.

Corporal Bess: The Story of a Boy and a Dog. il. Manning DeV. Lee. Dodd, 1952.

Drums along the Mohawk. Little, 1936; also in *Three Stalwarts*, below.

Erie Canal: The Story of the Digging of Clinton's Ditch. Munson-Williams-Proctor, 1960; also in *Three Stalwarts*, below.

First Hundred Years, 1848-1948; 1848, Oneida Community; 1880, Oneida Community, Limited; 1935 Oneida Limited. photographs by Samuel Chamberlain. Oneida Limited, 1948; revised, 1958.

Hound Dog Moses and the Promised Land. il. William Gropper. Dodd, 1953.

In the Hands of the Senecas. Little, 1947; a.k.a. *Captive Women*. Bantam, 1949.

Matchlock Gun. il. Paul Lantz. Dodd, 1941.

Mr. Benedict's Lion. il. Doris Lee. Dodd, 1950.

Moses. Charles Bush, 1939.

Mostly Canallers, Collected Stories. Little, 1934.

Musket and the Cross: The Struggle of France and England for North America. il. Samuel Bryant. Little, 1968.

Rome Haul. Little, 1929; also in *Three Stalwarts*, below.

Selected Short Stories. Editions for the Armed Services, 1943.

Seven American Stories. il. William S. Bock. Little, 1970.

Story of Richard Storm. il. William S. Bock. Little, 1974.

They Fought with What They Had: Story of the Army Air Forces in the Southwest Pacific, 1941-1942. Little, 1951.

They Had a Horse. il. Douglas Gorsline. Dodd, 1962.

Three Stalwarts: Drums along the Mohawk, Rome Haul, Erie Canal. Little, 1961; each issued separately, above.

Time to Go House. il. Joan B. Victor. Little, 1969.

Tom Whipple. il. Paul Lantz. Dodd, 1942.

Two Logs Crossing: John Haskell's Story. il. Tibor Gergely. Dodd, 1943.

Uncle Ben's Whale. il. William Gropper. Dodd, 1955.

Wedding Journey. il. Alan Tompkins. Little, 1947.

Wilderness Clearing. il. John S. DeMartelly. Dodd, 1944; also il. Marc Simont, 1954.

Wolf Hunt. il. William S. Bock. Little, 1970.

Young Ames. Little, 1942.

MEDIA

Bert Breen's Barn. (CB); Miller-Brody Productions, 1977 (C, R).

Big Barn. (BB).

Boyds of Black River. (BB, TB).

Chad Hanna. (BB, TB); Twentieth-Century Fox Film Corporation, 1940 (F).

Drums along the Mohawk. (BB, C, MT, TB); Twentieth-Century Fox Film Corporation, 1939 (F).

Erie Water. (BB).

Hound Dog Moses. (BB).

In the Hands of the Senecas. (BB, TB).

Matchlock Gun. (BB, TB); Miller-Brody Productions, 1969 (FSS); Newbery Award Records, 1969 (C, R).

Rome Haul. (TB). stage play, 1934; also as *Farmer Takes a Wife*, Twentieth-Century Fox Film Corporation, 1935 and 1953 (F).

Tom Whipple. (BB).

Two Logs Crossing. (BB).

COLLECTIONS

Harvard University Library. (Cambridge, Massachusetts).

Kerlan Collection, University of Minnesota. (Minneapolis, Minnesota).

Special Collections, Schaffer Library, Union College. (Schenectady, New York).

State Historical Society of Wisconsin Library. (Madison, Wisconsin).

BACKGROUND READING

Burke. *American Authors and Books, 1640 to the Present Day.*

Carmer, C. "Walter Edmonds of Black River Valley." *Publishers Weekly*, June 27, 1942.

Commire. *Something about the Author.*

Contemporary Authors.

Cournos. *Famous American Novelists.*

Current Biography.

Fuller. *More Junior Authors.*

Hart. *Oxford Companion to American Literature, Fourth Edition.*

Hopkins. *More Books by More People.*

Kirkpatrick. *Twentieth Century Children's Writers.*

Kunitz. *Authors Today and Yesterday.*

Kunitz. *Twentieth Century Authors.*

Kunitz. *Twentieth Century Authors, First Supplement.*

Miller. *Newbery Medal Books, 1922-1955.*

"Walter Edmonds" in *Writers on Writing.* Davidson Films/Silver Burdette, 1971 (F).

Ward. *Authors of Books for Young People, Second Edition.*

Warfel. *American Novelists of Today.*

FRITZ EICHENBERG, 1901-
author-illustrator

AWARDS

Ape in a Cape. Caldecott Honor Book, 1953.

(*"Have You Seen Tom Thumb?"* Newbery Honor Book, 1943.)

BIBLIOGRAPHY

Adventures of Sir Ignatious Tippitolio, Better Known to the World as Tippy, Proprietor of Tippitolio's Grand Imperial Hotel Oriella; by Glanville W. Smith. Harper, 1945.

All on a Summer's Day; by Marjorie Fischer. Random, 1941.

Animals to Africa; by Rosalys Hall. Holiday, 1939.

Anna Karenina; by Lev N. Tolstoi. Tr. Constance Garnett. Doubleday, 1944 (2 vols.), 1946 (1 vol.).

Anthology of Children's Literature, Third Edition; by Edna Johnson, et al. Houghton, 1959; il. with N. C. Wyeth, 1960.

Ape in a Cape: An Alphabet of Odd Animals. Harcourt, 1952.

Art and Faith. Pendle Hill, 1952.

Art of the Print: Art, Masterpiece, History, Technics. Abrams, 1976.

(ed.) *Artist's Proof, Volumes 1-11, 1961-1972: The Annual of Printmaking, Collector's Edition.* New York Graphic, 1971.

Ben Franklin of Old Philadelphia; by Margaret Cousins. Random, 1952.

Big Road Walker: Based on Stories Told by Alice Cannon; by Eula G. Duncan. Stokes, 1940.

Black Beauty: The Autobiography of a Horse; by Anna Sewell. Grosset, 1945.

Brothers Karamazov; by Feodor M. Dostoevski. Tr. Constance Garnett. Limited Editions, 1949.

BIBLIOGRAPHY (cont'd)

Cacoethes Scribendi; by Oliver W. Holmes. Brayers, 1946.

Characteristic Work of Fritz Eichenberg, Whose Technique in the Art of Wood-Engraving Has Given Added Charm and Vitality to the Printed Page. Haddon, n. d.

Childhood, Boyhood, Youth; by Lev N. Tolstoĭ. Tr. Leo Wiener. Limited Editions, 1972.

Child's Christmas in Wales; by Dylan Thomas. New Directions, 1969; also issued with portfolio.

Crime and Punishment; by Feodor Dostoevski. Tr. Constance Garnett. Heritage, 1938.

Dancing in the Moon: Counting Rhymes. Harcourt, 1955.

Devil and Daniel Webster; by Stephen V. Benét. Kingsport, 1945.

Dick Whittington and His Cat. Holiday, 1937.

Don't Blame Me!; by Richard A. Hughes. Harper, 1940.

Education in the Graphic Arts: A Symposium Held in the Wiggin Gallery, Boston Public Library, on May 5, 1967; with Ray Nash and Frederick Walkey. Boston Public Library, 1969.

Eugene Onegin; by Alexander Pushkin. Tr. Babette Deutsch. Limited Editions, 1943.

Fables with a Twist, and Twenty Twisted Tales. (Privately printed), 1977. (Portfolio).

Fathers and Sons; by Ivan S. Turgenev. Tr. Constance Garnett and Vassily Verestchagin. Limited Editions, 1941.

Favorite Animal Stories; by Felix Salten, *pseud*. (Siegmund Salzman). Messner, 1948.

Grand Inquisitor; by Feodor M. Dostoevski. Tr. Constance Garnett. Haddam, 1948.

Gulliver's Travels: An Account of the Four Voyages into Several Remote Nations of the World; by Jonathan Swift. Heritage, 1940.

(tr.) *H. A. P. Grieshaber: Woodcuts*; by Helmut A. P. Grieshaber. Tr. with William Hubben. Arts, 1965.

"Have You Seen Tom Thumb?"; by Mabel L. Hunt. Stokes, 1942.

Heroes of the Kalevala: Finland's Saga; by Babette Deutsch. Messner, 1940.

Idiot; by Feodor Dostoevski. Tr. Constance Garnett. Heritage, 1960.

(tr.) *In Praise of Folly*; by Desiderius Erasmus. Aquarius, 1972

Jane Eyre; by Charlotte Brontë. Random, 1943.

Jungle Book; by Rudyard Kipling. Grosset, 1950.

Littling of Gaywood; by Edna Turpin. Random, 1939.

Long Loneliness: Autobiography; by Dorothy Day. Harper, 1952.

Magic Shop; by Maurice Dolbier. Random, 1946.

Magic Type: A Christmas Parable; by Eli Canto. Composing Room, 1940.

Mime: The Art of Étienne Decroux. il. with Ronald Schwerin. Pratt Adlib, 1965.

Mischief in Fez; by Eleanor Hoffmann. Holiday, 1943.

Mystery of Dog Flip; by Thérèse Lenôtre. Tr. Simone Chamoud. Stokes, 1939.

Nantucket Woodcuts; with Naoko Matsubara. Barre, 1967.

No Room: An Old Story Retold; by Rose Dobbs. Coward, 1944.

Padre Porko, the Gentlemanly Pig; by Robert Davis. Holiday, 1939; enlarged, 1948.

Peaceable Kingdom, and Other Poems; by Elizabeth Coatsworth. Pantheon, 1958.

Phoebe-Belle; by Irmengarde Eberle. Graystone, 1941.

Portfolio of Drawings Appearing in "The Catholic Worker." Thistle, 1955.

(ed.) *Posada's Dance of Death, with 4 Relief Engravings by José G. Posada*; by Jean Charlot. Pratt Graphic Art Center, 1964.

Possessed; by Feodor Dostoevski. Tr. Constance Garnett. Heritage, 1960.

Puss in Boots. Holiday, 1936.

Raw Youth; by Feodor Dostoevski. Tr. Constance Garnett. Limited Editions, 1974.

Resurrection; by Lev N. Tolstoĭ. Tr. Leo Wiener. Limited Editions, 1963.

Rowena, the Skating Cow; by Stewart Schackne. Scribner, 1940.

Sancho and His Stubborn Mule; by Mark Keats. Scott, 1944.

Short Stories of Wilkie Collins; by Wilkie Collins, edited by Jerome I. Rodale. Rodale, 1950.

Sticks across the Chimney: A Story of Denmark; by Nora Burglon. Holiday, 1938.

Story of Peer Gynt; by Henrick Ibsen, adapted by E. V. Sandys. Crowell, 1941.

Story of Reynard the Fox; by Johann W. von Goethe. Tr. Thomas J. Arnold. Limited Editions, 1954.

Tale of King Midas and the Golden Touch; by Nathaniel Hawthorne. Limited Editions, 1943.

Tales of Edgar Allan Poe; by Edgar A. Poe. Random, 1944.

Tales of Living Playthings; by Antoniorobles (*i.e.*, Antonio Robles). Tr. Edward Haberman. Modern Age, 1938.

Tragedy of Richard the Third; by William Shakespeare. Limited Editions, 1940.

Tree That Ran Away; by Henry Beston. Macmillan, 1941.

Two Magicians: From an Ancient Ballad; adapted by John Langstaff. Atheneum, 1973.

Tyll Ulenspiegel's Merry Pranks; by Moritz Jagendorf. Vanguard, 1938.

Uncle Remus Stories; by Joel C. Harris. Peter Pauper, ca.1938.

War and Peace; by Lev N. Tolstoi. Tr. Louise and Aylmer Maude. Heritage, 1943 (2 vols.); 1951 (1 vol.).

Wide Fields: The Story of Henri Fabre; by Irmengarde Eberle. Crowell, 1943.

Witch of Ramoth; by Mark van Doren. Maple, 1950.

Wonderful House-Boat-Train; by Ruth S. Gannett. Random, 1946.

Wood and the Graver. Potter, 1977. (Limited edition); Crown, 1977.

EXHIBITIONS

Associated American Artists Gallery, 1966, 1977. (New York, New York).

Boston Public Library, 1976. (Boston, Massachusetts).

Klingspor Museum, 1975. (Offenbach, Germany).

Pratt Manhattan Center, 1972. (New York, New York).

COLLECTIONS

Bibliotheque National. (Paris, France).

Free Library of Philadelphia. (Philadelphia, Pennsylvania).

Hermitage Museum. (Leningrad, U.S.S.R.).

Kerlan Collection, University of Minnesota. (Minneapolis, Minnesota).

Metropolitan Museum of Art. (New York, New York).

Milwaukee Public Library. (Milwaukee, Wisconsin).

Museum of Modern Art. (New York, New York).

National Gallery of Art. (Washington, D.C.).

Prints and Photograph Division, Library of Congress. (Washington, D.C.).

Rare Book Room, Buffalo and Erie County Public Library. (Buffalo, New York).

BACKGROUND READING

Cahill, K. "Fritz Eichenberg, the Gentle Touch of Humanity." *American Artist*, October 1975.

Chewning, E. "Eichenberg's Confessions." *Print*, September 1976.

Commire. *Something about the Author*.

Contemporary Authors.

Eichenberg, F. "Artist's Career." *Idea Magazine* (Tokyo), January 1974.

Eichenberg, F. "Artist through the Looking Glass." *Horn Book*, May 1949.

Eichenberg, F. "Brothers Karamazov and I." *American Artist*, November 1950.

Eichenberg, F. "Education of an Artist." *Horn Book*, January 1960.

Eichenberg, F. "Illustrator's View of Illustration." *Print*, No. 3, 1943.

Ellis. *Book Illustration*.

"Fritz Eichenberg." *American Artist*, May 1967.

"Fritz Eichenberg." *Graphis*, No. 8, 1952.

Fuller. *Illustrators of Children's Books, 1967-1976*.

Fuller. *More Junior Authors*.

Kent, N. "Noted Bookman." *American Artist*, December 1944.

Kingman. *Illustrators of Children's Books, 1957-1966*.

Mahony. *Illustrators of Children's Books, 1744-1945*.

Miller. *Illustrators of Children's Books, 1946-1956*.

"Take a Bow." *Publishers Weekly*, February 4, 1957.

Ward. *Illustrators of Books for Young People, Second Edition*.

Zahn, C. "Fritz Eichenberg, the Artist and the Book." *New Boston Review*, No. 4, 1976.

EDWARD RANDOLPH EMBERLEY, 1931-
author-illustrator

AWARDS

Drummer Hoff. Caldecott Medal Book, 1968.

One Wide River to Cross. Caldecott Honor Book, 1967.

BIBLIOGRAPHY

American Inventions: A Book to Begin On; by Leslie Waller. Holt, 1963.

American West: A Book to Begin On; by Leslie Waller. Holt, 1966.

Big Dipper; by Franklyn Branley. Crowell, 1962.

Birds Eat and Eat and Eat; by Roma Gans. Crowell, 1963.

Birthday Wish. Little, 1977.

Bottom of the Sea; by Augusta Goldin. Crowell, 1966.

BIBLIOGRAPHY (cont'd)

Clothing, a Book to Begin On; by Leslie Waller. Holt, 1969.

Columbus Day; by Paul Showers. Crowell, 1965.

Drummer Hoff; adapted by Barbara Emberley. Prentice, 1967.

Ed Emberley's Drawing Book: Make a World. Little, 1972.

Ed Emberley's Drawing Book of Animals. Little, 1970.

Ed Emberley's Drawing Book of Faces. Little, 1975.

Ed Emberley's Great Thumbprint Drawing Book. Little, 1977.

Ed Emberley's Little Drawing Book of Birds. Little, 1973.

Ed Emberley's Little Drawing Book of Farms. Little, 1973.

Ed Emberley's Little Drawing Book of Trains. Little, 1973.

Ed Emberley's Little Drawing Book of Weirdos. Little, 1973.

Fifty-first Dragon; by Heywood Braun. Prentice, 1968.

Flag Day; by Dorothy LesTina. Crowell, 1965.

Flash, Crash, Rumble and Roll; by Franklyn Branley. Crowell, 1964; International Teaching Alphabet Edition, 1966.

Green Says Go. Little, 1968.

Klippity Klop. Little, 1974.

Krispin's Fair; by John Keller. Little, 1976.

Ladybug, Ladybug, Fly Away Home; by Judy Hawes. Crowell, 1967.

London Bridge Is Falling Down: The Song and the Game. Little, 1965.

Mommies Are for Loving; by Ruth B. Penn. Putnam, 1962.

Night's Nice; with Barbara Emberley. Doubleday, 1963.

One Wide River to Cross; adapted by Barbara Emberley. Prentice, 1966.

Parade Book. Little, 1962.

Punch and Judy: A Play for Puppets. Little, 1965.

Rhinoceros? Preposterous!; by Letta Schatz, Steck-Vaughan, 1965.

Rosebud. Little, 1966.

Simon's Song; adapted by Barbara Emberley. Prentice, 1969.

Story of Paul Bunyan; adapted by Barbara Emberley. Prentice, 1963.

Straight Hair, Curly Hair; by Augusta Goldin. Crowell, 1966; *a.k.a. Pelo Lacio, Pelo Rizo*. Tr. Richard Palmer, 1968.

Suppose You Met a Witch; by Ian Serraillier. Little, 1973.

What Is Symmetry? by Mindel and Harry Sitomer. Crowell, 1969.

White House: A Book to Begin On; by Mark K. Phelan. Holt, 1962.

Wing on a Flea: A Book about Shapes. Little, 1961.

Wizard of Op. Little, 1975; *a.k.a. Woo, the Wizard of Op*. Dent, 1976.

Yankee Doodle; by Richard Schackburg and Barbara Emberley. Prentice, 1965.

MEDIA

Drummer Hoff. (BB); Weston Woods Studios, 1968 (FSS); also in Weston Woods Studios Set No. 25, 1969 (FSS).

Night's Nice. Israel M. Berman/Sterling Educational Films, 1971 (F); also in *Night*. Bowmar Records, n. d. (R).

One Wide River to Cross. Bank Street College of Education, 1968 (F); Educational Enrichment Materials, n. d. (FSS); Westport Communications Group, 1969 (FS).

Simon's Song. Educational Enrichment Materials, 1969 (FSS); Westport Communications Group, 1969 (FS).

Story of Paul Bunyan. Educational Enrichment Materials, n. d. (FSS); Westport Communications Group, 1969 (FS).

Wing on a Flea. Weston Woods Studios, 1964 (FSS); also in Weston Woods Studios Set No. 20, 1965 (FSS).

Yankee Doodle. Educational Enrichment Materials, n. d. (FSS); Westport Communications Group, 1969 (FS).

COLLECTIONS

deGrummond Collection, University of Southern Mississippi. (Hattiesburg, Mississippi).

Free Library of Philadelphia. (Philadelphia, Pennsylvania).

Kerlan Collection, University of Minnesota. (Minneapolis, Minnesota).

Milwaukee Public Library. (Milwaukee, Wisconsin).

BACKGROUND READING

Commire. *Something about the Author*.

Contemporary Authors.

DeMontreville. *Third Book of Junior Authors*.

Hoffman. *Authors and Illustrators of Children's Books*.

Hopkins. *Books Are by People*.

Kingman. *Illustrators of Children's Books, 1957-1966*.

Kingman. *Illustrators of Children's Books, 1967-1976*.

Kingman. *Newbery and Caldecott Medal Books, 1966-1975*.

Reynolds, J. "Ed Emberley." *School Library Journal*, March 1968.

Smaridge. *Famous Literary Terms for Young People*.

Ward. *Authors of Books for Young People, Second Edition*.

Ward. *Illustrators of Books for Young People, Second Edition*.

Waugh, D. "Meteoric Career of Ed Emberley." *American Artist*, November 1966.

SYLVIA LOUISE ENGDAHL, 1933-
author

AWARDS

Enchantress from the Stars. Newbery Honor Book, 1971.

BIBLIOGRAPHY

(ed.) *Anywhere, Anywhen: Stories of Tomorrow*. Atheneum, 1976.

Beyond the Tomorrow Mountains. il. Richard Cuffari. Atheneum, 1973.

Enchantress from the Stars. il. Rodney Shackell. Atheneum, 1970.

Far Side of Evil. il. Richard Cuffari. Atheneum, 1971.

Journey between Worlds. il. James and Ruth McCrea. Atheneum, 1970.

Planet-Girded Suns: Man's View of Other Solar Systems. il. Richard Cuffari. Atheneum, 1974.

Subnuclear Zoo: New Discoveries in High Energy Physics; with Rick Roberson. Atheneum, 1977.

This Star Shall Abide. il. Richard Cuffari. Atheneum, 1972; *a.k.a. Heritage of the Star*. Gollancz, 1973.

(comp.) *Universe Ahead: Stories of the Future*; with Rick Roberson. il. Richard Cuffari. Atheneum, 1975.

MEDIA

Beyond the Tomorrow Mountains. (TB).

Enchantress from the Stars. (TB).

Far Side of Evil. (TB).

This Star Shall Abide. (TB).

BACKGROUND READING

Commire. *Something about the Author*.

Contemporary Authors.

DeMontreville. *Fourth Book of Junior Authors and Illustrators*.

Engdahl, S. "Changing Role of Science Fiction in Children's Literature." *Horn Book*, October 1971.

Engdahl, S. "Do Teenage Novels Fill a Need?" *English Journal*, February 1975.

Engdahl, S. "Perspective on the Future: The Quest of Space Age Young People." *School Media Quarterly*, Fall 1972.

Engdahl, S. "Why Write for Today's Teenagers?" *Horn Book*, June 1972.

Kirkpatrick. *Twentieth Century Children's Writers*.

+ELIZABETH ENRIGHT, 1909-1968
author-illustrator

AWARDS

Gone-Away Lake. Newbery Honor Book, 1958.

Thimble Summer. Newbery Medal Book, 1939.

BIBLIOGRAPHY

Amnon, a Lad of Palestine; by Marian King. Houghton, 1931.

Borrowed Summer: And Other Stories. Rinehart, 1946; *a.k.a. Maple Tree: And Other Stories*. Heinemann, 1947.

Christmas Tree for Lydia. Rinehart, 1951.

Crystal Locket; by Nellie M. Rowe. Whitman, 1935.

*Doublefields: Memories and Stories. Harcourt, 1966.

Four-Story Mistake. Rinehart, 1942; also in *Melendy Family*, below.

Gone-Away Lake. il. Beth and Joe Krush. Harcourt, 1957.

Kees; by Marian King. Harper, 1930.

Kees and Kleintje; by Marian King. Whitman, 1934.

Kintu: A Congo Adventure. Farrar, 1935.

Melendy Family: Containing The Saturdays, The Four-Story Mistake, and Then There Were Five. Rinehart, 1947; each also issued separately, above and below.

Moment before the Rain. Harcourt, 1955.

BIBLIOGRAPHY (cont'd)

Return to Gone-Away. il. Beth and Joe Krush. Harcourt, 1961.

Riddle of the Fly: And Other Stories. Harcourt, 1959.

Saturdays. Rinehart, 1941; also in *Melendy Family*, above.

Sea Is All Around. Rinehart, 1940.

Spiderweb for Two: A Melendy Maze. Rinehart, 1951.

Tatsinda. il. Irene Haas. Harcourt, 1963.

Then There Were Five. Rinehart, 1944; also in *Melendy Family*, above.

Thimble Summer. Rinehart, 1938.

Toys and Toy Makers; by James S. Tippett. Harper, 1931.

Zeee. il. Irene Haas. Harcourt, 1965.

MEDIA

Borrowed Summer. (BB).

Doublefields. (BB, CB, TB).

Four-Story Mistake. (BB, TB).

Gone-Away Lake. (BB, CB).

Return to Gone-Away. (BB).

Riddle of the Fly. (BB).

Saturdays. (BB, TB).

Spiderweb for Two. (BB).

Tatsinda. (TB).

Then There Were Five. (BB, TB).

Thimble Summer. (BB, TB); Miller-Brody Productions, 1969 (C, R).

COLLECTIONS

Arents Research Library, Syracuse University. (Syracuse, New York).

BACKGROUND READING

Burke. *American Authors and Books, 1640 to the Present Day*.

Commire. *Something about the Author*.

Contemporary Authors.

Current Biography.

Enright, E. "Realism in Children's Literature." *Horn Book*, April 1943.

Kirkpatrick. *Twentieth Century Children's Writers*.

Kunitz. *Junior Book of Authors, Second Edition Revised*.

Mahony. *Illustrators of Children's Books, 1744-1945*.

Miller. *Illustrators of Children's Books, 1946-1956*.

Miller. *Newbery Medal Books, 1922-1955*.

Obituary. *New York Times*, June 10, 1968.

Obituary. *Publishers Weekly*, June 17, 1968.

Smaridge. *Famous Modern Storytellers for Young People*.

Ward. *Authors of Books for Young People, Second Edition*.

ELEANOR RUTH ROSENFIELD ESTES, 1906-
author-illustrator

AWARDS

Ginger Pye. Newbery Medal Book, 1952.

Hundred Dresses. Newbery Honor Book, 1945.

Middle Moffat. Newbery Honor Book, 1943.

Rufus M. Newbery Honor Book, 1944.

BIBLIOGRAPHY

Alley. il. Edward Ardizzone. Harcourt, 1964.

Coat-Hanger Christmas Tree. il. Suzanne Suba. Atheneum, 1973.

Echoing Green: A Novel. Macmillan, 1947.

Ginger Pye. Harcourt, 1951; il. Margery Gill. Bodley Head, 1961.

Hundred Dresses. il. Louis Slobodkin. Harcourt, 1944.

Little Oven. Harcourt, 1955.

Lollipop Princess: A Play for Paper Dolls in One Act. Harcourt, 1967.

Middle Moffat. il. Louis Slobodkin. Harcourt, 1942.

Miranda the Great. il. Edward Ardizzone. Harcourt, 1967.

Moffats. il. Louis Slobodkin. Harcourt, 1941.

Pinky Pye. il. Edward Ardizzone. Harcourt, 1958.

Rufus M. il. Louis Slobodkin. Harcourt, 1943.

Sleeping Giant and Other Stories. Harcourt, 1948.

Sun and the Wind and Mr. Todd. il. Louis Slobodkin. Harcourt, 1943.

Tunnel of Hugsy Goode. il. Edward Ardizzone. Harcourt, 1972.

Witch Family. il. Edward Ardizzone. Harcourt, 1960.

MEDIA

Coat-Hanger Christmas Tree. (CB).

Ginger Pye. (BB); Miller-Brody Productions, 1975 (FSS); Newbery Award Records, 1969 (C, R).

Hundred Dresses. (BB).

Middle Moffat. (TB).

Moffats. (BB, TB).

Pinky Pye. (TB); Miller-Brody Productions, 1977 (C, R).

Rufus M. (BB).

COLLECTIONS

deGrummond Collection, University of Southern Mississippi. (Hattiesburg, Mississippi).

Kerlan Collection, University of Minnesota. (Minneapolis, Minnesota).

BACKGROUND READING

Alsetter, M. "Eleanor Estes and Her Books." *Elementary English*, May 1952.

Burke. *American Authors and Books, 1640 to the Present Day*.

Cameron, E. "Art of Eleanor Estes." *Horn Book*, December 1969; February 1970.

Commire. *Something about the Author*.

Contemporary Authors.

Current Biography.

Donnelly, E. " 'Way' of Eleanor Estes." *Ontario Library Review*, May 1956.

Eleanor Estes and Margaret McElderry. Profiles in Literature, 1975 (VT).

Estes, E. "Gathering Honey." *Horn Book*, December 1968.

Estes, E. "Inside Story of a Medal Recipient." *California Librarian*, September 1952.

Estes, E. "What Makes a Good Book?" *Writer*, November 1935.

Estes, E. "Writing for Children." *Writer*, April 1953.

Hopkins. *More Books by More People*.

Kirkpatrick. *Twentieth Century Children's Writers*.

Kunitz. *Junior Book of Authors, Second Edition Revised*.

Meet the Newbery Author: Eleanor Estes. Miller-Brody Productions, 1974 (FSS).

Miller. *Illustrators of Children's Books, 1946-1956*.

Miller. *Newbery Medal Books, 1922-1955*.

Montgomery. *Story behind Modern Books*.

Rice, M. "Eleanor Estes! A Study in Versatility." *Elementary English*, May 1968.

Salute to the Moffats on Their Twenty-fifth Birthday. Harcourt, (1965?).

Sayers, F. "Books of Eleanor Estes." *Horn Book*, August 1952.

Townsend. *Sense of Story*.

Ward. *Authors of Books for Young People, Second Edition*.

Warfel. *American Novelists of Today*.

MARIE HALL ETS, 1895-
author-illustrator

AWARDS

In the Forest. Caldecott Honor Book, 1945.

Just Me. Caldecott Honor Book, 1966.

Mister Penny's Race Horse. Caldecott Honor Book, 1957.

Mr. T. W. Anthony Woo. Caldecott Honor Book, 1952.

Nine Days to Christmas. Caldecott Medal Book, 1960.

Play with Me. Caldecott Honor Book, 1956.

BIBLIOGRAPHY

Another Day. Viking, 1953.

Automobiles for Mice. Viking, 1964.

Bad Boy, Good Boy. Crowell, 1967.

Beasts and Nonsense. Viking, 1952.

Cow's Party. Viking, 1958.

Elephant in a Well. Viking, 1972.

Gilberto and the Wind. Viking, 1963.

In the Forest. Viking, 1944.

Jay Bird. Viking, 1974.

Just Me. Viking, 1965.

Little Old Automobile. Viking, 1948.

Mister Penny. Viking, 1935.

Mister Penny's Circus. Viking, 1961.

Mister Penny's Race Horse. Viking, 1956.

Mr. T. W. Anthony Woo: The Story of a Cat and a Dog and a Mouse. Viking, 1951.

My Dog Rinty; with Ellen Tarry. il. Alexander and Alexandra Alland. Viking, 1946.

Nine Days to Christmas; with Aurora Labastida. Viking, 1959.

Oley, the Sea Monster. Viking, 1947.

Play with Me. Viking, 1955.

Rosa: The Life of an Italian Immigrant. University of Minnesota, 1970.

Story of a Baby. Viking, 1939.

Talking without Words: I Can, Can You? Viking, 1968.

MEDIA

Bad Boy, Good Boy. McGraw-Hill Company, 1973 (FSS).

Gilberto and the Wind. Bank Street College of Education, 1967 (F); Viking Press, 1974 (C); Weston Woods Studios, 1969 (FSS); also in Weston Woods Studios Set No. 24, 1969 (FSS).

In the Forest. Weston Woods Studios, 1959 (FSS), 1960 (F); also in Weston Woods Studios Set No. 5, 1965 (FSS).

Just Me. Weston Woods Studios, 1969 (FSS); also in Weston Woods Studios Set No. 25, 1969 (FSS).

Mr. T. W. Anthony Woo. (TB).

Nine Days to Christmas. (BB).

Play with Me. Viking Press, 1975 (C); Weston Woods Studios, 1963 (FSS); also in Weston Woods Studios Set No. 12, 1970 (FSS).

Talking without Words. Viking Press, 1970 (FSS).

Walk in the Forest. Young People's Records, 1951 (R).

EXHIBITIONS

American Federation of the Arts Gallery, 1945. (New York, New York).

Teachers College, Columbia University, 1963. (New York, New York).

COLLECTIONS

Collection of American Literature, Beinecke Library, Yale University. (New Haven, Connecticut).

deGrummond Collection, University of Southern Mississippi. (Hattiesburg, Mississippi).

Free Library of Philadelphia. (Philadelphia, Pennsylvania).

Gary Public Library. (Gary, Indiana).

Iowa City Public Library. (Iowa City, Iowa).

Kerlan Collection, University of Minnesota. (Minneapolis, Minnesota).

May Massee Collection, Emporia State College. (Emporia, Kansas).

Milwaukee Public Library. (Milwaukee, Wisconsin).

Special Collections, University Research Library, University of California. (Los Angeles, California).

BACKGROUND READING

Bader, B. *American Picturebooks from Noah's Ark to The Beast Within*.

Bianco, P. "Artist's Choice." *Horn Book*, June 1956.

Commire. *Something about the Author*.

Contemporary Authors.

Foremost Women in Communications.

Hoffman. *Authors and Illustrators of Children's Books*.

Hopkins. *Books Are by People*.

Irvine, E. "Marie Hall Ets, Her Picture Storybooks." *Elementary English*, May 1956.

Jenkins, W. "Educational Scene." *Elementary English*, May 1960.

Kingman. *Illustrators of Children's Books, 1957-1966*.

Kingman. *Illustrators of Children's Books, 1967-1976*.

Kingman. *Newbery and Caldecott Medal Books, 1956-1965*.

Kirkpatrick. *Twentieth Century Children's Writers*.

Kunitz. *Junior Book of Authors, Second Edition Revised*.

Mahony. *Illustrators of Children's Books, 1744-1945*.

"Marie Hall Ets." *Wilson Library Bulletin*, October 1965.

Miller. *Illustrators of Children's Books, 1946-1956*.

Smaridge. *Famous Author-Illustrators for Young People*.

Ward. *Authors of Books for Young People, Second Edition*.

Ward. *Illustrators of Books for Young People, Second Edition*.

+THOMAS FEELINGS, 1933-
author-illustrator

AWARDS

Jambo Means Hello. Caldecott Honor Book, 1975.

Moja Means One. Caldecott Honor Book, 1972.

(*To Be a Slave*. Newbery Honor Book, 1969.)

BIBLIOGRAPHY

African Crafts; by Jane Kerina and Marilyn Katzman. Lion, 1970.

*Black Feelings. Lothrop, 1972.

Black Folktales; by Julius Lester. Baron, 1969.

Black Is the Color; by Ruth D. Gibb. Center for Media Development, 1973.

Bola and the Oba's Drummers; by Letta Schatz. McGraw, 1967.

Congo: River of Mystery; by Robin McKown. McGraw, 1968.

Jambo Means Hello: Swahili Alphabet Book; by Muriel Feelings. Dial, 1974.

Moja Means One: Swahili Counting Book; by Muriel
Feelings. Dial, 1971.

*Nine Drawings from the Black Community, American
and African*. Drum and Spear, *ca*.1972. (Portfolio).

Panther's Moon; by Ruskin Bond. Random, 1969.

Quiet Place; by Rose Blue. Watts, 1969.

Song of the Empty Bottles; by Osmond Molarsky.
Walck, 1968.

Tales of Temba; by Kathleen Arnott. Walck, 1969.

To Be a Slave; by Julius Lester. Dial, 1968.

Tuesday Elephant; by Nancy Garfield. Crowell, 1968.

When Stones Were Soft: East African Fireside Tales;
by Eleanor Heady. Funk, 1968.

Zamani Goes to Market; by Muriel Feelings. Seabury,
1970.

BACKGROUND READING

Chandler. *Living Black American Authors*.

Commire. *Something about the Author*.

Contemporary Authors.

DeMontreville. *Third Book of Junior Authors*.

Dunbar. *Black Expatriots*.

Head and Heart. New Images, 1977 (F).

Hopkins. *Books Are by People*.

Kingman. *Illustrators of Children's Books, 1967-1976*.

Smaridge. *Famous Literary Teams for Young People*.

"This Month's Cover Artist." *Wilson Library Bulletin*,
September 1969.

Tom and Muriel Feelings. Profiles in Literature, 1971
(VT).

Ward. *Illustrators of Books for Young People, Second
Edition*.

+RACHEL LYMAN FIELD, 1894-1942
author-illustrator

AWARDS

Calico Bush. Newbery Honor Book, 1932.

Hitty. Newbery Medal Book, 1930.

(*Prayer for a Child*. Caldecott Medal Book, 1945.)

BIBLIOGRAPHY

All This, and Heaven Too. Macmillan, 1938.
(Announced as *Omitted Epitaph*.)

All through the Night. Macmillan, 1940; also il.
Shirley Hughes. Macmillan (England), 1955.

Alphabet for Boys and Girls. Doubleday, 1926.

(comp.) *American Folk and Fairy Tales*. il. Margaret
Freeman. Scribner, 1929.

And Now Tomorrow. Macmillan, 1942.

*At the Junction: A Fantasy for Railroad Stations in
One Act*. French, 1927; also in *Cross-Stitch Heart
and Other Plays*, below.

*Ave Maria: An Interpretation from Walt Disney's
"Fantasia"; Inspired by the Music of Franz
Schubert*. il. Walt Disney Studio. Random, 1940.

Bad Penny: A Drama in One Act. French, 1938.

Bargains in Cathay: A Comedy in One Act. French,
1927; also in *Cross-Stitch Heart and Other Plays*,
below.

Bird Began to Sing. il. Ilse Bischoff. Morrow, 1932.

Branches Green. il. Dorothy P. Lathrop. Macmillan,
1934.

Calico Bush. il. Allen Lewis. Macmillan, 1931.

Chimney Sweeps' Holiday. French, 1931; also in
Patchwork Plays, below.

Christmas in London. Aldus, 1946.

Christmas Time. Macmillan, 1941.

Cinderella Married: A Comedy in One Act. French,
1924; also in *Six Plays*, below.

Circus Garland: Poems. il. Prentiss Taylor. Winter
Wheat, 1930.

*Columbine in Business: A Modern Harlequinade in
One Act*. French, 1924; also in *Six Plays*, below.

Come Christmas; by Eleanor Farjeon. Stokes, 1927.

Cross-Stitch Heart: A Fantasy in One Act. French,
1934.

Cross-Stitch Heart and Other Plays. Scribner, 1927.
(Includes *At the Junction*, *Bargains in Cathay*,
Cross-Stitch Heart, Greasy *Luck*, *Londonderry
Air*, and *Nine Day's Queen*, issued separately,
above and below.)

Eliza and the Elves. il. Elizabeth MacKinstry.
Macmillan, 1926.

Fear Is the Thorn. Macmillan, 1936.

Fifteenth Candle: A Drama in One Act. French, 1921.

First Class Matter: A Comedy in One Act. French,
1936.

(adapt.) *Fortune's Caravan*; by Lily Juval. il. Maggie
Salcedo. Tr. Marion Saunders. Morrow, 1933.

*God's Pocket: The Story of Captain Samuel Hadlock,
Junior, of Cranbery Isles, Maine*. Macmillan, 1934.

Greasy Luck: A Drama in One Act. French, 1927;
also in *Cross-Stitch Heart and Other Plays*, above.

Hepatica Hawkes. il. Allen Lewis. Macmillan, 1932.

Hitty: Her First Hundred Years. il. Dorothy Lathrop.
Macmillan, 1929; *a.k.a. Hitty: The Life and Adventures of a Wooden Doll*. Routledge, 1932.

BIBLIOGRAPHY (cont'd)

House That Grew Smaller; by Margery Bianco. Macmillan, 1931.

How to Tell Stories to Children; by Sara C. Bryant. Houghton, 1924.

Just across the Street. Macmillan, 1933.

Little Book of Days. Doubleday, 1927.

Little Dog Toby. Macmillan, 1928.

Londonderry Air: A Play in One Act. French, *ca*.1933; also in *Cross-Stitch Heart and Other Plays*, above.

Magic Pawnshop: A New Year's Eve Fantasy. il. Elizabeth MacKinstry. Dutton, 1927.

Nine Day's Queen: An Historical Fantasy in One Act. French, 1927; also in *Cross-Stitch Heart and Other Plays*, above.

Patchwork Plays. Doubleday, 1930. (Includes *Chimney Sweeps' Holiday* and *Sentimental Scarecrow*, issued separately, above and below.)

Patchwork Quilt: A Fantasy in One Act. French, 1924; also in *Six Plays*, below.

(comp.) *People from Dickens: A Presentation of Leading Characters from the Books of Charles Dickens*. il. Thomas Fogarty. Scribner, 1935.

Pocket-Handkerchief Park. Doubleday, 1929; also in *Rachel Field Storybook*, below.

Poems. Macmillan, 1957.

Pointed People: Verses and Silhouettes. Yale, 1924.

Points East: Narratives from New England. Brewer, 1930.

Polly Patchwork. Doubleday, 1928; *a.k.a. Polly Patchwork (Comedy in Three Scenes) from the Story of the Same Title*. French, 1930; also in *Rachel Field Storybook*, below.

Prayer for a Child. il. Elizabeth O. Jones. Macmillan, 1944.

Punch and Robinetta; by Ethel M. Gate. Yale, 1923.

Rachel Field Storybook. il. Adrienne Adams. Doubleday, 1958. (Includes *Pocket-Handkerchief Park*, *Polly Patchwork*, and *Yellow Shop*, issued separately, above and below.)

Rise Up, Jennie Smith: A Play in One Act. French, 1918.

Sentimental Scarecrow: A Comedy in One Act. French, 1930; *a.k.a. Sentimental Scarecrow: A Musical Fantasy in One Act Based on Rachel Field's "Sentimental Scarecrow."* French, 1970; also in *Patchwork Plays*, above.

Six Plays. Scribner, 1924. (Includes *Cinderella Married*, *Columbine in Business*, *Patchwork Quilt*, *Theories and Thumbs*, and *Wisdom Teeth*, issued separately, above and below.)

Stories to Tell Children: 51 Stories with Suggestions for Telling; by Sara C. Bryant. Houghton, 1924.

Susanna B. and William C. Morrow, 1934.

Taxis and Toadstools. Doubleday, 1926.

Theories and Thumbs: A Fantasy for Museums in One Act. French, 1924; also in *Six Plays*, above.

Time out of Mind. Macmillan, 1935.

To See Ourselves; with Arthur Pederson. Macmillan, 1937.

(comp.) *White Cat and Other Old French Fairy Tales*; by Marie C. D'Aulnoy. il. Elizabeth MacKinstry. Macmillan, 1928.

Wisdom Teeth: A Comedy in One Act. French, 1924; also in *Six Plays*, above.

Yellow Shop. Doubleday, 1931; also in *Rachel Field Storybook*, above.

MEDIA

All This, and Heaven Too. (BB, TB); Warner Brothers Pictures, 1940 (F).

All through the Night. (BB).

And Now Tomorrow. (BB); Paramount Pictures, Inc., 1944 (F).

Calico Bush. (BB, TB).

Hitty. (BB).

Just across the Street. (BB).

Poems. (BB).

Prayer for a Child. (BB).

Taxis and Toadstools. (BB).

Time out of Mind. (BB); United Artists Corporation, 1947 (F); Universal International Pictures Company, 1951 (F).

COLLECTIONS

Collection of American Literature, Beinecke Library, Yale University. (New Haven, Connecticut).

Pack Memorial Library. (Asheville, North Carolina).

Saxon Collection, Howard-Tilton Memorial Library, Tulane University. (New Orleans, Louisiana).

Stockbridge Library Association. (Stockbridge, Massachusetts).

BACKGROUND READING

Barnes. *Children's Poets*.

Benét. *Famous Poets for Young People*.

Burke. *American Authors and Books, 1640 to the Present Day*.

Current Biography.

Fuller. *More Junior Authors.*

Hale, F. "Concerning Hitty: Her First Hundred Years." *Grade Teacher*, November 1930.

Hart. *Oxford Companion to American Literature, Fourth Edition.*

Horn Book, special issue, July 1942.

Kirkpatrick. *Twentieth Century Children's Writers.*

Kunitz. *American Authors.*

Kunitz. *Junior Book of Authors.*

Kunitz. *Junior Book of Authors, Second Edition Revised.*

Kunitz. *Living Authors.*

Kunitz. *Twentieth Century Authors.*

Kunitz. *Twentieth Century Authors, First Supplement.*

Mahony. *Contemporary Illustrators of Children's Books.*

Mahony. *Illustrators of Children's Books, 1744-1945.*

Miller. *Newbery Medal Books, 1922-1955.*

Montgomery. *Story behind Modern Books.*

Obituary. *New York Times*, March 16, 1942.

Quinnam, Barbara. *Rachel Field Collection of Old Children's Books in the District of Columbia Public Library: A Catalogue.* Washington, D.C., 1961 (thesis).

Randall. *Through Golden Windows.*

Ward. *Authors of Books for Young People, Second Edition.*

CHARLES JOSEPH FINGER, 1869-1941
author

AWARDS

Tales from Silver Lands. Newbery Medal Book, 1925.

BIBLIOGRAPHY

Adventure under Sapphire Skies. il. Helen Finger. Morrow, 1931.

Affair at the Inn as Seen by Phio the Innkeeper and the Taxgatherer of Rome. Georgina, 1931.

After the Great Companions: A Free Fantasia on a Lifetime of Reading. Dutton, 1934.

(ed.) *Autobiography of Benvenuto Cellini*; by Benvenuto Cellini. Haldeman, 1923.

Bobbie and Jock and the Mailman. il. Helen Finger. Holt, 1938.

Book of Real Adventures. Haldeman, 1924.

(ed.) *Boswell's Life of Johnson*; by James Boswell. Haldeman, 1923.

Bushrangers. il. Paul Honoré. McBride, 1924.

Cape Horn Snorter: A Story of the War of 1812, and of Gallant Days with Captain Porter of the U.S. Frigate, Essex. il. Henry C. Pitz. Houghton, 1939.

Choice of the Crowd: Being a Collection of These Poems Appearing in "All's Well" Which Met with the Approval of the Readers. Golden Horseshoe, 1922.

Courageous Companions. il. James Daugherty. Longmans, 1929.

David Livingstone: Explorer and Prophet. il. Arthur Zaidenberg. Doubleday, 1930.

Distant Prize: A Book about Rovers, Rangers and Rascals. il. Henry C. Pitz. Appleton, 1935.

Dog at His Heels: The Story of Jock, an Australian Sheep Dog, and What Befell Him and His Companions on a Great Drive. il. Henry C. Pitz. Winston, 1936.

Essence of Confucianism. Haldeman, 1923.

(ed.) *Five Weeks in a Balloon*; by Jules Verne. Haldeman, 1923.

*Footloose in the West: Being an Account of a Journey to Colorado and California and Other Western States. il. Helen Finger. Morrow, 1932.

Free Fantasia on Books and Reading. Haldeman, 1924.

Frontier Ballads: Heard and Gathered. il. Paul Honoré. Doubleday, 1927.

Gist of Burton's Anatomy of Melancholy. Haldeman, 1924.

Give a Man a Horse. il. Henry C. Pitz. Winston, 1938.

Golden Tales from Faraway. il. Helen Finger. Winston, 1940.

Great Pirates. Haldeman, 1924.

Henry David Thoreau: The Man Who Escaped from the Herd. Haldeman, 1922.

(ed.) *Heroes from Hakluyt*; by Richard Hakluyt. il. Paul Honoré. Holt, 1928.

High Water in Arkansas. il. Henry C. Pitz. Grosset, 1943.

Highwaymen: A Book of Gallant Rogues. il. Paul Honoré. McBride, 1923.

Hints on Writing One-Act Plays. Haldeman, 1923.

Hints on Writing Short Stories. Haldeman, 1922.

Historic Crimes and Criminals. Haldeman, 1922.

Ice Age. Haldeman, 1922.

In Lawless Lands. Golden Horseshoe, 1924.

Joseph Addison and His Time. Haldeman, 1922.

BIBLIOGRAPHY (cont'd)

Life of Barnum: The Man Who Lured the Herd. Haldeman, 1924.

Life of Napoleon. Haldeman, 1923.

Life of Theodore Roosevelt. Haldeman, 1924.

Lost Civilizations. Haldeman, 1922.

Magellan and the Pacific. Haldeman, 1923.

Magic Tower. il. Helen Finger. Kings Arm, 1938.

Mahomet. Haldeman, 1923.

Man for A'That: The Story of Robert Burns. Stratford, 1929.

Mark Twain: The Philosopher Who Laughed at the World. Haldeman, 1924.

My View of William Feather. Feather, 1923.

Note on Texas. Mayfield, 1927.

Oscar Wilde in Outline. Haldeman, 1923.

Our Navy: An Outline History for Young People. il. Henry C. Pitz. Houghton, 1926.

Ozark Fantasia; compiled and edited by Charles M. Wilson. il. Paul Honoré. Golden Horseshoe, 1927.

Paul Bunyan Geography: In Which Is an Account and Particular Relation of How That Master Logger So Wrought, with Babe, the Blue Ox, and His Companions, That Many Notable Things Were Done to Change the Face of These United States. Maple, 1931.

(ed.) *Pepys' Diary;* by Samuel Pepys. Haldeman, 1922.

(ed.) *Privateersman;* by Frederick Marryat. Haldeman, 1923.

Robin Hood and His Merry Men. Haldeman, 1924.

Romantic Rascals. il. Paul Honoré. McBride, 1927.

Sailor Chanties and Cowboy Songs. Haldeman, 1923.

*Seven Horizons. Doubleday, 1930.

Spreading Stain: A Tale for Boys and Men with Boys' Hearts. il. Paul Honoré. Doubleday, 1927.

Tales from Silver Lands. il. Paul Honoré. Doubleday, 1924.

Tales Worth Telling. il. Paul Honoré. Century, 1927.

(ed.) *Thirteenth Century Prose Tales;* by William Morris. Haldeman, 1923.

Tragic Story of Oscar Wilde's Life. Haldeman, 1923.

Travels of Marco Polo. Haldeman, 1924.

Valiant Vagabonds. Appleton, 1936.

(ed.) *Voyage to the Moon;* by Jules Verne. Haldeman, 1923.

When Guns Thundered at Tripoli. il. Henry C. Pitz. Holt, 1937.

Yankee Sea Captain in Patagonia. il. Henry C. Pitz. Grosset, 1941.

MEDIA

Adventure under Sapphire Skies. (BB).

Tales from Silver Lands. (TB); *a.k.a. Calabash Man and Other Tales from Silver Lands.* Miller-Brody Productions, 1973 (C, R); *a.k.a. Magic Ball and Other Tales from Silver Lands.* Miller-Brody Productions, 1972 (FSS); *a.k.a. Tale of the Lazy People from Tales from Silver Lands.* Miller-Brody Productions, ca.1972 (F).

COLLECTIONS

Baker Library, Dartmouth College. (Hanover, New Hampshire).

Bancroft Library, University of California. (Berkeley, California).

Conrad Collection, Beinecke Library, Yale University. (New Haven, Connecticut).

Harvard University Library. (Cambridge, Massachusetts).

University of Chicago Library. (Chicago, Illinois).

BACKGROUND READING

Burke. *American Authors and Books, 1640 to the Present Day.*

Coyle. *Ohio Authors and Their Books.*

Current Biography.

Kunitz. *Junior Book of Authors.*

Kunitz. *Junior Book of Authors, Second Edition Revised.*

Kunitz. *Living Authors.*

Kunitz. *Twentieth Century Authors.*

Miller. *Newbery Medal Books, 1922-1955.*

Murdoch, C. "Charles J. Finger: 'High-Hearted Adventurer.'" *Elementary English,* October 1926.

Obituary. *New York Times,* January 8, 1941.

Ward. *Authors of Books for Young People, Second Edition.*

Young Wings. *Writing Books for Boys and Girls.*

+CYRUS FISHER, *pseudonym*, 1904-
author

a.k.a. Darwin LeOra Teilhet

and as

William H. Fielding, *pseudonym*

AWARDS

Avion My Uncle Flew. Newbery Honor Book, 1947.

BIBLIOGRAPHY

as William H. Fielding:

Beautiful Humbug. Fawcett, 1964.

as Cyrus Fisher:

Ab Carmody's Treasure: Or, The Adventures of Absolute Carmody at the Minefree School, His Excape, His Flight to Guatemala. il. Lou Block. Holt, 1948.

Avion My Uncle Flew. il. Richard Floethe. Appleton, 1946.

Hawaiian Sword. Funk, 1956.

as Darwin L. Teilhet:

Big Runaround. Coward, 1964.

Bright Destination. Doubleday, 1935; *a.k.a. Bells on His Toes*. Methuen, 1937.

Broken Face Murders; with Hildegard Teilhet. Doubleday, 1940.

Crimson Hair Murders; with Hildegarde Teilhet. Doubleday, 1936.

Death Flies High. Morrow, 1931.

Double Agent; with Hildegarde Teilhet. Doubleday, 1945.

Fear Makers. Appleton, 1945.

Feather Cloak Murders: The Second Adventure of the Baron von Kaz. Doubleday, 1936.

First Adventure of the Brave Baron von Kaz in the Northern States of America: Ticking Terror Murders. Doubleday, 1935.

Happy Island. Sloane, 1950.

Hero by Proxy. Gollancz, 1943.

Journey to the West. Doubleday, 1938.

Lion's Skin. Sloane, 1955.

Murder in the Air. Morrow, 1931.

My True Love. Appleton, 1945.

Odd Man Pays. Little, 1944.

Private Undertaking. Coward, 1952.

Retreat from the Dolphin. Little, 1943.

Rim of Terror. Coward, 1950.

Road to Glory. Funk, 1956.

Skwee-Gee. il. Hardie Gramatky. Doubleday, 1940.

Something Wonderful to Happen: A Charivari. Appleton, 1947.

Steamboat on the River. il. John O. Cosgrave, II. Sloane, 1952.

Talking Sparrow Murders. Morrow, 1934.

Tough Guy, Smart Guy. Chapman, 1939.

Trouble Is My Master. Little, 1942.

MEDIA

Double Agent. (BB).

Hero by Proxy. (BB).

My True Love as *Room for the Groom*. Universal International Motion Pictures, 1952 (F).

Steamboat on the River. (BB, TB).

BACKGROUND READING

Warfel. *American Novelists of Today*.

+ESTHER FORBES, 1891-1967
author

AWARDS

Johnny Tremain. Newbery Medal Book, 1944.

BIBLIOGRAPHY

America's Paul Revere. il. Lynd Ward. Houghton, 1946.

Ann Douglas Sedgwick: An Interview. Houghton, 1928.

Boston Book. photographs by Arthur Griffin. Houghton, 1947.

General's Lady. Harcourt, 1938.

Johnny Tremain: A Novel for Old and Young. il. Lynd Ward. Houghton, 1943; large print edition, National Aid to the Visually Handicapped, 196?; *a.k.a. Johnny Tremain, a Novel for Old and Young, with Suggestions for Reading and Discussion*, by Ruth M. Stauffer, 1945.

Mirror for Witches: In Which Is Reflected the Life, Machinations, and Death of Famous Doll Bilby, Who, with a More Than Feminine Perversity, Preferred a Demon to a Mortal Lover. Here Is Also Told How and Why a Righteous and Most Awfull Judgement Befell Her, Destroying Both Corporeal Body and Immortal Soul. il. Robert Gibbings. Houghton, 1928.

Miss Marvel. Houghton, 1935.

O Genteel Lady! Houghton, 1926.

Paradise. Houghton, 1937.

Paul Revere and the World He Lived In. Houghton, 1942.

Rainbow on the Road. Houghton, 1954.

Running of the Tide. Houghton, 1948.

MEDIA

America's Paul Revere. (BB).

General's Lady. (BB).

Johnny Tremain. (BB, C, CB, MT, TB); Miller-Brody
Productions, 1969 (C, R); Walt Disney Produc-
tions, 1957 (F); *a.k.a. Johnny Tremain and the
Boston Tea Party* (excerpt from film). Walt Disney
Productions, 1966 (F), 19? (FSS); *a.k.a. Johnny
Tremain, Minuteman* (excerpt from film). Walt
Disney Productions, 1966 (F), 19? (FSS); *a.k.a.
Shot Heard 'round the World* (excerpt from film).
Walt Disney Productions, 19? (F), 19? (FSS).

Mirror for Witches. (BB); also basis for Sadler's Wells
ballet, London, 19?.

Paul Revere. (C, MT, TB).

Rainbow on the Road. (TB); *a.k.a. Come Summer*.
n. p., 1969 (F).

Running of the Tide. Metro-Goldwyn-Mayer, 1949 (F).

COLLECTIONS

American Antiquarian Society. (Worcester,
Massachusetts).

Clark University Library. (Worcester, Massachusetts).

Department of Rare Books and Manuscripts, Boston
Public Library. (Boston, Massachusetts).

BACKGROUND READING

Burke. *American Authors and Books, 1640 to the
Present Day*.

Commire. *Something about the Author*.

Contemporary Authors.

Fuller. *More Junior Authors*.

Hart. *Oxford Companion to Children's Literature,
Fourth Edition*.

Kirkpatrick. *Twentieth Century Children's Writers*.

Kunitz. *Twentieth Century Authors*.

Kunitz. *Twentieth Century Authors, First
Supplement*.

Miller. *Newbery Medal Books, 1922-1955*.

Obituary. *New York Times*, August 13, 1967.

Obituary. *Newsweek*, August 21, 1967.

Obituary. *Time*, August 25, 1967.

Ward. *Authors of Books for Young People, Second
Edition*.

Warfel. *American Novelists of Today*.

Warren, D. "Esther Forbes and the World She Lives
In." *Publishers Weekly*, May 13, 1944.

+LAUREN FORD, 1891-
author-illustrator

AWARDS

Ageless Story. Caldecott Honor Book, 1940.

BIBLIOGRAPHY

Ageless Story: With Its Antiphons; from the *Bible*.
Dodd, 1939.

Bells of Heaven: The Story of Joan of Arc; by
Christopher Bick. Dodd, 1949.

*Christmas Book: Scripture from the Gospel of St.
Luke*; from the *Bible*. Dodd, 1963.

(tr.) *Claude*; by Genevieve Fauconnier. Macmillan,
1937.

*Joan of Arc: Her Life as Told by Winston Churchill
in "A History of the English Speaking People"*;
by Winston Churchill. Dodd, 1969.

Little Book about God; from the *Bible*. Doubleday,
1934.

Memoirs of a Donkey; by Sophie DeSegur. Tr.
Marguerite Melcher. Macmillan, 1924.

Our Lady's Book. Dodd, 1962.

MEDIA

Little Book about God. (BB).

EXHIBITIONS

Feragil Gallery, 1930, 1932, 1935, 1938, 1945.
(New York, New York).

COLLECTIONS

Collection of American Literature, Beinecke Library,
Yale University. (New Haven, Connecticut).

Free Library of Philadelphia. (Philadelphia,
Pennsylvania).

Metropolitan Museum of Art. (New York, New York).

BACKGROUND READING

Contemporary Authors.

Mahony. *Illustrators of Children's Books, 1744-1945*.

Miller. *Illustrators of Children's Books, 1946-1956*.

O'Connor, J. "Presenting Miss Lauren Ford." *Carnegie
Magazine*, March 1939.

Ward. *Authors of Books for Young People, Second
Edition*.

+GENEVIEVE STUMP FOSTER, 1893-
author-illustrator

AWARDS

Abraham Lincoln's World. Newbery Honor Book, 1945.

Birthdays of Freedom. Newbery Honor Book, 1953.

George Washington. Newbery Honor Book, 1950.

George Washington's World. Newbery Honor Book, 1943.

BIBLIOGRAPHY

Abraham Lincoln: An Initial Biography. Scribner, 1950.

Abraham Lincoln's World. Scribner, 1944.

Andrew Jackson: An Initial Biography. Scribner, 1951.

Augustus Caesar's World: A Story of Ideas and Events from B.C. 44 to 14 A.D. Scribner, 1947.

Birthdays of Freedom: America's Heritage from the Ancient World. Scribner, 1952; also in *Birthdays of Freedom: From Early Man to July 4, 1776*, below.

Birthdays of Freedom, Book 2: From the Fall of Rome to July 4, 1776. Scribner, 1957; also in *Birthdays of Freedom: From Early Man to July 4, 1776*, below.

Birthdays of Freedom: From Early Man to July 4, 1776. Scribner, 1973. (Includes the two *Birthdays of Freedom* books, above.)

Boyhood Adventures of Our Presidents; by Frances Cavanah. Rand, 1938.

Children of the White House; by Frances Cavanah. Rand, 1936.

George Washington: An Initial Biography. Scribner, 1949.

George Washington's World. Scribner, 1942.

Mary Jane's Friends in Holland; by Clara I. Judson. Grosset, 1929.

Pioneer Girl: The Early Life of Frances Willard. Rand, 1939.

Theodore Roosevelt: An Initial Biography. Scribner, 1954.

When and Where in Italy: A Passport to Yesterday for Readers and Travelers of Today. Rand, 1955.

World of Captain John Smith, 1580-1631. Scribner, 1959.

World of Columbus and Sons. Scribner, 1965.

World of William Penn. Scribner, 1973.

Year of Columbus, 1492. Scribner, 1969.

Year of Independence, 1776. Scribner, 1970.

Year of Lincoln, 1861. Scribner, 1970.

Year of the Flying Machine. Scribner, 1977.

Year of the Horseless Carriage. Scribner, 1975.

Year of the Pilgrims, 1620. Scribner, 1969.

MEDIA

Abraham Lincoln. (CB, TB).

Abraham Lincoln's World. (BB, CB).

Augustus Caeser's World. (CB).

Birthdays of Freedom (Book 1). (BB, TB).

Birthdays of Freedom (Book 2). (BB, TB).

George Washington's World. (BB, TB).

Theodore Roosevelt. (BB).

World of Columbus and Sons. (BB, TB).

World of William Penn. (TB).

COLLECTIONS

Free Library of Philadelphia. (Philadelphia, Pennsylvania).

Kerlan Collection, University of Minnesota. (Minneapolis, Minnesota).

Prints and Manuscripts Division, Library of Congress. (Washington, D.C.).

University of Oregon Library. (Eugene, Oregon).

BACKGROUND READING

Burke. *American Authors and Books, 1640 to the Present Day*.

Commire. *Something about the Author*.

Contemporary Authors.

Dawson, M. "Genevieve Foster's Worlds." *Horn Book*, June 1952.

Fenwick, S. "Exploring History with Genevieve Foster." *Elementary English*, October 1954.

Foster, J. " Genevieve Foster." *Horn Book*, June 1952.

Genevieve Foster's World. Connecticut Films, Inc., 1971 (F).

Hoffman. *Authors and Illustrators of Children's Books*.

Hopkins. *More Books by More People*.

Kingman. *Illustrators of Children's Books, 1957-1966*.

Kingman. *Illustrators of Children's Books, 1967-1976*.

Kunitz. *Junior Book of Authors, Second Edition Revised*.

Miller. *Illustrators of Children's Books, 1946-1956*.

Townsend. *Sense of Story*.

Ward. *Authors of Books for Young People, Second Edition*.

PAULA FOX, 1923-
author

AWARDS

Slave Dancer. Newbery Medal Book, 1974.

BIBLIOGRAPHY

Blowfish Live in the Sea. Bradbury, 1970.

Dear Prosper. il. Steve McLachlin. White, 1968.

Desperate Characters. Harcourt, 1970.

Good Ethan. il. Arnold Lobel. Bradbury, 1973.

How Many Miles to Babylon? il. Paul Giovanopoulos. White, 1967.

Hungry Fred. il. Rosemary Wells. Bradbury, 1969.

King's Falcon. il. Eros Keith. Bradbury, 1969.

Likely Place. il. Edward Ardizzone. Macmillan, 1968.

Maurice's Room. il. Ingrid Fetz. Macmillan, 1966.

Poor George. Harcourt, 1967.

Portrait of Ivan. il. Saul Lambert. Bradbury, 1969.

Slave Dancer. il. Eros Keith. Bradbury, 1973.

Stone-Faced Boy. il. Donald A. McKay. Bradbury, 1968.

Western Coast. Harcourt, 1972.

Widow's Children. Dutton, 1976.

MEDIA

Blowfish Live in the Sea. (BB).

Desperate Characters. (BB); Independent Television Corporation, 1971 (F).

Good Ethan. (TB).

How Many Miles to Babylon? (BB, TB).

Maurice's Room. (BB).

Portrait of Ivan. (TB).

Slave Dancer. (BB, CB).

Stone-Faced Boy. (BB, MT).

Western Coast. (TB).

BACKGROUND READING

DeMontreville. *Fourth Book of Junior Authors and Illustrators.*

Kingman. *Newbery and Caldecott Medal Books, 1966-1975.*

Kirkpatrick. *Twentieth Century Children's Writers.*

Townsend. *Sense of Story.*

ANTONIO FRASCONI, 1919-
author-illustrator

AWARDS

House That Jack Built. Caldecott Honor Book, 1959.

BIBLIOGRAPHY

Appointment Calendar for 1966. Baltimore Museum of Art, 1966.

Bestiary/Bestiario: A Poem; by Pablo Neruda, *pseud.* (Neftalí R. R. Basulato). Tr. Elsa Neuberger. Harcourt, 1965.

Birds from My Homeland: Ten Hand-Colored Woodcuts with Notes from W. H. Hudson's "Birds of La Plata." Rodenko, 1958.

Cantilever Rainbow; by Ruth Krauss. Pantheon, 1955.

Crickets and Frogs, Grillos y Ranas: A Fable in Spanish and English; by Gabriela Mistral, *pseud.* (Lucila Godoy Alcayaga). Tr. and adapted by Doris Dana. Atheneum, 1972.

Elephant and His Secret, el Elefante y Su Secreto: Based on a Fable; by Gabriela Mistral, *pseud.* (Lucila Godoy Alcayaga). Tr. and adapted by Doris Dana. Atheneum, 1974.

Elijah the Slave: A Hebrew Legend Retold; by Isaac B. Singer. Tr. Isaac B. Singer and Elizabeth Shub. Farrar, 1970.

Face of Edgar Allan Poe: With a Note on Poe by Charles Baudelaire. Rodenko, 1959.

Frasconi against the Grain: The Woodcuts of Antonio Frasconi; by Nat Hentoff and Charles Parkhurst. Macmillan, 1975.

House That Jack Built: La Maison Que Jacques a Batie. Harcourt, 1958.

Kaleidoscope in Woodcuts. Harcourt, 1968.

Known Fables; by Aesop. Spiral, 1964.

Lied vom SA-Mann; by Bertoldt Brecht. Antonio Frasconi, 1961.

Love Lyrics; by Louis Untermeyer. Odyssey, 1965.

(ed.) *On the Slain Collegians: Selections from Poems;* by Herman Melville. Farrar, 1971.

(ed.) *Overhead the Sun: Lines from Walt Whitman;* by Walt Whitman. Farrar, 1969.

See Again, Say Again; Guarda di Nuovo, Parla di Nuoyo, Regarde et Parle: A Picture Book in Four Languages. Harcourt, 1964.

See and Say; Guada e Parla; Mira y Habla, Regarde et Parle: A Picture Book in Four Languages. Harcourt, 1955.

Six South American Folk Rhymes about Love: With Woodcuts. Spiral, 1964.

Six Spanish Nursery Rhymes. Crafton, 1960.

Snow and the Sun, La Nieve y el Sol: A South American Folk Rhyme in Two Languages. Harcourt, 1961.

Sunday in Monterrey. Harcourt, 1964.

12 Fables of Aesop; by Aesop. Tr. Glenway Wescott. Museum of Modern Art, 1954.

Unstill Life: Naturaleza Viva; by Mario Benedetti. Harcourt, 1969.

Whitman Portrait. Spiral, 1960.

Woodcuts. Spiral, 1957; *a.k.a. Woodcuts: With Comments by Antonio Frasconi* (et al.). Weyhe, 1957; *a.k.a. Woodcuts 1957: With Comments by Antonio Frasconi* (et al.). Typophiles, 1957.

MEDIA

Crickets and Frogs. (BB).

Neighboring Shore. Antonio Frasconi, 1960 (original F).

See and Say. Weston Woods Studios, 1964 (FSS); also in Weston Woods Studios Set No. 20, 1965 (FSS).

EXHIBITIONS

American Institute of Graphic Arts, 1976. (New York, New York).

Baltimore Museum of Art, 1951, 1963. (Baltimore, Maryland).

Bear Gallery, 1975. (Santa Barbara, California).

Brooklyn Museum of Arts and Sciences, 1946, 1964. (Brooklyn, New York).

Cleveland Museum of Art, 1952. (Cleveland, Ohio).

Dintenfass Gallery, 1962-63, 1966, 1971. (New York, New York).

Galleria Penelope, 1967. (Rome, Italy).

International Biennial Exhibition of Prints, 1975. (Tokyo, Japan).

Museo de Arte Moderno, 1976. (Cali, Colombia).

Museo del Libro, 1976. (San Juan, Puerto Rico).

Museum of Art, 1976. (Fribourg, Switzerland).

San Francisco Museum, 1975. (San Francisco, California).

Smithsonian Traveling Exhibition, 1953, 1964, 1976. (Europe).

Venice Biennele, 1968. (Venice, Italy).

Weyhe Gallery, 1948-49, 1950-54, 1956, 1960, 1964-65. (New York, New York).

COLLECTIONS

Arts Council of Great Britain. (London, England).

Bibliotheque National. (Paris, France).

Casa Americas. (Havana, Cuba).

Chicago Art Institute. (Chicago, Illinois).

Cleveland Museum of Art. (Cleveland, Ohio).

deGrummond Collection, University of Southern Mississippi. (Hattiesburg, Mississippi).

Detroit Art Institute. (Detroit, Michigan).

Honolulu Academy of Art. (Honolulu, Hawaii).

Metropolitan Museum of Art. (New York, New York).

Museo Nacional Bellas Arte. (Montevideo, Uruguay).

Museum of Modern Art. (New York, New York).

New York Public Library. (New York, New York).

Newark Museum. (Newark, New Jersey).

Philadelphia Museum of Art. (Philadelphia, Pennsylvania).

Prints and Photographs Division, Library of Congress. (Washington, D.C.).

Rhode Island School of Design. (Providence, Rhode Island).

San Diego Museum of Art. (San Diego, California).

BACKGROUND READING

Antonio Frasconi, Graphic Artist. Pablo Frasconi, 1975 (F).

Bader. *American Picturebooks from Noah's Ark to The Beast Within*.

Burke. *American Authors and Books, 1640 to the Present Day*.

Chernow, B. "Interview with Antonio Frasconi." *School Arts*, May 1966.

Commire. *Something about the Author*.

Contemporary Authors.

Current Biography.

DeMontreville. *Third Book of Junior Authors*.

"Frasconi's Brio with a Book." *Horizon*, March 1961.

Getlein, F. "Frasconi the Printmaker." *New Republic*, February 29, 1964.

Johnson, U. "Woodcuts of Antonio Frasconi." *Print*, Winter 1950.

Kingman. *Illustrators of Children's Books, 1957-1966*.

Kingman. *Illustrators of Children's Books, 1967-1976*.

Klemin. *Illustrated Book: Its Art and Craft*.

Lieberman, W. "Antonio Frasconi, Woodcutter." *Print*, July 1955.

Miller. *Illustrators of Children's Books, 1946-1956*.

Salsamendi, A. "Lively Art of Antonio Frasconi." *Américas*, May 1957.

Taylor, K. "Antonio Frasconi." *Graphis*, May 1958.

BACKGROUND READING (cont'd)

Varga, M. "Woodcuts by Antonio Frasconi." *American Artist*, October 1974.

Ward. *Authors of Books for Young People, Second Edition*.

"Wizard of the Woodcut." *Time*, December 20, 1963.

DON FREEMAN, 1908-
author-illustrator

AWARDS

Fly High, Fly Low. Caldecott Honor Book, 1958.

BIBLIOGRAPHY

Add-a-Line Alphabet. Golden Gate, 1968.

Beady Bear. Viking, 1954.

Bearymore. Viking, 1976.

Best of Friends; by Myra B. Brown. Golden Gate, 1967.

Best of Luck; by Myra B. Brown. Golden Gate, 1969.

Bill Bergson Lives Dangerously; by Astrid Lindgren. Viking, 1954.

Botts: The Naughty Otter, Golden Gate, 1963.

Burnish Me Bright; by Julia Cunningham. Pantheon, 1970.

California Indian Days; by Helen Bauer. Doubleday, 1963; new edition, 1968.

Chalk Box Story. Lippincott, 1976.

Christmas Strangers; by Marjorie Thayer. Childrens, 1976.

Chuggy and the Blue Caboose; with Lydia Freeman. Viking, 1951.

Circus in Peter's Closet; by Jane Randolph. Crowell, 1955.

Come Again, Pelican. Viking, 1961.

*Come One, Come All! Drawn from Memory. Rinehart, 1949.

Corduroy. Viking, 1968.

Cyrano the Crow. Viking, 1960.

Dandelion. Viking, 1964.

Diedrich Knickerbocker's History of New York; by Washington Irving. Heritage, 1940.

Don Freeman's Newstand: A Journal of One Man's Manhattan, Manhattan Sketchbook. Association of American Artists, 1940-41; also privately printed, 1936-1957.

Edward and the Night Horses; by Jacklyn Matthews. Golden Gate, 1971.

Far in the Day; by Julia Cunningham. Pantheon, 1972.

Flash the Dash. Golden Gate, 1973.

Fly High, Fly Low. Viking, 1957.

Forever Laughter. Golden Gate, 1970.

Ghost Town Treasure; by Clyde R. Bulla. Crowell, 1958.

Guard Mouse. Viking, 1967.

Hattie the Backstage Bat. Viking, 1970.

Human Comedy; by William Saroyan. Harcourt, 1943.

Inspector Peckitt. Viking, 1972.

It Shouldn't Happen. Harcourt, 1945.

Joey's Cat; by Robert Burch. Viking, 1969.

Mike's House; by Julia Sauer. Viking, 1954.

Monkeys Are Funny That Way; by Dorothy Koch. Holiday, 1962.

Monster Night at Grandma's House; by Richard Peck. Viking, 1977.

Mop Top. Viking, 1955.

My Name Is Aram; by William Saroyan. Harcourt, 1940.

Night the Lights Went Out. Viking, 1958.

Norman the Doorman. Viking, 1959.

Once around the Sun; by Brooks Atkinson. Harcourt, 1951.

Paper Party. Viking, 1974.

Penquins of All People! Viking, 1971.

Pet of the Met; with Lydia Freeman. Viking, 1953.

Quiet! There's a Canary in the Library. Golden Gate, 1969.

Rainbow of My Own. Viking, 1966.

Saroyan Special; by William Saroyan. Harcourt, 1948.

Sauce for the Gander; by Scott Corbett. Crowell, 1951.

Seal and the Slick. Viking, 1974.

Seven Days from Sunday; by Tom Galt. Crowell, 1956.

Seven in a Bed; by Ruth Sonneborn. Viking, 1968.

Sharp and Doane Advertisements. Sharp and Doane, 1943. (3 vols.).

Ski Pup. Viking, 1963.

Skitzy: The Story of Floyd W. Skitzafroid. Hooper, 1955.

Space Witch. Viking, 1959.

Third Monkey; by Ann N. Clark. Viking, 1956.

This for That; by Ann N. Clark. Golden Gate, 1965.

Tilly Witch. Viking, 1969.

Turtle and the Dove. Viking, 1964.

Uninvited Donkey; by Anne H. White. Viking, 1957.

Voltaire's Micromegas; by Elizabeth Hall. Golden Gate, 1967.

White Deer; by James Thurber. il. with James Thurber. Harcourt, 1945.

Whole Truth and Nothing but the Hole. McNally and Loftin, 1968.

Wild Cats of Rome; by Elizabeth Cooper. Golden Gate, 1972.

Will's Quill. Viking, 1975.

MEDIA

Baker. Children's Television Workshop, 1970 (original F).

Beady Bear. Viking Press, 1974 (C).

Corduroy. Taylor Associates, 1970 (FSS); Viking Press, 1970 (FSS).

Dandelion. Viking Press, 1970 (FSS).

Guard Mouse. Spoken Arts, 1971 (FSS).

Hattie the Backstage Bat. Taylor Associates, 1973 (FSS); Viking Press, 1971 (FSS).

Human Comedy. (BB).

Joey's Cat. Viking Press, 1970 (FSS).

Lollipop Opera. Pyramid Films, 1971 (original F).

Mop Top. Taylor Associates, 1970 (FSS); Viking Press, 1970 (FSS).

Norman the Doorman. (TB); Weston Woods Studios, 1966 (FSS), 1971 (F); also in Weston Woods Studios Set No. 15, 1965 (FSS).

Pet of the Met. (TB).

Rainbow of My Own. Bank Street College of Education, 1968 (F, FSS); Viking Press, 1975 (FSS).

Space Witch. (BB, TB).

Will's Quill. Viking Press, 1976 (C).

EXHIBITIONS

Associated American Artists Gallery, 1940. (New York, New York).

Fieden Gallery, 1976. (New York, New York).

COLLECTIONS

Arents Research Library, Syracuse University. (Syracuse, New York).

deGrummond Collection, University of Southern Mississippi. (Hattiesburg, Mississippi).

Kerlan Collection, University of Minnesota. (Minneapolis, Minnesota).

May Massee Collection, Emporia State College. (Emporia, Kansas).

BACKGROUND READING

Bader. *American Picturebooks from Noah's Ark to The Beast Within*.

Fuller. *More Junior Authors*.

Hopkins. *Books Are by People*.

Hutchens, J. "On an Author." *New York Herald Tribune Book Review*, May 17, 1953.

Kingman. *Illustrators of Children's Books, 1957-1966*.

Kingman. *Illustrators of Children's Books, 1967-1976*.

Kirkpatrick. *Twentieth Century Children's Writers*.

Miller. *Illustrators of Children's Books, 1946-1956*.

Storyteller. Churchill Films, 1972 (F).

Ward. *Authors of Books for Young People, Second Edition*.

WANDA HAZEL GÁG, 1893-1946
author-illustrator

AWARDS

ABC Bunny. Newbery Honor Book, 1934.

Millions of Cats. Newbery Honor Book, 1929.

Nothing at All. Caldecott Honor Book, 1942.

Snow White and the Seven Dwarfs. Caldecott Honor Book, 1939.

BIBLIOGRAPHY

ABC Bunny; hand-lettered by Howard Gág. Coward, 1933.

Day of Doom: Or, a Poetical Description of the Great and Last Judgement, with Other Poems; by Michael Wigglesworth. edited by Kenneth B. Murdock. Spiral, 1929.

Funny Thing. Coward, 1929; also in *Wanda Gág's Storybook*, below.

Gone Is Gone: Or, the Story of a Man Who Wanted to Do Housework. Coward, 1935.

*Growing Pains: Diaries and Drawings for the Years 1908-1917. Coward, 1940.

Mechanics of Written English; by Jean S. Rankin. Augsburg, 1917.

Millions of Cats. Coward, 1928; also issued in limited edition; also in *Wanda Gág's Storybook*, below.

(tr.) *More Tales from Grimm*; by Jacob and Wilhelm Grimm. Coward, 1947.

BIBLIOGRAPHY (cont'd)

Nothing at All. Coward, 1941.

Oak by the Waters of Rowan; by Spencer Kellogg, Jr. Aries, 1937.

Pound Image and Other Poems; by John Egilsrud. Lund, 1943.

Snippy and Snappy. Coward, 1931; also in *Wanda Gág's Storybook*, below.

(tr.) *Snow White and the Seven Dwarfs*; by Jacob and Wilhelm Grimm. Coward, 1938.

(tr.) *Tales from Grimm*; by Jacob and Wilhelm Grimm. Coward, 1936.

(tr.) *Three Gay Tales from Grimm*; by Jacob and Wilhelm Grimm. Coward, 1943.

Wanda Gág's Storybook. Coward, 1932. (Includes *Funny Thing*, *Millions of Cats*, and *Snippy and Snappy*, each issued separately, above.)

MEDIA

ABC Bunny. (TB).

Funny Thing. (TB).

Gone is Gone. (TB).

Millions of Cats. (BB); Weston Woods Studios, 1955 (F), 1956 (FSS); also in Weston Woods Studios Set No. 1, 1968 (FSS); a.k.a. *Millones de Gatos*. Weston Woods Studios, 1960 (F).

Nothing at All. (TB).

Snippy and Snappy. (TB).

Tales from Grimm. Weston Woods Studios, n. d. (R, F); a.k.a. *Fisherman and His Wife from Tales from Grimm*. Weston Woods Studios, 1970 (C, F, R).

EXHIBITIONS

Central Children's Room, New York Public Library, 1947. (New York, New York). (Memorial exhibition).

Weyhe Gallery, 1930. (New York, New York).

COLLECTIONS

Central Children's Room, Donnell Library Center, New York Public Library. (New York, New York).

Free Library of Philadelphia. (Philadelphia, Pennsylvania).

Kerlan Collection, University of Minnesota. (Minneapolis, Minnesota).

Minneapolis Institute of Art. (Minneapolis, Minnesota).

Special Collections, University Research Library, University of California. (Los Angeles, California).

BACKGROUND READING

Bader. *American Picturebooks from Noah's Ark to The Beast Within*.

Burke. *American Authors and Books, 1640 to the Present Day*.

Commire. *Yesterday's Authors of Books for Children*.

Current Biography.

Dobbs, R. "All Creation, Wanda Gág and Her Family." *Horn Book*, November 1935.

Gág, W. "I Like Fairy Tales." *Horn Book*, March 1939.

Garraty. *Dictionary of American Biography, Supplement 4*.

Hearn, Michael P. *50 Years of Wanda Gág's Millions of Cats 1928-1978*. Coward, 1978.

Horn Book, special issue, May 1947.

Hurley, B. "Wanda Gág: Artist, Author." *Elementary English*, October 1955.

Kirkpatrick. *Twentieth Century Children's Writers*.

Kunitz. *Junior Book of Authors*.

Kunitz. *Junior Book of Authors, Second Edition Revised*.

Kunitz. *Twentieth Century Authors*.

Kunitz. *Twentieth Century Authors, First Supplement*.

Mahony. *Contemporary Illustrators of Children's Books*.

Mahony. *Illustrators of Children's Books, 1744-1945*.

Obituary. *Art Digest*, August 1946.

Obituary. *New York Herald Tribune*, June 28, 1946.

Obituary. *New York Times*, June 28, 1946.

Scott, Alma. *Wanda Gág: The Story of an Artist*. University of Minnesota, 1949.

Smaridge. *Famous Author-Illustrators for Young People*.

Ward. *Authors of Books for Young People, Second Edition*.

+EVA ROE GAGGIN, 1879-1966
author

AWARDS

Down Ryton Water. Newbery Honor Book, 1942.

BIBLIOGRAPHY

All Those Buckles. il. Mildred Cloete. Viking, 1945.

Down Ryton Water. il. Elmer Hader. Viking, 1941.

Ear for Uncle Emil. il. Kate Seredy. Viking, 1939.

Jolly Animals. il. Keith Ward. Rand, 1930.

+PAUL GALDONE
author-illustrator

AWARDS

Anatole. Caldecott Honor Book, 1957.

Anatole and the Cat. Caldecott Honor Book, 1958.

(*Moccasin Trail*. Newbery Honor Book, 1953.)

(*Perilous Road*. Newbery Honor Book, 1959).

BIBLIOGRAPHY

Adventures of Egbert the Easter Egg; by Richard Armour. McGraw, 1965.

Adventures of Homer Fink; by Sidney Offit. St. Martin's, 1966.

All Sizes and Shapes of Monkeys and Apes; by Richard Armour. McGraw, 1970.

Anatole; by Eve Titus. McGraw, 1956.

Anatole and the Cat; by Eve Titus. McGraw, 1957.

Anatole and the Piano; by Eve Titus. McGraw, 1966.

Anatole and the Poodle; by Eve Titus. McGraw, 1965.

Anatole and the Robot; by Eve Titus. McGraw, 1960.

Anatole and the Thirty Thieves; by Eve Titus. McGraw, 1969.

Anatole and the Toyshop; by Eve Titus. McGraw, 1970.

Anatole in Italy; by Eve Titus. McGraw, 1973.

Anatole over Paris; by Eve Titus. McGraw, 1961.

(adapt.) *Androcles and the Lion*. McGraw, 1970.

Animals on the Ceiling; by Richard Armour. McGraw, 1966.

Anyone for Cub Scouts; by Henry G. Felsen. Scribner, 1954.

Audubon and His Sons; by Amy Hogeboom. Lothrop, 1956.

Ball of Fire; by Earl S. Miers. World, 1956.

Barbara Frietchie; by John G. Whittier. Crowell, 1965.

Bascombe, the Fastest Hound Alive; by George Goodman. Morrow, 1958.

Baseball Trick; by Scott Corbett. Atlantic, 1965.

Basil and the Pygmy Cats; by Eve Titus. McGraw, 1971.

Basil of Baker Street; by Eve Titus. McGraw, 1958.

Battle of the Kegs; by Frances Hopkinson. Crowell, 1964.

Because of the Sand Witches There; by Mary Q. Steele. Greenwillow, 1975.

Benjie Goes into Business; by Patricia M. Martin. Putnam, 1961.

Big Basketball Prize; by Marion Renick. Scribner, 1963.

Blind Men and the Elephants; by John Saxe. McGraw, 1963.

Boy at Bat; by Marion Renick. Scribner, 1961.

Boy with a Billion Pets; by Peggy Mann. Coward, 1960.

Bremen Town Musicians; by Jacob and Wilhelm Grimm. McGraw, 1968.

Brownie; by Hans Peterson. Lothrop, 1965.

Buckskin Scout and Other Ohio Stories; by Marion Renick and Margaret C. Tyler. World, 1953.

Budd's Noisy Wagon; by Richard Shaw. Warne, 1968.

Buffalo Knife; by William O. Steele. Harcourt, 1952.

Camel in the Sea; by Lee G. Goetz. McGraw, 1966.

Capital Ship: Or, The Walloping Window-Blind; by Charles Carryl. McGraw, 1963.

Clarence and the Burglar; by Ferdinand N. Monjo. Coward, 1973.

Cool Ride in the Sky; by Diane Wolkstein. Knopf, 1973.

Counting Carnival; by Feenie Ziner. Coward, 1962.

Dance of the Animals: A Puerto Rican Folk Tale; by Pura Belpré. Warne, 1972.

Deacon's Masterpiece: Or, The Wonderful One-Hoss Shay; by Oliver W. Holmes. McGraw, 1965.

Did You Feed My Cow? Rhymes and Games from City Streets and Country Lanes; by Margaret T. Burroughs. Crowell, 1966.

Different Dog; by Dale Everson. Morrow, 1960.

Disappearing Dog Trick; by Scott Corbett. Atlantic, 1963.

Dogs and Cats and Things Like That; by John Knoepfle. McGraw, 1971.

Down and Away: A Tale of Treasure and Adventure in the Emerald Lagoon; by Edwin Rols. Bobbs, 1956.

Dozen Dinosaurs; by Richard Armour. McGraw, 1967.

Elbert the Mind Reader; by Barbara Rinkoff. Lothrop, 1967.

Far Frontier; by William O. Steele. Harcourt, 1957.

First Seven Days: The Story of the Creation from Genesis; from the *Bible*. Crowell, 1962.

Fishing Cat; by Grace Meyers. Abingdon, 1953.

BIBLIOGRAPHY (cont'd)

Flaming Arrows; by William O. Steele. Harcourt, 1957.

Follow Your Nose; by Paul Showers. Crowell, 1963.

Frog Prince. McGraw, 1974.

Gaggle of Geese; by Eve Merriam. Knopf, 1960.

George Washington's Breakfast; by Jean Fritz. Coward, 1969.

Ghost of Five Owl Farm; by Wilson Gage, *pseud.* (Mary Q. Steele). World, 1966.

Golden Touch; by Nathaniel Hawthorne. McGraw, 1959.

Grandfather and I; by Helen E. Buckley. Lothrop, 1959.

Grandmother and I; by Helen E. Buckley. Lothrop, 1961.

Green Song; by Doris T. Plenn. McKay, 1954; *a.k.a. Canción Verde*. Tr. A. J. Colorado. Troutman, 1956.

Hairy Horror Trick; by Scott Corbett. Atlantic, 1969.

Hangman's Ghost Trick; by Scott Corbett. Atlantic, 1977.

Hans Brinker; by Mary M. Dodge. Doubleday, 1954.

Hare and the Tortoise; by Aesop. McGraw, 1962.

Hateful Plateful Trick; by Scott Corbett. Atlantic, 1971.

Henny Penny. Seabury, 1968.

Hereafterthis; by Joseph Jacobs. McGraw, 1973.

Heroines of the Early West; by Nancy W. Ross. Random, 1960.

High Sounds, Low Sounds; by Franklyn M. Branley. Crowell, 1967.

History of Little Tom Tucker. McGraw, 1970.

History of Mother Twaddle and the Marvelous Achievements of Her Son Jack. Seabury, 1974.

History of Simple Simon. McGraw, 1966.

Hockey Trick; by Scott Corbett. Atlantic, 1974.

Home Is If You Find It; by Harry Nye. Doubleday, 1947.

Home Run Trick; by Scott Corbett. Atlantic, 1973.

Horse, the Fox and the Lion: Adapted from The Fox and the Horse; by Jacob and Wilhelm Grimm. Seabury, 1968.

House That Jack Built. McGraw, 1961.

How Do You Travel?; by Miriam Schlein. Abingdon, 1954.

I Married a Redhead; by Morris M. Musselman. Crowell, 1949.

If It Does Not Meow, and Other Animal Riddle Rhymes; by Beatrice S. DeRegniers. Seabury, 1972.

Improbable Adventures of Marvelous O'Hara Soapstone; by Zibby Oneal. Viking, 1972.

Jack-O-Lantern; by Edna Barth. Seabury, 1974.

Jeff and Mr. James' Pond; by Esther Meeks. Lothrop, 1962.

Key of Gold; by Cora Cheney. Holt, 1955.

Kid Who Beat the Dodgers and Other Sports Stories; by Earl S. Miers. World, 1954.

Koko and the Ghosts; by Ivan Kušan. Harcourt, 1966.

Lemonade Trick; by Scott Corbett. Atlantic, 1960.

Liberation of Manhattan; by Edmund Demairte and Mark Applebaum. Doubleday, 1949.

Life of Jack Spratt, His Wife, and His Cat. McGraw, 1969.

Limerick Trick; by Scott Corbett. Atlantic, 196?.

Liselott and the Goloff; by Hans Peterson. Coward, 1964.

Little Boy and the Birthdays; by Helen E. Buckley. Lothrop, 1965.

Little Green Car; by Caroline Emerson. Grosset, 1946.

Little Red Hen. Seabury, 1973.

Little Red Riding Hood; by Jacob and Wilhelm Grimm. McGraw, 1974.

Little Tom Tucker. McGraw, 1970.

Little Truck; by Clara Baldwin. Doubleday, 1959.

Little Tuppen: An Old Tale. Seabury, 1967.

Lone Hunt; by William O. Steele. Harcourt, 1956.

Look at Your Eyes; by Paul Showers. Crowell, 1962.

Madcap Mystery; by Karin Anckarsvärd. Tr. Annabelle MacMillan. Harcourt, 1962.

Magic Porridge Pot. Seabury, 1976.

Mailbox Trick; by Scott Corbett. Atlantic, 1961.

Making the Mississippi Shout; by Mary Calhoun. Morrow, 1957.

Man in the Moon; by Margaret Otto. Holt, 1957.

Meshach and Abednego from the Book of Daniel; from the *Bible*. McGraw, 1965.

Miss Osborne-the-Mop; by Wilson Gage, *pseud.* (Mary Q. Steele). World, 1963.

Miss Pickerell and the Geiger Counter; by Ellen McGregor. McGraw, 1953.

Miss Pickerell Goes to Mars; by Ellen McGregor. McGraw, 1951.

Miss Pickerell Goes to the Arctic; by Ellen McGregor. McGraw, 1954.

Miss Pickerell Goes Undersea; by Ellen McGregor. McGraw, 1953.

Mr. Ferguson of the Fire Department; by Ellen McGregor. McGraw, 1956.

Mister Jim; by Rutherford G. Montgomery. World, 1957.

Mister Pringle and Mister Buttonhole; by Ellen McGregor. McGraw, 1957.

Mister Willowby's Christmas Tree; by Robert Barry. McGraw, 1963.

Mrs. Perrywinkle's Pets; by Jane Thayer, *pseud.* (Catherine Woolley). Morrow, 1955.

Moccasin Trail; by Eloise J. McGraw. Coward, 1952.

Monkey and the Crocodile: A Jataka Tale from India. Seabury, 1969.

Monkey Shines; by Earl S. Miers. World, 1955.

Moving Adventures of Old Dame Trot and Her Comical Cat. McGraw, 1973.

My Dog and I; by Nancy Lord. McGraw, 1958.

My Sister and I; by Helen E. Buckley. Lothrop, 1963.

Mysterious Schoolmaster; by Karin Anckarsvärd. Tr. Annabelle MacMillan. Harcourt, 1959.

Night Cat; by Irma S. Black. Holiday, 1957.

Nine Lives; by Edward Fenton. Pantheon, 1951.

Obedient Jack: An Old Tale. Watts, 1971.

Odd Old Mammals: Animals after the Dinosaurs; by Richard Armour. McGraw, 1968.

Old Charlie; by Clyde R. Bulla. Crowell, 1957.

Old Mother Hubbard and Her Dog; by Sarah C. Martin. McGraw, 1960.

Old Woman and Her Pig. McGraw, 1960; *a.k.a. Vieja y Su Cerdo.* Tr. Mary Finocchiaro, 1961; *a.k.a. Vielle Femme et Son Cochon*, 1961.

100 Hamburgers, the Getting Thin Book; by Mary Solot. Lothrop, 1972.

One Little Drum; by Margaret Hodges. Follett, 1958.

Oté: A Puerto Rican Folk Tale; by Pura Belpré. Pantheon, 1969.

Paddy, the Penquin. Crowell, 1959.

Pandora's Box: The Paradise of Children; by Nathaniel Hawthorne. McGraw, 1967.

Paul Revere's Ride; by Henry W. Longfellow. Crowell, 1963.

Peek the Piper; by Vitalil Bianki. Tr. S. K. Kederer. Braziller, 1964.

People Downstairs, and Other City Stories; by Rhoda Bacmeister. Coward, 1964.

People I'd Like to Keep; by Mary O'Neill. Doubleday, 1964.

Perilous Road; by William O. Steele. Harcourt, 1958.

Playing Possum; by Edward Eager. Putnam, 1955.

Queen Who Couldn't Bake Gingerbread; by Dorothy Van Woerkom. Knopf, 1975.

Rendezvous in Singapore; by Cora Cheney and Ben Partridge. Knopf, 1961.

Robber Ghost; by Karin Anckarsvärd. Tr. Annabelle MacMillan. Harcourt, 1961.

Rockets Away!; by Frances Frost. McGraw, 1953.

Rocking Chair Buck; by Cora Cheney. Holt, 1956.

Rusty Rings a Bell; by Franklyn M. Branley and Eleanor Vaughan. Crowell, 1957.

Sea Beach Adventure; by Gladys Saxon. Holt, 1956.

Secrets of Hidden Creek; by Wylly St. John. Viking, 1966.

Sidney's Ghost; by Carol Iden. World, 1969.

Silver Purse; by Elisa Bialk. World, 1952.

Small Clown; by Nancy Faulkner. Doubleday, 1960.

Sorry to Be So Cheerful; by Hildegarde Dolson. Random, 1955.

Space Cat; by Ruthven Todd. Scribner, 1952.

Space Cat and the Kittens; by Ruthven Todd. Scribner, 1958.

Space Cat Meets Mars; by Ruthven Todd. Scribner, 1957.

Space Cat Visits Venus; by Ruthven Todd. Scribner, 1955.

Speak Up, Edie!; by Johanna Johnston. Putnam, 1974.

Star of Wonder; by Robert Coles and Frances Frost. McGraw, 1953.

Star-Spangled Banner; by Frances S. Key. Crowell, 1966.

Strange Servant: A Russian Folktale; by Blanche Ross. Pantheon, 1977.

Sunlit Sea; by Augusta Goldin. Crowell, 1968.

Sunnyvale Fair; by Alice E. Goudey. Scribner, 1962.

Sword in the Tree; by Clyde R. Bulla. Crowell, 1956.

Table, the Donkey, and the Stick; by Jacob and Wilhelm Grimm. Seabury, 1976.

Tailypo; by Joanna Galdone. Seabury, 1977.

Tale of the Terrible Tiger, a Football Story; by Marion Renick. Scribner, 1959.

That's Right, Edie; by Johanna Johnston. Putnam, 1966.

Theodore Turtle; by Ellen McGregor. McGraw, 1955.

Three Aesop Fox Fables; by Aesop. Seabury, 1971.

Three Bears. Seabury, 1972.

Three Billy Goats Gruff; by Peter C. Asbjörnsen and Jörgen Moe. Seabury, 1973.

Three Little Pigs. Seabury, 1970.

BIBLIOGRAPHY (cont'd)

Three Poems of Edgar Allan Poe; by Edgar A. Poe. McGraw, 1966.

Three Wishes; by Joseph Jacobs. McGraw, 1961.

Timmy and the Tin-Can Telephone; by Franklyn M. Branley and Eleanor Vaughan. Lothrop, 1959.

To the Rescue; by Judy Van Der Veer. Harcourt, 1969.

Tom, Tom the Piper's Son. McGraw, 1964.

Tomahawks and Trouble; by William O. Steele. Harcourt, 1955.

Touchdown Trouble; by Earl S. Miers. World, 1953.

Town Mouse and the Country Mouse. McGraw, 1971.

Try It Again, Sam: Safety When You Walk; by Judith Viorst. Lothrop, 1970.

Tsar's Riddles: Or, The Wise Little Girl; by Guy Daniels. McGraw, 1967.

Turnabout Trick; by Scott Corbett. Atlantic, 1967.

Two and Me Makes Three; by Roberta Greene. Crowell, 1970.

Two Laughable Lyrics: The Pobble Who Has No Toes [and] The Quangle—Wangle's Hat; by Edward Lear. Putnam, 1966.

Two Old Bachelors; by Edward Lear. McGraw, 1962.

Varsity Double; by Al Hirshberg. Little, 1956.

Visit from St. Nicholas; by Clement C. Moore. McGraw, 1968.

Wallace the Wandering Pig; by Judy Van Der Veer. Harcourt, 1967.

Whales Go By; by Fred Phleger. Random, 1959.

What's New, Lincoln?; by Dale Fife. Coward, 1970.

What's the Prize, Lincoln?; by Dale Fife. Coward, 1971.

Where the Trail Divides; by Lorna Callahan. McGraw, 1957.

Whiskers, My Cat; by Letta Schatz. McGraw, 1967.

Who Goes There, Lincoln?; by Dale Fife. Coward, 1975.

Who'll Vote for Lincoln?; by Dale Fife. Coward, 1977.

Who's in Charge of Lincoln?; by Dale Fife. Coward, 1965.

Who's in Holes?; by Richard Armour. McGraw, 1971.

Wilderness Journey; by William O. Steele. Harcourt, 1953.

Winter Danger; by William O. Steele. Harcourt, 1954.

Wise Fool (Adapted from the Third Book of Pantagruel); by François Rabelais. Pantheon, 1968.

Woodrow Wilson; by Alfred Steinberg. Putnam, 1961.

Year Santa Went Modern; by Richard Armour. McGraw, 1964.

Your Skin and Mine; by Paul Showers. Crowell, 1965.

MEDIA

Anatole. Rembrandt Films, 1960 (F).

Anatole and the Piano. McGraw-Hill Publishing Company/Etude Films, 1968 (F, VC).

House That Jack Built. Weston Woods Studios, 1963 (FS).

Limerick Trick. McGraw-Hill Publishing Company, 1973 (FS).

Little Red Hen. Weston Woods Studios, 1974 (FSS).

Little Red Riding Hood. (BB).

Old Mother Hubbard and Her Dog. McGraw-Hill Publishing Company, 1963 (F); Weston Woods Studios, 1962 (FSS).

Old Woman and Her Pig. McGraw-Hill Publishing Company, 1963 (F); Weston Woods Studios, 1962 (FSS).

Wise Fool. Random House, n. d. (C).

EXHIBITIONS

Friedman Gallery, 1952. (New York, New York).

COLLECTIONS

Free Library of Philadelphia. (Philadelphia, Pennsylvania).

BACKGROUND READING

Contemporary Authors.

DeMontreville. *Third Book of Junior Authors*.

Hopkins. *Books Are by People*.

Kingman. *Illustrators of Children's Books, 1957-1966*.

Kingman. *Illustrators of Children's Books, 1967-1976*.

Miller. *Illustrators of Children's Books, 1946-1956*.

Ward. *Authors of Books for Young People, Second Edition*.

RUTH CHRISMAN GANNETT, 1896-
illustrator

AWARDS

(*Miss Hickory*. Newbery Medal Book, 1947.)

(*My Father's Dragon*. Newbery Honor Book, 1949.)

My Mother Is the Most Beautiful Woman in the World. Caldecott Honor Book, 1946.

BIBLIOGRAPHY

Cream Hill: Discoveries of a Weekend Countryman; by Lewis Gannett. Viking, 1949.

Dragons of Blueland; by Ruth S. Gannett. Random, 1951.

Elmer and the Dragon; by Ruth S. Gannett. Random, 1950.

Hi-Po the Hippo; by Dorothy Thomas. Random, 1942; *a.k.a. How the Baby Hippo Found a Home*, 1947.

Home Place; by Dorothy Thomas. Knopf, 1936.

Miss Hickory; by Carolyn S. Bailey. Viking, 1946.

My Father's Dragon; by Ruth S. Gannett. Random, 1948.

My Mother Is the Most Beautiful Woman in the World; by Becky Reyher. Howell, 1945.

Paco Goes to the Fair: A Story of Faraway Ecuador; by Richard Gill and Helen Hoke. Holt, 1940.

MEDIA

Dragons of Blueland. (BB, TB).

My Father's Dragon. (BB, TB).

My Mother Is the Most Beautiful Woman in the World. Stephen Bosustow Productions, 1969 (F); Film Associates, 1968 (FSS); McGraw-Hill Publishing Company, 1973 (FSS).

COLLECTION

Kerlan Collection, University of Minnesota. (Minneapolis, Minnesota).

BACKGROUND READING

Fuller. *More Junior Authors*.

Klemin. *Illustrated Book: Its Art and Craft*.

Miller. *Illustrators of Children's Books, 1946-1956*.

RUTH STILES GANNETT, 1923-
author

AWARDS

My Father's Dragon. Newbery Honor Book, 1949.

BIBLIOGRAPHY

Dragons of Blueland. il. Ruth C. Gannett. Random, 1951.

Elmer and the Dragon. il. Ruth C. Gannett. Random, 1950.

Katie and the Sad Noise. il. Ellie Simmons. Random, 1961.

My Father's Dragon. il. Ruth C. Gannett. Random, 1948.

Wonderful House-Boat-Train. il. Fritz Eichenberg. Random, 1949.

MEDIA

Dragons of Blueland. (BB, TB).

Elmer and the Dragon. (TB).

My Father's Dragon. (BB, TB).

COLLECTIONS

May Massee Collection, Emporia State College. (Emporia, Kansas).

Vassar College Library. (Poughkeepsie, New York).

BACKGROUND READING

Commire. *Something about the Author*.

Contemporary Authors.

DeMontreville. *Four Book of Junior Authors and Illustrators*.

Kirkpatrick. *Twentieth Century Children's Writers*.

Ward. *Authors of Books for Young People, Second Edition*.

DORIS GATES, 1901-
author

AWARDS

Blue Willow. Newbery Honor Book, 1941.

BIBLIOGRAPHY

Along Story Trails; with David Russell, et al. Ginn, 1962.

Becky and the Bandit. il. Paul Lantz. Ginn, 1955.

Blue Willow. il. Paul Lantz. Viking, 1940.

Cat and Mrs. Cary. il. Peggy Bacon. Viking, 1962; also il. Shirley Hughes. Methuen, 1964.

Down Story Roads; with David Russell, et al. Ginn, 1962.

Elderberry Bush. il. Lilian Obligado. Viking, 1967.

Fair Wind for Troy. il. Charles Mikolaycak. Viking, 1976.

Golden God, Apollo. il. Constantins CoConis. Viking, 1973.

BIBLIOGRAPHY (cont'd)

Helping Children Discover Books. il. Lois Axeman. Science Research Associates, 1956.

Lengthened Shadow, and Along the Road to Kansas. Kansas State Teachers College, 1954.

Little Vic. il. Kate Seredy. Viking, 1951.

May I Come In?; with Theodore Clymer, et al. Ginn, 1969.

Mightiest of Mortals. il. Richard Cuffari. Viking, 1976.

My Brother Mike. il. Wesley Dennis. Viking, 1948.

North Fork. Viking, 1945; il. Richard Kennedy. Mueller, 1950.

On Story Wings; with David Russell, et al. Ginn, 1962.

River Ranch. il. Jacob Landau. Viking, 1949.

Roads to Everywhere; with David Russell, et al. Ginn, 1961.

Sarah's Idea. il. Marjorie Torrey. Viking, 1938.

Sensible Kate: A Story. il. Marjorie Torrey. Viking, 1943.

Sun That Warms; with Theodore Clymer, et al. Ginn, 1970.

Trouble for Jerry. il. Marjorie Torrey. Viking, 1944; also il. F. Stocks May. Mueller, 1954.

Two Queens of Heaven, Aphrodite and Demeter. il. Trina S. Hyman. Viking, 1974.

Warrior Goddess, Athena. il. Don Bolognese. Viking, 1972.

MEDIA

Blue Willow. (BB); Viking Press, 1972 (FSS).

Cat and Mrs. Cary. (BB, TB); Pied Piper Productions, 1975 (FSS).

Little Vic. (BB).

May I Come In? (C, MT).

North Fork. (BB).

Roads to Everywhere. (C, MT).

Sun That Warms. (C, MT).

Warrior Goddess. (TB).

COLLECTIONS

Kerlan Collection, University of Minnesota. (Minneapolis, Minnesota).

May Massee Collection, Emporia State College. (Emporia, Kansas).

BACKGROUND READING

Alsetter, M. "Blue Willow." *Elementary English*, October 1959.

Commire. *Something about the Author*.

Contemporary Authors.

Gates, D. "Along the Road to Kansas." *Horn Book*, October 1955. See also *Lengthened Shadow, and Along the Road to Kansas* in bibliography, above.

Hoffman. *Authors and Illustrators of Children's Books*.

Kirkpatrick. *Twentieth Century Children's Writers*.

Kunitz. *Junior Book of Authors, Second Edition Revised*.

Montgomery. *Story behind Modern Books*.

Rollins, C. "Work of Doris Gates." *Elementary English*, December 1954.

Scott, J. "Artistry of 'Blue Willow.'" *Elementary English*, May 1973.

Ward. *Authors of Books for Young People, Second Edition*.

Young Wings. *Writing Books for Boys and Girls*.

JEAN CRAIGHEAD GEORGE, 1919-
author-illustrator

AWARDS

Julie of the Wolves. Newbery Medal Book, 1973.

My Side of the Mountain. Newbery Honor Book, 1960.

BIBLIOGRAPHY

All upon a Sidewalk. il. Don Bolognese. Dutton, 1974.

All upon a Stone. il. Don Bolognese. Crowell, 1971.

American Walk Book. Dutton, 1977.

Animals from A to Z: Marvels and Mysteries of Our Animal World. Reader's Digest, 1964.

Beastly Inventions: A Surprising Investigation into How Smart Animals Really Are. McKay, 1971; a.k.a. *Animals Can Do Anything*. Souvenir, 1972.

Bubo: The Great-Horned Owl; with John L. George. Dutton, 1954.

Coyote in Manhattan. il. John Kaufmann. Crowell, 1968.

Dipper of Copper Creek; with John L. George. Dutton, 1956.

Everglades Wildguide. il. Betty Fraser. United States Park Service, 1972.

Going to the Sun. Harper, 1976.

Gull Number 737. Crowell, 1964.

Hawks, Owls and Wildlife; by John Craighead. Dover, 1969.

Hold Zero! Crowell, 1966.

Hole in the Tree. Dutton, 1957.

Hook a Fish, Catch a Mountain. Dutton, 1975.

Julie of the Wolves. il. John Schoenherr. Harper, 1972; large print edition, Hall, 1973.

Masked Prowler: The Story of a Raccoon; with John L. George. Dutton, 1950.

Meph: The Pet Skunk; with John L. George. Dutton, 1952.

Moon of the Alligators. il. Adrina Zanazanian. Crowell, 1969.

Moon of the Bears. il. Mac Shepard. Crowell, 1967.

Moon of the Chickarees. il. John Schoenherr. Crowell, 1968.

Moon of the Deer. il. Jean Zallinger. Crowell, 1969.

Moon of the Fox Pups. il. Kiyoaki Komoda, Crowell, 1968.

Moon of the Gray Wolves. il. Lorence Bjorklund. Crowell, 1969.

Moon of the Moles. il. Robert Levering. Crowell, 1969.

Moon of the Monarch Butterflies. il. Murray Tinkleman. Crowell, 1968.

Moon of the Mountain Lions. il. Winifred Lubell. Crowell, 1968.

Moon of the Owls. il. Jean Zallinger. Crowell, 1967.

Moon of the Salamanders. il. John Kaufman. Crowell, 1967.

Moon of the Wild Pigs. il. Peter Parnall. Crowell, 1968.

Moon of the Winter Bird. il. Kazue Mizumura. Crowell, 1969.

My Side of the Mountain. Dutton, 1959.

Red Robin, Fly-Up. Reader's Digest, 1963.

Snow Tracks. Dutton, 1958.

Spring Comes to the Ocean. il. John F. Wilson. Crowell, 1965.

Summer of the Falcon. Crowell, 1962.

Vison: The Mink; with John L. George. Dutton, 1949.

Vulpes: The Red Fox; with John L. George. Dutton, 1948.

Wentletrap. il. Symeon Shimin. Dutton, 1977.

Who Really Killed Cock Robin? An Ecological Mystery. Dutton, 1971.

MEDIA

All upon a Stone. Miller-Brody Productions, 1974 (FSS).

Dipper of Copper Creek. (BB, TB).

Gull Number 737. (TB).

Julie of the Wolves. (BB, TB); Miller-Brody Productions, 1974 (FSS).

Masked Prowler. (TB).

Meph, the Pet Skunk. (BB).

My Side of the Mountain. (BB, C, CB, MT, TB); Paramount Pictures Corporation, 1968 (F).

Spring Comes to the Ocean. (BB, TB).

Summer of the Falcon. (TB).

Vulpes, the Red Fox. (BB, TB).

Who Really Killed Cock Robin? (BB).

Young American Filmstrips Series. Jam Handy, 19? (Original FS). (Includes Animals Grow; *Cheek, the Red Squirrel; Rings the Raccoon;* and *The Lazy Bear Cub.*)

COLLECTIONS

Free Library of Philadelphia. (Philadelphia, Pennsylvania).

Iowa City Public Library. (Iowa City, Iowa).

Kerlan Collection, University of Minnesota. (Minneapolis, Minnesota).

BACKGROUND READING

Burke. *American Authors and Books, 1640 to the Present Day.*

Commire. *Something about the Author.*

Contemporary Authors.

Fuller. *More Junior Authors.*

George, J. "Summer and Children and Birds and Bees and Books." *Horn Book,* June 1959.

Hopkins, L. "Jean George." *Elementary English,* October 1973.

Hopkins, L. *More Books by More People.*

Jean George. Profiles in Literature, 1974 (VT).

Kingman. *Newbery and Caldecott Medal Books, 1966-1975.*

Kirkpatrick. *Twentieth Century Children's Writers.*

Meet the Newbery Author: Jean George. Miller-Brody Productions, 1974 (FSS).

Miller. *Illustrators of Children's Books, 1946-1956.*

Ward. *Authors of Books for Young People, Second Edition.*

Young Wings. *Writing Books for Boys and Girls.*

TIBOR GERGELY, 1900-
author-illustrator

AWARDS

Wheel on the Chimney. Caldecott Honor Book, 1955.

BIBLIOGRAPHY

Animal Gym; by Beth G. Hoffman. Simon, 1956.

Animal Orchestra; by Ilo Orleans. Simon, 1958.

Animal Talk: A Pop-Up Alphabet Zoo, Based on an Idea by Robert Leydenfrost. Simon, 1960.

Animals: A Picture Book of Facts and Figures. McGraw, 1974.

Baby Wild Animals from A to Z. Western, 1973.

Bernard Shaw ane Kdoten und Aussprüche: Gesammelt und Ans Tageslicht Gefördert; by Ludwig Möllhausen. Phaidon, 1931.

Bobby and His Airplanes; by Helen Palmer. Simon, 1949.

Bobo the Barrage Balloon; by Margaret McConnell. Lothrop, 1943.

Busy Day, Busy People. Random, 1973.

Christopher and the Columbus; by Kathryn and Byron Jackson. Simon, 1951.

Circus Time; by Marion Conger. Simon, 1948.

Daddies; by Janet Frank. Simon, 1954.

Day at the Zoo; by Marion Conger. Simon, 1950.

Day in the Jungle; by Jeanette S. Lowrey. Artists' and Writers' Guild, 1943.

Deep Blue Sea; by Bertha M. Parker. Golden, 1958.

Eltévedt Litániák; by Anna Lesznai. Libelli, 1922.

Emily's Moon. Golden, 1969.

Exploring Space; by Rose Wyler. Golden, 1958.

Five Hundred Animals from A to Z; by Joseph A. Davis. American Heritage, 1970.

Five Little Firemen; by Margaret W. Brown and Edith T. Hurd. Simon, 1948.

Folding Father; by Heinrich Hauser. Tr. Barrows Mussey. Lothrop, 1942.

Forgetful Elephant; by Jean Greene. McKay, 1945.

From Then to Now; by John P. Leventhal. Simon, 1954.

Gergely's Golden Circus; by Peter Archer, *pseud.* (Kathryn and Byron Jackson). Simon, 1954.

Giant Little Golden Book about Dogs; by Kathleen Daly. Simon, 1957.

Golden Book of Nursery Tales; by Elsa J. Werner, *pseud.* (Jane W. Watson). Simon, 1948.

Golden Calendar; by Peggy Parish. Western, 1965.

Golden Grab Bag of Stories, Poems and Songs. Simon, 1951.

Golden 1966 Calendar; by John Peter. Golden, 1966.

Golden Picture Book of Questions and Answers: Hundreds of Questions about People, Animals and Places, with Facts and Surprises for Children on Every Page; by Horace Elmo. Simon, 1957.

Golden Story Book of River Bend; by Patricia Scarry. Simon, 1969.

Great Big Book of Bedtime Stories. Simon, 1967; *a.k.a. Tibor Gergely's Bedtime Stories*. Western, 1972.

Great Big Fire Engine Book. Simon, 1950.

Happy Little Whale; by Kenneth S. Norris. Simon, 1968.

Happy Man and His Dump Truck; by Miryam (Yardumiam). Simon, 1950.

Houses; by Elsa J. Werner, *pseud.* (Jane W. Watson). Simon, 1955.

Hundred Tuftys; by Jean Lilly. Dutton, 1940.

Jenny: The Bus That Nobody Loved; by Maurice Dolbier. Random, 1944.

Jokes; by George. Golden, 1961.

Jolly Barnyard; by Annie N. Bedford, *pseud.* (Jane W. Watson). Simon, 1950.

Jungle Books; by Rudyard Kipling. Golden, 1963.

Lion Cub's Busy Day; by Barbara S. Hazen. Golden, n. d.

Little Golden Book about the Seashore; by Kathleen N. Daly. Simon, 1957.

Little Golden Book of Dogs; by Nita Jonas. Simon, 1952.

Little Gray Donkey; by Alice Lunt. Norton (?), *ca.*1964.

Little Pond in the Woods; by Muriel Ward. Simon, 1948.

Little Red Caboose; by Miriam C. Potter. Simon, 1958.

Little Yip Yip and His Bark; by Kathryn and Bryon Jackson. Simon, 1950.

Magic Bus; by Maurice Dolbier. Random, 1948.

Make Way for the Thruway; by Caroline Emerson. Golden, 1961.

Me Book; by Jean Tyms. Western, 1974.

Merry Shipwreck; by Georges Duplaix. Harper, 1942.

Mister Puffer-Bill: Train Engineer; by Leone Arlandson. Golden, 1965.

My Little Golden Book about the Sky; by Rose Wyler. Simon, 1956.

My Little Golden Book about Travel; by Kathleen Daly. Simon, 1956.

No Room for the Baker; by Käthe Recheis. Four Winds, 1969.

Noah's Ark; by Jane Werner, *pseud.* (Jane W. Watson). Grosset, 1943; *a.k.a. Tibor Gergely's Noah's Ark Book.* Simon, 1966.

Parrot Book: Parrots and Other Exotic Birds. Simon, 1965.

Peewee the Mousedeer; by Hendrik DeLeeuw. McKay, 1943.

Red, White and Blue Auto; by Lucy S. Mitchell. Scott, 1943.

Richtige Himmelblau, 3 Märchen; by Bela Balazs. Masken, 1925.

Rupert the Rhinoceros; by Carl Memling. Golden, ca.1960.

Scuffy the Tugboat, and His Adventures down the River; by Gertrude Crampton. Simon, 1950.

Seven Little Postmen; by Margaret W. Brown and Edith T. Hurd. Simon, 1952.

Seven Sneezes; by Olga Cabral. Simon, 1948.

Storks Fly Home; by Jane Tompkins. Stokes, 1943.

Sweeney's Adventures: As Told by John Kieran in the Film "Sweeney Steps Out"; by Joseph Krumgold. Random, 1942.

Talking Typewriter; by Margaret Platt. Lothrop, 1940.

Taxi That Hurried; by Lucy S. Mitchell, et al. Simon, 1946.

Tell Me a Story . . . ; by Dorothy Canfield. University, 1940.

Tootle; by Gertrude Crampton. Simon, 1946.

Topsy Turvy Circus; by Georges Duplaix. Harper, 1940.

Train Stories; by Robert Garfield, *pseud.* (Kathryn and Byron Jackson) and Jessie Knittle. Simon, 1949.

Treasury of Little Golden Books; edited by Ellen L. Buell. Golden, 1960.

True Monkey Stories; by Frances M. Fox. Lothrop, 1941.

Two Logs Crossing: John Haskell's Story; by Walter D. Edmonds. Dodd, 1943.

"Watch Me!" Said the Jeep; by Helen Ferris. Garden City, 1944.

Wheel on the Chimney; by Margaret W. Brown. Lippincott, 1954.

When It Rained Cats and Dogs; by Nancy B. Turner. Lippincott, 1946.

Year in the City; by Lucy S. Mitchell. Simon, 1948.

MEDIA

Busy Day, Busy People. Random House, 1971 (C, FSS).

Wheel on the Chimney. Weston Woods Studios, 1966 (FSS); 1969 (F); also in Weston Woods Studios Set No. 16, 1965 (FSS).

COLLECTIONS

deGrummond Collection, University of Southern Mississippi. (Hattiesburg, Mississippi).

Ogle Collection, University of Oregon Library. (Eugene, Oregon).

Rare Book and Manuscript Library, Columbia University. (New York, New York).

Special Collections, University Research Library, University of California. (Los Angeles, California).

BACKGROUND READING

Mahony. *Illustrators of Children's Books, 1744-1945.*

Miller. *Illustrators of Children's Books, 1946-1956.*

Ward. *Illustrators of Books for Young People, Second Edition.*

+FREDERICK BENJAMIN GIPSON, 1903-1973
author

AWARDS

Old Yeller. Newbery Honor Book, 1957.

BIBLIOGRAPHY

Big Bend; with Oscar J. Langford. photographs by Harry DuPont and Joe Longford. University of Texas, 1952; second edition, 1973.

"Cow Killers," with the Aftosa Commission in Mexico. il. Bill Leftwich. University of Texas, 1962.

Cowhand: The Story of a Working Cowboy. Harper, 1953.

Fabulous Empire: Colonel Zack Miller's Story. Houghton, 1946.

Home Place. Harper, 1950; *a.k.a. Return to Texas.* Oliver, 1962.

Hound-Dog Man. Harper, 1949; *a.k.a. Circles round the Wagon.* Joseph, 1949.

Letter of Acceptance. Harper, 1960.

Old Yeller. il. Carl Burger. Harper, 1956; large print edition, Georgetown, 1966; *a.k.a. Walt Disney's Old Yeller, from the Walt Disney Motion Picture*

BIBLIOGRAPHY (cont'd)

Old Yeller (cont'd)
"Old Yeller" Based on the Novel of the Same Title, Told by Irwin Shapiro. il. Edwin Schmidt and E. Joseph Dreany. Simon, 1957; *a.k.a. Walt Disney's Old Yeller, Based on Old Yeller by Fred Gipson, Told by Willis Lindquist*. il. Walt Disney Studios, adapted by Robert Doremus. Simon, 1958.

Recollection Creek. il. Carl Burger. Harper, 1955; *a.k.a. Recollection Creek, Revised for Young People*, 1959.

Savage Sam. il. Carl Burger. Harper, 1962; *a.k.a. Walt Disney's Savage Sam, Told by Carl Memling, Based on the Novel by Fred Gipson*. il. Mel Crawford. Simon, 1963.

Trail-Driving Rooster. il. Marc Simont. Harper, 1955.

MEDIA

Brush Roper. n. p., n. d. (Original telecast, TV).

Circles round the Wagon see *Hound-Dog Man*, below.

Cowhand. (BB).

Home Place. (BB); *a.k.a. Return to Texas*. Twentieth-Century Fox Film Corporation, 1952 (F).

Hound-Dog Man. (TB); *a.k.a. Circles round the Wagon*. Twentieth-Century Fox Film Corporation, 1959 (F).

Old Yeller. (C, MT, TB); Miller-Brody Productions, 1973 (C, R); Walt Disney Productions, 1957 (F), 1964 (FSS); also in *Famous Stories Retold*, (C, MT).

Recollection Creek. (BB, TB).

Return to Texas see *Home Place*.

Savage Sam. (BB); Walt Disney Productions, 1963 (F).

Trail-Driving Rooster. (TB).

COLLECTIONS

Humanities Research Center, University of Texas. (Austin, Texas).

BACKGROUND READING

Burke. *American Authors and Books, 1640 to the Present Day*.

Commire. *Something about the Author*.

Contemporary Authors.

Current Biography.

DeMontreville. *Third Book of Junior Authors*.

Henderson, Sam. *Fred Gipson*. Steck-Vaughan, 1967.

Kirkpatrick. *Twentieth Century Children's Writers*.

New York Times Biographical Edition.

Ward. *Authors of Books for Young People, Second Edition*.

M. B. GOFFSTEIN, 1940-
author-illustrator
a.k.a. Marilyn Brooke Goffstein

AWARDS

Fish for Supper. Caldecott Honor Book, 1977.

BIBLIOGRAPHY

Across the Sea. Farrar, 1968.

Brookie and Her Lamb. Farrar, 1967.

Daisy Summerfield's Style. Delacorte, 1975.

Fish for Supper. Dial, 1976.

Gats! Pantheon, 1966.

Goldie the Dollmaker. Farrar, 1969.

Little Schubert. Harper, 1972. (Issued with recording of Schubert music by Peter Schaaf.)

Me and My Captain. Farrar, 1974.

My Crazy Sister. Dial, 1976.

Sleepy People. Farrar, 1966.

Two Piano Tuners. Farrar, 1970.

Underside of the Leaf. Farrar, 1972.

MEDIA

Daisy Summerfield's Style. (TB).

Two Piano Tuners. (BB).

Underside of the Leaf. (TB).

EXHIBITIONS

Kohn Gallery, 1966. (St. Paul, Minnesota).

St. Paul Art Institute, 1961. (St. Paul, Minnesota).

Wakefield Gallery, 1961-62, 1965. (New York, New York).

BACKGROUND READING

Commire. *Something about the Author*.

Contemporary Authors.

DeMontreville. *Fourth Book of Junior Authors and Illustrators*.

Kingman. *Illustrators of Children's Books, 1967-1976*.

MARGARET BLOY GRAHAM, 1920-
author-illustrator

AWARDS

All Falling Down. Caldecott Honor Book, 1952.

Storm Book. Caldecott Honor Book, 1953.

BIBLIOGRAPHY

All Falling Down; by Gene Zion. Harper, 1951.

Be Nice to Spiders. Harper, 1967.

Benjy and the Barking Bird. Harper, 1971.

Benjy's Boat Trip. Harper, 1977.

Benjy's Dog House. Harper, 1973.

Big Mose; by Katherine Shippen. Harper, 1953.

Crumb That Walked: More about Jane Jonquil; by
Charles Norman. Harper, 1951.

Dear Garbage Man; by Gene Zion. Harper, 1957;
a.k.a. Dear Dustman. Bodley Head, 1962.

Divine Torment; by Robert McDonald. Reynal, 1947.

Green Hornet Lunchbox; by Shirley Gordon.
Houghton, 1970.

Handy Guide to Grownups; by Jennifer Owlsey.
Random, 1950.

Harry and the Lady Next Door; by Gene Zion.
Harper, 1960.

Harry by the Sea; by Gene Zion. Harper, 1965.

Harry, the Dirty Dog; by Gene Zion. Harper, 1956.

Hide and Seek Day; by Gene Zion. Harper, 1954.

Hunch, Munch and Crunch: More about the Jonquils;
by Charles Norman. Harper, 1952.

Jeffie's Party; by Gene Zion. Harper, 1957.

Meanest Squirrel I Ever Met; by Gene Zion. Scribner,
1962.

*Mr. Upstairs and Mr. Downstairs: Introducing Jane
Jonquil and Her Father*; by Charles Norman.
Harper, 1950.

No Roses for Harry!; by Gene Zion. Harper, 1958.

Pack Rat's Day and Other Poems; by Jack Prelutsky.
Macmillan, 1974.

Plant Sitter; by Gene Zion. Harper, 1959.

Really Spring; by Gene Zion. Harper, 1956.

Storm Book; by Charlotte Zolotow. Harper, 1952.

Sugar Mouse Cake; by Gene Zion. Scribner, 1964.

Summer Snowman; by Gene Zion. Harper, 1955.

*To a Different Drum: The Story of Henry David
Thoreau*; by Charles Norman. Harper, 1954.

MEDIA

Be Nice to Spiders. (BB).

Benjy and the Barking Bird. Harper & Row, 1974
(FSS).

Harry and the Lady Next Door. Miller-Brody Productions, 1977 (FSS).

Harry by the Sea. Miller-Brody Productions, 1977
(FSS).

Harry, the Dirty Dog. Miller-Brody Productions,
1977 (FSS).

Meanest Squirrel I Ever Met. Miller-Brody Productions, 1974 (FSS); *a.k.a. Mas Pilla Ardilla*. Miller-
Brody Productions, 1974 (FSS).

No Roses for Harry! Miller-Brody Productions, 1977
(FSS).

Pack Rat's Day. (BB).

COLLECTIONS

Smith Collection, Toronto Public Library. (Toronto,
Ontario, Canada).

BACKGROUND READING

Bader. *American Picturebooks from Noah's Ark to
The Beast Within*.

Commire. *Something about the Author*.

Contemporary Authors.

Fuller. *More Junior Authors*.

Kingman. *Illustrators of Children's Books, 1957-1966*.

Kingman. *Illustrators of Children's Books, 1967-1976*.

Ward. *Illustrators of Books for Young People, Second
Edition*.

+ELIZABETH JANET GRAY, 1902-
author
a.k.a. Elizabeth Gray Vining

AWARDS

Adam of the Road. Newbery Medal Book, 1943.

Meggy MacIntosh. Newbery Honor Book, 1931.

Penn. Newbery Honor Book, 1939.

Young Walter Scott. Newbery Honor Book, 1936.

BIBLIOGRAPHY

as Elizabeth Janet Gray:

Adam of the Road. il. Robert Lawson. Viking, 1942;
National Aid to the Visually Handicapped, n. d.

BIBLIOGRAPHY (cont'd)

as Elizabeth Janet Gray (cont'd):

Anthology, with Comments. Pendle Hill, 1942.

Beppy Marlowe of Charles Town. il. Loren Barton. Viking, 1936.

Cheerful Heart. il. Kazue Mizumura. Viking, 1959.

Contributions of the Quakers. Pendle Hill, 1939.

Fair Adventure. il. Alice K. Reischer. Viking, 1940.

I Will Adventure. il. Corydon Bell. Viking, 1962; also il. Nigel Lambourne. Oliver, 1964.

Jane Hope. Viking, 1933.

Japanese Young People Today. Philadelphia Athenaeum, 1961.

May Massee Collection, Creative Publishing for Children; with Annis Duff. William Allen White Library, 1972.

Meggy MacIntosh. il. Marguerite de Angeli. Doubleday, 1930.

Meredith's Ann, an Out-of-Doors Story for Girls. il. G. B. Cutts. Doubleday, 1927; a.k.a. Meredith's Ann, Outdoor Adventures in New Hampshire, 1929.

Penn. il. George Whitney. Viking, 1938; a.k.a. Admiral Penn and Son William: A One-Act Play Based on Penn by Elizabeth Janet Gray; by Rosalie Regen. Friendship, 1956.

Sandy. il. Robert Hallock. Viking, 1945.

Tangle Garden: A Story for Girls. il. G. B. Cutts. Doubleday, 1928.

Tilly-Tod. il. Mary H. Frye. Doubleday, 1929.

William Penn, Mystic, as Reflected in His Writings. Pendle Hill, 1969.

Young Walter Scott. il. Kate Seredy. Viking, 1935.

as Elizabeth Gray Vining:

Flora: A Biography. Lippincott, 1966; a.k.a. Flora MacDonald: Her Life in the Highlands and America. Bles, 1967.

Friend of Life: The Biography of Rufus M. Jones. Lippincott, 1958.

I, Roberta. Lippincott, 1967.

*Quiet Pilgrimage. Lippincott, 1970.

*Return to Japan. Lippincott, 1960; excerpt as International Christian University, ca.1960.

Take Heed of Loving Me. Lippincott, 1963.

Taken Girl. Viking, 1972; large print edition, Hall, 1973.

Virginia Exiles. Lippincott, 1955.

*Windows for the Crown Prince. Lippincott, 1952.

World in Tune. Pendle Hill, 1952.

MEDIA

Adam of the Road. (BB, TB).

Cheerful Heart. (BB, TB).

I, Roberta. (TB).

Jane Hope. (BB).

Penn. (BB).

Return to Japan. (BB, TB).

Take Heed of Loving Me. (BB, TB).

Taken Girl. (TB).

Virginia Exiles. (BB).

Windows for the Crown Prince. (BB).

COLLECTIONS

deGrummond Collection, University of Southern Mississippi. (Hattiesburg, Mississippi).

May Massee Collection, Emporia State College. (Emporia, Kansas).

BACKGROUND READING

Breit, H. "Talk with Mrs. Vining." New York Times Book Review, June 18, 1952.

Burke. American Authors and Books, 1640 to the Present Day.

Commire. Something about the Author.

Contemporary Authors.

Current Biography.

Elizabeth Gray Vining. Profiles in Literature, 1969 (VT).

"Elizabeth Janet Gray." Library Journal, December 1, 1946.

"Fortune for Amos Fortune." Newsweek, March 12, 1951.

Gray, E. "In Search of a Boy." Horn Book, June 1939.

Hills, L. "Elizabeth Janet Gray and the Crown Prince of Japan." Reader's Digest, January 1948.

Hutchens, J. "On an Author." New York Herald Tribune Book Review, June 1, 1952.

Kirkpatrick. Twentieth Century Children's Writers.

Kunitz. Junior Book of Authors.

Kunitz. Junior Book of Authors, Second Edition Revised.

Miller. Newbery Medal Books, 1922-1955.

Montgomery. Story behind Modern Books.

"Royal Tutor." Newsweek, March 12, 1952.

Sayers, F. "Career of Elizabeth Janet Gray, Newbery Medal Winner." *Publishers Weekly*, June 19, 1943.

Sayers, F. "Elizabeth Janet Gray." *Junior Bookshelf*, July 1944.

Ward. *Authors of Books for Young People, Second Edition*.

"Window Openers." *Time*, May 26, 1952.

Young Wings. *Writing Books for Boys and Girls*.

+BETTE GREENE, 1934-
author

AWARDS

Philip Hall Likes Me. Newbery Honor Book, 1975.

BIBLIOGRAPHY

Philip Hall Likes Me. I Reckon Maybe. il. Charles Lily. Dial, 1974.

Summer of My German Soldier. Dial, 1973.

MEDIA

Philip Hall Likes Me. Miller-Brody Productions, 1976 (C, R).

Summer of My German Soldier. Miller-Brody Productions, 1976 (C, R); TV, *ca*.1976.

BACKGROUND READING

Commire. *Something about the Author*.

Contemporary Authors.

LEO GURKO, 1914-
author

AWARDS

Tom Paine. Newbery Honor Book, 1958.

BIBLIOGRAPHY

Angry Decade. Dodd, 1947.

Ernest Hemingway and the Pursuit of Heroism. Crowell, 1968.

Heroes, Highbrows and the Popular Mind. Bobbs, 1953; *a.k.a. Crisis of the American Mind*. Rider, 1956.

Joseph Conrad: Giant in Exile. Macmillan, 1962.

(tr.) *Six Wives of Henry VIII*; by Paul Rival. Putnam, 1936.

Thomas Wolfe: Beyond the Romantic Ego. Crowell, 1975.

Tom Paine: Freedom's Apostle. il. Fritz Kredel. Crowell, 1957.

Two Lives of Joseph Conrad. Crowell, 1965.

MEDIA

Ernest Hemingway. (C, MT).

Heroes, Highbrows and the Pursuit of Heroism. (BB).

Joseph Conrad. (TB).

Six Wives of Henry VIII. (CB).

Tom Paine. (BB, TB).

Lectures on tape:

Ambassadors; by Henry James. Edwards, 1970 (C).

Ship of Fools; by Katharine A. Porter. Edwards, 1970 (C).

U.S.A.; by John Dos Passos. Edwards, 1970 (C).

BACKGROUND READING

Commire. *Something about the Author*.

Contemporary Authors.

DeMontreville. *Third Book of Junior Authors*.

BERTA HOERNER HADER, 1891-1976
author-illustrator

and

ELMER STANLEY HADER, 1889-1973
author-illustrator

AWARDS

Big Snow. Caldecott Medal Book, 1949.

Cock-a-Doodle Doo. Caldecott Honor Book, 1940.

(*Down Ryton Water*. Newbery Honor Book, 1942.)

Mighty Hunter. Caldecott Honor Book, 1944.

BIBLIOGRAPHY

Elmer Hader:

Adventures of Theodore Roosevelt; by Edwin Emerson. Dutton, 1928.

Charm: A Book about It and Those Who Have It, for *Those Who Want It*; by Mary M. McBride and Alexander Williams. Henkle, 1927.

Down Ryton Water; by Eva R. Gaggin. Viking, 1941.

BIBLIOGRAPHY (cont'd)

Elmer Hader (cont'd):

Garden of the Lost Key; by Forrestine C. Hooker. Doubleday, 1929.

How Dear to My Heart; by Mary M. McBride. Macmillan, 1940.

Isle of Que; by Elsie Singmaster. Longmans, 1948.

Story of Health; by Hope K. Holway. Harper, 1931.

Story of Markets; by Ruth Camp. Harper, 1929.

Story of Water Supply; by Hope K. Holway. Harper, 1929.

Berta and Elmer Hader:

Baby Bear Story; by Hamilton Williamson. Doubleday, 1930.

Banana Tree House; by Phillis Garrard. Coward, 1938.

Berta and Elmer Hader's Picture Book of Mother Goose; from Mother Goose. Coward, 1930; new edition, 1944.

Berta and Elmer Hader's Picture Book of the States. Harper, 1932.

Big City. Macmillan, 1948.

Big Fellow at Work; by Dorothy Baruch. Harper, 1930.

Big Snow. Macmillan, 1948.

Billy Butter. Macmillan, 1936.

Bingo Is My Name; by Anne Stoddard. Century, 1931.

Cat and the Kitten. Macmillan, 1940.

Chicken Little and the Little Half Chick. Macmillan, 1927.

Chuck-a-Luck and His Reindeer. Houghton, 1933.

Cock-a-Doodle Doo: The Story of a Little Red Rooster. Macmillan, 1939.

Coming: Two Funny Clowns; hand-lettered by Howard Gág. Coward, 1929.

Cricket: The Story of a Little Circus Pony. Macmillan, 1938.

Ding, Dong, Bell, Pussy's in the Well. Macmillan, 1957.

Donald in Numberland; by Jean M. Peedie. Henkle, 1927.

Everyday Fun; by Julia L. Hahn. Houghton, 1935.

Farmer; by Henry B. Lent. Macmillan, 1937.

Farmer in the Dell. Macmillan, 1931.

Friendly Phoebe. Macmillan, 1953.

Good Little Dog; by Anne Stoddard. Century, 1930.

Green and Gold, the Story of the Banana. Macmillan, 1936.

Hansel and Gretel; by Jacob and Wilhelm Grimm. Macmillan, 1927.

Here, Bingo!; by Anne Stoddard. Century, 1932.

Home on the Range: Jeremiah Jones and His Friend Little Bear in the Far West. Macmillan, 1955.

Humpy: Son of the Sands; by Hamilton Williamson. Doubleday, 1937.

Jamaica Johnny. Macmillan, 1935.

Jimmy, the Groceryman; by Jane Miller. Houghton, 1934.

Lion Cub: A Jungle Tale. Doubleday, 1931.

Lions and Tigers and Elephants Too: Being an Account of Polly Patchin's Trip to the Zoo. Longmans, 1930.

Little Antelope, an Indian for a Day. Macmillan, 1962.

Little Appaloosa. Macmillan, 1949.

Little Chip of Willow Hill. Macmillan, 1958.

Little Elephant; by Hamilton Williamson. Doubleday, 1930.

Little Red Hen. Macmillan, 1928.

*Little Stone House: A Story of Building a House in the Country. Macmillan, 1944.

Little Town. Macmillan, 1941.

Little White Foot: His Adventures on Willow Hill. Macmillan, 1952.

Lost in the Zoo. Macmillan, 1951.

Marcos: A Mountain Boy of Mexico; by Melicent Lee. Whitman, 1937.

Midget and Bridget. Macmillan, 1934.

Mighty Hunter. Macmillan, 1943.

Mister Billy's Gun. Macmillan, 1960.

Mr. Peck's Pets; by Louise H. Seaman. Macmillan, 1947.

Monkey Tale; by Hamilton Williamson. Doubleday, 1929.

Old Woman and the Crooked Sixpence. Macmillan, 1928.

Picture Book of Travel: The Story of Transportation. Macmillan, 1928.

Play-Book of Words; by Prescott Lecky. Stokes, 1933.

Quack-Quack: The Story of a Little Wild Duck. Macmillan, 1961.

Rainbow's End. Macmillan, 1945.

Reading for Fun; by Julia L. Hahn. Houghton, 1939.

Reindeer Trail: A Long Journey from Lapland to Alaska. Macmillan, 1959.

Runaways: A Tale of the Woodlands. Macmillan, 1956.

Skyrocket. Macmillan, 1946.

Smiths and Rusty; by Alice Dalgliesh. Scribner, 1936.

Snow in the City: A Winter's Tale. Macmillan, 1963.

Sonny Elephant: A Jungle Tale; by Madge Bigham. Little, 1930.

Spunky. Macmillan, 1933.

Squirrely of Willow Hill. Macmillan, 1950.

Stop, Look, Listen. Longmans, 1936.

Story of Mr. Punch; by Octave Feuillet. Tr. J. Harris Gable. Dutton, 1929.

Story of Pancho and the Bull with the Crooked Tail. Macmillan, 1942; *a.k.a. Pancho*. Hale, 1947.

Story of the Three Bears. Macmillan, 1928.

Stripey: A Little Zebra; by Hamilton Williamson. Doubleday, 1939.

Timothy and the Blue Cart; by Elinor Whitney. Stokes, 1930.

Timothy Has Ideas; by Miriam E. Mason. Macmillan, 1943.

Tommy Thatcher Goes to Sea. Macmillan, 1937.

Tooky: The Story of a Seal Who Joined the Circus. Longmans, 1931.

Two Is Company, Three's a Crowd: A Wild Goose Tale. Macmillan, 1965.

Ugly Duckling; by Hans C. Andersen. Macmillan, 1927.

Under the Pig-Nut Tree, Spring. Knopf, 1930.

Under the Pig-Nut Tree, Summer. Knopf, 1931.

Visit from St. Nicholas; by Clement C. Moore. Macmillan, 1937.

Wee Willie Winkie and Some Other Girls and Boys from Mother Goose; from Mother Goose. Macmillan, 1927.

What'll You Do When You Grow Up??? A Book for Very Young People Who Haven't Made Up Their Minds. Longmans, 1929.

Whiffy McCann. Oxford, 1933.

Who Knows: A Little Primer; by Julia L. Hahn. Houghton, 1937.

Wish on the Moon. Macmillan, 1954.

Wonderful Locomotive; by Cornelia Meigs. Macmillan, 1928.

*Working Together: The Inside Story of the Hader Books Told and Pictured. Macmillan, 1937.

MEDIA

Big Snow. (BB); Weston Woods Studios, 1960 (FSS); also in Weston Woods Studios Set No. 8, 1965 (FSS).

Little Stone House. (BB).

Mighty Hunter. (BB, TB).

Story of Pancho as *Pancho*. Weston Woods Studios, 1959 (FSS), 1960 (F).

EXHIBITIONS

National Academy of Design, 19?. (New York, New York).

Salon Artistes Français, 19?. (Paris, France).

COLLECTIONS

deGrummond Collection, University of Southern Mississippi. (Hattiesburg, Mississippi).

Free Library of Philadelphia. (Philadelphia, Pennsylvania).

Gary Public Library. (Gary, Indiana).

Iowa City Public Library. (Iowa City, Iowa).

Kerlan Collection, University of Minnesota. (Minneapolis, Minnesota).

May Massee Collection, Emporia State College. (Emporia, Kansas).

San Francisco Art Museum. (San Francisco, California).

Special Collections, University Research Library, University of California. (Los Angeles, California).

BACKGROUND READING

Altsetter, M. "Berta and Elmer Hader." *Elementary English*, December 1955.

Burke. *American Authors and Books, 1640 to the Present Day*.

Contemporary Authors.

Hoffman. *Authors and Illustrators of Children's Books*.

Hopkins. *Books Are by People*.

Kemp, E., ed. Special issue. *Imprint: Oregon*, Spring-Fall 1977.

Kingman. *Illustrators of Children's Books, 1957-1966*.

Kingman. *Illustrators of Children's Books, 1967-1976*.

Kirkpatrick. *Twentieth Century Children's Writers*.

Kunitz. *Junior Book of Authors*.

Kunitz. *Junior Book of Authors, Second Edition Revised*.

Mahony. *Contemporary Illustrators of Children's Books*.

Mahony. *Illustrators of Children's Books, 1744-1945*.

Miller. *Illustrators of Children's Books, 1946-1956*.

Miller. *Caldecott Medal Books, 1938-1957*.

Smaridge. *Famous Literary Teams for Young People*.

BACKGROUND READING (cont'd)

Ward. *Authors of Books for Young People, Second Edition*.

Ward. *Illustrators of Books for Young People, Second Edition*.

"We Visit the Haders." *Instructor*, November 1951.

+GAIL EINHART HALEY, 1939-
author-illustrator

AWARDS

Story, a Story. Caldecott Medal Book, 1971.

BIBLIOGRAPHY

Abominable Snowman. Viking, 1975.

Altogether, One at a Time; by E. L. Konigsburg. Atheneum, 1971.

Costumes for Plays and Playing. Methuen, 1975.

Go Away, Stay Away. Scribner, 1977.

H.M.P.O. Cat. Bodley Head, 1975; *a.k.a. Post Office Cat*. Scribner, 1976.

Jack Jouett's Ride. Viking, 1973.

Koalas; by Berniece Kohn. Prentice, 1966.

My Kingdom for a Dragon. Crozet, 1962.

Noah's Ark. Atheneum, 1971.

One Two, Buckle My Shoe: A Book of Counting Rhymes. Doubleday, 1964.

P. S. Happy Anniversary; by Lois Wyse. World, 1966.

Peek-a-Boo Book of Kittens and Puppies; by Hannah Rush, *pseud*. (Hannahlore Rush). Nelson, 1965.

Round Stories, All about Growing Things. Follett, 1966. (Includes *The Acorn, The Dandelion, The Mistletoe*, and *The Mushroom*.)

Round Stories, All about Land Animals. Follett, 1966. (Includes *The Bird, The Butterfly, The Hare*, and *The Turtle*.)

Round Stories, All about Our World. Follett, 1966. (Includes *The Calendar, Night and Day, The Seasons*, and *The Week*.)

Round Stories, All about Water Animals. Follett, 1966. (Includes *The Lobster, The Salmon, The Starfish*, and *The Tadpole*.)

Skip Rope Book; by Francelia Butler. Dial, 1963.

Story, a Story: An African Tale Retold. Atheneum, 1970.

Three Wishes of Hu; by James Holding. Putnam, 1965.

Which Is Which; by Solveig P. Russell. Prentice, 1966.

Wonderful Magical World of Marguerite. McGraw, 1964.

MEDIA

Jack Jouett's Ride. (BB); Weston Woods Studios, 1975 (FSS).

Story, a Story. Weston Woods Studios, 1972 (FSS), 1973 (F).

COLLECTIONS

Kerlan Collection, University of Minnesota. (Minneapolis, Minnesota).

BACKGROUND READING

Contemporary Authors.

DeMontreville. *Third Book of Junior Authors*.

Kingman. *Illustrators of Children's Books, 1967-1976*.

Kingman. *Newbery and Caldecott Medal Books, 1966-1975*.

Kirkpatrick. *Twentieth Century Children's Writers*.

Ward. *Illustrators of Books for Young People, Second Edition*.

+ANNA GERTRUDE HALL, 1882-1967
author

AWARDS

Nansen. Newbery Honor Book, 1941.

BIBLIOGRAPHY

Cyrus Holt and the Civil War. il. Dorothy B. Morse. Viking, 1964.

Directions for the Librarian of a Small Library, Revised. Wilson, 1921.

Library Trustee. American Library Association, 1937.

Library Work with Children in Small Libraries. Hutting, *ca*.1921.

List of Books for School Libraries for the State of Oregon. Part 1, Books for Elementary Schools and for County Districts. (Salem, Oregon), 1932.

Nansen. il. Boris Artzybasheff. Viking, 1940.

MEDIA

Cyrus Holt and the Civil War. (TB).

Nansen. (BB, TB).

BACKGROUND READING

Commire. *Something about the Author.*

Contemporary Authors.

+GRACE TABER HALLOCK, 1893-1967
author

AWARDS

Boy Who Was. Newbery Honor Book, 1929.

BIBLIOGRAPHY

After the Rain: Cleanliness Customs of Children in Many Lands. il. Lou Rogers and Howard Smith. Cleanliness Institute, 1927; revised, 1937.

Around the World with Hob. il. Electra P. Depulous. Quaker Oats, 1931.

Bird in the Bush: Verses and Picture Maps. Dutton, 1930.

Boy Who Was. il. Harrie Wood. Dutton, 1928.

Dramatizing Child Health: A New Book of Health Plays, with Chapters on the Writing, the Producing, and the Educational Value of Dramatics. il. Harrie Wood. American Child Health, 1925.

Edward Jenner; with Clair E. Turner. Metropolitan Life Insurance, 1926.

Edward Livingston Trudeau; with Clair E. Turner. Metropolitan Life Insurance, 1926.

Florence Nightingale; with Clair E. Turner. Metropolitan Life Insurance, 1928.

Florence Nightingale and the Founding of Professional Nursing; with Clair E. Turner. Metropolitan Life Insurance, 1959.

Grain through the Ages; with Thomas D. Wood. il. Jessie Gillespie. Quaker Oats, 1927.

Growing Up; with Clair E. Turner. Heath, 1941.

Health and Physical Fitness; with Isidore H. Goldberger. Ginn, 1942; revised as *Understanding Health*, 1950; revised, 1955.

Health for Better Living Series; with Ross L. Allen and Eleanor Thomas. Ginn, 1954. (Includes *Growing Your Way* [revised, 1958]; *Health and Happy Days* [revised, 1958]; *Health in Work and Play* [revised, 1958]; *Health and Safety for You* [revised, 1958]; *Keeping Healthy and Strong* [revised, 1958]; *Teamwork for Health* [revised, 1958]. Added later were *Exploring Ways of Health* [1958] and *On Your Way* [1958].)

Health Heroes. Heath, 1929.

Health Observations of Schoolchildren: A Guide for Helping Teachers and Others to Observe and Understand the School Child in Health and Illness. il. Barbara Pfeiffer. McGraw, 1951; second edition, 1956.

Health through the Ages; with Charles E. A. Winslow. Metropolitan Life Insurance, 1933.

Hob o' the Mill; with Julia W. Abbot. il. Emma Clark. Quaker Oats, 1927.

Land of Health: How Children May Become Citizens of the Land of Health by Learning and Obeying Its Laws, with a Chapter on Exercise by Walter Camp; with Charles E. A. Winslow. Merrill, 1922; second edition, 1933.

Louis Pasteur; with Clair E. Turner. Metropolitan Life Insurance, 1925.

Marie Curie. Metropolitan Life Insurance, 1938.

(ed.) *May Day Festival Book.* American Child Health, 1925.

(ed.) *May Day Festival Book, 1927.* American Child Health, 1926.

(ed.) *May Day Festival Book, 1928.* American Child Health, 1927.

Petersham's Hill. il. Harrie Wood. Dutton, 1927.

Robert Koch; with Clair E. Turner. Metropolitan Life Insurance, 1932.

Safe and Healthy Living; with James M. Andress and Isidore H. Goldberger. Ginn, 1941.

School Health Programs for Parent-Teacher Associations and Women's Clubs. Child Health Association of America, 1922.

Spending the Days in China, Japan, and the Philippines; with Sally L. Jean. il. Jessie Gillespie. Harper, 1932.

Suggestions for Teachers in the Use of Hob o' the Mill: Historically Accurate Tales of Primitive, Ancient, Medieval and Colonial Children. Quaker Oats, 1927.

Suggestions from Teachers (of Grades II, IV and V) in the Use of After the Rain: Compiled from Classroom Reports of Teachers Whose Work Made This Publication Possible. Cleanliness Institute, 1932.

Tale of Soap and Water: The Historical Progress of Cleanliness. Cleanliness Institute, 1928; revised, 1937.

Travels of a Rolled Oat. il. Jessie Gillespie. Quaker Oats, 1931.

Tuberculosis: A Manual for Biology Teachers. Council of the Tuberculosis and Health Associations for Greater New York, 1947.

Voyage of Growing Up. Heath, 1928; revised, 1935; revised as *Growing Up*, 1941.

BIBLIOGRAPHY (cont'd)

Walter Reed; with Clair E. Turner. Metropolitan Life Insurance, 1926.

What to Do till the Doctor Comes, What to Know, What to Have Ready in the Home, and How to Deal with Sudden Illness, Accidental Injury or War Catastrophe: A Home Manual for Emergencies; with David B. Armstrong. il. Bernard Friedman. Simon, 1943.

MEDIA

Edward Livingston Trudeau. (BB).

Florence Nightingale. (BB).

Louis Pasteur. (BB).

Madame Curie. (BB).

Robert Koch. (BB).

Walter Reed. (BB).

BACKGROUND READING

Obituary. *New York Times*, August 19, 1967.

VIRGINIA HAMILTON, 1936-
author

AWARDS

M. C. Higgins, the Great. Newbery Medal Book, 1975.

Planet of Junior Brown. Newbery Honor Book, 1972.

BIBLIOGRAPHY

Arilla Sun Down. Greenwillow, 1976.

House of Dies Drear. il. Eros Keith. Macmillan, 1968.

Illusion and Reality. Library of Congress, 1976.

M. C. Higgins, the Great. Macmillan, 1974; large print edition, Hall, 1976.

Paul Robeson: The Life and Times of a Free Black Man. Harper, 1974.

Planet of Junior Brown. Macmillan, 1971.

Time-Ago Lost, More Tales of Jahdu. il. Ray Prather. Macmillan, 1973.

Time-Ago Tales of Jahdu. il. Nonny Hogrogian. Macmillan, 1969.

W. E. B. Du Bois: A Biography. Crowell, 1972.

(ed.) *Writings of W. E. B. Du Bois*; by William E. B. Du Bois. Crowell, 1975.

Zeely. il. Symeon Shimin. Macmillan, 1967.

MEDIA

House of Dies Drear. (TB).

M. C. Higgins. (BB, TB); Miller-Brody Productions, 1975 (C, R).

Paul Robeson. (TB).

Planet of Junior Brown. Miller-Brody Productions, 1977 (FSS).

Time-Ago Lost. (CB).

Time-Ago Tales of Jahdu. (TB).

W. E. B. Du Bois. (TB).

Zeely. (TB); a.k.a. *Virginia Hamilton Reads Zeely*. Caedmon, 1974 (R).

BACKGROUND READING

Commire. *Something about the Author*.

Contemporary Authors.

DeMontreville. *Fourth Book of Junior Authors and Illustrators*.

Hoffman. *Authors and Illustrators of Children's Books*.

Hopkins. *More Books by More People*.

Kingman. *Newbery and Caldecott Medal Books, 1966-1975*.

Kirkpatrick. *Twentieth Century Children's Writers*.

Langton, J. "Virginia Hamilton the Great." *Horn Book*, December 1974.

Meet the Newbery Author: Virginia Hamilton. Miller-Brody Productions, 1976 (FSS).

Nykoruk. *Authors in the News*.

"Profile of an Author: Virginia Hamilton." *Top of the News*, June 1969.

Rush. *Black American Writers Past and Present*.

Ward. *Authors of Books for Young People, Second Edition*.

+THOMAS SCHOFIELD HANDFORTH, 1897-1948
author-illustrator

AWARDS

Mei Lei. Caldecott Medal Book, 1939.

BIBLIOGRAPHY

Dragon and the Eagle: America Looks at China; by Delia Goetz. Foreign Policy Association, 1944.

Faraway Meadow. Doubleday, 1939.

Mei Lei. Doubleday, 1938.

Secret of the Porcelain Fish; by Margery Evernden. Random, 1947.

Toutou in Bondage; by Elizabeth Coatsworth. Macmillan, 1929.

Tranquilina's Paradise; by Susan Smith. Minton, 1930.

MEDIA

Mei Lei. McGraw-Hill Publishing Company, 1973 (FSS).

EXHIBITIONS

Kennedy Gallery, 1937, 1939. (New York, New York).

Walker Gallery, 1935. (New York, New York).

COLLECTIONS

Bibliotheque National. (Paris, France).

Capitol Museum. (Olympia, Washington).

Chicago Art Institute. (Chicago, Illinois).

Fogg Art Museum. (Cambridge, Massachusetts).

Handforth Collection, Tacoma Public Library. (Tacoma, Washington).

Kerlan Collection, University of Minnesota. (Minneapolis, Minnesota).

Metropolitan Museum of Art. (New York, New York).

Milwaukee Public Library. (Milwaukee, Wisconsin).

Minneapolis Art Institute. (Minneapolis, Minnesota).

Seattle Art Museum. (Seattle, Washington).

Tacoma Art Museum. (Tacoma, Washington).

Washington Historical Museum. (Tacoma, Washington).

BACKGROUND READING

Bader. *American Picturebooks from Noah's Ark to The Beast Within*.

Coatsworth, E. "Thomas Handforth's Mei Lei." *Horn Book*, May 1939.

Handforth, T. "Moon Bridge in Lily Pond." *Horn Book*, May 1939.

Horn Book, special issue, October 1950.

Kunitz. *Junior Book of Authors, Second Edition Revised*.

Lesser, M. "Thomas Handforth and Mei Lei." *Library Journal*, July 1939.

Mahony. *Illustrators of Children's Books, 1844-1945*.

Miller. *Caldecott Medal Books, 1938-1957*.

Miller. *Illustrators of Children's Books, 1946-1956*.

Obituary. *Art Digest*, January 1, 1949.

Ward. *Authors of Books for Young People, Second Edition*.

Ward. *Illustrators of Books for Young People, Second Edition*.

MARION BOYD HAVIGHURST, 1899-1974
author
   a.k.a. Marion Boyd
and
WALTER EDWIN HAVIGHURST, 1901-
author

AWARDS

Song of the Pines. Newbery Honor Book, 1950.

BIBLIOGRAPHY

Marion Boyd (Havighurst):

Murder in the Stacks. Lothrop, 1934.

Silver Wands. Yale University, 1923.

Strange Island. World, 1957.

Sycamore Tree. World, 1960.

Walter Havighurst:

Alexander Spotswood: Portrait of a Governor. Colonial Williamsburg, 1967.

Annie Oakley of the Wild West. Macmillan, 1954.

(ed.) *Approach to America*; with Robert Almy and Joseph M. Bachelor. Odyssey, 1942.

Buffalo Bill's Great Wild West Show. il. Jon Wonsetter. Random, 1957.

Designs for Writing; with Harold Haley. Dryden, 1939.

(ed.) *Exploring Literature*. Houghton, 1968.

First Book of Pioneers: Northwest Territory. il. Harvé Stein. Watts, 1959.

First Book of the California Gold Rush. il. Harvé Stein. Watts, 1962.

First Book of the Oregon Trail. il. Helen Borten. Watts, 1960.

George Rogers Clark: Soldier in the West. il. Jack Moment. McGraw, 1952.

Great Lakes Reader. Macmillan, 1966.

Heartland: Ohio, Indiana, Illinois. il. Grattan Condon. Harper, 1962; revised, 1974.

Land and the People. U.S. Department of Agriculture, 1941.

BIBLIOGRAPHY (cont'd)

Walter Havighurst (cont'd):

Land of Promise: The Story of the Northwest Territory. Macmillan, 1946.

(ed.) *Land of the Long Horizons*. Coward, 1960.

Life in America: The Great Plains. il. Charles P. Vanderwoud. Fiedler, 1951; second edition, 1955; *a.k.a. Great Plains*, 1964. (Available with *Unit of Teaching Pictures*, 1952 and 1967.)

Life in America: The Midwest. il. Jessie Miersma. Fiedler, 1951; second edition, 1955; *a.k.a. Midwest*, 1964. (Available with *Unit of Teaching Pictures*, 1951 and 1965); *a.k.a. Midwest and Great Plains*. Fiedler, 1967; second edition, 1972.

Life in America: The Northeast. il. Janet Croninger and Robert Poterack. Fiedler, 1955; second edition, 1960; *a.k.a. Northeast*, 1967; second edition, 1970. (Available with *Unit of Teaching Pictures*, 1955 and 1967.)

Long Ships Passing: The Story of the Great Lakes. il. John O. Cosgrove, II. Macmillan, 1942; enlarged, 1975.

(ed.) *Masters of the Modern Short Story*. Harcourt, 1945; second edition, 1955.

Men of Old Miami, 1809-1873: A Book of Portraits. Putnam, 1974.

Miami Years, 1809-1959. Putnam, 1958; revised, 1969.

No Homeward Course. Doubleday, 1941.

Ohio: A Bicentennial History. Norton, 1976.

Pier 17: A Novel. Macmillan, 1935.

Proud Prisoner. il. Leonard Vosburgh. Colonial Williamsburg, 1964.

Quiet Shore. Macmillan, 1937.

River to the West: Three Centuries of the Ohio. Putnam, 1970.

(ed.) *Selection: A Reader for College Writing*. Dryden, 1955.

Signature of Time. Macmillan, 1949.

Three Flags at the Straits: The Forts of Mackinac. Prentice, 1966.

Upper Mississippi: A Student's Guide to Localized History. Teacher's College, 1966.

Upper Mississippi: A Wilderness Saga. il. David and Lolita Granahan. Farrar, 1937; revised, 1944.

Vein of Iron: The Pickands-Mather Story. World, 1958.

Voices on the River: The Story of the Mississippi Waterways. Macmillan, 1964.

Winds of Spring. Macmillan, 1940.

Marion and Walter Havighurst:

Climb a Lofty Ladder: A Story of Swedish Settlements in Minnesota. il. Jill Elgin. Winston, 1952.

High Prairie. il. Gertrude Howe. Farrar, 1944.

Song of the Pines: A Story of Norwegian Lumbering in Wisconsin. il. Richard Floethe. Winston, 1949.

MEDIA

Annie Oakley. (BB, TB).

Buffalo Bill's Great Wild West Show. (BB, TB).

Climb a Lofty Ladder. (BB).

Exploring Literature. (C, MT).

George Rogers Clark. (BB).

Heartland. (BB, TB).

Land of Promise. (TB).

Life in America: The Midwest. (C, MT).

Long Ships Passing. (BB).

Masters of the Modern Short Story. (C, MT).

Midwest and the Great Plains. (C, MT).

Song of the Pines. (BB).

Voices on the River. (TB).

COLLECTIONS

Hillyer Collection, Arents Research Library, Syracuse University. (Syracuse, New York).

Kerlan Collection, University of Minnesota. (Minneapolis, Minnesota).

BACKGROUND READING

Commire. *Something about the Author*.

Contemporary Authors.

Coyle. *Ohio Authors and Their Books*.

Fuller. *More Junior Authors*.

Kunitz. *Twentieth Century Authors, First Supplement*.

Ward. *Authors of Books for Young People, Second Edition*.

Warfel. *American Novelists of Today*.

+CHARLES BOARDMAN HAWES, 1889-1923
author

AWARDS

Dark Frigate. Newbery Medal Book, 1924.

Great Quest. Newbery Honor Book, 1922.

BIBLIOGRAPHY

*Dark Frigate: Wherein Is Told the Story of Philip
Marsham Who Lived in the Time of King Charles
and Was Bred a Sailor but Came Home to England
after Many Hazards by Sea and Land and Fought
for the King at Newbury and Lost a Great Inheri-
tance and Departed for Barbadoes in the Same
Ship, by Curious Chance, in Which He Had Long
before Adventured with the Pirates.* il. Anton O.
Fischer. Atlantic, 1923; also il. Warren Chappell,
1971.

*Gloucester, by Land and Sea: The Story of a New
England Seacoast Town.* il. Lester G. Hornby.
Little, 1923; a.k.a. *Gloucester, by Land and Sea.*
Library Editions, 1970.

*Great Quest: A Romance of 1826, Wherein Are
Recorded the Experiences of Josiah Woods of
Topham, and of Those Others with Whom He
Sailed for Cuba and the Gulf of Guinea.* il.
George Varian. Little, 1921; also il. Anton O.
Fischer, 1934.

*Mutineers: A Tale of Old Days at Sea and Adventure
in the Far East as Benjamin Lathrop Set It Down
Some Sixty Years Ago.* il. Anton O. Fischer.
Little, 1920.

*Whaling: Wherein Are Discussed the Growth of the
European Whaling Industry, and of Its Offspring,
the American Whaling Industry, Primitive Whaling
among the Savages of North America, the Various
Manners and Means of Taking Whales in All Parts
of the World and in All Times of Its History.* il.
Clifford W. Ashley. Doubleday, 1924.

MEDIA

Dark Frigate. (BB, CB); Miller-Brody Productions,
1976 (FSS); Newbery Award Records, 1972
(C, R).

Great Quest. (BB).

Mutineers. (BB).

COLLECTIONS

New York Public Library. (New York, New York).

BACKGROUND READING

Burke. *American Authors and Books, 1640 to the
Present Day.*

Ernst, Clayton H. *Charles Boardman Hawes,
1889-1923: An Appreciation.* Little, 1927.

Johnson. *Dictionary of American Biography,
Supplement 4.*

Kunitz. *Authors Today and Yesterday.*

Kunitz. *Junior Book of Authors.*

Kunitz. *Twentieth Century Authors.*

Louis, M. "Charles Boardman Hawes—An Appreciation." *Elementary English*, June 1924.

Miller. *Newbery Medal Books, 1922-1955.*

Ward. *Authors of Books for Young People, Second
Edition.*

MARGUERITE BREITHAUPT HENRY, 1902-
author

AWARDS

Justin Morgan Had a Horse. Newbery Honor Book,
1946.

King of the Wind. Newbery Medal Book, 1949.

Misty of Chincoteague. Newbery Honor Book, 1948.

BIBLIOGRAPHY

Alaska in Story and Pictures. il. Kurt Wiese. Whitman,
1941.

Album of Horses. il. Wesley Dennis. Rand, 1951; see
also *Portfolio of Horses*, below.

All about Horses. il. Wesley Dennis and photographs.
Random, 1962; a.k.a. *Marguerite Henry's All
about Horses.* il. Walter D. Osborn and photographs, 1967.

Always Reddy. il. Wesley Dennis. McGraw, 1947;
a.k.a. *Shamrock Queen*, n. d.

Argentina in Story and Pictures. il. Kurt Wiese.
Whitman, 1941.

Auno and Tauno: A Story of Finland. il. Gladys
Blackwood. Whitman, 1940.

Australia in Story and Pictures. il. Kurt Wiese.
Whitman, 1946.

Bahamas in Story and Pictures. il. Kurt Wiese.
Whitman, 1946.

Benjamin West and His Cat Grimalkin. il. Wesley
Dennis. Bobbs, 1947.

Bermuda in Story and Pictures. il. Kurt Wiese.
Whitman, 1946.

Birds at Home. il. Jacob B. Abbot. Donohue, 1942;
new edition, Hubbard, 1972.

Black Gold. il. Wesley Dennis. Rand, 1957.

Born to Trot. il. Wesley Dennis. Rand, 1950.

Boy and a Dog. il. Diana Thorne and Ottilie Foy.
Wilcox, 1944.

Brazil in Story and Pictures. il. Kurt Wiese. Whitman,
1941.

Brighty of the Grand Canyon. il. Wesley Dennis.
Rand, 1953.

BIBLIOGRAPHY (cont'd)

British Honduras in Story and Pictures. il. Kurt Wiese. Whitman, 1946.

Canada in Story and Pictures. il. Kurt Wiese. Whitman, 1941.

Chile in Story and Pictures. il. Kurt Wiese. Whitman, 1941.

Cinnabar: The One O'Clock Fox. il. Wesley Dennis. Rand, 1956.

*Dear Readers and Riders. Rand, 1969.

Dilly Dally Sally. il. Gladys Blackwood. Saalfield, 1940.

Dominican Republic in Story and Pictures. il. Kurt Wiese. Whitman, 1946.

Five O'Clock Charlie. il. Wesley Dennis. Rand, 1962.

Gaudenzia, Pride of the Palio. il. Lynd Ward. Rand, 1960; *a.k.a. Wildest Horse in the World*, 1976.

Geraldine Belinda. il. Gladys Blackwood. Platt, 1942.

Hawaii in Story and Pictures. il. Kurt Wiese. Whitman, 1946.

Justin Morgan Had a Horse. il. Wesley Dennis. Wilcox, 1945; new edition, Rand, 1954.

King of the Wind. il. Wesley Dennis. Rand, 1948; also il. Sheila Rose. Constable, 1957.

Little Fellow. il. Diana Thorne. Winston, 1945; also il. Rich Rudish. Rand, 1975.

Little Long Ears and the Precious Oils. (Topeka, Kansas), 1956.

Little-or-Nothing from Nottingham. il. Wesley Dennis. McGraw, 1949.

Mexico in Story and Pictures. il. Kurt Wiese. Whitman, 1941.

Misty of Chincoteague. il. Wesley Dennis. Rand, 1947.

Misty, the Wonder Pony: By Misty Herself. il. Clare McKinley. Rand, 1956.

Muley-Ears, Nobody's Dog. il. Wesley Dennis. Rand, 1959.

Mustang: Wild Spirit of the West. il. Robert Lougheed. Rand, 1966.

New Zealand in Story and Pictures. il. Kurt Wiese. Whitman, 1946.

One Man's Meat. Rand, 1977.

Panama in Story and Pictures. il. Kurt Wiese. Whitman, 1941.

Pictorial Life Story of Misty. Rand, 1977.

Portfolio of Horse Paintings: With Commentary by Marguerite Henry; by Wesley Dennis. Rand, 1964.

Portfolio of Horses from Album of Horses: Commentary by Marguerite Henry; by Wesley Dennis. Rand, 1952; see also *Album of Horses*, above.

Robert Fulton: Boy Craftsman. il. Lawrence Dresser. Bobbs, 1945; also il. Robert Patterson, 1962.

San Domingo: The Medicine Hat Stallion. il. Robert Lougheed. Rand, 1972; *a.k.a. Peter Lundy and the Medicine Hat Stallion*, 1977.

Sea Star: Orphan of Chincoteague. il. Wesley Dennis. Rand, 1949.

(ed.) *Stories from around the World*. il. Krystyna Stasiak. Hubbard, 1974.

Stormy: Misty's Foal. il. Wesley Dennis. Rand, 1963.

Their First Igloo on Baffin Island; with Barbara True. il. Gladys Blackwood. Whitman, 1943.

Virgin Islands in Story and Pictures. il. Kurt Wiese. Whitman, 1946.

Wagging Tails: An Album of Dogs. il. Wesley Dennis. Rand, 1955; *a.k.a. Album of Dogs*, 1970.

West Indies in Story and Pictures. il. Kurt Wiese. Whitman, 1941.

White Stallion of Lipizza. il. Wesley Dennis. Rand, 1964.

MEDIA

Album of Horses. (BB).

Benjamin West and His Cat Grimalkin. (BB, TB).

Born to Trot. (BB).

Brighty of the Grand Canyon. (BB, TB); Feature Films/Paragon Productions, 1967 (F); Pied Piper Productions, 1975 (FS).

Cinnabar. (BB, TB).

Gaudenzia. (TB).

Justin Morgan Had a Horse. (BB, TB); Miller-Brody Productions, 1975 (FSS); Walt Disney Productions, 1975 (F).

King of the Wind. (BB, CB); Miller-Brody Productions, 1973 (FSS); Newbery Award Records, 1971 (C, R); Pied Piper Productions, 19? (FSS).

Little Fellow. (BB).

Misty of Chincoteague. (BB); Miller-Brody Productions, 1974 (FSS); Twentieth-Century Fox Film Corporation, 1961 (F).

Mustang. (BB).

Peter Lundy. National Broadcasting Corporation, 1977 (TV).

San Domingo see *Peter Lundy*.

Sea Star. (BB); Miller-Brody Productions, 1977 (C, R).

Stormy. (BB, CB, TB).

COLLECTIONS

Kerlan Collection, University of Minnesota. (Minneapolis, Minnesota).

BACKGROUND READING

Burke. *American Authors and Books, 1640 to the Present Day*.

Commire. *Something about the Author*.

Contemporary Authors.

Current Biography.

Henry, M. "How the Author of Children's Books Views Her Public." *Illinois Libraries*, January 1947.

Henry, M. "Weft of Truth and a Warp of Fiction." *Elementary English*, October 1974.

Hoffman. *Authors and Illustrators of Children's Books*.

Kirkpatrick. *Twentieth Century Children's Writers*.

Kunitz. *Junior Book of Authors, Second Edition Revised*.

Meet the Newbery Author: Marguerite Henry. Miller-Brody Productions, 1974 (FSS).

Miller. *Newbery Medal Books, 1922-1955*.

Odland, N. "Marguerite Henry, Mistress of Mole Meadows." *Elementary English*, January 1968.

Smaridge. *Famous Modern Storytellers for Young People*.

Ward. *Authors of Books for Young People, Second Edition*.

Wilt, M. "In Marguerite Henry, the Thread That Runs So True." *Elementary English*, November 1954.

Young Wings. *Writing Books for Boys and Girls*.

+VELINO SHIJE HERRERA, 1902-
illustrator

AWARDS

In My Mother's House. Caldecott Honor Book, 1942.

BIBLIOGRAPHY

In My Mother's House; by Ann N. Clark. Viking, 1941.

Young Hunter of Picuris; by Ann N. Clark. Office of Indian Affairs, 1943.

BACKGROUND READING

Mahony. *Illustrators of Children's Books, 1744-1945*.

+AGNES DANFORTH HEWES
author

AWARDS

Codfish Market. Newbery Honor Book, 1937.

Glory of the Seas. Newbery Honor Book, 1934.

Spice and the Devil's Cave. Newbery Honor Book, 1931.

BIBLIOGRAPHY

Anabel's Windows. il. Kurt Wiese. Dodd, 1949.

Boy of the Lost Crusade. il. Gustaf Tenggren. Houghton, 1923.

Codfish Market. il. Armstrong Sperry. Doubleday, 1936.

Glory of the Seas. il. Newell C. Wyeth. Knopf, 1933.

Golden Sleeve. il. Herbert M. Stoops. Doubleday, 1937.

Hundred Bridges to Go. Dodd, 1950.

Iron Doctor: A Story of Deep-Sea Diving. Houghton, 1940.

Jackhammer, Drill Runners of the Mountain Highways. Knopf, 1942.

Spice and the Devil's Cave. il. Lynd Ward. Knopf, 1930.

Spice Ho! A Story of Discovery. il. Wilfred Jones. Knopf, 1941; second edition, 1947.

Sword of Roland Arnot. il. Paul Strayer. Houghton, 1939.

Swords on the Sea. il. Lou Block. Knopf, 1928.

Two Oceans to Canton, the Story of the Old China Trade. il. Harry Roth. Knopf, 1944.

With the Will to Go. il. Don Lambo. Longmans, 1960.

MEDIA

Codfish Market. (BB).

Iron Doctor. (BB).

Swords on the Sea. (BB).

BACKGROUND READING

Burke. *American Authors and Books, 1640 to the Present Day*.

Dosch, Mary. *Girlhood in Syria, a Centennial Gift Volume Commemorating the American University of Beirut, 1867-1967*. Constance Spencer, 1967.

Hewes, A. "Way of All Spice." *Horn Book*, August 1930.

BACKGROUND READING (cont'd)

Kelly, E. "Through What Fair Field or Tossing Sea?" *Horn Book*, August 1930.

Kunitz. *Junior Book of Authors.*

Kunitz. *Junior Book of Authors, Second Edition Revised.*

Ward. *Authors of Books for Young People, Second Edition.*

+NONNY HOGROGIAN, 1932-
author-illustrator

AWARDS

Always Room for One More. Caldecott Medal Book, 1966.

Contest. Caldecott Honor Book, 1977.

(*Fearsome Inn.* Newbery Honor Book, 1968.)

One Fine Day. Caldecott Medal Book, 1972.

BIBLIOGRAPHY

About Wise Men and Simpletons: Twelve Tales from Grimm; by Jacob and Wilhelm Grimm. Macmillan, 1971.

Always Room for One More; by Sorche N. Leodhas, *pseud.* (Leclaire Alger). Holt, 1965.

Apples. Macmillan, 1972.

Arbor Day; by Aileen Fisher. Crowell, 1965.

Armenian Cookbook; by Rachel Hogrogian. Atheneum, 1971.

Bears Are Sleeping; by Yulya, *pseud.* (Julie Whitney). Scribner, 1967.

Billy Goat and His Well-Fed Friends. Harper, 1972.

Carrot Cake. Greenwillow, 1977.

Contest. Greenwillow, 1976.

Day Everybody Cried; by Beatrice S. DeRegniers. Viking, 1967.

Deirdre; by James Stephens. Macmillan, 1970.

Dog Writes on the Window with His Nose and Other Poems; by David Kheridan. Four Winds, 1977.

Down Come the Leaves; by Henrietta Bancroft. Crowell, 1961.

Favorite Fairy Tales Told in Greece; by Virginia Haviland. Little, 1970.

Fearsome Inn; by Isaac B. Singer. Tr. Isaac B. Singer and Elizabeth Shub. Scribner, 1967.

Gaelic Ghosts; by Sorche N. Leodhas, *pseud.* (Leclaire Alger). Holt, 1964.

Ghosts Go Haunting; by Sorche N. Leodhas, *pseud.* (Leclaire Alger). Holt, 1965.

Hand in Hand We'll Go: Ten Poems; by Robert Burns. Crowell, 1965.

Hermit and Harry and Me. Little, 1972.

In School: Learning in Four Languages; by Esther Hautzig. Macmillan, 1969.

King of the Kerry Fair; by Nicolette Meredith. Crowell, 1960.

Kitchen Knight; by Barbara Schiller. Holt, 1965.

Looking over Hills; by David Kheridan. Giligia, 1973.

Once There Was and Was Not: Armenian Folk Tales Retold; by Virginia Tashjian. Little, 1966.

One Fine Day. Macmillan, 1971.

One I Love, Two I Love and Other Loving Mother Goose Rhymes; from Mother Goose. Dutton, 1972.

Paz; by Cheli D. Ryan. Macmillan, 1971.

Poems of William Shakespeare; by William Shakespeare, selected by Lloyd Frankenberg. Crowell, 1966.

Renowned History of Little Red Riding Hood. Crowell, 1967.

Rooster Brother. Macmillan, 1974.

Sir Ribbeck of Ribbeck of Havelland; by Theodore Fontane. Tr. Elizabeth Shub. Macmillan, 1969.

Story of Prince Ivan, The Firebird, and The Gray Wolf; tr. Thomas Whitney. Scribner, 1968.

Tale of Stolen Time; by Eugeniie Shvarts. Tr. Lila Pargment and Estelle Titier. Prentice, 1966.

Thirteen Days of Yule. Crowell, 1968.

Three Apples Fell from Heaven: Armenian Tales Retold; by Virginia Tashjian. Little, 1971.

Three Sparrows and Other Nursery Poems; by Christian Morgenstern. Tr. Max Knight. Scribner, 1968.

Time-Ago Tales of Jahdu; by Virginia Hamilton. Macmillan, 1969.

Vasilisa the Beautiful; tr. Thomas Whitney. Macmillan, 1970.

Visions of America: By the Poets of Our Time; compiled by David Kheridan. Macmillan, 1973.

White Palace; by Mary O'Neill. Crowell, 1966.

MEDIA

Billy Goat. (BB).

One Fine Day. (TB); Weston Woods Studios, 1973 (FSS).

COLLECTIONS

Free Library of Philadelphia. (Philadelphia, Pennsylvania).

BACKGROUND READING

Commire. *Something about the Author.*

Contemporary Authors.

DeMontreville. *Third Book of Junior Authors.*

Hogrogian, N. "Story Sets the Pace: An Illustrator's View of Design." *Publishers Weekly*, February 21, 1966.

Hopkins. *Books Are by People.*

Kingman. *Illustrators of Children's Books, 1957-1966.*

Kingman. *Illustrators of Children's Books, 1967-1976.*

Kingman. *Newbery and Caldecott Medal Books, 1966-1975.*

Ward. *Authors of Books for Young People, Second Edition.*

Ward. *Illustrators of Books for Young People, Second Edition.*

Waugh, D. "Nonny Hogrogian, Decorator of Books for Children." *American Artist*, October 1966.

+HOLLING CLANCY HOLLING, 1900-
author-illustrator

AWARDS

Minn of the Mississippi. Newbery Honor Book, 1952.

Paddle-to-the-Sea. Caldecott Honor Book, 1942.

Seabird. Newbery Honor Book, 1949.

BIBLIOGRAPHY

Blot, Little City Cat; by Phyllis Crawford. Cape, 1930.

Book of Cowboys; with Lucille Holling. Platt, 1936.

Book of Indians; with Lucille Holling. Platt, 1935.

Children of Other Lands; by Watty Piper, *pseud.* (Frances M. Ford). Platt, 1943.

Choo-Me-Shoo; with Lucille Holling. Buzza, 1928.

Claws of the Thunderbird: A Tale of Three Lost Indians. Volland, 1928.

Little Buffalo Boy; with Lucille Holling. Garden City, 1939.

Little Bye-Bye- and-Bye. Volland, 1926.

Little Folks of Other Lands; edited by Watty Piper, *pseud.* (Frances M. Ford). Platt, 1932.

Magic Story Tree: A Collection of Fifteen Fairy Tales and Fables; with Lucille Holling. Platt, 1964.

Minn of the Mississippi. Houghton, 1951.

New Mexico Made Easy with Words of Modern Syllables. Clancy, 1923.

Paddle-to-the-Sea. Houghton, 1941.

Pagoo; with Lucille Holling. Houghton, 1957.

Road in Storyland; edited by Watty Piper, *pseud.* (Frances M. Ford). Platt, 1932.

Rocky Billy: The Story of the Bounding Career of a Rocky Mountain Goat. Macmillan, 1928.

Rum-Tum-Tummy: The Elephant Who Ate. Saalfield, 1928.

Seabird. Houghton, 1948.

Sun and Smoke: Verse and Woodcuts of New Mexico. (Privately printed), 1923.

Tree in the Trail. Houghton, 1942.

Twins Who Flew around the World. Platt, 1930.

MEDIA

Book of Indians. (TB).

Minn of the Mississippi. (BB).

Paddle-to-the-Sea. (BB); Julian Biggs/National Film Board of Canada, 1966 (F); Stillfilm, 1950 (4-part FSS).

Pagoo. Pied Piper Productions, n. d. (FSS); also in *Story of a Book*, Churchill Films, 1962 (F).

Seabird. (BB).

Tree in the Trail. (BB).

COLLECTIONS

Special Collections, University Research Library, University of California. (Los Angeles, California).

University of Oregon Library. (Eugene, Oregon).

BACKGROUND READING

Armstrong, M. "Holling C. Holling." *Horn Book*, April 1955.

Burke. *American Authors and Books, 1640 to the Present Day.*

Hoffman. *Authors and Illustrators of Children's Books.*

Kingman. *Illustrators of Children's Books, 1957-1966.*

Kirkpatrick. *Twentieth Century Children's Writers.*

Kunitz. *Junior Book of Authors, Second Edition Revised.*

Mahony. *Illustrators of Children's Books, 1744-1945.*

BACKGROUND READING (cont'd)

Miller. *Illustrators of Children's Books, 1946-1956.*

Ramsey, I. "Holling C. Holling: Author and Illustrator." *Elementary English*, February 1954.

Ward. *Authors of Books for Young People, Second Edition.*

Ward. *Illustrators of Books for Young People, Second Edition.*

+RALPH HUBBARD
author

AWARDS

Queer Person. Newbery Honor Book, 1931.

BIBLIOGRAPHY

Queer Person. il. Harold von Schmidt. Doubleday, 1930.

Wolf Song. il. Langdon Kihn. Doubleday, 1935.

IRENE HUNT, 1907-
author

AWARDS

Across Five Aprils. Newbery Honor Book, 1965.

Up a Road Slowly. Newbery Medal Book, 1967.

BIBLIOGRAPHY

Across Five Aprils. il. Albert J. Pucci. Follett, 1964.

Lottery Rose. Scribner, 1976.

No Promises in the Wind. Follett, 1970.

Trail of Apple Blossoms. il. Don Bolognese. Follett, 1968.

Up a Road Slowly. Follett, 1966.

William. Scribner, 1977.

MEDIA

Across Five Aprils. (BB, C, MT, TB). Miller-Brody Productions, 1974 (FSS).

No Promises in the Wind. (TB).

Up a Road Slowly. (C, MT, TB). Miller-Brody Productions, 1972 (FSS); Newbery Award Records, 1972 (C, R).

COLLECTIONS

deGrummond Collection, University of Southern Mississippi. (Hattiesburg, Mississippi).

Kerlan Collection, University of Minnesota. (Minneapolis, Minnesota).

BACKGROUND READING

Commire. *Something about the Author.*

Contemporary Authors.

DeMontreville. *Third Book of Junior Authors.*

Hopkins. *More Books by More People.*

Hunt, I. "Children's Literature from the Viewpoint of the Writer." *Illinois Libraries*, January 1966.

Irene Hunt. Pathways to Children's Literature, 196? (C).

Kingman. *Newbery and Caldecott Medal Books, 1966-1975.*

Kirkpatrick. *Twentieth Century Children's Writers.*

Ward. *Authors of Books for Young People, Second Edition.*

Writing for Children with Irene Hunt, University of Michigan Films, *ca.*1967 (F).

MABEL LEIGH HUNT, 1892-1971
author

AWARDS

Better Known as Johnny Appleseed. Newbery Honor Book, 1951.

"Have You Seen Tom Thumb?" Newbery Honor Book, 1943.

BIBLIOGRAPHY

Beggar's Daughter. Lippincott, 1963.

Benjie's Hat. il. Grace Paull. Stokes, 1938.

Better Known as Johnny Appleseed. il. James Daugherty. Lippincott, 1950.

Billy Button's Butter'd Biscuit. il. Katherine Milhous. Stokes, 1941.

Boy Who Had No Birthday. il. Cameron Wright. Stokes, 1935.

Corn-Belt Billy. il. Kurt Wiese. Grosset, 1942.

Cristy at Skippinghills. il. Velma Ilsley. Lippincott, 1958.

Cupola House. il. Nora S. Unwin. Lippincott, 1961.

Double Birthday Present. il. Elinore Blaisdell. Lippincott, 1947.

"Have You Seen Tom Thumb?" il. Fritz Eichenberg. Stokes, 1942.

John of Pudding Lane. il. Clotilde Funk. Stokes, 1941.

Johnny-Up and Johnny-Down. il. Harold Berson. Lippincott, 1962.

Ladycake Farm. il. Clotilde Funk. Lippincott, 1952.

Little Girl with Seven Names. il. Grace Paull. Stokes, 1936.

Little Grey Gown. il. Ilse Bischoff. Lippincott, 1939.

Lucinda: A Little Girl of 1860. il. Cameron Wright. Stokes, 1934.

Matilda's Buttons. il. Elinore Blaisdell. Lippincott, 1948.

Michel's Island. il. Kate Seredy. Stokes, 1940.

Miss Jellytot's Visit. il. Velma Ilsley. Lippincott, 1955.

Peddler's Clock. il. Elizabeth O. Jones, Grosset, 1943.

Peter Piper's Pickled Peppers. il. Katherine Milhous. Stokes, 1942.

Sibby Botherbox. il. Margery Collison. Lippincott, 1945.

Singing among Strangers. il. Irene Gibian. Lippincott, 1954.

69th Grandchild. il. Elinore Blaisdell. Lippincott, 1951.

Stars for Cristy. il. Velma Ilsley. Lippincott, 1956.

Such a Kind World. il. Edna Potter. Grosset, 1947.

Susan, Beware! il. Mildred Boyle. Stokes, 1937.

Tomorrow Will Be Bright. il. Tommy Shoemaker. Ginn, 1958.

Wonderful Baker. il. Grace Paull. Lippincott, 1950.

Young Man-of-the-House. il. Louis Slobodkin. Lippincott, 1944.

MEDIA

Benjie's Hat. (BB, TB).

Double Birthday Present. (BB, TB).

"Have You Seen Tom Thumb?" n. p., 19? (R); Columbia Broadcasting System, 19? (T.V.).

Ladycake Farm. (BB).

Little Girl with Seven Names. (BB).

Miss Jellytot's Visit. (TB); also in *Make-Believe Stories*. (TB).

Singing among Strangers. (BB).

Stars for Cristy. (BB).

COLLECTIONS

deGrummond Collection, University of Southern Mississippi, (Hattiesburg, Mississippi).

Kerlan Collection, University of Minnesota. (Minneapolis, Minnesota).

BACKGROUND READING

Burke. *American Authors and Books, 1640 to the Present Day*.

Commire. *Something about the Author*.

Contemporary Authors.

Current Biography.

Hunt, M. "Quaker Childhood in Indiana." *Horn Book*, January 1937.

Hunt, M. "Yeast in the Mind." *Horn Book*, May 1951.

Kirkpatrick. *Twentieth Century Children's Writers*.

Kunitz. *Junior Book of Authors, Second Edition Revised*.

Thompson. *Indiana Authors and Their Books, 1917-1966*.

Ward. *Authors of Books for Young People, Second Edition*.

+SULAMITH ISH-KISHOR, 1896-1977
author

AWARDS

Our Eddie. Newbery Honor Book, 1970.

BIBLIOGRAPHY

American Promise: A History of Jews in the New World. il. Grace Hick. Behrman, 1947.

Bible Story. United Synagogue, 1921.

Blessed Is the Daughter; with Meyer Wazman and Jacob Sloan. Shengold, 1960.

Boy of Old Prague. il. Ben Shahn. Pantheon, 1963.

Carpet of Solomon: A Hebrew Legend. il. Uri Shulevitz. Pantheon, 1966.

Children's History of Israel from the Creation to the Present Time: A New Presentation. Jordan, 19? (3 vols.). (Includes *From Creation to the Passing of Moses* [revised, 1933]; *From Joshua to the Second Temple* [revised, 1949]; *From the Second Temple to the Present Time* [revised, n. d.].)

Children's Story of the Bible: A Bible History for School and Home. Educational Stationery House, 1930.

BIBLIOGRAPHY (cont'd)

Drusilla: A Novel of the Emperor Hadrian. il. Thomas Morely. Pantheon, 1970.

Everyman's History of the Jews. Fell, 1948.

Friday Night Stories (Series 1-4): Adapted for Children from "The Legends of the Jews" by Louis Ginzberg. Tr. Henrietta Szold. United Synagogue, 1949.

Heaven on the Sea, and Other Stories: Together with Twenty Poems. il. Penina Ish-Kishor. Block, 1924.

How the Weatherman Came. il. Rebecca S. Andrews. Works Progress Administration, 1938.

How Theodor Herzl Created the Jewish National Fund: Together with an Album of Herzliana, a Chronology, and Excerpts from His Diary and Autobiography. Jewish National Fund, 1960.

Jews to Remember. il. Kyra Markham. Herbrew Printing, 1941.

Little Potato and Other Stories. il. J. Russack. Works Progress Administration, 1937.

Magnificent Hadrian: A Biography of Hadrian, Emperor of Rome. Minton, 1935; *a.k.a. Magnificent Hadrian.* Gollancz, 1935.

Master of Miracles: A New Novel of the Golem. il. Arnold Lobel. Harper, 1971.

Our Eddie. Pantheon, 1969.

Palace of Eagles and Other Stories. il. Alice Horodisch. Shoulson, 1948.

Pathways through the Jewish Holidays. il. Stuart Diamond. Ktav, 1967.

Stranger within Thy Gates, and Other Stories. il. Alice Horodisch. Shoulson, 1948.

Zalman Shazar: President of the People. Jewish National Fund, 1966.

MEDIA

Everyman's History of the Jews. (BB).

Jews to Remember. (BB).

COLLECTIONS

Dreiser Collection, Olin Library, Cornell University. (Ithaca, New York).

New York Public Library. (New York, New York).

BACKGROUND READING

Contemporary Authors.

Kirkpatrick. *Twentieth Century Children's Writers.*

New York Times Biographical Service.

Ward. *Authors of Books for Young People, Second Edition.*

WILL JAMES, *pseudonym*, 1892-1942
author-illustrator
a.k.a. Joseph Duffault

AWARDS

Smoky. Newbery Medal Book, 1927.

BIBLIOGRAPHY

All in the Day's Riding. Scribner, 1933.

American Cowboy. Scribner, 1942.

Big Enough. Scribner, 1931; also in *Young Cowboy*, below.

Book of Cowboy Stories. Scribner, 1951.

Cow Country. Scribner, 1927.

Cowboys North and South. Scribner, 1924.

Dark Horse. Scribner, 1939.

Drifting Cowboy. Scribner, 1925.

Flint Spears: Cowboy Rodeo Contestant. Scribner, 1938.

Home Ranch. Scribner, 1935.

Horses I've Known. Scribner, 1935.

In the Saddle with Uncle Bill. Scribner, 1935.

Jingle Bob; by Philip Rollins, Scribner, 1927.

*Lone Cowboy: My Life Story. Scribner, 1930; also issued in limited edition; *a.k.a. Cowboy in the Making: Arranged from the First Chapters of "Lone Cowboy."* Scribner, 1937.

Look-See with Uncle Bill. Scribner, 1938.

My First Horse. Scribner, 1940.

Sand. Scribner, 1929.

Scorpion: A Good Horse. Scribner, 1936.

Smoky: The Cowhorse. Scribner, 1926.

Sun Up: Tales of the Cow Camps. Scribner, 1931; also in *Young Cowboy*, below.

Three Mustangeers. Scribner, 1933.

Uncle Bill: A Tale of Two Kids and a Cowboy. Scribner, 1932.

Watched by Wild Animals; by Enos Mills. Doubleday, 1922.

Wild Animal Homestead; by Enos Mills. Doubleday, 1923.

Will James Cowboy Book; edited by Alice Dalgliesh. Scribner, 1938.

Young Cowboy: Arranged from "Big Enough" and "Sun Up." Scribner, 1935. (Includes selections from the two titles issued separately, above.)

MEDIA

Cow Country. (BB).

Cowboys North and South. (BB).

Drifting Cowboy. (BB).

Flint Spears. (BB).

Lone Cowboy. (BB, TB); Paramount Productions, Inc., 1933 (F).

Sand. Twentieth-Century Fox Film Corporation, 1949 (F).

Smoky. (BB, TB); Twentieth-Century Fox Film Corporation, 1933 (F), 1946 (F), 1966 (F); *a.k.a. Education of Smoky* (excerpt). Twentieth-Century Fox Film Corporation, 1946 (F).

Young Cowboy. (BB).

EXHIBITIONS

Macbeth Gallery, 1929. (New York, New York).

COLLECTIONS

Bancroft Library, University of California. (Berkeley, California).

Barrett Minor Authors Collection, Alderman Library, University of Virginia. (Charlottesville, Virginia).

Thomas Gilcrease Institute of American History and Art Library. (Tulsa, Oklahoma).

BACKGROUND READING

Amaral, A. "How Will James Got His Start." *Frontier Times*, June 1966.

Amaral, A. *Will James: The Gilt-edged Cowboy.* Westernlore, 1967.

Current Biography.

Flack, M. "Will James at Home." *Wilson Bulletin*, March 1938.

Hart. *Oxford Companion to American Literature, Fourth Edition.*

Hoofprints, special issue, Autumn 1972.

James. *Dictionary of American Biography, Supplement 3.*

Kirkpatrick. *Twentieth Century Children's Writers.*

Kunitz. *Junior Book of Authors.*

Kunitz. *Junior Book of Authors, Second Edition Revised.*

Kunitz. *Living Authors.*

Kunitz. *Twentieth Century Authors.*

Kunitz. *Twentieth Century Authors, First Supplement.*

Mahony. *Illustrators of Children's Books, 1744-1945.*

Miller. *Newbery Medal Books, 1922-1955.*

Obituary. *New York Times*, September 4, 1942.

Patterson. *On Our Way.*

Rollins, P. "Will James, Author of the Cowboy." *Elementary English*, January 1928.

Ward. *Authors of Books for Young People, Second Edition.*

Young Wings. *Writing Books for Boys and Girls.*

RANDALL JARRELL, 1915-1965
author

AWARDS

Animal Family. Newbery Honor Book, 1966.

(*Snow-White and the Seven Dwarfs.* Caldecott Honor Book, 1973.)

BIBLIOGRAPHY

(ed.) *Anchor Book of Stories.* Doubleday, 1958.

Animal Family. il. Maurice Sendak. Pantheon, 1965.

Bat Is Born. il. John Schoenherr. Doubleday, 1977.

(ed.) *Best Short Stories of Rudyard Kipling*; by Rudyard Kipling. Doubleday, 1961.

Blood for a Stranger. Harcourt, 1942.

Complete Poems. Farrar, 1969.

Death of the Ball Turret Gunner: A Poem. il. Robert A. Parker. David Lewis, 1969.

(ed.) *English in England*; by Rudyard Kipling. Doubleday, 1963.

(tr.) *Faust, Part I.*; by Goethe. Farrar, 1971.

Five American Young Poets; with others. New Directions, 1940.

Fly by Night. il. Maurice Sendak. Farrar, 1976.

(tr.) *Ghetto and the Jews of Rome* (tr. Moses Hadas) *and Lament of the Children* (tr. Randall Jarrell); by Ferdinand A. Gregorovius. Schocken, 1948.

Gingerbread Rabbit. il. Garth Williams. Macmillan, 1964.

(tr.) *Golden Bird and Other Fairy Tales of the Brothers Grimm*; by Jacob and Wilhelm Grimm. il. Sandro Nardini. Macmillan, 1962.

(ed.) *In the Vernacular: The English in India*; by Rudyard Kipling. Doubleday, 1963; *a.k.a. English in India: Short Stories.* Smith, 1964.

Jerome: The Biography of a Poem. il. woodcuts and Albrecht Dürer. Grossman, 1971.

(tr.) *Juniper Tree and Other Tales from Grimm*; by Jacob and Wilhelm Grimm. il. Maurice Sendak. Tr. with Lore Segal. Farrar, 1973; also issued in limited edition.

Little Friend, Little Friend. Dial, 1945.

Losses. Harcourt, 1948.

BIBLIOGRAPHY (cont'd)

Lost World. Macmillan, 1965; *a.k.a. Lost World: With an Appreciation by Robert Lowell*. Eyre, 1966.

Pictures from an Institution: A Comedy. Knopf, 1954.

Poetry and the Age. Knopf, 1953.

Poets, Critics, and Readers. (Charlottesville, Virginia), 1959.

(tr.) *Rabbit Catcher and Other Fairy Tales*; by Ludwig Bechstein. il. Ugo Fontana. Macmillan, 1962.

Sad Heart at the Supermarket: Essays and Fables. Atheneum, 1962.

Selected Poems. Knopf, 1955.

Selected Poems: Including the Woman at the Washington Zoo. Atheneum, 1964.

Seven-League Crutches. Harcourt, 1951.

(ed.) *Six Russian Short Novels: The Overcoat, Lady McBeth of the Mtsensk District, A Lear of the Steppes, Master and Man, The Death of Ivan Ilych, Ward No. 6*. Doubleday, 1963.

(tr.) *Snow-White and the Seven Dwarfs*; by Jacob and Wilhelm Grimm. il. Nancy Burkert. Farrar, 1972.

Third Book of Criticism. Farrar, 1969.

(tr.) *Three Sisters*; by Anton Chekov. Macmillan, 1969.

Uncollected Poems. (Cincinnati, Ohio), 1958.

War, War, War; written with others. University of Iowa, 1968.

Woman at the Washington Zoo: Poems and Translations. Atheneum, 1960.

MEDIA

Animal Family. (BB, TB).

Bat Poet: Randall Jarrell Reading. Caedmon, 19? (R).

Gingerbread Rabbit as *Randall Jarrell Reading The Gingerbread Rabbit*. Caedmon, 1972 (R).

Poems against War: Randall Jarrell Reading. Caedmon, 19? (R).

Poetry and the Age. (C, MT).

Sad Heart at the Supermarket. (BB).

COLLECTIONS

Bancroft Library, University of California. (Berkeley, California).

Berg Collection, New York Public Library. (New York, New York).

Clapp Library, Wellesley College. (Wellesley, Massachusetts).

Collection of American Literature, Beinecke Library, Yale University. (New Haven, Connecticut).

Harvard University Library. (Cambridge, Massachusetts).

Jackson Library, University of North Carolina. (Greensboro, North Carolina).

Manuscript Division, Library of Congress. (Washington, D.C.).

Rare Book Room, Buffalo and Erie County Public Library. (Buffalo, New York).

University of Chicago Library. (Chicago, Illinois).

BACKGROUND READING

Adams, Charles N. *Randall Jarrell: A Bibliography*. University of North Carolina Press, 1958.

Burke. *American Authors and Books, 1640 to the Present Day*.

Commire. *Something about the Author*.

Contemporary Authors.

DeMontreville. *Third Book of Junior Authors*.

Dunn, D. "Affable Misery." *Encounter*, October 1972.

Hart. *Oxford Companion to American Literature, Fourth Edition*.

Kirkpatrick. *Twentieth Century Children's Writers*.

Kunitz. *Twentieth Century Authors, First Supplement*.

Lowell, Robert, ed. *Randall Jarrell, 1914-1965*. Farrar, 1968.

Moore, M. "Randall Jarrell." *Atlantic Monthly*, September 1967.

Obituary. *National Review*, November 2, 1965.

Obituary. *New York Times*, October 15, 1965.

Obituary. *Newsweek*, October 25, 1965.

Obituary. *Publishers Weekly*, October 25, 1965.

Obituary. *Time*, October 22, 1965.

Rosenthal, Marie. *Randall Jarrell*. University of Minnesota Press, 1972.

Shapiro, Karl. *Randall Jarrell: A Lecture with a Bibliography of Jarrell Materials in the Library of Congress*. Library of Congress, 1967.

Ward. *Authors of Books for Young People, Second Edition*.

SUSAN JANE JEFFERS, 1942-
author-illustrator

AWARDS

Three Jovial Huntsmen. Caldecott Honor Book, 1974.

BIBLIOGRAPHY

All the Pretty Horses. Macmillan, 1974.

Buried Moon; by Joseph Jacobs. Bradbury, 1969.

Circus Detectives; by Harriette S. Abel. Ginn, 1971.

Everyhow Remarkable; by Victoria Lincoln. Crowell, 1967.

First of the Penguins; by Mary Q. Steele. Macmillan, 1973.

Shooting of Dan McGrew and The Cremation of Sam McGee; by Robert Service. il. with Rosemary Wells. Scott, 1969.

Spirit of Spring; by Penelope Proddow. Bradbury, 1970.

Three Jovial Huntsmen: A Mother Goose Rhyme; from Mother Goose. Bradbury, 1973.

Understanding Your Body; by Lawrence G. Blockman. Macmillan, 1968.

Why You Look Like You, Whereas I Tend to Look Like Me; by Charlotte Pomerantz. Scott, 1969.

Wild Robin. Dutton, 1976.

BACKGROUND READING

DeMontreville. *Fourth Book of Junior Authors and Illustrators*.

Kingman. *Illustrators of Children's Books, 1967-1976*.

Ward. *Illustrators of Books for Young People, Second Edition*.

ELEANORE MYERS JEWETT, 1890-1967
author

AWARDS

Hidden Treasure of Glaston. Newbery Honor Book, 1947.

BIBLIOGRAPHY

Big John's Secret. il. Frederick T. Chapman. Viking, 1962.

Charlemagne. Row, 1951.

Cobbler's Knob. il. Christine Price. Viking, 1956.

Egyptian Tales of Magic. il. Maurice Day. Little, 1924.

Felicity Finds a Way. Viking, 1952.

Feodora, a Story of Camp Kiloleet. il. John M. Foster. Barse, 1927.

Hidden Treasure of Glaston. il. Frederick T. Chapman. Viking, 1946; *a.k.a. Hidden Treasure of Glaston, with Study Material Prepared by C. M. Irwin*. Macmillan, 1966.

Judith and Jane. il. Charles L. Wrenn. Barse, 1925.

Mystery at Boulder Point. il. Jay H. Barnum. Viking, 1949.

Told on the King's Highway. il. Marie A. Lawson. Viking, 1943.

Which Was Witch? Tales of Ghosts and Magic from Korea. il. Taro Yashima, *pseud.* (Atushi J. Iwamatsu). Viking, 1953.

Wonder Tales from Tibet. il. Maurice Day. Little, 1922.

MEDIA

Big John's Secret. (BB).

Charlemagne. (TB).

Hidden Treasure of Glaston. (BB, TB).

Which Was Witch? (BB, TB).

BACKGROUND READING

Commire. *Something about the Author*.

Contemporary Authors.

Fuller. *More Junior Authors*.

+MARGARET ALISON JOHANSEN, 1896-1959
author

and

+ALICE ALISON LIDE, 1890-1956
author

AWARDS

Ood-Le-Uk. Newbery Honor Book, 1931.

BIBLIOGRAPHY

by Margaret A. Johansen:

From Sea to Shining Sea: How Americans Have Lived. il. Bernard Case. Washburn, 1960.

Hawk of Hawk Clan. il. William O'Brien. Longmans, 1941.

Voyagers West. il. William Ferguson. Washburn, 1959.

BIBLIOGRAPHY (cont'd)

by Alice A. Lide:

Aztec Drums. il. Carlos M. Sanchez. Longmans, 1931.

Inemak: The Little Greenlander. il. W. W. Clarke. Rand, 1927.

Johnny of the 4-H Club. il. C. E. B. Bernard. Little, 1941.

Princess of Yucatan. il. Carlos M. Sanchez. Longmans, 1939.

Tambalo and Other Stories of Far Lands; with Annie H. Alison. Beckley, 1930.

by Margaret A. Johansen and Alice A. Lide:

Dark Possession. Appleton, 1934.

History of St. Paul's Parish. Paragon, 1923.

Lapland Drum. il. Ursula Koering. Abingdon, 1955.

Magic Word for Elin. il. Cheslie D'Andrea. Abingdon, 1958.

Mystery of Mahteb, a Tale of Thirteenth-Century Ethiopia. il. Avery Johnson. Longmans, 1942.

Ood-Le-Uk: The Wanderer. il. Raymond Lufkin. Little, 1930.

Pearls of Fortune. il. Philip Cheney. Little, 1931.

Thord Firetooth. il. Henry C. Pitz. Lothrop, 1937.

Wooden Locket. il. Corydon Bell. Viking, 1953.

BACKGROUND READING

Kenan, R. "Twentieth Century Alabama Writers: The Writing Sisters, Alice Alison Lide and Margaret Alison Johansen." *Alabama Librarian*, January 1962.

Ward. *Authors of Books for Young People, Second Edition*.

Young Wings. *Writing Books for Boys and Girls*.

+GERALD WHITE JOHNSON, 1890-
author

AWARDS

America Is Born. Newbery Honor Book, 1960.

America Moves Forward. Newbery Honor Book, 1961.

BIBLIOGRAPHY

America Grows Up: A History for Peter. il. Leonard E. Fisher. Morrow, 1960.

America Is Born: A History for Peter. il. Leonard E. Fisher. Morrow, 1959.

America Moves Forward: A History for Peter. il. Leonard E. Fisher. Morrow, 1960.

American Heroes and Hero-Worship. Harper, 1943.

American Way: Together with Three Additional Discussions; with David C. Coyle, et al. Harper, 1938.

America's Silver Age: The Statecraft of Clay-Webster-Calhoun. Harper, 1939.

Andrew Jackson: An Epic in Homespun. Minton, 1927.

British Empire: An American View of Its History from 1776 to 1945. il. Leonard E. Fisher. Morrow, 1969.

By Reason of Strength. Minton, 1930; *a.k.a. Strength of Catherine Campbell*. Putnam, 1931.

Cabinet. il. Leonard E. Fisher. Morrow, 1966.

Communism: An American's View. il. Leonard E. Fisher. Morrow, 1964.

Congress. il. Leonard E. Fisher. Morrow, 1963.

Cosmopolitan Villager: A Birthday Souvenir, June 17, 1937. (Chapel Hill, North Carolina?), 1937.

Ethical Emphasis of Modern Historians. New York Society for Ethical Culture, 1955.

First Captain: The Story of John Paul Jones. Coward, 1947.

Franklin D. Roosevelt: Portrait of a Great Man. il. Leonard E. Fisher. Morrow, 1967.

Green Mount Cemetery One Hundreth Anniversary, 1838, 1938. Green Mount Cemetery, 1938.

Guilford's Worst Bad Egg Gets a Chance Instead of a Sentence. n. p., 1920.

Hod-Carrier: Notes on a Laborer of an Unfinished Cathedral. Morrow, 1964.

Honorable Titan: A Biographical Study of Adolph S. Ochs. Harper, 1946.

Imperial Republic: Speculation on the Future, If Any, of the Third U.S.A. Liveright, 1972.

Incredible Tale: The Odyssey of the Average American in the Last-Half Century. Harper, 1950.

Lectures Delivered at East Carolina College, November 11 and 12, 1958. East Carolina College, 1959 (?).

Liberal's Progress: Edward A. Filene, Shopkeeper to Social Statesman. Coward, 1948.

Lines Are Drawn: American Life since the First World War as Reflected in the Pulitzer-Prize Cartoons. Lippincott, 1958.

Little Night-Music: Discoveries in the Exploitation of an Art. il. Richard Q. Yardley. Harper, 1937.

Lunatic Fringe. Lippincott, 1957.

Making of a Southern Industrialist: A Biographical Study of Simpson Bobo Tanner. University of North Carolina, 1932.

Man Who Feels Left Behind. Morrow, 1961.

Maryland Act of Religious Toleration: An Interpretation. Committee for the 300th Anniversary of the Maryland Act of Toleration, 1949.

Mount Vernon, the Story of a Shrine: An Account of the Rescue and Rehabilitation of Washington's Home by the Mount Vernon Ladies' Association, Together with Pertinent Extracts from the Diaries and Letters of George Washington Concerning the Development of Mount Vernon, Selected and Annotated by Charles C. Wall. Random, 1953.

Number Thirty-six: A Novel. Minton, 1933.

Our English Heritage. Lippincott, 1949.

Patterns for Liberty: The Story of Old Philadelphia. McGraw, 1952.

Peril and Promise: An Inquiry into Freedom of the Press. Harper, 1958.

Personality in Journalism. University of Minnesota, 1958.

Politics, Party Competition, and the County Chairman in West Virginia: A Descriptive and Comparative Analysis of Political Party Chairmen and State Political Party Status. University of Tennessee, 1970.

Presidency. il. Leonard E. Fisher. Morrow, 1962.

Proud Tower in the Town: An Address Delivered before the Edgar Allan Poe Society of Baltimore. Furst, 1937.

Randolph of Roanoke: A Political Fantastic. Minton, 1929.

Republic's Second Chance? n. p., 1961.

Roosevelt: Dictator or Democrat? Harper, 1941; a.k.a. *Roosevelt: An American Study*. Hamilton, 1942.

Secession of the Southern States: Great Occasions. Putnam, 1933.

Senecute: A Paper Presented to the 14th Club, December 8th, 1960. 14th Street Hamilton Club, 1961.

Speech before the Democratic Congressional Wives Workshop, March 19, 1954. Democratic National Committee, 1954.

Story of Man's Work; with William R. Hayward. il. Philip Kappel. Minton, 1925; a.k.a. *Evolution of Labor: Past, Present and Future*. Duckworth, 1929.

Sunpapers of Baltimore; with Frank R. Kent, et al. Knopf, 1937.

Supreme Court. il. Leonard Everett Fisher. Morrow, 1962.

This American People. Harper, 1951.

Undefeated. Minton, 1927.

Wasted Land. University of North Carolina, 1937.

What Is News? A Tentative Outline. Knopf, 1926.

What Is the Law? (New York), 1930.

Woodrow Wilson: The Unforgettable Figure Who Has Returned to Haunt Us; with the editors of *Look Magazine*. Harper, 1944.

MEDIA

America Grows Up. (BB, TB).

America Is Born. (BB, TB).

America Moves Forward. (BB, TB).

Andrew Jackson. (BB).

British Empire. (TB).

Cabinet. (BB).

Communism. (BB).

Congress. (BB, TB).

Hod-Carrier. (BB).

Little Night-Music. (BB, TB).

Lunatic Fringe. (BB, TB).

Man Who Feels Left Behind. (TB).

Peril and Promise. (BB).

Presidency. (BB, TB).

Supreme Court. (BB, TB).

This American People. (BB).

COLLECTIONS

Barrett Minor Authors Collection, University of Virginia Library. (Charlottesville, Virginia).

Brown Collection, Arents Research Library, Syracuse University. (Syracuse, New York).

Manuscript Division, Library of Congress. (Washington, D.C.).

University of Iowa Library. (Iowa City, Iowa).

BACKGROUND READING

Burke. *American Authors and Books, 1640 to the Present Day*.

DeMontreville. *Third Book of Junior Authors*.

Hart. *Oxford Companion to American Literature, Fourth Edition*.

Hutchens, J. "On an Author." *New York Herald Tribune Book Review*, September 4, 1949.

BACKGROUND READING (cont'd)

Kunitz. *Twentieth Century Authors, First Supplement.*

Ward. *Authors of Books for Young People, Second Edition.*

+ELIZABETH ORTON JONES, 1910-
author-illustrator

AWARDS

Prayer for a Child. Caldecott Medal Book, 1945.

Small Rain. Caldecott Honor Book, 1944.

BIBLIOGRAPHY

Big Susan. Macmillan, 1947.

Brownies—Hush!; by Gladys Adshead. Oxford, 1938.

David; from the *Bible.* Macmillan, 1937.

How Far Is It to Bethlehem? Horn Book, 1955.

Little Child: The Christmas Miracle Told in Bible Verse; selected by Jessie O. Jones. Viking, 1946.

Little Red Riding Hood. Simon, 1948.

Lullaby for Eggs; by Elizabeth Bridgman. Macmillan, 1955.

Maminka's Children. Macmillan, 1940.

Mason, New Hampshire, 1768-1968. (Mason, New Hampshire?), 1969 (?).

Minnie the Mermaid; by Thomas O. Jones. Oxford, 1939.

Peddler's Clock; by Mabel L. Hunt. Grosset, 1943.

Prayer for a Child; by Rachel Field. Macmillan, 1944.

Prayer for Little Things; by Eleanor Farjeon. Houghton, 1945.

Ragman of Paris and His Ragamuffins. Oxford, 1937.

Scarlet Oak; by Cornelia Meigs. Macmillan, 1938.

Secrets; by Jessie O. Jones. Viking, 1945.

Small Rain: Verses from the Bible; selected by Jessie O. Jones. Viking, 1943.

Song of the Sun: From The Canticle of the Sun; by Francis of Assisi. Macmillan, 1952.

This Is the Way: Prayer and Precepts from World Religions; by Jessie O. Jones. Viking, 1951.

To Church We Go; by Cornelia Meigs. Follett, 1956.

Told under the Magic Umbrella: Modern Fanciful Stories for Young Children; by The Association for Childhood Education. Macmillan, 1939.

Twig. Macmillan, 1942.

What Miranda Knew; by Gladys Adshead. Oxford, 1938.

MEDIA

Big Susan. (BB).

Little Red Riding Hood. (BB).

Twig. (BB).

EXHIBITIONS

O'Brien Gallery, 19?. (Chicago, Illinois).

Smithsonian Institution, 19?. (Washington, D.C.).

COLLECTIONS

Kerlan Collection, University of Minnesota. (Minneapolis, Minnesota).

University of Oregon Library. (Eugene, Oregon).

BACKGROUND READING

Contemporary Authors.

Current Biography.

Kunitz. *Junior Book of Authors, Second Edition Revised.*

Mahony. *Illustrators of Children's Books, 1744-1945.*

Miller. *Caldecott Medal Books, 1938-1957.*

Miller. *Illustrators of Children's Books, 1946-1956.*

Ward. *Authors of Books for Young People, Second Edition.*

Ward. *Illustrators of Books for Young People, Second Edition.*

+IDWAL JONES, 1890-1964
author

AWARDS

Whistler's Van. Newbery Honor Book, 1937.

BIBLIOGRAPHY

Ark of Empire: San Francisco's Montgomery Block. il. Albert J. Camille. Doubleday, 1951.

Biscailuz: Sheriff of the New West; with Lindley Bynum. Morrow, 1950.

Black Bayou. Duell, 1941.

Chef's Holiday. il. Roger Duvoisin. Longmans, 1952.

China Boy, and Other Stories. Primavera, 1936.

High Bonnet. Prentice, 1945.

Splendid Shilling: A Novel. Doubleday, 1926.

Steel Chips. Knopf, 1929.

Vermilion. Prentice, 1947.

Vines in the Sun: A Journey through the California Vineyards. il. Albert J. Camille. Morrow, 1949.

Vineyard. Duell, 1942.

Whistler's Van. il. Zhenya Gay. Viking, 1936.

MEDIA

Vermilion. (BB).

COLLECTIONS

Bancroft Library, University of California. (Berkeley, California).

Special Collections, University Research Library, University of California. (Los Angeles, California).

BACKGROUND READING

Current Biography.

Obituary. *New York Times.* November 17, 1964.

Obituary. *Publishers Weekly*, November 30, 1964.

Warfel. *American Novelists of Today.*

Young Wings. *Writing Books for Boys and Girls.*

CLARA INGRAM JUDSON, 1879-1960
author

AWARDS

Abraham Lincoln: Friend of the People. Newbery Honor Book, 1951.

Mr. Justice Holmes. Newbery Honor Book, 1957.

Theodore Roosevelt. Newbery Honor Book, 1954.

BIBLIOGRAPHY

Abraham Lincoln. il. Polly Jackson. Follett, 1961.

Abraham Lincoln: Friend of People. il. Robert Frankenberg and photographs. Wilcox, 1950.

Alice Ann. il. John M. Foster. Barse, 1928.

Andrew Carnegie. il. Steele Savage. Follett, 1964.

Andrew Jackson: Frontier Statesman. il. Lorence Bjorklund. Follett, 1954.

Bed Time Tales. Adams Newspaper Service, n. d.

Benjamin Franklin. il. Robert Frankenberg. Follett, 1957.

Billy Robin and His Neighbors. Rand, 1917.

Boat Builder: The Story of Robert Fulton. il. Armstrong Sperry. Scribner, 1940.

Business Girl's Budget Book. American Bond and Mortgage, 1921.

Business Man's Budget Book. American Bond and Mortgage, 1923.

Camp at Gravel Point. Houghton, 1921.

Child Life Cook Book. Rand, 1926.

Christopher Columbus. il. Polly Jackson and Stan Williamson. Follett, 1960.

City Neighbor: The Story of Jane Addams. il. Ralph Ray. Scribner, 1951.

Cooking without Mother's Help: A Story Cook Book for Beginners. Nourse, 1918.

Donald McKay: Designer of Clipper Ships. il. John O. Cosgrave, II. Scribner, 1943.

Flower Fairies. il. Maginel W. Enright. Rand, 1915.

Foxy Squirrel. Rand, 1917.

Foxy Squirrel in the Garden. il. Frances Breem. Rand, 1921.

Garden Adventures in Winter. il. Frances Breem. Rand, 1923.

Garden Adventures of Tommy Tittlemouse. il. Frances Breem. Rand, 1922.

George Washington. il. Bob Patterson. Follett, 1961.

George Washington: Leader of the People. il. Robert Frankenberg. Wilcox, 1951.

Good-Night Stories. il. Clara P. Wilson. McClurg, 1916.

Green Ginger Jar: A Chinatown Mystery. il. Paul Brown. Houghton, 1949.

Household Budget Book. American Bond and Mortgage, 1922.

James Jerome Hill. il. Keith Ward. Row, 1950.

Jerry and Jean, Detectives. il. Dorothy L. Gregory. Rand, 1923.

John Jacob Astor. il. Milo Winter. Row, 1950.

Junior Cook Book. Barse, 1920.

Lost Violin: They Came from Bohemia. il. Margaret Bradfield. Houghton, 1947.

Mary Jane at School. il. Thelma Gooch. Barse, 1923.

Mary Jane down South. il. Frances White. Barse, 1919.

Mary Jane, Her Book. il. Frances White. Barse, 1918.

Mary Jane, Her Visit: Sequel to Mary Jane, Her Book. il. Frances White. Barse, 1918.

Mary Jane in Canada. il. Charles L. Wrenn. Barse, 1924.

Mary Jane in England. il. Charles L. Wrenn. Barse, 1928.

Mary Jane in France. il. Charles L. Wrenn. Barse, 1930.

Mary Jane in Italy. il. Marie Schubert. Grosset, 1933.

Mary Jane in New England. il. Thelma Gooch (?). Barse, 1921.

Mary Jane in Scotland. il. Charles L. Wrenn. Barse, 1929.

BIBLIOGRAPHY (cont'd)

Mary Jane in Spain. il. Marie Schubert. Grosset, 1937.

Mary Jane in Switzerland. il. Charles L. Wrenn (?). Barse, 1931.

Mary Jane's City Home. il. Thelma Gooch. Barse, 1920.

Mary Jane's Country Home. il. Thelma Gooch. Barse, 1922.

Mary Jane's Friends in Holland. il. Genevieve Foster. Grosset, 1929.

Mary Jane's Kindergarten: Sequel to Mary Jane, Her Visit. il. Frances White. Barse, 1918.

Mary Jane's Summer Fun. il. Charles L. Wrenn. Barse, 1925.

Mary Jane's Vacation. il. Charles L. Wrenn. Barse, 1927.

Mary Jane's Winter Sports. il. Charles L. Wrenn (?). Barse, 1926.

Mighty Soo: Five Hundred Years at Sault Ste. Marie. il. Robert Frankenberg. Follett, 1955.

Mr. Justice Holmes. il. Robert Todd. Follett, 1956.

People Who Come to Our House. il. Marjorie Peters. Rand, 1940.

People Who Work in the Country and in the City. il. Keith Ward. Rand, 1943.

People Who Work Near Our House. il. Keith Ward. Rand, 1942.

Picture Story and Biography of Admiral Christopher Columbus. il. Witold T. Mars. Follett, 1965.

Pioneer Girl: The Early Life of Frances Willard. il. Genevieve Foster. Rand, 1939.

Play Days. photographs by Arthur Daley. Grosset, 1937.

Railway Engineer: The Story of George Stephenson. il. Eric Simon. Scribner, 1941.

Reaper Man: The Story of Cyrus Hall. il. Paul Brown. Houghton, 1948.

St. Lawrence Seaway. il. Lorence F. Bjorklund and photographs. Follett, 1956; revised, 1964.

Sewing without Mother's Help: A Story Sewing Book for Beginners. Nourse, 1921.

Simon Bolivar. il. Henry C. Pitz. Row, 1953.

Soldier Doctor: The Story of William Gorgas. il. Robert Doremus. Scribner, 1942.

Summer Time. il. Polly Jackson. Broadman, 1948.

Sun Yat-Sen. il. Alexander Key. Row, 1953.

Theodore Roosevelt: Fighting Patriot. il. Lorence F. Bjorklund. Wilcox, 1953.

They Came from Dalmatia: Petrar's Treasure. il. Ursula Koering. Houghton, 1945; *a.k.a. Petrar's Treasure, They Came from Dalmatia*. Follett, 1958.

They Came from France. il. Lois Lenski. Houghton, 1943; *a.k.a. Pierre's Lucky Pouch: They Came From France*. Follett, 1957.

They Came from Ireland: Michael's Victory. il. Elmer Wexler. Houghton, 1946.

They Came from Scotland. il. Mary A. Reardon. Houghton, 1944; *a.k.a. Bruce Carries the Flag: They Came from Scotland*. Follett, 1957.

They Came from Sweden. il. Edward C. Caswell. Houghton, 1942; *a.k.a. Sod-House Winter: They Came from Sweden*. Follett, 1957.

Thomas Jefferson: Champion of the People. il. Robert Frankenberg. Wilcox, 1952.

Tommy Tittlemouse. Rand, 1918.

Virginia Lee. il. Charles L. Wrenn. Barse, 1926; *a.k.a. Virginia Lee's Bicycle Club*. Grosset, 1939.

What I Can Do with My Hands Series. Nourse, 1920.

Yankee Clippers: The Story of Donald McKay. il. Robert Frankenberg and Yukio Tashiro. Follett, 1965.

MEDIA

Abraham Lincoln, Friend of the People. (BB).

Andrew Jackson. (BB, TB).

Benjamin Franklin. (TB).

City Neighbor. (BB).

George Washington: Leader of the People. (BB).

Green Ginger Jar. (BB).

James Jerome Hill. (BB).

John Jacob Astor. (BB).

Lost Violin. Mercury Sound Books, 1957 (R).

Mighty Soo. (BB).

Mr. Justice Holmes. (BB, TB).

Simon Bolivar. (BB).

Soldier Doctor. (BB).

Sun Yat-Sen. (TB).

Theodore Roosevelt. (TB).

Thomas Jefferson. (BB, TB).

Yankee Clipper. (BB).

COLLECTIONS

Kerlan Collection, University of Minnesota. (Minneapolis, Minnesota).

Special Collections, University Research Library,
University of California. (Los Angeles,
California).

BACKGROUND READING

Banta. *Indiana Authors and Their Books, 1816-1916*.

Burke. *American Authors and Books, 1640 to the Present Day*.

Current Biography.

Hoffman. *Authors and Illustrators of Children's Books*.

Judson, C. "George Bought That Lantern." *ALA Bulletin*, September 1960.

Judson, C. "My Purpose in Writing." *Illinois Library Association Record*, September 1948.

Judson, C. "Writing Juveniles Isn't All Fun." *Library Journal*, August 1947.

Kunitz. *Junior Book of Authors, Second Edition Revised*.

McGuire, A. "Clara Ingram Judson." *Horn Book*, October 1960.

Obituary. *New York Times*, May 25, 1960.

Obituary. *Publishers Weekly*, June 13, 1960.

Rollins, C. "Clara Ingram Judson: Interpreter of America." *Elementary English*, December 1953.

Ward. *Authors of Books for Young People, Second Edition*.

Young Wings. *Writing Books for Boys and Girls*.

NICHOLAS KALASHNIKOFF, 1888-1961
author

AWARDS

Defender. Newbery Honor Book, 1952.

BIBLIOGRAPHY

Defender. il. Claire Louden and George Louden, Jr. Scribner, 1951; also il. Feodor Rojankovsky. Oxford, 1962.

Jumper: The Life of a Siberian Horse. il. Edward Shenton. Scribner, 1944; also il. Lionel Edwards. Lunn, 1948; *a.k.a. Jumper*. il. Victor G. Ambrus. Oxford, 1962; also il. Feodor Rojankovsky, 1963.

My Friend Yakub. il. Feodor Rojankovsky. Scribner, 1953.

They That Take Sword. Harper, 1939.

Toyon: A Dog of the North and His People. il. Arthur Markovia. Harper, 1950.

MEDIA

Defender. (BB, TB).

Jumper. (BB).

My Friend Yakub. (TB).

Toyon. (TB, MT).

BACKGROUND READING

Burke. *American Authors and Books, 1640 to the Present Day*.

Contemporary Authors.

Fuller. *More Junior Authors*.

Obituary. *New York Times*, August 8, 1961.

Obituary. *Publishers Weekly*, August 28, 1961.

FRANCIS KALNAY, 1899-
author

AWARDS

Chúcaro. Newbery Honor Book, 1959.

BIBLIOGRAPHY

Chúcaro, Wild Pony of the Pampa. il. Julian deMiskey. Harcourt, 1958.

Foglalj Helyet Péter. il. Candell Victor. Europa, 1936.

Handbook of Seasickness. Transatlantic, 1937.

It Happened in Chichipica. il. Charles Robinson. Harcourt, 1971.

New American: A Handbook of Necessary Information for Aliens, Rufugees and New Citizens; with Richard Collins. Greenberg, 1941.

Richest Boy in the World. il. Witold T. Mars. Harcourt, 1959.

MEDIA

Chúcaro. (TB); Miller-Brody Productions, 1976 (FSS).

Richest Boy in the World. (BB).

BACKGROUND READING

Commire. *Something about the Author*.

Contemporary Authors;

Current Biography.

Ward. *Authors of Books for Young People, Second Edition*.

EZRA JACK KEATS, 1916-
author-illustrator

AWARDS

Goggles. Caldecott Honor Book, 1970.

Snowy Day. Caldecott Medal Book, 1963.

BIBLIOGRAPHY

And Long Remember: Some Great Aericans Who Have Helped Me; by Dorothy C. Fisher. McGraw, 1959.

Apple Orchard; by Irmengarde Eberle. Walck, 1962.

Apt. 3. Macmillan, 1971.

Brave Riders; by Glenn Balch. Crowell, 1959.

Change of Climate: A More or Less Aimless and Amiable Account of Various Journeys and Encounters Abroad; by Jay Williams. Random, 1956.

Chester; by Eleanor Clymer. Dodd, 1954.

Chinese Knew; by Tillie S. Pine and Joseph Levine. McGraw, 1958.

Danny Dunn and the Anti-Gravity Paint; by Jay Williams and Raymond Abrashkin. McGraw, 1956.

Danny Dunn and the Homework Machine; by Jay Williams and Raymond Abrashkin. McGraw, 1958.

Danny Dunn and the Weather Machine; by Jay William Williams and Raymond Abrashkin. McGraw, 1959.

Danny Dunn on a Desert Island; by Jay Williams and Raymond Abrashkin. McGraw, 1957.

Dreams. Macmillan, 1974.

Egyptians Knew; by Tillie S. Pine and Joseph Levine. McGraw, 1962.

Eskimos Knew; by Tillie S. Pine and Joseph Levine. McGraw, 1962.

(ed.) *God Is in the Mountain*. Holt, 1966.

Goggles. Macmillan, 1969.

Grasses; by Irmengarde Eberle. Walck, 1960.

Hawaii: A Book to Begin On; by Juliet Swenson. Holt, 1963.

Hi, Cat! Macmillan, 1970.

In a Spring Garden; edited by Richard Lewis. Dial, 1965.

In the Night; by Paul Showers. Crowell, 1961.

In the Park: An Excursion in Four Languages; by Esther Hautzig. Macmillan, 1968.

Indians Knew; by Tillie S. Pine and Joseph Levine. McGraw, 1957.

Jennie's Hat. Harper, 1966.

John Henry: An American Legend. Pantheon, 1965.

Jubilant for Sure; by Elizabeth C. Lansing. Crowell, 1954.

King's Fountain; by Lloyd Alexander. Dutton, 1971.

Kitten for a Day. Watts, 1974.

Letter to Amy. Holt, 1968.

Little Drummer Boy; words and music by Katherine Davis, et al. Macmillan, 1968.

Louie. Greenwillow, 1975.

My Dog Is Lost!; with Pat Cherr. Crowell, 1960.

Mystery on the Isle of Skye; by Phyllis Whitney. Westminster, 1955.

Nature Detective; by Millicent Selsam. Scott, 1958; a.k.a. *How to Be a Nature Detective*. Harper, 1966.

Naughty Boy: A Poem; by John Keats. Viking, 1965.

(comp.) *Night*; photographs by Beverly Hall. Atheneum, 1969.

Nihal; by Eleanor A. Murphey. Crowell, 1960.

Our Rice Village in Cambodia; by Ruth Tooze. Viking, 1963.

(ed.) *Over in the Meadow*. Four Winds, 1971.

Peg-Legged Pirate of Sulu; by Cora Cheney. Knopf, 1960.

Penny Tunes and Princesses; by Myron Levoy. Harper, 1972.

Pet Show! Macmillan, 1972.

Peterkin Papers; by Lucretia Hale. Doubleday, 1963.

Peter's Chair. Harper, 1967.

Pilgrims Knew; by Tillie S. Pine and Joseph Levine. McGraw, 1957.

Psst! Doggie—. Watts, 1973.

Rice Bowl Pet; by Patricia M. Martin. Crowell, 1962.

Skates! Watts, 1973.

Snowy Day. Viking, 1962.

Speedy Digs Downside Up; by Maxine Kumin. Putnam, 1964.

Sure Thing for Shep; by Elizabeth Lansing. Coward, 1956.

Three Young Kings; by George Albee. Watts, 1956.

Tía María's Garden; by Ann N. Clark. Viking, 1963.

Tournament of the Lions; by Jay Williams. Walck, 1960.

Two Tickets to Freedom: The True Story of Ellen and William Craft, Fugitive Slaves; by Florence Freedman. Simon, 1971.

UNICEF Christmas cards. UNICEF, 1966.

Wee Joseph; by William MacKellar. McGraw, 1957.

What Good Is a Tail?; by Solveig P. Russell. Bobbs, 1962.

Whistle for Willie. Viking, 1964.

Wonder Tales of Dogs and Cats; by Frances Carpenter. Doubleday, 1955.

Zoo, Where Are You?; by Ann McGovern. Harper, 1964.

MEDIA

Apt. 3. (BB); Weston Woods Studios, 1977 (F, FSS); also in Weston Woods Studios Set No. 43, 1977 (FSS).

God Is in the Mountain. (BB).

Goggles. (BB, TB); Weston Woods Studios, 1974 (F, FSS).

Hi, Cat! Association-Sterling/Macmillan Films, 1974 (FS).

In a Spring Garden. Weston Woods Studios, 1967 (F, FSS).

John Henry. Guidance Associates, 1967 (FSS).

Letter to Amy. (BB); Weston Woods Studios, 1970 (F, FSS).

Little Drummer Boy. (BB). Weston Woods Studios, 1970 (F), 1971 (FSS).

My Dog Is Lost. (BB); Bank Street College of Education, 1967 (F).

Over in the Meadow. (TB).

Pet Show! (TB); Association-Sterling Films/Macmillan Films, 1975 (FS).

Peter's Chair. Weston Woods Studios, 1967 (FSS), 1971 (F); also in Weston Woods Studios Set No. 25, 1969 (FSS).

Snowy Day. Viking Press, 1974 (C); Weston Woods Studios, 1964 (F), 1965 (FSS); also in Weston Woods Studios Set No. 15, 1965 (FSS); also in *Lively Art of Picture Books*. Weston Woods Studios, 1964 (F).

Tía María's Garden. (BB, TB).

Whistle for Willie. (TB); Bank Street College of Education, 1967 (F); Viking Press, 1975 (C); Weston Woods Studios, 1965 (F, FSS); also in Weston Woods Studios Set No. 16, 1965 (FSS).

EXHIBITIONS

Associated American Artists Gallery, 1950, 1954. (New York, New York).

COLLECTIONS

deGrummond Collection, University of Southern Mississippi. (Hattiesburg, Mississippi).

Free Library of Philadelphia. (Philadelphia, Pennsylvania).

Gary Public Library. (Gary, Indiana).

Gutman Library, Harvard University. (Cambridge, Massachusetts).

Iowa City Public Library. (Iowa City, Iowa).

Kerlan Collection, University of Minnesota. (Minneapolis, Minnesota).

BACKGROUND READING

Bair. *Biography News*.

Commire. *Something about the Author*.

Contemporary Authors.

Ezra Jack Keats. Profiles in Literature, 1970 (VT); Weston Woods Studios, 1971 (F).

Freedman, F. B. "Ezra Jack Keats, Author and Illustrator." *Elementary English*, January 1969.

Fuller. *More Junior Authors*.

Hoffman. *Authors and Illustrators of Children's Books*.

Hopkins. *Books Are by People*.

Keats, E. "Artist at Work: Collage." *Horn Book*, June 1964.

Keats, E. "Dear Mr. Keats." *Horn Book*, June 1972.

Kingman. *Illustrators of Children's Books, 1957-1966*.

Kingman. *Illustrators of Children's Books, 1967-1976*.

Kingman. *Newbery and Caldecott Medal Books, 1956-1965*.

Kirkpatrick. *Twentieth Century Children's Writers*.

Mercier, J. "Ezra Jack Keats." *Publishers Weekly*, July 16, 1973.

Miller. *Illustrators of Children's Books, 1946-1956*.

Mykoruk. *Authors in the News*.

Perry, E. "Gentle World of Jack Keats." *American Artist*, September 1971.

Ward. *Authors of Books for Young People, Second Edition*.

Ward. *Illustrators of Books for Young People, Second Edition*.

HAROLD VERNE KEITH, 1903-
author

AWARDS

Rifles for Watie. Newbery Medal Book, 1958.

BIBLIOGRAPHY

Amos: A Play in Two Acts; written by students, based upon a plot by Harold Keith. Woman's Press, 1926.

BIBLIOGRAPHY (cont'd)

Bluejay Borders. il. Harold Berson. Crowell, 1972.

Boy's Life of Will Rogers. il. Karl S. Woerner. Crowell, 1937.

Brief Garland. Crowell, 1971.

Komantica. Crowell, 1965; il. Charles Keeping. Oxford, 1966.

Obstinate Land. Crowell, 1977.

Oklahoma Kickoff: An Informal History of the First Twenty-five Years of Football at the University of Oklahoma, and of the Amusing Hardships That Attended Its Pioneering. (Privately printed), 1948.

Pair of Captains. il. Mabel J. Woodbury. Crowell, 1951.

Rifles for Watie. Crowell, 1957.

Runt of Rodgers School. Lippincott, 1957.

Shotgun Shaw: A Baseball Story. il. Mabel J. Woodbury. Crowell, 1949.

Sports and Games. Crowell, 1941; revised, 1953; revised, 1960; revised, 1969.

Susy's Scoundrel. il. John Schoenherr. Crowell, 1974.

MEDIA

Komantica. (TB).

Rifles for Watie. (BB, CB, TB); Miller-Brody Productions, 1972 (FSS); Newbery Award Records, 1971 (C, R).

COLLECTIONS

deGrummond Collection, University of Southern Mississippi. (Hattiesburg, Mississippi).

Northwestern State College Library. (Alva, Oklahoma).

University of Oklahoma Library. (Norman, Oklahoma).

BACKGROUND READING

Burke. *American Authors and Books, 1640 to the Present Day*.

Commire. *Something about the Author*.

Contemporary Authors.

Current Biography.

Fuller. *More Junior Authors*.

Hopkins. *More Books by More People*.

Kingman. *Newbery and Caldecott Medal Books, 1956-1965*.

Kirkpatrick. *Twentieth Century Children's Writers*.

Painter, H. " 'Rifles for Watie': A Novel of the Civil War." *Elementary English*, May 1961.

Ward. *Authors of Books for Young People, Second Edition*.

Young Wings. *Writing Books for Boys and Girls*.

ERIC PHILBROOK KELLY, 1884-1960
author

AWARDS

Trumpeter of Krakow. Newbery Medal Book, 1929.

BIBLIOGRAPHY

Amazing Journey of David Ingram: Being the Story of Three White Men, David Ingram, Richard Twide, and Richard Browne, Who Crossed, in 1568-69, Those Lands of the New World Which Later Became the United States of America. Lippincott, 1949.

At the Sign of the Golden Compass: A Tale of the Printing House of Christopher Plantin in Antwerp, 1576. il. Raymond Lufkin. Macmillan, 1938.

Blacksmith of Vilno: A Tale of Poland in the Year 1832. il. Angela Pruszynska. Macmillan, 1930.

Christmas Nightingale: Three Christmas Stories from Poland. il. Marguerite de Angeli. Macmillan, 1932; variant as *Christmas Nightingale, Adapted from Eric P. Kelly's Book of That Name*; by Phyllis Groff. Children's Theater, 1935.

From Star to Star: A Story of Krakow in 1493. il. Manning DeV. Lee. Lippincott, 1943.

Girl Who Would Be Queen: The Story and the Diary of the Young Countess Krasinska; with Clara Hoffmanowa (*i.e.* Klementyna Hofmanowa). il. Vera Bock. McClurg, 1939.

Golden Star of Halich: A Tale of the Red Land in 1362. il. Angela Pruszynska. Macmillan, 1931.

Hand in the Picture: A Story of Poland. il. Irena Lorentowicz. Lippincott, 1947.

Hope of All the Poles in the World. Polish Catholic Union, 1941.

In Clean Hay: A Christmas Story. Aldus, 1940; il. Maud and Miska Petersham. Macmillan, 1953.

Land of the Polish People. Stokes, 1943; revised, Lippincott, 1952; *a.k.a. Land and People of Poland*. photographs by Dragŏs D. Kostich, 1964.

On Staked Plain: El Llano Estacado. il. Harvé Stein. Macmillan, 1940.

Polish Legends and Tales. Polish Publication Society, 1971.

Three Sides of Agiochook: A Tale of the New England Frontier in 1775. il. LeRoy Appleton. Macmillan, 1935.

Treasure Mountain. il. Raymond Lufkin. Macmillan, 1937.

Trumpeter of Krakow: A Tale of the Fifteenth Century. il. Angela Pruszynska. Macmillan, 1928; also il. Janina Domanska. Foreword by Louise Bechtel, 1966; Foreword by Naomi Lewis. Chatto, 1968.

MEDIA

Christmas Nightingale. (BB).

In Clean Hay. Intercontinental Audeo-Video Company, *ca*.1947 (R); Mercury Sound Books, 1957 (R).

Trumpeter of Krakow. (TB); Miller-Brody Productions, 1975 (FSS); Newbery Award Records, 1969 (R).

COLLECTIONS

Baker Library, Dartmouth College. (Hanover, New Hampshire).

BACKGROUND READING

Burke. *American Authors and Books, 1640 to the Present Day*.

Commire. *Yesterday's Authors of Books for Children*.

Hunt, M. "Eric P. Kelly: Interpreter of Poland." *Elementary English*, May 1940.

Kirkpatrick. *Twentieth Century Children's Writers*.

Kunitz. *Junior Book of Authors*.

Kunitz. *Junior Book of Authors, Second Edition Revised*.

Kunitz. *Living Authors*.

Miller. *Newbery Medal Books, 1922-1955*.

Obituary. *New York Times*, April 4, 1960.

Obituary. *Publishers Weekly*, January 8, 1960.

Obituary. *Wilson Library Bulletin*, March 1960.

Ward. *Authors of Books for Young People, Second Edition*.

Young Wings. *Writing Books for Boys and Girls*.

CAROL SEEGER KENDALL, 1917-
author

AWARDS

Gammage Cup. Newbery Honor Book, 1960.

BIBLIOGRAPHY

Baby-Snatcher. Lane, 1952.

Big Splash. il. Lilian Obligado. Viking, 1960.

Black Seven. Harper, 1946.

Gammage Cup. il. Erik Blegvad. Harcourt, 1959; *a.k.a. Minnipins*. Dent, 1960.

Other Side of the Tunnel. il. Lillian Buchanan. Abelard, 1956.

Whisper of Glocken. il. Imero Gobbato. Harcourt, 1965; Bodley Head, 1965. (British edition has a different first chapter than the American edition.)

MEDIA

Gammage Cup. (BB, TB); Miller-Brody Productions, 1976 (FSS).

Other Side of the Tunnel. (BB).

COLLECTIONS

Ohio State University Library. (Athens, Ohio).

BACKGROUND READING

Commire. *Something about the Author*.

Contemporary Authors.

Coyle. *Ohio Authors and Their Books*.

DeMontreville. *Third Book of Junior Authors*.

Foremost Women in Communications.

Kirkpatrick. *Twentieth Century Children's Writers*.

Ward. *Authors of Books for Young People, Second Edition*.

JULIET APPLEBY KEPES, 1919-
author-illustrator

AWARDS

Five Little Monkeys. Caldecott Honor Book, 1953.

BIBLIOGRAPHY

Beasts from a Brush: Imaginative Animal Drawings with Brief Verses. Pantheon, 1955.

Birds. Walker, 1968.

Boy Blue's Book of Beasts; by William J. Smith. Little, 1957.

Five Little Monkey Business. Houghton, 1965.

Five Little Monkeys. Houghton, 1952.

Frogs Merry. Pantheon, 1961.

BIBLIOGRAPHY (cont'd)

Give a Guess; by Mary B. Miller. Pantheon, 1957.

Lady Bird, Quickly. Little, 1967.

Laughing Time; by William J. Smith. Little, 1955.

Puptents and Pebbles: A Nonsense ABC; by William J. Smith. Little, 1959.

Run Little Monkeys! Run, Run, Run! Pantheon, 1974.

Seed That Peacock Planted. Little, 1967.

Seven Remarkable Bears; by Emilie McLeod. Houghton, 1954.

This Way Delight: A Book of Poetry for the Young; edited by Herbert Read. Pantheon, 1956.

Two Little Birds and Thee. Houghton, 1960.

MEDIA

Frogs Merry. Random House, Inc., 1961 (C).

COLLECTIONS

Harvard University. (Cambridge, Massachusetts).

Kerlan Collection, University of Minnesota. (Minneapolis, Minnesota).

BACKGROUND READING

Bader. *American Picturebooks from Noah's Art to The Beast Within*.

Commire. *Something about the Author*.

Contemporary Authors.

DeMontreville. *Third Book of Junior Authors*.

"Interiors' Cover Artist." *Interior and Industrial Design*, May 1949.

"Juliet Kepes." *Interior and Industrial Design*, October 1948.

Kingman. *Illustrators of Children's Books, 1957-1966*.

Kingman. *Illustrators of Children's Books, 1967-1976*.

Miller. *Illustrators of Children's Books, 1946-1956*.

Ward. *Authors of Books for Young People, Second Edition*.

Jennifer, Hecate, Macbeth, William McKinley, and Me, Elizabeth. Newbery Honor Book, 1968.

BIBLIOGRAPHY

About the B'nai Bagels. Atheneum, 1969.

Altogether, One at a Time. il. Gail E. Haley. Atheneum, 1971.

Dragon in the Ghetto Caper. Atheneum, 1974.

Father's Arcane Daughter. Atheneum, 1976.

From the Mixed-Up Files of Mrs. Basil E. Frankweiler. Atheneum, 1967.

(George). Atheneum, 1970; *a.k.a. Benjamin Dickinson Carr and His (George)*. Puffin, 1974.

Jennifer, Hecate, Macbeth, William McKinley, and Me, Elizabeth. Atheneum, 1967; *a.k.a. Jennifer, Hecate, Macbeth, and Me*. Macmillan (London), 1968.

Proud Taste for Scarlet and Miniver. Atheneum, 1973.

Second Mrs. Giaconda. Atheneum, 1975.

MEDIA

About the B'nai Bagels. (TB).

From the Mixed-Up Files of Mrs. Basil E. Frankweiler. (BB, C, MT, TB); Miller-Brody Productions, 1969 (C, R); Westfall Productions, 1973 (F; announced as *The Hideaways*).

BACKGROUND READING

Commire. *Something about the Author*.

Contemporary Authors.

DeMontreville. *Third Book of Junior Authors*.

Hoffman. *Authors and Illustrators of Children's Books*.

Hopkins. *More Books by More People*.

Kingman. *Newbery and Caldecott Medal Books, 1966-1975*.

Kirkpatrick. *Twentieth Century Children's Writers*.

Ward. *Authors of Books for Young People, Second Edition*.

E. L. KONIGSBURG, 1930-
author-illustrator
a.k.a. Elaine Lobol Konigsburg

AWARDS

From the Mixed-Up Files of Mrs. Basil E. Frankweiler. Newbery Medal Book, 1968.

+JOSEPH QUINCY KRUMGOLD, 1908-
author

AWARDS

...And Now Miguel. Newbery Medal Book, 1954.

Onion John. Newbery Medal Book, 1960.

BIBLIOGRAPHY

. . .*And Now Miguel*. il. Jean Charlot. Crowell, 1953.

Children's Crusade. Atheneum, 1971.

Henry 3. il. Alvin Smith. Atheneum, 1967.

Most Terrible Turk: A Story of Turkey. il. Michael Hampshire. Crowell, 1969.

Onion John. il. Symeon Shimin. Crowell, 1959.

Oxford Furnace 1741-1925. Warren County Historical Society, 1976.

Sweeny's Adventures: As Told by John Kieran in the Film "Sweeny Steps Out." il. Tibor Gergely. Random, 1942.

Thanks to Murder. Vanguard, 1935.

Where Do We Go from Here? An Essay on Children's Literature. Ahteneum, 1976.

MEDIA

Adventure in the Bronx. n. p., n. d. (original F).

. . .*And Now Miguel*. (BB, TB); Joseph Krumgold/ U.S. Information Agency, 1953 (F); Miller-Brody Productions, 1973 (C, R); Universal-International Motion Pictures, 1965 (F).

Henry 3. (TB).

Hidden Hunger. Industrial Patents Corporation, 1942 (original F).

Magic Iron; with Robert Riskin. Robert Riskin Productions, 1947 (original F).

Onion John. (BB, CB, TB); Miller-Brody Productions, 19? (C, R).

BACKGROUND READING

Commire. *Something about the Author*.

Contemporary Authors.

Fuller. *More Junior Authors*.

Jenkins, W. "Educational Scene." *Elementary English*, May 1960.

"Joseph Krumgold." *Wilson Library Bulletin*, March 1961.

Joseph Krumgold. Profiles in Literature, 1971 (VT).

Kayden, M. "Joseph Krumgold: Author and Film Producer." *Top of the News*, December 1960.

Kingman. *Newbery and Caldecott Medal Books, 1956-1966*.

Kirkpatrick. *Twentieth Century Children's Writers*.

Krumgold, J. "I'm New Here." *Wilson Library Bulletin*, April 1954.

Miller. *Newbery and Caldecott Medal Books, 1922-1955*.

Smaridge. *Famous Modern Storytellers for Young People*.

Ward. *Authors of Books for Young People, Second Edition*.

ANNE DEMPSTER KYLE, 1896-1966
author

AWARDS

Apprentice of Florence. Newbery Honor Book, 1934.

BIBLIOGRAPHY

Apprentice of Florence. il. Erick Berry, *pseud*. (Evangel A. Champlin). Houghton, 1933.

Crusader's Gold: A Story for Girls. Houghton, 1928.

Prince of the Pale Mountains. il. Maginel W. Barney. Houghton, 1929.

Red Sky over Rome. il. Marguerite de Angeli. Houghton, 1938.

COLLECTIONS

Modern Manuscript Collection, University of Notre Dame. (Notre Dame, Indiana).

BACKGROUND READING

Kunitz. *Junior Book of Authors*.

Kunitz. *Junior Book of Authors, Second Edition Revised*.

Kyle, A. "Closed Gates of the Guild of Silk." *Horn Book*, January 1934.

JEAN LEE LATHAM, 1902-
author
pseudonyms Janice Gard, Julian Lee

AWARDS

Carry On, Mr. Bowditch. Newbery Medal Book, 1956.

BIBLIOGRAPHY

as Janice Gard:

Depend on Me: A Farce in Three Acts. Dramatic, 1932.

Listen to Leon! A Farce in Three Acts. Dramatic, 1931.

BIBLIOGRAPHY (cont'd)

as Janice Gard (cont'd)

Lookin' Lovely: A Comedy in Three Acts. Dramatic, 1930.

as Jean Lee Latham:

Aladdin Retold. il. Pablo Ramirez. Bobbs, 1961.

Ali Baba Retold. il. Pablo Ramirez. Bobbs, 1961.

Alien Note: A One-Act Comedy for Girls. Dramatic, 1930.

Anchor's Aweigh: The Story of David Glasgow Farragut. il. Eros Keith. Harper, 1968.

And Then What Happened? A Book Appreciation Play in One Act. Dramatic, 1937.

Arms of the Law: A Mystery Play in Three Acts. Dramatic, 1940.

Bed of Petunias: A Comedy in One Act. Dramatic, 1937.

Blue Teapot: A Comedy in One Act. Dramatic, 1932.

Brave Little Tailor, Hansel and Gretel, Jack and the Beanstalk. il. Pablo Ramirez and José Correas. Bobbs, 1962; *a.k.a. Sastrecillo Valiénte, Hansel y Gretel, Jack y el Tallo de Haba*. Tr. Elsie Garciá, 1962; *a.k.a. Valliant Petit Tailleur, Hansel et Gretel, Jacques et le Haricot Géant*. Tr. Michèle Halverson, 1962.

Broadway Bound: A Comedy in Three Acts. Dramatic, 1933.

Carry On, Mr. Bowditch. il. John O. Cosgrave, II. Houghton, 1955.

Chagres: Power of the Panama Canal. il. Louis Glanzman and Fred Kilem. Garrard, 1964.

Children's Book: Containing Recitations, Songs, Drills, Exercises and Plays; with Harriette Wilbur and Nellie M. Linn. Dramatic, 1933.

Christmas Party: Dramatized from the Story by Zona Gale. Dramatic, 1930.

Christmas Programs for the Lower Grades: Recitations, Songs, Drills, Exercises, Plays and a Complete Program for the Lower Grades. Dramatic, 1937.

Christopher's Orphans: A One Act Play. Dramatic, 1931.

Columbia: Power House of North America. il. Fred Kilem. Garrard, 1967.

Crinoline and Candlelight: A Comedy in One Act. Dramatic, 1931.

Cuckoo That Couldn't Count; with Bee Lewi. il. Jacqueline Chwast. Macmillan, 1961; *a.k.a.* (tr.) *Cuco que no Podiá Contar*, 1961.

David Glasgow Farragut: Our First Admiral. il. Paul Frame. Garrard, 1967.

Dog That Lost His Family; with Bee Lewi. il. Karla Kuskin. Macmillan, 1961; *a.k.a.* (tr.) *Perro que Perdió a su Familia*, 1961.

Drake: The Man They Called a Pirate. il. Frederick Chapman. Harper, 1960.

Earl Der Biggers' The House without a Key: A Charlie Chan Mystery in Three Acts Dramatized from the Novel. Dramatic, 1942.

Eli Whitney. il. (Louis) Cary. Garrard, 1963.

Elizabeth Blackwell: Pioneer Woman Doctor. il. Ethel Gold. Garrard, 1975.

Far Voyager: The Story of James Cook. il. Karl W. Suecklen. Harper, 1970.

555 Pointers for Beginning Actors and Directors: Do's and Don't's of Drama. Dramatic, 1935.

Frightened Hero: A Story of the Siege of Latham House. il. Barbara Latham. Chilton, 1965.

George W. Goethals: Panama Canal Engineer. il. Hamilton Greene. Garrard, 1965.

Ghost of Rhodes Manor: A Mystery Play for Girls in Three Acts. Dramatic, 1939.

Giant and the Biscuits: A Comedy in One Act. Dramatic, 1934.

Gray Bread: A Drama in One Act. Row, 1941.

Have a Heart! Dramatic, 1937.

Here She Comes! A Farce-Comedy in Three Acts. Dramatic, 1937.

Hop O' My Thumb Retold. il. Arnalot. Bobbs, 1961; *a.k.a. Petit Poucet*. Tr. Michele Halverson, 1961; *a.k.a. Pulgarito*. Tr. Elsie Garciá, 1961.

Jack the Giant-Killer Retold. il. Pablo Ramirez. Bobbs, 1961; *a.k.a. Jack, le Tueur de Géants*. Tr. Jeanine B. Sebastian, 1961; *a.k.a. Jack, el Matador de Gigantes*. Tr. Elsie Garciá, 1961.

Just the Girl for Jimmy: A Comedy in Three Acts with a Director's Manual. Dramatic, 1937.

Magic Fishbone Retold; by Charles Dickens. il. Pablo Ramirez. Bobbs, 1961.

Man of the Monitor: The Story of John Ericsson. il. Leonard E. Fisher. Harper, 1962.

Man Who Never Snoozed; with Bee Lewi. il. Sheila Greenwald. Macmillan, 1961; *a.k.a.* (tr.) *Hombre que Nunca Dormitaba*, 1961.

Master of Solitaire. Dramatic, 1935.

Medals for Morse: Artist and Inventor. il. Douglas Gorsline. Aladdin, 1954.

Mickey the Mighty: A Health Play in One Act. Dramatic, 1937.

Minus a Million: Comedy in Three Acts. Dramatists, 1941.

Nightmare: A Drama in Three Acts. French, 1953.

Nine Radio Plays. Dramatic, 1940.

Nutcracker Retold; by Ernst T. A. Hoffman. il. José Carreas. Bobbs, 1961; *a.k.a. Casse-Noisette.* Tr. Jeanine B. Sebastian, 1961; *a.k.a. Cascanueces.* Tr. Elsie Garciá, 1961.

Old Doc: A Comedy-Drama in Three Acts, with Director's Manual in Back. Dramatic, 1940.

On Stage, Mr. Jefferson! il. Edward Shenton. Harper, 1958.

People Don't Change: A Christmas Comedy in One Act. Dramatic, 1941.

Playmaking Vs. Playwriting: Suggestions for Training Beginning Playwrights. (Chicago), 1933.

Prince and the Platters: A Comedy in One Act. Dramatic, 1934.

Puss in Boots Retold. il. Pablo Ramirez. Bobbs, 1961; *a.k.a. Chat Botté.* Tr. Michèle Halverson, 1961; *a.k.a. Gato con Botas.* Tr. Elsie Garciá, 1961.

Rachel Carson, Who Loved the Sea. il. Victor Mays. Garrard, 1973.

Retreat to Glory: The Story of Sam Houston. Harper, 1965.

Sam Houston: Hero of Texas. il. Ernest K. Barth and Hobe Hays. Garrard, 1965.

Señor Freedom: A Drama in One Act. Baker, 1941.

Sign unto You: A Christmas Drama in One Act. Dramatic, 1931.

Smile for the Lady! A Comedy in One Act. Dramatic, 1937.

Story of Eli Whitney. il. Fritz Kredel. Aladdin, 1953.

Thanks, Awfully! A Comedy in One Act. Dramatic, 1929.

Thanksgiving for All: A Collection of Plays, Recitations, Drills, Songs and Pageants. Dramatic, 1932.

They'll Never Look There! A Comedy in One Act. Dramatists, 1939.

This Dear-Bought Land. il. Jacob Landau. Harper, 1957.

Tommy Tomorrow: A Commencement Play in Three Acts. Dramatic, 1935.

Trail Blazer of the Seas. il. Victor Mays. Houghton, 1956.

Ugly Duckling, Goldilocks and the Three Bears, The Little Red Hen. il. José Correas and Pablo Ramirez. Bobbs, 1962; *a.k.a. Patito Feo, Rizitos de Oro y los Tres Osos, La Gallinita Roja.* Tr. Elsie Garciá, 1962; *a.k.a. Vilain Petit Canard, Boucles D'Or et les Trois Ours, La Petite Poule Rousse.* Tr. Michèle Halverson, 1962.

Wa O'Ka: Retold from the Spanish; by Pablo Ramirez. Bobbs, 1961.

Well Met by Moonlight: A Comedy in Three Acts. Dramatic, 1937.

What Are You Going to Wear? A Comedy in One Act. Dramatic, 1937.

What Tabbit the Rabbit Found. il. Bill Duggan. Garrard, 1974.

When Homer Honked; with Bee Lewi. il. Cyndy Szekeres. Macmillan, 1961; *a.k.a.* (tr.) *Cuando Domingo Granzó,* 1961.

Who Lives Here? il. Benton Mahan. Garrard, 1974.

Young Man in a Hurry, the Story of Cyrus W. Field. il. Victor Mays. Harper, 1958.

as Julian Lee:

Another Washington: A Pageant. Dramatic, 1931.

Big Brother Barges In. Dramatic, 1940.

Christmas Carol: A One-Act Dramatization of the Immortal Christmas Play. Dramatic, 1931.

Fiancé for Fanny: A Farce in One Act. Dramatic, 1931.

Ghost of Lone Cabin. Dramatic, 1940.

He Landed from London: A Comedy in Three Acts. Dramatic, 1935.

I Will! I Won't! A Comedy in Three Acts. Dramatic, 1931.

Just for Justin: A Farce. (Chicago), 1933.

Keeping Kitty's Dates: A Farce in One Act. Dramatic, 1931.

Lady to See You: A Farce in Three Acts. Dramatic, 1931.

Lincoln Yesterday and Today: Songs, Recitations, and Exercises. Dramatic, 1933.

Thanksgiving Programs for the Lower Grades: Recitations, Songs, Drills, Exercises, Plays, and a Complete Program. Dramatic, 1937.

Tiny Jim: A Christmas Play for Children. Dramatic, 1933.

Washington for All: Containing Recitations, Songs, Drills, Plays and a Tableau. Dramatic, 1931.

MEDIA

Carry On, Mr. Bowditch. (BB, C, MT, TB).

Drake. (BB, TB).

First Nighter. Original plays, 1938-1940 (Ra).

Grand Central Station. Original plays, 1938-1940 (Ra).

Man of the Monitor. (BB).

Old Doc. Kraft TV Theater, 1951 (T.V.).

On Stage. (BB, MT).

Rachel Carson. (TB).

MEDIA (cont'd)

Skippy Hollywood Theater. Original plays, 19? (Ra).

This Dear-Bought Land. (BB, TB).

Trail Blazer of the Seas. (BB, TB).

Young Man in a Hurry. (BB).

COLLECTIONS

deGrummond Collection, University of Southern Mississippi. (Hattiesburg, Mississippi).

Kerlan Collection, University of Minnesota. (Minneapolis, Minnesota).

West Virginia Collection, West Virginia University Library. (Morgantown, West Virginia).

BACKGROUND READING

Burke. *American Authors and Books, 1640 to the Present Day*.

Carlson, J. "Jean Lee Latham: A Memorable Person." *Elementary English*, February 1970.

Commire. *Something about the Author*.

Contemporary Authors.

Current Biography.

Fuller. *More Junior Authors*.

Hopkins. *More Books by More People*.

Kingman. *Newbery and Caldecott Medal Books, 1956-1965*.

Kirkpatrick. *Twentieth Century Children's Writers*.

Nykoruk. *Authors in the News*.

Ward. *Authors of Books for Young People, Second Edition*.

+DOROTHY PULIS LATHROP, 1891-
author-illustrator

AWARDS

Animals of the Bible. Caldecott Medal Book, 1938.

Fairy Circus. Newbery Honor Book, 1932.

(*Forgotten Daughter*. Newbery Honor Book, 1934.)

(*Hitty, Her First Hundred Years*. Newbery Medal Book, 1932.)

BIBLIOGRAPHY

Angel in the Woods. Macmillan, 1947.

Animals of the Bible; selected by Helen D. Fish from the *Bible*. Stokes, 1937.

Balloon Moon; by Elsie P. Cabot. Holt, 1927.

Bells and Grass; by Walter de la Mare. Viking, 1942.

Bouncing Betsey. Macmillan, 1936.

Branches Green; by Rachel Field. Macmillan, 1934.

Colt from Moon Mountain. Macmillan, 1941.

Corssings: A Fairy Play; by Walter de la Mare. Music by C. Armstrong Gibbs. Knopf, 1923.

Dog in the Tapestry Garden. Macmillan, 1962.

Down-Adown-Derry: A Book of Fairy Poems; by Walter de la Mare. Holt, 1922.

Dutch Cheese; by Walter de la Mare. Knopf, 1931.

Fairy Circus. Macmillan, 1931.

Fierce-Face: The Story of a Tiger; by Dhan G. Mukerji. Dutton, 1936.

Follow the Brook. Macmillan, 1960.

Forgotten Daughter; by Caroline D. Snedeker. Doubleday, 1933.

Grateful Elephant and Other Stories Translated from the Pāli; by Eugene W. Burlingame. Yale University, 1923.

Happy Flute; by Sant R. Mandal. Stokes, 1939.

Hide and Go Seek. Macmillan, 1938.

Hitty, Her First Hundred Years; by Rachel Field. Macmillan, 1929.

Let Them Live. Macmillan, 1951.

Light Princess; by George MacDonald. Macmillan, 1926.

Little Boy Lost; by William H. Hudson. Knopf, 1920.

Little Mermaid; by Hans C. Andersen. Macmillan, 1939.

Little White Goat. Macmillan, 1933.

Littlest Mouse. Macmillan, 1955.

Long Bright Land: Fairy Tales from Southern Seas. Little, 1929.

Lost Merry-Go-Round. Macmillan, 1934.

Made-to-Order Stories; by Dorothy Canfield. Harcourt, 1925.

Mr. Bumps and His Monkey; by Walter de la Mare. Winston, 1942.

Mopsa the Fairy; by Jean Ingelow. Harper, 1927.

Presents for Lupe. Macmillan, 1940.

Princess and Curdie; by George MacDonald. Macmillan, 1927.

Puffy and the Seven Leaf Clover. Macmillan, 1954.

Puppies for Keeps. Macmillan, 1943.

Silverhorn: The Hilda Conkling Book for Other Children; by Hilda Conkling. Stokes, 1924.

Skittle-Skattle Monkey. Macmillan, 1945.

Snail Who Ran. Stokes, 1934.

Snow Image; by Nathaniel Hawthorne. Macmillan, 1930.

Stars To-Night: Verses New and Old for Boys and Girls; by Sara Teasdale. Macmillan, 1930.

Sung under the Silver Umbrella; by the Association for Childhood Education. Macmillan, 1935.

Tales from the Enchanted Isles; by Ethel M. Gate. Yale University, 1926.

Three-Mulla-Mulgars; by Walter de la Mare. Knopf, 1919; *a.k.a. Three Royal Monkeys*, 1925.

Treasure of Carcassonne; by Albert Robida. Tr. F. T. Cooper. Longmans, 1928.

Who Goes There? Macmillan, 1935.

MEDIA

Who Goes There? (BB).

COLLECTIONS

Central Children's Room, Donnell Library Center, New York Public Library. (New York, New York).

Columbia University Library. (New York, New York).

Free Library of Philadelphia. (Philadelphia, Pennsylvania).

Kerlan Collection, University of Minnesota. (Minneapolis, Minnesota).

Special Collections, University Research Library, University of California. (Los Angeles, California).

BACKGROUND READING

Benét. *Famous Poets for Young People*.

Burke. *American Authors and Books, 1640 to the Present Day*.

Commire. *Something about the Author*.

Contemporary Authors.

Fay, H. "Dorothy Lathrop, Illustrator." *Publishers Weekly*, June 18, 1938.

Hopkins. *Books Are by People*.

Kingman. *Illustrators of Children's Books, 1957-1966*.

Kunitz. *Junior Book of Authors*.

Kunitz. *Junior Book of Authors, Second Edition Revised*.

Lathrop, D. "Illustrating De La Mare." *Horn Book*, May 1942.

Lathrop, D. "Test of Hitty's Patience." *Horn Book*, February 1930.

Mahony, B. "Artist's Triumph." *Horn Book*, July 1938.

Mahony, B. *Contemporary Illustrators of Children's Books*.

Mahony, B. *Illustrators of Children's Books, 1744-1945*.

Miller. *Caldecott Medal Books, 1938-1957*.

Miller. *Illustrators of Children's Books, 1946-1956*.

Renwick, S. "Dorothy Lathrop, Author and Illustrator of Children's Books." *American Artist*, October 1942.

Stoddard. *Topflight*.

Ward. *Authors of Books for Young People, Second Edition*.

Ward. *Illustrators of Books for Young People, Second Edition*.

+ROBERT LAWSON, 1892-1957
author-illustrator

AWARDS

(*Adam of the Road*. Newbery Medal Book, 1943.)

Four and Twenty Blackbirds. Caldecott Honor Book, 1938.

Great Wheel. Newbery Honor Book, 1958.

(*Mr. Popper's Penguins*. Newbery Honor Book, 1939.)

Rabbit Hill. Newbery Medal Book, 1945.

They Were Strong and Good. Caldecott Medal Book, 1941.

Wee Gillis. Caldecott Honor Book, 1939.

BIBLIOGRAPHY

Adam of the Road; by Elizabeth J. Gray. Viking, 1942.

Aesop's Fables: A New Version; by Munro Leaf. Heritage, 1941.

*At That Time. Viking, 1947.

Ben and Me: A New and Astonishing Life of Benjamin Franklin, as Written by His Good Mouse, Amos. Little, 1939; variant as *Walt Disney's Ben and Me, Based on the Book by Robert Lawson*. il. Walt Disney Studio, adapted by Campbell Grant. Simon, 1954.

Betsy Ross; by Helen D. Bates. McGraw, 1936.

Captain Kidd's Cat: Being the True and Dolorious Chronicle of William Kidd, Gent. & Merchant of New York, Late Captain of the Adventure Galley, of the Vicissitudes Attending His Unfortunate Cruise in Eastern Waters, of His Incarceration in Newgate Prison, of His Unjust Trial and Execution as Narrated by His Faithful Cat, McDermot, Who Ought to Know. Little, 1956.

BIBLIOGRAPHY (cont'd)

Country Colic: Being Sundry Remarks and Observations Concerning the Joys, Perils and Vexations of Rustic Residence, Together with Certain Other Suggestions of a Cautionary Nature for the Enlightenment and Guidance of the Inexperienced, Arranged as a Glossary and Lavishly Embellished with Numerous Diagrams Drawn from Life. Little, 1944.

Crock of Gold; by James Stephens. Limited Editions, 1942.

Dick Whittington and His Cat, Retold. Limited Editions, 1949.

Drums of Monmouth; by Emma G. Sterne. Dodd, 1935.

Edward, Hoppy and Joe, Knopf, 1952.

Fabulous Flight. Little, 1949.

Four and Twenty Blackbirds: Nursery Rhymes of Yesterday Recalled for Children of To-Day; compiled by Helen D. Fish. Lippincott, 1937.

Francis Scott Key; by Helen D. Bates. McGraw, 1936.

From the Horn of the Moon; by Arthur Mason. Doubleday, 1931.

Gaily We Parade: A Collection of Poems about People, Here, There, and Everywhere; compiled by John E. Brewton. Macmillan, 1948.

Golden Horseshoe; by Elizabeth Coatsworth. Macmillan, 1935; new edition, 1968.

Great Wheel. Viking, 1957.

Greylock and the Robins; by Tom Robinson. Viking, 1946.

Haven's End; by John Marquand. Little, 1933.

Hurdy-Gurdy Man; by Margery W. Bianco. Oxford, 1933.

I Discover Columbus: A True Chronicle of the Great Admiral and His Finding of the New World, Narrated by the Venerable Parrot Aurelio, Who Shared in the Glorious Adventure. Little, 1941.

I Hear America Singing: An Anthology of Folk Poetry; by Ruth Barnes. Winston, 1937.

Just for Fun: A Collection of Stories and Verses. Rand, 1943.

Little Woman Wanted Noise; by Valentine Teal. Rand, 1943.

Mathematics for Success; by Mary A. Potter. Ginn, 1952.

McWhinney's Jaunt. Little, 1951.

Miranda Is a Princess; by Emma G. Sterne. Dodd, 1937.

Mr. Popper's Penguins; by Richard and Florence Atwater. Little, 1938.

Mr. Revere and I: Being an Account of Certain Episodes in the Career of Paul Revere, Esq., as Recently Revealed by His Horse, Scheherazade, a Late Pride of His Royal Majesty's 14th Regiment of Foot. Little, 1953.

Mr. Twigg's Mistake. Little, 1947.

Mr. Wilmer. Little, 1945.

One Foot in Fairyland: Sixteen Tales; by Eleanor Farjeon. Stokes, 1938.

Peik; by Barbara Ring. Tr. Lorence M. Woodside. Little, 1932.

Pete the Pelican; by Rita Kissin. Lippincott, 1937.

Pilgrim's Progress: Retold and Shortened for Modern Readers; by Mary Godolphin, *pseud.* (Lucy Aikin). Stokes, 1939.

Poo-Poo and the Dragons; by C. S. Forester. Little, 1942.

Prince and the Pauper; by Mark Twain, *pseud.* (Samuel Clemens). Winston, 1937.

Prince Prigio; by Andrew Lang. Little, 1942.

Rabbit Hill. Viking, 1944.

Robbut, a Tale of Tails. Viking, 1948.

Roving Lobster; by Arthur Mason. Doubleday, 1931.

Seven Beads of Wampum; by Elizabeth Gale. Putnam, 1936.

Shoelace Robin; by William N. Hall. Crowell, 1945.

Slim; by William W. Haines. Little, 1934.

Smeller Martin. Viking, 1950.

Story of Ferdinand; by Munro Leaf. Viking, 1936; *a.k.a. Cuento de Ferdinando*. Tr. Pura Belpré, 1962; *a.k.a. Ferdinandus Taurus*. Tr. Elizabeth H. Redditus. McKay, 1962; variant as *Walt Disney's Ferdinand the Bull, from the Walt Disney Production, Based on "The Story of Ferdinand" by Munro Leaf and Robert Lawson*. il. Walt Disney Studio. Whitman, 1938.

Story of Jesus for Young People; by Walter R. Bowie. Scribner, 1937.

Story of Simpson and Sampson; by Munro Leaf. Viking, 1941.

Swords and Statues; by Clarence Stratton. Winston, 1937.

Tale of Two Cities; by Charles Dickens. Ginn, 1938.

They Were Strong and Good. Viking, 1940.

Tough Winter. Viking, 1954.

Treasure of the Isle of Mist; by William W. Tarn. Putnam, 1934.

Under the Tent of the Sky: A Collection of Poems about Animals, Large and Small; compiled by John E. Brewton. Macmillan, 1937.

Unicorn with Silver Shoes; by Ella Young. Longmans, 1932.

Watchwords of Liberty, a Pageant of American Quotations. Little, 1943.

Wee Gillis; by Munro Leaf. Viking, 1938; also issued in limited edition.

Wee Men of Ballywooden; by Arthur Mason. Doubleday, 1930.

Wind of the Vikings: A Tale of the Orkney Isles; by Maribelle Cormack. Appleton, 1937.

Wonderful Adventures of Little Prince Toofat; by George R. Chester. McCann, 1922.

MEDIA

Ben and Me. (TB); Walt Disney Productions, 1953 (F), 1971 (FSS).

Captain Kidd's Cat. (TB).

Fabulous Flight. (BB).

Great Wheel. (BB, TB).

Mr. Revere and I. (BB, TB).

Rabbit Hill. (BB, TB); Contemporary Films, Inc., 1967 (F); National Broadcasting Corporation/ Children's Theatre/McGraw Hill, 1968 (F, VC); Viking Press, 1972 (C, R).

They Were Strong and Good. Weston Woods Studios, 1968 (FSS).

Tough Winter. (BB, TB).

Watchwords of Liberty. (BB).

COLLECTIONS

Allentown Free Library. (Allentown, Pennsylvania).

Gardner Collection, Free Library of Philadelphia. (Philadelphia, Pennsylvania).

Kerlan Collection, University of Minnesota. (Minneapolis, Minnesota).

May Massee Collection, Emporia State College. (Emporia, Kansas).

Milwaukee Public Library. (Milwaukee, Wisconsin).

Special Collections, University Research Library, University of California. (Los Angeles, California).

BACKGROUND READING

Bader. *American Picturebooks from Noah's Ark to The Beast Within*.

Burke. *American Authors and Books, 1640 to the Present Day*.

Burns, M. " 'There Is Enough for All,' Robert Lawson's America." *Horn Book*, February, April, June, 1972.

Checklist of Drawings and Watercolors, 1922-1957, for Books Illustrated by Robert Lawson in the Frederick R. Gardner Collection. Free Library of Philadelphia, 1977.

Commire. *Yesterday's Authors of Books for Children*.

Current Biography.

Ellis. *Book Illustration*.

Gardner, Frederick R. *Robert Lawson on My Shelves*. Free Library of Philadelphia, 1977.

Fish, H. "Robert Lawson: Illustrator for Children." *Publishers Weekly*, June 21, 1941.

Hoffman. *Authors and Illustrators of Children's Books*.

Jones, Helen. *Robert Lawson, Illustrator: A Selection of His Characteristic Illustrations*. Little, 1972.

Kirkpatrick. *Twentieth Century Children's Writers*.

Kunitz. *Junior Book of Authors, Second Edition Revised*.

Lawson, R. "Make Me a Child Again." *Horn Book*, November 1940.

Mahony. *Contemporary Illustrators of Children's Books*.

Mahony. *Illustrators of Children's Books, 1744-1945*.

Miller. *Caldecott Medal Books, 1938-1957*.

Miller. *Illustrators of Children's Books, 1946-1956*.

Miller. *Newbery Medal Books, 1922-1955*.

Montgomery. *Story behind Modern Books*.

Obituary. Horn Book, August 1957.

Obituary. *New York Times*, May 28, 1957.

Obituary. *Publishers Weekly*, June 24, 1957.

Obituary. *Time*, June 10, 1957.

Obituary. *Wilson Library Bulletin*, June 24, 1957.

Sicherman, R. "Appreciation of Robert Lawson." *Elementary English*, December 1967.

Smaridge. *Famous Author-Illustrators for Young People*.

Ward. *Authors of Books for Young People, Second Edition*.

Ward. *Illustrators of Books for Young People, Second Edition*.

Weston, A. "Robert Lawson, Author and Illustrator." *Elementary English*, January 1970.

Young Wings. *Writing Books for Boys and Girls*.

+URSULA KROEBER LeGUIN, 1929-
author

AWARDS

Tombs of Atuan. Newbery Honor Book, 1972.

BIBLIOGRAPHY

City of Illusions. Ace, 1967.

Dispossessed: An Ambiguous Utopia. Harper, 1974.

Farthest Shore. il. Gail Garraty. Atheneum, 1972.

From Elfland to Poughkeepsie. Pendragon, 1973.

Lathe of Heaven. Scribner, 1971.

Left Hand of Darkness. Walker, 1969.

(ed.) *Nebula Award Stories II*. Harper, 1975.

New Atlantis and Other Novellas of Science Fiction; with Gene Wolfe. Hawthorn, 1975.

Orsinian Tales. Harper, 1976.

Planet of Exile. Ace, 1966.

Rocannon's World. Ace, 1964.

Tombs of Atuan. il. Gail Garraty. Atheneum, 1971.

Very Far from Anywhere Else. Atheneum, 1976.

Wild Angels. Capra, 1975.

Wind's Twelve Corners. Harper, 1975.

Wizard of Earthsea. il. Ruth Robbins. Parnassus, 1968.

Word for World Is Forest. Berkeley, 1976.

MEDIA

Dispossessed. (C, MT, TB).

Farthest Shore. (C, MT, TB).

Lathe of Heaven. (BB, MT).

Left Hand of Darkness. (C, MT, TB).

Tombs of Atuan. (C, MT, TB); Miller-Brody Productions, 1976 (C, R).

Wind's Quarters. (BB).

Wizard of Earthsea. (C, MT, TB).

Word for World Is Forest. (BB).

BACKGROUND READING

Bair. *Biography News*.

Cameron, E. "High Fantasy: A Wizard of Earthsea." *Horn Book*, April 1971.

Commire. *Something about the Author*.

Contemporary Authors.

DeMontreville. *Fourth Book of Junior Authors and Illustrators*.

Kirkpatrick. *Twentieth Century Children's Writers*.

Nykoruk. *Authors in the News*.

MADELEINE L'ENGLE, 1918-
author

AWARDS

Wrinkle in Time. Newbery Medal Book, 1963.

BIBLIOGRAPHY

And Both Were Young. Lothrop, 1949.

Arm of the Starfish. Farrar, 1965.

Camilla Dickinson: A Novel. Simon, 1951; a.k.a. *Camilla*. Crowell, 1965. (Announced as *Fourteen Days*.)

*Circle of Quiet. Farrar, 1972.

Dance in the Desert. il. Symeon Shimin. Farrar, 1969.

Dragons in the Water. Farrar, 1976.

18 Washington Square South: A Comedy in One Act. Baker, 1944.

Everyday Prayers. il. Lucile Butel. Morehouse-Barlow, 1974.

Ilsa. Vanguard, 1946.

Irrational Season. Seabury, 1977.

Journey with Jonah: One Act Play. il. Leonard E. Fisher. Farrar, 1967.

Lines Scribbled on an Envelope and Other Poems. Farrar, 1969.

Love Letters. Farrar, 1966.

Meet the Austins. Vanguard, 1960; il. Gillian Willett. Collins, 1968.

Moon by Night. Farrar, 1963.

Other Side of the Sun. Farrar, 1971.

Prelude. Vanguard, 1968. (First part of *Small Rain*, below.)

Small Rain. Vanguard, 1945.

(ed.) *Spiritual Light: Essays in Historical Theology*; with William Green. Seabury, 1976.

*Summer of the Great-Grandmother. Farrar, 1974.

Twenty-Four Days before Christmas. il. Inga. Farrar, 1964.

Wind in the Door. Farrar, 1973.

Winter's Love. Lippincott, 1957.

Wrinkle in Time. Farrar, 1962.

Young Unicorns. Farrar, 1968.

MEDIA

And Both Were Young. (BB).

Arm of the Starfish. (BB, TB).

Camilla. (TB).

Dragons in the Water. (TB).

Meet the Austins. (BB).

Moon by Night. (BB).

Summer of the Great-Grandmother. (CB).

Wind in the Door. (TB); Miller-Brody Productions, n. d. (FSS).

Wrinkle in Time. (BB, C, CB, MT, TB); Miller-Brody Productions, 1974 (FSS); Newbery Award Records, 1972 (C, R).

Young Unicorns. (BB, MT).

COLLECTIONS

deGrummond Collection, University of Southern Mississippi. (Hattiesburg, Mississippi).

Kerlan Collection, University of Minnesota. (Minneapolis, Minnesota).

L'Engle Collection, Wheaton College Library. (Wheaton, Illinois).

University of North Carolina Library. (Chapel Hill, North Carolina).

BACKGROUND READING

Burke. *American Authors and Books, 1640 to the Present Day.*

Commire. *Something about the Author.*

Contemporary Authors.

Fuller. *More Junior Authors.*

Hopkins. *More Books by More People.*

Kingman. *Newbery and Caldecott Medal Books, 1956-1965.*

Kirkpatrick. *Twentieth Century Children's Writers.*

L'Engle, M. "Before Babel." *Horn Book*, December 1966.

L'Engle, M. "Centipede and the Creative Spirit." *Horn Book*, August 1969.

L'Engle, M. "Danger of Wearing Glass Slippers." *Horn Book*, February 1964.

Madeleine L'Engle. Profiles in Literature, 1970 (VT).

"Madeleine L'Engle." *Wilson Library Bulletin*, May 1962.

Meet the Newbery Author: Madeleine L'Engle. Miller-Brody Productions, 1974 (FSS).

Nykoruk. *Authors in the News.*

Rausen, R. "Interview with Madeleine L'Engle." *Children's Literature in Education*, Winter 1975.

Townsend. *Sense of Story.*

Ward. *Authors of Books for Young People, Second Edition.*

Warfel. *American Novelists of Today.*

Wintle. *Pied Pipers.*

+LOIS LENORE LENSKI, 1893-1974
author-illustrator

AWARDS

Indian Captive. Newbery Honor Book, 1942.

Phebe Fairchild. Newbery Honor Book, 1937.

Strawberry Girl. Newbery Medal Book, 1946.

BIBLIOGRAPHY

Adventures in Understanding: Talks to Parents, Teachers, and Librarians, 1944-1966. Florida State University Library, 1968.

A-Going to the Westward. Stokes, 1937.

Alphabet People. Harper, 1928.

Animals for Me. Oxford, 1941.

Arabella and Her Aunt. Stokes, 1932.

At Our House. Music by Clyde R. Bulla. Walck, 1959.

Baby Car. Oxford, 1937.

Bayou Suzette. Stokes, 1943.

Bean Pickers: A Migrant Play. National Council of Churches, 1952.

Benny and His Penny. Knopf, 1931.

Berries in the Scoop: A Cape Code Cranberry Story. Lippincott, 1956.

Betsy and Tacy Go over the Big Hill; by Maud H. Lovelace. Crowell, 1942.

Betsy-Tacy; by Maud H. Lovelace. Crowell, 1930.

Betsy-Tacy and Tib; by Maud H. Lovelace. Crowell, 1941.

Big Little Davy. Oxford, 1956.

Blue Ridge Billy. Lippincott, 1946.

Blueberry Corners. Stokes, 1940.

Book of Enchantment; by Kathleen Adams and F. E. Atchinson. Dodd, 1928.

Book of Princess Stories; by Katheleen Adams and F. E. Atchinson. Dodd, 1927.

Boom Town Boy. Lippincott, 1948.

BIBLIOGRAPHY (cont'd)

Bound Girl of Cobble Hill. Stokes, 1938.

Candle-Light Stories; compiled by Veronica Hutchinson. Minton, 1928.

Change of Heart: A Migrant Play. National Council of Churches, 1952.

Children's Frieze Book to-Put-Together for Home Decoration. Platt, 1918.

Chimney Corner Fairy Tales; compiled by Veronica Hutchinson. Minton, 1926.

Chimney Corner Poems; compiled by Veronica Hutchinson. Minton, 1929.

Chimney Corner Stories: Tales for Little Children; compiled by Veronica Hutchinson. Minton, 1925.

Cinderella. Platt, 1922.

City Poems. Walck, 1971.

Coal Camp Girl. Stokes, 1959.

Corn-Farm Boy. Lippincott, 1954.

Cotton in My Sack. Lippincott, 1949.

Cowboy Small. Oxford, 1949; *a.k.a. Vaquero Pequeño*. Tr. Donald Worcestor. Walck, 1960; *a.k.a. Couboi Smaull,* 1967.

Davy and His Dog. Oxford, 1957.

Davy Goes Places. Walck, 1961.

Davy's Day. Oxford, 1943.

Debbie and Her Dolls. Walck, 1970.

Debbie and Her Family. Walck, 1969.

Debbie and Her Grandma. Walck, 1967.

Debbie and Her Pets. Walck, 1971.

Debbie Goes to Nursery School. Walck, 1970.

Debbie Herself. Walck, 1969.

Deer Valley Girl. Lippincott, 1968.

Dog Came to School: A Davy Book. Oxford, 1955.

Dolls from Fairyland: Cut-Outs. Nourse, 1921.

Dolls from the Land of Mother Goose: Cut-Outs. Platt, 1918.

Donkey Cart; by Clyde R. Bulla. Crowell, 1946.

Donkey-Town: A Betsy-Tacy Story; by Maud H. Lovelace. Crowell, 1943.

Dream Days; by Kenneth Grahame. Lane, 1922.

Easter Rabbit's Parade. Oxford, 1936.

Edgar, the 7:58; by Phil Strong. Farrar, 1938.

Fairy Tales Children Love; by Watty Piper, *pseud.* (Frances M. Ford). il. with Eulalie. Platt, 1932.

Fireside Poems; compiled by Veronica Hutchinson. Minton, 1930.

Fireside Stories; compiled by Veronica Hutchinson. Minton, 1927.

First Thanksgiving; by Lena Barksdale. Knopf, 1942.

Five and Ten; by Roberta Whitehead. Houghton, 1943.

Flood Friday. Lippincott, 1956.

Florida, My Florida: Poems. Florida State University Library, 1971.

Forgetful Tommy. Greenacres, 1943.

Golden Age; by Kenneth Grahame. Lane, 1921.

Golden Tales of Canada; by May L. Becker. Dodd, 1938.

Golden Tales of New England; by May L. Becker. Dodd, 1931.

Golden Tales of the Far West; by May L. Becker. Dodd, 1935.

Golden Tales of the Old South; by May L. Becker. Dodd, 1941.

Golden Tales of the Prairie States; by May L. Becker. Dodd, 1932.

Golden Tales of the Southwest; by May L. Becker. Dodd, 1939.

Gooseberry Garden. Harper, 1934.

Grandmother Tippytoe. Stokes, 1931.

Green-Faced Toad and Other Stories; by Vera Birch. Lane, 1921; Stokes, 1923.

Hat-Tub Tale: Or, On the Shores of the Bay of Fundy; by Caroline Emerson. Dodd, 1928.

High-Rise Secret. Lippincott, 1966.

Houseboat Girl. Lippincott, 1957.

I Like Winter. Oxford, 1950.

I Went for a Walk. Music by Clyde R. Bulla. Walck, 1958.

Ice Cream Is Good. National Dairy Council, 1948.

Indian Captive: The Story of Mary Jemison. Stokes, 1941; variant as *Indian Captive: The Story of Mary Jemison, Adapted by Gertrude Breen.* Coach-House, 1961; variant as *White Girl Captive: A Play in Three Acts for Boys and Girls, Based on the Book Indian Captive*, n. p., n. d.

Indigo Treasure; by Frances Rogers. il. with author. Stokes, 1941.

Jack Horner's Pie: A Book of Nursery Rhymes; from Mother Goose. Harper, 1927; *a.k.a. Lois Lenski's Mother Goose*, 1936.

Johnny Goes to the Fair: A Picture Book. Minton, 1932.

Jolly Rhymes of Mother Goose; edited by Watty Piper, *pseud.* (Frances M. Ford). il. with Eulalie. Platt, 1932.

Journey into Childhood: The Autobiography of Lois Lenski. Lippincott, 1972.

Judy's Journey. Lippincott, 1947.

Let's Play House. Oxford, 1944.

Letter to Popsey; by Mabel S. LaRue. Grosset, 1942.

Life I Live: Collected Poems. Walck, 1965.

Little Airplane. Oxford, 1938; *a.k.a. Little Aeroplane*. Oxford (London), 1939.

Little Auto. Oxford, 1934; *a.k.a. Baby Car*. Oxford (London), 1937; *a.k.a. Littl Autoe*. Walck, 1965; *a.k.a. Auto Pequeño*. Tr. Sandra Streepey, 1968.

Little Baby Ann. Oxford, 1935.

Little Engine That Could: Retold from the Pony Engine by Mabel C. Bragg; by Watty Piper, *pseud.* (Frances M. Ford). Platt, 1930.

Little Family: A Little Book. Doubleday, 1932.

Little Farm. Oxford, 1942; *a.k.a. Littl Farm*. Walck, 1965; *a.k.a. Granja Pequeña*. Tr. Sandra Streepey, 1968.

Little Fire Engine. Oxford, 1946.

Little Girl of 1900. Stokes, 1928.

Little Rag Doll; by Ethel C. Phillips. Houghton, 1930.

Little Sail Boat. Oxford, 1937; *a.k.a. Little Sailing-Boat*. Oxford (London), 1938.

Little Sioux Girl. Lippincott, 1958.

Little Train. Oxford, 1940.

Living with Others. Connecticut Council of Churches, 1952.

Lois Lenski's Christmas Stories. Lippincott, 1968.

Makio, 1915. Ohio State University, 1915.

Mama Hattie's Girl. Lippincott, 1953.

Merry-Go-Round of Modern Tales; by Caroline D. Emerson. Dutton, 1927.

Mr. and Mrs. Noah. Crowell, 1948.

Mr. Tip and Mr. Tuck; by Caroline D. Emerson. Dutton, 1930.

Monkey That Would Not Kill; by Henry Drummond. Dodd, 1925.

Mother Goose Rhymes; edited by Watty Piper, *pseud.* (Frances M. Ford). Platt, 1930; new edition, 1932; new edition, 1956.

Mother Makes Christmas; by Cornelia Meigs. Grosset, 1940.

My ABC Book. Platt, 1922.

My Friend the Cow. National Dairy Council, 1946.

Name for Obed; by Ethel C. Phillips. Houghton, 1941.

Now It's Fall. Oxford, 1948.

Ocean-Born Mary. Stokes, 1939.

Odysseus, Sage of Greece; by Alan L. Chidsey. Minton, 1931.

On a Summer Day. Oxford, 1953.

Once on Christmas; by Dorothy Thompson. Oxford, 1938.

Over the Big Hill: A Betsy-Tacy Story; by Maud H. Lovelace. Crowell, 1943.

Papa Small. Oxford, 1951; *a.k.a. Papa Pequeño*. Tr. Maria D. Lado. Walck, 1961; *a.k.a. Papa Petit*. Tr. Bernard Kaye, 1963; *a.k.a. Papa Smaull*, 1966.

Peanuts for Billy Ben. Lippincott, 1952.

Peep-Show Man; by Padraic Colum. Macmillan, 1924.

Phebe Fairchild, Her Book. Stokes, 1936.

Pinocchio: Adapted by Allen Chafee; by Carlo Collodi, *pseud.* (Carlo Lorenzini). Random, 1946.

Policeman Small. Walck, 1962.

Prairie School. Lippincott, 1951.

Project Boy. Lippincott, 1954.

Prudence and Peter and Their Adventures with Pots and Pans; by Elizabeth Robbins and Octavia Wilberforce. Morrow, 1928.

Puritan Adventure. Lippincott, 1944.

Read-to-Me Storybook; by The Child Study Association of America. Crowell, 1947.

Rustam: Lion of Persia; by Alan L. Chidsey. Minton, 1930.

San Francisco Boy. Lippincott, 1955.

Scotch Circus: The Story of Tammas Who Rode the Dragon; by Tom Powers. Houghton, 1934.

Shoo-Fly Girl. Lippincott, 1963.

Sing of Song of Sixpence; from Mother Goose. Harper, 1930.

Skipping Village: A Town of Not So Long Ago. Stokes, 1927.

Songs of Mr. Small. Music by Clyde R. Bulla. Walck, 1954.

Songs of the City. Music by Clyde R. Bulla. Marks Music, 1956.

Spinach Boy. Stokes, 1930.

Spring Is Here. Calligraphy by Hilda Scott. Oxford, 1945.

Strangers in a Strange Land: A Migrant Play. National Council of Churches, 1952.

Strawberry Girl. Lippincott, 1945.

Sugarplum House. Harper, 1935.

Surprise for Davy. Oxford, 1947.

Surprise for Mother. Stokes, 1937.

Surprise Place; by Mary G. Bonner. Knopf, 1945.

BIBLIOGRAPHY (cont'd)

Susie Mariar: An Old Folk Rhyme. Oxford, 1939.

Texas Tomboy. Lippincott, 1950.

They Came from France; by Clara I. Judson. Houghton, 1943; *a.k.a. Pierre's Lucky Pouch: They Came from France*. Follett, 1957.

Tick-Tock Tales; by Watty Piper, *pseud.* (Frances M. Ford). il. with Eulalie. Platt, 1931.

To Be a Logger. Lippincott, 1967.

Twenty-two Short Stories of America; edited by E. R. Mirrielees. Heath, 1937.

Twilight of Magic; by Hugh Lofting. Stokes, 1930.

Two Brothers and Their Animal Friends. Stokes, 1929.

Two Brothers and Their Baby Sister. Stokes, 1930.

Up to Six. Music by Clyde R. Bulla. Hansen Music, 1956.

Washington Picture-Book. Coward, 1930.

We Are Thy Children. Music by Clyde R. Bulla. Crowell, 1952; Hansen Music, 1956.

We Live by the River. Lippincott, 1956.

We Live in the City. Lippincott, 1954.

We Live in the Country. Lippincott, 1960.

We Live in the North. Lippincott, 1965.

We Live in the South. Lippincott, 1952.

We Live in the Southwest. Lippincott, 1952.

When I Grow Up. Music by Clyde R. Bulla. Walck, 1960.

Wonder City: A Picture Book of New York. Coward, 1929.

MEDIA

At Our House in *Songs of Mr. Small*, below.

Bayou Suzette. (TB); Intercontinental Audeo-Video Company, *ca.*1947 (R).

Boom-Town Boy. (TB).

Corn-Farm Billy. (BB).

Cotton in My Sack. (TB).

Cowboy Small. (BB).

Davy Goes Places. (BB).

Frank Luther Sings Lois Lenski Songs. Walck, 196? (R).

Houseboat Girl. (BB).

I Went for a Walk in *Songs of Mr. Small*, below.

Indian Captive. (BB, TB).

Judy's Journey. (BB).

Little Airplane. (BB).

Little Auto. (BB, TB).

Little Fire Engine. (BB).

Policeman Small. (BB).

Project Boy. (BB).

Shoo-Fly Girl. (BB).

Songs of Mr. Small. Walck, 1960 (R); (Includes *At Our House*, *I Went for a Walk*, and *When I Grow Up*.)

Strawberry Girl. (BB, CB, TB); Gloria Chandler Recordings, n. d. (R); Intercontinental Audeo-Video Company, *ca.*1947 (R); Miller-Brody Productions, 1973 (FSS); Newbery Award Records, 1970 (C, R).

Surprise for Davy. (BB).

When I Grow Up in *Songs of Mr. Small*, above.

EXHIBITIONS

Detroit Art Institute, n. d. (Detroit, Michigan).

Feragil Gallery, 1932. (New York, New York).

New York Water Color Show, n. d. (New York, New York).

Pennsylvania Water Color Show, 1922. (Philadelphia, Pennsylvania).

Weyhe Gallery, 1927, 1932. (New York, New York).

COLLECTIONS

Amos Memorial Public Library. (Sidney, Ohio).

Bizzell Memorial Library, University of Oklahoma. (Norman, Oklahoma).

Bobst Library, New York University. (New York, New York).

Butler Library, State University of New York. (Buffalo, New York).

Carnegie Library. (Liberty, Missouri).

Central Children's Room, Donnell Library Center, New York Public Library. (New York, New York).

Covey Collection, Southwestern College, Memorial Library. (Winfield, Kansas).

Curry Library, William Jewell College. (Liberty, Missouri).

Dallas Public Library. (Dallas, Texas).

deGrummond Collection, University of Southern Mississippi. (Hattiesburg, Mississippi).

Free Library of Philadelphia. (Philadelphia, Pennsylvania).

General University Library, New York University. (New York, New York).

Jackson Library, University of North Carolina. (Greensboro, North Carolina).

Kerlan Collection, University of Minnesota. (Minneapolis, Minnesota).

Lenski and Thompson Collections, Arents Research Library, Syracuse University. (Syracuse, New York).

May Massee Collection, Emporia State College. (Emporia, Kansas).

Milner Library, Illinois State University. (Normal, Illinois).

School of Library Science, University of Texas. (Austin, Texas).

Special Collections, University Research Library, University of California. (Los Angeles, California).

University of Florida Libraries. (Gainesville, Florida).

Warder Public Library. (Springfield, Ohio).

BACKGROUND READING

Bird, Nancy. *Lois Lenski Collection in the Florida State University Library*. Florida State University, 1966.

Commire. *Something about the Author*.

Contemporary Authors.

Coyle. *Ohio Authors and Their Books*.

Frank, C. "We Helped an Author." *Instructor*, January 1955.

Garvey, L. "Regional Stories." *Horn Book*, April 1951.

Giambra, Carolyn. *Lois Lenski Collection in the Edward H. Butler Library*. (Buffalo, New York), 1972.

Hoffman. *Authors and Illustrators of Children's Books*.

Hopkins. *Books Are by People*.

Jacobs, L. "Lois Lenski's Regional Literature." *Elementary English*, May 1953.

Kingman. *Illustrators of Children's Books, 1957-1966*.

Kingman. *Illustrators of Children's Books, 1967-1976*.

Kirkpatrick. *Twentieth Century Children's Writers*.

Kunitz. *Junior Book of Authors*.

Kunitz. *Junior Book of Authors, Second Edition Revised*.

Lenski, L. "Let Them Create." *Horn Book*, February 1952.

Lenski, L. "Out of a Paper Sack." *Horn Book*, July 1949.

Lenski, L. "Regional Children's Literature." *Wilson Library Bulletin*, December 1946.

Lenski, L. "Story of 'Phebe Fairchild, Her Book.'" *Horn Book*, December 1937.

Lois Lenski, Friend of Children. Lippincott, 1958.

Mahony. *Contemporary Illustrators of Children's Books*.

Mahony. *Illustrators of Children's Books, 1744-1945*.

Miller. *Illustrators of Children's Books, 1946-1956*.

Miller. *Newbery Medal Books, 1922-1955*.

Montgomery. *Story behind Modern Books*.

New York Times Biographical Service.

Obituary. *New York Times*, September 14, 1974.

Obituary. *Publishers Weekly*, September 30, 1974.

Obituary. *Time*, September 23, 1974.

Smaridge. *Famous Author-Illustrators for Young People*.

Titzell, J. "Lois Lenski: Serious Artist with a Sense of Humor." *Publishers Weekly*, March 29, 1930.

Ward. *Authors of Books for Young People, Second Edition*.

Witcher, Esther. *Lois Lenski Collection in the University of Oklahoma Library: With a Complete Bibliography of Her Works*. University of Oklahoma Library, 1963.

+BLAIR LENT, 1930-
author-illustrator
pseudonym Ernest Small

AWARDS

Angry Moon. Caldecott Honor Book, 1971.

Funny Little Woman. Caldecott Medal Book, 1973.

Wave. Caldecott Honor Book, 1965.

Why the Sun and the Moon Live in the Sky. Caldecott Honor Book, 1969.

BIBLIOGRAPHY

as Blair Lent:

Angry Moon, Retold; by William Sleator. Little, 1970.

Bear Teeth for Courage; by Florence Scull. Van Nostrand, 1964.

Christmas Sky; by Franklyn M. Branley. Crowell, 1966.

Favorite Fairy Tales Told in India; by Virginia Haviland. Little, 1973.

From King Boggen's Hall to Nothing-At-All: A Collection of Improbable House and Unusual Places Found in Traditional Rhymes and Limmericks. Little, 1967.

Funny Little Woman; by Arlene Mosel. Dutton, 1972.

John Tabor's Ride. Little, 1966.

BIBLIOGRAPHY (cont'd)

as Blair Lent (cont'd):

Little Match Girl; by Hans C. Andersen. Houghton, 1968.

May Horses; by Jan Wahl. Dial, 1969.

Miracle of the Talking Jungle; by Ruth Bartlett. Van Nostrand, 1965.

Oasis of the Stars; by Olga Economakis. Coward, 1965.

Pistachio. Little, 1964.

Telephone; by Kornei Chukovsky, adapted by William J. Smith. Delacorte, 1977.

Tikki-Tikki Tembo; by Arlene Mosel. Holt, 1968.

Wave: Adapted from Lafcadio Hearn's Gleanings in Buddha-Fields; by Margaret Hodges. Houghton, 1964.

Why the Sun and the Moon Live in the Sky; by Dayrell Elphinstone. Houghton, 1968.

as Ernest Small:

Baba Yaga. Houghton, 1966.

MEDIA

Funny Little Woman. Weston Woods Studios, 1973 (FSS).

John Tabor's Ride. Bank Street College of Education, 1968 (F).

Tikki-Tikki-Tembo. Weston Woods Studios, 1970 (FSS), 1974 (F).

Wave. BFA Productions, n. d. (F).

Why the Sun and the Moon Live in the Sky. ACI Films, 1970 (F), 1973 (FSS).

EXHIBITIONS

American Institute of Graphic Arts, 1964, 1967. (New York, New York).

Boston Arts Festival, 1953, 1955, 1956, 1957. (Boston, Massachusetts).

Boston Printmaker's Show, 1955-61, 1963. (Boston, Massachusetts).

BACKGROUND READING

Bader. *American Picturebooks from Noah's Ark to The Beast Within*.

Commire. *Something about the Author*.

Contemporary Authors.

DeMontreville. *Third Book of Junior Authors*.

Hopkins. *Books Are by People*.

Kingman. *Illustrators of Children's Books, 1957-1966*.

Kingman. *Illustrators of Children's Books, 1967-1976*.

Kingman. *Newbery and Caldecott Medal Books, 1966-1975*.

Lent, B., and Sleator, W. "Illustrator Talks." *Publishers Weekly*, February 17, 1969.

Ward. *Illustrators of Books for Young People, Second Edition*.

+SORCHE NIC LEODHAS, *pseudonym*, 1898-1968

author
a.k.a. Leclaire Gowans Alger

AWARDS

(*All in the Morning Early*. Caldecott Honor Book, 1964.)

(*Always Room for One More*. Caldecott Medal Book, 1966.)

Thistle and Thyme. Newbery Honor Book, 1963.

BIBLIOGRAPHY

as Leclaire Alger:

Dougal's Wish. il. Marc Simont. Harper, 1942.

Golden Summer. il. Aldren Watson. Harper, 1942.

Jan and the Wonderful Mouth-Organ. il. Charlotte Becker. Harper, 1939.

as Sorche Nic Leodhas:

All in the Morning Early. il. Evaline Ness. Holt, 1963.

Always Room for One More. il. Nonny Hogrogian. Holt, 1965.

By Loch and Lin: Tales from Scottish Ballads. il. Vera Bock. Holt, 1969.

Claymore and Kilt: Tales of Scottish Kings and Castles. il. Leo and Diane Dillon. Holt, 1967.

Gaelic Ghosts. il. Nonny Hogrogian. Holt, 1964; *a.k.a. Gaelic Ghosts: Tales of the Supernatural from Scotland*. Bodley Head, 1966.

Ghosts Go Haunting. il. Nonny Hogrogian. Holt, 1965.

Heather and Broom: Tales of the Scottish Highlands. il. Consuelo Joerns. Holt, 1960.

Kellyburn Braes. il. Evaline Ness. Holt, 1968.

Laird of Cockpen. il. Adrienne Adams. Holt, 1969.

Scottish Songbook. il. Evaline Ness. Holt, 1969.

Sea-Spell and Moor-Magic: Tales of the Western Isles. il. Vera Bock. Holt, 1968.

Thistle and Thyme: Tales and Legends from Scotland.
il. Evaline Ness. Holt, 1962; variant as *Thistle and
Thyme: Tales and Legends from Scotland.* Bodley
Head, 1965; (Includes stories from *Heather and
Broom,* and *Thistle and Thyme.*)

*Twelve Great Black Cats: And Other Eerie Scottish
Tales.* il. Vera Bock. Dutton, 1971.

MEDIA

All in the Morning Early. (BB, TB); BFA Educational
Media, 1969 (F); Stephen F. Bosustow Films,
n. d. (F).

Always Room for One More. (BB).

Gaelic Ghosts. (BB, TB).

Ghosts Go Haunting. (TB).

Heather and Broom. (TB).

Sea-Spell and Moor-Magic. (BB, TB).

Thistle and Thyme. (BB, TB).

BACKGROUND READING

Contemporary Authors.

DeMontreville. *Third Book of Junior Authors.*

Leodhas, S. "Scottish History Tales." *Horn Book,*
June 1967.

Ward. *Authors of Books for Young People, Second
Edition.*

+JULIUS B. LESTER, 1939-
author

AWARDS

To Be a Slave. Newbery Honor Book, 1969.

BIBLIOGRAPHY

Angry Children of Malcolm X. Southern Student
Organizing Committee, 1966.

Black Folktales. il. Tom Feelings. Baron, 1969.

Knee-High Man and Other Tales. il. Ralph Pinto.
Dial, 1972.

Long Journey Home: Stories from Black History.
Dial, 1972.

*Look Out, Whitey! Black Power's Gon' Get Your
Mama!* Dial, 1968.

Mud of Vietnam. Folklore Press, 1967.

(comp.) *Our Folk Tales: High John the Conqueror,
and Other Afro-American Tales.* il. Jennifer
Lawson. n. p., *ca.*1967.

Revolutionary Notes. Grove, 1969.

*Search for the New Land: History as a Subjective
Experience.* Dial, 1969.

(ed.) *Seventh Son: The Thought and Writing of
W. E. B. Du Bois*; by W. E. B. Du Bois. Random,
1971.

(ed.) *Sing Out.* Oak, 1964.

To Be a Slave. il. Tom Feelings. Dial, 1968.

(ed.) *To Praise Our Bridges: An Autobiography*;
by Fannie L. Hamer. KIPCO, 1967.

*12-String Guitar as Played by Leadbelly: An
Instruction Manual*; with Pete Seeger. Oak, 1965.

Two Love Stories. Dial, 1972.

Who I Am: Poems: photographs by David Gahr.
Dial, 1974.

MEDIA

Black Folktales. (C, MT).

Knee-High Man. (TB).

Long Journey Home. (TB).

Look Out, Whitey. (C, MT, TB).

Revolutionary Notes. (C, MT).

To Be a Slave. (C, MT, TB).

Two Love Stories. (TB).

COLLECTIONS

Bontemps Collection, Arents Research Library,
Syracuse University. (Syracuse, New York).

BACKGROUND READING

Burke. *American Authors and Books, 1640 to the
Present Day.*

Chandler. *Living Black American Authors.*

Commire. *Something about the Author.*

Contemporary Authors.

DeMontreville. *Fourth Book of Junior Authors and
Illustrators.*

Geller, E. "Julius Lester, Newbery Runner-Up."
School Library Journal, May 15, 1969.

Hoffman. *Authors and Illustrators of Children's Books.*

Rush. *Black American Writers Past and Present.*

Ward. *Authors of Books for Young People, Second
Edition.*

+ELIZABETH FOREMAN LEWIS, 1892-1958
author

AWARDS

Young Fu of the Upper Yangtze. Newbery Medal Book, 1933.

BIBLIOGRAPHY

China Quest. il. Kurt Wiese. Winston, 1937.

Ho-Ming: Girl of New China. il. Kurt Wiese. Winston, 1934.

Portraits from a Chinese Scroll. il. Virginia H. Stout. Calligraphy by Chen Caho-Ming. Winston, 1938.

Test Tubes and Scales; with George C. Basil. il. Raymond Creekmore. Winston, 1940.

To Beat a Tiger, One Needs a Brother's Help. il. John Huehnergarth. Holt, 1953; *a.k.a. To Beat a Tiger, One Needs a Brother's Help: With Study Material Prepared by P. W. Diebel and R. McBurney*. Macmillan (Canada), 1967.

When the Typhoon Blows. il. Kurt Wiese. Winston, 1942.

Young Fu of the Upper Yangtze. il. Kurt Wiese. Winston, 1932; also il. Ed Young. Holt, 1973.

MEDIA

China Quest. (BB).

Portraits from a Chinese Scroll. (BB).

To Beat a Tiger. (BB).

When the Typhoon Blows. (BB).

Young Fu of the Upper Yangtze. (BB); Miller-Brody Productions, 1973 (FSS); Newbery Award Records, 1972 (C, R).

BACKGROUND READING

Burke. *American Authors and Books, 1640 to the Present Day*.

Commire. *Yesterday's Authors of Books for Children*.

Kunitz. *Junior Book of Authors*.

Kunitz. *Junior Book of Authors, Second Edition Revised*.

Miller. *Newbery Medal Books, 1922-1955*.

Obituary. *New York Times*, August 8, 1958.

Obituary. *Publishers Weekly*, August 18, 1958.

Obituary. *Wilson Library Bulletin*, October 1958.

Ward. *Authors of Books for Young People, Second Edition*.

Young Wings. *Writing Books for Boys and Girls*.

+JENNIE DOROTHEA LINDQUIST, 1899-1977
author

AWARDS

Golden Name Day. Newbery Honor Book, 1956.

BIBLIOGRAPHY

(ed.) *Caroline M. Hewins, Her Book: Containing a Mid-Century Child and Her Books (and) Caroline M. Hewins and Books for Children*. Horn Book, 1954.

Crystal Tree. il. Mary Chalmers. Harper, 1966.

Golden Name Day. il. Garth Williams. Harper, 1955.

Little Silver House. il. Garth Williams. Harper, 1959.

MEDIA

Crystal Tree. (TB).

Golden Name Day. (BB, TB).

Little Silver House. (TB).

BACKGROUND READING

Commire. *Something about the Author*.

Contemporary Authors.

Fuller. *More Junior Authors*.

Lindquist, J. "Swedish Christmas in America." *Horn Book*, November 1948.

Miller, B. "Horn Book's New Editor." *Horn Book*, November 1950.

Miller, B. "Salute to Jennie D. Lindquist." *Horn Book*, June 1958.

Ward. *Authors of Books for Young People, Second Edition*.

LEONARD LIONNI, 1910-
author-illustrator

AWARDS

Alexander and the Wind-Up Mouse. Caldecott Honor Book, 1970.

Frederick. Caldecott Honor Book, 1968.

Inch by Inch. Caldecott Honor Book, 1961.

Swimmy. Caldecott Honor Book, 1964.

BIBLIOGRAPHY

Alexander and the Wind-Up Mouse. Pantheon, 1969.

Alphabet Tree. Pantheon, 1968.

Biggest House in the World. Pantheon, 1968.

Botanica Parallela. Adelphi, 1976; *a.k.a. Parallel Botany*. Tr. Patrick Creagh. Knopf, 1977.

Color of His Own. Pantheon, 1974; *a.k.a. Colour of His Own*. Schuman, 1975.

Designs for the Printed Page. Fortune, *ca.*1960.

Fish Is Fish. Pantheon, 1970.

Flea Story. Pantheon, 1977.

Frederick. Pantheon, 1967.

Greentail Mouse. Pantheon, 1973.

In the Rabbitgarden. Pantheon, 1974.

Inch by Inch. Astor-Honor, 1960; *a.k.a. Pouce par Pouce*. Tr. Micheline Schmitt, 1961; *a.k.a. Pulgada a Pulgada*. Tr. Teresa Haba, 1961.

Little Blue and Little Yellow: A Story for Pippo and Ann and Other Children. Astor-Honor, 1959.

On My Beach There Are Many Pebbles. Astor-Honor, 1961.

Swimmy. Pantheon, 1963; *a.k.a. Nageot*. Tr. Catherine David, 1963; *a.k.a. Suimi*. Tr. Teresa Haba, 1963.

Taccuino di Leo Lionni. Electa, 1972.

Theodore and the Talking Mushroom. Pantheon, 1971.

Tico and the Golden Wings. Pantheon, 1964.

MEDIA

Alexander and the Wind-Up Mouse. (TB).

Fish Is Fish. Random House, 1974 (C, FSS).

Frederick. (BB); Lionni-Gianini/Connecticut Films, Inc., 1970 (F); Random House, 1974 (C); Random House/Spectra Films, 1972 (F).

In the Rabbitgarden. (BB); Random House, 1976 (C, FSS).

Inch by Inch. (TB).

Little Blue and Little Yellow. David Hilberman/ Contemporary Films, Inc., 1961 (F); McGraw-Hill Company, 1961 (F, VC); Spectra Films, 1974 (FS).

Swimmy. Random House, 1974 (C, FSS).

Theodore and the Talking Mushroom. Random House/Spectra Films, 1974 (FS).

EXHIBITIONS

Ariete Museum, 1966. (Milan, Italy).

Biennale Bratislava, 1967. (Bratislava, Czechoslovakia).

Biennale di Venezia, 1973. (Venice, Italy).

Galleria CIAK, 1975. (Rome, Italy).

Galleria del Milione, 1972. (Milan, Italy).

Gaukunst Galerie, 1974. (Cologne, Germany).

I Portici, 1973. (Torino, Italy).

Klingspor Museum, 1972. (Offenbach, Germany).

Museum of Modern Art, 1953-54. (New York, New York).

Norlyst Gallery, 1947. (New York, New York).

Obelisco Gallery, 1964. (Rome, Italy).

Philadelphia Art Alliance, 1959. (Philadelphia, Pennsylvania).

Philadelphia Print Club, 1948. (Philadelphia, Pennsylvania).

Staempfli Gallery, 1977. (New York, New York).

Worcestor Museum, 1958. (Worcestor, Massachusetts).

BACKGROUND READING

Agee, R. "Lionni Artichokes." *Wilson Library Bulletin*, May 1970.

Agee, R. "We Meet Leo Lionni." *Top of the News*, October 1962.

Bader. *American Picturebooks from Noah's Ark to The Beast Within*.

Burke. *American Authors and Books, 1640 to the Present Day*.

Commire. *Something about the Author*.

Contemporary Authors.

DeMontreville. *Third Book of Junior Authors*.

Ettenberg, E. "Leo Lionni Interview." *American Artist*, April 1953.

Hoffman. *Authors and Illustrators of Children's Books*.

Hopkins. *Books Are by People*.

Kingman. *Illustrators of Children's Books, 1957-1966*.

Kingman. *Illustrators of Children's Books, 1967-1976*.

Kirkpatrick. *Twentieth Century Children's Writers*.

"Leo Lionni." *Gebrauschsgraphik*, August 1962.

Lionni, L. "Mrs. Sanborn, I Love You." *Publishers Weekly*, July 11, 1966.

Lionni, L. "My Books for Children." *Wilson Library Bulletin*, October 1964.

Oeris, G. "Leo Lionni." *Graphis*, May 1952.

Smaridge. *Famous Author-Illustrators for Young People*.

Ward. *Authors of Books for Young People, Second Edition*.

ARNOLD STARK LOBEL, 1933-
author-illustrator

AWARDS

Frog and Toad Are Friends. Caldecott Honor Book, 1971.

Frog and Toad Together. Newbery Honor Book, 1973.

Hildilid's Night. Caldecott Honor Book, 1972.

BIBLIOGRAPHY

All about Jewish Holidays and Customs; by Morris Epstein. Ktav, 1959; revised, 1970.

Ants Are Fun; by Mildred Myrick. Harper, 1968.

As I Was Crossing Boston Common; by Norma Farber. Dutton, 1973.

As Right as Right Can Be; by Ann Rose. Dial, 1976.

Bears of the Air. Harper, 1965.

Benny's Animals and How He Put Them in Order; by Millicent E. Selsam. Harper, 1966.

Bibletime: With 14 Full-Page Bible Pasteups and 84 Full-Color Perforated Bible Stamps; by Sol Scharfstein. Ktav, 1958.

Book of Chanukah: Poems, Riddles, Stories, Songs and Things to Do; by Edythe Scharfstein. il. with Ezekiel Schloss. Ktav, 1959.

Circus; by Jack Prelutsky. Macmillan, 1974.

Clay Pot Boy; by Cynthia Jameson. Coward, 1973.

Comic Adventures of Old Mother Hubbard and Her Dog; by Sarah C. Martin. Bradbury, 1968.

Dinosaur Time; by Peggy Parish. Harper, 1974.

Dudley Pippin; by Phil Ressner. Harper, 1965.

Four Little Children Who Went around the World; by Edward Lear. Macmillan, 1968.

Frog and Toad All Year. Harper, 1976.

Frog and Toad Are Friends. Harper, 1970.

Frog and Toad Together. Harper, 1972.

Giant John. Harper, 1964.

Good Ethan; by Paula Fox. Bradbury, 1973.

Great Blueness and Other Predicaments. Harper, 1968.

Greg's Microscope; by Millicent Selsam. Harper, 1963.

Hansel and Gretel; by Jacob and Wilhelm Grimm. Delacorte, 1971.

Hebrew Dictionary: Activity Funbook; by Sol Scharfstein. Ktav, 1958.

Hildilid's Night; by Cheli D. Ryan. Macmillan, 1971.

Holiday Dictionary: With 90 Religious Objects to Color and 84 Full-Page Color Perforated Religious Objects Stamps; by Sol Scharfstein. Ktav, 1958.

Holiday for Mister Muster. Harper, 1963.

How the Rooster Saved the Day. il. Anita Lobel. Greenwillow, 1977.

Ice-Cream Cone Coot and Other Rare Birds. Parents, 1971.

I'll Fix Anthony; by Judith Virst. Harper, 1969.

Junk Day on Juniper Street and Other Easy to Read Stories; by Lilian Moore. Parents, 1968.

Let's Be Early Settlers with Daniel Boone; by Peggy Parish. Harper, 1967.

Let's Be Indians; by Peggy Parish. Harper, 1962.

Let's Get Turtles; by Millicent Selsam. Harper, 1965.

Little Runner of the Longhouse; by Betty Baker. Harper, 1962.

Lucille. Harper, 1964.

Magic Spectacles and Other Easy to Read Stories; by Lilian Moore. Parents, 1966.

Man Who Took the Indoors Out. Harper, 1974.

Martha, the Movie Mouse. Harper, 1966.

Master of Miracles; by Sulamith Ish-Kishor. Harper, 1971.

Merry Merry FIBuary; by Doris Orgel. Parents, 1977.

Miss Suzy; by Miriam Young. Parents, 1964.

Miss Suzy's Birthday Present; by Miriam Young. Parents, 1974.

Miss Suzy's Easter Surprise; by Miriam Young. Parents, 1972.

Mouse Songs. Harper, 1977.

Mouse Tales. Harper, 1972.

My First Book of Prayers; by Edythe Scharfstein. il. with Ezekiel Schloss. Ktav, 1968.

New Vestments; by Edward Lear. Bradbury, 1970.

Nightmares: Poems to Trouble Your Sleep; by Jack Prelutsky. Greenwillow, 1976.

On the Day Peter Stuyvesant Sailed into Town. Harper, 1971.

Oscar Otter; by Nathaniel Benchley. Harper, 1966.

Prince Bertram the Bad. Harper, 1963.

Quarreling Book; by Charlotte Zolotow. Harper, 1963.

Red Fox and His Canoe; by Nathaniel Benchley. Harper, 1964.

Red Tag Comes Back; by Fred Phlegar. Harper, 1961.

Sam, the Minuteman; by Nathaniel Benchley. Harper, 1969.

Seahorse; by Robert A. Morris. Harper, 1972.

Secret Three; by Mildred Myrick. Harper, 1963.

Small Pig. Harper, 1969.

Someday; by Charlotte Zolotow. Harper, 1965.

Something Old, Something New; by Susan Oneacre. Harper, 1961.

Star Thief; by Andrea DiNoto. Macmillan, 1967.

Strange Disappearance of Arthur Cluck; by Nathaniel Benchley. Harper, 1967.

Terrible Tiger; by Jack Prelutsky. Macmillan, 1969.

Terry and the Caterpillars; by Millicent Selsam. Harper, 1962; *a.k.a. Teresita y la Orugas*. Tr. Pura Belpré, 1969.

Tom Totot and His Little Flute; by Laura Cathon. Macmillan, 1970.

Witch on the Corner; by Felice Holman. Norton, 1966.

Zoo for Mister Muster. Harper, 1962.

MEDIA

Dinosaur Time. (BB).

Frog and Toad All Year. (BB).

Frog and Toad Are Friends. (TB); Newbery Award Records, 1976 (C, R); *a.k.a. Letter from Frog and Toad Are Friends*. Miller-Brody Productions, 1976 (FSS); *a.k.a. Lost Button from Frog and Toad Are Friends*. Miller-Brody Productions, 1976 (FSS); *a.k.a. Spring from Frog and Toad Are Friends*. Miller-Brody Productions, 1976 (FSS); *a.k.a. Story from Frog and Toad Are Friends*. Miller-Brody Productions, 1976 (FSS); *a.k.a. Swim from Frog and Toad Are Friends*. Miller-Brody Productions, 1976 (FSS).

Frog and Toad Together. (TB); Newbery Award Records, 1976 (C, R); *a.k.a. Cookies from Frog and Toad Together*. Miller-Brody Productions, 1976 (FSS); *a.k.a. Dragons and Giants from Frog and Toad Together*. Miller-Brody Productions, 1976 (FSS); *a.k.a. Dream from Frog and Toad Together*. Miller-Brody Productions, 1976 (FSS); *a.k.a. Garden from Frog and Toad Are Friends*. Miller-Brody Productions, 1976 (FSS); *a.k.a. List from Frog and Toad Are Friends*. Miller-Brody Productions, 1976 (FSS).

Giant John. (BB).

Mouse Tales. (BB).

Prince Bertram the Bad. Harper & Row, 1974 (FSS).

Small Pig. (TB).

Someday in *Daydreams and Make Believe* by Charlotte Zolotow. Educational Enrichment Materials, 197? (FSS).

Strange Disappearance of Arthur Cluck. Harper & Row, 1974 (FSS).

COLLECTIONS

Free Library of Philadelphia. (Philadelphia, Pennsylvania).

Iowa City Public Library. (Iowa City, Iowa).

Kerlan Collection, University of Minnesota. (Minneapolis, Minnesota).

BACKGROUND READING

Arnold Lobel. Profiles in Literature, 1973 (VC).

"Authors and Editors." *Publishers Weekly*, May 17, 1971.

Commire. *Something about the Author*.

Contemporary Authors.

DeMontreville. *Third Book of Junior Authors*.

Hopkins. *Books Are by People*.

Kingman. *Illustrators of Children's Books, 1957-1966*.

Kingman. *Illustrators of Children's Books, 1967-1976*.

Kirkpatrick. *Twentieth Century Children's Writers*.

Natov, R., and DeLuca, G. "Interview with Arnold Lobel." *Lion and the Unicorn*, No. 1, 1977.

Nykoruk. *Authors in the News*.

Ward. *Authors of Books for Young People, Second Edition*.

HUGH JOHN LOFTING, 1886-1947
author-illustrator

AWARDS

Voyages of Doctor Dolittle. Newbery Medal Book, 1923.

BIBLIOGRAPHY

Doctor Dolittle: A Treasury; compiled by Olga Fricker. Lippincott, 1967.

Doctor Dolittle and the Green Canary; completed by Olga Michael. Lippincott, 1950.

Doctor Dolittle and the Secret Lake. Lippincott, 1948.

Doctor Dolittle in the Moon. Stokes, 1928.

Doctor Dolittle's Birthday Book. Stokes, 1936.

Doctor Dolittle's Caravan. Stokes, 1926.

Doctor Dolittle's Circus. Stokes, 1924.

Doctor Dolittle's Garden. Stokes, 1927.

Doctor Dolittle's Post Office. Stokes, 1923.

Doctor Dolittle's Puddleby Adventures; edited by Josephine Lofting. Lippincott, 1952.

Doctor Dolittle's Return. Stokes, 1923.

Doctor Dolittle's Zoo. Stokes, 1925.

Gub-Gub's Book: An Encyclopedia of Food in Twenty Volumes. Stokes, 1932. (1 vol.).

Noisy Nora. Stokes, 1929.

BIBLIOGRAPHY (cont'd)

Porridge Poetry: Cooked, Ornamented and Served Up. Stokes, 1924.

Story of Doctor Dolittle: Being the History of His Peculiar Life at Home and Astonishing Adventures in Foreign Parts. Cape, 1936.

Story of Mrs. Tubbs. Stokes, 1923; *a.k.a. Mesaventure de Madame Popotte*; adapted by Sarah J. Silberstein and Claire Brugell, 1930.

Tommy, Tilly and Mrs. Tubbs. Stokes, 1936.

Twilight of Magic. il. Lois Lenski. Stokes, 1930.

Victory for the Slain. Cape, 1942.

Voyages of Doctor Dolittle. Stokes, 1922; variant as *Hugh Lofting's Travels of Doctor Dolittle*; adapted by Al Perkins. il. Philip Wende. Random, 1967; *a.k.a. Viages de Doctor Dolittle*. Tr. Carlos Rivera, 1968; *a.k.a. Voyages du Docteur Dolittle*. Tr. Jean Vallier, 1968.

Related titles:

Doctor Dolittle and His Friends: A Special Motion Picture Edition, Adaptation from the Characters and Stories Created by Hugh Lofting; adapted by Polly Berrends. il. Leon Jason and photos. Random, 1967.

Doctor Dolittle and the Pirates; by Al Perkins. il. Philip Wende. Random, 1968.

Meet Doctor Dolittle; by Al Perkins. il. Leon Jason. Random, 1967.

MEDIA

Doctor Dolittle. H. M. Stone Productions, 1972 (unauthorized FSS); Twentieth Century Fox Film Corporation, 1967 (F).

Story of Doctor Dolittle. (BB, C, MT, TB).

Voyages of Doctor Dolittle. (BB, TB); Miller-Brody Productions, 1976 (FSS).

BACKGROUND READING

Burke. *American Authors and Books, 1640 to the Present Day*.

Chambers, D. "How, Now, Doctor Dolittle?" *Elementary Education*, April 1968.

Colwell, E. "Hugh Lofting: An Appreciation." *Junior Bookshelf*, December 1947.

Doyle. *Who's Who of Children's Literature*.

Fish, H. "Doctor Dolittle, His Life and Work." *Horn Book*, September 1948.

Fish, H. "Dr. Dolittle's Creator." *Saturday Review of Literature*, January 10, 1948.

Jones, M. "Connecticut's Puddleby-on-the-Marsh: Hugh Lofting." *Horn Book*, August 1968.

Kirkpatrick. *Twentieth Century Children's Writers*.

Kunitz. *Junior Book of Authors*.

Kunitz. *Junior Book of Authors, Second Edition Revised*.

Kunitz. *Living Authors*.

Kunitz. *Twentieth Century Authors*.

Kunitz. *Twentieth Century Authors, First Supplement*.

Lofting, C. "Mortifying Visit from a Dude Dad." *Life*, September 30, 1966.

Mahony. *Contemporary Illustrators of Children's Books*.

Mahony. *Illustrators of Children's Books, 1744-1945*.

Miller. *Illustrators of Children's Books, 1946-1956*.

Miller. *Newbery Medal Books, 1922-1955*.

Montgomery. *Story behind Great Books*.

Montgomery. *Story behind Modern Books*.

Obituary. *New York Times*, September 28, 1967.

Obituary. *Newsweek*, October 6, 1947.

Obituary. *Publishers Weekly*, October 11, 1947.

Obituary. *Time*, October 6, 1947.

Obituary. *Wilson Library Bulletin*, November 1947.

Schlegelmilch, W. "From Fairy Tale to Children's Novel." *Bookbird*, No. 4, 1970.

Shenk, D. "Hugh Lofting: Creator of Doctor Dolittle." *Elementary English*, April 1955.

Smaridge. *Famous Modern Storytellers for Young People*.

Ward. *Authors of Books for Young People, Second Edition*.

+ELOISE LOWNSBERY, 1888-
author

AWARDS

Out of the Flame. Newbery Honor Book, 1932.

BIBLIOGRAPHY

Alfred the Great. Row, 1951.

Boy Knight of Rheims. il. Elizabeth T. Wolcott. Houghton, 1927.

Camel for a Throne. il. Elizabeth T. Wolcott. Houghton, 1941.

Gift of the Forest; with Reginald L. Singh. il. Anne Vaughan. Longmans, 1942.

Lighting the Torch. il. Elizabeth T. Wolcott. Longman Longmans, 1934

Marta the Doll. il. Mayra Werten. Longmans, 1946.

Out of the Flame. il. Elizabeth T. Wolcott. Longmans, 1931.

Saints and Rebels. il. Elizabeth T. Wolcott. Longmans, 1937.

MEDIA

Alfred the Great. (BB).

Gift of the Forest. Mercury Sound Books, 1957 (R).

BACKGROUND READING

Current Biography.

Kunitz. *Junior Book of Authors, Second Edition Revised*.

Lownsbery, E. "Jean and Pierre." *Horn Book*, August 1932.

+DAVID MACAULAY, 1946-
author-illustrator

AWARDS

Cathedral. Caldecott Honor Book, 1974.

BIBLIOGRAPHY

Castle. Houghton, 1977.

Cathedral: The Story of Its Construction. Houghton, 1973.

City: A Story of Roman Planning and Construction. Houghton, 1974.

Pyramid. Houghton, 1975.

Underground. Houghton, 1976.

EXHIBITIONS

Montclair Art Museum, 1977. (Montclair, New Jersey).

Spaced Gallery of Architecture, 1977. (New York, New York).

BACKGROUND READING

Contemporary Authors.

Kingman. *Illustrators of Children's Books, 1967-1976*.

Mercier, J. "David Macaulay." *Publishers Weekly*, April 10, 1978.

+ALIDA SIMS MALKUS, 1895-
author

AWARDS

Dark Star of Itza. Newbery Honor Book, 1931.

BIBLIOGRAPHY

Along the Inca Highway. Heath, 1941.

Amazon: River of Promise. il. Bruno Leepin. McGraw, 1970.

Animals of the High Andes. il. Edward Osmond. Abelard, 1965.

Beloved Island: A Cuban Family's Flight for Freedom. Chilton, 1967.

Blue-Water Boundary: Epic Highway of the Great Lakes and the Saint Lawrence. Hastings, 1960.

Boys of the Andes: Stories; with Alice Desmond and Ednah Wood. il. Frank Dobias. Heath, 1941.

Caravans to Santa Fe. il. Marie A. Lawson. Harper, 1928.

Chula of the Magic Islands. Saalfield, 1948.

Citadel of a Hundred Stairways. il. Henry C. Pitz. Winston, 1941.

Colt of Destiny: A Story of the California Missions. il. Manning DeV. Lee. Winston, 1950.

Constancia Lona. Doubleday, 1947.

Dark Star of Itza: The Story of a Pagan Princess. il. Lowell Houser. Harcourt, 1930.

Dragon Fly of Zuñi. il. Erick Berry, *pseud*. (Evangel A. C. Best). Harcourt, 1928.

Eastward Sweeps the Current: A Saga of the Polynesian Seafarers. il. Dan Sweeney. Winston, 1937.

Exploring the Sky and Sea: Auguste and Jacques Piccard. il. Robert Boehmer. Kingston, 1961.

Fifth for the King: A Story of the Conquest of Yucatan and of the Discovery of the Amazon. il. Erick Berry, *pseud*. (Evangel A. C. Best). Harper, 1931.

Little Giant of the North: The Boy Who Won a Fur Empire. il. Jay H. Barnum. Winston, 1952.

Meadows in the Sea. il. Margaret Cosgrove. World, 1960.

Outpost of Peril. Day, 1961.

Pirates' Port: A Tale of Old New York. il. Lyle Justis. Harper, 1929.

Raquel of the Ranch Country. il. George F. Avison. Harcourt, 1927.

Sea and Its Rivers. Doubleday, 1956.

BIBLIOGRAPHY (cont'd)

Sidi: Boy of the Desert. il. Manning DeV. Lee. Winston, 1956.

Silver Llama. Winston, 1939.

Spindle Imp and Other Tales of Maya Myth and Folklore. il. Erick Berry, *pseud*. (Evangel A. C. Best). Harcourt, 1931.

Stone Knife Boy. il. Herbert M. Stoops. Harcourt, 1933.

Story of Good Queen Bess. il. Douglas Gorsline. Grosset, 1953.

Story of Jacqueline Kennedy. il. Michael Lowenbein. Grosset, 1967.

Story of Louis Pasteur. il. Jo Spier. Grosset, 1952; *a.k.a. True Book about Louis Pasteur*. Muller, 1954.

Story of Winston Churchill. il. Herman B. Vestal. Grosset, 1957.

Strange Voyagers. Chilton, 1966.

There Really Was a Hiawatha. il. Jon Neilson. Grosset, 1963.

Through the Wall: A Boy's Struggle for Freedom. Grosset, 1962.

Timber Line. il. Ruth King. Harcourt, 1929.

We Were There at the Battle of Gettysburg. il. Leonard Vosburgh. Grosset, 1955.

Young Inca Prince. il. William Moyers. Knopf, 1957.

COLLECTIONS

deGrummond Collection, University of Southern Mississippi. (Hattiesburg, Mississippi).

Kerlan Collection, University of Minnesota. (Minneapolis, Minnesota).

BACKGROUND READING

Contemporary Authors.

Kunitz. *Junior Book of Authors*.

Kunitz. *Junior Book of Authors, Second Edition Revised*.

Malkus, A. "Who Can It Best?" *Horn Book*, August 1929.

"Two Thousand Miles of Background." *Horn Book*, February 1929.

Ward. *Authors of Books for Young People, Second Edition*.

Young Wings. *Writing Books for Boys and Girls*.

+BERNARD GAY MARSHALL, 1875-
author

AWARDS

Cedric the Forester. Newbery Honor Book, 1922.

BIBLIOGRAPHY

Cedric the Forester. il. J. Scott Williams. Appleton, 1921.

Old Hickory's Prisoner: A Tale of the Second War for Independence. Appleton, 1925.

Redcoat and Minuteman. il. J. Scott Williams. Appleton, 1924.

Torch Bearers: A Tale of Cavalier Days. Appleton, 1923.

Walter of Tiverton. Appleton, 1923.

SHARON BELL MATHIS, 1937-
author

AWARDS

Hundred Penny Box. Newbery Honor Book, 1976.

BIBLIOGRAPHY

Brooklyn Story. il. Charles Bible. Hill, 1970.

Cartwheels. il. Norma Holt. Scholastic, 1977.

Hundred Penny Box. il. Leo and Diane Dillon. Viking, 1975.

Listen for the Fig Tree. Viking, 1974.

Ray Charles. il. George Ford. Crowell, 1973.

Sidewalk Story. il. Leo Carty. Viking, 1971.

Teacup Full of Roses. Viking, 1972; large print edition, Hall, 1973.

MEDIA

Hundred Penny Box. Miller-Brody Productions, 1977 (C, R).

Listen for the Fig Tree. (TB).

Ray Charles. (CB).

Teacup Full of Roses. (TB); Viking Press, 1977 (C, R).

BACKGROUND READING

Chandler. *Living Black American Authors*.

Commire. *Something about the Author*.

Contemporary Authors.

DeMontreville. *Fourth Book of Junior Authors and Illustrators.*

Kirkpatrick. *Twentieth Century Children's Writers.*

Rush. *Black American Writers Past and Present.*

+WILLIAM KEEPERS MAXWELL, 1908-
author

AWARDS

Heavenly Tenants. Newbery Honor Book, 1947.

BIBLIOGRAPHY

Ancestors. Knopf, 1971.

Bright Center of Heaven. Harper, 1934.

Château. Knopf, 1961.

Folded Leaf. Harper, 1945; a.k.a. *Folded Leaf: With Slight Revisions by the Author*. Vantage, 1959.

*Heavenly Tenants. il. Ilonka Karasz. Harper, 1946.

Old Man at the Railroad Crossing and Other Tales. Knopf, 1966.

Over by the River. Knopf, 1977.

They Came Like Swallows. Harper, 1937; a.k.a. *They Came Like Swallows: With Slight Revisions by the Author*. Vantage, 1960.

Time Will Darken It. Harper, 1948.

Writer as Illusionist: A Speech Delivered at Smith College, March 4, 1955. Unitelum, 1955.

MEDIA

Ancestors. (TB).

Château. (TB).

Folded Leaf. (BB).

They Came Like Swallows. (BB).

COLLECTIONS

American Academy of Arts and Letters Library. (New York, New York).

Harvard University Library. (Cambridge, Massachusetts).

Hillyer Collection, Arents Research Library, Syracuse University. (Syracuse, New York).

State Historical Society of Wisconsin Library. (Madison, Wisconsin).

BACKGROUND READING

Burke. *American Authors and Books, 1640 to the Present Day*.

Current Biography.

Hart. *Oxford Companion to American Literature, Fourth Edition*.

Kunitz. *Twentieth Century Authors, First Supplement*.

Ward. *Authors of Books for Young People, Second Edition*.

Warfel. *American Novelists of Today*.

ROBERT McCLOSKEY, 1914-
author-illustrator

AWARDS

Blueberries for Sal. Caldecott Honor Book, 1949.

Journey Cake, Ho! Caldecott Honor Book, 1954.

Make Way for Ducklings. Caldecott Medal Book, 1942.

One Morning in Maine. Caldecott Honor Book, 1953.

Time of Wonder. Caldecott Medal Book, 1958.

BIBLIOGRAPHY

Blueberries for Sal. Viking, 1948.

Burt Dow, Deep-Water Man: A Tale of the Sea in the Classic Tradition. Viking, 1963.

Centerburg Tales, or the Further Adventures of Homer. Viking, 1951.

George Washington Bicentennial Calendar. (Hamilton, Ohio), 1932.

Henry Reed, Inc.; by Keith Robertson. Viking, 1958.

Henry Reed's Baby-Sitting Service; by Keith Robertson. Viking, 1966.

Henry Reed's Big Show; by Keith Robertson. Viking, 1970.

Henry Reed's Journey; by Keith Robertson. Viking, 1963.

Homer Price. Viking, 1943; large print edition, National Aid to the Visually Handicapped, 19?.

Journey Cake, Ho!; by Ruth Sawyer. Viking, 1953.

Junket: The Dog Who Liked Everything "Just So"; by Anne H. White. Viking, 1955.

Lentil. Viking, 1940.

Make Way for Ducklings. Viking, 1941.

BIBLIOGRAPHY (cont'd)

Man Who Lost His Head; by Claire H. Bishop. Viking, 1942.

One Morning in Maine. Viking, 1952.

Time of Wonder. Viking, 1957.

Tree Toad: The Adventures of the Kid Brother; by Bob Davis. il. with Charles D. Gibson. Stokes, 1942.

Trigger John's Son; by Tom Robinson. Viking, 1949.

Yankee Doodle's Cousins; by Anne Malcolmson. Viking, 1941.

MEDIA

Blueberries for Sal. Weston Woods Studios, 1963 (FSS), 1967 (F).

Centerburg Tales. (BB).

Henry Reed, Inc. Viking Press, 1973 (FSS).

Homer Price. (BB, TB); Gloria Chandler Recordings, n. d. (R); Intercontinental Audeo-Video Company, *ca*.1947 (R); Viking Press, 1973 (FSS); *a.k.a. The Doughnuts from Homer Price*. Weston Woods Studios, 1963 (F); *a.k.a. The Case of the Cosmic Comics from Homer Price*. Weston Woods Studios, 1976 (F); *a.k.a. Homer Price Stories Read by Robert McCloskey*. Weston Woods Studios, n. d. (C).

Journey Cake, Ho! Weston Woods Studios, 1967 (F); also in Weston Woods Studios Set No. 18, 1968 (FSS).

Lentil. (BB, TB); Weston Woods Studios, 1957 (F), 1958 (FSS); also in Weston Woods Studios Set No. 3, 1965 (FSS); *a.k.a. Little Hero*. Young People's Records, 19? (R).

Make Way for Ducklings. (BB, TB); Viking Press, 1974 (C); Weston Woods Studios, 1955 (F), 1957 and 1968 (FSS); also in Weston Woods Studios Set No. 1, 1968 (FSS); Young People's Records, n. d. (R); also in *Lively Art of Picture Books*. Weston Woods Studios, 1964 (F).

One Morning in Maine. (BB, TB).

Time of Wonder. (BB, TB); Weston Woods Studios, 1960 (FSS); 1961 (F); also in Weston Woods Studios Set No. 7, 1965 (FSS).

COLLECTIONS

Free Library of Philadelphia. (Philadelphia, Pennsylvania).

Gary Public Library. (Gary, Indiana).

May Massee Collection, Emporia State College. (Emporia, Kansas).

Smith Collection, Toronto Public Library. (Toronto, Canada).

BACKGROUND READING

Archer, M. "Robert McCloskey: Student of Human Nature." *Elementary English*, May 1958.

Bader. *American Picturebooks from Noah's Ark to The Beast Within*.

Burke. *American Authors and Books, 1640 to the Present Day*.

Commire. *Something about the Author*.

Contemporary Authors.

Coyle. *Ohio Authors and Their Books*.

Current Biography.

Greig, E., and Gregler, D. "Homer Price." *Horn Book*, November 1943.

Harbage, M. "Robert McCloskey: He Doesn't Forget." *Horn Book*, May 1954.

Hoffman. *Authors and Illustrators of Children's Books*.

Hopkins. *Books Are by People*.

Hutchens, J. "On an Author." *New York Herald Tribune Book Review*, May 11, 1952.

Kingman. *Illustrators of Children's Books, 1957-1966*.

Kingman. *Illustrators of Children's Books, 1967-1976*.

Kingman. *Newbery and Caldecott Medal Books, 1956-1965*.

Kirkpatrick. *Twentieth Century Children's Writers*.

Kunitz. *Junior Book of Authors, Second Edition Revised*.

Larrick, N. "Robert McCloskey's Make Way for Ducklings." *Elementary English*, March 1960.

Mahony. *Illustrators of Children's Books, 1744-1945*.

Miller. *Caldecott Medal Books, 1938-1957*.

Miller. *Illustrators of Children's Books, 1946-1956*.

Montgomery. *Story behind Modern Books*.

Painter, H. "Robert McCloskey, Master of Humorous Realism." *Elementary English*, February 1968.

Robert McCloskey. Profiles in Literature, 1977 (VT); Weston Woods Studios, 1965 (F).

Sawyer, R. "Robert McCloskey: Good Craftsman and Fine Artist." *Publishers Weekly*, June 27, 1942.

Smaridge. *Famous Author-Illustrators for Young People*.

Stokes, R. "To America—with Draughts: In Search of Robert McCloskey." *Horn Book*, August 1967.

Ward. *Authors of Books for Young People, Second Edition*.

Ward. *Illustrators of Books for Young People, Second Edition*.

BEVERLY BRODSKY McDERMOTT
author-illustrator
a.k.a. Beverly Brodsky

AWARDS

Golem. Caldecott Honor Book, 1977.

BIBLIOGRAPHY

as Beverly Brodsky:

Jonah: An Old Testament Story; from the *Bible*. Lippincott, 1977.

as Beverly Brodsky McDermott:

Crystal Apple: A Russian Tale. Viking, 1974.

Forest of the Night; by John R. Townsend. Lippincott, 1975.

Golem: A Jewish Legend. Lippincott, 1976.

Sedna: An Eskimo Myth. Viking, 1975.

MEDIA

Crystal Apple. Weston Woods Studios, 1975 (FSS).

BACKGROUND READING

"Beverly McDermott." *Wilson Library Bulletin*, January 1976.

Commire. *Something about the Author*.

Contemporary Authors.

Kingman. *Illustrators of Children's Books, 1967-1976*.

Stevens, C. "Seeing Things à la Russe." *Print*, May 1974.

+GERALD McDERMOTT
author-illustrator

AWARDS

Anansi. Caldecott Honor Book, 1973.

Arrow to the Sun. Caldecott Medal Book, 1975.

BIBLIOGRAPHY

Anansi, the Spider: A Tale from the Ashanti. Holt, 1972.

Arrow to the Sun: A Pueblo Indian Tale, Adapted. Viking, 1974.

Knight of the Lion. Viking, 1976.

Magic Tree: A Tale from the Congo, Adapted. Holt, 1973.

Stonecutter: A Japanese Folktale, Adapted. Viking, 1975.

Voyage of Osiris: A Myth of Ancient Egypt. Windmill, 1977.

MEDIA

Anansi. Gerald McDermott Films/Landmark Educational Media, Inc., 1969 (F).

Arrow to the Sun. Weston Woods Studios, 1975 (F, FSS).

Magic Tree. Gerald McDermott Films/Texture Films, 19? (F).

Stone Cutter. Gerald McDermott Films/International Film Corporation, 1965 (F); Weston Woods Studios, 1975 (F, FSS).

EXHIBITIONS

Everson Art Museum, 1974. (Syracuse, New York).

BACKGROUND READING

DeMontreville. *Fourth Book of Junior Authors and Illustrators*.

Kingman. *Illustrators of Children's Books, 1967-1976*.

Kingman. *Newbery and Caldecott Medal Books, 1966-1975*.

Lanes, S. "Sign of the Times: The Caldecott Winner for 1975." *School Library Journal*, February 1976.

Nykoruk. *Authors in the News*.

Stevens, C. "Gerald McDermott: Animating Myth and Legend." *Print*, November 1973.

Ward. *Illustrators of Books for Young People, Second Edition*.

ELOISE JARVIS McGRAW, 1915-
author

AWARDS

Golden Goblet. Newbery Honor Book, 1962.

Moccasin Trail. Newbery Honor Book, 1953.

BIBLIOGRAPHY

Crown Fire. Coward, 1951; *a.k.a. Crown Fire, Edited for Schools by Jerome D. Shostak*. Oxford Book, 1957.

Golden Goblet. Coward, 1961; il. Owen Wood. Methuen, 1964.

Greensleeves. Harcourt, 1968.

Mara: Daughter of the Nile. il. Jack Myers. Coward, 1953.

Master Cornhill. Atheneum, 1973.

BIBLIOGRAPHY (cont'd)

Merry Go Round in Oz: Founded On and Continuing the Famous Oz Stories by L. Frank Baum; with Lauren M. Wagner. il. Dick Martin. Reilly, 1963.

Moccasin Trail. il. Paul Galdone. Coward, 1952.

Pharaoh. Coward, 1958.

Really Weird Summer. Atheneum, 1977.

Sawdust in His Shoes. il. Pers Crowell. Coward, 1950.

Steady Stephanie. Dramatic, 1961.

Techniques of Fiction Writing. Writer, 1959.

MEDIA

Greensleeves. (BB, TB).

Golden Goblet. Miller-Brody Productions, 1974 (FSS).

Mara. (TB).

Moccasin Trail. (BB); Miller-Brody Productions, 1976 (C, R).

Sawdust in His Shoes. (TB).

Techniques of Fiction Writing. (BB).

COLLECTIONS

Kerlan Collection, University of Minnesota. (Minneapolis, Minnesota).

University of Oregon Library. (Eugene, Oregon).

BACKGROUND READING

Burke. *American Authors and Books, 1640 to the Present Day*.

Commire. *Something about the Author*.

Contemporary Authors.

Current Biography.

Fuller. *More Junior Authors*.

Kirkpatrick. *Twentieth Century Children's Writers*.

Ward. *Authors of Books for Young People, Second Edition*.

+MARIAN HURD McNEELY, 1877-1930
author
a.k.a. Marian Kent Hurd

AWARDS

Jumping-Off Place. Newbery Honor Book, 1930.

BIBLIOGRAPHY

as Marian Kent Hurd:

Miss Billy: A Neighborhood Story; with Edith K. Stokely. il. Charles Copeland. Lothrop, 1905.

When She Came Home from College; with Jean B. Wilson. il. George Gibbs. Houghton, 1909.

as Marian Hurd McNeely:

Jumping-Off Place. il. William Siegel. Longmans, 1929.

Rusty Ruston: A Story for Brothers and Sisters. il. Eloise Burns. Longmans, 1928.

Way to Glory: And Other Stories. il. John Esley. Longmans, 1932.

Winning Out. il. Hattie L. Price. Longmans, 1931.

BACKGROUND READING

Fisher, D. "Marian Hurd McNeely." *Horn Book*, August 1932.

Kunitz. *Junior Book of Authors*.

Kunitz. *Junior Book of Authors, Second Edition Revised*.

+STEPHEN WARREN MEADER, 1892-
author-illustrator

AWARDS

Boy with a Pack. Newbery Honor Book, 1940.

BIBLIOGRAPHY

Away to Sea. il. Clinton Balmer. Harcourt, 1931.

Bat: The Story of a Bull Terrier. il. Edward Shenton. Harcourt, 1939.

Behind the Ranges. il. Edward Shenton. Harcourt, 1947.

Black Buccaneer. Harcourt, 1920; also il. Mead Schaeffer, 1929; also il. Edward Shenton, 1942.

Blow for Liberty. il. Victor Mays. Harcourt, 1965.

Blueberry Mountain. il. Edward Shenton. Harcourt, 1941.

Boy with a Pack. il. Edward Shenton. Harcourt, 1939.

Buckboard Stranger. il. Paul Calle. Harcourt, 1954.

Buffalo and Beaver. il. Charles Beck. Harcourt, 1960.

Bulldozer. il. Edwin Schmidt. Harcourt, 1951; *a.k.a. Bulldozer, School Edition Edited by Geraldine Murphy*, 1955.

Cape May Packet. il. Robert Frankenberg. Harcourt, 1969.

Cedar's Boy. il. Lee Townsend. Harcourt, 1949.

Clear for Action! il. Frank Beaudoin. Harcourt, 1940.

Commodore's Cup. il. Don Sibley. Harcourt, 1958.

Down the Big River. Harcourt, 1924.

Everglades Adventure. il. Charles Beck. Harcourt, 1957.

Fish Hawk's Nest. il. Edward Shenton. Harcourt, 1952.

Guns for the Saratoga. il. John O. Cosgrave, II. Harcourt, 1955.

Jonathan Goes West. il. Edward Shenton. Harcourt, 1946.

Keep 'Em Rolling. il. Al Savitt. Harcourt, 1967.

King of the Hills. il. Lee Townsend. Harcourt, 1933.

Lonesome End. il. Ned Butterfield. Harcourt, 1968.

Long Trains Roll. il. Edward Shenton. Harcourt, 1944.

Longshanks. il. Edward C. Caswell. Harcourt, 1928.

Lumberjack. il. Henry C. Pitz. Harcourt, 1934.

Muddy Road to Glory. il. George Hughes. Harcourt, 1963.

Phantom of the Blockade. il. Victor Mays. Harcourt, 1962.

Red Horse Hill. il. Lee Townsend. Harcourt, 1930.

River of the Wolves. il. Edward Shenton. Harcourt, 1948.

Sabre Pilot. il. John Polgreen. Harcourt, 1956.

Sea Snake. il. Edward Shenton. Harcourt, 1943.

Shadow in the Pines. il. Edward Shenton. Harcourt, 1942.

Skippy's Family. il. Elizabeth Korn. Harcourt, 1945.

Snow on Blueberry Mountain. il. Don Sibley. Harcourt, 1961.

Sparkplug of the Hornets. il. Don Sibley. Harcourt, 1953.

Stranger on Big Hickory. il. Don Lambo. Harcourt, 1964.

T-Model Tommy. il. Edward Shenton. Harcourt, 1938; *a.k.a. T-Model Tommy, Edited by Blanche J. Thompson*, 1940.

Topsail Island Treasure. il. Marbury Brown. Harcourt, 1966.

Trap-Lines North: A True Story of the Canadian Woods. il. Enos B. Comstock. Dodd, 1936.

Voyage of the Javelin. il. John O. Cosgrave, II. Harcourt, 1959.

Whaler 'round the Horn. il. Edward Shenton. Harcourt, 1950.

Who Rides in the Dark? il. James MacDonald. Harcourt, 1937.

Wild Pony Island. il. Charles Beck. Harcourt, 1959.

Will to Win and Other Stories. il. John Gincano. Harcourt, 1936.

MEDIA

Boy with a Pack. (BB, TB).

Buckboard Stranger. (BB).

Buffalo and Beaver. (MT).

Bulldozer. (BB).

Clear for Action. (BB).

Long Trains Roll. (BB).

Phantom of the Blockade. (BB).

Red Horse Hill. (BB).

River of the Wolves. (BB).

Sea Snake. (BB).

Trap Lines North. Intercontinental Audeo-Video Company, *ca.*1947 (R).

Who Rides in the Dark? (BB, C, MT).

COLLECTIONS

deGrummond Collection, University of Southern Mississippi. (Hattiesburg, Mississippi).

BACKGROUND READING

Burke. *American Authors and Books, 1640 to the Present Day*.

Commire. *Something about the Author*.

Contemporary Authors.

Kirkpatrick. *Twentieth Century Children's Writers*.

Kunitz. *Junior Book of Authors*.

Kunitz. *Junior Book of Authors, Second Edition Revised*.

"Racetrack and Riverbank, the Books of Stephen Meader." *Horn Book*, November 1930.

Ward. *Authors of Books for Young People, Second Edition*.

FLORENCE CRANNELL MEANS, 1891-
author

AWARDS

Moved-Outers. Newbery Honor Book, 1946.

BIBLIOGRAPHY

Across the Fruited Plain. il. Janet Smalley. Missionary Education, 1940.

Adella Mary in New Mexico. Houghton, 1939.

Alicia. il. William Barss. Houghton, 1953.

All 'round Me Shinin'. Baptist Board of Education, ca. 1940.

Assorted Sisters. il. Helen Blair. Houghton, 1947.

At the End of Nowhere. il. David Hendrickson. Houghton, 1940.

Biography of Frederick Douglass. Imperial International, 1969.

Black Tents: A Junior Play of Life among the Bedouins in Syria. Missionary Education, 1926.

Borrowed Brothers. il. Dorothy B. Morse. Houghton, 1958.

Bowlful of Stars: A Story of the Pioneer West. il. Henry C. Pitz. Houghton, 1934.

But I Am Sara. Houghton, 1961.

Candle in the Mist: A Story for Girls. il. Marguerite de Angeli. Houghton, 1931; *a.k.a. Candle in the Mist: A Story for Girls; Edited with an Introduction and Reading Aids by Alice Brandinger*, 1968.

Carvers' George: A Biography of George Washington Carver. il. Harvé Stein. Houghton, 1952.

Children of the Great Spirit: A Course on the American Indian for Primary Children; with Frances S. Riggs. Missionary Education, 1932.

Children of the Promise. il. Janet Smalley. Missionary Education, 1941.

Dusky Day: A College Story. il. Manning DeV. Lee. Houghton, 1933.

Emmy and the Blue Door. il. Frank Nicholas. Houghton, 1959.

Frankie and Willie Go a Far Piece. Baptist Board of Education, ca.1940.

Great Day in the Morning. il. Helen Blair. Houghton, 1949.

Hetty of the Grande Deluxe. il. Helen Blair. Houghton, 1951.

House under the Hill. il. Helen Blair. Houghton, 1949.

It Takes All Kinds. Houghton, 1964.

Knock at the Door, Emmy. il. Paul Lantz. Houghton, 1956.

Moved-Outers. il. Helen Blair. Houghton, 1945.

Our Cup Is Broken. Houghton, 1969.

Penny for Luck: A Story of the Rockies. il. Paul Quinn. Houghton, 1935.

Pepita's Adventures in Friendship: A Play for Juniors about Mexicans in the United States. Missionary Education, 1929.

Peter of the Mesa. il. Janet Smalley. Friendship, 1944.

Rafael and Consuelo: Stories and Studies about Mexicans in the United States for Primary Children; with Harriet L. Fullen. Missionary Education, 1929.

Rainbow Bridge. il. Eleanor F. Lattimore. Missionary Education, 1934.

Rains Will Come. il. Fred Kabotie. Houghton, 1954.

Ranch and Ring: A Story of the Pioneer West. il. Harvey J. Peck. Houghton, 1932.

Reach for a Star. Houghton, 1957.

Sagebrush Surgeon. Friendship, 1955.

Shadow over Wide Ruin. il. Lorence F. Bjorklund. Houghton, 1942.

Shuttered Windows. il. Armstrong Sperry. Houghton, 1938.

Silver Fleece: A Story of the Spanish in New Mexico; with Carl Means. il. Edwin L. Schmidt. Winston, 1950.

Singing Wood: A College Story. il. Manning DeV. Lee. Houghton, 1937.

Smith Valley. Houghton, 1973.

Some California Puppies and How They Grew. Baptist Board of Education, ca.1940.

Sunlight on the Hopi Mesas: The Story of Abigail E. Johnson. Judson, 1960.

Tangled Waters: A Navajo Story. il. Herbert M. Stoops. Houghton, 1936.

Tara Finds the Door to Happiness: A Play for Juniors. Missionary Education, 1926.

Teresita of the Valley. il. Nicholas Panesis. Houghton, 1943.

That Girl Andy. Houghton, 1962.

Tolliver. Houghton, 1963.

Us Maltbys. Houghton, 1966.

Whispering Girl: A Hopi Indian Story of Today. il. Oscar Howard. Houghton, 1941.

Wither the Tribes Go Up. Northern Baptist Convention, 1944.

MEDIA

Alicia. (BB).

Borrowed Brothers. (BB).

Candle in the Mist. (BB, C, MT).

Rains Will Come. (BB).

Shuttered Windows. (BB, TB).

Smith Valley. (CB).

COLLECTIONS

Bontemps Collection, Arents Research Library,
Syracuse University. (Syracuse, New York).

University of Colorado Library. (Boulder, Colorado).

BACKGROUND READING

Andrews, S. "Florence Crannell Means." *Horn Book*,
January 1946.

Burke. *American Authors and Books, 1640 to the
Present Day*.

Commire. *Something about the Author*.

Contemporary Authors.

Foremost Women in Communications.

Kirkpatrick. *Twentieth Century Children's Writers*.

Kunitz. *Junior Book of Authors*.

Kunitz. *Junior Book of Authors, Second Edition
Revised*.

Means, F. "Mosaic." *Horn Book*, January 1940.

Pease, H. "Without Evasion." *Horn Book*,
January 1945.

Smaridge. *Story behind Modern Books*.

Ward. *Authors of Books for Young People,
Second Edition*.

Young Wings. *Writing Books for Boys and Girls*.

+CORNELIA LYNDE MEIGS, 1884-1972
author
pseudonym Adair Aldon

AWARDS

Clearing Weather. Newbery Honor Book, 1929.

Invincible Louisa. Newbery Medal Book, 1934.

Swift Rivers. Newbery Honor Book, 1933.

Windy Hill. Newbery Honor Book, 1922.

BIBLIOGRAPHY

as Adair Aldon:

At the Sign of the Two Heroes. il. S. Gordon Smyth.
Century, 1920.

Hill of Adventure. il. J. Clinton Shepherd. Century,
1922.

Island of Appledore. il. W. B. King. Macmillan, 1917.

Pirate of Jasper Peak. Macmillan, 1918.

as Cornelia Meigs:

As the Crow Flies. Macmillan, 1927.

Call of the Mountain. il. James Daugherty. Little,
1940.

Clearing Weather. il. Frank Dobias. Little, 1928.

Covered Bridge. il. Marguerite de Angeli. Macmillan,
1926.

(ed.) *Critical History of Children's Literature: A
Survey of Children's Books in English from
Earliest Times to the Present*; with Anne T.
Eaton, et al. il. Vera Bock. Macmillan, 1953;
revised, 1969.

Crooked Apple Tree. il. Helen M. Grose. Little, 1929.

Dutch Colt. il. George and Doris Hauman. Macmillan,
1952.

Fair Wind to Virginia. il. Jon C. Wonsetler. Macmillan,
1955.

(ed.) *Glimpses of Louisa: A Centennial Sampling of
the Best Short Stories*; by Louisa M. Alcott.
Little, 1968.

*Great Design: Men and Events in the United Nations
from 1945 to 1963*. Little, 1964.

*Helga and the White Peacock: A Play in Three Acts
for Young People*. il. Ruth Bigham. photographs
by Margaret Browne. Macmillan, 1922.

*Invincible Louisa: Story of the Author of Little
Women*. Little, 1933; *a.k.a. Invincible Louisa:
The Story of Louisa Alcott*, 1935; *a.k.a.
Invincible Louisa, the Story of the Author of
Little Women, with a New Introduction*, 1968.

Jane Addams: Pioneer for Social Justice. Little, 1970.

Kingdom of the Winding Road. il. Frances White.
Macmillan, 1915; il. Willy Pogány, 1928.

(ed.) *Little Women: Or, Meg, Jo, Beth and Amy*; by
Louisa M. Alcott. il. Jessie W. Smith. Little, 1968.

Louisa May Alcott: A Bibliography; with Lucile
Gulliver. Little, 1932.

Louisa May Alcott and the American Family Story.
Bodley Head, 1970; Walck, 1971.

Master Simon's Garden: A Story. il. Frances White.
Macmillan, 1916; also il. John Rae, 1929.

Mother Makes Christmas. il. Lois Lenski. Grosset,
1940.

Mounted Messenger. il. Jon C. Wonsetler. Macmillan,
1943.

Mystery at the Red House. il. Robert MacLean.
Macmillan, 1961.

*New Moon: The Story of Dick Martin's Courage, His
Silver Sixpence and His Friends in the New World*.
il. Marguerite de Angeli. Macmillan, 1924.

BIBLIOGRAPHY (cont'd)

Pool of Stars. Macmillan, 1919; il. John Rae, 1929.

Railroad West: A Novel. il. Helen H. Bencker. Little, 1937.

Rain on the Roof. il. Edith B. Price. Macmillan, 1925.

Saint John's Church, Havre De Grace, Md., 1809-1959. Democratic-Ledger, 1959.

Steadfast Princess: A Play for Young People. Macmillan, 1916.

Swift Rivers. il. Forest W. Orr. Little, 1932; also il. Peter Hurd, 1937.

To Church We Go. il. Elizabeth O. Jones. Follett, 1956.

Trade Wind. il. Henry C. Pitz. Little, 1927.

Two Arrows: A Story. Macmillan, 1949.

Vanished Island. il. Dorothy Bayley. Macmillan, 1941.

Violent Men: A Study of Human Relations in the First American Congress. Macmillan, 1949.

What Makes a College? A History of Bryn Mawr. Macmillan, 1956.

Wild Geese Flying. il. Charles Geer. Macmillan, 1957.

Willow Whistle. il. E. Boyd Smith. Macmillan, 1931.

Wind in the Chimney. il. Louise Mansfield. Macmillan, 1934.

Windy Hill. Macmillan, 1921.

Wonderful Locomotive. il. Berta and Elmer Hader. Macmillan, 1928.

Young Americans: How History Looked to Them While It Was in the Making; A Collection of Stories. Ginn, 1936.

MEDIA

Dutch Colt. (BB).

Great Design. (BB, TB).

Invincible Louisa. (BB, CB, TB); Miller-Brody Productions, 1969 (C, R).

Jane Addams. (TB).

Wild Geese Flying. (BB).

Willow Whistle. (BB).

Wonderful Locomotive. (BB).

COLLECTIONS

Bryn Mawr College Library. (Bryn Mawr, Pennsylvania).

deGrummond Collection, University of Southern Mississippi. (Hattiesburg, Mississippi).

University of Iowa Library. (Iowa City, Iowa).

BACKGROUND READING

Burke. *American Authors and Books, 1640 to the Present Day*.

Commire. *Something about the Author*.

Contemporary Authors.

Foremost Women in Communications.

Kirkpatrick. *Twentieth Century Children's Writers*.

Kunitz. *Junior Book of Authors*.

Kunitz. *Junior Book of Authors, Second Edition Revised*.

Kunitz. *Living Authors*.

Kunitz. "Writing for Children Today." *Horn Book*, September 1949.

Meigs, C. "How 'The Wonderful Locomotive' Happened." *Horn Book*, August 1928.

Miller. *Newbery Medal Books, 1922-1955*.

Montgomery. *Story behind Modern Books*.

New York Times Biographical Edition.

Patee, D. "Cornelia Meigs." *Horn Book*, September 1944.

Sauer, J. "Books of Cornelia Meigs." *Horn Book*, September 1944.

Ward. *Authors of Books for Young People, Second Edition*.

Young Wings. *Writing Books for Boys and Girls*.

MISKA MILES, *pseudonym*, 1899-
author
a.k.a. Patricia Miles Martin

AWARDS

Annie and the Old One. Newbery Honor Book, 1972.

BIBLIOGRAPHY

as *Patricia Miles Martin*:

Abraham Lincoln. il. Gustav Schrotter. Putnam, 1964.

Andrew Jackson. il. Salem Tamer. Putnam, 1966.

Be Brave, Charlie. il. Bonnie Johnson. Putnam, 1972.

Benjie Goes into Business. il. Paul Galdone. Putnam, 1961.

Birthday Present. il. Margot Locke. Abingdon, 1963.

Bony Pony. il. Glen Dines. Putnam, 1965.

Broomtail Bronc. il. Margot Locke. Abingdon, 1965.

Calvin and the Cub Scouts. il. Tom Hamil. Putnam, 1964.

Cat. il. Jonathan Goell. Ginn, 1974.

Chandler Chipmunk's Flying Lesson and Other Stories. il. Margot Locke. Abingdon, 1960.

Chicanos: Mexicans in the U.S. il. Robert Frankenberg. Parents, 1971.

Daniel Boone. il. Glen Dines. Putnam, 1965.

Dog and the Boat Boy. il. Earl Thollander. Putnam, 1969.

Dog Next Door and Other Stories; with Theodore Clymer, et al. Ginn, 1969.

Dolley Madison. il. Unada (Gliewe). Putnam, 1967.

Dolls from Cheyenne. il. Don Almquist. Putnam, 1967.

Eskimos: People of Alaska. il. Robert Frankenberg. Parents, 1970.

Friend of Miguel. il. Genia (Wennerstrom). Rand, 1967.

Grandma's Gun. il. Robert Corey. Golden Gate, 1968.

Greedy One. il. Kazue Mizumura. Rand, 1964.

Happy Piper and the Goat. il. Kurt Werth. Lothrop, 1960.

Hide. il. Dick Rogers. Ginn, 1974.

How Can You Hide an Elephant? il. George M. Ulrich. Ginn, 1974.

Indians: The First Americans. il. Robert Frankenberg. Parents, 1970.

Jacqueline Kennedy Onassis. il. Paul Frame. Putnam, 1969.

James Madison. il. Richard Cuffari. Putnam, 1970.

Jefferson Davis. il. Salem Tamer. Putnam, 1966.

John Fitzgerald Kennedy. il. Paul Frame. Putnam, 1964.

John Marshall. il. Salem Tamer. Putnam, 1967.

Jump Frog Jump. il. Earl Thollander. Putnam, 1965.

Kumi and the Pearl. il. Tom Hamil. Putnam, 1968.

Little Brown Hen. il. Harper Johnson. Crowell, 1960.

Little Two and the Peach Tree. il. Joan Berg. Atheneum, 1963.

Long Ago Christmas. il. Albert Orbaan. Putnam, 1968.

Lucky Little Porcupine. il. Lee Smith. Putnam, 1963.

May I Come In?; with Theodore Clymer, et al. Ginn, 1976.

Mrs. Grumble and Fire Engine Number 7. il. Earl Thollander. Putnam, 1967.

Navajo Pet. il. John Hamberger. Putnam, 1971.

No, No Rosina. il. Earl Thollander. Putnam, 1964.

One Special Dog. il. Johnny and Lucy Hawkinson. Rand, 1968.

Pocahontas. il. Portia Takajian. Putnam, 1963.

Pointed Brush. il. Roger Duvoisin. Lothrop, 1959.

Pumpkin Patch. il. Tom Hamil. Putnam, 1966.

Raccoon and Mrs. McGinnis. il. Leonard Weisgard. Putnam, 1961.

Rice Bowl Pet. il. Ezra J. Keats. Crowell, 1962.

Rolling the Cheese. il. Alton Raible. Atheneum, 1966.

Show and Tell. il. Tom Hamil. Putnam, 1962.

Sing, Sailor, Sing. il. Graham Booth. Golden Gate, 1966.

Stanley, the Dog Next Door; with Theodore Clymer, et al. Ginn, 1976.

Suzu and the Bride Doll. il. Kazue Mizumura. Rand, 1960.

Sylvester Jones and the Voice in the Forest. il. Leonard Weisgard. Lothrop, 1958.

"That Cat! 1-2-3." il. Unada (Gliewe). Putnam, 1969.

There Goes the Tiger! il. Tom Hamil. Putnam, 1970.

Thomas Alva Edison. il. Fermin Rocker. Putnam, 1971.

Trina's Boxcar. il. Robert L. Jefferson. Abingdon, 1967.

Two Plays about Foolish People. il. Gabriel Lisowski. Putnam, 1972.

Woody's Big Trouble. il. Paul Galdone. Putnam, 1967.

Zachary's Taylor. il. Tran Mawicke. Putnam, 1969.

as Miska Miles:

Aaron's Door. il. Alan E. Cober. Atlantic, 1977.

Annie and the Old One. il. Peter Parnall. Atlantic, 1971.

Apricot ABC. il. Peter Parnall. Atlantic, 1969.

Chicken Forgets. il. Jim Arnosky. Atlantic, 1976.

Dusty and the Fiddlers. il. Erik Blegvad. Atlantic, 1962.

Eddie's Bear. il. John Schoenherr. Atlantic, 1970.

Fox and the Fire. il. John Schoenherr. Atlantic, 1966.

Gertrude's Pocket. il. Emily McCully. Atlantic, 1970.

Hoagie's Rifle Gun. il. John Schoenherr. Atlantic, 1970.

Kickapoo. il. Wesley Dennis. Atlantic, 1961.

Mississippi Possum. il. John Schoenherr. Atlantic, 1965.

Nobody's Cat. il. John Schoenherr. Atlantic, 1969.

Otter in the Cove. il. John Schoenherr. Atlantic, 1974.

Pieces of Home. il. Victor Ambrus. Atlantic, 1967.

Pony in the Schoolhouse. il. Erik Blegvad. Atlantic, 1964.

Rabbit Garden. il. John Schoenherr. Atlantic, 1967.

BIBLIOGRAPHY (cont'd)

as Miska Miles (cont'd):

See a White Horse. il. Wesley Dennis. Atlantic, 1963.

Small Rabbit. il. Jim Arnosky. Atlantic, 1977.

Somebody's Dog. il. John Schoenherr. Atlantic, 1973.

Swim, Little Duck. il. Jim Arnosky. Atlantic, 1976.

Teacher's Pet. il. Fen Lassell. Atlantic, 1966.

Tree House Town. il. Emily McCully. Atlantic, 1974.

Uncle Fonzo's Ford. il. Wendy Watson. Atlantic, 1968.

Wharf Rat. il. John Schoenherr. Atlantic, 1972.

MEDIA

Annie and the Old One. (BB); BFA Educational Media, 1977 (F); Greenhouse Films, 19? (F).

Calvin and the Cub Scouts. (BB).

Gertrude's Pocket. (BB).

Mississippi Possum. (BB).

One Special Dog. Stephen Bosustow Productions, 19? (F).

Pony in the Schoolhouse. (BB).

Somebody's Dog. (BB, TB); a.k.a. *William's Dog*. Xerox Films/Lumin Films, 1975 (FSS).

Uncle Fonzo's Ford. (TB).

COLLECTIONS

deGrummond Collection, University of Southern Mississippi. (Hattiesburg, Mississippi).

Kerlan Collection, University of Minnesota. (Minneapolis, Minnesota).

BACKGROUND READING

Commire. *Something about the Author*.

Contemporary Authors.

DeMontreville. *Fourth Book of Junior Authors and Illustrators*.

Foremost Women in Communications.

Kirkpatrick. *Twentieth Century Children's Writers*.

Ward. *Authors of Books for Young People, Second Edition*.

KATHERINE MILHOUS, 1894-1977
author-illustrator

AWARDS

Egg Tree. Caldecott Medal Book, 1951.

(*Silver Pencil*. Newbery Honor Book, 1945.)

BIBLIOGRAPHY

Along Janet's Road; by Alice Dalgliesh. Scribner, 1946.

Appolonia's Valentine. Scribner, 1954.

Billy Button's Butter'd Biscuit; by Mabel L. Hunt. Stokes, 1941.

Book for Jennifer: A Story of London Children in the Eighteenth Century and of Mr. Newbery's Juvenile Library; by Alice Dalgliesh, also il. with woodcuts. Scribner, 1940.

Brownies: Adapted from the Story; by Juliana Ewing. Scribner, 1946.

Corporal Keeperupper. Scribner, 1943.

Egg Tree and How It Grew. Scribner, 1950.

First Christmas Crib. Scribner, 1944.

Happily Ever After: Fairy Tales; compiled by Alice Dalgliesh. Scribner, 1939.

Herodia, the Lovely Puppet. Scribner, 1943.

Little Angel: A Story of Old Rio; by Alice Dalgliesh. Scribner, 1943.

Lovina: A Story of the Pennsylvania Country. Scribner, 1940.

"Old Abe," American Eagle; by Lorraine Sherwood. Scribner, 1946.

Patrick and the Golden Slippers. Scribner, 1951.

Peter Piper's Pickled Peppers; by Mabel L. Hunt. Stokes, 1942.

Silver Pencil; by Alice Dalgliesh. Scribner, 1944.

Snow over Bethlehem. Scribner, 1945.

They Live in South America; by Alice Dalgliesh. il. with Frances Lichten. Scribner, 1942.

Through These Arches: The Story of Independence Hall. Lippincott, 1964.

Wings around South America; by Alice Dalgliesh. Scribner, 1955.

With Bells On: A Christmas Story. Scribner, 1955.

MEDIA

Appolonia's Valentine. (BB).

Egg Tree. (BB).

Through These Arches. (TB).

EXHIBITIONS

New York World's Fair, 1939. (New York, New York).

COLLECTIONS

Central Children's Room, Donnell Library Center,
New York Public Library. (New York, New York).

deGrummond Collection, University of Southern
Mississippi. (Hattiesburg, Mississippi).

Free Library of Philadelphia. (Philadelphia,
Pennsylvania).

Kerlan Collection, University of Minnesota.
(Minneapolis, Minnesota).

Milwaukee Public Library. (Milwaukee, Wisconsin).

Special Collections, University Research Library,
University of California. (Los Angeles, California).

BACKGROUND READING

Burke. *American Authors and Books, 1640 to the
Present Day*.

Dalgliesh, A. "Two Illustrators: Katherine Milhous
and Hildegard Woodward." *Horn Book*,
January 1945.

Hoffman. *Authors and Illustrators of Children's Books*.

Hopkins. *Books Are by People*.

Kingman. *Illustrators of Children's Books, 1957-1966*.

Kirkpatrick. *Twentieth Century Children's Writers*.

Kunitz. *Junior Book of Authors, Second Edition
Revised*.

Mahony. *Illustrators of Children's Books, 1744-1945*.

Miller. *Caldecott Medal Books, 1938-1957*.

Miller. *Illustrators of Children's Books, 1946-1956*.

Templin, E. "Enjoying Festivals with Katherine
Milhous." *Elementary English*, November 1957.

Ward. *Authors of Books for Young People, Second
Edition*.

Ward. *Illustrators of Books for Young People, Second
Edition*.

Young Wings. *Writing Books for Boys and Girls*.

+ELIZABETH CLEVELAND MILLER,
1889-1936
author

AWARDS

Pran of Albania. Newbery Honor Book, 1930.

BIBLIOGRAPHY

Children of the Mountain Eagle. il. Maud and Miska
Petersham. Doubleday, 1927.

Pran of Albania. il. Maud and Miska Petersham.
Doubleday, 1929.

Young Trajan. il. Maud and Miska Petersham.
Doubleday, 1931.

BACKGROUND READING

Kunitz. *Junior Book of Authors*.

Kunitz. *Junior Book of Authors, Second Edition
Revised*.

Seabury, F. "Elizabeth Cleveland Miller, Joyous
Explorer." *Horn Book*, May 1937.

Young Wings. *Writing Books for Boys and Girls*.

+RUTHERFORD GEORGE MONTGOMERY,
1896-
author
>   *pseudonyms* A. A. Avery
>   Al Avery
>   Everitt Proctor

AWARDS

Kildee House. Newbery Honor Book, 1950.

BIBLIOGRAPHY

as A. A. Avery:

Anything for a Quiet Life. Farrar, 1942.

as Al Avery:

Yankee Flier in Italy. il. Paul Laune. Grosset, 1944.

Yankee Flier in Normandy. il. Clayton Knight.
Grosset, 1945.

Yankee Flier in North Africa. il. Paul Laune. Grosset,
1943.

Yankee Flier in the Far East. il. Paul Laune. Grosset,
1942.

Yankee Flier in the South Pacific. il. Paul Laune.
Grosset, 1943.

Yankee Flier on a Rescue Mission. il. Clayton Knight.
Grosset, 1945.

Yankee Flier over Berlin. il. Paul Laune. Grosset, 1944.

Yankee Flier under Secret Orders. il. Clayton Knight.
Grosset, 1946.

Yankee Flier with the R. A. F. il. Paul Laune. Grosset,
1941.

as Rutherford G. Montgomery:

Amikuk. il. Marie Nonnast. World, 1955.

BIBLIOGRAPHY (cont'd)

as Rutherford G. Montgomery (cont'd):

Beaver Water. il. Robert Doremus. World, 1956.

Big Brownie. il. Jacob Landau. Holt, 1944.

Big Red: A Wild Stallion. il. Pers Crowell. Caxton, 1971.

Black Powder Empire. Little, 1955.

Blue Streak and Doctor Medusa. il. Frances Kirn. Whitman, 1946.

Broken Fang. il. Lynn B. Hunt. Donohue, 1935.

Call of the West. Grosset, 1933.

Capture of the West Wind. Duell, 1962.

Carcajou. il. L. D. Cram. Caxton, 1936.

Claim Jumpers of Marble Canyon. il. William Moyers. Knopf, 1956.

Corey's Sea Monster. il. Harvey Kidder. World, 1969.

Crazy Kill Range. il. Lorence Bjorklund. World, 1963.

Defiant Heart. Duell, 1963.

Dolphins as They Are. Duell, 1967.

Ghost Town Adventure. il. Russell Sherman. Holt, 1942.

Ghost Town Gold. il. Lorence Bjorklund. World, 1965.

Golden Stallion. il. Al Brulé. Grosset, 1962.

Golden Stallion and the Mysterious Feud. il. Albert Michini. Little, 1967.

Golden Stallion and the Wolf Dog. il. Percy Leason. Little, 1959.

Golden Stallion's Adventures at Redstone. il. Percy Leason. Little, 1959.

Golden Stallion's Revenge. il. George Giguère. Little, 1953.

Golden Stallion's Victory. il. George Giguère. Little, 1956.

Gray Wolf. il. Jacob B. Abbott. Houghton, 1938.

High Country. Derrydale, 1938.

Hill Ranch. il. Barbara Cooney. Doubleday, 1951.

Horse for Claudia and Dennis; with Natlee Kenoyer. Duell, 1958.

Hurricane Yank. il. James Shimer. McKay, 1942.

Husky: Co-Pilot of the Pilgrim. il. Jacob Landau. Holt, 1942; also il. Nina S. Langley. Ward, 1949.

Iceblink. il. Rudolf Freund. Holt, 1941; *a.k.a. Iceblink: With Questions and Related Activities by Jennifer Harvey*. Book Society of Canada, 1969.

In Happy Hollow. il. Harold Berson. Doubleday, 1958.

Into the Groove: A Story about Sports Car Racing. Dodd, 1966.

Jet Navigator, Strategic Air Command. il. Grover Heiman. Dodd, 1959.

Jets Away! Dodd, 1957.

Kent Barstow Aboard the Dyna Soar. Duell, 1964.

Kent Barstow and the Commando Flight. Duell, 1963.

Kent Barstow on a B-70 Mission. Duell, 1963.

Kent Barstow, Space Man. Duell, 1961.

Kent Barstow, Special Agent. Duell, 1958.

Kildee House. il. Barbara Cooney. Doubleday, 1949.

King of the Castle: The Story of a Kangaroo Rat. il. Russell F. Pedersen. World, 1961.

Kinkajou on the Town. il. Lorence F. Bjorklund. World, 1967.

Klepty. il. Polly Hecathorn. Duell, 1961.

Living Wilderness as Seen by Rutherford Montgomery. il. Campbell Grant. Dodd, 1964.

McGonnigle's Lake. il. Garry McKenzie. Doubleday, 1953.

McNulty's Holiday. il. Charles Geer. Duell, 1963.

Midnight. il. Jacob B. Abbott. Holt, 1940.

Missile Away: A Kent Barstow Adventure. Duell, 1959.

Mission Intruder: A Kent Barstow Adventure. Duell, 1960.

Mister Jim. il. Paul Galdone. World, 1957.

Monte, the Bear Who Became a Celebrity: Based on a Story by H. L. Coggins. il. Charles Geer. Duell, 1962.

Mountain Man. World, 1957.

Mystery of Crystal Canyon. il. Taylor Oughton. Winston, 1951.

Mystery of the Turquoise Frog. il. Millard McGee. Messner, 1946.

Orphans of the Wild. il. L. Dean. Black, 1939.

Out of the Sun. il. Clayton Knight. McKay, 1943.

Pekan the Shadow. il. Jerome D. Menninger. Caxton, 1970.

Posted Water. Ward, 1959.

Rough Riders Ho! il. E. Franklin Wittmack. McKay, 1946.

Rufus. il. Jerome D. Meininger. Caxton, 1973.

(ed.) *Saddlebag of Tales: A Collection of Stories Told by Members of the Western Writers of America*; by the Western Writers of America. il. Sam Savitt. Dodd, 1959.

Sea Raiders Ho! il. E. Franklin Wittmack. McKay, 1945.

Seecatch: A Story of a Fur Seal. il. Ralph C. Smith. Ginn, 1955.

Sex Isn't Everything. il. Armand Weston. Dodd, 1961.

Silver Hills. il. Robert Frankenberg. World, 1958.

Smoky Trails. Ward, 1967.

Snowman. Duell, 1962.

Spike Kelly of the Commandos. il. J. R. White. Whitman, 1942.

Stan Ball of the Rangers. il. Jacob B. Abbott. McKay, 1941.

Stubborn One. Duell, *ca.*1966.

Thornbush Jungle. il. Lorence Bjorklund. World, 1966.

Thumbs Up! il. E. Franklin Wittmack. McKay, 1942.

Thunderboats Ho! il. E. Franklin Wittmack. McKay, 1945.

Timberline Tales. il. Jacob B. Abbott. McKay, 1939.

Tim's Mountain. il. Julian DeMiskey. World, 1959.

Tom Pittman, U.S.A.F. Duell, 1957.

Trail of the Buffalo. il. Kurt Wiese. Houghton, 1939.

Trappers' Trail. il. Harold Cressingham. Holt, 1943. (Identified as "Rutherford *B*. Montgomery").

Troopers Three. il. Zhenya Gay. Doubleday, 1932.

Walt Disney's Cougar: A Fact-Fiction Nature Story, Based on a Walt Disney Film. il. Robert Magnusen. Simon, 1961; *a.k.a. Cougar: A Fact-Fiction Nature Story, Based on a Walt Disney Film*. Purnell, 1962.

Walt Disney's El Blanco: The Legend of the White Stallion; A Fact-Fiction Nature Story, Based on a "Walt Disney Presents" Television Show. il. Gloria Stevens. Simon, 1961; *a.k.a. El Blanco: The Legend of the White Stallion, Based on a "Walt Disney Presents" Television Show*. Purnell, 1962.

Walt Disney's The Odyssey of an Otter: A Fact-Fiction Nature Story, Based on a Walt Disney Film Presentation. il. Hamilton Greene. Simon, 1960; *a.k.a. Odyssey of an Otter: A Fact-Fiction Nature Story, Based on a Walt Disney Film Presentation*. Purnell, 1962.

Walt Disney's Weecha the Raccoon: A Fact-Fiction Nature Story, Based on a Walt Disney Film Presentation. il. Lawrence T. Dresser. Simon, 1960; *a.k.a. Weecha the Raccoon: A Fact-Fiction Nature Story, Based on a Walt Disney Film Presentation*. Purnell, 1962.

Wapiti the Elk. il. Gardell D. Christensen. Little, 1952.

War Wings. il. Clayton Knight. McKay, 1943.

Warhawk Patrol. il. Clayton Knight. McKay, 1944.

White Mountaineer. il. Gardell D. Christensen. Little, 1953.

Whitetail: The Story of a Prairie Dog. il. Marie Nonnast. World, 1958.

Yellow Eyes. il. L. D. Cram. Caxton, 1937.

as Everitt Proctor:

Last Cruise of the Jeanette. Westminster, 1944.

Men against the Ice. il. Ilsa Barnett. Westminster, 1946.

Thar She Blows. il. David Hendrickson. Westminster, 1945.

MEDIA

Beaver Water. (BB, TB).

Flash, the Teenaged Otter. Walt Disney Productions, n. d. (Original screenplay, F).

Golden Stallion's Victory. (BB, TB).

Hound Who Thought He Was a Raccoon. Walt Disney Productions, n. d. (Original screenplay, F).

Kildee House. (TB).

Killers of the High Country. Walt Disney Productions, n. d. (Original screenplay, F).

Legend of El Blanco. Walt Disney Productions, 1966 (TV).

Living Wilderness. (BB).

Missile Away. (BB).

Monte, the Bear Who Became a Celebrity. (BB).

Old Sancho, the Homing Steer. Walt Disney Productions, n. d. (Original screenplay, F).

COLLECTIONS

deGrummond Collection, University of Southern Mississippi. (Hattiesburg, Mississippi).

Kerlan Collection, University of Minnesota. (Minneapolis, Minnesota).

University of Oregon Library. (Eugene, Oregon).

BACKGROUND READING

Burke. *American Authors and Books, 1640 to the Present Day*.

Commire. *Something about the Author*.

Contemporary Authors.

Fuller. *More Junior Authors*.

Kirkpatrick. *Twentieth Century Children's Writers*.

Ward. *Authors of Books for Young People, Second Edition*.

Young Wings. *Writing Books for Boys and Girls*.

+BENI MONTRESOR, 1926-
author-illustrator

AWARDS

(*Belling the Tiger*. Newbery Honor Book, 1962.)

May I Bring a Friend? Caldecott Medal Book, 1965.

BIBLIOGRAPHY

A for Angel: Beni Montresor's ABC Picture-Stories. Knopf, 1969.

Belling the Tiger; by Mary Stolz. Harper, 1961.

Cinderella: From the Opera; by Gioacchino Rossini. Knopf, 1965.

Great Rebellion; by Mary Stolz. Harper, 1961.

House of Flowers, House of Stars. Knopf, 1962.

I Saw a Ship A-Sailing: Or, The Wonderful Games That Only Little Flower-Plant Children Can Play. Knopf, 1967.

Last Savage; by Gian-Carlo Menotti. New York Graphic, 1964.

Magic Flute; by Wolfgang Mozart; retold by Stephen Spender. Pantheon, 1966.

May I Bring a Friend?; by Beatrice S. deRegniers. Atheneum, 1964.

Mommies at Work; by Eve Merriam. Knopf, 1961.

Old Neapolitan Fairy Tales; by Rose L. Mincieli. Knopf, 1963.

On Christmas Eve; by Margaret W. Brown. Scott, 1961.

Princesses: Sixteen Stories about Princesses, with Biographical Notes on Each Author; by Sally P. Johnson. Harper, 1962.

Siri the Conquistador; by Mary Stolz. Harper, 1963.

Sounds of a Summer Night; by May Garelick. Scott, 1963.

Willy O'Dwyer Jumped in the Fire: Variations on a Folk Rhyme; by Beatrice S. deRegniers. Atheneum, 1968.

Witches of Venice. Knopf, 1963.

MEDIA

Cinderella. Random House, 1972 (C).

May I Bring a Friend? Weston Woods Studios, 1973 (FSS).

Pilgrimage. n. p. (Original co-authored screenplay, F), n. d.

EXHIBITIONS

Kroedler Gallery, 1965. (New York, New York).

COLLECTIONS

Kerlan Collection, University of Minnesota. (Minneapolis, Minnesota).

BACKGROUND READING

Commire. *Something about the Author*.

Contemporary Authors.

Current Biography.

DeMontreville. *Third Book of Junior Authors*.

Hopkins. *Books Are by People*.

Kingman. *Illustrators of Children's Books, 1957-1966*.

Kingman. *Newbery and Caldecott Medal Books, 1956-1966*.

Kirkpatrick. *Twentieth Century Children's Writers*.

Masti, D. "Stage Designs of Beni Montresor." *Connoisseur*, February 1966.

Stevenson, F. "Gentleman of Verona." *Opera News*, February 8, 1964.

Ward. *Authors of Books for Young People, Second Edition*.

Ward. *Illustrators of Books for Young People, Second Edition*.

+GRACE PURDIE MOON, 1877-1947
author-illustrator

AWARDS

Runaway Papoose. Newbery Honor Book, 1929.

BIBLIOGRAPHY

Arrow of Tee-May. il. Carl Moon. Doubleday, 1931.

Book of Nah-Wee; with Carl Moon. Doubleday, 1932.

Chi-Weé and Loki of the Desert. il. Carl Moon. Doubleday, 1926.

Chi-Weé: The Adventures of a Little Indian Girl. il. Carl Moon. Doubleday, 1925.

Daughter of Thunder. il. Carl Moon. Macmillan, 1942.

Far-Away Desert. il. Carl Moon. Doubleday, 1932.

Indian Legends in Rhyme. il. Carl Moon. Stokes, 1917. (Identified as "Karl Moon.")

Lost Indian Magic: A Mystery Story of the Red Man as He Lived before the White Man Came. il. Carl Moon. Stokes, 1918.

Magic Trail. il. Carl Moon. Doubleday, 1929.

Missing Katchina. il. Carl Moon. Doubleday, 1930.

Nadita (Little Nothing). il. Carl Moon. Doubleday, 1927; *a.k.a. Nadita*, 1946.

One Little Indian. il. Carl Moon. Whitman, 1950; revised, 1967.

Runaway Papoose. il. Carl Moon. Doubleday, 1928.

Shanty Ann. il. Carl Moon. Stokes, 1935.

Singing Sands. il. Carl Moon. Stokes, 1936.

Solita. il. Carl Moon. Doubleday, 1938.

Tita of Mexico. il. Carl Moon. Stokes, 1934.

White Indian. Doubleday, 1937.

Wongo and the Wise Old Crow. il. Carl Moon. Reilly, 1923.

BACKGROUND READING

Burke. *American Authors and Books, 1640 to the Present Day*.

Kunitz. *Junior Book of Authors*.

Kunitz. *Junior Book of Authors, Second Edition Revised*.

Obituary. *New York Times*, September 8, 1947.

Obituary. *Publishers Weekly*, September 27, 1947.

Obituary. *Wilson Library Bulletin*, November 1947.

Thompson. *Indiana Authors and Their Books, 1917-1966*.

Ward. *Authors of Books for Young People, Second Edition*.

Young Wings. *Writing Books for Boys and Girls*.

+ANNE CARROLL MOORE, 1871-1961
author

AWARDS

Nicholas. Newbery Honor Book, 1925.

BIBLIOGRAPHY

Art of Beatrix Potter: With an Appreciation by Anne Carroll Moore. Warne, 1955.

(ed.) *Bold Dragoon and Other Ghostly Tales*; by Washington Irving. il. James Daugherty. Knopf, 1930.

Century of Kate Greenaway. Warne, 1946.

Children's Books of Yesterday: An Exhibition from Many Countries. New York Public Library, 1933.

Choice of a Hobby: A Unique Descriptive List of Books Offering Inspiration and Guidance to Hobby Riders and Hobby Hunters; A Springboard for Personal Adventure. Compton's, 1934.

*Cross Roads to Childhood. Doran, 1926; also in *My Roads to Childhood*, below.

Joseph A. Altsheler and American History. n. p., 1919.

(ed.) *Knickerbocker's History of New York*; by Washington Irving. il. James Daugherty. Doubleday, 1928.

List of Books Recommended for a Children's Library, Compiled for the Iowa Library Commission. Iowa Printing, 1903.

*My Roads to Childhood: Views and Reviews of Children's Books. il. Arthur Lougee, 1939; with new introduction by Frances C. Sayers. Horn Book, 1961. (Includes *Cross Roads to Childhood*, *New Roads to Childhood*, and *Roads to Childhood*, issued separately, above and below.)

*New Roads to Childhood. Doran, 1923; also in *My Roads to Childhood*, above.

Nicholas: A Manhattan Christmas Story. il. Jay Van Everen. Putnam, 1924.

Nicholas and the Golden Goose. il. Jay Van Everen. Putnam, 1932.

Reading for Pleasure: A Descriptive List of Books Prepared for Compton's Pictured Encyclopedia. Compton's, 1935.

*Roads to Childhood: Views and Reviews of Children's Books. Doran, 1920; also in *My Roads to Childhood*, above.

Seven Stories High. Compton's, 1932. (Various revisions followed.)

Three Owls: A Book about Children's Books, Their Authors, Artists and Critics. Macmillan, 1925.

Three Owls, Second Book: Contemporary Criticism of Children's Books. Coward, 1928.

Three Owls, Third Book: Contemporary Criticism of Children's Books. Coward, 1931.

Training for the Work of a Children's Librarian. American Library Association, 1914.

Writing and Criticism: A Book for Margery Bianco; with Bertha E. Mahony. il. Valenti Angelo. Horn Book, 1951.

COLLECTIONS

American Jewish Archives. (Cincinnati, Ohio).

BACKGROUND READING

Burke. *American Authors and Books, 1640 to the Present Day*.

Commire. *Something about the Author*.

Contemporary Authors.

D'Aulaire, I. "Miss Moore: A Reminiscence." *Horn Book*, October 1964.

BACKGROUND READING (cont'd)

Evans, E. "Miss Moore Fills Eighty Years." *Publishers Weekly*, July 28, 1951.

Heins, E. "Anne Carroll Moore." *Horn Book*, October 1971.

Hogarth, G. "Anne Carroll Moore: A Tribute." *Junior Bookshelf*, March 1961.

Horn Book, special issue, June 1960.

Horovitz, C., and Sayers, F. "Remembrance and Re-Creation: Some Talk about Writing a Biography." *Horn Book*, October 1972.

Kunitz. *Junior Book of Authors*.

Kunitz. *Junior Book of Authors, Second Edition Revised*.

Miller, B. "Anne Carroll Moore, Doctor of Humane Letters." *Horn Book*, January 1942.

New York Public Library Bulletin, special issue, November 1956.

Obituary. *Bulletin of the New York Public Library*, February 1961.

Obituary. *Horn Book*, April 1961.

Obituary. *New York Times*, January 21, 1961.

Obituary. *Publishers Weekly*, January 30, 1961.

Obituary. *Wilson Library Bulletin*, March 1961.

Sawyer, R. "Anne Carroll Moore of Limerick, Maine, Minister without a Portfolio." *Horn Book*, July 1950.

Sayers, Frances C. *Anne Carroll Moore: A Biography*. Atheneum, 1972.

Sayers, Frances C. "Postscript: The Later Years." *Horn Book*, April 1961.

Ward. *Authors of Books for Young People, Second Edition*.

Wessell, M. "Anne Carroll Moore." *Catholic Library World*, January 1960.

Williams, M. "Anne Carroll Moore." *Bulletin of Bibliography*, May 1946.

JANET GAYLORD MOORE, 1905-
author

AWARDS

Many Ways of Seeing. Newbery Honor Book, 1970.

BIBLIOGRAPHY

Introduction to the Art of China in the Cleveland Museum of Art. Cleveland Museum of Art, 1971.

Many Ways of Seeing: An Introduction to the Pleasures of Art. World, 1969.

BACKGROUND READING

Contemporary Authors.

Ward. *Illustrators of Books for Young People, Second Edition*.

+NICOLAS MORDVINOFF, 1911-1973
author-illustrator
a.k.a. Nicolas

AWARDS

Finders Keepers. Caldecott Medal Book, 1952.

Two Reds. Caldecott Honor Book, 1951.

BIBLIOGRAPHY

as Nicolas:

Alphonse, That Bearded One; by Natalie S. Carlson. Harcourt, 1954.

Bear's Land. Coward, 1955.

Big Steve: The Doubled Quick Tunnelman; by Marie H. Bloch. Coward, 1952.

Billy the Kid; with Will (Lipkind). Harcourt, 1961.

Boy and the Forest; with Will (Lipkind). Harcourt, 1964.

Cezar and the Music-Maker; by Earland and Marjorie Schwalje. Knopf, 1951.

Chaga; with Will (Lipkind). Harcourt, 1955.

Christmas Bunny; with Will (Lipkind). Harcourt, 1953.

Circus Ruckus; with Will (Lipkind). Harcourt, 1954.

Coral Island. Doubleday, 1957.

Daniel Boone's Echo; by William O. Steele. Harcourt, 1957.

Davy Crockett's Earthquake; by William O. Steele. Harcourt, 1956.

Evangeline: Pigeon of Paris; by Natalie S. Carlson. Harcourt, 1960.

Even Steven; with Will (Lipkind). Harcourt, 1952.

Finders Keepers; with Will (Lipkind). Harcourt, 1951.

Four-Leaf Clover; with Will (Lipkind). Harcourt, 1959.

Hortense: The Cow for a Queen; by Natalie S. Carlson. Harcourt, 1957.

Just So Stories; by Rudyard Kipling. Garden City, 1952.

Little Tiny Rooster; with Will (Lipkind). Harcourt, 1960.

Magic Feather Duster; with Will (Lipkind). Harcourt, 1958.

Panchito; by Loren D. Good. Coward, 1955.

Perry the Imp; with Will (Lipkind). Harcourt, 1954.

Russet and the Two Reds; with Will (Lipkind). Harcourt, 1962.

Sleepyhead; with Will (Lipkind). Harcourt, 1957.

Thunder Island; by William Stone. Knopf, 1942.

Two Reds; with Will (Lipkind). Harcourt, 1950.

as Nicolas Mordvinoff:

Boy of the Islands; by Will (Lipkind). Harcourt, 1954.

Boy with a Harpoon; by Will (Lipkind). Harcourt, 1952.

Burma Boy; by Willis Lindquist. McGraw, 1953.

Pépé Was the Saddest Bird; by William Stone. Knopf, 1944.

Ship of Flame: A Saga of the South Seas; by William Stone. Knopf, 1945.

Tahiti Landfall; by William Stone. also il. with photographs by Prudence and Igor A. Allen. Morrow, 1946.

MEDIA

Finders Keepers. Weston Woods Studios, 1960 (FSS); also in Weston Woods Studios Set No. 7, 1965 (FSS).

EXHIBITIONS

Galerie 9, 1970. (Paris, France).

Luyber Gallery, 1949. (New York, New York).

COLLECTIONS

Kerlan Collection, University of Minnesota. (Minneapolis, Minnesota).

BACKGROUND READING

Bader. *American Picturebooks from Noah's Ark to The Beast Within*.

Contemporary Authors.

Eichenberg, F. "Artist's Choice." *Horn Book*, July 1951.

(Foster), Mariana. "Artist's Choice." *Horn Book*, October 1958.

Fuller. *More Junior Authors*.

Hopkins. *Books Are by People*.

Kingman. *Illustrators of Children's Books, 1957-1966*.

Mahony. *Illustrators of Children's Books, 1744-1945*.

Miller. *Caldecott Medal Books, 1938-1957*.

Miller. *Illustrators of Children's Books, 1946-1956*.

Obituary. *New York Times*, May 15, 1973.

Obituary. *Publishers Weekly*, May 28, 1973.

Ward. *Authors of Books for Young People, Second Edition*.

Ward. *Illustrators of Books for Young People, Second Edition*.

+DHAN GOPAL MUKERJI, 1890-1936
author

AWARDS

Gay-Neck. Newbery Medal Book, 1928.

BIBLIOGRAPHY

Bunny, Hound and Clown. il. Kurt Wiese. Dutton, 1931.

*Caste and Outcast. Dutton, 1923.

Chief of the Herd. il. Mahlon Blaine. Dutton, 1929.

Chintamini: A Symbolic Drama by Girish Ghose; with Carolyn C. Davies. Badger, 1914.

Daily Meditation: Or, The Practice of Repose. Dutton, 1933.

(tr.) *Devotional Passages from the Hindu Bible: Adapted into English*; from the *Upanishads*. Dutton, 1929.

Disillusioned India. Dutton, 1930.

Face of Silence. Dutton, 1926.

Fierce-Face: The Story of a Tiger. il. Dorothy Lathrop. Dutton, 1936.

Gay-Neck: The Story of a Pigeon. il. Boris Artzybasheff. Dutton, 1927.

Ghond: The Hunter. il. Boris Artzybasheff. Dutton, 1928.

Hari: The Jungle Lad. il. Morgan Steinmetz. Dutton, 1924.

Hindu Fables for Little Children. il. Kurt Wiese. Dutton, 1929.

Jungle Beasts and Man. il. J. E. Allen. Dutton, 1923.

Kari: The Elephant. il. J. E. Allen. Dutton, 1922.

Layla-Majnu: A Musical Play in Three Acts. Elder, 1916.

Master Monkey. il. Florence Weber. Dutton, 1932.

My Brother's Face. Dutton, 1924.

Path of Prayer. Dutton, 1932.

BIBLIOGRAPHY (cont'd)

Rajani: Songs of the Night. Elder, 1916.

(ed.) *Rama, the Hero of India: Done into a Short English Version for Boys and Girls*; from the Valmīki. il. Edgar P. D'Aulaire. Dutton, 1930.

Sandhya: Songs of Twilight. Elder, 1917.

Secret Listeners of the East. Dutton, 1926.

Son of Mother India Answers. Dutton, 1928.

(tr.) *Song of God: Translation of the Bhagavad-Gita*. Dutton, 1931.

Visit India with Me. Dutton, 1929.

MEDIA

Gay-Neck. (BB, TB); Miller-Brody Productions, 1973 (FSS).

Jungle Beasts and Man. (TB).

Kari. (BB, TB).

BACKGROUND READING

Hamilton, A. "Friend's Tribute." *Horn Book*, May 1937.

Horn Book, special issue, July 1937.

Kirkpatrick. *Twentieth Century Children's Writers*.

Kunitz. *Junior Book of Authors*.

Kunitz. *Junior Book of Authors, Second Edition Revised*.

Kunitz. *Living Authors*.

Kunitz. *Twentieth Century Authors*.

Miller. *Newbery Medal Books, 1922-1955*.

Ward. *Authors of Books for Young People, Second Edition*.

+EVALINE MICHELOW NESS, 1911-
author-illustrator

AWARDS

All in the Morning Early. Caldecott Honor Book, 1964.

Pocketful of Cricket. Caldecott Honor Book, 1965.

Sam, Bangs and Moonshine. Caldecott Medal Book, 1967.

(*Thistle and Thyme*. Newbery Honor Book, 1963.)

Tom Tit Tot. Caldecott Honor Book, 1966.

BIBLIOGRAPHY

Across from Indian Shore; by Barbara Robinson. Lothrop, 1962.

All in the Morning Early; by Sorche N. Leodhas, pseud. (Leclaire G. Alger). Holt, 1963.

Amelia Mixed the Mustard and Other Poems. Scribner, 1975.

American Colonial Paper House to Cut Out and Color. Scribner, 1975.

Bridge; by Charlton Ogburn. Houghton, 1960.

Candle Tales; by Julia Cunningham. Pantheon, 1963.

Coll and His White Pig; by Lloyd Alexander. Holt, 1965.

Do You Have the Time, Lydia? Dutton, 1971; a.k.a. ¿Tienes Tiempo, Lydia?, 1976.

Don't You Remember?; by Lucille Clifton. Dutton, 1973.

Double Discovery. Scribner, 1965.

Everett Anderson's Christmas Coming; by Lucille Clifton. Holt, 1971.

Exactly Alike. Scribner, 1964.

Favorite Fairy Tales Told in Italy; by Virginia Haviland. Little, 1965.

Four Rooms from the Metropolitan Museum of Art. Scribner, 1977.

Funny Town; by Eve Merriam. Collier, 1963.

Gift for Sula Sula. Scribner, 1963.

Girl and the Goatherd: Or, This and That and Thus and So. Scribner, 1970.

Joey and the Birthday Present; by Maxine Kumin and Anne Sexton. McGraw, 1971.

Josefina February. Scribner, 1963.

Josie and the Snow; by Helen E. Buckley. Lothrop, 1964.

Josie's Buttercup; by Helen E. Buckley. Lothrop, 1967.

Kellyburn Braes; by Sorche N. Leodhas, pseud. (Leclaire G. Alger). Holt, 1968.

Lives of My Cat Alfred; by Nathan Zimelman. Dutton, 1976.

Lonely Maria; by Elizabeth Coatsworth. Pantheon, 1960.

Long, Broad and Quickeye: Adapted. Scribner, 1969.

Macaroon; by Julia Cunningham. Pantheon, 1962.

Mr. Miacca: An English Folk Tale; by Joseph Jacobs. Holt, 1967.

Old Mother Hubbard and Her Dog; by Sarah C. Martin. Holt, 1972.

Ondine; by Maurice Osborne. Houghton, 1960.

Paper Palace to Cut Out and Color. Scribner, 1976.

Pavo and the Princess. Scribner, 1964.

Pierino and the Bell; by Sylvia Cassedy. Doubleday, 1966.

Pocketful of Cricket; by Rebecca Caudill. Holt, 1964.

Princess and the Lion; by Elizabeth Coatsworth. Pantheon, 1963.

Sam, Bangs and Moonshine. Holt, 1966.

Scottish Songbook; by Sorche N. Leodhas, *pseud.* (Leclaire G. Alger). Holt, 1969.

Sherwood Ring; by Elizabeth M. Pope. Houghton, 1958.

Some of the Days of Everett Anderson; by Lucille Clifton. Holt, 1970.

Steamroller: A Fantasy; by Margaret W. Brown. Walker, 1974.

Story of Ophelia; by Mary Gibbons. Doubleday, 1954.

This Is an American Colonial Paper House to Cut and Color. Scribner, 1975.

Thistle and Thyme: Tales and Legends from Scotland; by Sorche N. Leodhas, *pseud.* (Leclaire G. Alger). Holt, 1962.

Tom Tit Tot: An English Folk Tale; by Joseph Jacobs. Scribner, 1965.

Too Many Crackers; by Helen E. Buckley. Lothrop, 1966.

Trace through the Forest; by Barbara Robinson. Lothrop, 1965.

Truthful Harp; by Lloyd Alexander. Holt, 1967.

Warmint: A Poem; by Walter De La Mare. Scribner, 1976.

Where Did Josie Go?; by Helen E. Buckley. Lothrop, 1962.

Wizard's Tears; by Maxine Kumin. McGraw, 1975.

Woman of the Wood; by Algernon Blackwood. Holt, 1973.

Yeck Eck. Dutton, 1974.

MEDIA

Amelia Mixed the Mustard. (CB).

Do You Have the Time, Lydia? (CB).

Exactly Alike. (TB).

Josefina February. (TB).

Josie and the Snow. Weston Woods Studios, 1968 (FSS); also in Weston Woods Studios Set No. 22, 1968 (FSS).

Sam, Bangs and Moonshine. (BB); BFA, Inc., 1976 (F); Miller-Brody Productions, 1976 (FSS).

COLLECTIONS

deGrummond Collection, University of Southern Mississippi. (Hattiesburg, Mississippi).

Free Library of Philadelphia. (Philadelphia, Pennsylvania).

Iowa City Public Library. (Iowa City, Iowa).

Kerlan Collection, University of Minnesota. (Minneapolis, Minnesota).

BACKGROUND READING

Commire. *Something about the Author.*

Contemporary Authors.

DeMontreville. *Third Book of Junior Authors.*

Durrell, A. "Evaline Ness." *Library Journal*, March 15, 1967.

Hopkins. *Books Are by People.*

Kingman. *Illustrators of Children's Books, 1957-1966.*

Kingman. *Illustrators of Children's Books, 1967-1976.*

Kingman. *Newbery and Caldecott Medal Books, 1966-1975.*

Kirkpatrick. *Twentieth Century Children's Writers.*

Lloyd Alexander, Evaline Ness and Anne Durrell. Profiles in Literature, 1972 (VT).

Michel, J. "Evaline Ness, the Caldecott Medalist for 1967." *American Artist*, June 1967.

Ward. *Authors of Books for Young People, Second Edition.*

Ward. *Illustrators of Books for Young People, Second Edition.*

Watson, E. "Evaline Ness: Rising Young Star in the Illustration Firmament." *American Artist*, January 1956.

EMILY CHENEY NEVILLE, 1919-
author

AWARDS

It's Like This, Cat. Newbery Medal Book, 1964.

BIBLIOGRAPHY

Berries Goodman. Harper, 1965.

Fogarty. Harper, 1969.

Garden of Broken Glass. Delacorte, 1975.

It's Like This, Cat. il. Emil Weiss. Harper, 1963; large print edition, 1967.

Reader for Adults. Bank Street, 1968.

Reader for Fourth, Fifth and Sixth Grades. Bank Street, 1974.

BIBLIOGRAPHY (cont'd)

Seventeenth Street Gang. il. Emily McCully. Harper, 1966.

*Traveler from a Small Kingdom. il. George Mocniak. Harper, 1968.

MEDIA

Berries Goodman. (BB, TB).

Fogarty. (TB).

It's Like This, Cat. (BB, C, MT, TB); Miller-Brody Productions, 1970 (C, R); Profiles in Literature, 1975 (excerpt, VT).

Seventeenth Street Gang. (BB).

COLLECTIONS

Free Library of Philadelphia. (Philadelphia, Pennsylvania).

Kerlan Collection, University of Minnesota. (Minneapolis, Minnesota).

BACKGROUND READING

Commire. *Something about the Author*.

Contemporary Authors.

DeMontreville. *Third Book of Junior Authors*.

"Emily Cheney Neville." *Wilson Library Bulletin*, November 1964.

Foremost Women in Communications.

Hopkins. *More Books by More People*.

Kingman. *Newbery and Caldecott Medal Books, 1956-1965*.

Kirkpatrick. *Twentieth Century Children's Writers*.

Ward. *Authors of Books for Young People, Second Edition*.

+CLARE TURLAY NEWBERRY, 1903-1970
author-illustrator

AWARDS

April's Kittens. Caldecott Honor Book, 1941.

Barkis. Caldecott Honor Book, 1939.

Marshmallow. Caldecott Honor Book, 1943.

T-Bone. Caldecott Honor Book, 1951.

BIBLIOGRAPHY

April's Kittens. Harper, 1940.

Babette. Harper, 1937.

Barkis. Harper, 1938.

Cats: A Portfolio. Harper, 1943.

Cats and Kittens: A Portfolio. Harper, 1956.

Cousin Toby. Harper, 1939.

Drawing a Cat. Studio, 1940; *a.k.a. Drawing Cats*, 1959.

Frosty. Harper, 1961.

Herbert the Lion. Brewer, 1931.

Ice Cream for Two. Harper, 1953.

Kitten's ABC. Harper, 1946; new edition, 1965.

Lambert's Bargain. Harper, 1941.

Marshmallow. Harper, 1942.

Mittens. Harper, 1936.

Pandora. Harper, 1944.

Percy, Polly, and Pete. Harper, 1952.

Smudge. Harper, 1948.

T-Bone, the Baby Sitter. Harper, 1950.

What's That? Harper, 1946.

Widget. Harper, 1958.

COLLECTIONS

deGrummond Collection, University of Southern Mississippi. (Hattiesburg, Mississippi).

Free Library of Philadelphia. (Philadelphia, Pennsylvania).

Kerlan Collection, University of Minnesota. (Minneapolis, Minnesota).

University of Oregon Library. (Eugene, Oregon).

BACKGROUND READING

Commire. *Something about the Author*.

Contemporary Authors.

Kirkpatrick. *Twentieth Century Children's Writers*.

Kunitz. *Junior Book of Authors, Second Edition Revised*.

Mahony. *Illustrators of Children's Books, 1744-1945*.

Miller. *Illustrators of Children's Books, 1946-1956*.

Newberry, C. "Cats and Kittens." *Horn Book*, March 1936.

Obituary. *Publishers Weekly*, March 23, 1970.

Ward. *Authors of Books for Young People, Second Edition*.

STERLING NORTH, 1906-1974
author

AWARDS

Rascal. Newbery Honor Book, 1964.

BIBLIOGRAPHY

Abe Lincoln: Log Cabin to White House. il. Lee Ames. Random, 1956.

Being a Literary Map of These United States: Depecting a Renaissance No Less Astonishing Than That of Periclean Athens or Elizabethan London; with Gladys North. Putnam, 1942.

Birthday of Little Jesus. il. Valenti Angelo. Grosset, 1952.

Book of Lyric Poems, Poems of Chicago. n. p., 1952.

Captured by the Mohawks and Other Adventures of Radisson. il. Victor Mays. Houghton, 1960.

First Steamboat on the Mississippi. il. Victor Mays. Houghton, 1962.

Five Little Bears. il. Hazel Frazee. Rand, 1935; also il. Jean Tamburine, 1955.

George Washington: Frontier Colonel. il. Lee Ames. Random, 1957.

Greased Lightning. il. Kurt Wiese. Winston, 1940.

Hurry, Spring! il. Carl Burger. Dutton, 1966.

Little Rascal. il. Carl Burger. Dutton, 1965.

Mark Twain and the River. il. Victor Mays. Random, 1957.

Midsummer Madness. Grosset, 1933; il. Kurt Wiese, 1943.

Night Outlasts the Whippoorwill. Macmillan, 1936.

Pedro Gorino: The Adventures of a Negro Sea-Captain in Africa and on the Seven Seas in His Attempts to Found an Ethiopian Empire; An Autobiographical Narrative; with Harry Dean. Houghton, 1929; *a.k.a. Umbala.* Harrarp, 1929.

Plowing on Sunday. Macmillan, 1933.

(Poems). University of Chicago, 1925.

**Raccoons Are the Brightest People.* Dutton, 1966; *a.k.a. Raccoons in My Life.* Hodder, 1967.

**Rascal: A Memoir of a Better Era.* il. John Schoenherr. Dutton, 1963; large print edition, Watts, 1970; *a.k.a. Rascal: The True Story of a Pet Raccoon.* Hodder, 1960.

Reunion on the Wabash. il. Brad Holland. Doubleday, 1952.

Seven against the Years. Macmillan, 1939.

So Dear to My Heart. Doubleday, 1947; il. Brad Holland, 1948; variant as *So Dear to My Heart: A Novel of Lamplight Days on the Farm, the Story of the Walt Disney Motion Picture.* Dell, 1949; variant as *Walt Disney's So Dear to My Heart: Adapted by Helen Palmer from the Motion Picture.* il. Walt Disney Studio, adapted by Bill Peet. Simon, 1950; variant as *Runaway Lamb at the County Fair, from the Walt Disney Motion Picture So Dear to My Heart Based on the Novel by Sterling North.* il. Walt Disney Studio, adapted by Julius Svendsen. Grosset, 1949.

So Red the Nose: Or, Breath in the Afternoon; with Carl Koch. il. Roy C. Nelson. Farrar, 1935.

Son of the Lamp Maker: The Story of a Boy Who Knew Jesus. il. Manning DeV. Lee. Rand, 1956.

Speak of the Devil: An Anthology of the Appearances of the Devil in the Literature of the Western World; with Clarence B. Boutell. Doubleday, 1945.

Thoreau of Walden Pond. il. Harvé Stein. Houghton, 1959.

Wolfling: A Documentary Novel of the 1870's. il. John Schoenherr. Dutton, 1969.

Writings of Mazlo de la Roche. Little, *ca.* 1940.

Young Thomas Edison. il. William Barss and photographs. Houghton, 1958.

Zipper ABC Book. il. Keith Ward. Rand, 1937.

MEDIA

Abe Lincoln. Educational Enrichment Records, 1963 (R).

First Steamboat on the Mississippi. (BB).

George Washington. (BB); Educational Enrichment Records, 1964 (R).

Little Rascal. Walt Disney Productions, 1969 (F, FSS).

Plowing on Sunday. (BB).

Raccoons are the Brightest People. (BB, C, MT, TB).

Rascal. (C, MT).

Seven against the Years. (BB).

So Dear to My Heart. (TB); RKO Radio Pictures, 1948 (F); Walt Disney Productions, 1940 (F), 1973 (FS, FSS).

COLLECTIONS

Dillon Collection, Arents Research Library, Syracuse University. (Syracuse, New York).

Mugar Memorial Library. Boston University. (Boston, Massachusetts).

State Historical Society of Wisconsin Library. (Madison, Wisconsin).

University of Chicago Library. (Chicago, Illinois).

BACKGROUND READING

Burke. *American Authors and Books, 1640 to the Present Day.*

Commire. *Something about the Author.*

Contemporary Authors.

Current Biography.

DeMontreville. *Third Book of Junior Authors.*

Kirkpatrick. *Twentieth Century Children's Writers.*

Kunitz. *Twentieth Century Authors.*

Kunitz. *Twentieth Century Authors, First Supplement.*

MacMaster, J. "Sterling North Brings Books Alive." *Editor and Publisher*, September 24, 1949.

New York Times Biographical Service.

Obituary. *New York Times*, December 23, 1974.

Obituary. *Publishers Weekly*, January 13, 1975.

Ward. *Authors of Books for Young People, Second Edition.*

Warfel. *American Novelists of Today.*

"You Meet Such Interesting People." *Publishers Weekly*, March 15, 1964.

Young Wings. *Writing Books for Boys and Girls.*

+ROBERT C. O'BRIEN, *pseudonym*, 1918-1973
author
a.k.a. Robert Leslie Conly

AWARDS

Mrs. Frisby and the Rats of NIMH. Newbery Medal Book, 1972.

BIBLIOGRAPHY

Mrs. Frisby and the Rats of NIMH. il. Zena Bernstein. Atheneum, 1971.

Report from Group 17. Atheneum, 1972.

Silver Crown. il. Dale Payson. Atheneum, 1968.

Z for Zachariah. Atheneum, 1975.

MEDIA

Mrs. Frisby and the Rats of NIMH. (CB, TB); Miller-Brody Productions, 1973 (FSS); Newbery Award Records, 1972 (C, R).

Porpoises: Friends of the Sea. (BB). (Based on a *National Geographic Magazine* article).

Report from Group 17. (TB).

Z for Zachariah. (TB).

BACKGROUND READING

Contemporary Authors.

DeMontreville. *Fourth Book of Junior Authors and Illustrators.*

Kingman. *Newbery and Caldecott Medal Books, 1966-1977.*

Kirkpatrick. *Twentieth Century Children's Writers.*

Obituary. *New York Times*, March 8, 1973.

Obituary. *Publishers Weekly*, March 12, 1973.

Obituary. *Time*, March 19, 1973.

SCOTT O'DELL, 1902-
author

AWARDS

Black Pearl. Newbery Honor Book, 1968.

Island of the Blue Dolphins. Newbery Medal Book, 1961.

King's Fifth. Newbery Honor Book, 1967.

Sing Down the Moon. Newbery Honor Book, 1971.

BIBLIOGRAPHY

Black Pearl. il. Milton Johnson. Houghton, 1967; also il. Graham Humphreys. Longmans, 1968.

Carlota. Houghton, 1977.

Child of Fire. Houghton, 1974.

Country of the Sun, Southern California: An Informal History and Guide. Crowell, 1957.

Cruise of the Arctic Star. il. Samuel Bryant. Houghton, 1973; large print edition, Hall, 1976.

Dark Canoe. il. Milton Johnson. Houghton, 1968.

Hawk That Dare Not Hunt by Day. Houghton, 1975.

Hill of the Hawk. Bobbs, 1947.

Island of the Blue Dolphins. Houghton, 1960; large print edition, Hall, 1974.

Journey to Jericho. il. Leonard Weisgard. Houghton, 1969.

King's Fifth. il. Samuel Bryant. Houghton, 1966.

Man Alone; with William Doyle. Bobbs, 1953.

Psychology of Children's Art; with Rhoda Kellogg. CRM, 1967.

Representative Photoplays Analyzed. Palmer Institute, 1924.

Sea Is Red: A Novel. Holt, 1958.

Sing Down the Moon. Houghton, 1970.

Treasure of Topo-el-Bampo. il. Lynd Ward. Houghton, 1972.

290. Houghton, 1976.

Woman of Spain: A Story of Old California. Houghton, 1934.

Zia. Houghton, 1976.

MEDIA

Black Pearl. (BB); Miller-Brody Productions, 1974 (FSS).

Child of Fire. (TB); Miller-Brody Productions, 1976 (C, R).

Cruise of the Arctic Star. (TB).

Dark Canoe. (BB).

Island of the Blue Dolphins. (BB, C, MT, TB); Pied Piper Productions, 19? (FSS); Universal-International Motion Pictures, 1964 (F); *a.k.a. Island of the Blue Dolphins, an Introduction*. Teaching Films, 1965 (excerpt, F).

King's Fifth. (BB, TB); Miller-Brody Productions 1976 (FSS).

Sing Down the Moon. (TB); Miller-Brody Productions, 1975 (FSS).

Zia. (TB); Miller-Brody Productions, 1977 (C, R).

COLLECTIONS

deGrummond Collection, University of Southern Mississippi. (Hattiesburg, Mississippi).

Free Library of Philadelphia. (Philadelphia, Pennsylvania).

University of Oregon Library. (Eugene, Oregon).

BACKGROUND READING

"Authors and Editors." *Publishers Weekly*, November 15, 1971.

Bearwood, S. "Scott O'Dell and Island of the Blue Dolphins." *Elementary English*, October 1961.

Bragg, P. "Scott O'Dell." *Publishers Weekly*, November 15, 1971.

Burke. *American Authors and Books, 1640 to the Present Day*.

Commire. *Something about the Author*.

Contemporary Authors.

Fuller. *More Junior Authors*.

Hoffman. *Authors and Illustrators of Children's Books*.

Keenan, S. "Scott O'Dell." *Wilson Library Bulletin*, December 1961.

Kingman. *Newbery and Caldecott Medal Books, 1956-1965*.

Kirkpatrick. *Twentieth Century Children's Writers*.

McCormick, E. "Scott O'Dell: Immortal Writer." *American Libraries*, June 1973.

Meet the Newbery Author: Scott O'Dell. Miller-Brody Productions, 1974 (FSS).

O'Dell, S. "Acceptance Speech: Hans Christian Andersen Award." *Horn Book*, October 1972.

"Outdoor Man." *New York Times Book Review*, October 12, 1947.

Scott O'Dell. Profiles in Literature, 1976 (VT).

Townsend. *Sense of Story*.

Ward. *Authors of Books for Young People, Second Edition*.

Warfel. *American Novelists of Today*.

Wintle. *Pied Pipers*.

+ELIZABETH OLDS, 1897-
author-illustrator

AWARDS

Feather Mountain. Caldecott Honor Book, 1952.

BIBLIOGRAPHY

Another Tiny Tim. Institute, 1941.

Big Fire. Houghton, 1945.

Deep Treasure: A Story of Oil. Houghton, 1958.

Feather Mountain. Houghton, 1951.

Little Una. Scribner, 1953.

Plop Plop Ploppie. Scribner, 1962.

Riding the Rails. Houghton, 1948.

EXHIBITIONS

ACA Gallery, 1950, 1952, 1955, 1960, 1961. (New York, New York).

Metropolitan Museum of Art, 1942. (New York, New York).

Museum of Modern Art, 1949. (New York, New York).

Staten Island Museum, 1969. (New York, New York).

Whitney Museum, 1947. (New York, New York).

COLLECTIONS

Baltimore Museum. (Baltimore, Maryland).

COLLECTIONS (cont'd)

Brooklyn Museum of Arts and Sciences. (Brooklyn, New York).

deGrummond Collection, University of Southern Mississippi. (Hattiesburg, Mississippi).

Free Library of Philadelphia. (Philadelphia, Pennsylvania).

Kerlan Collection, University of Minnesota. (Minneapolis, Minnesota).

Metropolitan Museum of Art. (New York, New York).

Minneapolis Institute of Art. (Minneapolis, Minnesota).

Philadelphia Museum of Art. (Philadelphia, Pennsylvania).

San Francisco Museum of Art. (San Francisco, California).

BACKGROUND READING

Burke. *American Authors and Books, 1640 to the Present Day.*

Commire. *Something about the Author.*

Contemporary Authors.

Kingman. *Illustrators of Children's Books, 1957-1966.*

Miller. *Illustrators of Children's Books, 1946-1956.*

Ward. *Authors of Books for Young People, Second Edition.*

Young Wings. *Writing Books for Boys and Girls.*

+ANTHONY D. PALAZZO, 1905-1970
author-illustrator

AWARDS

Timothy Turtle. Caldecott Honor Book, 1947.

BIBLIOGRAPHY

Aesop's Fables: Selected by Laura Harris; from Aesop. Doubleday, 1954.

Alphabet. Meredith, 1966.

Amerigo, the Wandering Tortoise. Duell, 1965.

Animal Babies. Garden City, 1960.

Animal Family Album; edited by Robin Fox. Lion, 1967.

Animal Folk Tales of America, Retold. Doubleday, 1961.

Animals of the Night. Lion, 1970.

Anna Sewell's Black Beauty, Retold; by Anna Sewell. Garden City, 1959.

Beagle Named Bertram; by Amalie Sharfman. Crowell, 1954.

Bianco and the New World. Viking, 1957.

Biggest and Littlest Animals. Lion, 1971.

Bird Alphabet. Duell, 1966.

Cat Alphabet. Duell, 1966.

Charley, the Horse. Viking, 1950.

Chicken in a Tunnel; by Jane Thayer, *pseud.* (Catherine Woolley). Morrow, 1956.

Conversation Clinic; by Loren Carroll. Esquire-Coronet, 1938.

Did You Say Dogs? Garrard, 1964.

Dinosaur Alphabet. Duell, 1963.

Down with Dinosaurs! Verses; by Al Graham. Duell, 1963.

Edward Lear's Nonsense Book; by Edward Lear. Garden City, 1956.

Elephant Alphabet. Duell, 1961.

Federico, the Flying Squirrel. Viking, 1951.

Fireman: Save My Cat! Abelard, 1964.

Forest Patrol; by Jim Kjelgaard. Holiday, 1941.

Four Musicians; by Jacob and Wilhelm Grimm. Doubleday, 1962.

Giant Nursery Book. Garden City, 1957.

Giant Playtime Book. Garden City, 1959.

Golden Girl. Garrard, 1963.

Goldilocks and the Three Bears, Retold. Garden City, 1959.

Great Othello: The Story of a Seal. Viking, 1952.

Henny-Penny and Chicken Little, Retold. Garden City, 1960.

Hey, Horses!; by Elizabeth Graves. Garrard, 1965.

Jan and the Reindeer. Garrard, 1963.

Let's Go to the Circus. Doubleday, 1961.

Let's Go to the Jungle. Doubleday, 1962.

Lord Is My Shepherd: The Twenty-third Psalm; from the *Bible.* Walck, 1965.

Lost Halo; by H. Winslow. Esquire-Coronet, 1941.

Magic Crayon: Drawing from Simple Shapes and Forms. Lion, 1967.

Mr. Whistle's Secret. Viking, 1953.

Monkey Alphabet. Duell, 1962.

Mother Goose Nursery Almanac; from Mother Goose. Garden City, 1960.

Mouse with a Small Guitar; by Al Graham. Welch, 1947.

Old Bet; by Anne Colver. Knopf, 1957.

Otter's Story; by Emil Liers. Viking, 1953.

Passel of Possums and Other Animal Families; by Robin Fox. Lion, 1968.

Pied Piper, Retold; with Al Graham, from Robert Browning. Duell, 1963.

Pig for Tom. Garrard, 1963.

Ramona Knew What She Wanted. Abelard, 1964.

Rhymes around the Year. Oldhams, 1961.

Rhymes of Squire O'Squirrel. Duell, 1963.

Runaway House; by P. K. Thomajan. Rittenhouse, 1941.

Secret of Alexander's Horse. Duell, 1965.

Simple Simon, Retold. Doubleday, 1959.

Songs for a Small Guitar; by Al Graham. Duell, 1962.

Story of Noah's Ark, Retold; from the *Bible*. Garden City, 1955.

Story of Peter and the Wolf; by Serge Prokofieff. Doubleday, 1961.

Story of Seraphina; by Anne H. White. Viking, 1951.

Story of Snowman: The Cinderella Horse. Duell, 1962.

Susie, the Cat. Viking, 1949.

Tales of Don Quixote and His Friends, Retold; from Cervantes. Garden City, 1958.

Thai, Kao and Tone: An Elephant Story. Abelard, 1966.

Three Little Kittens, Retold. Doubleday, 1961.

Time for All Things: Ecclesiastes, Chapter 3, Verses 1-8; from the *Bible*. Walck, 1966.

Timothy Turtle; by Al Graham. Welch, 1946.

Ugly Duckling; by Hans C. Andersen. Doubleday, 1962.

Villages Are the Heart of Spain. Esquire-Coronet, 1937.

Waldo the Woodchuck. Garrard, 1964.

Wings of the Morning: Verses from the Bible; edited by Robin Palmer. Walck, 1968.

MEDIA

Charley, the Horse. (BB).

Mr. Whistle's Secret. (TB).

EXHIBITIONS

Chicago Art Institute, n. d. (Chicago, Illinois).

Museum of Modern Art, n. d. (New York, New York).

Paris Gallery, 1936. (New York, New York).

Pennsylvania Academy of Fine Art, n. d. (Philadelphia, Pennsylvania).

COLLECTIONS

Kerlan Collection, University of Minnesota. (Minneapolis, Minnesota).

BACKGROUND READING

Angelo, V. "Artist's Choice." *Horn Book*, March 1950.

Commire. *Something about the Author*.

Contemporary Authors.

DeMontreville. *Third Book of Junior Authors*.

Kingman. *Illustrators of Children's Books, 1957-1966*.

Miller. *Illustrators of Children's Books, 1946-1956*.

Obituary. *New York Times*, September 12, 1970.

Obituary. *Publishers Weekly*, October 5, 1970.

Ward. *Authors of Books for Young People, Second Edition*.

Young Wings. *Writing Books for Boys and Girls*.

ROBERT ANDREW PARKER, 1927-
illustrator

AWARDS

Pop Corn and Ma Goodness. Caldecott Honor Book, 1970.

BIBLIOGRAPHY

Book of Animal Poems; by William Cole. Viking, 1973.

Book of Nature Poems; by William Cole. Viking, 1969.

Collected Prose; by Marrianne Moore. Viking, 19?.

Death of the Ball Turret Gunner; by Randall Jarrell. David Lewis, 1969.

Eight Poems; by Marianne Moore. Museum of Modern Art, 1962.

Great Jazz Artists; by James L. Collier. Four Winds, 1977.

Guess Who My Favorite Person Is; by Byrd Baylor. Scribner, 1977.

Hoofprint on the Wind; by Ann N. Clark. Viking, 1972.

Izzie; by Susan Pearson. Dial, 1975.

King Fox: And Other Old Tales, Retold; by Freya Littledale. Doubleday, 1971.

Liam's Catch; by Dorothy D. Parker. Viking, 1972.

Mermaid and the Whale; by Georgess McHargue. Holt, 1973.

BIBLIOGRAPHY (cont'd)

Pop Corn and Ma Goodness; by Edna M. Preston. Viking, 1969.

Trees Stand Shining, Poetry of the North American Indians; edited by Hettie Jones. Dial, 1971.

When Light Turns into Night; by Crescent Dragonwagon. Harper, 1975.

Winter Wife: An Abenaki Folktale, Retold; by Anne C. Crompton. Little, 1975.

Zeek Silver Moon; by Amy Ehrlich. Dial, 1972.

MEDIA

Days of Wilfred Owen. Bob Bach, 1966. (Original illustrations, F).

How to Kill; by Keith Douglas. Walter Goodman, 1970. (Original illustrations, F).

EXHIBITIONS

Brooklyn Museum of Arts and Sciences, 1967. (Brooklyn, New York).

Dintenfass Gallery, 1966-67, 1969-77. (New York, New York).

Hudson Gallery, 1963. (Detroit, Michigan).

Laon Museum, 1956. (Paris, France).

Metropolitan Museum of Art, 1952. (New York, New York).

Museum of Modern Art, 1953, 1957. (New York, New York).

New School for Social Research, 1965. (New York, New York).

Roko Gallery, 1954-56, 1958. (New York, New York).

School of Visual Arts, 1965. (New York, New York).

Whitney Museum, 1957. (New York, New York).

World House Gallery, 1960-61, 1964. (New York, New York).

COLLECTIONS

American Academy of Arts and Letters Library. (New York, New York).

Arents Research Library, Syracuse University. (Syracuse, New York).

Brooklyn Museum of Arts and Sciences. (Brooklyn, New York).

Dublin Museum. (Dublin, Ireland).

Los Angeles County Museum. (Los Angeles, California).

Morgan Library. (New York, New York).

Museum of Modern Art. (New York, New York).

Whitney Museum. (New York, New York).

BACKGROUND READING

American Federation of the Arts. *Forty Artists under Forty*.

DeMontreville. *Fourth Book of Junior Authors and Illustrators*.

Kingman. *Illustrators of Children's Books, 1967-1976*.

"New Talent in the U.S.A.: With Note by the Artist." *Art in America*, February 1956.

Ward. *Illustrators of Books for Young People, Second Edition*.

PETER PARNALL, 1936-
author-illustrator

AWARDS

(*Annie and the Old One*. Newbery Honor Book, 1972.)

Desert Is Theirs. Caldecott Honor Book, 1976.

Hawk, I'm Your Brother. Caldecott Honor Book, 1977.

BIBLIOGRAPHY

Alfalfa Hill. Doubleday, 1975.

Annie and the Old One; by Miska Miles, *pseud.* (Patricia M. Martin). Atlantic, 1971.

Apricot ABC; by Miska Miles, *pseud.* (Patricia M. Martin). Atlantic, 1969.

Beastly Circus; by Peggy Parish. Simon, 1969.

Beyond Your Doorstep; by Hal Borland. Knopf, 1962.

Big Frog, Little Pond. McCall, 1971.

But Ostriches . . . ; by Aileen Fisher. Crowell, 1970.

Cheechakoes; by Wayne Short. Random, 1962.

Desert Is Theirs; by Byrd Baylor. Scribner, 1975.

Desert Solitaire; by Edward Abbey. Simon, 1968.

Doctor Rabbit; by Jan Wahl. Delacorte, 1970.

Dog's Book of Birds. Scribner, 1977.

Dog's Book of Bugs; by Elizabeth Griffen. Atheneum, 1967.

Emma's Search for Something; by Mary Anderson. Atheneum, 1973.

Everybody Needs a Rock; by Byrd Baylor. Scribner, 1974.

Farewell to Texas; by William O. Douglas. Simon, 1967.

Fire Bringer; by Margaret Hodges. Little, 1972.

Fireside Song Book of Birds and Beasts; by Jane Yolen. Simon, 1972.

Gifts of an Eagle; by Kent Durden. Simon, 1972.

Great Fish. Doubleday, 1973.

Gruesome Green Witch; by Patricia Coffin. Walker, 1969.

Hawk, I'm Your Brother; by Byrd Baylor. Scribner, 1976.

Inspector; by George Mendoza. Doubleday, 1970.

Kavik the Wolf Dog; by Walt Morey. Dutton, 1968.

Knee Deep in Thunder; by Sheila Moon. Atheneum, 1967.

Little Book of Little Beasts; by Mary A. Hoberman. Simon, 1973.

Little Italian Cookbook; by Chris Lindsay. Walker, 1968.

Malachi Mudge; by Edward Cecil, *pseud.* (Cecil Maiden). McGraw, 1968.

Moon of the Wild Pigs; by Jean George. Crowell, 1968.

Moonfish and Owl Scratchings; by George Mendoza. Grosset, 1971.

Mountain. Doubleday, 1971.

Natural History of Marine Mammals; by Victor Scheffer. Scribner, 1976.

Nightwatchers; with Angus Cameron. Four Winds, 1971.

Of Houses and Cats; by Eunice de Chazeau. Random, 1965.

One Hundred Great Guns; by Merrill Lindsay. Walker, 1967.

Peregrine Falcons; by Alice Schick. Dial, 1975.

Pig with One Nostril; by Millard Lampell. Doubleday, 1975.

Psychology of Birds; by Harold Burtt. Macmillan, 1967.

Rabbit's World; by Miriam Schlein. Four Winds, 1973.

Seven Houses; by Josephine W. Johnson. Simon, 1973.

Six Voyages of Pleasant Fieldmouse; by Jan Wahl. Delacorte, 1971.

Tale of Middle Length; by Mary F. Shura. Atheneum, 1966.

Tales of Myrtle the Turtle; by Keith Robertson. Viking, 1974.

Tall Tales of the Catskills; by Frank L. DuMond. Atheneum, 1968.

Twilight Seas; by Sally Carrighar. Weybright, 1975.

Twist, Wiggle, and Squirm: A Book about Earthworms; by Laurence Pringle. Crowell, 1973.

Underground Hideaway; by Murray Goodwin. Harper, 1968.

When the Porcupine Moved In; by Cora Annett. Watts, 1971.

Year on Muskrat Marsh; by Berniece Freschet. Scribner, 1974.

MEDIA

Twilight Seas. (BB).

BACKGROUND READING

DeMontreville. *Third Book of Junior Authors*.

Kingman. *Illustrators of Children's Books, 1957-1966*.

Kingman. *Illustrators of Children's Books, 1967-1976*.

Ward. *Illustrators of Books for Young People, Second Edition*.

+ANNE PARRISH, 1888-1957
author-illustrator

AWARDS

Dream-Coach. Newbery Honor Book, 1925.

Floating Island. Newbery Honor Book, 1931.

Story of Appleby Capple. Newbery Honor Book, 1951.

BIBLIOGRAPHY

All Kneeling Down. Harper, 1928.

And Have Not Love. Harper, 1954; *a.k.a. And Have Not Charity*. Hutchinson, 1955.

Clouded Star. Harper, 1948.

Dream-Coach: Fare, Forty Winks; Coach Leaves Every Night for No One Knows Where, and Here Is Told How a Princess, a Little Chinese Emperor, a French Boy and a Norwegian Boy Took Trips in This Great Coach; with (George) Dillwyn Parrish. Macmillan, 1924.

Floating Island. Harper, 1930.

Golden Wedding. Harper, 1936.

Knee-High to a Grasshopper; with (George) Dillwyn Parrish. Macmillan, 1923.

Loads of Love. Harper, 1932.

Lucky One. Harper, 1958.

Lustres; with (George) Dillwyn Parrish. Doran, 1924.

Methodist Faun. Harper, 1929.

Mr. Despondency's Daughter. Harper, 1938.

Perennial Bachelor. Harper, 1925.

Pocketful of Poses. Doran, 1923.

BIBLIOGRAPHY (cont'd)

Poor Child. Harper, 1945.

Pray for a Tomorrow. Harper, 1941.

Sea Level. Harper, 1934.

Semi-Attached. Doran, 1924.

Story of Appleby Capple. Harper, 1950.

To-Morrow Morning. Harper, 1956.

MEDIA

All Kneeling Down as *Born to Be Bad*. RKO Radio
   Pictures, 1950 (F).

And Have Not Love. (BB).

Clouded Star. (TB).

Golden Wedding. (BB).

Lucky One. (BB).

Perennial Bachelor. (BB, TB).

Poor Child. (BB).

Pray for a Tomorrow. (BB).

Sea Level. (BB).

COLLECTIONS

Harvard University Library. (Cambridge,
   Massachusetts).

New York Public Library. (New York, New York).

Pack Memorial Public Library. (Asheville,
   North Carolina).

Wadsworth Museum. (Hartford, Connecticut).

BACKGROUND READING

"Anne Parrish Tizell: With a Catalog of Her Drawings
   and Paintings She Collected." *Wadsworth
   Atheneum Bulletin*, Winter 1958.

Burke. *American Authors and Books, 1640 to the
   Present Day*.

Current Biography.

Davis, L. "Anne Parrish as a Writer of Children's
   Books." *Horn Book*, February 1960.

Hart. *Oxford Companion to American Literature,
   Fourth Edition*.

Kunitz. *Junior Book of Authors*.

Kunitz. *Living Authors*.

Kunitz. *Twentieth Century Authors*.

Kunitz. *Twentieth Century Authors, First
   Supplement*.

Mahony, B. "Anne Parrish's Memorable Nonsense
   Story." *Horn Book*, January 1951.

Mahony, B. *Illustrators of Children's Books,
   1744-1945*.

Miller. *Illustrators of Children's Books, 1946-1956*.

Obituary. *New York Times*, September 7, 1957.

Obituary. *Publishers Weekly*, September 23, 1957.

Obituary. *Time*, September 16, 1957.

Obituary. *Wilson Library Bulletin*, November 5, 1957.

Parrish, A. "Writing for Children." *Horn Book*,
   March 1951.

Ward. *Authors of Books for Young People, Second
   Edition*.

Warfel. *American Novelists of Today*.

MAUD SYLVIA FULLER PETERSHAM, 1890-1971
author-illustrator
a.k.a. Maud Fuller

and

MISKA PETERSHAM, 1888-1960
author-illustrator

AWARDS

American ABC. Caldecott Honor Book, 1942.

(*Pran of Albania*. Newbery Honor Book, 1930.)

Rooster Crows. Caldecott Medal Book, 1946.

BIBLIOGRAPHY

as Maud Fuller:

Cambridge Book of Poetry for Young People. Putnam,
   1916.

as Maud Petersham:

*Shepherd Psalm: Psalm XXIII from the Book of
   Psalms*; from the *Bible*. Macmillan, 1962.

as Maud and Miska Petersham:

Albanian Wonder Tales; by Post Wheeler. Doubleday,
   1936.

American ABC. Macmillan, 1941.

*America's Stamps: The Story of One Hundred Years
   of U.S. Postage Stamps*. Macmillan, 1947.

Ark of Father Noah and Mother Noah. Doubleday,
   1930.

Auntie and Celia Jane and Miki. Doubleday, 1932.

Beckoning Road; by Sydney Rowland, et al. Winston, 1931.

Billy Bang's Book; by Mabel S. G. LaRue. Macmillan, 1927.

Bird in Hand: Sayings from Poor Richard's Almanac, by the Wise American; by Benjamin Franklin. Macmillan, 1951.

Box with Red Wheels: A Picture Book. Macmillan, 1955.

Boy Who Had No Heart. Macmillan, 1955.

Broom Fairies and Other Stories. Yale, 1917.

Children of Ancient Britain; by Louise Lamprey. Little, 1921.

Children of the Mountain Eagle; by Elizabeth C. Miller. Doubleday, 1927.

Child's Own Book of Verse; by Ada M. Skinner and Frances G. Wicker. Macmillan, 1917. (3 vols.).

Christ Child, as Told by Matthew and Luke; from the *Bible*. Doubleday, 1931.

Circus Baby: A Picture Book. Macmillan, 1950.

David: From the Story Told in the First Book of Samuel and the First Book of Kings; from the *Bible*. Winston, 1938; also in *Stories from the Old Testament*, below.

Enchanted Forest; by William Bowen. Macmillan, 1920.

Everyday Canadian Primer; by Elsie S. Eells. Macmillan, 1928.

Faraway Hills; by Wilhelmina Harper and A. J. Hamilton. Macmillan, 1929.

Five Little Friends; by Sherred W. Adams. Macmillan, 1928.

Four and Lena; by Marie Barringer. Doubleday, 1938.

F-U-N Book; by Mabel S. G. LaRue. Macmillan, 1924.

Get-a-Way and Háry János. Viking, 1933.

Guld: The Cavern King; by Mary L. Branch. Penn, 1917.

Heidi; by Johanna Spyri. Garden City, 1932.

Heights and Highways; by Wilhelmina Harper and A. J. Hamilton. Macmillan, 1929.

History Stories for Primary Grades; by John Wayland. Macmillan, 1925.

In Animal Land; by Mabel S. G. LaRue. Macmillan, 1924; revised, 1929.

In Clean Hay; by Eric Kelly. Macmillan, 1953.

Jesus' Story: A Little New Testament, Bible Text Selected from the King James Version; from the *Bible*. Macmillan, 1942.

Joseph and His Brothers: From the Story Told in the Book of Genesis; from the *Bible*. Winston, 1938; also in *Stories from the Old Testament*, below.

Language Garden: A Primary Language Book; by Inez Howard, et al. Macmillan, 1924.

Literature: A Series of Anthologies; by Ethel A. Cross, et al. Macmillan, 1943-46. (Includes *Book 1, Appreciating Literature* [revised, 1951]; *Book 2, Understanding Literature* [revised, 1951]; *Book 3, Interpreting Literature* [revised, 1951]; *Book 4, Types of Literature* [revised, 1954]; *Book 5, Heritage of American Literature* [revised, 1954]; *Book 6, Heritage of British Literature* [revised, 1954]; *Book 7, Heritage of World Literature* [revised, 1954].)

Little Book of Prayers: With the Addition of Prayers from the Bible; by Emilie Johnson. Viking, 1941.

Little Indians; by Mabel S. G. LaRue. Macmillan, 1930; new edition, 1934.

Little Ugly Face: And Other Indian Tales; by Florence C. Coolidge. Macmillan, 1925.

Long-Ago Peopie: How They Lived in Britain before History Began. Little, 1921.

Magic Doll of Roumania: A Wonder Story in Which East and West Do Meet; Written for American Children; by Maria, Queen of Roumania. Stokes, 1929.

Marquette Readers; by the Sisters of Mercy. Macmillan, 1924-26. (Includes *Pre-Primer Chart* [1925]; *Primer* [1929]; *First Reader* [1925]; *Second Reader* [1926]; *Teacher's Manual* [1925].)

Martin the Goose Boy; by Marie Barringer. Doubleday, 1932.

Miki and Mary: Their Search for Treasures. Viking, 1934.

Miki: The Book of Maud and Miska Petersham. Doubleday, 1929.

Miss Posy Longlegs; by Miriam E. Mason. Macmillan, 1955.

Moses: From the Story Told in the Old Testament; from the *Bible*. Winston, 1938; also in *Stories from the Old Testament*, below.

My Very First Book. Macmillan, 1925.

Number Friends: A Primary Arithmetic; by Inez Howard, et al. Macmillan, 1927.

Nursery Friends from France; by Olive B. Miller. Book House, 1925. (Volume 1 of *My Travelship* series.)

Off to Bed: Seven Stories for Wide-Awakes. Macmillan, 1954.

Pathway to Reading: Primer; by Bessie B. Coleman and J. F. H. Uhl. Silver, 1925.

Pathway to Reading: Teacher's Manual; by Bessie B. Coleman and J. F. H. Uhl. Silver, 1925.

Peppernuts. Macmillan, 1958.

BIBLIOGRAPHY (cont'd)

Philippine Literature Series; by Harriott Fansler and Isidoro Panlasigul. il. with Violet M. Higgins. Macmillan, 1923.

Philippine National Literature, Volume 2; by Harriott Fansler and Isidoro Panlasigul. il. with Violet M. Higgins. Macmillan, 1925.

Picnic Book; by Jean Ayer. Macmillan, 1934.

Pinocchio; by Carlo Collodi, *pseud.* (Carlo Lorenzini). Garden City, 1932.

Pleasant Pathways; by Wilhelmina Harper and A. J. Hamilton. Macmillan, 1928.

Poppy Seed Cakes; by Margery Clark, *pseud.* (Mary Clark and Margery Quigley). Doubleday, 1924.

Pran of Albania; by Elizabeth C. Miller. Doubleday, 1929.

Rich Cargoes; by Sydney Rowland, et al. Winston, 1931.

Rip Van Winkle and the Legend of Sleepy Hollow; by Washington Irving. Macmillan, 1951.

Rooster Crows: A Book of American Rhymes and Jingles. Macmillan, 1945.

Rootabaga Pigeons; by Carl Sandburg. Harcourt, 1923.

Rootabaga Stories; by Carl Sandburg. Harcourt, 1922.

Ruth: From the Story Told in the Old Testament; from the *Bible*. Winston, 1938; also in *Stories from the Old Testament*, below.

Silver Mace: A Story of Old Williamsburg. Macmillan, 1956.

Stories from the Old Testament: Joseph, Moses, Ruth, David. Winston, 1938; also issued separately, above.

Story Book of Aircraft. Winston, 1935; also in *Story Book of Wheels, Ships, Trains, Aircraft*, below.

Story Book of Clothes. Winston, 1933; also in *Story Book of Things We Use*, below.

Story Book of Coal. Winston, 1935; also in *Story Book of Earth's Treasures*, below.

Story Book of Corn. Winston, 1936; also in *Story Book of Foods from the Field*, below.

Story Book of Cotton. Winston, 1939; also in *Story Book of Things We Wear*, below.

Story Book of Earth's Treasures: Gold, Coal, Iron and Steel. Winston, 1935; also issued separately, above and below.

Story Book of Foods. Winston, 1933; also in *Story Book of Things We Use*, below.

Story Book of Foods from the Field: Wheat, Corn, Rice, Sugar. Winston, 1936; also issued separately, above and below.

Story Book of Gold. Winston, 1935; also in *Story Book of Earth's Treasures*, above.

Story Book of Houses. Winston, 1933; also in *Story Book of Things We Use*, below.

Story Book of Iron and Steel. Winston, 1935; also in *Story Book of Earth's Treasures*, above.

Story Book of Oil. Winston, 1935; also in *Story Book of Earth's Treasures*, above.

Story Book of Rayon. Winston, 1939; also in *Story Book of Things We Wear*, below.

Story Book of Rice. Winston, 1936; also in *Story Book of Foods from the Field*, above.

Story Book of Ships. Winston, 1935; also in *Story Book of Wheels, Ships, Trains, Aircraft*, below.

Story Book of Silk. Winston, 1939; also in *Story Book of Things We Wear*, below; *a.k.a. Let's Learn about Silk*. il. James E. Barry. Harvey, 1967.

Story Book of Sugar. Winston, 1936; also in *Story Book of Foods from the Field*, above; *a.k.a. Let's Learn about Sugar*. il. James E. Barry. Harvey, 1969.

Story Book of Things We Use: Houses, Clothes, Food, Transportation. Winston, 1939; also issued separately, above and below.

Story Book of Things We Wear: Wool, Cotton, Silk, Rayon. Winston, 1939; also issued separately, above and below.

Story Book of Trains. Winston, 1935; also in *Story Book of Wheels, Ships, Trains, Aircraft*, below.

Story Book of Transportation. Winston, 1933; also in *Story Book of Things We Use*, above.

Story Book of Wheat. Winston, 1936; also in *Story Book of Foods from the Field*, above.

Story Book of Wheels. Winston, 1935; also in *Story Book of Wheels, Ships, Trains, Aircraft*, below.

Story Book of Wheels, Ships, Trains, Aircraft. Winston, 1935; also issued separately, above.

Story Book of Wool. Winston, 1939; also in *Story Book of Things We Wear*, above.

Story of Jesus: A Little New Testament, Bible Text Selected from the Confraternity Christian Doctrine Edition; from the *Bible*. Macmillan, 1944; *a.k.a. Story of Jesus: A Little New Testament, Bible Text Selected from the Revised Standard Version*, 1967.

Story of the Presidents of the United States of America. Macmillan, 1953; new edition, 1966.

Susannah, the Pioneer Cow; by Miriam E. Mason. Macmillan, 1941.

Tales from Shakespeare; by Charles and Mary Lamb. Macmillan, 1923.

Tales of Enchantment from Spain, Retold; by Elsie S. Eels. Harcourt, 1920.

Tales Told in Holland; by Olive B. Miller. Book House, 1925. (Volume 3 of My Travelship series.)

Thinking and Reading Practice Cards; by Bessie B. Coleman and J. F. H. Uhl. Silver, 1927.

Told under the Christmas Tree; by The Association for Childhood Education. Macmillan, 1948.

Treasure Trove; by Sydney Rowland, et al. Winston, 1931.

Twenty-four Unusual Stories; by Anna C. Tyler. Harcourt, 1921.

Under the Story Tree; by Mabel S. G. LaRue. Macmillan, 1923.

Voyage of the Wee Red Cap; by Ruth Sawyer. Macmillan, 1948.

Where Was Bobby?; by Marguerite Clement. Doubleday, 1928.

Winding Roads: Stories by Various Authors; compiled by Wilhelmina Harper and A. J. Hamilton. Macmillan, 1932.

Wings of Adventure; by Sydney Rowland, et al. Winston, 1931.

Young Trajan; by Elizabeth C. Miller. Doubleday, 1931.

Zip, the Toy Mule: And Other Stories; by Mabel S. G. LaRue. Macmillan, 1932.

MEDIA

Box with Red Wheels. (CB); Association-Sterling Films/Macmillan Films, 1974 (FSS).

Christ Child. (BB).

Circus Baby. (TB); Weston Woods Studio, 1956 (F), 1958 (FSS); also in Weston Woods Studios Set No. 3, 1965 (FSS).

Joseph and His Brothers. (BB).

Rooster Crows. (BB, CB).

COLLECTIONS

deGrummond Collection, University of Southern Mississippi. (Hattiesburg, Mississippi).

Free Library of Philadelphia. (Philadelphia, Pennsylvania).

Gary Public Library. (Gary, Indiana).

Kerlan Collection, University of Minnesota. (Minneapolis, Minnesota).

Special Collections, University Research Library, University of California. (Los Angeles, California).

University of Oregon Library. (Eugene, Oregon).

Vassar College Library. (Poughkeepsie, New York).

BACKGROUND READING

Bader. American Picturebooks from Noah's Ark to The Beast Within.

Burke. American Authors and Books, 1640 to the Present Day.

Contemporary Authors.

Hopkins. Books Are by People.

Kingman. Illustrators of Children's Books, 1957-1966.

Kingman. Illustrators of Children's Books, 1967-1976.

Kirkpatrick. Twentieth Century Children's Writers.

Kunitz. Junior Book of Authors.

Kunitz. Junior Book of Authors, Second Edition Revised.

Mahony. Contemporary Illustrators of Children's Books.

Mahony. Illustrators of Children's Books, 1744-1945.

Miller. Caldecott Medal Books, 1938-1957.

Miller. Illustrators of Children's Books, 1946-1956.

Montgomery. Story behind Modern Books.

Obituary. (Maud Petersham)

Obituary. New York Times, November 30, 1971.

Obituary. Publishers Weekly, December 13, 1971.

Obituary. (Miska Petersham)

Obituary. Horn Book, August 1960.

Obituary. Library Journal, September 15, 1960.

Obituary. New York Times, May 16, 1960.

Obituary. Publishers Weekly, May 23, 1960.

Smaridge. Famous Literary Teams for Young People.

Ward. Authors of Books for Young People, Second Edition.

Ward. Illustrators of Books for Young People, Second Edition.

Young Wings. Writing Books for Boys and Girls.

LEO POLITI, 1908-
author-illustrator

AWARDS

Juanita. Caldecott Honor Book, 1949.

AWARDS (cont'd)

Pedro. Caldecott Honor Book, 1947.

Song of the Swallows. Caldecott Medal Book, 1950.

BIBLIOGRAPHY

All Things Bright and Beautiful: A Hymn; by Cecil F. Alexander. Scribner, 1962.

Angelo, the Naughty One; by Helen Garrett. Viking, 1944.

Aqui Se Habla Español; by Margarita Lopez. Heath, 1942.

At the Palace Gates; by Helen R. Parish. Viking, 1949.

Boat for Peppé. Scribner, 1950.

Bunker Hill, Los Angeles: Reminiscences of Bygone Days. Desert-Southwest, 1964.

Butterflies Come. Scribner, 1957.

Columbus Story; by Alice Dalgliesh. Scribner, 1955.

Coyote the Rebel; by Louis Perez. Holt, 1947.

Emmet. Scribner, 1971.

Juanita. Scribner, 1948.

Least One; by Ruth Sawyer. Viking, 1941.

Lito and the Clown. Scribner, 1964.

Little Leo. Scribner, 1951.

Little Pancho. Viking, 1938.

Looking-for-Something: The Story of a Stray Burro of Ecuador; by Ann N. Clark. Viking, 1952.

Magic Money; by Ann N. Clark. Viking, 1950.

Mieko. Golden Gate, 1969.

Mission Bell. Scribner, 1953.

Moy, Moy. Scribner, 1960.

Nicest Gift. Scribner, 1973.

Noble Doll; by Elizabeth Coatsworth. Viking, 1961.

Pedro, the Angel of Olvera Street. Scribner, 1946; a.k.a. *Pedro, el Ángel de la Calle Olvera*, 1961.

Piccolo's Prank Scribner, 1965.

Poinsetta. Best-West, 1969.

Rosa. Scribner, 1963; also Spanish edition, 1963.

Saint Francis and the Animals. Scribner, 1959.

Song of the Swallows. Scribner, 1949.

Stories from the Americas. Tr. Frank Henius. Scribner, 1944.

Tales of the Los Angeles Parks. Best-West, 1966.

Three Miracles; by Catherine Blanton. Day, 1946.

Three Stalks of Corn. Scribner, 1976.

Vamos a Hablar Español; by Margarita Mesas and Esther Brown. Heath, 1949.

Young Giotto. Horn Book, 1947.

MEDIA

Juanita. (BB).

Little Leo. (BB).

Pedro. (TB).

Song of the Swallows. (TB); Miller-Brody Productions, 1974 (FSS), a.k.a. *Canción de los Golondrinas*, 1974 (FSS).

COLLECTIONS

Free Library of Philadelphia. (Philadelphia, Pennsylvania).

Kerlan Collection, University of Minnesota. (Minneapolis, Minnesota).

May Massee Collection, Emporia State College. (Emporia, Kansas).

Special Collections, University Research Library, University of California. (Los Angeles, California).

BACKGROUND READING

Bader. *American Picturebooks from Noah's Ark to The Beast Within*.

Commire. *Something about the Author*.

Contemporary Authors.

English, G. "Leo Politi." *Horn Book*, July 1950.

Hoffman. *Authors and Illustrators of Children's Books*.

Hopkins. *Books Are by People*.

Kingman. *Illustrators of Children's Books, 1957-1966*.

Kingman. *Illustrators of Children's Books, 1967-1976*.

Kirkpatrick. *Twentieth Century Children's Writers*.

Kunitz. *Junior Book of Authors, Second Edition Revised*.

Mahony. *Illustrators of Children's Books, 1744-1945*.

McCreedy, M. "Leo Politi." *Catholic Library World*, February 1966.

Miller. *Caldecott Medal Books, 1938-1957*.

Miller. *Illustrators of Children's Books, 1946-1956*.

Nichols, R. "To the Children with Love, From Leo Politi." *Horn Book*, April 1966.

Schreiber, G. "Artist's Choice." *Horn Book*, April 1953.

Templin, E. "Leo Politi: Children's Historian." *Elementary English*, October 1956.

Ward. *Authors of Books for Young People, Second Edition*.

Ward. *Illustrators of Books for Young People, Second Edition*.

Young Wings. *Writing Books for Boys and Girls*.

ELIZABETH MARIE POPE, 1917-
author

AWARDS

Perilous Gard. Newbery Honor Book, 1975.

BIBLIOGRAPHY

Paradise Regained: The Tradition and the Poem. Russell, 1947.

Perilous Gard. il. Richard Cuffari. Houghton, 1974; large print edition, Hall, 1976.

Sherwood Ring. il. Evaline Ness. Houghton, 1958.

MEDIA

Perilous Gard. (CB).

Sherwood Ring. (TB).

COLLECTIONS

Kerlan Collection, University of Minnesota. (Minneapolis, Minnesota).

BACKGROUND READING

Contemporary Authors.

+LOUISE SPIEKER RANKIN, 1897-1951
author

AWARDS

Daughter of the Mountains. Newbery Honor Book, 1949.

BIBLIOGRAPHY

American Cookbook for India. il. R. D. Thompson. Thacker, 1944.

Daughter of the Mountains. il. Kurt Wiese. Viking, 1948.

Gentling of Jonathan. il. Lee Townsend. Viking, 1950.

MEDIA

Daughter of the Mountains. (BB, TB).

BACKGROUND READING

Fuller, *More Junior Authors*.

Obituary. *New York Times*, November 22, 1951.

Obituary. *Wilson Library Bulletin*, January 1952.

ELLEN RASKIN, 1928-
author-illustrator

AWARDS

Figgs & Phantoms. Newbery Honor Book, 1975.

BIBLIOGRAPHY

A & The: Or William T. C. Baumgarten Comes to Town. Atheneum, 1970.

And It Rained. Atheneum, 1969.

Books: A Book to Begin On; by Susan Bartlett. Holt, 1968.

Child's Christmas in Wales; by Dylan Thomas. New Directions, 1959.

Circles and Curves; by Arthur Razzell and K. G. O. Watts. Doubleday, 1964.

Come Along!; by Rebecca Caudill. Holt, 1969.

Elidor; by Alan Garner. Walck, 1967.

Ellen Grae; by Vera and Bill Cleaver. Lippincott, 1967.

Figgs & Phantoms. Dutton, 1974.

Franklin Stein. Atheneum, 1972.

Ghost in a Four-Room Apartment. Atheneum, 1969.

Goblin Market; by Christina B. Rossetti. Dutton, 1970.

Happy Christmas; by Claire H. Bishop. Daye, 1956.

Inatuck's Friend; by Suzanne S. Morrow. Little, 1968.

Jewish Sabbath; by Molly Cone. Crowell, 1966.

King of Men; by Olivia Coolidge. Houghton, 1966.

Mama I Wish I Was Snow: Child You'll Be Very Cold; by Ruth Krauss. Atheneum, 1962.

Moe Q. McGlutch: He Smoked Too Much. Parents, 1973.

Moose, Goose and Little Nobody. Parents, 1974.

Mysterious Disappearance of Leon (I Mean Noel). Dutton, 1971.

BIBLIOGRAPHY (cont'd)

Nothing Ever Happens on My Block. Atheneum, 1966.

Paper Zoo; by Reneé K. Weiss. Macmillan, 1968.

Piping Down the Valleys Wild: Poetry for the Young of All Ages; by Nancy Larrick. Delacorte, 1968.

Poems by Robert Herrick; edited by Winifred Scott. Crowell, 1967.

Poems for Young People by D. H. Lawrence; selected by William Cole. Viking, 1967.

Poems of Edgar Allan Poe; by Edgar A. Poe. Crowell, 1965.

Probability: The Science of Chance; by Arthur Razzell and K. G. O. Watts. Doubleday, 1964.

Shrieks at Midnight: Macabre Poems, Eerie and Humorous; by Sara Brewton. Crowell, 1969.

Silly Songs and Sad. Crowell, 1967.

Songs of Innocence; by William Blake. Doubleday, 1966. (2 vols.: Vol. 1, *Poetry*; Vol. 2, *Songs*).

Spectacles. Atheneum, 1968.

Symmetry; by Arthur Razzell and K. G. O. Watts. Doubleday, 1968.

Tatooed Potato and Other Clues. Dutton, 1975.

This Is 4: The Idea of a Number; by Arthur Razzell and K. G. O. Watts. Doubleday, 1964.

Three and the Shape of Three; by Arthur Razzell and K. G. O. Watts. Doubleday, 1964.

Twenty-two, Twenty-three. Atheneum, 1976.

We Alcotts: The Story of Louisa May Alcott's Family as Seen through the Eyes of Marmee; by Aileen Fisher and Olive Rabe. Atheneum, 1968.

We Dickinsons: The Life of Emily Dickinson as Seen through the Eyes of Her Brother, Austin; by Aileen Fisher and Olive Rabe. Atheneum, 1965.

Who Said, Sue, Said Whoo? Atheneum, 1973.

World's Greatest Freak Show. Atheneum, 1971.

MEDIA

Spectacles. (TB).

Tatooed Potato. (CB).

World's Greatest Freak Show. Stephen Bosustow Productions/Xerox Films, 1972 (F, FSS).

EXHIBITIONS

Biennale Bratislava, 1969. (Bratislava, Czechoslovakia).

COLLECTIONS

Cooperative Children's Book Center, University of Wisconsin. (Madison, Wisconsin).

Kerlan Collection, University of Minnesota. (Minneapolis, Minnesota).

Milwaukee Public Library. (Milwaukee, Wisconsin).

BACKGROUND READING

Bader. *American Picturebooks from Noah's Ark to The Beast Within*.

Commire. *Something about the Author*.

Contemporary Authors.

DeMontreville. *Third Book of Junior Authors*.

Hopkins. *Books Are by People*.

Kingman. *Illustrators of Children's Books, 1957-1966*.

Kingman. *Illustrators of Children's Books, 1967-1976*.

Kirkpatrick. *Twentieth Century Children's Writers*.

"Profile of an Author, Ellen Raskin." *Top of the News*, June 1972.

Raskin, E. "Creative Spirit and Children's Literature." *Wilson Library Bulletin*, October, 1978.

Ward. *Illustrators of Books for Young People, Second Edition*.

MARJORIE KINNAN RAWLINGS, 1896-1953
author

AWARDS

Secret River. Newbery Honor Book, 1956.

BIBLIOGRAPHY

*Cross Creek. il. Edward Shenton. Scribner, 1942.

Cross Creek Cookery. il. Robert Camp. Scribner, 1942; *a.k.a. Marjorie Kinnan Rawlings Cookbook: Cross Creek Cookery*. Hammond, 1960.

Golden Apples. Scribner, 1935.

Jacob's Ladder. il. Jessie Ayers. University of Miami, 1950.

Marjorie Kinnan Rawlings Reader; selected and edited by Julia S. Bigham. Scribner, 1956.

Secret River. il. Leonard Weisgard. Scribner, 1955.

Sojourner. Scribner, 1953.

South Moon Under. Scribner, 1933.

When the Whippoorwill---. Scribner, 1940.

Yearling. il. Edward Shenton. Scribner, 1938; also il. Newell C. Wyeth, 1939; also il. Leonard Weisgard, 1955; large print edition, Watts, 1965; *a.k.a. Yearling: With a Study Guide by Mary L. Flagg and Edith Cowles*. il. Edward Shenton, 1962.

MEDIA

Cross Creek. (BB, CB, TB).

Cross Creek Cookery. (BB, CB).

Golden Apples. (BB).

Sojourner. (BB, TB).

South Moon Under. (CB); as *Sun Comes Up*. Metro-Goldwyn-Mayer, Inc., 1948 (F).

When the Whippoorwill---. (BB, CB).

Yearling. (BB, TB); Caedmon Records, 1974 (R); Metro-Goldwyn-Mayer, Inc., 1946 (F).

COLLECTIONS

American Academy of Arts and Letters Library. (New York, New York).

Baker Memorial Library, Dartmouth College. (Hanover, New Hampshire).

Collection of American Literature, Beinecke Library, Yale University. (New Haven, Connecticut).

Marjorie Kinnan Rawlings State Museum. (Cross Creek, Florida).

Modern Manuscript Collection, University of Notre Dame. (Notre Dame, Indiana).

Princeton University Library. (Princeton, New Jersey).

University of Florida Libraries. (Gainesville, Florida).

BACKGROUND READING

Bellman, Samuel J. *Marjorie Kinnan Rawlings*. Twayne, 1974.

Bigelow, Gordon E. *Frontier Eden: The Literary Career of Marjorie Kinnan Rawlings*. University of Florida, 1966.

Bigelow, Gordon E. "Marjorie Kinnan Rawlings' Wilerness." *Sewanee Review*, Spring 1965.

Burke. *American Authors and Books, 1640 to the Present Day*.

Commire. *Yesterday's Authors of Books for Children*.

Cournos. *Famous American Novelists*.

Current Biography.

DeMontreville. *Third Book of Junior Authors*.

Hart. *Oxford Companion to American Literature, Fourth Edition*.

Kirkpatrick. *Twentieth Century Children's Writers*.

Kunitz. *Twentieth Century Authors*.

Kunitz. *Twentieth Century Authors, First Supplement*.

Montgomery. *Story behind Modern Books*.

Nichols, L. "Talk with Mrs. Rawlings." *New York Times Book Review*, February 1, 1953.

Obituary. *New York Times*, December 15, 1953.

Obituary. *Newsweek*, December 28, 1953.

Obituary. *Publishers Weekly*, December 26, 1953.

Obituary. *Saturday Review of Literature*, January 16, 1954.

Obituary. *Time,* December 25, 1953.

Obituary. *Wilson Library Bulletin*, February 1954.

Warfel. *American Novelists of Today*.

Williams, W. "To the Ghost of Marjorie Kinnan Rawlings." *Virginia Quarterly*, Autumn 1960.

+PHILIP G. REED, 1908-
illustrator

AWARDS

Mother Goose. Caldecott Honor Book, 1964.

BIBLIOGRAPHY

Christmas Carol in Prose: Being a Ghost Story of Christmas; by Charles Dickens. Holiday, 1940.

How to Sell a Consulting Engineer; by Consulting Engineer, *ca.*1957.

Many Moons; by James Thurber. Roe, 1958.

Mother Goose and Nursery Rhymes; from Mother Goose. Atheneum, 1963.

Seven Voyages of Sindbad the Sailor; from the Arabian Nights. Holiday, 1939.

BACKGROUND READING

Current Biography.

DeMontreville. *Third Book of Junior Authors*.

DeNoto, A. "Philip Reed." *Library Journal*, March 14, 1964.

Kingman. *Illustrators of Children's Books, 1957-1966*.

Mahony. *Illustrators of Children's Books, 1744-1945*.

Ogg, O. "Illustrator, Designer, Master Printer." *American Artist*, May 1948.

Ward. *Illustrators of Books for Young People, Second Edition*.

+JOHANNA REISS
author

AWARDS

Upstairs Room. Newbery Honor Book, 1973.

BIBLIOGRAPHY

Journey Back. Crowell, 1976.

Upstairs Room. Crowell, 1972; large print edition, Hall, 1973.

MEDIA

Upstairs Room. Miller-Brody Productions, 1976 (FSS).

+DOROTHY MARY RHOADS, 1895-
author

AWARDS

Corn Grows Ripe. Newbery Honor Book, 1957.

BIBLIOGRAPHY

Bright Feather and Other Maya Tales. il. Lowell Houser. Doubleday, 1932.

Corn Grows Ripe. il. Jean Charlot. Viking, 1956.

Story of Chan Yuc. il. Jean Charlot. Viking, 1941.

MEDIA

Corn Grows Ripe. (BB).

BACKGROUND READING

Contemporary Authors.

Ward. *Authors of Books for Young People, Second Edition*.

+MABEL LOUISE ROBINSON, 1874-1962
author

AWARDS

Bright Island. Newbery Honor Book, 1938.

Runner of the Mountain Tops. Newbery Honor Book, 1940.

BIBLIOGRAPHY

All by Ourselves. il. Mary S. Wright. Dutton, 1924.

All the Year Round. il. Aldren Watson. Harper, 1954.

Art of Writing Prose; with Helen R. Hull and Roger S. Loomis. Smith, 1930; revised, Farrar, 1936.

Back-Seat Driver. il. Leonard Shortall. Random, 1949.

Bitter Forfeit. Bobbs, 1947.

(ed.) *Blue Ribbon Stories: The Best Children's Stories of 1929, Selected by the Juvenile Writing Class of Columbia University*. Appleton, 1929.

(ed.) *Blue Ribbon Stories: The Best Magazine Stories for Boys and Girls*. Macmillan, 1932.

Bright Island. il. Lynd Ward. Random, 1937.

Course in Juvenile Story Writing and in the Study of Juvenile Literature. Columbia University, 1923.

Creative Writing: The Story Form; with Helen R. Hull. American Book, 1932.

Curriculum of the Woman's College. U.S. Bureau of Education, 1918.

Deepening Year. Westminster, 1950.

Dr. Tam O'Shanter. Dutton, 1921.

Gordon of Sesame Street Storybook. Random, 1951.

Home Study Course in Juvenile Story Writing: Prepared under the Supervision of the Department of English, Columbia University. Columbia University, 1930.

Island Noon. Random, 1942.

Juvenile Story Writing. Dutton, 1922; revised as *Writing for Young People*. il. Béla Dankovszky. Nelson, 1950.

King Arthur and His Knights. il. Douglas Gorsline. Random, 1953.

Little Lucia. Dutton, 1923.

Little Lucia and Her Puppy. Dutton, 1923.

Little Lucia's Island Camp. Dutton, 1924.

Little Lucia's School. il. Sophia T. Balcom. Dutton, 1926.

Riley Goes to Obedience School. il. Leonard Shortall. Random, 1956.

Robin and Angus. il. Eloise B. Wilkin. Macmillan, 1931.

Robin and Heather. il. Eunice Vibberts. Macmillan, 1932.

Robin and Tito. il. Eloise Burns. Macmillan, 1930.

Runner of the Mountain Tops: The Life of Louis Agassiz. il. Lynd Ward. Random, 1939.

Sarah's Daikin. il. Julie Brown. Dutton, 1927; *a.k.a. Sarah and Her Dog, Daikin*, 1931.

(ed.) *Second Book of Blue Ribbon Stories: The Best Children's Stories of 1930, Selected by the Juvenile Writing Class of Columbia University*. il. Decie Merwin. Appleton, 1930.

Skipper Riley: The Terrier Dog. il. Leonard Shortall. Random, 1955.

Strong Wings. il. Lynd Ward. Random, 1951.

MEDIA

All the Year Round. (BB).

Bright Island. (BB).

Writing for Young People. (BB).

COLLECTIONS

Rare Book and Manuscript Library, Columbia University. (New York, New York).

BACKGROUND READING

Burke. *American Authors and Books, 1640 to the Present Day*.

Kunitz. *Junior Book of Authors, Second Edition Revised*.

Maine Writers Research Club. *Maine Writers of Juvenile Fiction*.

Obituary. *New York Times*, February 22, 1962.

Obituary. *Publishers Weekly*, March 5, 1962.

Petry, A. "Mabel Louise Robinson." *Horn Book*, August 1962.

"She'd Rather Be Ignored." *Saturday Evening Post*, April 5, 1947.

Stoddard. *Topflight*.

Warfel. *American Novelists of Today*.

Young Wings. *Writing Books for Boys and Girls*.

FEODOR STEPANOVICH ROJANKOVSKY, 1891-1970
author-illustrator
pseudonym Rojan

AWARDS

(*All Alone*. Newbery Honor Book, 1954.)

Frog Went a-Courtin'. Caldecott Medal Book, 1956.

BIBLIOGRAPHY

as *Rojan:*

ABC du Père Castor. Flammarion, 1936.

ABC Jeux du Père Castor. Flammarion, 1936.

Bourru l'Ours Brun; by Lida. Flammarion, 1936; a.k.a. *Bourru, the Brown Bear*. Tr. Rose Fyleman; Allen, 1939; a.k.a. *Bruin, the Brown Bear*. Tr. Lily Duplaix. Harper, 1937; new edition, Golden. 1966.

Calendreir des Enfants; by Y. Lacôte. Flammarion, 1936. (Three different editions issued.); a.k.a. *Children's Year: Adapted by Margaret W. Brown*. Harper, 1937; a.k.a. *Petites Joies de Chaque Mois*, 1964.

Coucou; by Lida. Flammarion, 1939; a.k.a. *Cuckoo*. Tr. Rose Fyleman. Allen, 1938; a.k.a. *Cuckoo*. Tr. Lily Duplaix. Harper, 1942.

Dnevnik Foksa Mikki; by Sasha Cernyj. Moscow-Logos, *ca.*1926.

Froux le Lièvre; by Lida. Flammarion, 1935; a.k.a. *Fluff, the Little White Rabbit*. Tr. Georges Duplaix. Harper, 1937; a.k.a. *Froux, the Hare*. Tr. Rose Fyleman. Allen, 1938.

Globusnyj Celovecik; by Natal'ja Kodrjanskaja. Imprimerie Union, 1954.

Grande Maison de Blanc. n. p., 1929.

Kosac'ja Sanatorija; by Sasha Cernyj. (Paris, France), 1928.

Maly Lord; by Frances H. Burnett. Tr. M. J. Zaleska. Naklad Begethnera I Wolffa, 1925.

Marja; by Antoni Malczewski. Wydawnictwo Polskie, 1922.

Martin Pêcheur; by Lida. Flammarion, 1938; a.k.a. *Martin the Kingfisher*. Tr. Rose Fyleman. Allen, 1938; a.k.a. *Kingfisher*. Tr. Lily Duplaix. Harper, 1940.

Molodaja Rosija; edited by Sasha Cernyj. Zemgor, 1927.

Panache l'Ecrureuil; by Lida. Flammarion, 1934; a.k.a. *Pompom, the Little Red Squirrel*. Tr. Georges Duplaix. Harper, 1936; a.k.a. *Mischief, the Squirrel*. Tr. Rose Fyleman. Allen, 1938.

Petits Père Castor Series. Flammarion, 1941-48. (Includes *Animaux du Zoo*, by Lida [1941]; *Cendrillon*, by Charles Perrault [1942]; *Drôles de Bêtes*, by Paul François [1941]; *Histoire du Chien de Brisquet*, by Charles Nodier [1942]; *Histoire due Nègre Zo'Hio et de l'Oiseau Moqueur*, by Marie Colmont, *pseud.* [Marie deB. Delavand] [1941]; *Mes Amis*, by Paul Francois [1941]; *Musiciens de la Ville de Brême*, by Jacob and Wilhelm Grimm [1942]; and *Royaume de la Mer*, [author unknown], [1948].)

Pic et Pic et Colégram; by Marie Colmont, *pseud.* (Marie deB. Delavand). Flammarion, 1941.

Plouf Canard Sauvage; by Lida. Flammarion, 1935; a.k.a. *Plouf, the Little Wild Duck*. Tr. Georges Duplaix. Harper, 1936; new edition as *Ploof, the Little Wild Duck*. Golden, 1966; a.k.a. *Ploof, the Little Wild Duck*. Tr. Rose Fyleman. Allen, 1938.

Przygody Tomka Sawyera; by Mark Twain, *pseud.* (Samuel L. Clemens). Tr. Jana Bilinskiego. Wydawnictwo Polskie, *ca.*1925.

BIBLIOGRAPHY (cont'd)

as Rojan (cont'd):

Quipic le Hérisson; by Lida. Flammarion, 1937; *a.k.a.
Quipic, the Hedgehog*. Tr. Rose Fyleman. Allen,
1938; *a.k.a. Spiky the Hedgehog*. Tr. Lily Duplaix.
Harper, 1938; new edition, Golden, 1966.

Renine Wierszyki; by Ewa Szelburg. Towarzystwo
Wydawnjcze Warszawje, *ca*.1925.

Scaf le Phoque; by Lida. Flammarion, 1936; *a.k.a.
Scuff the Seal*. Tr. Lily Duplaix. Harper, 1937;
a.k.a. Scaf the Seal. Tr. Rose Fyleman. Allen, 1939;
new edition, Golden, 1966.

Slon Birara; by F. Antoni Ossendowski.
Wydawnictwo Polskie, *ca*.1925.

Sonety Krymskie; by Adam Mickiewicz.
Wydawnictwo Polskie, 1922.

Zivaja Azbuka; by Sasha Cernyj. Karbasnikoff, 1926.

as Feodor Rojankovsky:

All Alone; by Claire H. Bishop. Viking, 1953.

Animal Dictionary; by Jane W. Watson. Golden, 1960.

Animal Stories; by Georges Duplaix. Simon, 1944;
a.k.a. Animal Tales, Original Stories. Golden, 1971.

Animals in the Zoo. Knopf, 1962.

Animals on the Farm. Knopf, 1967.

Balboa, Swordsman and Conquistador; by Felix
Riesenberg, Jr. Random, 1956.

Big Elephant; by Kathryn and Byron Jackson. Simon,
1949; *a.k.a. Kathryn and Byron Jackson's Big
Elephant*. Golden, 1973.

Big Farmer Big; by Kathryn and Byron Jackson.
Simon, 1948. (Includes smaller volume inserted
on cover titled *Little Farmer Little*.)

Butterfly That Stamped; by Rudyard Kipling. Garden
City, 1947.

Cabin Faced West; by Jean Fritz. Coward, 1958.

Cat That Walked by Himself; by Rudyard Kipling.
Garden City, 1947.

Cortez, the Conqueror; by Covelle Newcomb.
Random, 1947.

Cow Went over the Mountain; by Jeanette Krinsley.
Golden, 1963.

Cricket in a Thicket; by Aileen Fisher. Scribner,
1963.

Crowd of Cows; by John Graham. Harcourt, 1968.

*Daniel Boone: Les Aventures d'un Chasseur Ameri-
cain Parmi les Peaux-Rouges*. Domino, 1931; also
issued as limited portfolio edition; *a.k.a. Daniel
Boone: Historic Adventures of an American

Hunter among the Indians*. Tr. Esther Averill and
Lila Stanley, 1931; *a.k.a. Daniel Boone*. Harper,
1945.

Dog and Cat Book: Stories and Poems. Simon, 1963.

Elephant's Child; by Rudyard Kipling. Garden City,
1942.

En Famille; by Marguerite Reynier. Flammarion,
1934.

Experiment with St. George; by J. W. Dunne. Faber,
1939.

*Falcon under the Hat: Russian Merry Tales and
Fairy Tales*; by Guy Daniels. Funk, 1969.

Favorite Fairy Tales. Simon, 1949.

*Feodor Rojankovsky's ABC: An Alphabet of Many
Things*. Golden, 1970.

*Flash: The Story of a Horse, a Coachdog and the
Gypsies*; by Esther Averill. Smith, 1934; *a.k.a.
Eclair, Known to English-Speaking Children as
Flash*. Domino, 1938.

Frog Went a-Courtin', Retold; by John Langstaff.
Harcourt, 1955.

Gaston and Josephine; by Georges Duplaix. Simon,
1948.

Giant Golden Book of Cat Stories; by Elizabeth
Coatsworth. Simon, 1953; also in *Giant Golden
Book of Dogs, Cats and Horses*, below.

Giant Golden Book of Dog Stories; by Elizabeth
Coatsworth. Simon, 1953; also in *Giant Golden
Book of Dogs, Cats and Horses*, below.

*Giant Golden Book of Dogs, Cats and Horses, 61
Stories and Poems*; by Elizabeth Coatsworth and
Kate Barnes. Golden, 1957. (Includes *Giant
Golden Book of Cat Stories*, . . .*Dog Stories*,
and . . .*Horse Stories*, above and below.)

Giant Golden Book of Horse Stories; by Elizabeth
Coatsworth and Kate Barnes. Simon, 1954; also
in *Giant Golden Book of Dogs, Cats and Horses*,
above.

*Golden Bible: From the King James Version of the
Old Testament*; by Elsa J. Werner, *pseud.* (Jane W.
Watson). Simon, 1946; *a.k.a. Golden Book of the
Bible: Stories of the Old Testament*, 1953; *a.k.a.
Golden Bible: Stories from the Old Testament*.
Hamlyn, 1970.

Golden Book of Birds; by Hazel Lockwood. Simon,
1943.

Great Big Animal Book. Golden, 1950.

Great Big Wild Animal Book. Golden, 1951.

Holy Bible: The Old Testament; by Jane W. Watson
and Charles Hartman. il. with Alice and Martin
Provensen. Guild, 1960, (2 vols.); *a.k.a. Catholic
Children's Bible*, Golden, 1958.

Hop, Little Kangaroo; by (?). Western, 1965.

How the Camel Got His Hump; by Rudyard Kipling. Garden City, 1942.

How the Leopard Got His Spots; by Rudyard Kipling. Garden City, 1942.

How the Rhinoceros Got His Skin; by Rudyard Kipling. Garden City, 1942.

I Can Count; by Carl Memling. Simon, 1963.

I Play at the Beach; by Dorothy Koch. Holiday, 1955.

Kitten's Surprise; by Nina. Simon, 1951.

Little Golden Mother Goose: 75 Favorite Rhymes; from Mother Goose. Simon, 1957.

Little River; by Ann Rand. Harcourt, 1959.

Michka; by Marie Colmont, *pseud.* (Marie deB. Delavand). Flammarion, 1941; *a.k.a. Christmas Bear*. Tr. Constance Hirsch. Golden, 1966.

More Mother Goose Rhymes: 57 Favorite Rhymes; from Mother Goose. Simon, 1958.

Mulberry Tree; by Jan Wahl. Norton, 1970.

Music for Living Series; by James L. Mursell, et al. Silver, 1956. (Includes *I Like the City, I Like the Country, Music in Our Town, Music Near and Far*, and *Music Now and Long Ago*.)

My Friend Yakub; by Nicholas Kalashnikoff. Scribner, 1953.

Name for Kitty; by Phyllis McGinley. Simon, 1948.

Old Man Is Always Right; by Hans C. Andersen. Harper, 1940.

Our Puppy; by Elsa R. Nast, *pseud.* (Jane W. Watson). Simon, 1948.

Outside Cat; by Jane Thayer, *pseud.* (Catherine Woolley). Morrow, 1957.

Over in the Meadow; by John Langstaff. Music by Marshall Woodbridge. Harcourt, 1957.

Petits et les Grands; by Rose Celli. Flammarion, 1933; *a.k.a. Wild Animals and Their Little Ones*. Artists and Writers Guild, 1935.

Pictures from Mother Goose: A Golden Portfolio Containing Jack and Jill; Mary Had a Little Lamb; Little Boy Blue; Old Woman in the Shoe; Little Tommy Tittlemouse; Rain, Rain Go Away; Little Miss Muffet, and *Pussy Cat, Pussy Cat*; from Mother Goose. Simon, 1945.

Powder: The Story of a Colt, a Duchess and the Circus; by Esther Averill. Smith, 1933; *a.k.a. Poudre, Known to English-Speaking Children as Powder*; with Lila Stanley. Domino, 1938.

Quand Cigalou s'en va Dans la Montagne; by Marie Colmont, *pseud.* (Marie deB. Delavand). n. p. 19?.

Robinson Crusoe; by Daniel Defoe, adapted by Anne T. White. Golden, 1960.

Rojankovsky's Wonderful Picture Book: An Anthology; edited by Nina Rojankovsky. Golden, 1972.

So Small; by Ann Rand. Harcourt, 1962.

Tales of Poindi; by Jean Mariotti. Tr. Esther Averill. Domino, 1938.

Tall Book of Mother Goose; from Mother Goose. Harper, 1942.

Tall Book of Nursery Rhymes. Artists and Writers Guild, 1944.

10 Little Animals; by Carl Memling. Golden, 1965.

Three Bears; adapted by Kathleen N. Daly. Golden, 1948.

To Make a Duck Happy; by Carol E. Lester. Harper, 1969.

Treasure Trove of the Sun; by Mikhail Prishvin. Tr. Tatiana Balkoff-Drowne. Viking, 1952.

Trouble at Beaver Dam; by Florence Tchaika. Messner, 1953.

True Story of Smokey the Bear; by Jane W. Watson. Golden, 1969.

Ugly Duckling; by Hans C. Andersen. Grosset, 1945.

Voyages of Jacques Cartier; by Esther Averill. Domino, 1937; *a.k.a. Cartier Sails the St. Lawrence*. Harper, 1956.

Whirly Bird; by Dimitry Varley. Knopf, 1961.

White Bunny with the Magic Nose; by Georges Duplaix. Golden, n. d.

White Drake and Other Tales; by Ann S. Moncrieff. Methuen, 1936.

Wild Animal Babies; by Kathleen N. Daly. Western, 1958.

Year in the Forest; by Bill Hall. McGraw, 1973.

MEDIA

Frog Went a-Courtin'. Weston Woods Studios, 1961 (F), 1960 (FSS); also in Weston Woods Studios Set No. 8, 1965 (FSS).

Over in the Meadow. Weston Woods Studios, 1969 (F), 1965 (FSS); also in Weston Woods Studios Set No. 4, 1965 (FSS).

COLLECTIONS

Kerlan Collection, University of Minnesota. (Minneapolis, Minnesota).

May Massee Collection, Emporia State College. (Emporia, Kansas).

Ogle Collection, University of Oregon Library. (Eugene, Oregon).

Special Collections, University Research Library, University of California. (Los Angeles, California).

BACKGROUND READING

Averill, E. "Feodor Rojankovsky and Les Peaux-Rouges." *Horn Book*, February 1930.

Averill, E. "Feodor Rojankovsky, Illustrator." *Horn Book*, May 1934.

Averill, E. "Publisher's Odyssey." in *Horn Book Sampler on Children's Books and Reading*. Horn Book, 1959.

Bader. *American Picturebooks from Noah's Ark to The Beast Within*.

Contemporary Authors.

Doyle. *Who's Who in Children's Literature*.

Eichenberg, F. "Feodor Rojankovsky: Friend of American Children." *American Artist*, January 1957.

"Feodor Rojankovsky." *Junior Bookshelf*, November 1945.

"Feodor Rojankovsky, Paris." *Gebrauchsgraphik*, December 1932.

Hopkins. *Books Are by People*.

Kingman. *Illustrators of Children's Books, 1957-1966*.

Kingman. *Illustrators of Children's Books, 1967-1976*.

Kingman. *Newbery and Caldecott Medal Books, 1956-1965*.

Kunitz. *Junior Book of Authors, Second Edition Revised*.

Mahony. *Illustrators of Children's Books, 1744-1945*.

Miller. *Caldecott Medal Books, 1938-1957*.

Miller. *Illustrators of Children's Books, 1946-1956*.

New York Times Biographical Edition.

Obituary. *New York Times*, October 13, 1970.

Obituary. *Publishers Weekly*, November 9, 1970.

"Rojankovsky and His Books for Children." *Publishers Weekly*, October 28, 1944.

Ward. *Authors of Books for Young People, Second Edition*.

Ward. *Illustrators of Books for Young People, Second Edition*.

+CONSTANCE MAYFIELD ROURKE, 1885-1941
author

AWARDS

Audubon. Newbery Honor Book, 1937.

Davy Crockett. Newbery Honor Book, 1935.

BIBLIOGRAPHY

American Humor: A Study of the National Character. Doubleday, 1931.

Audubon: With 12 Colored Plates from Original Audubon Prints. il. James MacDonald. Harcourt, 1936; large print edition, Watts, 1966.

Charles Sheeler: Artist in the American Tradition. il. Charles Sheeler. Harcourt, 1938.

Davy Crockett. il. James MacDonald. Harcourt, 1934; also il. Walter J. Seaton. Jr. Deluxe Editions, 1956; *a.k.a. Davy Crockett, Introduced and with Study Guides by Geraldine Murphy*. Harcourt, 1955.

Roots of American Culture: And Other Essays; edited by Van W. Brooks. Harcourt, 1942.

Troupers of the Gold Coast: Or, The Rise of Lotta Crabtree. Harcourt, 1928.

Trumpets of Jubilee: Lyman Beecher, Harriet Beecher Stowe, Henry Ward Beecher, Horace Greeley, P. T. Barnum. Harcourt, 1927.

MEDIA

American Humor. (C, MT).

Audubon. (BB, TB).

Davy Crockett as *Davy Crockett and the River Pilots*. United Artists, 1955 (F); *Davy Crockett, Indian Scout*. United Artists, 1950 (F); *Davy Crockett, King of the Wild Frontier*. Walt Disney Productions, (1950s, TV series); *Davy Crockett, Part I: Frontiersman*. Walt Disney Productions, n.d. (FSS); *Davy Crockett, Part II: Politician*. Walt Disney Productions, n. d. (FSS); *Three Adventures of Davy Crockett*. Walt Disney Productions, n. d. (R).

Trumpets of Jubilee. (C, MT).

COLLECTIONS

Bancroft Library, University of California. (Berkeley, California).

New York Public Library. (New York, New York).

Vassar College Library. (Poughkeepsie, New York).

BACKGROUND READING

Burke. *American Authors and Books, 1640 to the Present Day*.

Commire. *Yesterday's Authors of Books for Children*.

Coyle. *Ohio Authors and Their Books*.

Current Biography.

Fuller. *More Junior Authors*.

Hart. *Oxford Companion to American Literature, Fourth Edition*.

James. *Dictionary of American Biography, Supplement 3.*

Kunitz. *Twentieth Century Authors.*

Kunitz. *Twentieth Century Authors, First Supplement.*

Obituary. *New York Times*, March 24, 1941.

MARI SUZETTE SANDOZ, 1896-1966
author

AWARDS

Horsecatcher. Newbery Honor Book, 1958.

BIBLIOGRAPHY

Area of the Richer Beaver Harvest of North America: Some Penetrations of the Beaver Men to the Heart of the Continent, Their Concentration on the Upper Missouri, and the Drive to the Western Sea, 1604-1834. il. with Doyle Waugh. Carr, 1934.

Battle of the Little Big Horn. Lippincott, 1966.

Beaver Men, Spearheads of Empire. Hastings, 1964.

Buffalo Catchers: The Story of the Hide Men. Hastings, 1954; *a.k.a. Buffalo Hunters: The Slaughter of the Great Buffalo Herds.* Eyre, 1960.

Capital City. Little, 1939.

Cattlemen: From the Rio Grande across the Far Marias. Hastings, 1958.

Cheyenne Autumn. McGraw, 1953.

Christmas of the Phonograph Records: A Recollection. il. James W. Brown. University of Nebraska, 1966.

Crazy Horse, the Strange Man of the Oglalas: A Biography. Knopf, 1942.

Farlooker. Buffalo Head, 1962.

Great Council. Pifer, 1970.

Horsecatcher. Westminster, 1957.

Hostiles and Friendlies: Selected Short Writings. University of Nebraska, 1959.

Love Song to the Plains. il. Bryan Forsyth. Harper, 1961.

Miss Morissa: Doctor of the Gold Trail, a Novel. McGraw, 1955.

New Introduction by Mari Sandoz to The Cheyenne Indians, Their History and Ways of Life by George Bird Grinnell. Buffalo Head, 1962.

Old Jules. Little, 1935; *a.k.a. . . .20th Anniversary Edition.* Hastings, 1955; *a.k.a. Old Jules Country: A Selection from Old Jules and Thirty Years of Writing since the Book Was Published, with Eleven Illustrations by Bryan Forsyth, of the Author and of People and Scenes of Her Books, a Finding Map of the Old Jules Home Region and a Section of Analytical Notes on the Author's Seventeen Books,* 1965.

Old Jules Home Region. Carr, 1962.

Ossie and the Sea Monster and Other Stories. Pifer, 1974.

*Sandhill Sundays: And Other Recollections. University of Nebraska, 1970.

Slogum House. Little, 1937.

Son of the Gamblin' Man: The Youth of an Artist. Potter, 1960.

Story Catcher. il. Elsie J. McCorkell. Westminster, 1963.

These Were the Sioux. Hastings, 1961.

Tom-Walker: A New Novel. Dial, 1947.

Winter Thunder. Westminster, 1954.

MEDIA

Battle of the Little Bighorn. (BB).

Crazy Horse. (C, MT).

Horsecatcher. (BB, C, MT, TB); Miller-Brody Productions, 1974 (FSS).

Love Song to the Plains. (BB).

Miss Morissa. (BB).

Story Catcher. (C, MT).

Winter Thunder. (BB).

COLLECTIONS

Arents Research Library, Syracuse University. (Syracuse, New York).

DeGolyer Foundation Library. (Dallas, Texas).

Mari Sandoz Museum. (Gordon, Nebraska).

Sandoz Collection, University of Nebraska Library. (Lincoln, Nebraska).

BACKGROUND READING

Burke. *American Authors and Books, 1640 to the Present Day.*

Commire. *Something about the Author.*

Contemporary Authors.

DeMontreville. *Third Book of Junior Authors.*

BACKGROUND READING (cont'd)

Hart. *Oxford Companion to American Literature, Fourth Edition*.

Kunitz. *Twentieth Century Authors*.

Kunitz. *Twentieth Century Authors, First Supplement*.

Nichols, L. "Cowgirl." *New York Times Book Review*, June 22, 1958.

Nicoll, B. "Mari Sandoz, Nebraska Loner." *American West*, Spring 1965.

Obituary. *New York Times*, March 11, 1966.

Obituary. *Publishers Weekly*, March 21, 1966.

Obituary. *Time*, March 18, 1966.

Sandoz. "How I Came to Write." *Baltimore Bulletin of Education*, May 1958.

Ward. *Authors of Books for Young People, Second Edition*.

+JULIA LINA SAUER, 1891-
author

AWARDS

Fog Magic. Newbery Honor Book, 1944.

Light at Tern Rock. Newbery Honor Book, 1952.

BIBLIOGRAPHY

Fog Magic. il. Lynd Ward. Viking, 1943.

Light at Tern Rock. il. Georges Schreiber. Viking, 1951.

Mike's House. il. Don Freeman. Viking, 1954.

(ed.) *Radio Roads to Reading: Library Book Talks Broadcast to Boys and Girls*. Wilson, 1939.

MEDIA

Fog Magic. (BB).

Light at Tern Rock. (BB).

Mike's House. (BB).

COLLECTIONS

Kerlan Collection, University of Minnesota. (Minneapolis, Minnesota).

BACKGROUND READING

Fuller. *More Junior Authors*.

Sauer, J. "So Close to the Gulls." *Horn Book*, September 1949.

+RUTH SAWYER, 1880-1970
author

AWARDS

(*Christmas Anna Angel*. Caldecott Honor Book, 1945.)

(*Journey Cake, Ho!* Caldecott Honor Book, 1954.)

Roller Skates. Newbery Honor Book, 1937.

BIBLIOGRAPHY

Annabel. Falmouth, 1941.

Child's Yearbook: With Cut-Out Pictures by the Author. Harper, 1917.

Christmas Anna Angel. il. Kate Seredy. Viking, 1944; Aldus, 1949 . (Limited edition).

Christmas Apple, a Play in Two Scenes: Adapted from the Story of "The Christmas Apple" Originally Published in This Way to Christmas; by Margaret D. Williams. French, 1939.

Cottage for Betsy. il. Vera Bock. Harper, 1954.

Daddles: The Story of a Plain Hound-Dog. il. Robert Frankenberg. Little, 1964.

Dietrich of Berne and the Dwarf King Laurin: Hero Tales of the Austrian Tyrol, Collected and Retold; with Emmy Mollès. il. Frederick T. Chapman. Viking, 1963.

Doctor Danny. il. J. Scott Williams. Harper, 1918.

Enchanted Schoolhouse. il. Hugh Troy. Viking, 1956.

*Folkhouse: The Autobiography of a Home. il. Allan McNab. Appleton, 1932.

Four Ducks on a Pond. Harper, 1928.

Gallant: The Story of Storm Veblen. Appleton, 1936.

Gladiola Murphy. Harper, 1923.

Gold of Bernardino. il. D. M. Goodwin. Aldus, 1952. (Limited edition).

Herself, Himself and Myself: A Romance. Harper, 1917.

How to Tell a Story. Compton, 1962.

Journey Cake, Ho! il. Robert McCloskey. Viking, 1953.

Joy to the World: Christmas Legends. il. Trina S. Hyman. Little, 1966.

Least One. il. Leo Politi. Viking, 1941.

Leerie. il. Clinton Balmer. Harper, 1920.

Little Red Horse. il. Jay H. Barnum. Viking, 1950.

Long Christmas: Old Tales Interspersed with Carols and Christmas Rhymes. il. Valenti Angelo. Viking, 1941; a.k.a. *Long Christmas: Stories and Carols for Christmas*. il. William Stobbs. Bodley Head, 1964.

Luck of the Road. Appleton, 1934.

Maggie Rose: Her Birthday Christmas. il. Maurice Sendak. Harper, 1952.

My Spain: A Storyteller's Year of Collecting. Viking, 1967.

Old Con and Patrick. il. Cathal O'Toole. Viking, 1946.

Oscar. Falmouth, 1939.

Picture Tales from Spain. il. Carlos Sanchez. Stokes, 1936.

Primrose Ring. il. Fanny Munsell. Harper, 1915.

Roller Skates. il. Valenti Angelo. Viking, 1936; also il. Shirley Hughes. Bodley Head, 1964.

Seven Miles to Arden. Harper, 1915.

Sidhe of Ben-Mor: An Irish Folk Play. Badger, 1910.

Silver Sixpence. il. James H. Crank. Harper, 1921.

(comp.) *Story Parade Rainbow Book: A Collection of Modern Stories for Boys and Girls*. Winston, 1942.

Tale of the Enchanted Bunnies. Harper, 1923.

This Is the Christmas: A Serbian Folk Tale. Horn Book, 1945.

This Way to Christmas. Harper, 1916; il. Maginel W. Barney, 1924.

Toño Antonio. il. F. Luis Mora. Viking, 1934.

Voyage of the Wee Red Cap. il. Maud and Miska Petersham. Macmillan, 1948.

Way of the Storyteller. Viking, 1942; enlarged, 1962.

Year of Jubilo. il. Edward Shenton. Viking, 1940; a.k.a. *Lucinda's Year of Jubilo*. il. Shirley Hughes. Bodley Head, 1965.

Year of the Christmas Dragon. il. Hugh Troy. Viking, 1960.

MEDIA

Chinese Fairy Tales. (TB).

Christmas Legends Told by Ruth Sawyer. Weston Woods Studios, 1968 (R). (Includes *Joy to the World*.)

Cottage for Betsy. (BB).

Dietrich of Berne. (TB).

Enchanted Schoolhouse. (BB, TB).

Folkhouse. (BB).

Frog in *Folk Tale Records*, American Library Association, n. d. (R).

Heart of a Boy (short story). (BB).

Journey Cake. (BB, TB); Weston Woods Studios, 1967 (FSS); also in Weston Woods Studios Set No. 18, 1968 (FSS).

Joy to the World. (BB); Weston Woods Studios, n. d. (C, R); also in *Christmas Legends Told by Ruth Sawyer*, above.

Long Christmas. (TB); a.k.a. *Carols from Long Christmas*. Gloria Chandler Recordings, n. d. (R); a.k.a. *Schnitzel, Schnatzel and Schnotzel from Long Christmas*. American Library Association, 1970 (R).

Luck of the Road. (BB).

Old Con and Patrick. (TB).

Peddler of Ballaghadereen. (TB).

Primrose Ring. (BB); Jessie L. Lasky Feature Play Company, 1917 (F).

Roller Skates. (BB, TB).

Ruth Sawyer Relates. (TB).

Schnitzel, Schnatzel and Schnotzel in *Folk Tales Retold*. American Library Association, 1970 (C); also in *Long Christmas*, above.

Seven Miles to Arden. (BB).

This Way to Christmas. (BB).

Voyage of the Wee Red Cap in *Ruth Sawyer Storyteller*, below.

Way of the Storyteller. (C, MT).

COLLECTIONS

College of St. Catherine Library. (St. Paul, Minnesota).

May Massee Collection, Emporia State College. (Emporia, Kansas).

BACKGROUND READING

Background of (Ruth Sawyer's) Stories. (BB).

Burke. *American Authors and Books, 1640 to the Present Day*.

Contemporary Authors.

Haviland, Virginia. *Ruth Sawyer*. Walck, 1965.

Heins, P. "Ruth Sawyer." *Horn Book*, August 1970.

Horn Book, special issue, October 1965.

Jewett, E. "Ruth Sawyer Durand." *Catholic Library World*, February 1965.

Kirkpatrick. *Twentieth Century Children's Writers*.

Kunitz. *Junior Book of Authors, Second Edition Revised*.

Kunitz. *Twentieth Century Authors*.

Kunitz. *Twentieth Century Authors, First Supplement*.

Miller. *Newbery Medal Books, 1922-1955*.

BACKGROUND READING (cont'd)

Moore, A. "Ruth Sawyer, Storyteller." *Horn Book*, January 1936.

Overton, J. "This Way to Christmas with Ruth Sawyer." *Horn Book*, November 1944.

Ruth Sawyer Comments about Storytelling. (TB).

Ruth Sawyer Relates. (TB).

Ruth Sawyer, Storyteller. Weston Woods Studios, 1968 (R).

Sawyer, R. "On Reading the Bible Aloud." *Horn Book*, March 1945.

Sawyer, R. "Remarks upon Receiving the Newbery Award." *ALA Bulletin*, October 1937.

Sullivan, S. "Fairy Gold in a Storyteller's Yarns." *Elementary English*, December 1958.

Ward. *Authors of Books for Young People.*

Young Wings. *Writing Books for Boys and Girls.*

JACK WARNER SCHAEFER, 1907-
author

AWARDS

Old Ramon. Newbery Honor Book, 1961.

BIBLIOGRAPHY

Adolphe Francis Alphonse Bandelier. Press of the Territorian, 1966.

American Bestiary. il. Linda K. Powell. Houghton, 1975.

Big Range: Short Stories. Houghton, 1953.

Canyon. Houghton, 1953; il. Richard Willson. Heineman, 1963; *a.k.a. Canyon, and Other Stories.* Deutsch, 1955.

Collected Stories of Jack Schaefer. Houghton, 1966.

Company of Cowards. Houghton, 1957.

First Blood. Houghton, 1953; large print edition, Watts, 1968.

Great Endurance Horse Race: 600 Miles on a Single Mount, 1908, from Evanston, Wyoming to Denver. il. Sol B. Fielding. Stagecoach, 1963.

Heroes without Glory: Some Good Men of the Old West. Houghton, 1964.

Kean Land: And Other Stories. Houghton, 1959.

Mavericks. il. Lorence F. Bjorklund. Houghton, 1967.

Monte Walsh. Houghton, 1963.

New Mexico. Coward, 1967.

Old Ramon. il. Harold West. Houghton, 1960; also il. Jill Bennett. Deutsch, 1962.

(ed.) *Out West: An Anthology of Stories.* Houghton, 1955; *Out West: A Western Omnibus.* Deutsch, 1959.

Pioneers, Short Stories. Houghton, 1954.

Plainsmen. il. Lorence F. Bjorklund. Houghton, 1963.

Shane. Houghton, 1949. il. John McCormack, 1954; *a.k.a. Shane, Edited with an Introduction and Reading Aids by Margaret Early,* 1964; *a.k.a. Shane, and Other Stories.* Deutsch, 1953; large print edition, Ulverscroft, 1965.

Short Novels of Jack Schaefer. Houghton, 1967.

Stubby Pringle's Christmas. il. Lorence F. Bjorklund. Houghton, 1964.

MEDIA

Big Range as *Silver Whip.* Twentieth Century Fox Film Corporation, 1953 (F).

Canyon. (BB).

Collected Stories of Jack Schaefer. (TB).

Company of Cowards. Metro-Goldwyn-Mayer, Inc., 1965 (F).

Heroes without Glory. (BB, CB, TB).

Mavericks. (BB, MT).

Monte Walsh. (TB); Cinema Centre Films, 1969 (F).

Old Ramon. (BB); Miller-Brody Productions, 1974 (FSS).

Pioneers. (TB).

Plainsmen. (TB).

Shane. (BB, C, MT); Ebenezer Bayliss and Sons, 1973 (MT); Paramount Pictures Corporation, 1953 (F).

Short Novels of Jack Schaefer. (BB).

COLLECTIONS

Coe Library, University of Wyoming. (Laramie, Wyoming).

University of New Mexico Library. (Albuquerque, New Mexico).

BACKGROUND READING

Burke. *American Authors and Books, 1640 to the Present Day.*

Commire. *Something about the Author.*

Contemporary Authors.

Coyle. *Ohio Authors and Their Books.*

DeMontreville. *Third Book of Junior Authors.*

Kirkpatrick. *Twentieth Century Children's Writers.*

Schaefer, J. "Story behind Old Ramon." *Top of the News*, May 1962.

Ward. *Authors of Books for Young People, Second Edition*.

+SARAH LINDSAY SCHMIDT
author

AWARDS

New Land. Newbery Honor Book, 1934.

BIBLIOGRAPHY

Hurricane Mystery. Random, 1943.

New Land: A Novel for Boys and Girls. il. Frank Dobias. McBride, 1933.

Ranching on Eagle Eye. il. Paul Laune. McBride, 1936.

Secret of Silver Peak. il. Hans Kreis. Random, 1938.

Shadow over Winding Ranch. il. Rafaello Busoni. Random, 1940.

This Is My Heritage. Abelard, 1953.

BACKGROUND READING

Young Wings. *Writing Books for Boys and Girls*.

GEORGES SCHREIBER, 1904-1977
author-illustrator

AWARDS

Bambino, the Clown. Caldecott Honor Book, 1948.

(*Light at Tern Rock*. Newbery Honor Book, 1952.)

(*Pancakes-Paris*. Newbery Honor Book, 1948.)

BIBLIOGRAPHY

Bambino Goes Home. Viking, 1959.

Bambino the Clown. Viking, 1947.

Light at Tern Rock; by Julia L. Sauer. Viking, 1951.

Pancakes-Paris; by Claire H. Bishop. Viking, 1947.

(ed.) *Portraits and Self-Portraits*. Hall, 1936.

Professor Bull's Umbrella; with Will Lipkind. Viking, 1954.

Ride on the Wind: Told from "The Spirit of St. Louis" by Charles A. Lindbergh; edited by Alice Dalgliesh. Scribner, 1956.

That Jud!; by Elspeth Bragdon. Viking, 1957.

War Posters. United States Treasury Department, *ca*.1943.

EXHIBITIONS

ACA Gallery, 1938. (New York, New York).

Associated American Artists Gallery, 1939, 1946, 1953, 1955. (New York, New York).

Kennedy Gallery, 1971, 1973. (New York, New York).

Milch Gallery, 1966. (New York, New York).

New School Associates Gallery, 1968. (New York, New York).

Wellon Gallery, 1956. (New York, New York).

COLLECTIONS

Bibliotheque National. (Paris, France).

Kerlan Collection, University of Minnesota. (Minneapolis, Minnesota).

May Massee Collection, Emporia State College. (Emporia, Kansas).

Metropolitan Museum of Art. (New York, New York).

Whitney Museum. (New York, New York).

BACKGROUND READING

Burke. *American Authors and Books, 1640 to the Present Day*.

Current Biography.

"Georges Schreiber." *American Artist*, April 1943; *Art Digest*, June 1940.

Miller. *Illustrators of Children's Books, 1946-1956*.

Ward. *Illustrators of Books for Young People, Second Edition*.

Young Wings. *Writing Books for Boys and Girls*.

ELIZABETH SEEGER, 1889-1973
author

AWARDS

Pageant of Chinese History. Newbery Honor Book, 1935.

BIBLIOGRAPHY

Eastern Religions. il. photographs. Crowell, 1973.

Five Brothers: The Story of the Mahabharata, Adapted from the English Translation of Kisari M. Granguli. il. Cyrus L. Baldridge. Day, 1948; *a.k.a. Five Sons of King Pandu: The Story of the*

BIBLIOGRAPHY (cont'd)

Five Brothers (cont'd)
Mahabharata, Adapted from the English Transla-
tion of Kisari Mohan Granguli. il. Gordon Laite.
Scott, 1967.

Open Letter to Anne Morrow Lindbergh. (New York?),
1941 (?).

Orient Past and Present. il. Roberta Paflin. American
Council of the Institute of Pacific Relations, 1946.

Pageant of Chinese History. il. Bernard C. Watkins.
Longmans, 1934; second edition, 1944; third
edition, 1947; fourth edition, 1962.

Pageant of Russian History. il. Bernard C. Watkins
and Erik Magons. McKay, 1950.

Peter the Great. il. Harold Price. Row, 1953.

Ramayana: Adapted from the English of Hari Prasad
Shastri. il. Gordon Laite. Scott, 1969.

MEDIA

Five Brothers. (BB).

Pageant of Chinese History. (C, MT).

BACKGROUND READING

Contemporary Authors.

GEORGE SELDEN, *pseudonym*, 1929-
author
a.k.a. George Selden Thompson

AWARDS

Cricket in Times Square. Newbery Honor Book, 1961.

BIBLIOGRAPHY

Children's Story, Adapted; by James Clavell.
Dramatists, 1966.

Cricket in Times Square. il. Garth Williams. Farrar,
1960.

Dog That Could Swim Underwater: Memoirs of a
Springer Spaniel. il. Morgan Dennis. Viking, 1956.

Dunkard. il. Peter Lippman. Harper, 1968.

Garden under the Sea. il. Garry MacKenzie. Viking,
1957; a.k.a. Oscar Lobster's Fair Exchange. il.
Peter Lippman. Harper, 1966.

Genie of Sutton Place. Farrar, 1973.

Harry Cat's Pet Puppy. il. Garth Williams. Farrar,
1974.

Heinrich Schliemann: Discoverer of Buried Treasure.
il. Lorence F. Bjorklund. Macmillan, 1964.

I See What I See! il. Robert Galster. Farrar, 1962.

Mice, the Monks and the Christmas Tree. il. Jan
Balet. Macmillan, 1963.

Sir Arthur Evans: Discoverer of Knossos. il. Lee
Ames. Macmillan, 1964.

Tucker's Countryside. il. Garth Williams. Farrar,
1969.

MEDIA

Cricket in Times Square. (CB, TB); American
Broadcasting Corporation, 19? (TV); Educational
Enrichment Materials, 19? (F, VC); Chuck Jones,
1973 (F), 19? (FSS); Miller-Brody Productions,
1975 (FSS); Pied Piper Productions, 19? (FSS).

Dunkard. (BB, TB).

Harry Cat's Pet Puppy. Miller-Brody Productions,
1977 (C, R).

Heinrich Schliemann. (BB).

Sparrow Socks. (BB).

Tucker's Countryside. (TB); Miller-Brody Productions,
1973 (C, R).

COLLECTIONS

deGrummond Collection, University of Southern
Mississippi. (Hattiesburg, Mississippi).

BACKGROUND READING

Commire. Something about the Author.

Contemporary Authors.

DeMontreville. Fourth Book of Junior Authors and
Illustrators.

Hopkins. More Books by More People.

Kirkpatrick. Twentieth Century Children's Writers.

Ward. Authors of Books for Young People, Second
Edition.

MAURICE BERNARD SENDAK, 1928-
author-illustrator

AWARDS

(Along Came a Dog. Newbery Honor Book, 1959.)

(Animal Family. Newbery Honor Book, 1966.)

(House of Sixty Fathers. Newbery Honor Book, 1957.)

(Hurry Home, Candy. Newbery Honor Book, 1954.)

In the Night Kitchen. Caldecott Honor Book, 1971.

Little Bear's Visit. Caldecott Honor Book, 1962.

Mr. Rabbit and the Lovely Present. Caldecott Honor Book, 1963.

Moon Jumpers. Caldecott Honor Book, 1960.

Very Special House. Caldecott Honor Book, 1954.

What Do You Say, Dear? Caldecott Honor Book, 1959.

(*Wheel on the School*. Newbery Medal Book, 1955.)

Where the Wild Things Are. Caldecott Medal Book, 1964.

(*Zlateh the Goat*. Newbery Honor Book, 1967.)

BIBLIOGRAPHY

Along Came a Dog; by Meindert DeJong. Harper, 1958.

Animal Family; by Randall Jarrell. Pantheon, 1965.

Atomics for the Millions; by Maxwell C. Eidinoff and Hyman Ruchlis. McGraw, 1947.

Bat-Poet; by Randall Jarrell. Macmillan, 1964.

Bee-Man of Orn; by Frank Stockton. Holt, 1964.

Big Green Book; by Robert Graves. Macmillan, 1962.

Birthday Party; by Ruth Krauss. Harper, 1957.

Charlotte and the White Horse; by Ruth Krauss. Harper, 1955.

Circus Girl; by Jack Sendak. Harper, 1957.

Dwarf Long-Nose; by Wilhelm Hauff. Tr. Doris Orgel. Random, 1960.

Fantasy Drawings. Rosenbach Foundation, 1970.

Father Bear Comes Home; by Else H. Minarik. Harper, 1959.

Fly by Night; by Randall Jarrell. Farrar, 1976.

Fortunia; by Marie D'Aulnoy. (Privately Printed, 1974.)

Giant Story; by Beatrice S. deRegniers. Harper, 1953.

Golden Key; by George MacDonald. Farrar, 1967.

Good Shabbos Everybody!; by Robert Garvey. United Synagogue Commission, 1951.

Griffin and the Minor Canon; by Frank Stockton. Holt, 1963.

Happy Hanukkah Everybody; by Hyman and Alice Chanover. United Synagogue Commission, 1954.

Happy Rain; by Jack Sendak. Harper, 1956.

Hector Protector, and As I Went over the Water: Two Nursery Rhymes with Pictures. Harper, 1965.

Higglety Pigglety Pop! Or, There Must Be More to Life. Harper, 1967.

Hole Is to Dig: A First Book of First Definitions; by Ruth Krauss. Harper, 1952.

House of Sixty Fathers; by Meindert DeJong. Harper, 1956.

How Little Lori Visited Times Square; by Amos Vogel. Harper, 1963.

Hurry Home, Candy; by Meindert DeJong. Harper, 1953.

I Want to Paint My Bathroom Blue; by Ruth Krauss. Harper, 1956.

I'll Be You and You Be Me; by Ruth Krauss. Harper, 1954.

In the Night Kitchen; lettered by Diana Blair. Harper, 1970; variant as *In the Night Kitchen Coloring Book*, 1971.

Juniper Tree and Other Tales from Grimm; by Jacob and Wilhelm Grimm; selected with Lore Segal. Tr. Randall Jarrell and Lore Segal. Farrar, 1973; also issued in limited edition.

Kenny's Window. Harper, 1956.

King Grisly-Beard; by Jacob and Wilhelm Grimm. Tr. Edgar Taylor. Farrar, 1973.

Kiss for Little Bear; by Else H. Minarik. Harper, 1968.

Let's Be Enemies; by Janice M. Udry. Harper, 1961.

Light Princess; by George MacDonald. Farrar, 1969.

Little Bear; by Else H. Minarik. Harper, 1957.

Little Bear's Friend; by Else H. Minarik. Harper, 1960.

Little Bear's Visit; by Else H. Minarik. Harper, 1961.

Little Cow and the Turtle; by Meindert DeJong. Harper, 1955.

Lullabies and Night Songs; edited by William Engvick. Music by Alec Wilder. Harper, 1965.

Maggie Rose: Her Birthday Christmas; by Ruth Sawyer. Harper, 1952.

Magic Pictures; More about the Wonderful Farm; by Marcel Aymé. Tr. Norman Denny. Harper, 1954.

Mr. Rabbit and the Lovely Present; by Charlotte Zolotow. Harper, 1962.

Mrs. Piggle-Wiggle's Farm; by Betty MacDonald. Lippincott, 1954.

Moon-Jumpers; by Janice M. Udry. Harper, 1959.

Nikolenka's Childhood; by Leo Tolstoy. Tr. Louise and Aylmer Maude. Pantheon, 1963.

No Fighting, No Biting!; by Else H. Minarik. Harper, 1958.

Nutshell Library. Harper, 1962. (Includes *Alligators All Around: An Alphabet; Chicken Soup with Rice: A Book of Months; One Was Johnny: A Counting Book*; and *Pierre: A Cautionary Tale in Five Chapters and a Prologue*.)

Open House for Butterflies; by Ruth Krauss. Harper, 1960.

Pictures by Maurice Sendak. Harper, 1971. (Portfolio).

BIBLIOGRAPHY (cont'd)

Pleasant Fieldmouse; by Jan Wahl. Harper, 1964.

Randall Jarrell, 1914-1965; edited Robert Lowell. Farrar, 1968.

Poems from William Blake's "Songs of Innocence." Bodley Head, 1967.

Really Rosie, Starring the Nutshell Kids. Music by Carole King. Harper, 1975.

Sarah's Room; by Doris Orgel. Harper, 1963.

Schoolmaster Whackwell's Wonderful Sons; by Clemens Brentano. Random, 1962.

Seven Little Monsters. Harper, 1977

Seven Tales; by Hans C. Andersen. Tr. Eva LeGallienne. Harper, 1959.

Shadrach; by Meindert DeJong. Harper, 1953.

She Loves Me, She Loves Me Not; by Robert Keeshan. Harper, 1963.

Sign on Rosie's Door. Harper, 1960.

Singing Hill; by Meindert DeJong. Harper, 1962.

Some Swell Pup: Or, Are You Sure You Want a Dog?; with Matthew Margolis. Farrar, 1976.

Somebody Else's Nut Tree and Other Tales for Children; by Ruth Krauss. Harper, 1958.

Tale of Gockel, Hinkel and Gackeliah; by Clemens Brentano. Random, 1961.

Ten Little Rabbits: A Counting Book with Mino the Magician. Rosenbach Foundation, 1970.

Tin Fiddle; by Edward Tripp. Oxford, 1954.

Very Far Away. Harper, 1957.

Very Special House; by Ruth Krauss. Harper, 1953.

What Can You Do With a Shoe?; by Beatrice S. deRegniers. Harper, 1955.

What Do You Do, Dear?; by Seslye Joslin. Scott, 1961; *a.k.a. Qu'est-ce qu'on Dit, Mon Petit?*, 1966.

What Do You Say, Dear?; by Seslye Joslin. Scott, 1958; *a.k.a. Que se Dice, Niño?*, 1961.

Wheel on the School; by Meindert DeJong. Harper, 1954.

Where the Wild Things Are. Harper, 1963.

Wonderful Farm; by Marcel Aymé. Tr. Norman Denny. Harper, 1951.

You Can't Get There from Here; by Ogden Nash. Little, 1957.

Zlateh the Goat, and Other Stories; by Isaac B. Singer. Tr. Elizabeth Shub. Farrar, 1966.

MEDIA

Alligators All Around. Weston Woods Studios, 1976 (FSS).

Charlotte and the White Horse. Weston Woods Studios, 1967 (FSS).

Chicken Soup with Rice. Weston Woods Studios, 1976 (FSS).

Higglety Pigglety Pop. (BB); Caedmon Records, 19? (R).

Hole Is to Dig. Weston Woods Studios, 1968 (FSS); also in Weston Woods Studios Set No. 23, 1968 (FSS).

In the Night Kitchen. (TB).

Kiss for Little Bear. Weston Woods Studios, 1972 (FSS).

Let's Be Enemies. Weston Woods Studios, 1970 (FSS).

Little Bear's Visit. Weston Woods Studios, 1967 (FSS).

Maurice Sendak's Really Rosie Starring the Nutshell Kids and the Sign on Rosie's Door. Weston Woods Studios, 1976 (F, TV).

One Was Johnny. Weston Woods Studios, 1976 (FSS).

Pierre. Weston Woods Studios, 1976 (FSS).

Really Rosie. n. p., 1975 (TV).

What Do You Do, Dear? Weston Woods Studios, 1964 (FSS).

What Do You Say, Dear? Weston Woods Studios, 1964 (FSS); also in Weston Woods Studios Set No. 21, 1965 (FSS).

Where the Wild Things Are. (BB, TB); Weston Woods Studios, 1968 (FSS), 1976 (F); also in *Lively Art of Picture Books*. Weston Woods Studios, 1964 (F).

EXHIBITIONS

Ashmolean Museum, 1975. (Oxford, England).

Galerie Daniel Keel, 1974. (Zurich, Switzerland).

New School for Visual Arts, 1964. (New York, New York).

Rosenbach Foundation, 1970, 1975. (Philadelphia, Pennsylvania).

Trinity College, 1972. (Hartford, Connecticut).

COLLECTIONS

Kerlan Collection, University of Minnesota. (Minneapolis, Minnesota).

Rosenbach Foundation. (Philadelphia, Pennsylvania).

BACKGROUND READING

Bader. *American Picturebooks from Noah's Ark to The Beast Within*.

Bell, A. "Affectionate Analysis of Higglety Pigglety Pop!" *Horn Book*, April 1968.

Braun, S. "Sendak Raises the Shade on Childhood." *New York Times Magazine*, June 7, 1970.

Burke. *American Authors and Books, 1640 to the Present Day*.

Chrystie, F. "Maurice Sendak: An Artist Best Understood by Children." *Publishers Weekly*, February 24, 1964.

Commire. *Something about the Author*.

Contemporary Authors.

Cooney, B. "Artist's Choice." *Horn Book*, August 1956.

Current Biography.

Davis, D. "Wrong Recipe Used in the Night Kitchen." *Elementary English*, November 1971.

Fuller. *More Junior Authors*.

Harris, M. "My Impressions of Sendak." *Elementary English*, November 1971.

Haviland, V. "Questions to an Artist Who Is Also an Author: A Conversation between Maurice Sendak and Virginia Haviland." *Quarterly Journal of the Library of Congress*, October 1971; also issued separately, 1972.

Hentoff, N. "Among the Wild Things." *New Yorker*, January 22, 1966.

Hoffman. *Authors and Illustrators of Children's Books*.

Hopkins. *Books Are by People*.

Hürlimann, B. "Maurice Sendak." *Graphis*, No. 25, 1969.

Kingman. *Illustrators of Children's Books, 1957-1966*.

Kingman. *Illustrators of Children's Books, 1967-1976*.

Kingman. *Newbery and Caldecott Medal Books, 1956-1965*.

Kirkpatrick. *Twentieth Century Children's Writers*.

Lanes, S. "Art of Maurice Sendak: A Diversity of Influences Inform an Art for Children." *Artforum*, May 1971.

Maurice Sendak. Profiles in Literature, 1977 (VT); Weston Woods Studios, 1966 (F).

Michel, J. "Maurice Sendak: Illustrator of the Child's World." *American Artist*, September 1964.

Miller. *Illustrators of Children's Books, 1946-1956*.

O'Doherty, B. "Portrait of the Artist as a Young Alchemist." *New York Times Book Review*, May 12, 1963.

Ryder. *Artists of a Certain Line*.

Sendak, M. "(Hans Christian Andersen) Acceptance Speech." *Bookbird*, No. 2, 1970.

Sendak, M. "I Don't Write Children's Books—I Just Know What Is in My Head." *Yale Alumni Review*, May 1972.

Smaridge. *Famous Author-Illustrators for Young People*.

Smith, Jeffrey C. *Conversation with Maurice Sendak*. (Elmhurst, Illinois), 1974.

Swanton, A. "Maurice Sendak's Picture Books." *Children's Literature in Education*, November 1971.

Taylor, M. "In Defense of the Wild Things." *Horn Book*, December 1970.

Ward. *Authors of Books for Young People, Second Edition*.

Ward. *Illustrators of Books for Young People, Second Edition*.

Wintle. *Pied Pipers*.

+KATE SEREDY, 1899-1975
author-illustrator

AWARDS

(*Caddie Woodlawn*. Newbery Medal Book, 1936.)

Christmas Anna Angel. Caldecott Honor Book, 1945.

Good Master. Newbery Honor Book, 1936.

Singing Tree. Newbery Honor Book, 1940.

White Stag. Newbery Medal Book, 1938.

(*Winterbound*. Newbery Honor Book, 1937.)

(*Wonderful Year*. Newbery Honor Book, 1947.)

(*Young Walter Scott*. Newbery Honor Book, 1936.)

BIBLIOGRAPHY

Adopted Jane; by Helen F. Daringer. Harcourt, 1947.

Bible Children: Stories from the Bible; edited by Blanche J. Thompson. Dodd, 1937.

Brand-New Uncle. Viking, 1961.

Broken Song; by Sonia Daugherty. Nelson, 1934.

Caddie Woodlawn; by Carol R. Brink. Macmillan, 1935.

Candle Burns for France; by Blanche J. Thompson. Bruce, 1946.

Chestry Oak. Viking, 1948.

Christmas Anna Angel; by Ruth Sawyer. Viking, 1944; Aldus, 1949. (Limited edition).

BIBLIOGRAPHY (cont'd)

Dog Named Penny; by Clyde R. Bulla. Crowell, 1955.

Ear for Uncle Emil; by Eva R. Gaggin. Viking, 1939.

Finnegan II: His Nine Lives; by Carolyn S. Bailey. Viking, 1953.

Fun at the Playground; by Bernice O. Frissell and Mary L. Friebele. Macmillan, 1946.

Good Master. Viking, 1935.

Gunniwolf: And Other Merry Tales; compiled by Wilhelmina Harper. McKay, 1936.

Gypsy. Viking, 1951.

Hoot-Owl; by Mabel S. G. LaRue. Macmillan, 1946.

House for Ten; by Miriam E. Mason. Ginn, 1949.

Lazy Tinka. Viking, 1962.

Listening. Viking, 1936.

Little Vic; by Doris Gates. Viking, 1951.

Living Together at Home and School; by Prudence Cutright, W. W. Charters, and Mae K. Clark. Macmillan, 1944.

Mademoiselle Misfortune; by Carol R. Brink. Macmillan, 1936.

Mary Montgomery: Rebel; by Helen F. Daringer. Harcourt, 1948.

Michael's Island; by Mabel L. Hunt. Stokes, 1940.

Oldest Story: The Story of the Bible for Young People; by Blanche J. Thompson. Bruce, 1943.

Open Gate. Viking, 1943.

Philomena. Viking, 1955.

Pilgrim Kate; by Helen F. Daringer. Harcourt, 1949.

Prince Commands: Being Sundry Adventures of Michael Karl, Sometime Prince and Pretender to the Throne of Moravia; by Andre Norton. Appleton, 1934.

Selfish Giant: And Other Stories; compiled by Wilhelmina Harper. McKay, 1935.

Singing Tree. Viking, 1939.

Smiling Hill Farm; by Miriam E. Mason. Ginn, 1937.

Tenement Tree. Viking, 1959.

Tree for Peter. Viking, 1941.

White Stag. Viking, 1937.

(tr.) *Who Is Johnny?*; by Leopold Gëdo. il. Leopold Gëdo. Viking, 1930.

Winterbound; by Margery Bianco. Viking, 1936.

With Harp and Lute; by Blanche J. Thompson. Macmillan, 1935.

Wonderful Year; by Nancy Barnes, *pseud.* (Helen S. Adams). Messner, 1946.

Young Walter Scott; by Elizabeth J. Gray. Viking, 1935.

MEDIA

Brand-New Uncle. (BB).

Good Master. (BB, TB).

Philomena. (BB).

Singing Tree. (BB, TB); Intercontinental Audeo-Video Company, *ca.*1947 (R).

Tree for Peter. (BB, TB).

White Stag. (BB, TB).

COLLECTIONS

Department of Rare Books and Manuscripts, Boston Public Library. (Boston, Massachusetts).

May Massee Collection, Emporia State College. (Emporia, Kansas).

BACKGROUND READING

Commire. *Something about the Author*.

Contemporary Authors.

Current Biography.

Higgins, J. "Kate Seredy: Storyteller." *Horn Book*, August 1968.

Hoffman. *Authors and Illustrators of Children's Books*.

Kassen, A. "Kate Seredy: A Person Worth Knowing." *Elementary English*, March 1968.

Kirkpatrick. *Twentieth Century Children's Writers*.

Kunitz. *Junior Book of Authors, Second Edition Revised*.

Mahony. *Illustrators of Children's Books, 1744-1945*.

Markey, L. "Kate Seredy's World." *Elementary English*, December 1952.

Miller. *Illustrators of Children's Books, 1946-1956*.

Miller. *Newbery Medal Books, 1922-1955*.

Montgomery. *Story behind Modern Books*.

Obituary. *New York Times*, March 11, 1975.

Seredy, K. "Country of 'The Good Master.'" *Elementary English*, May 1936.

Seredy, K. "Letter about Her Books and Her Life." *Horn Book*, July 1935.

Seredy, K. "Small Eternal Flame." *Horn Book*, February 1957.

Ward. *Authors of Books for Young People, Second Edition*.

Young Wings. *Writing Books for Boys and Girls*.

+DR. SEUSS, *pseudonym*, **1904-**
author-illustrator
a.k.a. Theodor Seuss Geisel

and as

pseudonym Theo LeSeig

AWARDS

Bartholomew and the Oobleck. Caldecott Honor Book, 1950.

If I Ran the Zoo. Caldecott Honor Book, 1951.

McElligot's Pool. Caldecott Honor Book, 1948.

BIBLIOGRAPHY

as Theo LeSeig:

Come Over to My House. il. Richard Erdoes. Random, 1966.

Eye Book. il. Roy McKie. Random, 1968.

Hooper Humperdink...? Not Him! il. Charles E. Martin. Random, 1976.

I Can Write! By Me, Myself. il. Roy McKie. Random, 1971.

I Wish That I Had Duck Feet. il. Barney Tobey. Random, 1965.

In a People House. il. Roy McKie. Random, 1972.

Many Mice of Mr. Brice. il. Roy McKie. Random, 1973.

Please Try to Remember the First of Octember. il. Arthur Cummings. Random, 1977.

Ten Apples up on Top! il. Roy McKie. Random, 1961.

Wacky Wednesday. il. George Booth. Random, 1974.

Would You Rather Be a Bullfrog? il. Roy McKie. Random, 1975.

as Dr. Seuss:

And To Think That I Saw It on Mulberry Street. Vanguard, 1937.

Bartholomew and the Oobleck. Random, 1949.

Boners, Being a Collection of Schoolboy Wisdom: Or Knowledge as It Is Sometimes Written, Compiled from Classrooms and Examination Papers; by Alexander Abingdon, *pseud.* (Viking Press editors). Viking, 1931; also in *Boners Omnibus*, below.

Boners Omnibus: Boners, More Boners, Still More Boners; Being a Collection of Schoolboy Wisdom, or Knowledge as It Is Sometimes Written, Compiled from Classrooms and Examination Papers. il. with Virginia Huget. Sun Dial, 1942. (Includes *Boners*, above, and *More Boners*, below.)

Cat in the Hat. Random, 1957; *a.k.a. Chat au Chapeau*. Tr. Jean Vallier, 1967; *a.k.a. El Gato Ensomberado*. Tr. Carlos Rivera, 1967.

Cat in the Hat Comes Back. Random, 1958.

Cat in the Hat Songbook. Music by Eugene Poddany. Random, 1967.

Cat's Quizzer. Random, 1976.

Did I Ever Tell You How Lucky You Are? Random, 1973.

Dr. Seuss's ABC. Random, 1963.

Dr. Seuss's Lost World Revisited: A Forward-Looking Back Glance. Award, 1967.

Dr. Seuss's Sleep Book. Random, 1962.

500 Hats of Bartholomew Cubbins. Vanguard, 1938.

Foot Book. Random, 1968.

Fox in Socks. Random, 1965.

Great Day for Up! il. Quentin Blake. Random, 1974.

Green Eggs and Ham. Random, 1960.

Happy Birthday to You! Random, 1959.

Hop on Pop. Random, 1963.

Horton Hatches the Egg. Random, 1940.

Horton Hears a Who! Random, 1954.

How the Grinch Stole Christmas. Random, 1957.

I Can Draw It Myself by Me, Myself. Random, 1970.

I Can Lick 30 Tigers Today: And Other Stories. Random, 1969.

I Had Trouble Getting to Solla Sellew. Random, 1965.

If I Ran the Circus. Random, 1956.

If I Ran the Zoo. Random, 1950.

King's Stilts. Random, 1939.

Lorax. Random, 1971.

Marvin K. Mooney, Will You Please Go Now? Random, 1972.

McElligot's Pool. Random, 1947.

Mr. Brown Can Moo: Can You? Random, 1970.

More Boners: Compiled from Classroom and Examination Papers; by Alexander Abingdon, *pseud.* (Viking Press editors). Viking, 1931; also in *Boners Omnibus*, above.

My Book about Me by Me, Myself. I Write It! I Drew It! With a Little Help from My Friends Dr. Seuss and Roy McKie. Random, 1959.

Oh, the Thinks You Can Think! Random, 1975.

On beyond Zebra. Random, 1955.

One Fish, Two Fish, Red Fish, Blue Fish. Random, 1960.

Scrambled Eggs Super! Random, 1953.

Seven Lady Godivas. Random, 1939.

BIBLIOGRAPHY (cont'd)

as Dr. Seuss (cont'd):

Shape of Me and Other Stuff. Random, 1973.

Signs of Civilization. LaJolla Town Council, 1956.

Sneetches and Other Stories. Random, 1961.

There's a Wocket in My Pocket. Random, 1974.

Thidwick: The Big-Hearted Moose. Random, 1948.

Yertle the Turtle: And Other Stories. Random, 1958.

related titles:

Cat in the Hat Dictionary: By the Cat Himself; with
P. D. Eastman. Random, 1964; *a.k.a. Cat in the
Hat Beginner Book Dictionary in French*. Tr.
Odette Filloux, 1965; *a.k.a. Cat in the Hat
Beginner Book Dictionary in Spanish*. Tr.
Robert R. Nardelli, 1966.

MEDIA

And to Think That I Saw It on Mulberry Street. (TB).
Paramount Pictures, Inc., 1946 (F); performed by
Deems Taylor, Carnegie Hall, 1943; also in *Happy
Birthday to You*, below.

Bartholomew and the Oobleck. Beginner Books
Filmstrips, n. d. (FSS); RCA Camden, n. d. (C, R);
Random House, Inc., 1972 (C).

Big Brag. Caedmon Records, 1970 (R); also in *Happy
Birthday to You*, below.

Cat in the Hat. (BB, TB); Columbia Broadcasting
System/BFA Educational Media, 1972 (F, Tele-
cast); Beginner Books Filmstrip Set No. 2, Random
House/Paratore Pictures, 1974 (FSS); also in
Dr. Seuss's Nonsense Tales, below.

Cat in the Hat Comes Back. (BB, TB); Beginner Books
Filmstrip Set No. 4. Random House/Paratore
Pictures, 1974 (FSS); also in *Dr. Seuss's Nonsense
Tales*, below.

Cat in the Hat Songbook as *Dr. Seuss Presents the Cat
in the Hat Songbook*. RCA Camden, 1967 (C, R).

Design for Death. RKO Radio Pictures, Inc., 1947
(original F).

Dr. Seuss on the Loose. Columbia Broadcasting
System/DePatie-Freleng Enterprises, 1974 (F).
(Includes *Green Eggs and Ham*, *The Sneetches*,
and *The Zax*.)

*Dr. Seuss Presents Fox in Socks and Green Eggs and
Ham*. RCA Camden, 1965 (R).

*Dr. Seuss Presents Horton Hatches the Egg, The
Sneetches, and Other Stories*. RCA Camden, 1962
(R). (Includes *Too Many Daves*, *What Was I
Scared Of?*, and *The Zax*.)

Dr. Seuss's ABC. (BB); Beginner Books Filmstrip Set
No. 3, Random House/Paratore Pictures, 1974
(FSS).

Dr. Seuss's Nonsense Tales. (BB, TB). (Includes *Cat in
the Hat*, *Cat in the Hat Comes Back*, *Green Eggs
and Ham*, *Horton Hatches the Egg*, *If I Ran the
Circus*, *On beyond Zebra*, *Thidwick*, and *Yertle
the Turtle*.)

Dr. Seuss's Sleep Book and If I Ran the Zoo. RCA
Camden, 1969 (C, R).

Eye Book. Beginner Book Filmstrip Set No. 1.
Random House/Paradore Pictures, 1974 (FSS).

500 Hats of Bartholomew Cubbins. (BB, TB); Bluebird Records, *ca.*1947 (R); Paramount Pictures,
Inc., 1943 (F); RCA Camden, n. d. (C, R).

5000 Fingers of Dr. T. n. p., n. d. (original F).

Foot Book. Beginner Books Filmstrip Set No. 1.
Random House/Paradore Pictures, 1974 (FSS).

Fox in Socks. Beginner Books Filmstrip Set No. 4.
Random House/Paradore Pictures, 1974 (FSS);
RCA Camden, n. d. (C, R); also in *Dr. Seuss on
the Loose*, above; also in *Dr. Seuss Presents Fox
in Socks and Green Eggs and Ham*, above.

Gerald McBoing Boing. Stephen F. Bosustow, n. d.
(F); UPA, Inc., 1950 (original F).

Great Day for Up. Random House, 1975 (FSS).

Green Eggs and Ham. Beginner Books Filmstrip Set
No. 1, n. d. (FSS); BFA Educational Media, 1974
(F); Random House/Paratore Pictures, 1974
(FSS); also in *Dr. Seuss on the Loose*, above; also
in *Dr. Seuss Presents Fox in Socks* and *Green
Eggs and Ham*, above; *a.k.a. Green Eggs and Ham
from Dr. Seuss on the Loose*. Columbia Broad-
casting System/DePatie-Freleng Enterprises, 1974
(F).

Happy Birthday to You. (TB); Caedmon, 196? (C);
1970 (R); (Includes *And To Think That I Saw It
on Mulberry Street*, *Big Brag*, and *Gertrude
McFuzz*.)

Hoober Bloob Highway. BFA Educational Media,
1975 (F); Columbia Broadcasting System/
DePatie-Freleng Enterprises, 1975 (TV).

Hop on Pop. (BB); Columbia Broadcasting System,
n. d. (TV); Leo the Lion Records, 1966 (R);
RCA Camden, n. d. (C, R); also in *Dr. Seuss
Presents Horton Hatches the Egg*, above; also in
Dr. Seuss's Nonsense Tales, above.

Horton Hears a Who & Horton Hatches an Egg.
Random House, 1976 (FSS); also in *Dr. Seuss
Presents Horton Hatches an Egg*, above.

How the Grinch Stole Christmas. (TB); Columbia
Broadcasting System, n. d. (TV); Random House,
1976 (FSS); also in *Dr. Seuss's Nonsense Tales*,
above; *a.k.a. Songs from How the Grinch Stole
Christmas*. RCA Camden, n. d. (R).

I Wish I Had Duck Feet. Random House, 1976 (C, FSS).

If I Ran the Circus. (BB, TB); with *If I Ran the Zoo*. Random House, 1977 (FSS); also in *Dr. Seuss's Nonsense Tales*, above.

If I Ran the Zoo. (BB, TB); RCA Camden, 1966 (C, R); also in *Dr. Seuss's Sleep Book*, above; also with *If I Ran the Circus*, above.

Lorax. BFA Educational Media, 1973 (F); Columbia Broadcasting System/DePatie Freleng Enterprises, 1972 (R, TV); Random House, 1977 (FSS).

Marvin K. Mooney. Random House, 1975 (C, FSS).

McElligot's Pool. (BB).

Mr. Brown Can Moo. Beginner Books Filmstrip Set No. 4. Random House/Paratore Pictures, 1974 (FSS).

Oh, the Thinks You Can Think! Random House, 1975 (C, FSS).

On beyond Zebra. (TB); also in *Dr. Seuss's Nonsense Tales*, above.

One Fish, Two Fish. Beginner Books Filmstrip Set No. 3. Random House/Paratore Pictures, 1974 (FSS).

Sneetches. RCA Camden, n. d. (C, R); also in *Dr. Seuss on the Loose*, above; a.k.a. *Sneetches and Other Stories*. Random House, 1976 (Includes *Too Many Daves*, *What Was I Scared Of?*, and *The Zax*.); a.k.a. *Sneetches from Dr. Seuss On the Loose*. Columbia Broadcasting System/ DePatie-Freleng Enterprises, 1974 (F).

Ten Apples up on Top. Beginner Books Filmstrip Set No. 2. Random House/Paratore Pictures, 1974 (FSS).

There's a Wocket in My Pocket. Random House, 1975 (C, FSS).

Thidwick. (TB); also in *Dr. Seuss's Nonsense Tales*, above.

Yertle the Turtle. (CB, TB); RCA Camden, 1961 (C, R); a.k.a. *Yertle the Turtle and Other Stories*. Random House, 1977 (FSS). (Includes *Big Brag* and *Gertrude McFuzz*.); also in *Dr. Seuss's Nonsense Tales*, above.

Your Job in Germany (Hitler Lives). United States Army/Warner Brothers, Inc., 1946 (original F).

Zax. BFA Educational Media, 1974 (F); also in *Dr. Seuss Presents Horton Hatches the Egg*, above; also in *Dr. Seuss on the Loose*, above; also in *Sneetches and Other Stories*, above; a.k.a. *Zax from Dr. Seuss on the Loose*. Columbia Broadcasting System/DePatie-Freleng Enterprises, 1974 (F).

EXHIBITIONS

Dartmouth College, 1975. (Hanover, New Hampshire).

Fine Arts Gallery, 1958. (San Diego, California).

LaJolla Museum of Contemporary Art, 1976. (LaJolla, California).

Toledo Museum of Art, 1975. (Toledo, Ohio).

COLLECTIONS

Baker Library, Dartmouth College. (Hanover, New Hampshire).

Humanities Research Center, University of Texas. (Austin, Texas).

Special Collections, University Research Library, University of California. (Los Angeles, California).

BACKGROUND READING

"Authors and Editors." *Publishers Weekly*, December 2, 1968.

Bader. *American Picturebooks from Noah's Ark to The Beast Within*.

Bailey, J., Jr. "Three Decades of Dr. Seuss." *Elementary English*, January 1962.

Burke. *American Authors and Books, 1640 to the Present Day*.

Cohn, R. "Wonderful World of Dr. Seuss." *Saturday Evening Post*, July 6, 1957.

Commire. *Something about the Author*.

Contemporary Authors.

Current Biography.

Dempsey, D. "Significance of Dr. Seuss." *New York Times Book Review*, May 11, 1958.

Diehl, D. "Dr. Seuss and the Naked Ladies." *Esquire*, June 1974.

"Dr. Seuss' Success." *Times Educational Supplement*, October 19, 1962.

Dohm, Jr. "Curious Case of Dr. Seuss: A Minority Report from America." *Junior Bookshelf*, December 1963.

Doyle. *Who's Who of Children's Literature*.

Fadiman, C. "Party of One." *Holiday*, April 1959.

Fuller. *More Junior Authors*.

"He Makes C-A-T Spell Big Money." *Business Week*, July 18, 1974.

Hoffman. *Authors and Illustrators of Children's Books*.

Hopkins. *Books Are by People*.

BACKGROUND READING (cont'd)

Jennison, C. "Dr. Seuss: What Am I Doing Here?" *Saturday Evening Post*, October 23, 1965.

Kann, E. "Children's Friend." *New Yorker*, December 17, 1960.

Kasindorf, M. "Happy Accident." *Newsweek*, February 28, 1972.

Kingman. *Illustrators of Children's Books, 1957-1966.*

Kingman. *Illustrators of Children's Books, 1967-1976.*

Kirkpatrick. *Twentieth Century Children's Writers.*

Kunitz. *Twentieth Century Authors.*

Kunitz. *Twentieth Century Authors, First Supplement.*

"Logical Insanity of Dr. Seuss." *Time*, August 11, 1967.

Mahony. *Illustrators of Children's Books, 1744-1945.*

Miller. *Illustrators of Children's Books, 1946-1956.*

"Name—Ted Geisel." *Newsweek*, June 20, 1960.

Nichols, L. "Seuss Sweep." *New York Times Book Review*, May 8, 1960.

Ort, L. "Theodor Seuss Geisel: The Children's Dr. Seuss." *Elementary English*, March 1955.

Stewart, G. "Dr. Seuss: Fanciful Sage of Childhood." *Reader's Digest*, April 1972.

"25th Anniversary of Dr. Seuss." *Publishers Weekly*, December 17, 1962.

"Wacky World of Dr. Seuss." *Life*, April 6, 1959.

Ward. *Authors of Books for Young People, Second Edition.*

Wintle. *Pied Pipers.*

Young Wings. *Writing Books for Boys and Girls.*

HELEN MOORE SEWELL, 1896-1957
author-illustrator

AWARDS

(*Bears on Hemlock Mountain*. Newbery Honor Book, 1953.)

(*By the Shores of Silver Lake*. Newbery Honor Book, 1940.)

(*Little Town on the Prairie*. Newbery Honor Book, 1942.)

(*Long Winter*. Newbery Honor Book, 1941.)

(*On the Banks of Plum Creek*. Newbery Honor Book, 1938.)

Thanksgiving Story. Caldecott Honor Book, 1955.

(*These Happy Golden Years*. Newbery Honor Book, 1944.)

BIBLIOGRAPHY

ABC for Everyday. Macmillan, 1930.

Anne Frances; by Eliza O. White. Houghton, 1935.

Away Goes Sally; by Elizabeth Coatsworth. Macmillan, 1934.

Azor; by Maude Crowley. Oxford, 1948.

Azor and the Blue-Eyed Cow; by Maude Crowley. Oxford, 1951.

Azor and the Haddock; by Maude Crowley. Oxford, 1949.

Baby Island; by Carol R. Brink. Macmillan, 1937.

Bears on Hemlock Mountain; by Alice Dalgliesh. Scribner, 1952.

Bee in Her Bonnett; by Eva Kristofferson. Crowell, 1944.

Belinda the Mouse. Oxford, 1944.

Big Green Umbrella; by Elizabeth Coatsworth. Grosset, 1944.

Birthdays for Robin. Macmillan, 1943.

Blue Barns: The Story of Two Big Geese and Seven Little Ducks. Macmillan, 1933.

Bluebonnets for Lucinda; by Frances C. Sayers. Viking, 1934.

Blue-Eyed Lady; by Ferenc Molnar. Viking, 1942.

Boat Children of Canton; by Marion B. Ward. McKay, 1944.

Book of Myths: Selections from Bulfinch's Age of Fables; by Thomas Bulfinch. Macmillan, 1942.

Brave Bantam; by Louise Seaman. Macmillan, 1946.

Broomstick and Snowflake; by Johan Falkberget. Tr. Tekla Welhaven. Macmillan, 1933.

Building a House in Sweden; by Marjorie Cautley. Macmillan, 1931.

By the Shores of Silver Lake; by Laura I. Wilder. il. with Mildred Boyle. Harper, 1939.

Christmas Magic; by James S. Tippett. Grosset, 1944.

Christmas Tree in the Woods; by Susan C. Smith. Minton, 1932.

Cinderella. Macmillan, 1934. (Also issued as a portfolio.)

Colonel's Squad; by Alf Evers. Macmillan, 1952.

Cruise of the Little Dipper; by Susan Langer. Norcross, 1924.

Dream Keeper and Other Poems; by Langston Hughes. Knopf, 1932.

Fair American; by Elizabeth Coatsworth. Macmillan, 1940.

Farmer Boy; by Laura I. Wilder. Harper, 1933.

First Bible; selected and arranged by J. W. Maury. Oxford, 1934.

Five Bushel Farm; by Elizabeth Coatsworth. Macmillan, 1939.

Golden Christmas Manger. Golden, 1948; new edition, 1953.

Grimm's Tales; by Jacob and Wilhelm Grimm. il. with Madeline Gekiere. Oxford, 1954.

Head for Happy. Macmillan, 1931.

In the Beginning; by Alf Evers. Macmillan, 1954.

Jane Eyre; by Charlotte Brontë. Oxford, 1938.

Jimmy and Jemima. Macmillan, 1940.

Little House in the Big Woods; by Laura I. Wilder. il. with Mildred Boyle. Harper, 1932.

Little House on the Prairie; by Laura I. Wilder. il. with Mildred Boyle. Harper, 1935.

Little Town on the Prairie; by Laura I. Wilder. il. with Mildred Boyle. Harper, 1941.

Long Winter; by Laura I. Wilder. il. with Mildred Boyle. Harper, 1940.

Magic Hill, and Other Stories; by Alan A. Milne. Grosset, 1937.

Menagerie; by Mary B. Miller. Macmillan, 1928.

Ming and Mehitable. Macmillan, 1936.

Mr. Hermit Crab: A Tale for Children; by Mimpsy Rhys. Macmillan, 1929.

Mrs. McThing: A Play; by Mary E. Chase. il. with Madeline Gekiere. Oxford, 1952.

Old John; by Mairin Cregan. Macmillan, 1936.

On the Banks of Plum Creek; by Laura I. Wilder. il. with Mildred Boyle. Harper, 1937.

Once There Was a Little Boy; by Dorothy Kunhardt. Viking, 1946.

Peggy and the Pony. Oxford, 1936.

Peggy and the Pup. Oxford, 1941.

Peter and Gretchen of Old Nuremburg; by Viola M. Jones. Whitman, 1935; new edition, 1940.

Pinocchio: Edited to Fit the Interests and Abilities of Young Readers; by Carlo Collodi, *pseud.* (Carlo Lorenzini), edited by Edward L. Thorndike. Appleton, 1935.

Poems; by Emily Dickinson, edited by Louis Untermeyer. Limited Editions, 1952.

Pride and Prejudice; by Jane Austen. Limited Editions, 1940.

Princess and the Apple Tree and Other Stories; A. A. Milne. Grosset, 1937.

Round of Carols; compiled by Thomas T. Noble. Music by George Beaverson. Oxford, 1935.

Sally Gabble and the Fairies; by Miriam S. Potter. Macmillan, 1929.

Secrets and Surprises; by Irmengarde Eberle. Heath, 1951.

Tag-along Tooloo; by Frances C. Sayers. Viking, 1941.

Ten Saints; by Eleanor Farjeon. Oxford, 1936.

Thanksgiving Story; by Alice Dalgliesh. Scribner, 1954.

These Happy Golden Years; by Laura I. Wilder. il. with Mildred Boyle. Harper, 1943.

Three Kings of Saba; by Alf Evers. Lippincott, 1955.

Three Tall Tales; with (Elena) Eleska. Macmillan, 1947.

Where Is Adelaide?; by Eliza O. White. Houghton, 1933.

White Horse; by Elizabeth Coatsworth. Macmillan, 1942.

Wonderful Day; by Elizabeth Coatsworth. Macmillan, 1946.

(comp.) *Words to the Wise: A Book of Proverbs for Boys and Girls*. Dodd, 1932.

Young Brontës: Charlotte, Emily, Branwell and Anne; by Mary L. Jarden. Viking, 1938.

MEDIA

Book of Myths. (BB).

EXHIBITIONS

Central Children's Room, New York Public Library, 1959. (New York, New York).

Kohn and Son Gallery, 1933. (New York, New York).

Passedoit Gallery, 1939. (New York, New York).

Vendome Gallery, 1943. (New York, New York).

COLLECTIONS

May Massee Collection, Emporia State College. (Emporia, Kansas).

BACKGROUND READING

Bader. *American Picturebooks from Noah's Ark to The Beast Within*.

Bechtel, L. "About Helen Sewell." *Horn Book*, July 1934.

Bechtel, L. "Helen Sewell and Her Art for Children." *Horn Book*, March 1946.

Bechtel, L. "Helen Sewell, 1896-1956: The Development of a Great Illustrator." *Horn Book*, October 1957.

BACKGROUND READING (cont'd)

Burke. *American Authors and Books, 1640 to the Present Day*.

Ellis. *Book Illustration*.

Kirkpatrick. *Twentieth Century Children's Writers*.

Kunitz. *Junior Book of Authors, Second Edition Revised*.

MacKenzie, G. "Artist's Choice." *Horn Book*, October 1956.

Mahony. *Contemporary Illustrators of Children's Books*.

Mahony. *Illustrators of Children's Books, 1744-1945*.

Miller. *Illustrators of Children's Books, 1946-1956*.

Obituary. *New York Times*, February 26, 1957.

Pitz, H. "Book Illustrations of Helen Sewell." *American Artist*, January 1958.

Sewell, H. "Illustrator Meets the Comics." *Horn Book*, March 1948.

Ward. *Authors of Books for Young People, Second Edition*.

+MONICA SHANNON
author

AWARDS

Dobry. Newbery Medal Book, 1935.

BIBLIOGRAPHY

California Fairy Tales. il. C. E. Millard. Doubleday, 1926.

California in Print. (Los Angeles, California), 1919 (?).

Dobry. il. Atanas Katchanakoff. Viking, 1934.

Eyes for the Dark. Doubleday, 1928; *a.k.a. More Tales from California*. il. C. E. Millard, 1935.

Goose Grass Rhymes. il. Neva K. Brown. Doubleday, 1930.

Tawnymore. il. Jean Charlot. Doubleday, 1931.

MEDIA

California Fairy Tales as *Artistic Pig from California Fairy Tales*. Spoken Arts, 1972 (C); *a.k.a. Bean Boy from California Fairy Tales*. Spoken Arts, 1972 (C); *a.k.a. Enchanted Gypsy from California Fairy Tales*. Spoken Arts, 1972 (C); *a.k.a. First Hat from California Fairy Tales*. Spoken Arts, 1972 (C).

Dobry. (BB, TB).

BACKGROUND READING

Burke. *American Authors and Books, 1640 to the Present Day*.

Kirkpatrick. *Twentieth Century Children's Writers*.

Kunitz. *Junior Book of Authors, Second Edition Revised*.

Miller, E. "Monica Shannon." *Horn Book*, March 1935.

Shannon, M. "Goat Who Owned Me." *Horn Book*, March 1934.

Ward. *Authors of Books for Young People, Second Edition*.

+KATHERINE BINNEY SHIPPEN, 1892-
author

AWARDS

Men, Microscopes and Living Things. Newbery Honor Book, 1956.

New Found World. Newbery Honor Book, 1946.

BIBLIOGRAPHY

Andrew Carnegie and the Age of Steel. il. Ernest K. Barth and photographs. Random, 1958.

Big Mose. il. Margaret B. Graham. Harper, 1953.

Bridle for Pegasus. il. Charles B. Falls. Viking, 1951.

Bright Design: Electrical Energy and the Men Who Have Traced Its Pattern. il. Charles M. Daugherty. Viking, 1949.

Discovery, Exploration, Settlement: Unit of Teaching Pictures. Informative Classroom Pictures, 1949.

Great Heritage. il. Charles B. Falls. Viking, 1947.

Heritage of Music; with Anna Seidlova. il. Otto van Ersel. Viking, 1963.

I Know a City: The Story of New York's Growth. il. Robin King. Viking, 1954.

Leif Eriksson: First Voyager to America. Harper, 1951.

Lightfoot: The Story of an Indian Boy. il. Tom Two-Arrows. Viking, 1950.

Men, Microscopes and Living Things. il. Anthony Ravielli. Viking, 1955; *a.k.a. So Many Marvels*. Angus, 1968.

Men of Medicine. il. Anthony Ravielli. Viking, 1957.

Milton S. Hershey. Random, 1959.

Miracle in Motion: The Story of America's Industry. Harper, 1955.

Mr. Bell Invents the Telephone. il. Richard Floethe. Random, 1952.

Moses. il. Lili Cassel. Harper, 1949.

New Found World. il. Charles B. Falls. Viking, 1945.

Passage to America: The Story of the Great Migrations. Harper, 1950.

Pool of Knowledge: How the United Nations Share Their Skills. il. photographs. Harper, 1954; revised, 1965.

Portals to the Past, the Story of Archaeology. il. Mel Silverman. Harper, 1963; *a.k.a. Men of Archaeology.* il. Sally Mellersh. Dobson, 1964.

This Union Cause: The Growth of Organized Labor in America. Harper, 1958.

MEDIA

Andrew Carnegie and the Age of Steel. (BB); Educational Enrichment Materials, 1964 (R).

Bridle for Pegasus. (TB).

Bright Design. (BB).

Heritage of Music. (BB, TB).

Men, Microscopes and Living Things. (BB, TB).

Men of Medicine. (BB).

Mr. Bell Invents the Telephone. (BB); Educational Enrichment Materials, 1964 (R).

Moses. (BB).

Passage to America. (TB).

Pool of Knowledge. (BB).

COLLECTIONS

deGrummond Collection, University of Southern Mississippi. (Hattiesburg, Mississippi).

May Massee Collection, Emporia State College. (Emporia, Kansas).

BACKGROUND READING

Commire. *Something about the Author.*

Contemporary Authors.

Current Biography.

Fuller. *More Junior Authors.*

Ward. *Authors of Books for Young People.*

Young Wings. *Writing Books for Boys and Girls.*

URI SHULEVITZ, 1935-
author-illustrator

AWARDS

Fool of the World. Caldecott Medal Book, 1969.

BIBLIOGRAPHY

Carpet of Solomon: A Hebrew Legend; by Sulamith Ish-Kishor. Pantheon, 1966.

Charley Sang a Song; by H. R. and Daniel Hays. Harper, 1964.

Dawn. Farrar, 1974.

Fool of the World and the Flying Ship: A Russian Tale Retold; by Arthur Ransome. Farrar, 1968.

Fools of Chelm and Their History; by Isaac B. Singer. Tr. Isaac B. Singer and Elizabeth Shub. Farrar, 1973.

Magician: Adapted from the Yiddish of Isaac L. Peretz. Macmillan, 1973.

Maximilian's World; by Mary Stolz. Harper, 1966.

Month Brothers; by Dorothy Nathan. Dutton, 1967.

Moon in My Room. Harper, 1963.

My Kind of Verse; compiled by John Smith. Macmillan, 1968.

Mystery of the Woods; by Mary Stolz. Harper, 1964.

Oh, What a Noise! Macmillan, 1971.

One Monday Morning. Scribner, 1967.

Rain Rain Rivers. Farrar, 1969.

Rose, a Bridge, and a Wild Black Horse; by Charlotte Zolotow. Harper, 1964.

Runaway Jonah, and Other Tales; by Jan Wahl. Macmillan, 1968.

Second Witch; by Jack Sendak. Harper, 1965.

Silkspinners; by Jean R. Larson. Scribner, 1967.

Soldier and Tsar in the Forest: A Russian Tale; by Afanasyev. Tr. Richard Lowrie. Farrar, 1972.

Touchstone; by Robert L. Stevenson. Greenwillow, 1976.

Twelve Dancing Princesses; by Jacob and Wilhelm Grimm. Tr. Elizabeth Shub. Scribner, 1966.

Who Knows Ten?; by Molly Cone. Union of Hebrew Congregations, 1965.

Wonderful Kite; by Jan Wahl. Delacorte, 1970.

MEDIA

Oh, What a Noise! Association-Sterling/Macmillan Films, 1975 (FSS).

One Monday Morning. (BB); Weston Woods Studios, 1971 (FSS).

BACKGROUND READING

Commire. *Something about the Author*.

Contemporary Authors.

DeMontreville. *Third Book of Junior Authors*.

Hopkins. *Books Are by People*.

Kingman. *Illustrators of Children's Books, 1957-1966*.

Kingman. *Illustrators of Children's Books, 1967-1976*.

Kingman. *Newbery and Caldecott Medal Books, 1966-1975*.

"Month's Cover Artist, Uri Shulevitz." *Wilson Library Bulletin*, May 1970.

Shulevitz, U. "Within the Margins of a Picture Book." *Horn Book*, June 1971.

Ward. *Authors of Books for Young People, Second Edition*.

Ward. *Illustrators of Books for Young People, Second Edition*.

+NICHOLAS SIDJAKOV, 1924-
illustrator

AWARDS

Baboushka and the Three Kings. Caldecott Medal Book, 1961.

BIBLIOGRAPHY

Baboushka and the Three Kings: Adapted from a Russian Folktale; by Ruth Robbins. Parnassus, 1960.

Emperor and the Drummer Boy; by Ruth Robbins. Parnassus, 1962; *a.k.a. Emperem et le Tambour*. Tr. Marie Byrne, n. d.

Friendly Beasts: Adapted from an Old English Carol of the Same Title; by Laura N. Baker. Parnassus, 1957.

Harlequin and Mother Goose: Or, The Magic Stick; by Ruth Robbins. Parnassus, 1965.

Lodestone and Toadstone; by Irene Elmer. Knopf, 1969.

Staffan: An Old Christmas Folk Song; by Ross Shideler. Parnassus, 1970.

COLLECTIONS

Gary Public Library. (Gary, Indiana).

Kerlan Collection, University of Minnesota. (Minneapolis, Minnesota).

BACKGROUND READING

Fuller. *More Junior Authors*.

Kingman. *Illustrators of Children's Books, 1957-1966*.

Kingman. *Newbery and Caldecott Medal Books, 1956-1965*.

Ward. *Authors of Books for Young People, Second Edition*.

Ward. *Illustrators of Books for Young People, Second Edition*.

MARC SIMONT, 1915-
author-illustrator

AWARDS

Happy Day. Caldecott Honor Book, 1950.

Tree Is Nice. Caldecott Medal Book, 1957.

BIBLIOGRAPHY

Afternoon in Spain. Morrow, 1965.

American Riddle Book; by Carl Withers and Sula Benét. Abelard, 1954.

Backward Day; by Ruth Krauss. Harper, 1950.

Big World and the Little House; by Ruth Krauss. Schuman, 1949.

Billy and the Unhappy Bull; by Meindert DeJong. Harper, 1946.

Castle in the Silver Woods: And Other Scandinavian Fairy Tales, Retold; by Ruth Owen. Dodd, 1939.

Child's Eye View of the World; with The Boston Children's Medical Center Staff. Delacorte, 1972.

Contest at Paca. Harper, 1959.

Deer Mountain Hideaway; by Elizabeth Lansing. Crowell, 1953.

Deer River Raft; by Elizabeth Lansing. Crowell, 1955.

Dougal's Wish; by Leclaire Alger. Harper, 1942.

Every Time I Climb a Tree; by David McCord. Little, 1967.

First Christmas; by Robbie Trent. Harper, 1948.

First Story; by Margaret W. Brown. Harper, 1947.

Fish Head; by Jean Fritz. Coward, 1954.

Flying Ebony; by Iris Vinton. Dodd, 1947.

Glenda; by Janice M. Udry. Harper, 1969.

Good Luck Duck; by Meindert DeJong. Harper, 1950.

Good Man and His Good Wife; by Ruth Krauss. Harper, 1962.

Happy Day; by Ruth Krauss. Harper, 1949.

How Come Elephants? Harper, 1949.

How to Get to First Base: A Picture Book of Baseball; with Red Smith. Schuman, 1952.

I Know a Magic House; by Julius Schwartz. McGraw, 1956.

Jareb; by Miriam Powell. Crowell, 1952.

(tr.) *Lieutenant Colonel and the Gypsy*; by Federico Garcia-Lorca. Doubleday, 1971.

Lovely Summer. Harper, 1952.

Men of Power: A Book of Dictators; by Albert Carr. Viking, 1940.

Mimi. Harper, 1954.

Nate the Great. Coward, 1972.

Nate the Great and the Lost List; by Marjorie W. Sharmat. Coward, 1976.

Nate the Great Goes Undercover. Coward, 1974.

Nellie and Her Flying Crocodile; by Chad Walsh. Harper, 1956.

Now I Know; by Julius Schwartz. McGraw, 1955.

Opera Soufflé: 60 Pictures in Bravura. Schuman, 1950.

Pigeon, Fly Home!; by Thomas Liggett. Holiday, 1956.

Plumber out of the Sea. Harper, 1955.

Polly's Oats. Harper, 1951.

Rainbow Book of American Folk Tales and Legends; by Maria Leach. World, 1958.

Red Fairy Book; by Andrew Lang. Longmans, 1948.

Robert Louis Stevenson, Teller of Tales; by Eulalie O. Grover. Dodd, 1940.

Sarah Deborah's Day; by Charlotte Jackson. Dodd, 1941.

Seal That Couldn't Swim; by Alexis Ladas. Little, 1959.

Star in the Pail; by David McCord. Little, 1976.

Thirteen Clocks; by James Thurber. Simon, 1950. (Identified as "Mark Simont.")

Trail-Driving Rooster; by Fred Gipson. Harper, 1955.

Tree Is Nice; by Janice M. Udry. Harper, 1956.

Welcome; by Babette Deutsch. Harper, 1942.

What to Do When "There's Nothing to Do": 601 Tested Play Ideas for Young Children; by Elizabeth M. Gregg and the staff of the Boston Medical Center. Delacorte, 1969.

Wilderness Clearing; by Walter D. Edmonds. Little, 1954.

Wolfie; by Janet Chenery. Harper, 1969.

Wonderful O; by James Thurber. Simon, 1957.

MEDIA

Happy Day. Weston Woods Studios, 1968 (FSS); also in Weston Woods Studios Set No. 22, 1968 (FSS).

Nate the Great. (BB).

Tree Is Nice. Weston Woods Studio, 1960 (FSS); also in Weston Woods Studios Set No. 7, 1965 (FSS).

EXHIBITIONS

Rutgers University Art Gallery, 1974. (New Brunswick, New Jersey).

COLLECTIONS

Kerlan Collection, University of Minnesota. (Minneapolis, Minnesota).

May Massee Collection, Emporia State College. (Emporia, Kansas).

BACKGROUND READING

Bader. *American Picturebooks from Noah's Ark to The Beast Within*.

Burke. *American Authors and Books, 1640 to the Present Day*.

Commire. *Something about the Author*.

Contemporary Authors.

Fuller. *More Junior Authors*.

Hopkins. *Books Are by People*.

Kingman. *Illustrators of Children's Books, 1957-1966*.

Kingman. *Newbery and Caldecott Medal Books, 1956-1965*.

Klemin. *Illustrated Book: Its Art and Craft*.

Miller. *Caldecott Medal Books, 1938-1957*.

Miller. *Illustrators of Children's Books, 1946-1956*.

Ward. *Authors of Books for Young People, Second Edition*.

Ward. *Illustrators of Books for Young People, Second Edition*.

ISAAC BASHEVIS SINGER, 1904-
author
a.k.a. Isaac Bashevis
Isaac Singer
Itzhak Bashevis Singer

AWARDS

Fearsome Inn. Newbery Honor Book, 1968.

AWARDS (cont'd)

When Shlemiel Went to Warsaw. Newbery Honor Book, 1969.

Zlateh the Goat. Newbery Honor Book, 1967.

BIBLIOGRAPHY

as Isaac Bashevis:

Familie Mushkat. (New York), 1950; a.k.a. *Family Moskat*. Tr. A. H. Gross. Knopf, 1950.

as Isaac Bashevis Singer:

(tr.) *All Quiet on the Western Front*; by Erich M. Remarque. Tr. to Yiddish. (Wilno), 1930.

Alone in the Wild Forest. il. Margot Zemach. Tr. with Elizabeth Shub. Farrar, 1971.

Crown of Feathers and Other Stories. Farrar, 1973.

**Day of Pleasure: Stories of a Boy Growing Up in Warsaw*. photographs by Roman Vishniac. Farrar, 1969.

Elijah the Slave: A Hebrew Legend Retold. il. Antonio Frasconi. Tr. with Elizabeth Shub. Farrar, 1970.

Enemies: A Love Story. Tr. Aliza Sherrin and Elizabeth Shub. Farrar, 1972.

Estate. Tr. with Elaine Gottlieb. Farrar, 1968.

Fearsome Inn. il. Nonny Hogrogian. Tr. with Elizabeth Shub. Farrar, 1967.

Fools of Chelm and Their History. il. Uri Shulevitz. Tr. with Elizabeth Shub. Farrar, 1973.

Friend of Kafka: And Other Stories. Farrar, 1970.

(tr.) *From Moscow to Jerusalem*; by Leon S. Glaser. Tr. to Yiddish. (New York), 1938.

Gimpel the Fool: And Other Stories. Tr. Saul Bellow, et al. Noonday, 1957.

Hasidim: Paintings, Drawings and Etchings; with Ira Moskowitz. Crown, 1973.

Isaac Bashevis Singer Reader. Farrar, 1971.

Joseph and Koza: Or the Sacrifice to the Vistula. il. Symeon Shimin. Tr. with Elizabeth Shub. Farrar, 1970.

Little Boy in Search of God: Mysticism in a Personal Light; with Ira Moskowitz. Doubleday, 1976.

(tr.) *Magic Mountain*; by Thomas Mann. Tr. to Yiddish. (Wilno), 1930. (4 vols.).

Magician of Lublin. Tr. Elaine Gottlieb and Joseph Singer. Noonday, 1960.

Manor. Tr. Joseph Singer. Farrar, 1967.

**Mayn Taten's Bes-din Shtub*. (New York), 1956; a.k.a. *In My Father's Court*. Tr. Channah Klinerman-Goldstein. Farrar, 1966; large print edition, National Aid to the Visually Handicapped, 1968.

Mazel and Shlimazel: Or the Milk of a Lioness. il. Margot Zemach. Tr. Elizabeth Shub. Farrar, 1967.

Naftali the Story Teller and His Horse, Sus. il. Margot Zemach. Farrar, 1976.

(tr.) *Pan*; by Knut Hamsun. Tr. to Yiddish. (Wilno), 1928.

Passions: And Other Stories. Farrar, 1975.

(ed.) *Prism 2*; with Elaine Gottlieb. Twayne, 1965.

(tr.) *Road Back*; by Erich M. Remarque. Tr. to Yiddish. (Wilno), 1931.

Seance: And Other Stories. Tr. Elizabeth Shub and Aliza Sherrin. Farrar, 1968.

Selected Short Stories; edited by Irving Howe. Random, 1966.

Short Friday: And Other Stories. Farrar, 1964; large print edition, National Aid to the Visually Handicapped, n. d.

Slave. Tr. with Cecil Hemley. Farrar, 1962.

Soton in Goray. (Warsaw, Poland), 1935; a.k.a. *Satan in Goray and Other Stories*. Tr. Jacob Sloan. Noonday, 1955.

Spinoza of Market Street, Short Stories. Tr. Elaine Gottlieb, et al. Farrar, 1961.

Tale of Three Wishes; with Irene Lieblich. Farrar, 1976.

Topsy-Turvy Emperor of China. il. William P. du Bois. Harper, 1971.

(tr.) *Victoria*; by Knut Hamsun. Tr. to Yiddish. (Wilno), n. d.

Visit to the Rabbinical Seminary in Cincinnati. (New York), 1965.

When Shlemiel Went to Warsaw and Other Stories. il. Margot Zemach. Tr. with Elizabeth Shub. Farrar, 1968.

Why Noah Chose the Dove. il. Eric Carle. Tr. Elizabeth Shub. Farrar, 1973.

Wicked City. Farrar, 1972.

Zlateh the Goat: And Other Stories. il. Maurice Sendak. Tr. Elizabeth Shub. Harper, 1966.

MEDIA

Alone in the Wild Forest. (BB).

Crown of Feathers. (TB).

Day of Pleasure. (BB, TB).

Elijah the Slave. (BB, TB).

Enemies. (TB).

Estate. (BB, TB).

Family Moskat. (C, MT).

Fearsome Inn. (BB, TB).

Friend of Kafka. (BB).

In My Father's Court. (BB, C, MT, TB).

Isaac Bashevis Singer Reads in Yiddish. Caedmon Records, Inc., 1970 (C, R).

Isaac Singer and Mrs. Pupko's Beard. New Yorker, 1973 (F).

Joseph and Koza. (BB).

Magician of Lublin. (BB); Walter Reade Organization, n. d. (F).

Manor. (BB).

Passions. (BB, CB).

Rabbi Leib and the Witch Cunnegunde. Miller-Brody Productions, 1976 (FSS).

Satan in Goray. (C, MT).

Seance. (BB, TB).

Selected Short Stories. (BB).

Short Friday. (BB, TB).

Shrewd Toadie and Lyzer the Miser. Miller-Brody Productions, 1976 (FSS).

Slave. (BB, C, MT); AVCO, Inc., n. d. (F).

Spinoza of Market Street. (BB).

When Shlemiel Went to Warsaw. (BB); Miller-Brody Productions, 1975 (FSS).

Why Noah Chose the Dove. (BB, TB); Miller-Brody Productions, 1975 (FSS).

Wicked City. (BB, TB).

Zlateh the Goat. (BB, TB); Miller-Brody Productions, 1975 (FSS). Includes *First Shlemiel*. Weston Woods Studios, n. d. (F).

COLLECTIONS

Elman Collection, Arents Research Library, Syracuse University. (Syracuse, New York).

BACKGROUND READING

Allentuck, Marcia, ed. *Achievement of Isaac Bashevis Singer*. Southern Illinois University, 1969.

Anderson, D. "Isaac Bashevis Singer: Conversations in California; Interview." *Modern Fiction Studies*, Winter 1970.

"Authors and Editors." *Publishers Weekly*, October 16, 1967.

Blocker, J., and Elman, R. "Interview with Isaac Bashevis Singer." *Commentary*, November 1963.

Bluchen, Irving H. *Isaac Bashevis Singer and the Eternal Past*. New York University, 1968.

Burke. *American Authors and Books, 1640 to the Present Day*.

Christensen, B. "Isaac Bashevis Singer: A Bibliography." *Bulletin of Bibliography*, January 1969.

Commire. *Something about the Author*.

Contemporary Authors.

Current Biography.

DeMontreville. *Third Book of Junior Authors*.

Flender, H. "Isaac Bashevis Singer, Interview." *Paris Review*, Fall 1968.

Hopkins. *More Books by More People*.

Kimmel, E. "I. B. Singer's 'Alone in the Wild Forest': A Kabbalistic Parable." *Children's Literature in Education*, Fall 1975.

Kirkpatrick. *Twentieth Century Children's Writers*.

Lottman, H. "I. B. Singer, Storyteller." *New York Times Book Review*, June 25, 1972.

Malin, Irving. *Critical Views of Isaac Bashevis Singer*. New York University, 1969.

Malin, Irving. *Isaac Bashevis Singer*. Ungar, 1972.

Meet the Newbery Author: Isaac B. Singer. Miller-Brody Productions, 1976 (FSS).

Mildwood, B. "Short Visits with Five Writers and One Friend." *Esquire*, November 1970.

New York Times Biographical Edition.

"Note on Isaac Bashevis Singer." *Children's Literature in Education*, Fall 1975.

Nykoruk. *Authors in the News*.

Pinsker, S. "Isaac Bashevis Singer: An Interview." *Critique*, No. 2, 1969.

Pondrom, C. "Isaac Bashevis Singer." *Contemporary Literature*, Winter 1969.

Reicheck, M. "Storyteller." *New York Times Magazine*, March 23, 1975.

Siegel, Ben. *Isaac Bashevis Singer*. University of Minnesota, 1969.

Singer, I. "Are Children the Ultimate Literary Critics?" *Top of the News*, November 1972.

"Special from No Man's Land." *Time*, October 10, 1967.

Wakeman. *World Authors*.

Ward. *Authors of Books for Young People, Second Edition*.

Wolkstein, D. "Stories behind the Stories: An Interview with Isaac Bashevis Singer." *Children's Literature in Education*, Fall 1975.

+ELSIE SINGMASTER, 1879-1958
author

AWARDS

Swords of Steel. Newbery Honor Book, 1934.

BIBLIOGRAPHY

Basil Everman. Houghton, 1920.

Bennett Malin. Houghton, 1922.

Book of the Colonies. Doubleday, 1927.

Book of the Constitution. Doran, 1926.

Book of the United States. Doubleday, 1926.

Boy at Gettysburg. Houghton, 1924.

Bred in the Bone: And Other Stories. il. Elizabeth S. Green. Houghton, 1925.

Cloud of Witnesses. Leavis, 1930.

Common Service Book and Hymnal. n. p., 1918 (?).

Ellen Leavis: A Novel. Houghton, 1921.

Emmeline. Houghton, 1916.

Gettysburg: Stories of the Red Harvest and the Aftermath. Houghton, 1913; enlarged, 1930.

Hidden Road. Houghton, 1923.

High Wind Rising. Houghton, 1942.

I Heard of a River: The Story of the Germans in Pennsylvania. il. Henry C. Pitz. Winston, 1948.

I Speak for Thaddeus Stevens. Houghton, 1947.

Isle of Que. il. Elmer Hader. Longmans, 1948.

John Baring's House. Houghton, 1920.

Katy Gaumer. Houghton, 1913.

Keller's Anna Ruth. Houghton, 1925.

Little Money Ahead. il. Hubert Rogers. Houghton, 1930.

Long Journey. Houghton, 1917.

Loving Heart. il. Hubert Rogers. Houghton, 1937.

Magic Mirror. Houghton, 1934.

Martin Luther: The Story of His Live. Houghton, 1917.

Pennsylvania's Susquehanna: Interesting History, Legends, and Descriptions of the "Heart River" of Pennsylvania, Its Surrounding Hills and Mountains, Its Broad Valleys and Narrow Gorges, Its Canals and Railroads, Its Towns and Cities, and, above All, Its Beauty. McFarland, 1950.

Rifles for Washington. il. Frank E. Schoonover. Houghton, 1938.

'Sewing Susie': A Story of Gettysburg. Houghton, 1927.

Stories of Pennsylvania. il. Aldren Turner. Pennsylvania Book, 1937. (2 vols.); vol. 3, 1938; vol. 4, 1940.

Stories to Read at Christmas. Houghton, 1940.

Story of Lutheran Missions. Women's Missionary Societies, 1917.

Suggestions to Leaders of Study Classes Using Under Many Flags; with Katerine D. Cronk and E. D. Glen. Missionary Education, 1921.

Swords of Steel: The Story of a Gettysburg Boy. il. David Hendrickson. Houghton, 1933.

Under Many Flags; with Katerine D. Cronk. Missionary Education, 1921.

Virginia's Bandit. Houghton, 1929.

What Everybody Wanted. Houghton, 1928.

When Sarah Saved the Day. Houghton, 1909.

When Sarah Went to School. Houghton, 1910.

You Make Your Own Luck. il. Bernard Westmacott. Longmans, 1929.

Young Ravenals. il. Hattie L. Price. Houghton, 1922.

MEDIA

Boy at Gettysburg. (BB).

Bred in Bone. (BB, TB).

Hidden Road. (BB).

Keller's Anna Ruth. (BB).

Magic Mirror. (BB).

You Make Your Own Luck. (BB).

COLLECTIONS

Adams County Historical Society Library. (Gettysburg, Pennsylvania).

Franklin and Marshall College Library. (Lancaster, Pennsylvania).

Harvard University Library. (Cambridge, Massachusetts).

New York Public Library. (New York, New York).

Pennsylvania Historical and Museum Commission Library. (Harrisburg, Pennsylvania).

BACKGROUND READING

Burke. *American Authors and Books, 1640 to the Present Day*.

Hart. *Oxford Companion to American Literature, Fourth Edition*.

Kunitz. *Authors Today and Yesterday*.

Kunitz. *Junior Book of Authors*.

Kunitz. *Twentieth Century Authors*.

Kunitz. *Twentieth Century Authors, First Supplement*.

Obituary. *New York Times*, October 1, 1958.

Obituary. *Publishers Weekly*, October 27, 1958.

Obituary. *Wilson Library Bulletin*, November 1958.

Warfel. *American Novelists of Today*.

+LOUIS SLOBODKIN, 1903-1975
author-illustrator

AWARDS

(*Hundred Dresses*. Newbery Honor Book, 1945.)

Many Moons. Caldecott Medal Book, 1944.

(*Middle Moffat*. Newbery Honor Book, 1943.)

(*Rufus M.* Newbery Honor Book, 1944.)

BIBLIOGRAPHY

Adventures of Arab. Macmillan, 1946.

Adventures of Tom Sawyer; by Mark Twain, *pseud.* (Samuel L. Clemens). World, 1946.

Alhambra: Palace of Mystery and Splendor; by Washington Irving. Selected and arranged by Mabel Williams. Macmillan, 1953.

Amiable Giant. Macmillan, 1955.

Bixxy and the Secret Message. Macmillan, 1949.

Circus: April 1st. Macmillan, 1953.

Clean Clarence; by Priscilla and Otto Friedrich. Lothrop, 1959.

Clear the Track for Michael's Magic Train. Macmillan, 1945.

Colette and the Princess. Dutton, 1965.

Cowboy Twins; with Florence Slobodkin. Vanguard, 1960.

Dinny and Danny. Macmillan, 1951.

Evie and Cooky; by Irmengarde Eberle. Knopf, 1957.

Evie and the Wonderful Kangaroo; by Irmengarde Eberle. Knopf, 1955.

Excuse Me! Certainly! Vanguard, 1959.

First Book of Drawing. Watts, 1958.

Fo'Castle Waltz. Vanguard, 1945.

Friendly Animals. Vanguard, 1944.

Garibaldi; by Nina B. Baker. Vanguard, 1944.

Gertie the Horse Who Thought and Thought; by Margaret Glendinning. McGraw, 1951.

Gogo: The French Seagull. Macmillan, 1960.

Good Place to Hide. Macmillan, 1961.

Horse with the High-Heeled Shoes. Vanguard, 1954.

Hundred Dresses; by Eleanor Estes. Harcourt, 1944.

Hustle and Bustle. Macmillan, 1948.

Io Sono: I Am Italian; with Florence Slobodkin. Vanguard, 1962.

Jonathan and the Rainbow; by Jacob Blanck. Houghton, 1948.

King and the Noble Blacksmith; by Jacob Blanck. Houghton, 1950.

King's Shoes; by Helen Bill. Watts, 1956.

Late Cuckoo. Vanguard, 1962.

Lenin; by Nina B. Baker. Vanguard, 1945.

Little Mermaid Who Could Not Sing. Macmillan, 1956.

Little O; by Edith Unnerstad. Macmillan, 1957.

Love and Knishes; by Sara Kasdan. Vanguard, 1956.

Lovely Culpeppers; by Margaret Uppington. Watts, 1963.

Luigi and the Long-Nosed Soldier. Macmillan, 1963.

Magic Fishbone: A Romance from the Pen of Miss Alice Rainbird (Aged 7); by Charles Dickens. Vanguard, 1953.

Magic Michael. Macmillan, 1944.

Many Moons; by James Thurber. Harcourt, 1943.

Marshmallow Ghosts; by Priscilla and Otto Friedrich. Lothrop, 1960.

Martin's Dinosaur; by Reda Davis. Crowell, 1959.

Mazel Tov Y'All; by Sara Kasdan. Vanguard, 1968.

Melvin the Moose Child. Macmillan, 1957.

Middle Moffat; by Eleanor Estes. Harcourt, 1942.

Millions and Millions and Millions! Vanguard, 1955.

Mr. Mushroom. Macmillan, 1950.

Mr. Papadilly and Willy; with Florence Slobodkin. Vanguard, 1964.

Mr. Petersand's Cats and Kittens. Macmillan, 1954.

Mr. Spindles and the Spiders; by Andrew Packard. McGraw, 1961.

Moffats; by Eleanor Estes. Harcourt, 1941.

Moon Blossom and the Golden Penny. Vanguard, 1963.

Nomi and the Lovely Animals. Vanguard, 1960.

One Is Good, but Two Are Better. Vanguard, 1956.

Our Friendly Animals. Vanguard, 1951.

Peter the Great; by Nina B. Baker. Vanguard, 1943.

Picco: The Sad Italian Pony. Vanguard, 1961.

Polka-Dot Goat. Macmillan, 1964.

BIBLIOGRAPHY (cont'd)

Pysen; by Edith Unnerstad. Tr. Inger Boye. Macmillan, 1955.

Read about the Busman. Watts, 1967.

Read about the Fireman. Watts, 1967.

Read about the Policeman. Watts, 1966.

Read about the Postman. Watts, 1966.

Red Head; by Edward Eager. Houghton, 1951.

Robin Hood and His Merry Outlaws; by Joseph W. McSpadden. World, 1946.

Round-Trip Space Ship. Macmillan, 1968.

Rufus M; by Eleanor Estes. Harcourt, 1943.

Russia & America: Old Friends—New Neighbors. Foreign Policy Association, 1945.

Sarah Somebody; with Florence Slobodkin. Vanguard, 1969.

Saucepan Journey; by Edith Unnerstad. Tr. James Harker. Macmillan, 1951.

Sculpture: Principles and Practice. Macmillan, 1949.

Seaweed Hat. Macmillan, 1947.

Space Ship Returns to the Apple Tree. Macmillan, 1958.

Space Ship under the Apple Tree. Macmillan, 1952.

Sun, the Wind and Mr. Todd; by Eleanor Estes. Harcourt, 1943.

Thank You, You're Welcome. Vanguard, 1957.

Three-Seated Space Ship: The Latest Model of the Space Ship under the Apple Tree. Macmillan, 1962.

Too Many Mittens; with Florence Slobodkin. Vanguard, 1958.

Trick or Treat. Macmillan, 1959.

Up High and Down Low. Macmillan, 1960.

Upside-Down Town. Little, 1958.

Warm-Hearted Polar Bear; by Robert Murphy. Little, 1957.

Wilbur the Warrior. Vanguard, 1972.

Yasu and the Strangers. Macmillan, 1965.

Young Man of the House; by Mabel L. Hunt. Lippincott, 1944.

MEDIA

Adventures of Arab. (BB).

Amiable Giant. (BB).

Circus: April 1st. (BB).

Magic Michael. Weston Woods Studios, 1960 (F), 1965 (FSS); also in Weston Woods Studios Set No. 6, 1965 (FSS).

Many Moons. H. M. Stone Productions, 1972 (FSS).

Mr. Petersand's Cats and Kittens. (BB).

Read about the Postman. (BB).

Space Ship Returns to the Apple Tree. (BB).

COLLECTIONS

deGrummond Collection, University of Southern Mississippi. (Hattiesburg, Mississippi).

Free Library of Philadelphia. (Philadelphia, Pennsylvania).

Kerlan Collection, University of Minnesota. (Minneapolis, Minnesota).

Milwaukee Public Library. (Milwaukee, Wisconsin).

Special Collections, University Research Library, University of California. (Los Angeles, California).

BACKGROUND READING

Burke. *American Authors and Books, 1640 to the Present Day*.

Commire. *Something about the Author*.

Contemporary Authors.

Current Biography.

Hopkins. *Books Are by People*.

Kingman. *Illustrators of Children's Books, 1957-1966*.

Kingman. *Illustrators of Children's Books, 1967-1976*.

Kirkpatrick. *Twentieth Century Children's Writers*.

Kunitz. *Junior Book of Authors, Second Edition Revised*.

Mahony. *Illustrators of Children's Books, 1744-1945*.

Miller. *Caldecott Medal Books, 1938-1957*.

Miller. *Illustrators of Children's Books, 1946-1956*.

New York Times Biographical Service.

Obituary. *New York Times*, May 9, 1975.

Slobodkin, L. "Notes on a Sculptor's Life." *Magazine of Art*, June 1939.

Ward. *Authors of Books for Young People, Second Edition*.

Ward. *Illustrators of Books for Young People, Second Edition*.

CAROLINE DALE SNEDEKER, 1871-1956
author
a.k.a. Caroline Dale Owen

AWARDS

Downright Dencey. Newbery Honor Book, 1928.

Forgotten Daughter. Newbery Honor Book, 1934.

BIBLIOGRAPHY

as Caroline Dale Owen:

Seth Way: A Romance of the New Harmony Community. il. Franklin Booth. Houghton, 1917.

as Caroline Dale Snedeker:

Beckoning Road. il. Manning DeV. Lee. Doubleday, 1929.

Black Arrowhead: Legends of Long Island. il. Manning DeV. Lee. Doubleday, 1929.

Coward of Thermopylae. Doubleday, 1911; *a.k.a. Spartan,* 1912.

(ed.) *Diaries: 1824-1826;* by Donald Macdonald. Indiana Historical Society, 1942.

Downright Dencey. il. Maginel W. Barney. Doubleday, 1927.

Forgotten Daughter. il. Dorothy P. Lathrop. Doubleday, 1933.

Luke's Quest. il. Nora S. Unwin. Doubleday, 1947.

Lysis Goes to the Play. il. Reisie Lonette. Lothrop, 1962.

Perilous Seat. il. Manning DeV. Lee. Doubleday, 1923.

Theras and His Town. il. Mary W. Harting. Doubleday, 1924; also il. Dimitri Davis, 1961.

Town of the Fearless. il. Manning DeV. Lee. Doubleday, 1931.

Triumph for Flavius. il. Cedric Rogers. Lothrop, 1955.

Uncharted Ways. il. Manning DeV. Lee. Doubleday, 1935.

White Isle. il. Fritz Kredel. Doubleday, 1940.

MEDIA

Downright Dencey. (BB); Gloria Chandler Recordings, n. d. (R); Intercontinental Audeo-Video Company, *ca.*1947 (R); Mercury Sound Books, 1957 (R).

Forgotten Daughter. (TB).

Triumph for Flavius. (TB).

COLLECTIONS

Working Men's Institute and Library. (New Harmony, Indiana).

BACKGROUND READING

Banta. *Indiana Authors and Their Books, 1816-1916.*

Burke. *American Authors and Books, 1640 to the Present Day.*

Commire. *Yesterday's Authors of Books for Children.*

Coyle. *Ohio Authors and Their Books.*

Fish, H. "Caroline Dale Snedeker: An Appreciation." *Horn Book,* October 1935.

Kirkpatrick. *Twentieth Century Children's Writers.*

Kunitz. *Junior Book of Authors.*

Kunitz. *Junior Book of Authors, Second Edition Revised.*

Montgomery. *Story behind Modern Books.*

Obituary. *Publishers Weekly,* February 11, 1956.

Obituary. *Wilson Library Bulletin,* February 11, 1956.

Snedeker, C. "Rome and Ourselves." *Horn Book,* March 1934.

Snedeker, C. "Tribolite Door, Chapters from My Life." *Horn Book,* September 1947; January 1948.

Snedeker, C. "White Isle: Writing for Children." *Elementary English Review,* October 1941.

Ward. *Authors of Books for Young People, Second Edition.*

Young Wings. Writing Books for Boys and Girls.

ZILPHA KEATLEY SNYDER, 1927-
author

AWARDS

Egypt Game. Newbery Honor Book, 1968.

Headless Cupid. Newbery Honor Book, 1972.

Witches of Worm. Newbery Honor Book, 1973.

BIBLIOGRAPHY

And All Between. il. Alton Raible. Atheneum, 1976.

Below the Root. il. Alton Raible. Atheneum, 1975.

Black and Blue Magic. il. Gene Holtan. Atheneum, 1966.

Changeling. il. Alton Raible. Atheneum, 1970.

Egypt Game. il. Alton Raible. Atheneum, 1967.

Eyes in the Fishbowl. il. Alton Raible. Atheneum, 1968.

Headless Cupid. il. Alton Raible. Atheneum, 1971.

Princess and the Giants. il. Beatrice Darwin. Atheneum, 1973.

Season of Ponies. il. Alton Raible. Atheneum, 1964.

Today Is Saturday: Poems. photographs by John Arms. Atheneum, 1969.

BIBLIOGRAPHY (cont'd)

Truth about Stone Hollow. il. Alton Raible. Atheneum, 1974.

Until the Celebration. il. Alton Raible. Atheneum, 1977.

Velvet Room. il. Alton Raible. Atheneum, 1965.

Witches of Worm. il. Alton Raible. Atheneum, 1972.

MEDIA

Black and Blue Magic. Pied Piper Productions, 1975 (FSS).

Changeling. (TB).

Egypt Game. (TB); Miller-Brody Productions, 1975 (C, R).

Eyes in the Fishbowl. (TB).

Headless Cupid. (TB); Miller-Brody Productions, 1976 (C, R).

Season of Ponies. (BB).

Velvet Room. (BB).

Witches of Worm. (TB).

COLLECTIONS

Kerlan Collection, University of Minnesota. (Minneapolis, Minnesota).

BACKGROUND READING

Commire. *Something about the Author*.

Contemporary Authors.

DeMontreville. *Third Book of Junior Authors*.

Hopkins. *More Books by More People*.

Karl, J. "Zilpha Keatley Snyder." *Elementary English*, September 1974.

Kirkpatrick. *Twentieth Century Children's Writers*.

Ward. *Authors of Books for Young People, Second Edition*.

VIRGINIA EGGERTSEN SORENSON, 1912-
author

AWARDS

Miracles on Maple Hill. Newbery Medal Book, 1957.

BIBLIOGRAPHY

Around the Corner. il. Robert Weaver. Harcourt, 1971.

Curious Missie. il. Marilyn Miller. Harcourt, 1953.

Evening and the Morning. Harcourt, 1949.

House Next Door: Utah, 1896. il. Lili Cassel. Scribner, 1954.

Kingdom Come. Harcourt, 1960.

Little Lower Than the Angels. Knopf, 1942.

Lotte's Locket. il. Fermin Rocker. Harcourt, 1964.

Man with the Key. Harcourt, 1974.

Many Heavens: A New Mormon Novel. Harcourt, 1954.

Miracles on Maple Hill. il. Beth and Joe Krush. Harcourt, 1956.

Neighbors: A Novel. Reynal, 1947.

On This Star. Reynal, 1946.

Plain Girl. il. Charles Geer. Harcourt, 1955.

Proper Gods. Harcourt, 1951.

*Where Nothing Is Long Ago: Memories of a Mormon Childhood. Harcourt, 1963.

MEDIA

Around the Corner. (TB).

Little Lower Than the Angels. (BB).

Lotte's Locket. (BB).

Miracles on Maple Hill. (BB, TB); Miller-Brody Productions, 1972 (C, R).

Plain Girl. (BB).

Where Nothing Is Long Ago. (BB, TB).

COLLECTIONS

Kerlan Collection, University of Minnesota. (Minneapolis, Minnesota).

Mugar Memorial Library, Boston University. (Boston, Massachusetts).

BACKGROUND READING

Burke. *American Authors and Books, 1640 to the Present Day*.

Commire. *Something about the Author*.

Contemporary Authors.

Current Biography.

Fuller. *More Junior Authors*.

Hopkins. *More Books by More People*.

Kingman. *Newbery and Caldecott Medal Books, 1956-1965*.

Kirkpatrick. *Twentieth Century Children's Writers*.

Kunitz. *Twentieth Century Authors, First Supplement*.

Ward. *Authors of Books for Young People, Second Edition*.

Warfel. *American Novelists of Today*.

ELIZABETH GEORGE SPEARE, 1908-
author

AWARDS

Bronze Bow. Newbery Medal Book, 1962.

Witch of Blackbird Pond. Newbery Medal Book, 1959.

BIBLIOGRAPHY

Anchor: A Play in One Act for Four Women. Baker, 1953.

Bronze Bow. Houghton, 1961.

Calico Captive. il. Witold T. Mars. Houghton, 1957.

Child Life in New England, 1790-1840. Old Sturbridge Village, 1961.

Life in Colonial America. il. Charles Walker and old prints. Random, 1963.

Prospering. Houghton, 1967.

Seasonal Verses Gathered by Elizabeth George Speare from the Connecticut Almanack for the Year of the Christian Era 1773. il. Barbara Cooney. American Library Association, 1959.

Stranger: A One Act Play of Bible Times. Baker, 1955.

Witch of Blackbird Pond. Houghton, 1958.

MEDIA

Bronze Bow. (BB, CB, TB); Miller-Brody Productions, 1972 (C, R); Newbery Award Records, 1972 (R).

Calico Captive. (BB, TB).

Life in Colonial America. (TB).

Witch of Blackbird Pond. (BB, C, MT, TB); Miller-Brody Productions, 1970 (C, R); Newbery Award Records, 1970 (C, R); Profiles in Literature, 1975 (VT, excerpt).

COLLECTIONS

Kerlan Collection, University of Minnesota. (Minneapolis, Minnesota).

BACKGROUND READING

Burke. *American Authors and Books, 1640 to the Present Day*.

Commire. *Something about the Author*.

Contemporary Authors.

Current Biography.

Elizabeth George Speare. Profiles in Literature, 1975 (VT).

Foremost Women in Communications.

Fuller. *More Junior Authors*.

Hopkins. *More Books by More People*.

Kingman. *Newbery and Caldecott Medal Books, 1956-1965*.

Kirkpatrick. *Twentieth Century Children's Writers*.

Ward. *Authors of Books for Young People, Second Edition*.

+ARMSTRONG W. SPERRY, 1897-1976
author-illustrator

AWARDS

All Sail Set. Newbery Honor Book, 1936.

Call It Courage. Newbery Medal Book, 1941.

(*Codfish Market*. Newbery Honor Book, 1937.)

BIBLIOGRAPHY

All about the Arctic and Antarctic. Random, 1957.

All about the Jungle. Random, 1959.

All Sail Set: A Romance of the "Flying Cloud." Winston, 1935.

Amazon: River Sea of Brazil. il. with Sam Galhil. Garrard, 1962.

Bamboo: The Grass Tree. Macmillan, 1942.

Black Falcon: A Story of Piracy and Old New Orleans. Winston, 1949.

Boat Builder: The Story of Robert Fulton; by Clara I. Judson. Scribner, 1940.

Boy Who Was Afraid. Lane, 1942; also il. William Stobbs. Bodley Head, 1963.

Call It Courage. Macmillan, 1940.

Captain Cook Explores the South Seas. Random, 1955; *a.k.a. All about Captain Cook*. Allen, 1960.

Captain James Cook. Row, 1953.

Carmen: Silent Partner; by Mabel Kahmann. Dodd, 1934.

Clipper Ship Men; by Alexander Liang. Duell, 1944.

Coconut: The Wonder Tree. Macmillan, 1942.

Codfish Market; by Agnes D. Hewes. Doubleday, 1936.

Courage over the Andes; by Frederic A. Kummer. Winston, 1940.

BIBLIOGRAPHY (cont'd)

Danger to the Windward. Winston, 1947.

Dogie Boy; by Edith H. Berrien. Whitman, 1943.

Frozen Fire. Doubleday, 1956.

Great River, Wide Land: The Rio Grande through History. Macmillan, 1967.

House Afire!; by Helen T. Follett. Scribner, 1941.

Hull-Down for Action. Doubleday, 1945.

John Paul Jones: Fighting Sailor. Random, 1953.

Jungle River; by Howard Pease. Doubleday, 1948.

Klondike Gold; by Hubert Coryell. Macmillan, 1938.

Little Eagle: A Navajo Boy. Winston, 1938.

Lost Lagoon: A Pacific Adventure. Doubleday, 1939.

Magic Portholes; by Helen T. Follett. Macmillan, 1932.

Nicholas Arnold, Toolmaker; by Marion Lansing. Doubleday, 1941.

No Brighter Glory. Macmillan, 1942.

Ocean Outposts; by Helen T. Follett. Scribner, 1942.

One Day with Jambi in Sumatra. Winston, 1934.

One Day with Manu. Winston, 1933.

One Day with Tuktu, an Eskimo Boy. Winston, 1935.

Pacific Islands Speaking. Macmillan, 1955.

Rain Forest. Macmillan, 1947.

River of the West: The Story of the Boston Men. il. Henry C. Pitz. Winston, 1952.

Secret of the Congo; by Charlie M. Simon. Ginn, 1956.

Shuttered Windows; by Florence C. Means. Houghton, 1938.

Sky Highways: Geography from the Air; by Trevor Lloyd. Houghton, 1945.

South of Cape Horn: A Saga of Nat Palmer and Early Antarctic Exploration. Holt, 1958.

Stars to Steer By; by Helen T. Follett. Macmillan, 1934.

Storm Canvas. Winston, 1944.

Story of Hiawatha; by Henry W. Longfellow, adapted by Allen Chaffee. Random, 1951.

(comp.) *Story Parade, Gold Book: A Collection of Modern Stories for Boys and Girls*. Winston, 1939-42. (5 vols.).

Tall Timber; by Stewart H. Holbrook. Macmillan, 1941.

Teri Taro from Bora Bora; by William Stone. Knopf, 1940.

Thunder Country. Macmillan, 1952.

Thunderbolt House; by Howard Pease. Doubleday, 1944.

Two Children of Brazil; by Rose Brown. Lippincott, 1940.

Voyages of Christopher Columbus. Random, 1950.

Wagons Westward: The Old Trail to Santa Fe. Winston, 1936.

Winabojo: Master of Life; by James C. Bowman. Whitman, 1941.

MEDIA

All about the Arctic. (TB).

Amazon. (BB).

Black Falcon. (BB, TB).

Call It Courage. (BB, TB); Miller-Brody Productions, 1972 (FSS); Newbery Award Records, 1969 (C, R); Pied Piper Productions, n. d. (FSS).

Hull-Down for Action. (BB).

John Paul Jones. (BB, TB); Educational Enrichment Materials, 1964 (R).

Storm Canvas. (BB).

Thunder Country. (BB).

Voyages of Christopher Columbus. (BB); Educational Enrichment Materials, 1964 (R).

Wagons Westward. (BB).

When the Typhoon Blows. Intercontinental Audeo-Video Company, *ca*.1947 (R).

COLLECTIONS

deGrummond Collection, University of Southern Mississippi. (Hattiesburg, Mississippi).

Kerlan Collection, University of Minnesota. (Minneapolis, Minnesota).

BACKGROUND READING

Commire. *Something about the Author*.

Contemporary Authors.

Current Biography.

Follett, H. "Armstrong Sperry and His Work." *Publishers Weekly*, June 21, 1941.

Kirkpatrick. *Twentieth Century Children's Writers*.

Kunitz. *Junior Book of Authors, Second Edition Revised*.

Mahony. *Illustrators of Children's Books, 1744-1945*.

Miller. *Illustrators of Children's Books, 1946-1956*.

Miller. *Newbery Medal Books, 1922-1955*.

Montgomery. *Story behind Modern Books*.

Sperry, A. ''Part of Victory.'' *Horn Book*, May 1943.

Ward. *Authors of Books for Young People, Second Edition*.

Young Wings. *Writing Books for Boys and Girls*.

PETER EDWARD SPIER, 1927-
author-illustrator

AWARDS

Fox Went Out on a Chilly Night. Caldecott Honor Book, 1962.

BIBLIOGRAPHY

Adventurers All; by Louis Untermeyer. Golden, 1953.

Ancient Rome; by R. Butterfield. Odyssey, 1964.

And So My Garden Grows; from Mother Goose. Doubleday, 1969.

Animals You Will Never Forget. Reader's Digest, 1969.

Archaeology; by C. W. Ceram, *pseud*. (Kurt Marek). Odyssey, 1964.

Architecture; by M. Valmarana. Odyssey, 1965.

Betty Crocker's Guide to Easy Entertaining. Golden, 1959.

Boss Chombale; by Margaret Hubbard. Crowell, 1957.

Boy Overboard!; by George H. Grant. Little, 1961.

Cabin for the Mary Christmas; by Vera A. Amrein. Harcourt, 1955.

Cargo for Jennifer; by Marjorie Vetter. Longmans, 1954.

Cocoa; by Margaret Otto. Holt, 1953.

Cow Who Fell in the Canal; by Phyllis Krasilovsky. Doubleday, 1957.

Crash! Bang! Boom! Doubleday, 1972.

Elizabethan England; by Anthony West. Odyssey, 1965.

Empty Moat; by Margaretha Shemin. Coward, 1969.

England. Ginn, 1957.

Erie Canal. Doubleday, 1970.

Esmeralda Ahoy!; by Elizabeth Fairholme and Pamela Powell. Doubleday, 1959.

Fast-Slow, High-Low: A Book of Opposites. Doubleday, 1972.

Favorite Christmas Carols: Fifty-nine Yuletide Songs Both Old and New; by Margaret B. Boni, arranged by Norman Lloyd. Simon, 1957.

Fox Went Out on a Chilly Night: An Old Song. Doubleday, 1961.

Frederica: Colonial Fort and Town; by T. R. Reese. United States National Park Service, 1969.

Gobble, Growl, Grunt. Doubleday, 1971.

Golden Book Encyclopedia, Volume 1. Golden, 1970.

Golden Garden Guide: A Practical Handbook of Gardening and Outdoor Living; by John L. Strohm. Golden, 1960.

Golden Guide to Flowers: Annuals, Perennials, Bulbs, and a Special Section on Roses; by John L. Strohm, et al. Golden, 1962.

Golden Guide to Lawns, Shrubs, and Trees; by John L. Strohm. Golden, 1961.

Great Furniture Styles, 1660-1830; by Donald D. MacMillan. Odyssey, 1965.

Hans Brinker: Or, The Silver Skates; by Mary M. Dodge. Doubleday, 1960.

Hector the Stowaway Dog: A True Story; by Kenneth Dodson. Little, 1958.

Here and There: One Hundred Poems about Places; edited by Elinor Parker. Crowell, 1967.

Hippolyte: Crab King; by Joy Anderson. Harcourt, 1956.

History of the Theater; by Kurt Marek. Odyssey, 1964.

Hurrah: We're Outward Bound!; from Mother Goose. Doubleday, 1967.

Island City; by Lavinia Davis. Doubleday, 1961.

Italy; by Paul Friedlander and Joseph Brooks. il. with Emil Lowenstein. Simon, 1955.

Jessica's Journal; by Jessica Reynolds. Holt, 1958.

Last Hurdle; by Frieda Brown. Crowell, 1953.

Level Land; by Dola DeJong. Scribner, 1961.

Lions Fed the Tigers; by Douglas Angus. Houghton, 1958.

Little Lord Fauntleroy; by Frances H. Burnett. Doubleday, 1954.

Little Riders; by Margaretha Shemin. Coward, 1963.

Logboek van de Gratias; by P. Bakker. Elsevier, 1948.

London Bridge Is Falling Down; from Mother Goose. Doubleday, 1967.

Mantel; by Nikolai Gogol. (Holland), 1946.

My Antarctic Honeymoon: A Year at the Bottom of the World; by Jennie Darlington and Jane McIlvaine. Doubleday, 1956.

Mystery of Mont Saint-Michel; by Michel Rouzé. Tr. George Libaire. Holt, 1965; *a.k.a. Forest of Quokelunde*. Parrish, 1956.

BIBLIOGRAPHY (cont'd)

Mystery of Willet; by Richard Watkins. Nelson, 1959.

Noah's Ark; from the *Bible*. Doubleday, 1977.

Of Dikes and Windmills. Doubleday, 1969.

One Hundred More Story Poems; edited by Elinor Perker. Crowell, 1960.

Op Reis Met Prins Bernhard; by E. Elias. Bezige Bij, 1951.

Prince and the Pauper; by Mark Twain, *pseud*. (Samuel L. Clemens). Doubleday, 1954.

Sailing Ship; by Jan de Hartog. Odyssey, 1964.

Science and Living in Today's World Series, Volumes 6, 7, 8. Doubleday, 1955-56.

Sea Broke Through; by Ardo Flakkeberg. Knopf, 1960.

Star-Spangled Banner; by Frances S. Key. Doubleday, 1973.

Straten Schrijven Historie; by Steussy. Schoonderbeek, 1951.

Tam Morgan, the Liveliest Girl in Salem; by Ruth L. Holberg. Doubleday, 1953.

Teenage Tales, Volume 4; by Ruth Strang, et al. Heath, 1957.

Thunder Hill; by Elmer Reynolds. Doubleday, 1953.

Tin Lizzie. Doubleday, 1975.

To Market! To Market!; from Mother Goose. Doubleday, 1967.

Traveler's Tale of Tikal. National Geographic, 1975.

Virgin Diplomats; by Elmer Bendiner. Knopf, 1975.

Wonder Tales of Ships and Seas; by Frances Carpenter. Doubleday, 1959.

Wonders of the World; by H. J. Berkhard. Simon, 1953.

Works of Ann Frank; by Ann Frank. Doubleday, 1959.

World of Michelangelo. Time-Life, 1966.

MEDIA

Cow Who Fell in the Canal. Weston Woods Studios, 1965 (FSS), 1970 (F); also in Weston Woods Studios Set No. 4, 1965 (FSS).

Erie Canal. Weston Woods Studios, 1974 (FSS), 1976 (F).

Fox Went Out on a Chilly Night. Weston Woods Studios, 1965 (FSS); also in Weston Woods Studios Set No. 14, 1965 (FSS).

London Bridge Is Falling Down. Weston Woods Studios, 1969 (F), 1971 (FSS).

Star-Spangled Banner. Weston Woods Studios, 1975 (F).

COLLECTIONS

deGrummond Collection, University of Southern Mississippi. (Hattiesburg, Mississippi).

Kerlan Collection, University of Minnesota. (Minneapolis, Minnesota).

Port Washington Public Library. (Port Washington, New York).

BACKGROUND READING

Commire. *Something about the Author*.

Contemporary Authors.

"Cover Artist." *Wilson Library Bulletin*, October 1974.

DeMontreville. *Third Book of Junior Authors*.

Hopkins. *Books Are by People*.

Kingman. *Illustrators of Children's Books, 1957-1966*.

Kingman. *Illustrators of Children's Books, 1967-1976*.

Michel, J. "Illustrations of Peter Spier." *American Artist*, October 1969.

Miller. *Illustrators of Children's Books, 1946-1956*.

Ward. *Illustrators of Books for Young People, Second Edition*.

MARY QUINTARD GOVAN STEELE, 1922-
author
pseudonym Wilson Gage

AWARDS

Journey Outside. Newbery Honor Book, 1970.

BIBLIOGRAPHY

as Wilson Gage:

Big Blue Island. il. Glen Rounds. World, 1964.

Dan and Miranda. il. Glen Rounds. World, 1962.

Down in the Boondocks. il. Glen Rounds. Greenwillow, 1977.

Ghost of Five Owl Farm. il. Paul Galdone. World, 1956.

Mike's Toads. il. Glen Rounds. World, 1970.

Miss-Osborne-the-Mop. il. Paul Galdone. World, 1963.

Secret of Crossbone Hill. il. Mary Stevens. World, 1959.

Secret of Fiery Gorge. il. Mary Stevens. World, 1961.

Secret of Indian Mound. il. Mary Stevens. World, 1958.

Squash Pie. il. Glen Rounds. Greenwillow, 1976.

Wild Goose Tale. il. Glen Rounds. World, 1961.

as Mary Q. Steele:

Because of the Sand Witches There. il. Paul Galdone. Greenwillow, 1975.

Eye in the Forest; with William O. Steele. Dutton, 1975.

First of the Penguins. il. Susan Jeffers. Macmillan, 1973.

Journey Outside. il. Rocco Negri. Viking, 1969.

Living Year: An Almanac for My Survivors. Viking, 1973.

True Men. Greenwillow, 1976.

MEDIA

Big Blue Island. (BB).

Dan and Miranda. (BB).

Ghost of Five Owl Farm. (BB, TB).

Journey Outside. (CB); Viking Press, 1976 (C, R).

Living Year. (CB).

Mike's Toads. (TB).

Miss-Osborne-the-Mop. (BB).

Secret of Crossbone Hill. (BB).

Secret of Fiery Gorge. (BB).

Wild Goose Tale. (BB).

COLLECTIONS

deGrummond Collection, University of Southern Mississippi. (Hattiesburg, Mississippi).

Kerlan Collection, University of Minnesota. (Minneapolis, Minnesota).

BACKGROUND READING

Commire. _Something about the Author_.

Contemporary Authors.

DeMontreville. _Third Book of Junior Authors_.

Kirkpatrick. _Twentieth Century Children's Writers_.

Meet the Authors. Imperial International, 1969 (CT).

Steele, M. Q. "As Far as You Can See." _Horn Book_, June 1975.

Steele, M. Q. "Realism and Honesty." _Horn Book_, February 1971.

Ward. _Authors of Books for Young People, Second Edition_.

WILLIAM OWEN STEELE, 1917-
author

AWARDS

Perilous Road. Newbery Honor Book, 1959.

BIBLIOGRAPHY

Andy Jackson's Water Well. il. Michael Ramus. Harcourt, 1959.

Buffalo Knife. il. Paul Galdone. Harcourt, 1952.

Daniel Boone's Echo. il. Nicolas (Mordvinoff). Harcourt, 1957.

Davy Crockett's Earthquake. il. Nicolas (Mordvinoff). Harcourt, 1956.

DeSoto, Child of the Sun: The Search for Gold. il. Lorence Bjorklund. Aladdin, 1956.

Eye in the Forest; with Mary Q. Steele. Dutton, 1975.

Far Frontier. il. Paul Galdone. Harcourt, 1959.

Flaming Arrows. il. Paul Galdone. Harcourt, 1957.

Francis Marion, Young Swamp Fox. il. Dirk Gringhuis. Bobbs, 1954; also il. Frank Nicholas, 1962.

Golden Root. il. Fritz Kredel. Aladdin, 1951.

Henry Woodward of Carolina: Surgeon Trader, Indian Chief. il. Hoyt Simmons. Sandlapper, 1972.

Hound Dog Zip to the Rescue. il. Mimi Korach. Garrard, 1970.

John Sevier, Pioneer Boy. il. Sandra James. Bobbs, 1953.

John's Secret Treasure. Macmillan, 1975.

Lone Hunt. il. Paul Galdone. Harcourt, 1956.

Man with the Silver Eyes. Harcourt, 1976.

No-Name Man of the Mountain. il. Jack Davis. Harcourt, 1964.

Old Wilderness Road: An American Journey. Harcourt, 1968.

Over-Mountain Boy. il. Fritz Kredel. Aladdin, 1952.

Perilous Road. il. Paul Galdone. Harcourt, 1958.

Spooky Thing. il. Paul Coker. Harcourt, 1958.

Story of Daniel Boone. il. Warren Baumgartner. Grosset, 1953; also il. Gerald Facey. Muller, 1957.

Story of Leif Ericson. il. Panas Lapé. Grosset, 1954.

Story of . . . Reflection Riding (with Addenda): A Scenic, Historic, Botanic Drive-Thru. (Chattanooga, Tennessee), 1955.

Tomahawk Border. il. Vernon Wooten. Colonial Williamsburg, 1966.

BIBLIOGRAPHY (cont'd)

Tomahawks and Trouble. il. Paul Galdone. Harcourt, 1955.

Trail through Danger. il. Charles Beck. Harcourt, 1965.

Triple Trouble for Hound Dog Zip. il. Mimi Korach. Garrard, 1972.

Wayah of the Real People. il. Ilsa Barnett. Colonial Williamsburg, 1964.

We Were There on the Oregon Trail. il. Jo Polseno. Grosset, 1955.

We Were There with the Pony Express. il. Frank Vaughn. Grosset, 1956.

Westward Adventure: The True Stories of Six Pioneers. il. Kathleen Voute. Harcourt, 1962.

Wilderness Journey. il. Paul Galdone. Harcourt, 1953.

Wilderness Tatoo: A Narrative of Jean Ortiz. Harcourt, 1972.

Winter Danger. il. Paul Galdone. Harcourt, 1954.

Year of the Bloody Sevens. il. Charles Beck. Harcourt, 1963.

MEDIA

Daniel Boone's Echo. (TB).

Far Frontier. (BB, TB).

Flaming Arrows. (TB).

Francis Marion. (BB).

Lone Hunt. (BB, TB).

Old Wilderness Road. (BB).

Perilous Road. (TB); Miller-Brody Productions, 1976 (FSS); Pied Piper Productions, n. d. (FSS).

Tomahawk Border. (BB).

Tomahawks and Trouble. (BB).

Westward Adventure. (BB).

Wilderness Tatoo. (TB).

Winter Danger. (TB).

Year of the Bloody Sevens. (TB).

COLLECTIONS

Kerlan Collection, University of Minnesota. (Minneapolis, Minnesota).

Mississippi Valley Collection, Brisler Library, Memphis State University. (Memphis, Tennessee).

BACKGROUND READING

Burke. *American Authors and Books, 1640 to the Present Day*.

Burns, P., and Hines, R. "Tennessee's Teller of Tall Tales, William O. Steele." *Elementary English*, December 1961.

Commire. *Something about the Author*.

Contemporary Authors.

Fuller. *More Junior Authors*.

Kirkpatrick. *Twentieth Century Children's Writers*.

Meet the Authors. Imperial International, 1969 (CT).

Steele, W. "Last Buffalo Killed in Tennessee." *Horn Book*, April 1969.

Steele, W. "Long Hunter and the Tall Tale." *Horn Book*, February 1958.

Ward. *Authors of Books for Young People, Second Edition*.

WILLIAM STEIG, 1907-
author-illustrator

AWARDS

Abel's Island. Newbery Honor Book, 1977.

Amazing Bone. Caldecott Honor Book, 1977.

Sylvester and the Magic Pebble. Caldecott Medal Book, 1970.

BIBLIOGRAPHY

Abel's Island. Farrar, 1976.

About People: A Book of Symbolical Drawings. Random, 1939; also in *Steig Album*, below.

Agony in the Kindergarten. Duell, 1950; also in *Steig Album*, below.

All Embarrassed. Duell, 1944; also in *Steig Album*, below.

Amazing Bone. Farrar, 1976.

Amos and Boris. Farrar, 1971.

Bad Island. Windmill, 1969.

Bad Speller. Windmill, 1970.

Caleb and Kate. Farrar, 1977.

C D B! Windmill, 1968.

Continuous Performance. Duell, 1963.

Decline and Fall of Practically Everybody; by Will Cuppy, edited by Fred Feldkamp. Holt, 1950.

Dominic. Farrar, 1972.

Dreams of Glory, and Other Drawings. Knopf, 1953.

Eye for Elephants. Windmill, 1970.

Farmer Palmer's Wagon Ride. Farrar, 1974.

Giggle Box: Funny Stories for Boys and Girls; by Phyllis Fenner. Knopf, 1950.

Great Bustard and Other People: Containing How to Tell Your Friends from the Apes and How to Become Extinct; by Will Cuppy. il. with Jacks. Farrar, 1944.

How to Become Extinct; by Will Cuppy. Farrar, 1941; also in *Great Bustard*, above.

Listen Little Man! A Document from the Archives of the Orgone Institute; by Wilhelm Reich. Tr. Theodore Wolfe. Orgone Institute, 1948.

Lonely Ones. Duell, 1942; also in *Steig Album*, below.

Male/Female. Farrar, 1971.

Man about Town. Smith, 1932.

Mr. Blanding Builds His Dream House; by Eric Hodgins. Simon, 1947.

Persistent Faces. Duell, 1945; also in *Steig Album*, below.

Poker for Fun and Profit; by Irwin Steig. McDowell, 1959.

Real Thief. Farrar, 1973.

Rejected Lovers. Knopf, 1951.

Roland: The Minstrel Pig. Windmill, 1968.

Small Fry. Duell, 1944; revised and enlarged, 1951; also in *Steig Album*, below.

Steig Album: Seven Complete Books. Duell, 1953. (Includes *About People, Agony in the Kindergarten, All Embarrassed, Lonely Ones, Persistent Faces, Small Fry*, and *Till Death Do Us Part*, above and below.)

Sylvester and the Magic Pebble. Windmill, 1969; a.k.a. *Silvestre y la Piedrita*, 1977.

Till Death Do Us Part: Some Ballet Notes on Marriage. Duell, 1947; also in *Steig Album*, above.

MEDIA

Amos and Boris. (TB); Miller-Brody Productions, 1975 (FSS).

Farmer Palmer's Wagon Ride. (TB).

Real Thief. (TB).

Roland the Minstrel Pig. Caedmon Records, n. d. (R).

Sylvester and the Magic Pebble. (TB).

EXHIBITIONS

Downtown Gallery, 1934, 1939, 1942. (New York, New York).

Smith College, 1940. (Northampton, Massachusetts).

Weyhe Gallery, 1971. (New York, New York).

COLLECTIONS

Brooklyn Museum of Arts and Sciences. (Brooklyn, New York).

Free Library of Philadelphia. (Philadelphia, Pennsylvania).

Kerlan Collection, University of Minnesota. (Minneapolis, Minnesota).

Rhode Island Museum. (Providence, Rhode Island).

Smith College. (Northampton, Massachusetts).

BACKGROUND READING

Bader. *American Picturebooks from Noah's Ark to The Beast Within*.

Burke. *American Authors and Books, 1640 to the Present Day*.

Current Biography.

DeMontreville. *Third Book of Junior Authors*.

Higgins, J. "William Steig, Champion for Romance." *Children's Literature in Education*, No. 1, 1978.

Kingman. *Illustrators of Children's Books, 1967-1976*.

Kingman. *Newbery and Caldecott Medal Books, 1966-1975*.

Kirkpatrick. *Twentieth Century Children's Writers*.

New York Times Biographical Edition.

Nykoruk. *Authors in the News*.

Ward. *Authors of Books for Young People, Second Edition*.

Ward. *Illustrators of Books for Young People, Second Edition*.

"William Steig in Three Parts." *American Artist*, March 1943.

MARY SLATTERY STOLZ, 1920-
author

AWARDS

Belling the Tiger. Newbery Honor Book, 1962.

Noonday Friends. Newbery Honor Book, 1966.

BIBLIOGRAPHY

And Love Replied. Harper, 1958.

Beautiful Friend, and Other Stories. Harper, 1960.

Because of Madeline. Harper, 1957.

Belling the Tiger. il. Beni Montresor. Harper, 1961.

Bully of Barkham Street. il. Leonard Shortall. Harper, 1963; large print edition, 1967.

BIBLIOGRAPHY (cont'd)

By the Highway Home. Harper, 1971.

Cat in a Mirror. Harper, 1975.

Day and the Way We Met. Harper, 1956.

Dog on Barkham Street. il. Leonard Shortall. Harper, 1960.

Dragons of the Queen. il. Edward Frascino. Harper, 1969.

Edge of Next Year. Harper, 1974.

Emmett's Pig. il. Garth Williams. Harper, 1959.

Ferris Wheel. Harper, 1976.

Frédou. il. Tomi Ungerer. Harper, 1962.

Good-by My Shadow. Harper, 1957.

Great Rebellion. il. Beni Montresor. Harper, 1961.

Hospital Zone. Harper, 1956.

In a Mirror. Harper, 1953.

Juan. il. Louis S. Glanzman. Harper, 1970.

Leap before You Look. Harper, 1971.

Leftover Elf. il. Peggy Bacon. Harper, 1952.

Maximilian's World. il. Uri Shulevitz. Harper, 1966.

Mystery of the Woods. il. Uri Shulevitz. Harper, 1964.

Noonday Friends. il. Louis S. Glanzman. Harper, 1965.

Organdy Cupcakes. Harper, 1951.

Pigeon Flight. il. Murray Tinkleman. Harper, 1962.

Pray Love, Remember. Harper, 1954.

Ready or Not. Harper, 1953.

Rosemary. Harper, 1955.

Say Something. il. Edward Frascino. Harper, 1968.

Sea Gulls Woke Me. Harper, 1951.

Second Nature. Harper, 1958.

Siri the Conquistador. il. Beni Montresor. Harper, 1963.

Some Merry-Go-Round Music. Harper, 1959.

Story of a Singular Hen and Her Peculiar Children. il. Edward Frascino. Harper, 1969.

To Tell Your Love. Harper, 1950.

Truth and Consequence. Harper, 1953.

Two by Two. Houghton, 1954; *a.k.a. Love, or a Season*. Harper, 1964.

Wait for Me, Michael. Harper, 1961.

Who Wants Music on Monday? Harper, 1963.

Wonderful Terrible Time. il. Louis S. Glanzman. Harper, 1967.

MEDIA

And Love Replied. (BB).

Because of Madeline. (BB, TB).

Belling the Tiger. (TB).

By the Highway Home. (BB).

Day and the Way We Met. (BB, TB).

Dog on Barkham Street. (BB).

Edge of Next Year. (CB).

Frédou. (TB).

Good-by My Shadow. (TB).

Leap before You Look. (TB).

Noonday Friends. (BB, TB); Miller-Brody Productions, 1977 (FSS).

Ready or Not. (BB).

Rosemary. (BB).

Say Something. Harper & Row, 1974 (FSS).

Sea Gulls Woke Me. (BB).

Second Nature. (BB, MT).

Some Merry-Go-Round Music. (BB).

To Tell Your Love. (TB).

Wait for Me, Michael. (BB).

Who Wants Music on Monday? (BB, TB).

Wonderful Terrible Time. (TB).

COLLECTIONS

Kerlan Collection, University of Minnesota. (Minneapolis, Minnesota).

BACKGROUND READING

Bair. *Biography News.*

Burke. *American Authors and Books, 1640 to the Present Day.*

Commire. *Something about the Author.*

Contemporary Authors.

Current Biography.

Foremost Women in Communications.

Fuller. *More Junior Authors.*

Hopkins. *More Books by More People.*

Nykoruk. *Authors in the News.*

Ward. *Authors of Books for Young People, Second Edition.*

HELEN TODD STONE, 1904-
illustrator

AWARDS

All around the Town. Caldecott Honor Book, 1949.

Most Wonderful Doll in the World. Caldecott Honor Book, 1951.

BIBLIOGRAPHY

All around the Town; by Phyllis McGinley, Lippincott, 1948.

Bundle Book; by Ruth Krauss. Harper, 1951.

Cats and People; by Frances L. Lockridge. Lippincott, 1950.

Exciting Adventures of Waldo the Duck; by Earl and Linette Burton. McGraw, 1945.

Horse Who Had His Picture in the Paper; by Phyllis McGinley. Lippincott, 1951.

Horse Who Lived Upstairs; by Phyllis McGinley. Lippincott, 1944.

Let It Rain!; by Dorothy Koch. Holiday, 1959.

Little Ballet Dancer; by Monica Stirling. Lothrop, 1952.

Little Flower Girl; by Elizabeth Tate. Lothrop, 1956.

Little Witch; by Anna E. Bennett. Lippincott, 1953.

Lucy McLockett; by Phyllis McGinley. Lippincott, 1945.

Most Wonderful Doll in the World; by Phyllis McGinley. Lippincott, 1950.

Plain Princess; by Phyllis McGinley. Lippincott, 1945.

Pussycat's Christmas; by Margaret W. Brown. Crowell, 1949.

Sally Saucer; by Edna Weiss. Houghton, 1956.

Snow Is Falling; by Franklyn M. Branley. Crowell, 1963.

Taffy and Joe; by Earl and Linette Burton. McGraw, 1947.

Tell Me, Mister Owl; by Doris Foster. Lothrop, 1957.

Tree for Me; by Norma Simon. Lippincott, 1956.

Twirly Skirt; by Martha Goldberg. Holiday, 1954.

Violets Are Blue; by Mary Kennedy. Lothrop, 1951.

Watch Honeybees with Me; by Judy Hawes. Crowell, 1964.

Young Miss Burney; by Anna B. Stewart. Lippincott, 1947.

COLLECTIONS

Kerlan Collection, University of Minnesota. (Minneapolis, Minnesota).

Special Collections, University Research Library, University of California. (Los Angeles, California).

BACKGROUND READING

Commire. *Something about the Author*.

Contemporary Authors.

Current Biography.

Foremost Women in Communications.

Fuller. *More Junior Authors*.

Kingman. *Illustrators of Children's Books, 1957-1966*.

Mahony. *Illustrators of Children's Books, 1744-1945*.

Miller. *Illustrators of Children's Books, 1946-1956*.

Stone, H. "Hallowe'en Birthday." *Horn Book*, October 1953.

Stone, H. "Princess Goes to Press." *Horn Book*, January 1946.

Ward. *Illustrators of Books for Young People, Second Edition*.

+PHILIP DUFFIELD STONG, 1899-1957
author

AWARDS

Honk, the Moose. Newbery Honor Book, 1936.

BIBLIOGRAPHY

Adventure of "Horse" Barnsby. Doubleday, 1956.

Beast Called an Elephant. il. Kurt Wiese. Dodd, 1955.

Blizzard. Doubleday, 1955.

Buckskin Breeches. Farrar, 1937.

Captain Kidd's Cow. il. Kurt Wiese. Dodd, 1941.

Career. Harcourt, 1936.

Censored, the Goat. il. Kurt Wiese. Dodd, 1945.

County Fair. photographs by Josephine von Miklos, et al. Stackpole, 1938.

Cowhand Goes to Town. il. Kurt Wiese. Dodd, 1939.

Edgar: The 7:58. il. Lois Lenski. Farrar, 1938.

Farm Boy: A Hunt for Indian Treasure. il. Kurt Wiese. Dodd, 1934; also in *Phil Stong's Big Book*, below.

Farmer in the Dell. Harcourt, 1935.

Forty Pounds of Gold. il. Arthur Shilstone. Doubleday, 1951.

Gold in Them Hills: Being an Irreverant History of the Great 1849 Gold Rush. Doubleday, 1957.

BIBLIOGRAPHY (cont'd)

Hawkeyes: A Biography of the State of Iowa. Dodd, 1940.

High Water. il. Kurt Wiese. Dodd, 1937; also in *Phil Stong's Big Book*, below.

Hired Man's Elephant. il. Doris Lee. Dodd, 1939.

Hirum, the Hillbilly. il. Kurt Wiese. Dodd, 1950.

Honk, the Moose. il. Kurt Wiese. Dodd, 1935.

Horses and Americans. il. Kurt Wiese, prints and photographs. Stokes, 1939; Garden City, 1939. (Limited edition).

If School Keeps. il. F. E. Warren. Farrar, 1940.

Iron Mountain. Farrar, 1942.

Ivanhoe Keeler. Farrar, 1939.

Jessamy John. Doubleday, 1947.

Long Lane. il. F. E. Warren. Farrar, 1939.

Marta of Muscovy: The Fabulous Life of Russia's First Empress. Doubleday, 1945.

Mike: The Story of a Young Circus Acrobat. il. Kurt Wiese. Dodd, 1957.

Mississippi Pilot: With Mark Twain on the Great River. Dodd, 1954.

Missouri Canary. il. Kurt Wiese. Dodd, 1943.

No-Sitch, the Hound. il. Kurt Wiese. Dodd, 1936; also in *Phil Stong's Big Book*, below.

One Destiny. Reynal, 1942.

(ed.) *Other Worlds: An Anthology of 25 Fantastic Stories*. Funk, 1941; *a.k.a. 25 Modern Stories of Mystery and Imagination*. Garden City, 1942.

Phil Stong's Big Book: Farm Boy, High Water, No-Sitch, the Hound. il. Kurt Wiese. Dodd, 1961; each issued separately, above and below.

Positive Pete! il. Kurt Wiese. Dodd, 1947.

Prince and the Porker. il. Kurt Wiese. Dodd, 1950.

Princess. Farrar, 1941. (Announced as *Miss Edison*.)

Rebellion of Lennie Barlow. Farrar, 1937.

Return in August. Doubleday, 1953.

Shake 'Em Up! A Practical Handbook of Polite Drinking; with Virginia Elliott. Harcourt, 1930.

State Fair. Century, 1932; il. U. Hyde. Barker, 1933; variant as *State Fair, a 3 Act Comedy, Dramatized from the Book by Phil Stong*; by Luella McMahon. Dramatic, 1953.

Stranger's Return. Harcourt, 1933.

Village Tale. Harcourt, 1934.

Way Down Cellar. il. Kurt Wiese. Dodd, 1942.

Week-End. Harcourt, 1935.

Young Settler. il. Kurt Wiese. Dodd, 1938.

MEDIA

Blizzard. (TB).

Buckskin Breeches. (TB).

Captain Kidd's Cow. Intercontinental Audeo-Video Company, *ca.*1947 (R); Mercury Sound Books, 1957 (R).

Career. RKO Radio Pictures, 1939 (F).

High Water. (BB).

Honk, the Moose. (TB).

Long Lane. (BB).

Mike. (BB).

Mississippi Pilot. (BB).

State Fair. (BB); Twentieth Century Fox Film Corporation, 1933, 1945, 1962 (F).

Stranger's Return. (BB).

Way Down Cellar. Walt Disney Productions, 1967 (TV).

COLLECTIONS

New York Public Library. (New York, New York).

Princeton University Library. (Princeton, New Jersey)

University of Iowa Library. (Iowa City, Iowa).

BACKGROUND READING

Burke. *American Authors and Books, 1640 to the Present Day*.

Fuller. *More Junior Authors*.

Hart. *Oxford Companion to American Literature, Fourth Edition*.

Kirkpatrick. *Twentieth Century Children's Writers*.

Kunitz. *Twentieth Century Authors*.

Kunitz. *Twentieth Century Authors, First Supplement*.

Montgomery. *Story behind Modern Books*.

Obituary. *New York Times*, August 27, 1957.

Stong, P. "Phil Stong on Keosaqua, Iowa." Voice of America, 1955 (Ra).

Ward. *Authors of Books for Young People, Second Edition*.

Warfel. *American Novelists of Today*.

Young Wings. *Writing Books for Boys and Girls*.

+HILDEGARDE HOYT SWIFT, 1890?-1977
author

AWARDS

Little Blacknose. Newbery Honor Book, 1930.

Railroad to Freedom. Newbery Honor Book, 1932.

BIBLIOGRAPHY

Edge of April: A Biography of John Burroughs. il. Lynd Ward. Morrow, 1957.

From the Eagle's Wing: A Biography of John Muir. il. Lynd Ward. Morrow, 1962.

House by the Sea. il. Lynd Ward. Harcourt, 1938.

Little Blacknose: The Story of a Pioneer. il. Lynd Ward. Harcourt, 1929.

Little Red Lighthouse and the Great Gray Bridge; with Lynd Ward. Harcourt, 1942.

North Star Shining: A Pictorial History of the American Negro. il. Lynd Ward. Morrow, 1947.

Railroad to Freedom: A Story of the Civil War. il. Lynd Ward. Harcourt, 1932.

MEDIA

Edge of April. (BB).

From the Eagle's Wing. (BB).

Little Red Lighthouse. Weston Woods Studios, 1956 (F), 1965 (FSS); also in Weston Woods Studios Set No. 3, 1965 (FSS); *a.k.a. Pequeño Faro Rojo y el Gran Puente Gris*. Weston Woods Studios, 1960 (F).

North Star Shining. (BB).

Railroad to Freedom. (BB).

BACKGROUND READING

Contemporary Authors.

Kunitz. *Junior Book of Authors, Second Edition Revised*.

Ward. *Authors of Books for Young People, Second Edition*.

Warfel. *American Novelists of Today*.

+MILDRED D. TAYLOR
author

AWARDS

Roll of Thunder. Newbery Medal Book, 1977.

BIBLIOGRAPHY

Roll of Thunder, Hear My Cry. Dial, 1976.

Song of the Trees. il. Jerry Pickney. Dial, 1975.

BACKGROUND READING

Taylor, M. "Newbery Award Acceptance." *Horn Book*, August 1977; *a.k.a.* "Newbery Acceptance Speech." *Top of the News*, Summer 1977.

+EUNICE STRONG HAMMOND TIETJENS, 1884-1944
author

AWARDS

Boy of the South Seas. Newbery Honor Book, 1932.

BIBLIOGRAPHY

Adventure in Friendship, un Vuelo Hacia la Amistad, uma Cruzada de Amizade; with Phyllis Murray. Pan-American, 1936.

Body and Raiment. Knopf, 1919.

Boy of the Desert. il. Will Hollingsworth. Coward, 1928.

Boy of the South Seas. il. Myrtle Sheldon. Coward, 1931.

China; with Louise S. Hammond. photographs by Burton Holmes. Wheeler, 1930.

Gingerbread Boy. il. Nina R. Jordan. Whitman, 1932.

Jakie. Boni, 1921.

Japan, Korea and Formosa; ed. and il. by Burton Holmes. Wheeler, 1924; revised, Reilly, 1941.

Jaw-Breaker's Alphabet; with Janet Tietjens. il. Hermann Post. Boni, 1930.

Leaves in Windy Weather. Knopf, 1929.

(ed.) *Manga Reva: The Forgotten Islands*; by Robert Eskridge. Bobbs, 1931.

(ed.) *Poetry of the Orient: An Anthology of the Classic Secular Poetry of the Major Eastern Nations*. Knopf, 1928.

Profiles from China: Sketches in Verse of People & Things Seen in the Interior. Seymour, 1917; *a.k.a. Profiles from China: Sketches in Free Verse of People & Things Seen in the Interior*. Knopf, 1919.

Profiles from Home: Sketches in Free Verse of People & Things Seen in the United States. Knopf, 1925.

BIBLIOGRAPHY (cont'd)

Romance of Antar. il. Samuel Glanckoff. Coward, 1929.

*World at My Shoulder. Macmillan, 1938.

COLLECTIONS

Harvard University Library. (Cambridge, Massachusetts).

Newberry Library. (Chicago, Illinois).

Tietjens Collection, Manuscript Division, Library of Congress. (Washington, D.C.).

University of Chicago Libraries. (Chicago, Illinois).

Yale University Library. (New Haven, Connecticut).

BACKGROUND READING

Burke. *American Authors and Books, 1640 to the Present Day*.

Current Biography.

Hart. *Oxford Companion to American Literature, Fourth Edition*.

Kunitz. *Junior Book of Authors*.

Kunitz. *Twentieth Century Authors*.

Kunitz. *Twentieth Century Authors, First Supplement*.

Obituary. *New York Times*, September 7, 1944.

Young Wings. *Writing Books for Boys and Girls*.

+MARJORIE TORREY, *pseudonym*, 1899-
author-illustrator
a.k.a. Marjorie Torrey Hood Chanslor
pseudonyms Torrey Chanslor
Torrey Hood

AWARDS

Sing in Praise. Caldecott Honor Book, 1947.

Sing Mother Goose. Caldecott Honor Book, 1946.

BIBLIOGRAPHY

as Torrey Chanslor:

Our First Murder. Stokes, 1940.

Our Second Murder. Stokes, 1941.

as Torrey Hood:

Saturday Night Is My Delight. Putnam, 1952.

as Marjorie Torrey:

Alice's Adventures in Wonderland; by Lewis Carroll, *pseud.* (Charles L. Dodgson). Random, 1955.

Artie and the Princess. Howell, 1945.

Far from Marlborough Street; by Elizabeth Philbrook. Viking, 1944.

Favorite Nursery Songs; by Phyllis Obanian. Random, 1956.

Merriweathers. Viking, 1949.

Penny. Howell, 1944; *a.k.a. Penny, the Story of a Little Girl*. Harrap, 1948.

Peter Pan; by James M. Barrie, edited by Josette Frank. Random, 1957.

Sarah's Idea; by Doris Gates. Viking, 1938.

Sensible Kate; by Doris Gates. Viking, 1943.

Sing in Praise: A Collection of the Best-Loved Hymns, Stories of the Hymns and Musical Arrangements; by Opal Wheeler. Dutton, 1946.

Sing Mother Goose; by Opal Wheeler. Dutton, 1945.

Three Little Chipmunks. Grosset, 1947.

Trouble for Jerry; by Doris Gates. Viking, 1944.

MEDIA

Artie and the Princess. (BB).

COLLECTIONS

deGrummond Collection, University of Southern Mississippi. (Hattiesburg, Mississippi).

May Massee Collection, Emporia State College. (Emporia, Kansas).

BACKGROUND READING

Fuller. *More Junior Authors*.

Miller. *Illustrators of Children's Books, 1946-1956*.

Ward. *Illustrators of Books for Young People, Second Edition*.

CAROLYN TREFFINGER
author

AWARDS

Li Lun. Newbery Honor Book, 1948.

BIBLIOGRAPHY

Jimmy's Shoes. il. Ruth C. Collings. Penn, 1934.

Li Lun: Lad of Courage. il. Kurt Wiese. Abingdon, 1947.

Rag-Doll Jane. il. Fern B. Peat. Saalfield, 1930.

MEDIA

Li Lun. (BB).

ELIZABETH BORTON DE TREVIÑO, 1904-
author
a.k.a. Elizabeth Borton

AWARDS

I, Juan de Pareja. Newbery Medal Book, 1966.

BIBLIOGRAPHY

as Elizabeth Borton:

Our Little Aztec Cousin of Long Ago: Being the Story of a Coyote and How He Won Honor under His King. il. Harold Cue. Page, 1934.

Our Little Ethiopian Counsin: Children of the Queen of Sheba. il. photographs. Page, 1935.

Pollyanna and the Secret Mission. il. Harold Cue. Page, 1951.

Pollyanna in Hollywood. il. H. Weston Taylor. Page, 1931.

Pollyanna's Castle in Mexico. il. Harold Cue. Page, 1934.

Pollyanna's Door to Happiness. il. Harold Cue. Page, 1936.

Pollyanna's Golden Horseshoe. il. Griswold Tyng. Page, 1939.

as Elizabeth Borton de Treviño:

About Bellamy. il. Jessie Robinson. Harper, 1940.

Beyond the Gates of Hercules: A Tale of Lost Atlantis. Farrar, 1971.

Carpet of Flowers. il. Alan H. Crane. Crowell, 1955.

Casilda of the Rising Moon: A Tale of Magic and of Faith, of Knights and a Saint in Medieval Spain. Farrar, 1967.

Even as You Love. Crowell, 1957.

Fourth Gift. Doubleday, 1966.

Greek of Toledo: A Narrative of El Greco. Crowell, 1959.

*Hearthstone of My Heart. Doubleday, 1977.

Here Is Mexico. Farrar, 1970.

House on Bitterness Street. Doubleday, 1970.

I, Juan de Pareja. Farrar, 1965.

Juarez, Man of Law. Farrar, 1974.

Music Within. Doubleday, 1973.

*My Heart Lies South: The Story of My Mexican Marriage. Crowell, 1953; revised as *My Heart Lies South: The Story of My Mexican Marriage, with Epilog*, 1972.

Nacar, the White Deer. il. Enrico Arno. Farrar, 1963.

Turi's Poppa. il. Enrico Arno. Farrar, 1968; *a.k.a. Turi's Papa*. Gollancz, 1969.

Where the Heart Is. Farrar, 1962.

MEDIA

Carpet of Flowers. (BB).

Even as You Love. (BB).

Fourth Gift. (BB).

I, Juan de Pareja. (TB); Miller-Brody Productions, 1975 (FSS).

Music Within. (TB).

My Heart Lies South. (TB).

Turi's Poppa. (TB).

COLLECTIONS

Mugar Memorial Library, Boston University. (Boston, Massachusetts).

BACKGROUND READING

Commire. *Something about the Author*.

Contemporary Authors.

DeMontreville. *Third Book of Junior Authors*.

Elizabeth Borton de Treviño. Profiles in Literature, 1977 (VT, produced in Spanish and in English).

Foremost Women in Communications.

Hoffman. *Authors and Illustrators of Children's Books*.

Hopkins. *More Books by More People*.

Kingman. *Newbery and Caldecott Medal Books, 1966-1975*.

Kirkpatrick. *Twentieth Century Children's Writers*.

Ward. *Authors of Books for Young People, Second Edition*.

TASHA TUDOR, 1915-
author-illustrator

AWARDS

Mother Goose. Caldecott Honor Book, 1945.

1 Is One. Caldecott Honor Book, 1957.

BIBLIOGRAPHY

A Is for Annabelle. Oxford, 1954.

Adventures of a Beagle; by Thomas McCready, Jr. Ariel, 1959.

Alexander the Gander. Oxford, 1939; enlarged, 1961.

Amanda and the Bear. Oxford, 1951.

And It Was So; selected by Sara K. Clarke. Westminster, 1958.

Around the Year. Oxford, 1957.

Becky's Birthday. Viking, 1960.

Becky's Christmas. Viking, 1961.

Betty Crocker's Kitchen Garden; by Mary M. Campbell. Golden, 1971.

Biggity Bantam; by Thomas McCready, Jr. Ariel, 1954.

Brite and Fair. Noone, 1968.

Child's Garden of Verses; by Robert L. Stevenson. Oxford, 1947.

Christmas Cat; by Efner T. Holmes. Crowell, 1976.

Corgiville Fair. Crowell, 1971.

County Fair. Oxford, 1940; enlarged, Walck, 1964.

Dolls' Christmas. Walck, 1950.

Doll's House; by Rumer Godden. Georgian Webb, 1947; Viking, 1962; also in *Tasha Tudor Sampler*, below.

Dorcas Porkus. Oxford, 1942; enlarged, Walck, 1963.

Edgar Allen Crow. Oxford, 1953.

Fairy Tales from Hans Christian Andersen; by Hans C. Andersen. Oxford, 1945.

First Delights: A Book about the Five Senses. Platt, 1966.

First Graces. Oxford, 1955.

First Poems of Childhood. Platt, 1967.

First Prayers. Oxford, 1952. (Issued in Catholic and Protestant editions.)

Increase Rabbit; by Thomas McCready, Jr. Ariel, 1958.

Jackanapes; by Juliana H. Ewing. Oxford, 1948.

Linsey Woolsey. Oxford, 1946.

Little Princess; by Frances H. Burnett. Lippincott, 1963.

Little Women; by Louisa M. Alcott. World, 1969.

Lord Will Love Thee; selected by Sara K. Clarke. Westminster, 1959.

Mr. Stubbs; by Thomas McCready, Jr. Ariel, 1956.

More Prayers. Walck, 1967.

Mother Goose: Seventy Seven Verses with Pictures; from Mother Goose. Oxford, 1944.

My Brimful Book: Favorite Poems of Childhood, Mother Goose Rhymes, Animal Stories; edited by Dana Bruce. Platt, 1960.

New England Butt'ry Shelf Almanac; by Mary M. Campbell. World, 1970.

Night before Christmas; by Clement C. Moore. St. Onge, 1962; reillustrated, Rand, 1975.

1 Is One. Oxford, 1956.

Pekin White; by Thomas McCready, Jr. Ariel, 1955.

Pumpkin Moonshine. Oxford, 1938; enlarged, 1962; also in *Tasha Tudor Sampler*, below.

Real Diary of a Real Boy; by Henry A. Shute. Smith, 1967.

Round Dozen; by Louisa M. Alcott, edited by Anne T. Eaton. Viking, 1963.

Secret Garden; by Frances H. Burnett. Lippincott, 1962.

Snow before Christmas. Oxford, 1941.

(ed.) *Take Joy! The Tasha Tudor Christmas Book*. World, 1966.

Tale for Easter. Oxford, 1941; also in *Tasha Tudor Sampler*, below.

(ed.) *Tasha Tudor Book of Fairy Tales*. Platt, 1961.

Tasha Tudor Sampler. McKay-Walck, 1977. (Includes *Dolls' Christmas, Pumpkin Moonshine*, and *Tale for Easter*, issued separately, above.)

Tasha Tudor's Bedtime Book; edited by Kate Klimo. Platt, 1977.

Tasha Tudor's Favorite Stories. Lippincott, 1965.

Thistly B. Oxford, 1949.

Twenty-third Psalm; from the *Bible*. St. Onge, 1965.

White Goose. Farrar, 1943.

(comp.) *Wings from the Wind: An Anthology of Poems*. Lippincott, 1964.

MEDIA

Alexander the Gander. (BB).

Becky's Birthday. (BB).

Becky's Christmas. (BB).

Mother Goose. (BB, TB).

COLLECTIONS

Free Library of Philadelphia. (Philadelphia, Pennsylvania).

Kerlan Collection, University of Minnesota. (Minneapolis, Minnesota).

Milwaukee Public Library. (Milwaukee, Wisconsin).

Special Collections, University Research Library, University of California. (Los Angeles, California).

BACKGROUND READING

Burke. *American Authors and Books, 1640 to the Present Day.*

Kingman. *Illustrators of Children's Books, 1957-1966.*

Kingman. *Illustrators of Children's Books, 1967-1976.*

Kirkpatrick. *Twentieth Century Children's Writers.*

Kunitz. *Junior Book of Authors, Second Edition Revised.*

Mahony. *Illustrators of Children's Books, 1744-1945.*

Miller. *Illustrators of Children's Books, 1946-1956.*

New York Times Biographical Service.

Ward. *Authors of Books for Young People, Second Edition.*

EDWIN BURDETT TUNIS, 1897-1973
author-illustrator

AWARDS

Frontier Living. Newbery Honor Book, 1962.

BIBLIOGRAPHY

Chipmunks on the Doorstep. Crowell, 1971.

Colonial Craftsmen and the Beginnings of Modern Industry. World, 1965.

Colonial Living. World, 1957.

Frontier Living. World, 1961.

Historical and Literary Map of the Old State of Maryland: Showing Forth Divers Curious and Notable Facts Relating to Scenes, Incidents, and Persons Worthy to be Recalled on the State's Three-Hundreth Anniversary. Enoch Pratt Free Library, 1931.

Indians. World, 1959.

Oars, Sails and Steam: A Picture Book of Ships. World, 1952.

Seventeen: A Tale of Youth and Summer Time and the Baxter Family, Especially William; by Booth Tarkington. Harper, 1932.

Shaw's Fortune: The Picture Story of a Colonial Plantation. World, 1966.

Tavern at the Ferry. Crowell, 1973.

Weapons: A Pictorial History. World, 1954.

Wheels: A Pictorial History. World, 1955.

You Will Find It in Maryland; by Stirling Graham. Records, 1945.

Young United States, 1783-1830: A Time of Change and Growth, a Time of Learning Democracy, a Time of New Ways of Living, Thinking and Doing. World, 1969.

MEDIA

Colonial Craftsmen. (BB).

Colonial Living. (TB).

Frontier Living. (TB).

Shaw's Fortune. (BB).

Tavern at the Ferry. (TB).

Young United States. (TB).

COLLECTIONS

Kerlan Collection, University of Minnesota. (Minneapolis, Minnesota).

University of Oregon Library. (Eugene, Oregon).

BACKGROUND READING

Commire. *Something about the Author.*

Contemporary Authors.

Fuller. *More Junior Authors.*

Kingman. *Illustrators of Children's Books, 1957-1966.*

Kingman. *Illustrators of Children's Books, 1967-1976.*

Miller. *Illustrators of Children's Books, 1946-1956.*

Tunis, E. "Some Problems of a Writer-Illustrator." *Horn Book,* December 1966.

Ward. *Authors of Books for Young People, Second Edition.*

+BRINTON CASSADAY TURKLE, 1915-
author-illustrator

AWARDS

Thy Friend, Obadiah. Caldecott Honor Book, 1970.

BIBLIOGRAPHY

Adventures of Obadiah. Viking, 1972.

BIBLIOGRAPHY (cont'd)

Anna and the Baby Buzzard; by Helga Sandburg. Dutton, 1970.

Aunt-Sitter; by Quail Hawkins. Holiday, 1958.

Ballad of William Sycamore, 1790-1871; by Stephen V. Benét. Little, 1959.

Belinda and Me; by Bettye H. Braucher. Viking, 1966.

Boy Who Didn't Believe in Spring; by Lucille Clifton. Dutton, 1973.

C Is for Circus; by Bernice Chardiet. Walker, 1971.

Cat That Clumped; by Paul Annixter, *pseud*. (Howard Sturtzel). Holiday, 1966.

Catch a Little Fox: Variations on a Folk Rhyme; by Beatrice S. deRegniers. Seabury, 1970.

Danny Dunn and the Fossil Cave; by Jay Williams and Raymond Abrashkin. McGraw, 1961.

Danny Dunn on the Ocean Floor; by Jay Williams and Raymond Abrashkin. McGraw, 1960.

Deep in the Forest. Dutton, 1976.

Doll in the Bakeshop; by Carol B. York. Watts, 1965.

Elves and the Shoemaker; by Freya Littledale. Four Winds, 1975.

Far-Off Land; by Rebecca Caudill. Viking, 1964.

Fiddler of High Lonesome. Viking, 1968.

Four Paws into Adventure; by Claude Cenac. Watts, 1965.

Granny and the Indians; by Peggy Parish. Macmillan, 1969.

High-Noon Rocket; by Charles P. May. Holiday, 1966.

How Joe the Bear and Sam the Mouse Got Together; by Beatrice S. deRegniers. Parents, 1965.

Hunt the Mountain Lion; by Gus Tavo, *pseud*. (Martha M. P. and Gustave Ivan). Knopf, 1959.

If You Grew Up with Abraham Lincoln; by Ann McGovern. Four Winds, 1966.

If You Lived in Colonial Times; by Ann McGovern. Four Winds, 1964.

In the Clearing; by Robert Frost. Holt, 1962.

Indian Children of America: A Book to Begin On; by Margaret C. Farquhar. Holt, 1964.

Island Time; by Bette Lamont. Lippincott, 1976.

It's Only Arnold. Viking, 1973.

Jake; by Tamara Kitt. Abelard, 1969.

Just Suppose; by May Garelick. Four Winds, 1969.

Larry; by Edith Agnew. Friendship, 1960.

Leo of Alaska; by Edith Agnew. Friendship, 1958.

Lollipop Party; by Ruth Sonneborn. Viking, 1967.

Lucky and the Giant; by Benjamin Elkin.

Magic of Millicent Musgrave. Viking, 1967.

Miracle of Sage Valley; by Jan Young. Longmans, 1958.

Mr. Blue; by Margaret Embry. Holiday, 1963.

Mooncoin Castle: Or, Skullduggery Rewarded. Viking, 1970.

Mystery of the Red Tide; by Frank Bonham. Dutton, 1966.

New Boy; by Mary Urmstrom. Doubleday, 1950.

Obadiah the Bold. Viking, 1965.

Over the River and through the Wood; by Lydia M. Child. Coward, 1974.

Peter's Tent; by Norah Smaridge. Viking, 1965.

Poor Richard in France; by F. N. Monjo. Holt, 1973.

Sam and the Impossible Thing; by Tamara Kitt. Norton, 1967.

Sky Dog. Viking, 1969.

Special Birthday Present for Someone Very Special; by Tamara Kitt. Norton, 1966.

Story of Ben Franklin; by Eve Merriam. Four Winds, 1965.

That's What Friends Are For; by Florence P. Heide and Sylvia Van Clief. Four Winds, 1968.

Thy Friend, Obadiah. Viking, 1969.

Timberline Treasure; by Adrien Stoutenberg. Westminster, 1952.

Treasure for Tomás; by Edith Agnew. Friendship, 1964.

Troublesome Tuba; by Barbara Rinkoff. Lothrop, 1967.

War Cry of the West; by Nathaniel Burt. Holt, 1964.

Who Likes It Hot?; by May Garelick. Four Winds, 1972.

You Say You Saw a Camel?; by Elizabeth Coatsworth. Row, 1958.

Yvette of the Ballet Opera; by Leon Harris. McGraw, 1970.

MEDIA

Adventures of Obadiah. (TB).

Fiddler of High Lonesome. (BB).

Obadiah the Bold. (TB); Viking Press, 1970 (FSS).

Sky Dog. Viking Press, n. d. (C, R).

Thy Friend, Obadiah. (BB); Viking Press, 1971 (FSS).

BACKGROUND READING

Commire. *Something about the Author*.

Contemporary Authors.

DeMontreville. *Third Book of Junior Authors.*

Hopkins. *Books Are by People.*

Kingman. *Illustrators of Children's Books, 1957-1966.*

Kingman. *Illustrators of Children's Books, 1967-1976.*

Kirkpatrick. *Twentieth Century Children's Writers.*

Smaridge. *Famous Author-Illustrators for Young People.*

Turkle, B. "Confessions of a Leprechaun: An Author and Illustrator of Children's Books." *Publishers Weekly*, July 14, 1969.

Ward. *Illustrators of Books for Young People, Second Edition.*

+JAMES RAMSEY ULLMAN, 1907-1971
author

AWARDS

Banner in the Sky. Newbery Honor Book, 1955.

BIBLIOGRAPHY

Age of Mountaineering. Lippincott, 1954; enlarged, 1964; *a.k.a. Age of Mountaineering: With a Chapter on British Mountains by W. H. Murray.* Collins, 1956.

(ed.) *Americans on Everest: The Official Account of the Ascent Led by Norman G. Dyhrenfurth.* Lippincott, 1964.

And Not to Yield. Doubleday, 1970; large print edition, National Aid to the Physically Handicapped, n. d.

Banner in the Sky. Lippincott, 1954; *a.k.a. Third Man on the Mountain.* Pocket Books, 1959; *a.k.a. Banner in the Sky: With Notes and Questions by John M. Bassett.* McClelland, 1966.

Caribbean Here & Now: The Complete Vacation Guide to 52 Sunny Islands in the Caribbean Sea; with Al Dinhofer. Macmillan, 1968; revised to *Caribbean Here & Now: The Complete Vacation Guide to 52 Sunny Islands and Vacation Lands in the Caribbean Sea,* 1969; revised to *Caribbean Here & Now: The Complete 1971-72 Guide to the Sunny Islands and Vacation Lands,* 1970.

Day on Fire: A Novel Suggested by the Life of Arthur Rimbaud. World, 1958.

Down the Colorado with Major Powell. il. Nicholas Eggenhofer. Houghton, 1960.

Fia Fia: A Novel of the South Pacific. World, 1962; *a.k.a. Island below the Wind.* Collins, 1962.

High Conquest: The Story of Mountaineering. Lippincott, 1941.

Is Nothing Sacred? A "Success" Story in Three Acts; with Arnold L. Scheuer, Jr. Baker, 1934.

Island of the Blue Macaws, and Sixteen Other Stories. Lippincott, 1953.

(ed.) *Kingdom of Adventure: Everest, a Chronicle of Man's Assault on the Earth's Highest Mountain, Narrated by the Participants with an Accompanying Text.* Sloane, 1947.

Mad Shelley. Princeton University, 1930.

Other Side of the Mountain: An Escape to the Amazon. Carrick, 1938.

River of the Sun. Lippincott, 1951.

Sands of Karakorum. Lippincott, 1953.

Silver Sword, and Other Stories. Collins, 1954.

Tiger of the Snows: The Autobiography of Tenzig of Everest; with Norkey Tenzig. Putnam, 1955; *a.k.a. Tiger of Everest.* (New York), 1955; *a.k.a. Man of Everest: The Autobiography of Tenzig.* Harrap, 1955; enlarged, Severn House, 1975.

Where the Bong Tree Grows: The Log of One Man's Journey in the South Pacific. World, 1963.

White Tower. Lippincott, 1945.

Windom's Way. Lippincott, 1952.

MEDIA

Americans on Everest. Dyhrenfurth/Pyramid Films. 1967 (F).

Banner in the Sky. (BB, CB, TB); Miller-Brody Productions, 1972 (C, R); Newbery Award Records, 1972 (C, R); *a.k.a. Third Man on the Mountain.* Walt Disney Productions, 1959 (F).

High Conquest. Monogram Pictures Corporation, 1947 (F).

River of the Sun. (TB).

Tiger of the Snows. (TB).

White Tower. (TB); RKO Radio Pictures, Inc., 1950 (F).

Windom's Way. J. A. Rank, 1957 (F).

COLLECTIONS

Princeton University Library. (Princeton, New Jersey).

BACKGROUND READING

Breit, H. "Talk with Mr. Ullman." *New York Tribune Book Review*, January 21, 1951.

Burke. *American Authors and Books, 1640 to the Present Day.*

Commire. *Something about the Author.*

BACKGROUND READING (cont'd)

Contemporary Authors.

Current Biography.

DeMontreville. *Fourth Book of Junior Authors and Illustrators.*

Hutchens, J. "On an Author." *New York Herald Tribune Book Review*, January 21, 1951.

Kunitz. *Twentieth Century Authors, First Supplement.*

New York Times Biographical Edition.

Ward. *Authors of Books for Young People, Second Edition.*

+HENDRIK WILLEM VAN LOON, 1882-1944
author-illustrator

AWARDS

Story of Mankind. Newbery Medal Book, 1922.

BIBLIOGRAPHY

Adventures and Escapes of Gustavus Vasa, and How They Carried Him from His Rather Obscure Origin to the Throne of Sweden. Dodd, 1945.

Air-Storming: A Collection of 40 Radio Talks over the Stations of the National Broadcasting Company. also il. with photographs. Harcourt, 1935; *a.k.a. Van Loon on the Air: Broadcasts from the Studio of the National Broadcasting Corporation.* Harrap, 1936.

America. Boni, 1927; *a.k.a. Story of America.* Garden City, 1934.

Ancient Man and the Beginning of Civilizations. Boni, 1920.

Around the World with the Alphabet and Hendrik Van Loon: To Teach Little Children Their Letters and at the Same Time Give Their Papas and Mamas Something to Think About. Simon, 1935.

Arts. Simon, 1937; *a.k.a. Arts and Mankind.* Harrap, 1938.

Christmas Carols: Illustrated and Done Up into Simple Music; with Grace Castagnetta. Simon, 1937; new edition, 1950.

Christmas Songs; with Grace Castagnetta. American Artist, 1942.

Fall of the Dutch Republic. Houghton, 1913.

Folk Songs of Many Lands. Simon, 1938.

Golden Book of Dutch Navigators; also il. with old prints. Century, 1916; new edition, Appleton, 1938.

Good Tidings: Words from St. Luke; from the *Bible*, with Grace Castagnetta. American Artist, 1941.

Here and Now Storybook: Two-through-Seven -Year Olds. il. with Christine Price. Dutton, 1936; revised and enlarged, 1948.

History with a Match: Being an Account of the Earliest Navigators and the Discovery of America. McKay, 1917; *a.k.a. Romance of Discovery: Being an Account of the Earliest Navigators and the Discovery of America.* Carlton, 1937.

How to Look at Pictures: A Short History of Painting. Modern Age, 1938.

Indiscreet Itinery: Or, How the Unconventional Traveler Should See Holland by One Who Was Actually Born There. Harcourt, 1933.

*Invasion: Being the Personal Recollection of What Happened to Our Own Family, and to Some of Our Friends during the First Forty-eight Hours of That Terrible Incident in Our History Which Is Now Known as the Great Invasion and How We Escaped with Our Lives and the Strange Adventures Which Befell Us before the Nazis Were Driven from Our Territories; Written Down at the Time and Now for the First Time Presented to the Public at Large. Harcourt, 1940.

Last of the Troubadors: Carl Michael Bellamm, 1740-1795, His Life and His Music. Simon, 1939.

Life and Times of Johann Sebastian Bach: Described and Depicted; music by Grace Castagnetta. Simon, 1940. (Issued with four records in a box; book and records also issued separately.)

Life and Times of Peter Styvesant. Holt, 1926.

Life and Times of Rembrandt, R. V. R., Is an Account of the Last Years and Death of One Rembrandt Harmenszoon van Rijn, a Painter and Etcher of Some Renown Who Lived and Worked in the Town of Amsterdam, and Died of General Neglect and Diverse Other Unfortunate Circumstances on the Fourth Day of October of the Year of Grace, 1699, Who Was Attended in His Afflictions by One Joannis Van Loon, Doctor Mediciane and Chirugeon in Extraordinary, Who during a Most Busy Life Yet Found Time to Write Down These Personal Recollections of the Greatest of His Fellow-Citizens and Which Are Now for the First Time Presented (Provided with as Few Notes, Emendations and Critical Observations as Possible), by His Great-Great-Grandson, Nine Times Removed. Liveright, 1930; *a.k.a. ...Authorized Abridgement.* Bantam, 1957.

Life and Times of Simon Bolivar: This Is the Story of Simon Bolivar, Liberator of Venezuela, the Man Who First of All Had the Vision of a United States for the Whole of the American Continent. Dodd, 1942; *a.k.a. Fighters for Freedom: Jefferson and Bolivar.* Dodd, 1962; *a.k.a. Jefferson* and Bolivar: New World Fighters for Freedom. Harrap, 1966. (The last two titles also include Thomas Jefferson, below.)

Man: The Miracle Maker. Liveright, 1928; a.k.a. Multiplex Man: Or, the Story of Survival through Invention. Cape, 1928; a.k.a. Story of Inventions: Man the Miracle Maker. Garden City, 1932.

Message of the Bells: Or, What Happened to Us on Christmas Eve; music by Grace Castagnetta. Garden City, 1942.

*My School Books: From the Unpublished Autobiography of Hendrik Van Loon. E. I. DuPont deNemours, 1939.

Observations on the Mystery of Print and the Work of Johann Gutenberg. Book Manufacturers Institute, 1938.

Our Battle: Being One Man's Answer to My Battle by Adolf Hitler. Simon, 1938.

(ed.) Praise of Folly: With a Short Life of the Author; by Erasmus Desiderius. Black, 1942.

Re: Elephant up a Tree: This Is the True Story of Sir John, Or Why Elephants Have Decided to Remain Elephants, as Told by One of Them. Simon, 1933.

Ships and How They Sailed the Seven Seas, 5,000 B.C.–A.D. 1935. Simon, 1935.

Short History of Discovery from the Earliest Times to the Founding of the Colonies. McKay, 1917.

Songs America Sings; with Grace Castagnetta. Simon, 1939.

Songs We Sing: A Small Collection of Songs That Have Been Sung for a Great Many Years by the Children of All Lands; music by Grace Castagnetta. Simon, 1936.

Story of America. Garden City, 1934; revised, Liveright, 1942.

Story of Mankind. Boni, 1921; school edition, Macmillan, 1924; revised, Boni, 1926; enlarged and revised, Liveright, 1936, 1951, 1967 (by Gerard Van Loon); updated, 1972 (by Gerard Van Loon); a.k.a. Story of Mankind, Including a New Final Chapter Which Brings the Material up to the European War of 1939. Pocket Books, 1939.

Story of Rabelais and Voltaire: With Selections from the Works of Rabelais and Voltaire. Bantam, 1940.

Story of the Bible. Boni, 1946.

Story of the Pacific. Harcourt, 1940.

Story of Wilbur the Hat: Being a True Account of Strange Things Which Sometimes Happen in a Part of the World Which Does Not Exist. Boni, 1925.

Thomas Jefferson: The Serene Fellow from Monticello Who Gave Us an American Way of Thinking and Who Gained World-Wide Renown by His Noble Understanding of That Most Difficult of All the Arts, the Art of Living, as He Felt That It Should be Practiced in the Republic of Which He Was One of the Founders. Dodd, 1943; a.k.a. Fighters for Freedom: Jefferson and Bolivar, 1962; a.k.a. Jefferson and Bolivar: New World Fighters for Freedom. Harrap, 1966. (The last two titles include Life and Times of Simon Bolivar, above.)

To Have—Or To Be: Take Your Choice. Day, 1932.

Tolerance. Boni, 1925.

Van Loon's Geography: The Story of the World We Live In. Simon, 1932; a.k.a. Home of Mankind: The Story of the World We Live In. Harrap, 1936.

Van Loon's Lives: Being a True and Faithful Account of a Number of Highly Interesting Meetings with Certain Historical Personages, from Confucius and Plato to Voltaire and Thomas Jefferson, about Whom We Had Always Felt a Great Deal of Curiosity, and Who Came to See Us as Our Dinner Guests in a Bygone Year. Simon, 1942.

World Divided Is a World Lost. Cosmos, 1935.

MEDIA

Ancient Man. (BB).

Arts. (TB).

Indiscreet Itinery. (BB).

Life and Times of Johann Sebastian Bach. (TB).

Life and Times of Rembrandt. (BB).

Our Battle. (BB).

Story of Mankind. (BB, C, MT, TB); Miller-Brody Productions, 1973 (C); Warner Brothers Pictures, 1957 (F).

Story of the Pacific. (BB).

Tolerance. (BB).

Van Loon's Geography. (BB).

Van Loon's Lives. (TB).

EXHIBITIONS

Feragil Gallery, 1937, 1940. (New York, New York).

COLLECTIONS

American Academy of Arts and Letters Library. (New York, New York).

Central Children's Room, Donnell Library Center, New York Public Library. (New York, New York).

COLLECTIONS (cont'd)

Collection of American Literature, Beinecke Library, Yale University. (New Haven, Connecticut).

Department of Manuscripts and University Archives, Cornell University Library. (Ithaca, New York).

Department of Rare Books and Manuscripts, Boston Public Library. (Boston, Massachusetts).

Free Library of Philadelphia. (Philadelphia, Pennsylvania).

Harvard University Library. (Cambridge, Massachusetts).

Kerlan Collection, University of Minnesota. (Minneapolis, Minnesota).

New York Public Library. (New York, New York).

Newark Public Library. (Newark, New Jersey).

Olin Library, Cornell University. (Ithaca, New York).

Pack Memorial Public Library. (Asheville, North Carolina).

Rare Book and Manuscript Library, Columbia University. (New York, New York).

Smith Collection, Toronto Public Library. (Toronto, Ontario).

Special Collections, University Research Library, University of California. (Los Angeles, California).

State Historical Society of Wisconsin Library. (Madison, Wisconsin).

BACKGROUND READING

Bond, F. "Hendrik and the Gate of Heaven." *Saturday Review of Literature*, June 15, 1946.

Burke. *American Authors and Books, 1640 to the Present Day*.

Current Biography.

Ellis. *Book Illustration*.

James. *Dictionary of American Biography, Supplement Three*.

Kunitz. *Junior Book of Authors*.

Kunitz. *Junior Book of Authors, Second Edition Revised*.

Kunitz. *Living Authors*.

Kunitz. *Twentieth Century Authors*.

Kunitz. *Twentieth Century Authors, First Supplement*.

Mahony. *Illustrators of Children's Books, 1744-1945*.

Miller. *Newbery Medal Books, 1922-1955*.

Obituary. *Art News*, March 15, 1944.

Obituary. *New York Times*, March 12, 1944.

Van Loon, Gerard. *Story of Hendrik Willem Van Loon*. Lippincott, 1972.

Van Ryan, F. "Most Unforgettable Character I've Ever Met." *Reader's Digest*, September 1952.

Ward. *Authors of Books for Young People, Second Edition*.

+HILDA GERARDA VAN STOCKUM, 1908-
author-illustrator

AWARDS

Day on Skates. Newbery Honor Book, 1935.

BIBLIOGRAPHY

Afke's Ten; by Ninke van Hichtum, *pseud.* (Sjowkje Troelstra-Bokma deBoer). Tr. Marie K. Pidgeon. Lippincott, 1936.

Andries. Viking, 1942; *a.k.a. Andries: Edited by S. H. Burton*. Longmans, 1959.

Angel's Alphabet. Viking, 1950.

Beggars' Penny; by Catherine C. Coblentz. Longmans, 1943.

Bells of Leyden Sing; by Catherine C. Coblentz. Longmans, 1944.

Bennie and the New Baby. Constable, 1964.

Borrowed House. Farrar, 1975.

(tr.) *Bruno*; by Achim Börger. il. Ronald Himler. Morrow, 1975.

Burro of Burnegat Road; by Delia Goetz. Harcourt, 1945.

Canadian Summer. Viking, 1948.

(tr.) *Corso the Donkey*; by Pothast Gimbery. il. Elly Beek. Dutton, 1963.

Cottage at Bantry Bay. Viking, 1938.

(tr.) *Curse of Laguna Grande*. by Siny R. Van Iterson. Morrow, 1973.

Day on Skates: The Story of a Dutch Picnic. Harper, 1934.

Francie on the Run. Viking, 1939.

Friendly Gables. Viking, 1960.

Gerrit and the Organ. Viking, 1943.

Hans Brinker: Or, The Silver Skates; by Mary M. Dodge. World, 1946.

(tr.) *In the Spell of the Past*; by Siny R. VanIterson. Morrow, 1975.

Jeremy Bear. Constable, 1963.

(tr.) *Kasimir*; by Achim Börger. Morrow, 1976.

Kersti and St. Nicholas. Viking, 1940.

King Oberon's Forest. il. Brigid Marlin. Viking, 1957.

Little Men; by Louisa M. Alcott. World, 1950.

Little Old Bear. Viking, 1962.

Little Women; by Louisa M. Alcott. World, 1946.

(tr.) *Marian and Marion*; by J. M. Selleger-Elout. il. B. Midderigh-Bokhorst. Viking, 1949.

Mitchells. Viking, 1945.

Mogo's Flute. il. Robin Jacques. Viking, 1966.

New Baby Is Lost. Constable, 1964.

Patsy and the Pup. Viking, 1950.

Pegreen. Viking, 1941.

Penengro. Farrar, 1972.

Rainbow Book of Bible Stories: The Old Testament and the New Testament; from the *Bible*, edited by May L. Becker. World, 1948.

Rufus Round and Round. il. Joanna Worth. Longmans, 1973.

(tr.) *Smugglers of Buenaventura*; by Siny R. VanIterson. Morrow, 1974.

Stryd Voor Een Molen; by Jan Den Tex. n. p., 1952.

(tr.) *Tilio: A Boy of Papua*; by Rudolf Vorrhoeve. Lippincott, 1937.

Willow Brook Farm; by Katherine D. Christ. Heath, 1948.

Winged Watchman. Farrar, 1962.

MEDIA

Cottage at Bantry Bay. (BB, TB).

Francie on the Run. (TB).

Mogo's Flute. (TB).

Winged Watchman. (BB).

EXHIBITIONS

DeKuyl Gallery, 1964. (Bilthoven, Netherlands).

Den Arts Gallery, 1974. (Ottawa, Canada).

Difas Gallery, 1964. (Geneva, Switzerland).

Montreal Museum of Fine Arts, 1957. (Montreal, Canada).

Painters Gallery, 1953. (Dublin, Ireland).

Royal Academy, 1961, 1977. (London, England).

Van Der Straeten Gallery, 1973. (New York, New York).

COLLECTIONS

deGrummond Collection, University of Southern Mississippi. (Hattiesburg, Mississippi).

Kerlan Collection, University of Minnesota. (Minneapolis, Minnesota).

May Massee Collection, Emporia State College. (Emporia, Kansas).

Special Collections, University Research Library, University of California. (Los Angeles, California).

BACKGROUND READING

Commire. *Something about the Author*.

Contemporary Authors.

Kingman. *Illustrators of Children's Books, 1957-1966*.

Kingman. *Illustrators of Children's Books, 1967-1976*.

Kirkpatrick. *Twentieth Century Children's Writers*.

Kunitz. *Junior Book of Authors, Second Edition Revised*.

Mahony. *Illustrators of Children's Books, 1744-1945*.

Miller. *Illustrators of Children's Books, 1946-1956*.

Van Stockum, H. "Birthdays in an Artist's Family." *Horn Book*, November 1944.

Van Stockum, H. "Holland during Invasion." *Horn Book*, January 1946.

Van Stockum, H. "Through an Illustrator's Eyes." *Horn Book*, May 1944.

Ward. *Authors of Books for Young People, Second Edition*.

Young Wings. *Writing Books for Boys and Girls*.

+LYND KENDALL WARD, 1905-
author-illustrator

AWARDS

America's Ethan Allen. Caldecott Honor Book, 1950.

Biggest Bear. Caldecott Medal Book, 1953.

(*Bright Island*. Newbery Honor Book, 1938.)

(*Cat Who Went to Heaven*. Newbery Medal Book, 1931.)

(*Fog Magic*. Newbery Honor Book, 1944.)

(*Johnny Tremain*. Newbery Medal Book, 1944.)

(*Little Blacknose*. Newbery Honor Book, 1930.)

(*Railroad to Freedom*. Newbery Honor Book, 1933.)

AWARDS (cont'd)

(*Runner of the Mountain Tops*. Newbery Honor Book, 1940.)

(*Spice and the Devil's Cave*. Newbery Honor Book, 1931.)

BIBLIOGRAPHY

Alaska Gold Rush; by May McNeer. Random, 1960.

Almanac for Moderns; by Donald C. Peatti. Random, 1935.

American Indian Story; by May McNeer. Farrar, 1963.

America's Abraham Lincoln; by May McNeer. Houghton, 1957.

America's Ethan Allen; by Stewart H. Holbrook. Houghton, 1949.

America's Mark Twain; by May McNeer. Houghton, 1962.

America's Paul Revere; by Esther Forbes. Houghton, 1946.

America's Robert E. Lee; by Henry S. Commager. Houghton, 1951.

Armed with Courage; with May McNeer. Abingdon, 1957.

Ballad of Reading Gaol; by Oscar Wilde. Macy-Masius, 1928.

Begging Deer: And Other Stories of Japanese Children; by Dorothy Rowe. Macmillan, 1928.

Beowulf. Heritage, 1939.

Bible Readings for Boys and Girls: Selected Passages from the Revised Standard Version of the Holy Bible. Nelson, 1959.

Biggest Bear. Houghton, 1952; *a.k.a. Biggest Baer*. Scholastic, 1965.

Birds against Men; by Louis Halle. Viking, 1938.

Black Sombrero; by Nanda Ward. Pelligrini, 1952.

Book of Hours; by Donald C. Peatti. Putnam, 1937.

Brady; by Jean Fritz. Coward, 1960.

Bright Island; by Mabel L. Robinson. Random, 1937.

Cadaver of Gideon Wyck; by Alexander Laing. Farrar, 1934.

California Gold Rush; by May McNeer. Random, 1950.

Can Prayer Be Answered?; by Mary Austin. Farrar, 1934.

Canadian Story; by May McNeer. Farrar, 1958.

Cat Who Went to Heaven; by Elizabeth Coatsworth. Macmillan, 1930; new edition, 1958.

Children of the New Forest; by Frederick Marryat, edited by May McNeer. Macmillan, 1930.

Ching-Li and the Dragons; by Alice Howard. Macmillan, 1931.

Christmas Poem; by Thomas Mann. Tr. Henny Hart. Equinox, 1932.

Cloister and the Hearth; by Charles Reade. Limited Editions, 1932. (2 vols.).

Comte de Monte-Cristo; by Alexandre Dumas. Limited Editions, 1941. (2 vols.).

Conquest of the North and South Poles: Adventures of the Perry and Byrd Expeditions. Random, 1952; *a.k.a. Conquest of the Poles: By Sled and Air*. Hale, 1952.

Czardas; by Jenö Heltai. Houghton, 1932.

Dragon Run; by Carley Dawson. Houghton, 1955.

Dream of the Blue Heron; by Victor Barnouw. Delacorte, 1966.

Early Thunder; by Jean Fritz. Coward, 1967.

Edge of April: A Biography of John Burroughs; by Hildegarde H. Smith. Morrow, 1957.

Explorer's Digest; by Leonard Clark. Houghton, 1959.

Faust: A Tragedy; by Johann W. von Goethe. Tr. Alice Raphael. Ballou, 1930.

Five Plays from Shakespeare; by William Shakespeare edited by Katherine Miller. Houghton, 1964.

Flutter of an Eyelid; by Myron Brinig. Farrar, 1933.

Fog Magic; by Julia Sauer. Viking, 1943.

For Whom the Bell Tolls; by Ernest Hemingway. Princeton, 1942.

Frankenstein; by Mary Shelley. Smith, 1934.

From the Eagle's Wing: A Biography of John Muir; by Hildegarde H. Swift. Morrow, 1962.

Gargantua and Pantagruel: The Five Books; by François Rabelais. Tr. Jacques LeClerq. Heritage, 1942.

Gaudenzia: Pride of the Palio; by Marguerite Henry. Rand, 1960; *a.k.a. Wildest Horse in the World*, 1976.

Give Me Freedom; by May McNeer. Abingdon, 1964.

God's Man: A Novel in Woodcuts. Cape, 1929; also in *Storyteller without Words*, below.

Gold Rush; by May McNeer. Grosset, 1944.

Golden Flash; by May McNeer. Viking, 1947.

Green Bough; by William Faulkner. Smith, 1933.

Haunted Omnibus; edited by Alexander K. Laing. Farrar, 1936; *a.k.a. Great Ghost Stories of the World: The Haunted Omnibus*. Garden City, 1939.

Hi, Tom; by Nanda Ward. Hastings, 1962.

High Flying Hat; by Nanda Ward. Farrar, 1956.

Horn That Stopped the Band; by Arthur Parsons. Watts, 1954.

Hot Countries; by Alec Waugh. Farrar, 1930.

House by the Sea; by Hildegarde H. Swift. Harcourt, 1938.

Idylls of the King; by Alfred Tennyson. Limited Editions, 1952.

Impassioned Clay; by Llewelyn Powys. Longmans, 1931.

In Place of Profit: Social Incentives in the Soviet Union; by Henry F. Ward. Scribner, 1933.

Innocent Voyage; by Richard A. W. Hughes. Heritage, 1944.

Jockeys, Crooks and Kings: The Story of Winnie O'Connor's Life as Told to Earl Chapin May; by Winifred S. O'Connor. Cape, 1930.

John Wesley; with May McNeer. Abingdon, 1951.

Johnny Tremain: A Novel for Young and Old; by Esther Forbes. Houghton, 1943. *a.k.a. Johnny Tremain: A Novel for Young and Old, with Suggestions for Reading and Discussion by Ruth M. Stauffer*, 1945.

Kidnapped; by Robert L. Stevenson. Grosset, 1948.

Last Hunt; by Maurice Genevois. Tr. Warre B. Wells. Random, 1940.

Life and Strange Surprizing Adventures of Robinson Crusoe; by Daniel Defoe. Grosset, 1946.

Little Baptiste; by May McNeer. Houghton, 1954.

Little Blacknose: The Story of a Pioneer; by Hildegarde H. Swift. Harcourt, 1929.

Little Red Lighthouse and the Great Gray Bridge; with Hildegarde H. Swift. Harcourt, 1942.

Lola the Bear; by Henry M. Rideout. Duffield, 1928.

Madman's Drum: A Novel in Woodcuts. Cape, 1930; also in *Storyteller without Words*, below.

Man with Four Lives; by William J. Cowen. Farrar, 1934.

Many Mansions from the Bible: Interpretations; by Jessie O. Jones. Viking, 1947.

Martin Luther; with May McNeer. Abingdon, 1953.

Master of Ballantrae; by Robert L. Stevenson. Heritage, 1965.

Mexican Story; by May McNeer. Farrar, 1953.

Midsummer Night; by Carl Wilhelmson. Farrar, 1953.

Miserables; by Victor Hugo. Tr. Lascelles Wraxall. Limited Editions, 1938 (5 vols.); Heritage, 1960. (2 vols.).

Mr. Wicker's Window; by Carley Dawson. Houghton, 1952.

Moriae Enocomium: Or, The Praise of Folly; by Desiderius Erasmus. Limited Editions, 1943.

"Most Women..."; by Alec Waugh. Farrar, 1931.

Motives of Nicholas Holtz; by Thomas Painter and Alexander K. Laing. Farrar, 1936.

My Friend Mac: The Story of Little Baptiste and the Moose; by May McNeer. Houghton, 1960.

Nic of the Woods. Houghton, 1965.

Nocturnes; by Thomas Mann. Tr. H. T. Lowe-Porter. Equinox, 1934.

North Star Shining: A Pictorial History of the American Negro; by Hildegarde H. Swift. Morrow, 1947.

Now That the Gods Are Dead; by Llewelyn Powys. Equinox, 1932.

One of Us: The Story of John Reed; by Granville Hicks. Equinox, 1935.

Palomino Boy; by Donald L. Emblem and Betty J. Mitchell. Viking, 1948.

Peculiar Magic; by Annabel and Edgar Johnson. Houghton, 1965.

Porpoise of Pirate Bay; by F. Martin Howard. Random, 1938.

Prelude to a Million Years: A Book of Wood Engravings. Equinox, 1933; also in *Storyteller without Words*, below.

Primer of Economics; by Stuart Chase. Random, 1941.

Prince Bantam: Being the Adventures of Yositsune and His Faithful Henchman Great Benkei of the Western Pagoda; with May McNeer. Macmillan, 1929.

Pursuer; by Louis Golding. Farrar, 1936.

Railroad to Freedom; by Hildegarde Swift. Harcourt, 1932.

Reunion in Poland; by Jean Karsavina. International, 1945.

Rights of Man; by Thomas Paine. Heritage, 1961.

Runner of the Mountain Tops: The Life of Louis Agassiz; by Mabel L. Robinson. Random, 1939.

Sangamon; by Edgar L. Masters. Farrar, 1942.

Santiago; by Ann N. Clark. Viking, 1955.

Secret of the Silver Reindeer; by Lee Kingman. Doubleday, 1968.

Sign of the Seven Seas; by Carley Dawson. Houghton, 1954.

Silver Pony: A Story in Pictures. Houghton, 1973.

Sir Bob; by Salvador DeMadariaga. Harper, 1930.

Song without Words: A Book of Engravings on Wood. Random, 1936; also in *Storyteller without Words*, below.

Southern Mail; by Antoine de Saint-Exupéry. Tr. Stuart Gilbert. Smith, 1933.

Spice and the Devil's Cave; by Agnes D. Hewes. Knopf, 1930.

BIBLIOGRAPHY (cont'd)

Stallion; by Margarite Steen. Little, 1932.

Stallion from the North; by Thomas Rourke, *pseud.* (Daniel J. Clifton). Farrar, 1932.

Stop Tim! The Tale of a Car; with May McNeer. Farrar, 1930.

Stories from the Bible: Retold; by Alvin Tresselt. Abingdon, 1973.

Story of George Washington; by May McNeer. Abingdon, 1973.

Story of Odysseus; by Homer. Tr. W. H. D. Rouse. Modern Age, 1937.

Story of Siegfried; by Richard Wagner, arranged by Angela Diller. Smith, 1931.

Story of Ulysses S. Grant; by Jeanette C. Nolan. Grosset, 1952.

Storyteller without Words: The Wood Engravings of Lynd Ward. Abrams, 1974. (Includes *God's Man*, *Madman's Drum*, *Prelude to a Million Years*, *Song without Words*, *Vertigo*, and *Wild Pilgrimage*, issued separately, above and below.)

Stranger in the Pines; by May McNeer. Houghton, 1971.

Strong Wings; by Mabel L. Robinson. Random, 1951.

Swiss Family Robinson; by Johann Wysss, edited by William H. G. Kingston. il. with Lee Gregori. Grosset, 1949.

Tales of Wonder and Magnificence; from the *Arabian Nights*, selected and edited by Padraic Colum. Macmillan, 1953.

Thirteen Such Years; by Alec Waugh. Farrar, 1932.

Topgallant: A Herring Gull; by Marjorie Medary. Random, 1935.

Traveling Ships: Stories of Chinese Children; by Dorothy Rowe. Macmillan, 1929.

Treasure Island; by Robert L. Stevenson. American Education, 1970.

Treasure of Topo-el-Bampo; by Scott O'Dell. Houghton, 1972.

Up a Crooked River; by May McNeer. Viking, 1952.

Vertigo: A Novel in Woodcuts. Random, 1937; also in *Storyteller without Words*, above.

Waif Maid; by May McNeer. Macmillan, 1930.

War Chief of the Seminoles; by May McNeer. Random, 1954; *a.k.a. Osceola and the Seminole War*. Hale, 19?.

White Sparrow; by Padraic Colum. Macmillan, 1933.

Wild Pilgrimage. Smith, 1932; also in *Storyteller without Words*, above.

Wolf of Lambs Lane; by May McNeer. Houghton, 1967.

Wonder Flights of Long Ago; edited by Mary E. Barry and Paul Hanna. Appleton, 1930.

Writings of Thomas Jefferson; by Thomas Jefferson. Limited Editions, 1967.

MEDIA

Biggest Bear. (BB, TB); Weston Woods Studios, 1968 (FSS); also in Weston Woods Studios Set No. 4, 1968 (FSS).

Little Red Lighthouse. (BB); Weston Woods Studios, 1956 (F), 1965 (FSS); also in Weston Woods Studios Set No. 3, 1965 (FSS); *a.k.a. Pequeño Faro Rojo y el Gran Puente Gris*. Weston Woods Studios, 1960 (F).

Silver Pony. Weston Woods Studios, 1975 (FSS).

EXHIBITIONS

National Academy of Design, 19?. (New York, New York).

New York World's Fair, 1939. (New York, New York).

COLLECTIONS

Archives of American Art. (Detroit, Michigan).

deGrummond Collection, University of Southern Mississippi. (Hattiesburg, Mississippi).

Department of Rare Books and Manuscripts, Boston Public Library. (Boston, Massachusetts).

Free Library of Philadelphia. (Philadelphia, Pennsylvania).

Gary Public Library. (Gary, Indiana).

Kent and Wickey Collections, Arents Research Library, Syracuse University. (Syracuse, New York).

Kerlan Collection, University of Minnesota. (Minneapolis, Minnesota).

May Massee Collection, Emporia State College. (Emporia, Kansas).

Metropolitan Museum of Art. (New York, New York).

Newark Museum. (Newark, New Jersey).

Rare Book and Manuscript Library, Columbia University. (New York, New York).

University of Iowa Library. (Iowa City, Iowa).

Victoria and Albert Museum. (London, England).

BACKGROUND READING

Bannon, L. "Artist's Choice." *Horn Book*, April 1961.

Burke. *American Authors and Books, 1640 to the Present Day*.

Commire. *Something about the Author*.

Contemporary Authors.

DeMontreville. *Fourth Book of Junior Authors and Illustrators*.

Ellis. *Book Illustration*.

George, C. "Master Printer." *American Artist*, May 1976.

Hoffman. *Authors and Illustrators of Children's Books*.

Hopkins. *Books Are by People*.

Kingman. *Illustrators of Children's Books, 1957-1966*.

Kingman. *Illustrators of Children's Books, 1967-1976*.

Klemin. *Illustrated Book: Its Art and Craft*.

Kunitz. *Junior Book of Authors*.

Kunitz. *Junior Book of Authors, Second Edition Revised*.

Lynd Ward and May McNeer. Profiles in Literature, 1974 (VT).

Mahony. *Contemporary Illustrators of Children's Books*.

Mahony. *Illustrators of Children's Books, 1744-1945*.

Miller. *Caldecott Medal Books, 1938-1957*.

Miller. *Illustrators of Children's Books, 1946-1956*.

Painter, H. "Lynd Ward: Artist, Writer, Scholar." *Elementary English*, November 1962.

Pitz, H. "Illustrations of Lynd Ward." *American Artist*, March 1955.

Smaridge. *Famous Literary Teams for Young People*.

Truesdell, W. "Woodcuts of Lynd Ward." *Print Connoisseur*, October 1930.

Ward. *Authors of Books for Young People, Second Edition*.

Ward. *Illustrators of Books for Young People, Second Edition*.

Ward, L. "Book Artist, Today and Tomorrow." *Horn Book*, May 1944.

Ward, L. "Book Artist, Today and Tomorrow and the Twenty-Five Years." *Horn Book*, September 1949.

Ward, L. "Building a Lincoln Book." *American Artist*, February 1959.

Ward, L. "Contemporary Book Illustration." *Horn Book*, February 1930.

Ward, L. "Doing a Book in Lithography." *Horn Book*, February 1964.

Ward, L. "Graphic Arts and Children's Books." *Horn Book*, April 1956.

Ward, L. "Illustrating a Book in Lithography." *American Artist*, November 1965.

Ward, L. "When I Illustrate a Book." *Instructor*, November 1953.

MARY HAYS WEIK, 1898-
author

AWARDS

Jazz Man. Newbery Honor Book, 1967.

BIBLIOGRAPHY

Adventure: A Book of Verse. Badger, 1919.

Atoms on Campus. Committee to End Radiological Hazards, 1969.

Community Centers for Living: A New Kind of Adult Education to Lessen the Tensions of Present-Day Life. American Registry of World Citizens, 1954.

Hot Spots in Prospect for America: Nuclear Plans for Chicago and the Connecticut River Valley. Committee to End Radiological Hazards, 1967.

House at Cherry Hill. il. (Vladimir) Bobri. Knopf, 1958.

House on Liberty Street. il. Ann Grifalconi. Atheneum, 1972.

How Safe Are "Plowshare" Atomic Blasts? Committee to End Radiological Hazards, 1967.

How to Use Government Statistics to Find Local Health Conditions. Committee to End Radiological Hazards, 1967.

Jazz Man. il. Ann Grifalconi. Atheneum, 1966.

Let's Talk It Over: A Handbook for Discussion Groups on U.N. Charter Reform. American Federation of World Citizens, 1955.

Montrose Catastrophe: Outbreak of Cancer Deaths Downwind from Indian Point Power Plant. Committee to End Radiological Hazards, 1969.

Parliament for Man: A Handbook for Discussion Groups on U.N. Charter Reform. American Federation of World Citizens, 1959.

Pollution of Waterways by Atomic Wastes. Committee to End Radiological Hazards, 1967.

Report to the People: On the Need to Curb Abuses of the U.S. Public Hearing System, and Notes on Effects of Atomic Development Observed in Other Countries. Committee to End Radiological Hazards, 1971.

Scarlet Thread: A Group of One-Act Plays for Young People. il. Barbara Remington. Atheneum, 1968.

Search for World Community. American Federation of World Citizens, 1955.

Should a Nuclear Reactor Be Allowed on a College Campus? Committee to End Radiological Hazards, 1971.

BIBLIOGRAPHY (cont'd)

Story Nobody Prints: Health Conditions around U.S. Atomic Plants and What the Citizen Can Do about It. Committee to End Radiological Hazards, 1965; second edition, 1968.

Tampering with the Food We Eat. Committee to End Radiological Hazards, 1967.

Time-Bomb at Indian Point. Committee to End Radiological Hazards, 1966.

Towards a New World: A Bibliography of United Nations and World Affairs. American Federation of World Citizens, 1955.

U.N. Charter for Man?; with John Grifalconi. American Federation of World Citizens, 1954.

United Nations Force to Guard World Peace: An Analysis of the Safeguards Needed in Its Control. American Federation of World Citizens, 1958.

Weekend New York Almost Lost. Committee to End Radiological Hazards, 1967.

World Set Free. American Registry of World Citizens, 1954.

Your Community and the World: Building Responsible Citizens for the New World Community. American Registry of World Citizens, 1955.

COLLECTIONS

Kerlan Collection, University of Minnesota. (Minneapolis, Minnesota).

BACKGROUND READING

Commire. *Something about the Author*.

Contemporary Authors.

Hopkins. *More Books by More People*.

Mayo, A. "Defusing the Atomic Establishment." *MS. Magazine*, October 1973.

Thompson. *Indiana Authors, 1917-1966*.

+ANN YEZNER WEIL, 1908-1969
author

AWARDS

Red Sails to Capri. Newbery Honor Book, 1953.

BIBLIOGRAPHY

Animal Families. il. Roger Vernam. Greenberg, 1946.

Betsy Ross: Girl of Old Philadelphia. il. Sandra James. Bobbs, 1954; also il. Al Fiorentino. Bobbs, 1961.

Eleanor Roosevelt: Courageous Girl. il. Gray Morrow. Bobbs, 1965.

Franklin Roosevelt: Boy of the Four Freedoms. il. Syd Browne. Bobbs, 1947; also il. Robert Doremus, 1962.

John Phillip Sousa: Marching Boy. il. Katherine Sampson. Bobbs, 1959.

John Quincy Adams: Boy Patriot. il. Paul Laune. Bobbs, 1945; also il. William Moyers, 1963.

My Dear Patsy: A Novel of Jefferson's Daughter. il. Jessie Robinson. Bobbs, 1941.

Pussycat's Breakfast. il. Mary Barton. Greenberg, 1944.

Red Sails to Capri. il. Charles B. Falls. Viking, 1952.

Silver Fawn. il. E. Leon. Bobbs, 1939.

Very First Day. il. Jessie Robinson. Appleton, 1946.

MEDIA

Franklin Roosevelt. (BB).

John Quincy Adams. (BB).

COLLECTIONS

deGrummond Collection, University of Southern Mississippi. (Hattiesburg, Mississippi).

May Massee Collection, Emporia State College. (Emporia, Kansas).

BACKGROUND READING

Commire. *Something about the Author*.

Contemporary Authors.

Thompson. *Indiana Authors, 1917-1966*.

LEONARD JOSEPH WEISGARD, 1916-
author-illustrator
pseudonym Adam Green

AWARDS

(*Courage of Sarah Noble*. Newbery Honor Book, 1955.)

Little Island. Caldecott Medal Book, 1947.

Little Lost Lamb. Caldecott Honor Book, 1946.

Rain Drop Splash. Caldecott Honor Book, 1947.

(*Secret River*. Newbery Honor Book, 1956.)

BIBLIOGRAPHY

as Adam Green:

Baby's Playthings. McLoughlin, 1956.

Funny Bunny Factory. Grosset, 1950.

Just Like Me. Treasure, 1954.

Let's Play. World, 1951.

Let's Play Train. Treasure, 1953.

Most Beautiful Tree in the World. Wonder, 1956.

Who Dreams of Cheese? Scribner, 1950.

as Leonard Weisgard:

Abner's Cabin; by Alf Evers. Watts, 1957.

Adam and the Golden Cock; by Alice Dalgliesh. Scribner, 1959.

Adult's Guide to My Book of Prayer; by Hyman Chanover. United Synagogue Commission, 1959.

Alice's Adventures in Wonderland (and) Through the Looking-Glass; by Lewis Carroll, *pseud.* (Charles L. Dodgson). Harper, 1949.

Americans Every One; by Lavinia Davis. Doubleday, 1942.

And It Came to Pass; by Jean Slaughter. Macmillan, 1971.

Athenians in the Classical Period. Coward, 1963.

Baby Elephant; by Sesyle Joslin. Harcourt, 1960.

Baby Elephant and the Secret Wishes; by Sesyle Joslin. Harcourt, 1962.

Baby Elephant Goes to China; by Sesyle Joslin. Harcourt, 1963.

Baby Elephant's Baby Book; by Sesyle Joslin. Harcourt, 1964.

Baby Elephant's Trunk; by Sesyle Joslin. Harcourt, 1961.

Beach before Breakfast; by Maxine Kumin. Putnam, 1964.

Beginnings of Cities: Re-Creation in Pictures and Text of Mesopotamian Life, from Farming to Early City Building. Coward, 1968.

Beloved Friend; by Marguerite Vance. Holt, 1963.

Big Book of Train Stories. Grosset, 1955.

Big Dog, Little Dog; by Margaret W. Brown. Doubleday, 1943.

Big Treasure Book of Fairy Tales Retold; by Evelyn Andreas. Grosset, 1954.

Big Treasure Book of Nursery Tales Retold; by Evelyn Andreas. Grosset, 1954.

Boat That Mooed; by Christopher Fry. Macmillan, 1965.

Book about God; by Florence M. Fitch. Lothrop, 1953.

Brave Baby Elephant; by Sesyle Joslin. Harcourt, 1960.

Bucky Bear Who Would Not Take His Nap; by Elaine Wayne. Lothrop, 1944.

Calf, Goodnight; by Nancy Jewell. Harper, 1973.

Child Jesus; by Florence M. Fitch. Lothrop, 1955.

Cinderella, Retold. Garden City, 1939.

City Country ABC; by Morrell Gipson. Garden City, 1946.

City Noisy Book; by Margaret W. Brown. Scott, 1946.

Clean Pig. Scribner, 1952.

Comical Tragedy or Tragical Comedy of Punch and Judy; adapted by Margaret W. Brown. Scott, 1940.

Country Noisy Book; by Margaret W. Brown. Scott, 1940.

Courage of Sarah Noble; by Alice Dalgliesh. Scribner, 1954.

Cozy Hour Storybook; by Nora Kramer. Random, 1960.

Cynthia and the Unicorn; by Jean T. Freeman. Norton, 1967.

Dark Wood of the Golden Birds; by Margaret W. Brown. Harper, 1950.

Deer in the Snow; by Miriam Schlein. Abelard, 1956.

Do You Want to Hear a Secret?; by Sylvia Redman. Lothrop, 1960.

Doctor Proctor and Mrs. Merriweather; by Irma S. Black. Whitman, 1971.

Dorinda; by Elizabeth Howard. Lothrop, 1944.

Down Huckleberry Hill. Scribner, 1947.

Elephant's Child; by Rudyard Kipling. Garden City, 1945.

Fairy Tales; by Hans C. Andersen. Doubleday, 1958.

Family Mother Goose; from Mother Goose. Harper, 1951. (3 vols.).

Favorite Fairy Tales Told in Norway: Retold from Norse Folklore; by Virginia Haviland. Little, 1961.

Favorite Poems Old and New; by Helen Ferris. Doubleday, 1957.

First Days of the World; by Gerald Ames and Rose Wyler. Harper, 1958; also in *How Things Began*, below.

First Doll in the World; by Lee Pape. Lothrop, 1961.

First Farmers in the New Stone Age. Coward, 1966.

First People in the World; by Gerald Ames and Rose Wyler. Harper, 1958; also in *How Things Began*, below.

French Are Coming; by Wilma P. Hays. Holt, 1965.

Giving Away Suzanne; by Lois Duncan, *pseud.* (Lois S. Arquette.) Dodd, 1963.

BIBLIOGRAPHY (cont'd)

as Leonard Weisgard (cont'd):

Golden Bunny and 17 Other Stories; by Margaret W. Brown. Simon, 1953.

Golden Egg Book; by Margaret W. Brown. Simon, 1947.

Good Hunting, Little Indian; by Peggy Parish. Scott, 1962.

Grab Bag: Stories for Each and Every One; by Lavinia Davis and Marjorie Fischer. Doubleday, 1941.

Grimm's Fairy Tales; by Jacob and Wilhelm Grimm. Garden City, 1954.

Growing Time; by Sandol S. Warburg. Houghton, 1969.

Gulliver's Travels; by Jonathan Swift. Grosset, 1954.

Hailstones and Halibut Bones: Adventures in Color; by Mary O'Neill. Doubleday, 1961.

Half-as-Big and the Tiger; by Bernice Frankel. Watts, 1961.

Hawaiian Myths of the Earth, Sea and Sky; by Vivian L. Thompson. Holiday, 1966.

Heidi; by Johanna Spyri. World, 1946.

High Trail; by Vivian Breck, *pseud.* (Vivian Breckenfield). Doubleday, 1948.

How the Rhinoceros Got His Skin; by Rudyard Kipling. Walker, 1974.

How Things Began; by Gerald Ames and Rose Wyler. Blackie, 1969. (Issued separately as *First Days of the World* and *First People of the World*, above.)

Important Book; by Margaret W. Brown. Harper, 1949.

Indian, Indian; by Charlotte Zolotow. Simon, 1952.

Indoor Noisy Book; by Margaret W. Brown. Scott, 1942.

Jesus Christ, Son of God; by Mary L. Ellis. Knox, 1967.

Journey to Jericho; by Scott O'Dell. Houghton, 1969.

Just for Fun: Humorous Stories and Poems; by Alice Hazeltine and Elva S. Smith. Lothrop, 1948.

Like Nothing At All; by Aileen Fisher. Crowell, 1962.

Little Chicken; by Margaret W. Brown. Harper, 1943.

Little Eskimo; by Charlotte Jackson. Simon, 1952.

Little Frightened Tiger; by Golden MacDonald, *pseud.* (Margaret W. Brown). Doubleday, 1953.

Little Island; by Golden MacDonald, *pseud.* (Margaret W. Brown). Doubleday, 1946.

Little Joe; by Dorothy Clark. Lothrop, 1940.

Little Lost Lamb; by Golden MacDonald, *pseud.* (Margaret W. Brown). Doubleday, 1945.

Little Lost Squirrel; by Alvin Tresselt. Grosset, 1950.

Little Woodcock; by Berniece Freschet. Scribner, 1967.

Look at the Moon; by May Garelick. Scott, 1969.

Lost Prince; by Frances H. Burnett. Lippincott, 1967.

Louis of New Orleans; by Frances Cavanah. McKay, 1941.

Macmillan Life-Science Readers; by John D. Barnard, et al. Macmillan, 1959. (9 vols.).

Magic Ringlet; by Konstantin Paustovskii. Tr. Thomas P. Whitney. Scott, 1971.

McCall's Read-Me-a-Story Book; by Margaret Bevans. Putnam, 1961.

Midnight Alarm: The Story of Paul Revere's Ride; by Mary K. Phelan. Crowell, 1968.

Mr. Peaceable Paints. Scribner, 1956.

Mrs. Goose's Green Trailer; by Miriam C. Potter. Wonder, 1956.

Mrs. Mallard's Ducklings; by Celia Delafield. Lothrop, 1946.

Mouse and the Lion; by Eve Titus. Parents, 1962.

My Book of Prayer; by Hyman Chanover. United Synagogue Commission, 1959.

My First Picture Book. Grosset, 1953.

Nails to Nickels: The Story of American Coins, Old and New; by Elizabeth A. Campbell. Little, 1960.

Nannabah's Friend; by Mary Perrine. Houghton, 1970.

New Wizard of Oz; by Frank L. Baum. Doubleday, 1955.

Nibble, Nibble: Poems for Children; by Margaret W. Brown. Scott, 1959.

Night and Day; by Margaret W. Brown. Harper, 1942.

Night before Christmas; by Clement C. Moore. Grosset, 1949.

Noisy Bird Book; by Margaret W. Brown. also il. with Audubon prints. Scott, 1943.

Noisy Book; by Margaret W. Brown. Scott, 1939.

Noon Balloon; by Margaret W. Brown. Harper, 1952.

On the Sand Dune; by Doris Orgel. Harper, 1968.

Pedro of Santa Fe; by Frances Cavanah. McKay, 1941.

Pelican Here, Pelican There. Scribner, 1948.

Penguin's Way; by Joanna Jonston. Doubleday, 1962.

Peter Rabbit; by Beatrix Potter. Grosset, 1955.

Peter's Brownstone House; by Hila Colman. Morrow, 1963.

Pick the Vegetables; by Esther Reno. Lothrop, 1944.

Picture Book of Musical Instruments; by Marion Lacey. Lothrop, 1942.

Pilgrim Thanksgiving; by Wilma P. Hays. Coward, 1955.

Plymouth Thanksgiving. Doubleday, 1967.

Poodle and the Sheep; by Margaret W. Brown. Dutton, 1941.

Pup Called Cinderella; by Esther Reno. Bobbs, 1939.

Pussy Willow; by Margaret W. Brown. Simon, 1951.

Quiet Noisy Book; by Margaret W. Brown. Harper, 1950.

Rabbit Story; by Alvin Tresselt. Lothrop, 1957.

Raccoon and Mrs. McGinnis; by Patricia M. Martin. Putnam, 1961.

Rain Drop Splash; by Alvin Tresselt. Lothrop, 1946.

Red Light, Green Light; by Golden MacDonald, *pseud.* (Margaret W. Brown). Doubleday, 1944.

Round the Afternoon; by Charlotte Jackson. Dodd, 1946.

Salt Boy; by Mary Perrine. Houghton, 1968.

Scarab for Luck: A Story of Ancient Egypt; by Enid L. Meadowcroft. Crowell, 1964.

Seashore Noisy Book; by Margaret W. Brown. Scott, 1941.

Secret River; by Majorie K. Rawlings. Scribner, 1955.

See along the Shore; by Millicent Selsam. Harper, 1956.

Señor Baby Elephant; by Sesyle Joslin. Harcourt, 1962.

Shepherdess of France: Remembrances of Jeanne D'Arc; by John Masefield. Coward, 1969.

Silly Willy Nilly. Scribner, 1953.

Sir Kevin of Devon; by Adelaide Holl. Lothrop, 1963.

Snowflake and the Starfish; by Robert Nathan. Knopf, 1959.

Something for Now: Something for Later; by Miriam Schlein. Harper, 1956.

Son of God: Adapted from The Son of God by Edric Weld and William Sydor; by Mary L. Ellis. Seabury, 1957.

Stories of Love; by Alice Hazeltine and Elva S. Smith. Lothrop, 1951.

Story of Valentine; by Wilma P. Hays. Coward, 1956.

SuAn; by Doris Johnson. Follett, 1968.

Suki: The Siamese Pussy. Nelson, 1937.

Summer Noisy Book; by Margaret W. Brown. Harper, 1951.

Susie Is a Kitten; by Nettie King. Garden City, 1945.

Sylvester Jones and the Voice in the Forest; by Patricia M. Martin. Lothrop, 1958.

Tales from Shakespeare; by Charles and Mary Lamb. Grosset, 1955.

Three and Domingo; by Marguerite Bro. Doubleday, 1953.

Through the Harbor from Everywhere; by Irmengarde Eberle. Bobbs, 1938.

Timid Timothy: The Kitten Who Learned to Be Brave; by Gweneira Williams. Scott, 1944.

Toby Tyler; by James Kaler, *pseud.* (James K. Otis). Doubleday, 1961.

Tom Sawyer; by Mark Twain, *pseud.* (Samuel L. Clemens). American Education, 1970.

Treasures to See: A Museum Picture-Book. Harcourt, 1956.

Try and Catch Me; by Nancy Jewell. Harper, 1972.

Try on a Shoe; by Jane Moncure. Child's World, 1973.

Under the Greenwood Tree: Songs from the Plays; by William Shakespeare, selected by Julia L. Reynolds. Oxford, 1940.

Valentine Cat; by Clyde R. Bulla. Crowell, 1959.

Wake Up and Goodnight; by Charlotte Zolotow. Harper, 1971.

Watch That Watch; by Hila Colman. Morrow, 1962.

Water-Carrier's Secrets; by Maria Chambers. Oxford, 1942.

Whale's Way; by Joanna Johnston. Doubleday, 1965.

What Is for My Birthday?; by Isabel and Frederick Eberstadt. Little, 1961.

What Makes a Bird a Bird?; by May Garelick. Follett, 1969.

Wheels; by Charlotte Jackson. Simon, 1952.

When a Boy Goes to Bed at Night; by Faith McNulty. Knopf, 1962.

When a Boy Wakes Up in the Morning; by Faith McNulty. Knopf, 1962.

When I Go to the Moon; by Claudia Lewis. Macmillan, 1961.

Where Did Tuffy Hide?; by Isabel and Frederick Eberstadt. Little, 1957.

Where Does the Butterfly Go When It Rains?; by May Garelick. Scott, 1961.

Whistle for the Train; by Golden MacDonald, *pseud.* (Margaret W. Brown). Doubleday, 1956.

White Bird; by Clyde R. Bulla. Crowell, 1966.

Who Ever Heard of Kangaroo Eggs?; by Samuel Vaughan. Doubleday, 1957.

Who Is at the Door?; by Isabel and Frederick Eberstadt. Little, 1959.

BIBLIOGRAPHY (cont'd)

as Leonard Weisgard (cont'd):

Whose Little Bird Am I? Crowell, 1944.

Willa; by Ruth Franchere. Crowell, 1958.

Would You Like to Be a Monkey? Crowell, 1945.

Wreath of Christmas Legends; by Phyllis McGinley. Macmillan, 1967.

MEDIA

Little Island. Weston Woods Studios, 1964 (F), 1965 (FSS); also in Weston Woods Studios Set No. 8, 1965 (FSS).

Plymouth Thanksgiving. (BB).

Rain Drop Splash. Weston Woods Studios, 1968 (FSS).

Where Does the Butterfly Go When It Rains? Weston Woods Studio, 1968 (FSS); also in Weston Woods Studios Set No. 22, 1968 (FSS).

EXHIBITIONS   EXHIBITIONS

Metropolitan Museum of Art, 19?. (New York, New York).

Museum of Modern Art, 19?. (New York, New York).

Waterbury Museum, 19?. (Waterbury, Massachusetts).

Worcester Museum, 19?. (Worcester, Massachusetts).

COLLECTIONS

Kerlan Collection, University of Minnesota. (Minneapolis, Minnesota).

Milwaukee Public Library. (Milwaukee, Wisconsin).

Special Collections, University Research Library, University of California. (Los Angeles, California).

BACKGROUND READING

Commire. *Something about the Author*.

Contemporary Authors.

Floethe, R. "Artist's Choice." *Horn Book*, April 1962.

Hopkins. *Books Are by People*.

Jones, E. "Artist's Choice." *Horn Book*, November 1950.

Kingman. *Illustrators of Children's Books, 1957-1966*.

Kingman. *Illustrators of Children's Books, 1967-1976*.

Kunitz. *Junior Book of Authors, Second Edition Revised*.

Mahony. *Illustrators of Children's Books, 1744-1945*.

Miller. *Caldecott Medal Books, 1938-1957*.

Miller. *Illustrators of Children's Books, 1946-1956*.

Painter, H. "Leonard Weisgard: Exponent of Beauty." *Elementary English*, October 1970.

Ward. *Authors of Books for Young People, Second Edition*.

Ward. *Illustrators of Books for Young People, Second Edition*.

Weisgard, L. "Influences and Applications." *Horn Book*, August 1964.

+CHRISTINE GOUTIERE WESTON, 1904-
author

AWARDS

Bhimsa. Newbery Honor Book, 1946.

BIBLIOGRAPHY

Afghanistan. Scribner, 1962.

Be Thou the Bride. Scribner, 1940.

Bhimsa, the Dancing Bear. il. Roger Duvoisin. Scribner, 1945.

Ceylon. il. photographs Rafael Palacios. Scribner, 1960.

Dark Wood. Scribner, 1946.

Devil's Foot. Scribner, 1942. (Announced as *Pigeon Hill*.)

Hoopoe. Harper, 1970.

Indigo. Scribner, 1943.

There and Then. il. George DeGoutiere. Scribner, 1947.

Wise Children. Scribner, 1957.

World Is a Bridge. Scribner, 1950.

MEDIA

Bhimsa. (BB).

Indigo. (BB).

There and Then. (TB).

Wise Children. (BB).

BACKGROUND READING

Breit, H. "Talk with Mrs. Weston." *New York Tribune Book Review*, April 19, 1950.

Kunitz. *Twentieth Century Authors, First Supplement*.

E. B. WHITE, 1899-
author
a.k.a. Elwyn Brooks White

AWARDS

Charlotte's Web. Newbery Honor Book, 1953.

BIBLIOGRAPHY

Alice through the Cellophane. Day, 1933.

Another Ho Hum. Farrar, 1932.

Charlotte's Web. il. Garth Williams. Harper, 1952; large print edition, 1969.

E. B. White Reader: Edited with Commentary and Questions; edited by William P. Watt and R. W. Bradford. Harper, 1966.

(ed.) *Elements of Style, with Revisions and a Chapter on Writing by E. B. White*; by William Strunk, Jr. Macmillan, 1959; second edition, 1972.

Essays of E. B. White. Harper, 1977.

Evening on Ice. (New York?), 1967.

Every Day Is Saturday. Harper, 1934.

Farewell to Model T; with R. L. Strout. Putnam, 1936.

Fox of Peapack and Other Poems. Harper, 1938.

Here Is New York. Harper, 1949.

Ho Hum: Newsbreaks from the New Yorker. Farrar, 1931.

Is Sex Necessary? Or, Why You Feel the Way You Do; with James Thurber. Harper, 1929.

Lady Is Cold: Poems. Harper, 1929.

*Letters of E. B. White; edited by Dorothy L. Guth. Harper, 1976.

One Man's Meat. Harper, 1942; enlarged, 1944.

*Points of My Compass: Letters from the East, the West, the North, the South. Harper, 1962.

Quo Vadimus? Or, The Case for the Bicycle. Harper, 1939.

Second Tree from the Corner. Harper, 1954; *a.k.a. Second Tree from the Corner: With Critical and Biographical Material by W. W. Watt*, 1962.

Stuart Little. il. Garth Williams. Harper, 1945.

Subtreasury of American Humor; with Katharine S. White. Coward, 1941; enlarged, 1944.

Topics: Our New Countryman at the U.N. Congressional, 1968.

Trumpet of the Swan. il. Edward Frascino. Harper, 1970.

(ed.) *Walden*; by Henry D. Thoreau. Houghton, 1964.

Wild Flag: Editorials from the New Yorker on Federal World Matters. Houghton, 1946.

MEDIA

Charlotte's Web. (BB, C, MT, TB); Paramount Pictures, Inc./Hanna-Barbera, 1972 (F); Paramount Records, 1972 (R); Pathways of Sound, 1970 (R); RCA Camden; 19? (C); *a.k.a. Charlotte's Web (Introductory Set)*, Stephen F. Bosustow Productions, 1974 (FSS, excerpt).

Elements of Style. (BB, C, MT).

Here Is New York. (BB).

One Man's Meat. (TB).

Points of My Compass. (BB, TB).

Second Tree from the Corner. (BB, TB).

Stuart Little. (BB, MT, TB); McGraw-Hill, Inc., 19? (F, VC); National Broadcasting Company Children's Theatre/Contemporary Films, 1967 (F, TV); Pathways of Sound, 19? (R); Pied Piper Productions, 19? (FSS).

Subtreasury of American Humor. (BB, C, MT, TB).

Trumpet of the Swan. (C, MT).

COLLECTIONS

American Academy of Arts and Letters Library. (New York, New York).

Baker Memorial Library, Dartmouth College. (Hanover, New Hampshire).

Children's Book Section and Manuscript Division, Library of Congress. (Washington, D.C.).

McGinley and Mercury Collections, Arents Research Library, Syracuse University. (Syracuse, New York).

Miller Library, Colby College. (Waterville, Maine).

Olin Library, Cornell University. (Ithaca, New York).

Princeton University Library. (Princeton, New Jersey).

BACKGROUND READING

Benét. *Famous English and American Essayists*.

Breit, H. "Visit." *New York Herald Tribune Book Review*, January 17, 1954.

Burke. *American Authors and Books, 1640 to the Present Day*.

Commire. *Something about the Author*.

Contemporary Authors.

Current Biography.

Doyle. *Who's Who in Children's Literature*.

Fuller. *More Junior Authors*.

Glastonbury, M. "E. B. White's Unexpected Items of Enchantment." *Children's Literature in Education*, May 1973.

BACKGROUND READING (cont'd)

Hart. *Oxford Companion to American Literature, Fourth Edition*.

Hoffman. *Authors and Illustrators of Children's Books*.

Hopkins. *More Books by More People*.

Kirkpatrick. *Twentieth Century Children's Writers*.

Kunitz. *Twentieth Century Authors*.

Kunitz. *Twentieth Century Authors, First Supplement*.

New York Times Biographical Service.

Nykoruk. *Authors in the News*.

Sampson, Edward C. *E. B. White*. Twayne, 1974.

Smaridge. *Famous Modern Storytellers for Young People*.

"Typewriter Man." Newsweek, February 22, 1960.

Ward. *Authors of Books for Young People, Second Edition*.

White, E. B. "Laura Ingalls Wilder Acceptance." *Horn Book*, August 1970.

Wintle. *Pied Pipers*.

ELINOR WHITNEY, 1889-
author
a.k.a. Elinor Whitney Field

AWARDS

Tod of the Fens. Newbery Honor Book, 1929.

BIBLIOGRAPHY

as Elinor Whitney:

(ed.) *Jester's Purse by Nydia E. Minchin: And Other Plays for Boys and Girls*. il. Lorraine Coombs. Harcourt, 1926.

Mystery Club. il. William Siegel. Stokes, 1933.

Timothy and the Blue Cart. il. Berta and Elmer Hader. Stokes, 1930.

Tod of the Fens. il. Warwick Goble. Macmillan, 1928.

Try All Ports. il. Bernard Westmacott. Longmans, 1931.

Tyke-y: His Book and His Mark. Macmillan, 1925.

as Elinor Whitney Field:

(ed.) *Caldecott Medal Books, 1938-1957: With the Artists' Acceptance Papers & Related Material*

Chiefly from the Horn Book Magazine; with Bertha M. Miller. Horn Book, 1957.

(ed.) *Contemporary Illustrators of Children's Books*; with Bertha E. Mahony. Women's Educational and Industrial Union, 1930.

(ed.) *Five Years of Children's Books: A Supplement to Realms of Gold*; with Bertha E. Mahony. Doubleday, 1936.

(ed.) *Horn Book Reflections on Children's Books and Reading: Selections from Eighteen Years of the Horn Book Magazine, 1949-1966*. Horn Book, 1969.

(ed.) *Illustrators of Children's Books, 1744-1945*; with Bertha E. Mahony, et al. Horn Book, 1946.

(ed.) *Newbery Medal Books, 1922-1955: With Their Authors' Acceptance Papers & Related Material Chiefly from the Horn Book Magazine*; with Bertha E. Mahony. Horn Book, 1957.

(ed.) *Realms of Gold in Children's Books: The Fifth Edition of Books for Boys and Girls, a Suggestive Purchase List Previously Published by The Bookshop for Boys and Girls, Women's Educational and Industrial Union*; with Bertha E. Mahony. Doubleday, 1929.

BACKGROUND READING

Burke. *American Authors and Books, 1640 to the Present Day*.

Kunitz. *Junior Book of Authors*.

Kunitz. *Junior Book of Authors, Second Edition Revised*.

ESTER ALBERTI WIER, 1910-
author

AWARDS

Loner. Newbery Honor Book, 1964.

BIBLIOGRAPHY

Action at Paradise Marsh. il. Earl R. Blust. Stackpole, 1968.

Answer Book on Air Force Social Customs; with Dorothy C. Hickey. il. Grace W. Harrison. Military Service, 1957.

Answer Book on Naval Social Customs; with Dorothy C. Hickey. il. Grace W. Harrison. Military Service, 1956; second edition, 1957.

Army Social Customs. Military Service, 1958; il. J. Franklin Whitman, Jr., 1960.

Barrel. il. Carl Kidwell. McKay, 1966.

Easy Does It. il. Witold T. Mars. Vanguard, 1965.

Gift of the Mountains. il. Richard W. Lewis. McKay, 1963.

Hunting Trail. il. Richard Cuffari. Walck, 1974.

King of the Mountain. Walck, 1975.

Loner. il. Christine Price. McKay, 1963; also il. Anthony Maitland. Constable, 1966.

Long Year. il. Ursula Koering. McKay, 1969.

Partners. il. Anna M. Ahl. McKay, 1972.

Rumptydoolers. il. Witold T. Mars. Vanguard, 1964.

Space Hut. il. Leo Summers. Stackpole, 1967.

Straggler: Adventures of a Sea Bird. il. Leonard Vosburgh. McKay, 1970.

What Every Air Force Wife Should Know. Military Service, 1958; second edition, 1963; third edition, 1966.

White Oak. il. Anne M. Jauss. McKay, 1971.

Wind Chasers. il. Kurt Werth. McKay, 1967; also il. A. R. Whitear. Constable, 1968.

Winners. il. Ursula Koering. McKay, 1967.

MEDIA

Barrel. (BB).

Loner. (BB, C, MT); Miller-Brody Productions, 1975 (FSS); Newbery Award Records, 19? (R); *a.k.a. Young Loners*. Walt Disney Productions, 1968 (TV).

Rumptydoolers. (BB, TB).

COLLECTIONS

deGrummond Collection, University of Southern Mississippi. (Hattiesburg, Mississippi).

Kerlan Collection, University of Minnesota. (Minneapolis, Minnesota).

BACKGROUND READING

Commire. *Something about the Author*.

Contemporary Authors.

DeMontreville. *Third Book of Junior Authors*.

Kirkpatrick. *Twentieth Century Children's Writers*.

Ward. *Authors of Books for Young People, Second Edition*.

+KURT WIESE, 1887-1974
author-illustrator

AWARDS

(*Daughter of the Mountains*. Newbery Honor Book, 1949.)

Fish in the Air. Caldecott Honor Book, 1949.

(*Honk, the Moose*. Newbery Honor Book, 1936.)

(*Li Lun: Lad of Courage*. Newbery Honor Book, 1948.)

You Can Write Chinese. Caldecott Honor Book, 1946.

(*Young Fu of the Upper Yangtze*. Newbery Medal Book, 1933.)

BIBLIOGRAPHY

Abandoned Orchard; by Eleanor Risley. Little, 1932.

Abraham: The Itinerant Mouse; by Donald Hutter. Dodd, 1947.

Abraham Lincoln; by Enid L. Meadowcroft. Crowell, 1942.

Abschied von Paradies: Ein Roman unter Kindern; by Frank Thies, edited by O. G. Boetzkes. Heath, 1930.

Adventure in Black and White; by Attilio Gatti. Scribner, 1943.

Adventures of Duc of Indochina; by Albert J. Nevins. Dodd, 1955.

Adventures of Kenji of Japan; by Albert J. Nevins. Dodd, 1952.

Adventures of Mario; by Waldemar Bonsels. Bond, 1930.

Adventures of Monkey; by Wu Ch'êng-ên, adapted by Arthur Waley. Doubleday, 1944.

Adventures of Pancho of Peru; by Albert J. Nevins. Dodd, 1953.

Adventures of Ramón of India; by Albert J. Nevins. Dodd, 1954.

Adventures of Wu Han of Korea; by Albert J. Nevins. Dodd, 1951.

Alaska in Story and Pictures; by Marguerite Henry. Whitman, 1941.

Alaskan Hunter; by Florence Hayes. Houghton, 1959.

Albert Elephant; by Marjorie A. Hayes. Little, 1938.

Alexander: The Tale of a Monkey; by Marion and Edith Brown. Bobbs, 1934.

All about Great Rivers of the World; by Anne T. White. Random, 1957.

All about Volcanoes and Earthquakes; by Frederick Pough. Random, 1953.

BIBLIOGRAPHY (cont'd)

All the Mowgli Stories; by Rudyard Kipling. Double-day, 1936.

Amandus, Who Was Much Too Big; by Elsie and Morris Glenn. Macrae, 1939.

Amat and the Water-Buffalo; by Jeanette Guillaume and Mary L. Bachmann. Coward, 1962.

Amos: The Beagle with a Plan; by John Parke. Pantheon, 1953.

Anabel's Windows; by Agnes D. Hewes. Dodd, 1949.

Angleworms on Toast; by MacKinlay Kantor. Coward, 1942.

Animal Babies; by Alice Pratt. Beacon, 1941.

Animal Pioneers; by Catherine C. Coblentz. Little, 1936.

Animals of a Sage Brush Ranch; by Alice Pratt. Rand, 1938.

Argentina in Story and Pictures; by Marguerite Henry. Whitman, 1941.

Attack and Other Stories; by Burdette Buckingham. Ginn, 1936.

Australia Calling; by Margaret Macpherson. Dodd, 1946.

Australia in Story and Pictures; by Marguerite Henry. Whitman, 1946.

Back of Time; by Margaret I. Ross. Harper, 1932.

Bahamas in Story and Pictures; by Marguerite Henry. Whitman, 1946.

Bambi: A Life in the Woods; by Felix Salten, *pseud.* (Siegmund Salzman). Tr. Whitaker Chambers. Simon, 1928; *a.k.a. Bambi: Eine Lebensge Shicte aus dem Walde.* Tr. Clair H. Bell. Heath, 1932.

Bambi's Children; by Felix Salten, *pseud.* (Siegmund Salzman). Tr. Barthold Fles. il. with Erna Pinner. Grosset, 1941.

Beast Called an Elephant; by Phil Strong. Dodd, 1955.

Beggars of Dreams; by Mary B. Hollister. also il. with Chinese woodcuts. Dodd, 1937.

Bells of the Harbor; by Meindert DeJong. Harper, 1941.

Biene Maja und Ihre Abenteuer; by Waldemar Bonsels, edited by Franz Schneider and Martha J. Boyd. Heath, 1929.

Black Bear Twins; by Jane Tompkins. Lippincott, 1952.

Blackfellow of Bundi: A Native Australian Boy; by Lela and Walter Harris. Whitman, 1931.

Blue Butterfly Goes to South America; by Ruth H. Hutchinson. Whitman, 1940.

Blue Junk; by Priscilla Holtan. Grosset, 1931.

Blue Mittens; by Mary Reely. Hale, 1935.

Boating Is Fun; by Ruth Brindze. Dodd, 1949.

Bob Clifton, African Planter; by Wilbur O. Hoague. Holt, 1953.

Bob Clifton, Congo Crusader; by Wilbur O. Hoague. Holt, 1951.

Bob Clifton, Elephant Hunter; by Wilbur O. Hoague. Holt, 1949.

Bob Clifton, Jungle Traveler; by Wilbur O. Hoague. Holt, 1950.

Bolivia in Story and Pictures; by Bernadine Bailey. Whitman, 1942.

Book of Mysteries, Three Baffling Tales: The River Acres Riddle, Cat's Cradle, The Hexagonal Chest; by Augusta Seaman. Doubleday, 1929.

Brazil in Story and Pictures; by Marguerite Henry. Whitman, 1941.

Bright Pathways; by Esma Booth. Friendship, 1955.

British Honduras in Story and Pictures; by Marguerite Henry. Whitman, 1946.

Buddy the Bear. Coward, 1936.

Bunny, Hound and Clown; by Dhan G. Mukerji. Dutton, 1931.

Camel Bells: A Boy of Baghdad; by Anna Ratzesberger. Whitman, 1935.

Canada in Story and Pictures; by Marguerite Henry. Whitman, 1941.

Captain Kidd's Cow; by Phil Stong. Dodd, 1941.

Carnival Time at Ströbeck; by May Harris. Whitman, 1938.

Cats for the Tooseys; by Mabel S. G. LaRue. Nelson, 1939.

Censored, the Goat; by Phil Stong. Dodd, 1945.

Central American Roundabout; by Agnes Rothery. Dodd, 1944.

Cheeky: A Prairie Dog; by Josephine Lau. Whitman, 1937.

Children of the Blizzard; by Heluiz Washburne and Anuata Blackmore. Day, 1952.

Chile in Story and Pictures; by Marguerite Henry. Whitman, 1941.

China Quest; by Elizabeth F. Lewis. Winston, 1937.

Chinese Ink Stick. Doubleday, 1929.

Circus of Our Own; by Irmengarde Eberle. Dodd, 1948.

Clockwork Twin; by Walter R. Brooks. Knopf, 1937.

Collected Poems of Freddy the Pig; by Walter R. Brooks. Knopf, 1953.

Columbia in Story and Pictures; by Lois Donaldson. Whitman, 1944.

Copydog in India; by Jene Barr. Viking, 1955.

Corn-Belt Billy; by Mabel L. Hunt. Grosset, 1942.

Corporal Corey of the Royal Canadian Mounted; by Jack O'Brien, *pseud.* (John S. O'Brien). Winston, 1936.

Costa Rica in Story and Pictures; by Lois Donaldson. Whitman, 1943.

Cowhand Goes to Town; by Phil Stong. Dodd, 1939.

Cradle of the Deep; by Joan Lowell. Simon, 1929.

Crunch: The Squirrel; by Elizabeth A. Bond and Joan E. Rabin. Dodd, 1939.

Cuddle Bear of Piney Forest; by Elizabeth Hamilton. Coward, 1948.

Cunning Turtle. Viking, 1956.

Daughter of the Mountains; by Louise S. Rankin. Viking, 1948.

Day after Tomorrow; by Alice H. Lewis. Friendship, 1956.

Deliveryman; by Charlotte Kuh. Macmillan, 1929.

Dike against the Sea; by Mary B. Hollister. Friendship, 1948. (Includes *Junior Teacher's Guide on China*, 1948.)

Dirk's Dog Bello; by Meindert DeJong. Harper, 1939.

Dog, the Fox, and the Fleas. McKay, 1953.

Dogs; by Albert P. Terhune. Saalfield, 1940.

Dominican Republic in Story and Pictures; by Marguerite Henry. Whitman, 1946.

Don: The Story of a Lion Dog; by Zane Grey. Harper, 1928.

Donkey Beads: A Tale of a Persian Donkey; by Anna Ratzesberger. Whitman, 1938.

Down in the Grass; by Harold Kellock. Coward, 1929.

Down the Road with Johnny; by Irene Smith. McGraw, 1951.

Dragon Treasure; by Adolph Paschang. Longmans, 1932.

Dumblebum; by Elsie and Morris Glenn. Macrae, 1947.

Each in His Own Way: Stories of Famous Animals; by Alice Gall and Fleming H. Crew. Oxford, 1937.

Early Old Testament Stories; by Ethel L. Smither. Abingdon, 1954.

Ecuador in Story and Pictures; by Bernadine Bailey. Whitman, 1942.

Eight Rings on His Tail: A Round Meadow Story; by John Oldrin. Viking, 1956.

Ekhorn; by Haakon Lie. Tr. Claes L. Hultgren. Whitman, 1931.

Ella the Elephant. Coward, 1931; also in *Kurt Wiese's Picture Book of Animals*, below.

Engineer; by Charlotte Kuh. Macmillan, 1928.

Eskimo Hunter; by Florence Hayes. Random, 1945.

Etuk: The Eskimo Hunter; by Miriam MacMillan. Dodd, 1950.

Fables of Aesop; by Joseph Jacobs. Macmillan, 1950.

Famous Bridges of the World; by David B. Steinman. Random, 1953.

Farm Boy: A Hunt for Indian Treasure; by Phil Stong. Doubleday, 1934; also in *Phil Stong's Big Book*, below.

Favorite Stories Old and New; by Sidonie Gruenberg. Doubleday, 1942; revised and enlarged, 1955.

Feeling Better? Amusements and Occupations for Convalescents; by Cornelia Trowbridge. Dodd, 1936.

Ferryman; by Claire H. Bishop. Coward, 1941.

Fifteen Rabbits; by Felix Salten, *pseud.* (Siegmund Salzman). Tr. Whittaker Chambers. Grosset, 1942.

Fireman; by Charlotte Kuh. Macmillan, 1929.

First to Be Called Christians; by Ethel L. Smither. Abingdon, 1955.

Fish in the Air. Viking, 1948.

Five Chinese Brothers; by Claire H. Bishop. Coward, 1938; *a.k.a. Cinq Frères Chinois*, 1960; *a.k.a. Fiev Chinees Bruthers*. Scholastic, 1965.

Flowered Donkey; by Margaret MacKay. Day, 1950.

Flute Players of Beppu; by Kathryn Gallant. Coward, 1960.

Four Friends; by Eleanor Hoffman. Macmillan, 1946.

14th Street: A Novel in Verse; by Percy Shostac. Simon, 1930.

Freddy and Mr. Camphor; by Walter R. Brooks. Knopf, 1944.

Freddy and Simon the Dictator; by Walter R. Brooks. Knopf, 1956.

Freddy and the Baseball Team from Mars; by Walter R. Brooks. Knopf, 1955.

Freddy and the Bean Home News; by Walter R. Brooks. Knopf, 1943.

Freddy and the Ignoramus; by Walter R. Brooks. Knopf, 1945.

Freddy and the Men from Mars; by Walter R. Brooks. Knopf, 1954.

Freddy and the Perilous Adventure; by Walter R. Brooks. Knopf, 1942.

Freddy and the Popinjay; by Walter R. Brooks. Knopf, 1945.

Freddy and the Spaceship; by Walter R. Brooks. Knopf, 1953.

Freddy Goes Camping; by Walter R. Brooks. Knopf, 1948.

BIBLIOGRAPHY (cont'd)

Freddy Goes to Florida; by Walter R. Brooks. Knopf, 1949.

Freddy Goes to the North Pole; by Walter R. Brooks. Knopf, 1951.

Freddy Plays Football; by Walter R. Brooks. Knopf, 1949.

Freddy Rides Again; by Walter R. Brooks. Knopf, 1951.

Freddy the Cowboy; by Walter R. Brooks. Knopf, 1950.

Freddy the Detective; by Walter R. Brooks. Knopf, 1932.

Freddy the Magician; by Walter R. Brooks. Knopf, 1947.

Freddy the Pied Piper; by Walter R. Brooks. Knopf, 1946.

Freddy the Pilot; by Walter R. Brooks. Knopf, 1952.

Freddy's Cousin Weedly; by Walter R. Brooks. Knopf, 1940.

Gay Pippo; by Eleanor Pease and Beatrice deMelik. Whitman, 1936.

Gipsy Bridle; by Leonora M. Weber. Little, 1930.

Go West, Young Bear; by Elizabeth Hamilton. Coward, 1948.

Golden Door: A Story of Liberty's Children; by Hertha Pauli. Knopf, 1949.

Goldfish under the Ice; by Christopher Moley. Dodd, 1932.

Good Wind and Good Water; by Alice C. Gardiner and Nancy Osborne. Viking, 1934.

Grandson of Yen-Foh: Adapted from the Chinese; by Ethel Eldridge. Whitman, 1936.

Greased Lightning; by Sterling North. Winston, 1940.

Great All-Star Animal League Ball Game; by Vincent Starrett. Dodd, 1957.

Great Gravity the Cat; by Johanna Johnston. Knopf, 1958.

Great Kipling Stories: Together with a Life of Rudyard Kipling; edited by Lowell Thomas. Winston, 1936.

Greenland in Story and Pictures; by Bernadine Bailey. Whitman, 1942.

Groundhog and His Shadow. Viking, 1959.

Guatemala in Story and Pictures; by Bernadine Bailey. Whitman, 1942.

Guiana in Story and Pictures; by Lois Donaldson. Whitman, 1944.

Hamlet: A Cocker Spaniel; by Irma S. Black. Holiday, 1938.

Happy Easter. Viking, 1952.

Hawaii in Story and Pictures; by Bernadine Bailey. Whitman, 1946.

Hello, Alaska!; by Sarah Litchfield. Whitman, 1945.

Here's Howie; by Mary Malone. Dodd, 1962.

Hidden Valley; by Laura Benét. Dodd, 1938.

High Water; by Phil Stong. Dodd, 1950; also in *Phil Stong's Big Book*, below.

Hindu Fables for Little Children; by Dhan G. Mukerji. Dutton, 1929.

Hirum the Hillbilly; by Phil Stong. Dodd, 1950.

His Excellency and Peter; by Theodore A. and Mary M. H. Harper. Doubleday, 1930.

Home-Builders; by Warren H. Miller. Winston, 1946.

Ho-Ming: Girl of New China; by Elizabeth F. Lewis. Winston, 1934.

Honduras in Story and Pictures; by Bernadine Bailey. Whitman, 1942.

Honk, the Moose; by Phil Stong. Dodd, 1935.

Hoppity; by Miriam E. Mason. Macmillan, 1947.

Horse and Americans; by Phil Stong. also il. with old prints and photographs. Stokes, 1939.

Hound of Florence; by Felix Salten, *pseud*. (Siegmund Salzman). Tr. Huntley Patterson. Simon, 1930.

House with Red Sails; by Leone Adelson. McKay, 1951.

Iceland in Story and Pictures; by Bernadine Bailey. Whitman, 1942.

If You Should Want to Write: A Handbook for Beginning Authors; by Alice Colver. Dodd, 1939.

Igor's Summer: A Story of Our Russian Friends; by Lorraine and Jerrold Beim. Russian War Relief, 1943.

In Defense of Mothers: How to Bring Up Children in Spite of More Zealous Psychologists; by Leo Kamer. Dodd, 1941.

Jamba the Elephant; by Theodore Waldeck. Viking, 1942.

Jasmine: A Story of Present Day Persia; by Anna Ratzesberger. Whitman, 1937.

Jasper the Gypsy Dog; by Mabel Kahmann. Messner, 1938.

Java Jungle Tales; by Hendrik DeLeeuw. Doubleday, 1933.

Joan and the Three Deer; by Marjorie Medary. Random, 1939.

Joe Buys Nails. Doubleday, 1931.

Jothy: A Story of the South Indian Jungle; by Charlotte Wyckoff. Longmans, 1933.

Juneau: The Sleigh Dog; by West Lathrop. Random, 1942.

Jungle Book; by Rudyard Kipling. Doubleday, 1932.

Jungle Monkey; by JoBessie Waldeck. Viking, 1946.

Jungle Twins; by Irma Roberts. Coward, 1951.

Karoo the Kangaroo. Coward, 1929; also in *Kurt Wiese's Picture Book of Animals*, below.

Kee-Kee and Company: A Story of American Children in China; by Mary B. Hollister. Dodd, 1938.

Ki-Ki: A Circus Trouper; by Edith Craine. Whitman, 1937.

Kim of Korea; by Faith Norris and Peter Lumm. Messner, 1955.

King and the Princess; by Jack O'Brien, *pseud.* (John S. O'Brien). Grosset, 1940.

Kip: A Young Rooster; by Irma S. Black. Holiday, 1939.

Ki-Yu: A Story of Panthers; by Roderick Haig-Brown. Houghton, 1934; *a.k.a. Panther*. Cape, 1934.

Kurt Wiese's Picture Book of Animals. Coward, 1947. (Includes *Ella the Elephant*, *Karoo the Kangaroo*, and *Wallie the Walrus*, issued separately, above and below.)

Later Old Testament Stories; by Ethel L. Smither. Abingdon, 1956.

Laughing Matter; by Helen Smith. Scribner, 1949.

Laurie; by Estelle Clapp. Doubleday, 1953.

Li Lun: Lad of Courage; by Carolyn Treffinger. Abingdon, 1947.

Liang and Lo. Doubleday, 1930.

Limpy: Tale of a Monkey Hero; by Hyde Matzdorff. Day, 1957.

Lions in the Barn; by Virginia Voight. Holiday, 1955.

Lions on the Hunt; by Theodore Waldeck. Viking, 1942.

Little Boy Lost in Brazil. Dodd, 1942.

Little Circus Dog; by Jene Barr. Whitman, 1949.

Little Ones; by Dorothy Kunhardt. Viking, 1935.

Little Prairie Dog; by Jene Barr. Whitman, 1949.

Little Tooktoo: The Story of Santa Claus' Youngest Reindeer; by Marie A. Stafford. Morrow, 1930.

Livingstone the Pathfinder; by Basil J. Mathews. Friendship, 1955.

Lost Horizon; by James Hilton. World, 1948.

Lucky Days for Johnny; by Irene Smith. McGraw, 1950.

Made in China: The Story of China's Expression; by Cornelia Spencer, *pseud.* (Grace Yaukey). Knopf, 1943; second edition, 1952.

Magic Firecracker; by Mitchell Dawson. Viking, 1949.

Many Hands in Many Lands; by Alice G. Kelsey. Friendship, 1953.

Me an' Pete; by Wendell McKown. Doubleday, 1934.

Mexico in Story and Pictures; by Marguerite Henry. Whitman, 1941.

Midnight and Jeremiah; by Sterling North. Winston, 1943.

Midsummer Madness; by Sterling North. Winston, 1943.

Mike: The Story of a Young Circus Acrobat; by Phil Stong. Knopf, 1957.

Missouri Canary; by Phil Stong. Dodd, 1943.

Mr. Piper's Bus; by Eleanor Clymer. Dodd, 1961.

Mr. Red Squirrel; by Tom Robinson. Viking, 1943.

Mr. Z of Everything; by M. S. Klutch. Coward, 1946.

Mrs. Piggle-Wiggle's Magic; by Betty McDonald. Lippincott, 1949.

Moffats; by Ethel Hubbard. Friendship, 1952.

Moo-Wee: The Musk-Ox; by Jane Tompkins. Stokes, 1938.

Most Beautiful House; by Hertha Pauli. Knopf, 1949.

Motorman; by Charlotte Kuh. Macmillan, 1929.

Mpengo of the Congo; by Grace W. McGarran. Friendship, 1945. (Includes *Teacher's Guide on Africa*; by Armilda B. Keiser, 1946.)

Muffy: The Tale of a Muskrat; by Zenobia Bird. Whitman, 1941.

Mulberry Village: A Story of Country Life in China; by Mary B. Hollister. Dodd, 1936.

Muskox: Little Tooktoo's Friend; by Marie A. Stafford. Morrow, 1931.

Mystery Dogs of Glen Hazard; by Maristan Chapman, *pseud.* (Mary and John Chapman). Grosset, 1941.

New York Nights; by Stephen Graham. Doran, 1927.

New Zealand in Story and Pictures; by Marguerite Henry. Whitman, 1946.

Newfoundland in Story and Pictures; by Lois Donaldson. Whitman, 1944.

Nibby; by Ann Meyer. Coward, 1952.

Nibs: The Orphan Deer of the Adirondacks; by Don Lang. Grosset, 1942.

Nicaragua in Story and Pictures; by Lois Donaldson. Whitman, 1943.

Ning's Pong; by Hester Hawkes. Coward, 1953.

North America: The Land They Live in for the Children Who Live There; by Lucy S. Mitchell. Macmillan, 1931.

BIBLIOGRAPHY (cont'd)

No-Sitch, the Hound; by Phil Stong. Dodd, 1936; also in *Phil Stong's Big Book*, below.

Odie Seeks a Friend; by Julius King. Coward, 1934.

On Safari; by Theodore Waldeck. Viking, 1940.

Ootah and His Puppy; by Marie A. Stafford. Morrow, 1931.

Oswald's Pet Dragon; by Carl Glick. Coward, 1943.

Otter Twins; by Jane Tompkins. Lippincott, 1955.

Our Country; by Lucy S. Mitchell and Dorothy Stall. Heath, 1945.

Our Planet the Earth: Then and Now; by Lillian Rifkin. Lothrop, 1934.

Paddy's Christmas; by Helen Monsell. Knopf, 1942.

Pal: The Story of an Airedale; by Alexandra Jenkins. Appleton, 1930.

Panama in Story and Pictures; by Marguerite Henry. Whitman, 1941.

Panther Magic; by Olaf Baker. Dodd, 1928.

Paraguay in Story and Pictures; by Lois Donaldson. Whitman, 1944.

Parrot Dealer. Coward, 1932.

Pecos Bill and Lightning; by Leigh Peck. Houghton, 1940.

Peetie: The Story of a Real Cat; by Inis Jones. McBride, 1935.

Penguin Twins; by Jane Tompkins. Stokes, 1939.

Peru in Story and Pictures; by Bernadine Bailey. Whitman, 1942.

Phil Stong's Big Book: Farm Boy, High Water (and) No-Sitch, the Hound. Dodd, 1961. (Each also issued separately, above.)

Picture Book of Alabama; by Bernadine Bailey. Whitman, 1953.

Picture Book of Alaska; by Bernadine Bailey. Whitman, 1959; revised, 1965.

Picture Book of Arizona; by Bernadine Bailey. Whitman, 1957.

Picture Book of Arkansas; by Bernadine Bailey. Whitman, 1957.

Picture Book of California; by Bernadine Bailey. Whitman, 1949; revised, 1966.

Picture Book of Colorado; by Bernadine Bailey. Whitman, 1950; revised, 1966.

Picture Book of Connecticut; by Bernadine Bailey. Whitman, 1955; revised, 1966.

Picture Book of Delaware; by Bernadine Bailey. Whitman, 1960.

Picture Book of Florida; by Bernadine Bailey. Whitman, 1949.

Picture Book of Georgia; by Bernadine Bailey. Whitman, 1953.

Picture Book of Hawaii; by Bernadine Bailey. Whitman, 1960; revised, 1964.

Picture Book of Idaho; by Bernadine Bailey. Whitman, 1962.

Picture Book of Illinois; by Bernadine Bailey. Whitman, 1940; revised, 1964.

Picture Book of Indiana; by Bernadine Bailey. Whitman, 1950; revised, 1966.

Picture Book of Iowa; by Bernadine Bailey. Whitman, 1952; revised, 1966.

Picture Book of Kansas; by Bernadine Bailey. Whitman, 1954; revised, 1965.

Picture Book of Kentucky; by Bernadine Bailey. Whitman, 1955; revised, 1963.

Picture Book of Louisiana; by Bernadine Bailey. Whitman, 1954.

Picture Book of Maine; by Bernadine Bailey. Whitman, 1957.

Picture Book of Maryland; by Bernadine Bailey. Whitman, 1955; revised, 1966.

Picture Book of Massachusetts; by Bernadine Bailey. Whitman, 1949; revised, 1965.

Picture Book of Michigan; by Bernadine Bailey. Whitman, 1950; revised, 1965.

Picture Book of Minnesota; by Bernadine Bailey. Whitman, 1953.

Picture Book of Mississippi; by Bernadine Bailey. Whitman, 1956.

Picture Book of Missouri; by Bernadine Bailey. Whitman, 1951.

Picture Book of Montana; by Bernadine Bailey. Whitman, 1961.

Picture Book of Nebraska; by Bernadine Bailey. Whitman, 1956.

Picture Book of Nevada; by Bernadine Bailey. Whitman, 1961.

Picture Book of New Hampshire; by Bernadine Bailey. Whitman, 1961; revised, 1965.

Picture Book of New Jersey; by Bernadine Bailey. Whitman, 1951; revised, 1965.

Picture Book of New Mexico; by Bernadine Bailey. Whitman, 1960.

Picture Book of New York; by Bernadine Bailey. Whitman, 1950; revised, 1966.

Picture Book of North Carolina; by Bernadine Bailey. Whitman, 1950; revised, 1966.

Picture Book of North Dakota; by Bernadine Bailey. Whitman, 1960.

Picture Book of Ohio; by Bernadine Bailey. Whitman, 1950.

Picture Book of Oklahoma; by Bernadine Bailey. Whitman, 1952.

Picture Book of Oregon; by Bernadine Bailey. Whitman, 1954.

Picture Book of Pennsylvania; by Bernadine Bailey. Whitman, 1950; revised, 1966.

Picture Book of Rhode Island; by Bernadine Bailey. Whitman, 1960; revised, 1966.

Picture Book of South Carolina; by Bernadine Bailey. Whitman, 1956; revised, 1966.

Picture Book of South Dakota; by Bernadine Bailey. Whitman, 1960.

Picture Book of Tennessee; by Bernadine Bailey. Whitman, 1952; revised, 1966.

Picture Book of Texas; by Bernadine Bailey. Whitman, 1950; revised, 1964.

Picture Book of Virginia; by Bernadine Bailey. Whitman, 1956; revised, 1965.

Picture Book of Washington; by Bernadine Bailey. Whitman, 1962.

Picture Book of West Virginia; by Bernadine Bailey. Whitman, 1956; revised, 1965.

Picture Book of Wisconsin; by Bernadine Bailey. Whitman, 1951; revised, 1964.

Picture Book of Wyoming; by Bernadine Bailey. Whitman, 1960; revised, 1966.

Picture Story of China; by Emily Hahn. McKay, 1946.

Pierre of the Big Top; by Col. S. P. Meeker. Dodd, 1957.

Pika and the Roses; by Elizabeth Coatsworth. Pantheon, 1959.

Pinocchio: The Story of a Puppet; by Carlo Collodi, *pseud.* (Carlo Lorenzini). Tr. M. A. Murray. Nelson, 1938.

Poetic Parrot; by Margaret MacKay. Day, 1951.

Polar Bear Twins; by Jane Tompkins. Stokes, 1937.

Policeman; by Charlotte Kuh. Macmillan, 1929.

Poodle-Ooodle of Doodle Farm; by Lawton and Ruth Mackall. Stokes, 1929.

Porcupine Twins; by Jane Tompkins. Lippincott, 1954.

Positive Pete!; by Phil Stong. Dodd, 1947.

Postman; by Charlotte Kuh. Macmillan, 1929.

Prince and the Porker; by Phil Stong. Dodd, 1950.

Puppy for Keeps; by Quail Hawkins. Holiday, 1943.

Quest in the Desert; by Roy C. Andrews. Viking, 1950.

Quest of the Snow Leopard; by Roy C. Andrews. Viking, 1955.

Rabbit Bros. Circus: One Night Only. Viking, 1963.

Rabbits' Revenge. Coward, 1940.

Raccoon Twins; by Jane Tompkins. Stokes, 1942.

Ranger: Sea Dog of the Royal Canadian Mounted; by Charles S. Strong. Winston, 1948.

Ranger's Arctic Patrol; by Charles S. Strong. Winston, 1952.

Red Rajah; by Louise A. Kent. Houghton, 1933.

Red Squirrel Twins; by Jane Tompkins. Stokes, 1937.

Reindeer Twins; by Jane Tompkins. Lippincott, 1956.

Return of Silver Chief; by Jack O'Brien, *pseud.* (John S. O'Brien). Winston, 1943.

River Children: A Story of Boat Life in China; by Mary B. Hollister. Dodd, 1935.

Rocco Came In; by John Beecroft. Dodd, 1959.

Roger and the Fishes; by Charlotte Jackson. Dodd, 1943.

Rolling Snow; by Virginia Voight. Holiday, 1956.

Rosie the Rhino; by Marion Conger. Abingdon, 1948.

Round Meadow; by John Oldrin. Viking, 1951.

Roundhouse Cat and Other Railroad Animals; by Freeman Hubbard. McGraw, 1951.

Royal Red; by Jack O'Brien, *pseud.* (John S. O'Brien). Winston, 1951.

Salvador in Story and Pictures; by Lois Donaldson. Whitman, 1943.

Saranga the Pygmy; by Attilio Gatti. Scribner, 1939.

Sheep; by Arthur Gilfillan. Little, 1929.

Silk and Satin Lane; by Esther Wood. Longmans, 1939.

Silver Chief, Dog of the North; by Jack O'Brien, *pseud.* (John S. O'Brien). Winston, 1933.

Silver Chief to the Rescue; by Jack O'Brien, *pseud.* (John S. O'Brien). Winston, 1937.

Silver Chief's Revenge; by Jack O'Brien, *pseud.* (John S. O'Brien). Winston, 1955.

Skeeter: The Story of an Arabian Gazelle; by Robert Shaffer. Dodd, 1952.

Snow for Christmas; by Vernon Bowen. McKay, 1953.

Snowshoe Twins; by Jane Tompkins. Stokes, 1941.

Snowy for Luck; by Arthur Goode. Whitman, 1934.

Spike of Swift River; by Jack O'Brien, *pseud.* (John S. O'Brien). Winston, 1942.

Stories of Jesus; by Ethel L. Smither. Abingdon, 1954.

Story about Ping; by Marjorie Flack. Viking, 1933.

Story of Freginald; by Walter R. Brooks. Knopf, 1936; *a.k.a. Freddy and Freginald*. Lane, 1956.

BIBLIOGRAPHY (cont'd)

Story of Little Black Sambo; by Helen Bannerman. Animated by A. V. Warren. Garden City, 1933.

Streamlined Pig; by Margaret W. Brown. Harper, 1938.

Su-Mei's Golden Year; by Marguerite Bro. Doubleday, 1950.

Tale of Two Horses; by Aimé Tschiffely. Simon, 1935.

Tapiola's Brave Regiment; by Robert Nathan. Knopf, 1941.

Tents in the Wilderness: A Story of a Labrador Indian Boy; by Julius E. Lips. Stokes, 1942.

Thames, London's River; by Noel Streatfeild. il. with Fred Klein. Garrard, 1964.

Thief in the Attic. Viking, 1965.

This Is the Moon; by Marion B. Cothren. Coward, 1946.

Three Little Kittens. Macmillan, 1928.

Three Seeds; by Hester Hawkes. Coward, 1956.

Three Sisters: The Story of the Soong Family of China; by Cornelia Spencer, *pseud.* (Grace Yaukey). Day, 1939.

Tito: The Pig of Guatemala; by Charlotte Jackson. Dodd, 1940.

Toby: A Curious Cat; by Irma S. Black. Holiday, 1948.

Toco Toucan; by William Bridges. Harper, 1940.

Tommy's Wonderful Airplane; by Eleanor Clymer. Dodd, 1951.

Too Many Bears and Other Stories; by Burdette Buckingham. Ginn, 1936.

Too Many Dogs; by Quail Hawkins. Holiday, 1946.

Tooseys; by Mabel S. G. LaRue. Nelson, 1938.

Trail of the Buffalo; by Rutherford Montgomery. Houghton, 1939.

Train That Never Came Back: And Other Railroad Stories; by Freeman Hubbard. McGraw, 1952.

Tramp: The Sheep Dog; by Don Lang. Grosset, 1943.

Truffle Pig; by Claire H. Bishop. Coward, 1971.

Twenty Thousand Leagues under the Sea; by Jules Verne. World, 1946.

Twenty-two Bears; by Claire H. Bishop. Viking, 1964.

Untold Story of Exploration; by Lowell Thomas. Dodd, 1935.

Uruguay in Story and Pictures; by Lois Donaldson. Whitman, 1943.

Valiant, Dog of the Timberline; by Jack O'Brien, *pseud.* (John S. O'Brien). Winston, 1935.

Venezuela in Story and Pictures; by Bernadine Bailey. Whitman, 1942.

Very Special Pet; by Lavinia Davis. Grosset, 1940.

Viennese Noveletts; by Arthur Schnitzler. Simon, 1931.

Virgin Islands in Story and Pictures; by Marguerite Henry. Whitman, 1946.

Wagtail; by Alice Gall and Fleming H. Crew. Oxford, 1932.

Walking Hat; by William N. Hall. Knopf, 1950.

Wallie the Walrus. Coward, 1930; also in *Kurt Wiese's Picture Book of Animals*, above.

Way Down Cellar; by Phil Stong. Dodd, 1942.

West Indies in Story and Pictures; by Marguerite Henry. Whitman, 1941.

What? Another Cat!; by John Beecroft. Dodd, 1960.

What Every Young Rabbit Should Know; by Carol Denison. Dodd, 1948.

When the Typhoon Blows; by Elizabeth F. Lewis. Winston, 1942.

Where Any Young Cat Might Be; by Carol Denison and Jane Cummin. Dodd, 1956.

White Leopard: A Tale of the African Bush; by Inglis Fletcher. Bobbs, 1931.

White Panther; by Theodore Waldeck. Viking, 1941.

White Stars of Freedom; by Miriam Isasi and Melcena B. Denny. Whitman, 1942.

Wiggins for President; by Walter R. Brooks. Knopf, 1937; a.k.a. *Freddy the Politician*, 1948.

Wild West Bill Rides Home; by Muriel F. Millen. Whitman, 1946.

Wind on the Prairie; by Leonora M. Weber. Little, 1929.

With Love and Irony; by Yu-T'ang Lin. Day, 1940.

Wizard and His Magic Powder: Tales of the Channel Islands; by Alfred Campbell. Knopf, 1945.

Wolf-Tracker; by Zane Grey. Harper, 1930.

Wonderful Adventures of Ting Ling; by Vernon Bowen. McKay, 1952.

World Song; by Ann N. Clark. Viking, 1960.

Wreck of the Dumaru: A Story of Cannibalism in an Open Boat; by Lowell Thomas. also il. with Photographs. Doubleday, 1930.

Yangtze: China's River Highway; by Cornelia Spencer, *pseud.* (Grace Yaukey). il. with Fred Klein. Garrard, 1964.

Yen-Foh, a Chinese Boy: Adapted from the Chinese; by Ethel Eldridge. Whitman, 1935.

Yinka-Tu the Yak; by Alice Lide. Viking, 1938.

You Can Write Chinese. Viking, 1945.

Young Fu of the Upper Yangtze; by Elizabeth F. Lewis. Winston, 1932.

Young Settler; by Phil Stong. Dodd, 1938.

Your Breakfast and the People Who Made It; by Benjamin Gruenberg and Leone Adelson. Doubleday, 1954.

MEDIA

Fish in the Air. Weston Woods Studios, 1967 (FSS); also in Weston Woods Studios Set No. 18, 1968 (FSS).

Five Chinese Brothers. Weston Woods Studios, 1958 (F), 19? (FSS); also in Weston Woods Studios Set No. 5, 1965 (FSS); *a.k.a. Cinco Hermanos Chinos*. Weston Woods Studios, 1960 (F); *a.k.a. Cinq Fréres Chinois*. Weston Woods Studios, 1960 (F).

Happy Easter. (BB).

Story about Ping. Weston Woods Studios, 1955 (F), 1957 (FSS); also in Weston Woods Studios Set No. 2, 1965 (FSS).

EXHIBITIONS

World's Fair, 1937. (Paris, France).

COLLECTIONS

deGrummond Collection, University of Southern Mississippi. (Hattiesburg, Mississippi).

Free Library of Philadelphia. (Philadelphia, Pennsylvania).

Kerlan Collection, University of Minnesota. (Minneapolis, Minnesota).

May Massee Collection, Emporia State College. (Emporia, Kansas).

Milwaukee Public Library. (Milwaukee, Wisconsin).

Special Collections, University Research Library, University of California. (Los Angeles, California).

University of Oregon Library. (Eugene, Oregon).

BACKGROUND READING

Bader. *American Picturebooks from Noah's Ark to The Beast Within*.

Bertram, J. "Kurt Wiese, Prolific Artist." *Elementary English*, April 1956.

Burke. *American Authors and Books, 1640 to the Present Day*.

Commire. *Something about the Author*.

Contemporary Authors.

Kingman. *Illustrators of Children's Books, 1957-1966*.

Kingman. *Illustrators of Children's Books, 1967-1976*.

Kirkpatrick. *Twentieth Century Children's Writers*.

Kunitz. *Junior Book of Authors*.

Kunitz. *Junior Book of Authors, Second Edition Revised*.

"Kurt Wiese, Busiest Illustrator, Has 14 Juveniles on Fall List." *Publishers Weekly*, October 28, 1950.

Mahony. *Contemporary Illustrators of Children's Books*.

Mahony. *Illustrators of Children's Books, 1744-1945*.

Miller. *Illustrators of Children's Books, 1946-1956*.

Ward. *Authors of Books for Young People, Second Edition*.

Young Wings. *Writing Books for Boys and Girls*.

LAURA INGALLS WILDER, 1867-1957
author

AWARDS

By the Shores of Silver Lake. Newbery Honor Book, 1940.

Little Town on the Prairie. Newbery Honor Book, 1942.

Long Winter. Newbery Honor Book, 1941.

On the Banks of Plum Creek. Newbery Honor Book, 1938.

These Happy Golden Years. Newbery Honor Book, 1943.

BIBLIOGRAPHY

*By the Shores of Silver Lake. il. Helen Sewell and Mildred Boyle. Harper, 1939; also il. Garth Williams, 1953.

*Farmer Boy. il. Helen Sewell. Harper, 1933; also il. Garth Williams, 1953.

*First Four Years. il. Garth Williams. Harper, 1971.

*Little House in the Big Woods. il. Helen Sewell and Mildred Boyle. Harper, 1932; also il. Garth Williams, 1953; large print edition, 19?.

*Little House on the Prairie. il. Helen Sewell and Mildred Boyle. Harper, 1935; also il. Garth Williams, 1953.

*Little Town on the Prairie. il. Helen Sewell and Mildred Boyle. Harper, 1941; also il. Garth Williams, 1953; variant as *Little Town on the Prairie Color Book*. APB, 1976.

*Long Winter. il. Helen Sewell and Mildred Boyle. Harper, 1940; also il. Garth Williams, 1953.

*On the Banks of Plum Creek. il. Helen Sewell and Mildred Boyle. Harper, 1937; also il. Garth Williams, 1953.

BIBLIOGRAPHY (cont'd)

On the Way Home: The Diary from a Trip from South Dakota to Mansfield, Missouri in 1894, with a Setting by Rose Wilder Lane. Harper, 1962.

These Happy Golden Years. il. Helen Sewell and Mildred Boyle. Harper, 1942; also il. Garth Williams, 1953.

West from Home: Laura Ingalls Wilder's Letters to Alonzo Wilder, San Francisco, 1915; edited by Roger McBride, historical setting by Margot P. Doss. Harper, 1974.

related titles:

Laura Ingalls Wilder Songbook: Favorite Songs from the "Little House" Books; edited Eugenia Garson, music arranged Herbert Haufrecht. il. Garth Williams. Harper, 1968.

Prairie Recipes and Kitchen Antiques: A Delightful Collection of Recipes and Antiques from the Site of the Original Little House on the Prairie; by Wilma Kurtis and Anita Gold. il. photographs Wallace-Homestead, *ca.*1977.

MEDIA

By the Shores of Silver Lake. (BB, TB).

Farmer Boy. (BB, TB).

First Four Years. (TB).

Little House in the Big Woods. (BB, TB); Miller-Brody Productions, 1977 (C, R; includes *Little House on the Prairie*); Pathways of Sound, 19? (R); RCA, Inc., 19? (C).

Little House on the Prairie. (BB, TB); Miller-Brody Productions, 1977 (C, R; includes *Little House in the Big Woods*); National Broadcasting Company, *ca.*1975+ (TV series).

Little Town on the Prairie. (BB, TB).

On the Banks of Plum Creek. (BB, TB).

On the Way Home. (BB).

These Happy Golden Years. (BB, TB).

West from Home. (TB).

COLLECTIONS

DeSmet Public Library. (DeSmet, South Dakota).

Laura Ingalls Wilder Home and Museum. (Mansfield, Missouri).

Pomona Public Library. (Pomona, California).

BACKGROUND READING

Anderson, D. "Little More about Laura, Her Relatives in Wisconsin." *Elementary English*, March, May, 1964.

Anderson, William. *Story of the Ingalls.* Laura Ingalls Wilder Home and Museum Association, 1967; revised and enlarged edition, 1971.

Anderson, William. *Story of the Wilders.* Laura Ingalls Wilder Home and Museum Association, 1971.

Anderson, William. *Laura Wilder of Mansfield.* Laura Ingalls Wilder Home and Museum Association, 1968.

Colwell, E. "Laura Ingalls Wilder." *Junior Bookshelf*, November 1962.

Cooper, B. "Authenticity of the Historical Background of the "Little House" Books." *Elementary English*, November 1963.

Current Biography.

Doyle. *Who's Who of Children's Literature.*

Eddins, Doris K. *Teacher's Tribute to Laura Ingalls Wilder.* National Education Association, 1967.

Flanagan, F. "Tribute to Laura Ingalls Wilder." *Elementary English*, April 1957.

Getting to Know Laura. Missouri Library Association, Children's Services Roundtable, 1976.

Horn Book, special issues, December 1953 and October 1965.

Kies, C. "Laura and Mary and the Three R's." *Peabody Journal of Education*, September 1965.

Kirkpatrick. *Twentieth Century Children's Writers.*

Kunitz. *Junior Book of Authors, Second Edition Revised.*

Lane, R. "Who's Who and Why." *Saturday Evening Post*, July 6, 1935.

Laura Ingalls Wilder Lore, Vol. 1, 1976+.

Lichty, Irene, and Lichty, L. D. *Ingalls Family from Plum Creek to Walnut Grove via Burr Oak, Iowa.* Laura Ingalls Wilder Home and Museum Association, 1970.

Long, H. "Laura Ingalls Wilder Award." *Top of the News*, January 1965.

Montgomery. *Story behind Modern Books.*

Mortenson, L. "Little Houses and Magnificent Mansions." *Elementary English*, May 1968.

Obituary. *New York Times*, February 12, 1957.

Obituary. *Publishers Weekly*, February 25, 1957.

Obituary. *Wilson Library Bulletin*, April 1957.

Smaridge. *Famous Modern Storytellers for Young People.*

Smith, D. "Farmer Boy." *Franklin Historical Review*, August 1964.

Smith, I. "Laura Ingalls Wilder and the Little House Books." *Horn Book*, September 1943.

Stromdahl, J. "Lasting Contribution." *Top of the News*, January 1965.

Thurman, E. "On the Trail of Laura Ingalls Wilder." *Instructor*, February 1975.

Top of the News, special issue, April 1967.

Walker, B. "Trail of History Refreshingly Free of Violence." *New York Times*, September 21, 1969.

Ward. *Authors of Books for Young People, Second Edition*.

Ward, N. "Laura Ingalls Wilder: An Appreciation." *Elementary English*, October 1973.

Wenzel, E. " 'Little House' Books of Laura Ingalls Wilder." *Elementary English*, February 1952.

Zochert, Donald. *Laura: The Life of Laura Ingalls Wilder*. Regnery, 1976.

MAIA TERESA WOJCIECHOWSKA, 1927-
author
a.k.a. Maia Rodman

AWARDS

Shadow of a Bull. Newbery Medal Book, 1965.

BIBLIOGRAPHY

as Maia Rodman:

Loved Look: International Hairstyling Guide. American Hairdresser, 1960.

Market Day for 'Ti Andre. il. Wilson Bigaud. Viking, 1952.

as Maia Wojciechowska:

(tr.) *Bridge to the Other Side*; by Monika Kotowska. Doubleday, 1970.

"Don't Play Dead before You Have To." Harper, 1970.

"Hey, What's Wrong With This One?" il. Joan Sandin. Harper, 1969.

Hollywood Kid. Harper, 1966.

Kingdom in a Horse. Harper, 1965.

Life and Death of a Brave Bull. il. John Groth. Harcourt, 1972.

Odyssey of Courage: The Story of Alvar Nuñez Cabez da Vaca. il. Alvin Smith. Atheneum, 1965.

Rotten Years. Doubleday, 1971.

Shadow of a Bull. il. Alvin Smith. Atheneum, 1964.

Single Light. Harper, 1968; large print edition, 1969.

Through the Broken Mirror with Alice: Including Parts of Through the Looking-Glass, by Lewis Carroll. Harcourt, 1972.

Tuned-Out. Harper, 1968.

Winter Tales from Poland. il. Laslo Kubinyi. Doubleday, 1973.

MEDIA

Shadow of a Bull. (TB); Miller-Brody Productions, 1970 (C, R).

Single Light. (BB); Recording for the Blind, n. d. (C, MT).

Till the Break of Day. (BB).

Tuned Out. Recording for the Blind, n. d. (C, MT).

COLLECTIONS

Berrigan Collection, Olin Library, Cornell University. (Ithaca, New York).

deGrummond Collection, University of Southern Mississippi. (Hattiesburg, Mississippi).

Kerlan Collection, University of Minnesota. (Minneapolis, Minnesota).

BACKGROUND READING

Burke. *American Authors and Books, 1640 to the Present Day*.

Commire. *Something about the Author*.

Contemporary Authors.

Current Biography.

DeMontreville. *Third Book of Junior Authors*.

Frankel, H. "Say I'm Eccentric." *Saturday Review*, March 25, 1965.

Hoffman. *Authors and Illustrators of Children's Books*.

Hopkins. *More Books by More People*.

Kingman. *Newbery and Caldecott Medal Books, 1956-1965*.

Kirkpatrick. *Twentieth Century Children's Writers*.

Ward. *Authors of Books for Young People, Second Edition*.

Wintle. *Pied Pipers*.

+HILDEGARD WOODWARD, 1898-
author-illustrator

AWARDS

Roger and the Fox. Caldecott Honor Book, 1948.

Wild Birthday Cake. Caldecott Honor Book, 1950.

BIBLIOGRAPHY

America Travels: The Story of a Hundred Years of Travel in America; by Alice Dalgliesh. Scribner, 1933; revised, 1961.

Blue Teapot: Sandy Cove Stories; by Alice Dalgliesh. Macmillan, 1931.

Chosen Baby; by Virginia Wasson. Lippincott, 1950.

Christmas: A Book of Stories Old and New; edited by Alice Dalgliesh. Scribner, 1934; revised, 1950.

Country Neighborhood; by Elizabeth Coatsworth. Macmillan, 1944.

Danny's Luck; by Lavinia Davis. Doubleday, 1953.

Everyday Children. Oxford, 1935.

Heidi: Edited to Fit the Interests and Abilities of Young Readers by Edward L. Thorndike; by Johanna Spyri. Appleton, 1935.

Here's Juggins; by Amy Stone. Lothrop, 1936.

House on Grandfather's Hill. Scribner, 1961.

Jared's Blessing. Scribner, 1942.

Philippe's Hill; by Lee Kingman. Doubleday, 1950.

P-Penny and His Little Red Cart; by Amy Stone. Lothrop, 1934.

Relief's Rocker: A Story of Sandy Cove and the Sea; by Alice Dalgliesh. Macmillan, 1932.

Roger and the Fox; by Lavinia Davis. Doubleday, 1947.

Round Robin; by Lavinia Davis. Scribner, 1943.

Roundabout: Another Sandy Cove Story; by Alice Dalgliesh. Macmillan, 1934.

Summer Is Fun; by Lavinia Davis. Doubleday, 1951.

Time Was. Scribner, 1941.

Wild Birthday Cake; by Lavinia Davis. Doubleday, 1949.

Wonderful Story of How You Were Born; by Sidonie Gruenberg. Doubleday, 1952.

Yammy Buys a Bicycle; by Bernice Bryant. Whitman, 1940.

COLLECTIONS

Kerlan Collection, University of Minnesota. (Minneapolis, Minnesota).

BACKGROUND READING

Contemporary Authors.

Dalgliesh, A. "Two Illustrators: Katherine Milhous and Hildegard Woodward." *Horn Book*, January 1945.

Foremost Women in Communications.

Mahony. *Illustrators of Children's Books, 1744-1945*.

Miller. *Illustrators of Children's Books, 1946-1956*.

Ward. *Authors of Books for Young People, Second Edition*.

TARO YASHIMA, *pseudonym*, 1908-
author-illustrator
a.k.a. Atushi Jun Iwamatsu

AWARDS

Crow Boy. Caldecott Honor Book, 1956.

Seashore Story. Caldecott Honor Book, 1968.

Umbrella. Caldecott Honor Book, 1959.

BIBLIOGRAPHY

Crow Boy. Viking, 1955.

Fisherman and the Goblet; by Mark Taylor. Golden Gate, 1971.

Golden Footprints; with Hotoju Muku. World, 1960.

Horizon Is Calling. Holt, 1947.

Momo's Kitten; with Mitsu Yashima, *pseud.* (Tomoe Iwamatsu). Viking, 1961.

New Sun. Holt, 1943.

Plenty to Watch; with Mitsu Yashima, *pseud.* (Tomoe Iwamatsu). Viking, 1954.

Seashore Story. Viking, 1967.

Soo Ling Finds a Way; by June Behrens. Golden Gate, 1965.

Sugar Pear Tree; by Clyde R. Bulla. Crowell, 1961.

Umbrella. Viking, 1958.

Which Was Witch? Tales of Ghosts and Magic from Korea; by Eleanore M. Jewett. Viking, 1953.

Youngest One. Viking, 1962.

MEDIA

Crow Boy. (BB); Viking Press, 1975 (C); Weston Woods Studios, 1963 (FSS), 1971 (F); also in Weston Woods Studios Set No. 11, 1968 (FSS).

Golden Village as *Taro Yashima's Golden Village*. Gerald Johnson/Pyramid Films, 1972 (F).

Momo's Kitten. Viking Press, 1974 (C).

Umbrella. (BB, TB). Weston Woods Studios, 1968 (FSS); also in Weston Woods Studios Set No. 25, 1969 (FSS).

Village Tree. Viking Press, 1972 (C); Weston Woods Studios, 1973 (FSS).

EXHIBITIONS

ACA Gallery, 1944. (New York, New York).

COLLECTIONS

deGrummond Collection, University of Southern Mississippi. (Hattiesburg, Mississippi).

Kerlan Collection, University of Minnesota. (Minneapolis, Minnesota).

BACKGROUND READING

Commire. *Something about the Author.*

Contemporary Authors.

Fuller. *More Junior Authors.*

Hopkins. *Books Are by People.*

Johnson, G. "Golden Village: Taro Yashima's Book." *Horn Book*, April 1967.

Kingman. *Illustrators of Children's Books, 1957-1966.*

Kingman. *Illustrators of Children's Books, 1967-1976.*

Miller. *Illustrators of Children's Books, 1946-1956.*

Mordvinoff, N. "Artist's Choice." *Horn Book*, December 1952.

Smaridge. *Famous Literary Teams for Young People.*

Ward. *Illustrators of Books for Young People, Second Edition.*

Yashima, T. "On Making a Book for a Child." *Horn Book*, February 1955.

ELIZABETH YATES, 1905-
author

AWARDS

Amos Fortune, Free Man. Newbery Medal Book, 1951.

Mountain Born. Newbery Honor Book, 1944.

BIBLIOGRAPHY

Amos Fortune: Free Man. il. Nora S. Unwin. Aladdin, 1950.

Around the Year in Ireland. il. Jon Nielsen. Heath, 1942.

Beloved Bondage. Coward, 1948.

Book of Hours. Seabury, 1976.

Brave Interval. Coward, 1952.

Call It Zest. Stephen Greene, 1977.

Carey Girl. il. Georg Hartmann. Coward, 1956.

Carolina's Courage. il. Nora S. Unwin. Dutton, 1964; a.k.a. *Carolina and the Indian Doll.* Methuen, 1965.

Children of the Bible. il. Nora S. Unwin. Aladdin, 1950.

(ed.) *Christmas Story;* from the *Bible.* il. Nora S. Unwin. Aladdin, 1949.

Climbing Higher: An Iceland Adventure. Black, 1939.

David Livingstone. Row, 1952.

(ed.) *Doll Who Came Alive;* by Enys Tregarthen, *pseud.* (Nellie Sloggett). il. Nora S. Unwin. Day, 1942.

Easter Story. il. Nora S. Unwin. Dutton, 1967.

(ed.) *Gathered Grace: A Short Selection of George MacDonald's Poems with a Biographical Sketch;* by George MacDonald. il. Nora S. Unwin. Heffer, 1938.

Gifts of the True Love: Based on the Old Carol, The Twelve Days of Christmas. il. Nora S. Unwin. Pendle Hill, 1958; new edition, Countryman, 1976.

Guardian Heart. Coward, 1950.

Hans and Frieda in the Swiss Mountains. Nelson, 1939.

Haven for the Brave. Knopf, 1941.

High Holiday. Black, 1938; second edition, 1946.

Howard Thurman: Portrait of a Practical Dreamer. Day, 1964.

Hue and Cry. Coward, 1953.

Is There a Doctor in the Barn? A Day in the Life of Forrest F. Tenney, D.V.M. il. Guy Fleming. Dutton, 1966; new edition, Bauhan, 1977.

(ed.) *Joseph: The King James Version of a Well-Loved Tale;* from the *Bible.* il. Nora S. Unwin. Knopf, 1947.

Lighted Heart. il. Nora S. Unwin. Dutton, 1960; fourth edition, Bauhaun, 1974.

Mountain Born. il. Nora S. Unwin. Coward, 1943.

Nearby: A Novel. Coward, 1947.

New Hampshire. Coward, 1969.

Next Fine Day: A Novel. il. Nora S. Unwin. Day, 1962.

On That Night. il. James Barkley. Dutton, 1969.

Once in the Year: A Christmas Story. il. Nora S. Unwin. Coward, 1947.

Patterns on the Wall. il. Warren Chappell. Knopf, 1943.

Pebble in a Pool: The Widening Circles of Dorothy Canfield Fisher's Life. il. photographs. Dutton, 1958; a.k.a. *Lady from Vermont: Dorothy Canfield Fisher's Life and World.* Stephen Green, 1971.

BIBLIOGRAPHY (cont'd)

(ed.) *Piskey Folk: A Book of Cornish Legends*; by Enys Tregarthen, *pseud.* (Nellie Sloggett). photographs by William McGreal. Day, 1940.

Place for Peter. il. Nora S. Unwin. Coward, 1952.

Prudence Crandall: Woman of Courage. il. Nora S. Unwin. Dutton, 1955.

Quest in the North-Land: An Iceland Adventure. Knopf, 1940.

Rainbow 'round the World: A Story of UNICEF. il. Dirk Gringhuis and Betty Alden. Bobbs, 1954.

Road through Sandwich Notch. il. Nora S. Unwin. Stephen Greene, 1973.

Sam's Secret Journal. il. Allan Eitzen. Friendship, 1964.

Sarah Whitcher's Story. il. Nora S. Unwin. Dutton, 1971.

(ed.) *Sir Gibbie*; by George MacDonald. Dutton, 1963.

Skeezer: Dog with a Mission. il. Joan Drescher. Harvey, 1972.

Someday You'll Write. Dutton, 1962.

Under the Little Fir: And Other Stories. Coward, 1942.

Up the Golden Stair. Dutton, 1966.

We, the People. il. Nora S. Unwin. Countryman, 1974.

(ed.) *White Ring*; by Enys Tregarthen, *pseud.* (Nellie Sloggett). Harcourt, 1949.

Wind of Spring. Coward, 1945.

With Pipe, Paddle, and Song: A Story of the French-Canadian Voyageurs Circa 1750. il. Nora S. Unwin. Dutton, 1968.

Young Traveler in the U.S.A. Phoenix, 1948.

(ed.) *Your Prayers and Mine*. il. Nora S. Unwin. Houghton, 1954.

MEDIA

Amos Fortune. (BB, TB); Miller-Brody Productions, 19? (C, R).

Carolina's Courage. (TB).

David Livingstone. (TB).

Howard Thurman. (TB).

Hue and Cry. (BB, TB).

Lighted Heart. (BB, TB).

Mountain Born. Miller-Brody Productions, 1977 (C, R).

Next Fine Day. (BB).

On That Night. (BB).

Patterns on the Wall. (BB, TB).

Pebble in a Pool. (BB).

Prudence Crandall. (BB).

Rainbow 'round the World. (BB).

Someday You'll Write. (BB).

COLLECTIONS

deGrummond Collection, University of Southern Mississippi. (Hattiesburg, Mississippi).

Kerlan Collection, University of Minnesota. (Minneapolis, Minnesota).

May Massee Collection, Emporia State College. (Emporia, Kansas).

Mugar Memorial Library, Boston University. (Boston, Massachusetts).

Rare Book Room, Buffalo and Erie County Public Library. (Buffalo, New York).

BACKGROUND READING

Burke. *American Authors and Books, 1640 to the Present Day*.

Chapin, R. "Miss Yates on the Novel's Goal." *Christian Science Monitor*, October 8, 1950.

Commire. *Something about the Author*.

Contemporary Authors.

Current Biography.

Hoffman. *Authors and Illustrators of Children's Books*.

Hopkins. *More Books by More People*.

Kirkpatrick. *Twentieth Century Children's Writers*.

Kunitz. *Junior Book of Authors, Second Edition Revised*.

Kunitz. *Twentieth Century Authors, First Supplement*.

MacCampbell, J. "Work of Elizabeth Yates." *Elementary English*, November 1952.

Meet the Newbery Author, Elizabeth Yates. Miller-Brody Productions, 1976 (FS).

Miller. *Newbery Medal Books, 1922-1955*.

Painter, H. "Elizabeth Yates: Artist with Words." *Elementary English*, October 1965.

Ward. *Authors of Books for Young People, Second Edition*.

Warfel. *American Novelists of Today*.

Yates, E. "Please Answer This." *Horn Book*, April 1963.

Yates, E. "Why Did You End Your Story That Way?" *Horn Book*, December 1967.

Young Wings. *Writing Books for Boys and Girls.*

LAURENCE MICHAEL YEP, 1948-
author

AWARDS

Dragonwings. Newbery Honor Book, 1976.

BIBLIOGRAPHY

Child of the Owl. Harper, 1977.

Dragonwings. Harper, 1975.

Seademons. Harper, 1977.

Sweetwater. il. Julia Noonan. Harper, 1973.

MEDIA

Dragonwings. (CB); Miller-Brody Productions, 1977 (C, R).

Sweetwater. (BB, TB).

COLLECTIONS

Galaxy Publishing Company Collection, Arents Research Library, Syracuse University. (Syracuse, New York).

BACKGROUND READING

Commire. *Something about the Author.*

Contemporary Authors.

Yep, L. "Fantasy and Reality." *Horn Book*, April 1978.

Yep, L. "Writing Dragonwings." *Reading Teacher*, January 1977.

ED DJR-CHÙNG YOUNG, 1931-
illustrator

AWARDS

Emperor and the Kite. Caldecott Honor Book, 1968.

BIBLIOGRAPHY

Bird from the Sea; by Renee K. Weiss. Crowell, 1970.

Chinese Mother Goose Rhymes; edited by Robert Hyndman. World, 1968.

Cricket Boy; by Feenie Ziner. Doubleday, 1977.

8,000 Stones: A Chinese Folktale; by Diane Wolkstein. Doubleday, 1971.

Emperor and the Kite; by Jane Yolen. World, 1967.

Girl Who Loved the Wind; by Jane Yolen. Crowell, 1972.

Golden Swans: A Picture Story from Thailand, Retold; by Kermit Krueger. World, 1969.

Horse from Nowhere; edited by L. C. Hunt. Holt, 1973.

Mean Mouse and Other Mean Stories; by Janice M. Udry. Harper, 1962.

Poetry for Young Scientists; edited by Leland Jacobs and Sally Nohelty. Holt, 1964.

Red Lion, Adapted; by Diane Wolkstein. Crowell, 1977.

Seventh Mandarin; by Jane Yolen. Seabury, 1970.

Tiniest Sound; by Melvin Evans. Doubleday, 1969.

Yellow Boat; by Margaret Hillert. Follett, 1966.

Young Fu of the Upper Yangtze; by Elizabeth F. Lewis. Holt, 1973.

MEDIA

Seventh Mandarin. Xerox Filmstrips/Stephen F. Bosustow Productions, 1973 (F, FSS).

COLLECTIONS

Kerlan Collection, University of Minnesota. (Minneapolis, Minnesota).

BACKGROUND READING

Commire. *Something about the Author.*

DeMontreville. *Third Book of Junior Authors.*

Kingman. *Illustrators of Children's Books, 1967-1976.*

Ward. *Illustrators of Books for Young People, Second Edition.*

+ELLA YOUNG, 1867-1956
author

AWARDS

Tangle-Coated Horse. Newbery Honor Book, 1930.

Wonder Smith and His Son. Newbery Honor Book, 1928.

BIBLIOGRAPHY

Celtic Wonder Tales Retold. il. Maud Gonne. Dutton, 1923.

Coming of Laugh: A Celtic Wonder-Tale Retold. il. Maud Gonne. Maunsel, 1909.

*Flowering Dusk: Things Remembered Accurately and Inaccurately. Longmans, 1945.

Marzilian and Other Poems. n. p., 1949.

Seed of Pomegranate: And Other Poems. n. p., 1950.

Tangle-Coated Horse and Other Tales: Episodes from the Fionn Saga. il. Vera Bock. Longmans, 1929.

To the Little Princess: An Epistle. Seeger, 1930.

Unicorn with Silver Shoes. il. Robert Lawson. Longmans, 1932.

Wonder Smith and His Son: A Tale from the Golden Childhood of the World, Retold. il. Boris Artzybasheff. Longmans, 1927.

COLLECTIONS

Special Collections, University Research Library, University of California. (Los Angeles, California).

BACKGROUND READING

Colum, Padraic. *Ella Young: An Appreciation*. Longmans, 1931.

Eaton, A. "Ella Young's Unicorns and Kyelins." *Horn Book*, August 1933.

Flanagan, S. "Ella Young at Home." *Horn Book*, March 1939.

Horn Book, special issue, May 1939.

Kunitz. *Junior Book of Authors*.

Kunitz. *Junior Book of Authors, Second Edition Revised*.

Kunitz. *Living Authors*.

Kunitz. *Twentieth Century Authors*.

Kunitz. *Twentieth Century Authors, First Supplement*.

Obituary. *New York Times*, July 25, 1956.

Obituary. *Publishers Weekly*, September 3, 1956.

Obituary. *Wilson Library Bulletin*, September 1956.

Sayers, F. "Flowering Dusk of Ella Young." *Horn Book*, May 1945.

Ward. *Authors of Books for Young People, Second Edition*.

Young, E. "Faerie Music (Ceol Sidhe)." *Horn Book*, May 1945.

MARGOT ZEMACH, 1931-
author-illustrator

AWARDS

Duffy and the Devil. Caldecott Medal Book, 1974.

Judge. Caldecott Honor Book, 1970.

(*When Shlemiel Went to Warsaw*. Newbery Honor Book, 1969.)

BIBLIOGRAPHY

Alone in the Wild Forest; by Isaac B. Singer. Tr. Isaac B. Singer and Elizabeth Shub. Farrar, 1971.

Awake and Dreaming; by Harve Zemach, *pseud.* (Harvey Fischtrom). Farrar, 1970.

Duffy and the Devil: A Cornish Tale, Retold; by Harve Zemach, *pseud.* (Harvey Fischtrom). Farrar, 1973.

Favorite Fairy Tales Told in Denmark; by Virginia Haviland. Little, 1971.

Fisherman and His Wife; by Jacob and Wilhelm Grimm. Norton, 1966.

Foundling and Other Tales of Pyrdain; by Lloyd Alexander. Holt, 1973.

Frogs Who Wanted a King and Other Songs from La Fontaine; by Jean De La Fontaine, edited by Edward Smith. Four Winds, 1977.

Harlequin; by Rose L. Mincielli. Knopf, 1968.

Hat with a Rose; by Harve Zemach, *pseud.* (Harvey Fischtrom). Dutton, 1961.

Hush, Little Baby. Dutton, 1976.

It Could Always Be Worse. Farrar, 1977.

Judge: An Untrue Tale; by Harve Zemach, *pseud.* (Harvey Fischtrom). Farrar, 1969.

King of the Hermits: And Other Stories; by Jack Sendak. Farrar, 1967.

Last Dragon; by Fleming L. Blitch. Lippincott, 1964.

Little Tiny Woman. Bobbs, 1965.

Mazel and Schlimazel: Or, The Milk of a Lioness; by Isaac B. Singer. Tr. Elizabeth Shub. Farrar, 1967.

Mommy, Buy Me a China Doll: Adapted from an Ozark Children's Song; by Harve Zemach, *pseud.* (Harvey Fischtrom). Follett, 1966; new edition, Farrar, 1976.

Naftali the Story Teller and His Horse, Sus; by Isaac B. Singer. Farrar, 1976.

Nail Soup: A Swedish Folktale, Retold; by Harve Zemach, *pseud.* (Harvey Fischtrom). Follett, 1965.

Penny a Look: An Old Story Retold; by Harve Zemach, *pseud.* (Harvey Fischtrom). Follett, 1971.

Princess and Froggie; by Kaethe and Harve Zemach, *pseud.* (Kaethe and Harvey Fischtrom). Farrar, 1975.

Question Box; by J. Williams. Norton, 1965.

Salt: A Russian Tale from a Literal Translation by Benjamin Zemach; adapted by Harve Zemach, *pseud.* (Harvey Fischtrom). Follett, 1965; new edition, Farrar, 1977.

Simon Broom Gives a Wedding; by Uri Suhl. Four Winds, 1972.

Small Boy Is Listening; by Harve Zemach, *pseud.* (Harvey Fischtrom). Houghton, 1959.

Speckled Hen: A Russian Nursery Rhyme; by Harve Zemach, *pseud.* (Harvey Fischtrom). Holt, 1966.

Take a Giant Step; by Hannelore Hahn. Little, 1960.

Three Sillies: A Folk Tale. Holt, 1963.

To Hilda for Helping. Farrar, 1977.

Too Much Nose: An Italian Tale, Adapted; by Harve Zemach. *pseud.* (Harvey Fischtrom). Holt, 1967.

Tricks of Master Dabble; by Harve Zemach, *pseud.* (Harvey Fischtrom). Holt, 1965.

When Shlemiel Went to Warsaw and Other Stories; by Isaac B. Singer. Tr. Isaac B. Singer and Elizabeth Shub. Farrar, 1968.

Why Don't You Draw a Dog; by Marguerite Melcher. Little, 1962.

MEDIA

Duffy and the Devil. Miller-Brody Productions, 1975 (FSS).

Judge. Miller-Brody Productions, 1975 (FSS).

Little Tiny Woman. Weston Woods Studios, 19? (R).

Mazel and Schlimazel. Miller-Brody Productions, 1976 (FSS).

Mommy, Buy Me a China Doll. Weston Woods Studios, 1970 (FSS).

Nail Soup. Weston Woods Studios, 19? (FSS).

Princess and Froggie. Random House, 1977 (FSS).

Salt. Weston Woods Studios, 19? (FSS); also in Weston Woods Studios Set No. 18, 1968 (FSS).

COLLECTIONS

Free Library of Philadelphia. (Philadelphia, Pennsylvania).

Kerlan Collection, University of Minnesota. (Minneapolis, Minnesota).

BACKGROUND READING

Bader. *American Picturebooks from Noah's Ark to The Beast Within*.

DeMontreville. *Third Book of Junior Authors*.

Kingman. *Illustrators of Children's Books, 1956-1966*.

Kingman. *Illustrators of Children's Books, 1967-1976*.

Kingman. *Newbery and Caldecott Medal Books, 1966-1975*.

Ward. *Illustrators of Books for Young People, Second Edition*.

Zemach, M. and H. "I Liked the Part Where the Mother Fell in the Mud." *Publishers Weekly*, February 26, 1968.

Appendix A
NEWBERY MEDAL AND HONOR BOOKS,
1922-1977

Honor Book listings in these appendixes are in alphabetical order within the award year. Readers will note that some years have the notation "No record" in the Honor Books listing. This indicates that Honor Books for that year, if any, are not known and records do not exist to indicate that any books received the Honor Book designation for that year.

1922

MEDAL BOOK

Story of Mankind, by Hendrik Van Loon

HONOR BOOKS

Cedric the Forester, by Bernard Marshall

Golden Fleece and the Heroes Who Lived before Achilles, by Padraic Colum

Great Quest, by Charles B. Hawes

Old Tobacco Shop, by William Bowen

Windy Hill, by Cornelia Meigs

1923

MEDAL BOOK

Voyages of Dr. Dolittle, by Hugh Lofting

HONOR BOOK

No record

1924

MEDAL BOOK

Dark Frigate, by Charles B. Hawes

HONOR BOOK

No record

1925

MEDAL BOOK

Tales from Silver Lands, by Charles Finger

HONOR BOOKS

Dream Coach, by Anne Parrish

Nicholas, by Anne C. Moore

1926

MEDAL BOOK

Shen of the Sea, by Arthur B. Chrisman

HONOR BOOK

Voyagers, by Padraic Colum

1927

MEDAL BOOK

Smoky, the Cowhorse, by Will James

HONOR BOOK

No record

1928

MEDAL BOOK

Gayneck: The Story of a Pigeon, by Dhan G. Mukerji

HONOR BOOKS

Downright Dencey, by Caroline D. Snedeker

Wonder Smith and His Son, by Ella Young

1929

MEDAL BOOK

Trumpeter of Krakow, by Eric Kelly

HONOR BOOKS

Boy Who Was, by Grace Hallock

Clearing Weather, by Cornelia Meigs

Millions of Cats, by Wanda Gág

Pigtail of Ah Lee Ben Loo, by John Bennett

Runaway Papoose, by Grace Moon

Tod of the Fens, by Elinor Whitney

1930

MEDAL BOOK

Hitty, by Rachel Field

HONOR BOOKS

Daughter of the Seine, by Jeanette Eaton

Jumping-Off Place, by Marian H. McNeely

Little Blacknose, by Hildegarde H. Swift

Pran of Albania, by Elizabeth Miller

Tangle-Coated Horse and Other Tales, by Ella Young

Vaino, by Julia D. Adams

1931

MEDAL BOOK

Cat Who Went to Heaven, by Elizabeth Coatsworth

HONOR BOOKS

Dark Star of Itza, by Alida Malkus

Floating Island, by Anne Parrish

Garram the Hunter, by Herbert Best

Meggy Macintosh, by Elizabeth J. Gray

Mountains Are Free, by Julia D. Adams

Ood-Le-Uk the Wanderer, by Alison Lide and Margaret Johansen

Queer Person, by Ralph Hubbard

Spice and the Devil's Cave, by Agnes Hewes

1932

MEDAL BOOK

Waterless Mountain, by Laura A. Armer

HONOR BOOKS

Boy of the South Seas, by Eunice Tietjens

Calico Bush, by Rachel Field

Fairy Circus, by Dorothy Lathrop

Jane's Island, by Marjorie H. Allee

Out of the Flame, by Eloise Lownsbery

Truce of the Wolf and Other Tales of Old Italy, by Mary G. Davis

1933

MEDAL BOOK

Young Fu of the Upper Yangtze, by Elizabeth F. Lewis

HONOR BOOKS

Children of the Soil, by Nora Burglon

Railroad to Freedom, by Hildegarde H. Swift

Swift Rivers, by Cornelia Meigs

1934

MEDAL BOOK

Invincible Louisa, by Cornelia Meigs

HONOR BOOKS

ABC Bunny, by Wanda Gág

Apprentice of Florence, by Anne Kyle

Big Tree of Bunlahy, by Padraic Colum

Forgotten Daughter, by Caroline D. Snedeker

Glory of the Seas, by Agnes Hewes

New Land, by Sarah Schmidt

Swords of Steel, by Elsie Singmaster

Winged Girl of Knossos, by Erick Berry

1935

MEDAL BOOK

Dobry, by Monica Shannon

HONOR BOOKS

Davy Crockett, by Constance Rourke

Day on Skates, by Hilda Van Stockum

Pageant of Chinese History, by Elizabeth Seeger

1936

MEDAL BOOK

Caddie Woodlawn, by Carol R. Brink

HONOR BOOKS

All Sail Set, by Armstrong Sperry

Good Master, by Kate Seredy

Honk, the Moose, by Phil Stong

Young Walter Scott, by Elizabeth J. Gray

1937

MEDAL BOOK

Roller Skates, by Ruth Sawyer

HONOR BOOKS

Audubon, by Constance Rourke

Codfish Market, by Agnes Hewes

Golden Basket, by Ludwig Bemelmans

Phebe Fairchild, Her Book, by Lois Lenski

Whistler's Van, by Idwal Jones

Winterbound, by Margery Bianco

1938

MEDAL BOOK

White Stag, by Kate Seredy

HONOR BOOKS

Bright Island, by Mabel L. Robinson

On the Banks of Plum Creek, by Laura I. Wilder

Pecos Bill, by James C. Bowman

1939

MEDAL BOOK

Thimble Summer, by Elizabeth Enright

HONOR BOOKS

"Hello, the Boat!," by Phyllis Crawford

Leader by Destiny, by Jeanette Eaton

Mr. Popper's Penguins, by Richard and Florence Atwater

Nino, by Valenti Angelo

Penn, by Elizabeth J. Gray

1940

MEDAL BOOK

Daniel Boone, by James Daugherty

HONOR BOOKS

Boy with a Pack, by Stephen Meader

By the Shores of Silver Lake, by Laura I. Wilder

Runner of the Mountain Tops, by Mabel L. Robinson

Singing Tree, by Kate Seredy

1941

MEDAL BOOK

Call It Courage, by Armstrong Sperry

HONOR BOOKS

Blue Willow, by Doris Gates

Long Winter, by Laura I. Wilder

Nansen, by Anna G. Hall

Young Mac of Fort Vancouver, by Mary Jane Carr

1942

MEDAL BOOK

Matchlock Gun, by Walter D. Edmonds

HONOR BOOKS

Down Ryton Water, by Eva R. Gaggin

George Washington's World, by Genevieve Foster

Indian Captive, by Lois Lenski

Little Town on the Prairie, by Laura I. Wilder

1943

MEDAL BOOK

Adam of the Road, by Elizabeth J. Gray

HONOR BOOKS

"Have You Seen Tom Thumb?", by Mabel L. Hunt

Middle Moffatt, by Eleanor Estes

1944

MEDAL BOOK

Johnny Tremain, by Esther Forbes

HONOR BOOKS

Fog Magic, by Julia Sauer

Mountain Born, by Elizabeth Yates

Rufus M, by Eleanor Estes

These Happy Golden Years, by Laura I. Wilder

1945

MEDAL BOOK

Rabbit Hill, by Robert Lawson

HONOR BOOKS

Abraham Lincoln's World, by Genevieve Foster

Hundred Dresses, by Eleanor Estes

Lone Journey, by Jeanette Eaton

Silver Pencil, by Alice Dalgliesh

1946

MEDAL BOOK

Strawberry Girl, by Lois Lenski

HONOR BOOKS

Bhimsa, the Dancing Bear, by Christine Weston

Justin Morgan Had a Horse, by Marguerite Henry

Moved-Outers, by Florence C. Means

New Found World, by Katherine Shippen

1947

MEDAL BOOK

Miss Hickory, by Carolyn S. Bailey

HONOR BOOKS

Avion My Uncle Flew, by Cyrus Fisher

Big Tree, by Mary and Conrad Buff

Heavenly Tenants, by William Maxwell

Hidden Treasure of Glaston, by Eleanore Jewett

Wonderful Year, by Nancy Barnes

1948

MEDAL BOOK

Twenty-one Balloons, by William P. Du Bois

HONOR BOOKS

Cow-Tail Switch and Other West African Stories, by Harold Courlander

Li Lun, by Carolyn Treffinger

Misty of Chincoteague, by Marguerite Henry

Pancakes—Paris, by Claire H. Bishop

Quaint and Curious Education of Johnny Longfoot, by Catherine Besterman

1949

MEDAL BOOK

King of the Wind, by Marguerite Henry

HONOR BOOKS

Daughter of the Mountains, by Louise Rankin

My Father's Dragon, by Ruth S. Gannett

Seabird, by Holling C. Holling

Story of the Negro, by Arna Bontemps

1950

MEDAL BOOK

Door in the Wall, by Marguerite de Angeli

HONOR BOOKS

Blue Cat of Castletown, by Catherine C. Coblentz

George Washington, by Genevieve Foster

Kildee House, by Rutherford B. Montgomery

Song of the Pines, by Walter and Marion Havighurst

Tree of Freedom, by Rebecca Caudill

1951

MEDAL BOOK

Amos Fortune, Free Man, by Elizabeth Yates

HONOR BOOKS

Abraham Lincoln: Friend of the People, by Clara I. Judson

Better Known as Johnny Appleseed, by Mabel L. Hunt

Gandhi: Fighter without a Sword, by Jeanette Eaton

Story of Appleby Capple, by Anne Parrish

1952

MEDAL BOOK

Ginger Pye, by Eleanor Estes

HONOR BOOKS

Americans before Columbus, by Elizabeth C. Baity

Apple and the Arrow, by Mary and Conrad Buff

Defender, by Nicholas Kalashnikoff

Light at Tern Rock, by Julia Sauer

Minn of the Mississippi, by Holling C. Holling

1953

MEDAL BOOK

Secret of the Andes, by Ann N. Clark

HONOR BOOKS

Bears on Hemlock Mountain, by Alice Dalgliesh

Birthdays of Freedom, Volume 1, by Genevieve Foster

Charlotte's Web, by E. B. White

Moccasin Trail, by Eloise J. McGraw

Red Sails to Capri, by Ann Weil

1954

MEDAL BOOK

. . . And Now Miguel, by Joseph Krumgold

HONOR BOOKS

All Alone, by Claire H. Bishop

Hurry Home, Candy, by Meindert DeJong

Magic Maize, by Mary and Conrad Buff

Shadrach, by Meindert DeJong

Theodore Roosevelt, by Clara I. Judson

1955

MEDAL BOOK

Wheel on the School, by Meindert DeJong

HONOR BOOKS

Banner in the Sky, by James R. Ullman

Courage of Sarah Noble, by Alice Dalgliesh

1956

MEDAL BOOK

Carry On, Mr. Bowditch, by Jean L. Latham

HONOR BOOKS

Golden Name Day, by Jennie D. Lindquist

Men, Microscopes and Living Things, by Katherine Shippen

Secret River, by Marjorie K. Rawlings

1957

MEDAL BOOK

Miracles on Maple Hill, by Virginia Sorensen

HONOR BOOKS

Black Fox of Lorne, by Marguerite de Angeli

Corn Grows Ripe, by Dorothy Rhoads

House of Sixty Fathers, by Meindert DeJong

Mr. Justice Holmes, by Clara I. Judson

Old Yeller, by Fred Gipson

1958

MEDAL BOOK

Rifles for Watie, by Harold Keith

HONOR BOOKS

Gone-Away Lake, by Elizabeth Enright

Great Wheel, by Robert Lawson

Horsecatcher, by Mari Sandoz

Tom Paine: Freedom's Apostle, by Leo Gurko

1959

MEDAL BOOK

Witch of Blackbird Pond, by Elizabeth G. Speare

HONOR BOOKS

Along Came a Dog, by Meindert DeJong

Chúcaro, by Frances Kalnay

Family under the Bridge, by Natalie S. Carlson

Perilous Road, by William O. Steele

1960

MEDAL BOOK

Onion John, by Joseph Krumgold

HONOR BOOKS

America Is Born, by Gerald W. Johnson

Gammage Cup, by Carol Kendall

My Side of the Mountain, by Jean George

1961

MEDAL BOOK

Island of the Blue Dolphins, by Scott O'Dell

HONOR BOOKS

America Moves Forward, by Gerald W. Johnson

Cricket in Times Square, by George Selden

Old Ramon, by Jack Schaefer

1962

MEDAL BOOK

Bronze Bow, by Elizabeth G. Speare

HONOR BOOKS

Belling the Tiger, by Mary Stolz

Frontier Living, by Edwin Tunis

Golden Goblet, by Eloise J. McGraw

1963

MEDAL BOOK

Wrinkle in Time, by Madeleine L'Engle

HONOR BOOKS

Men of Athens, by Olivia Coolidge

Thistle and Thyme, by Sorche N. Leodhas

1964

MEDAL BOOK

It's Like This, Cat, by Emily C. Neville

HONOR BOOKS

Loner, by Ester Wier

Rascal, by Sterling North

1965

MEDAL BOOK

Shadow of a Bull, by Maia Wojciechowska

HONOR BOOK

Across Five Aprils, by Irene Hunt

1966

MEDAL BOOK

I, Juan de Pareja, by Elizabeth B. de Treviño

HONOR BOOKS

Animal Family, by Randall Jarrell

Black Cauldron, by Lloyd Alexander

Noonday Friends, by Mary Stolz

1967

MEDAL BOOK

Up a Road Slowly, by Irene Hunt

HONOR BOOKS

Jazz Man, by Mary H. Weik

King's Fifth, by Scott O'Dell

Zlateh the Goat, by Isaac B. Singer

1968

MEDAL BOOK

From the Mixed-Up Files of Mrs. Basil E. Frankweiler, by E. L. Konigsburg

HONOR BOOKS

Black Pearl, by Scott O'Dell

Egypt Game, by Zilpha K. Snyder

Fearsome Inn, by Isaac B. Singer

Jennifer, Hecate, Macbeth, William McKinley, and Me, Elizabeth, by E. L. Konigsburg

1969

MEDAL BOOK

High King, by Lloyd Alexander

HONOR BOOKS

To Be a Slave, by Julius Lester

When Shlemiel Went to Warsaw & Other Stories, by Isaac B. Singer

1970

MEDAL BOOK

Sounder, by William H. Armstrong

HONOR BOOKS

Journey Outside, by Mary Q. Steele

Many Ways of Seeing, by Janet G. Moore

Our Eddie, by Sulamith Ish-Kishor

1971

MEDAL BOOK

Summer of the Swans, by Betsy Byars

1971 (cont'd)

HONOR BOOKS

Enchantress from the Stars, by Sylvia L. Engdahl

Knee-Knock Rise, by Natalie Babbitt

Sing Down the Moon, by Scott O'Dell

1972

MEDAL BOOK

Mrs. Frisby and the Rats of NIMH, by Robert C. O'Brien

HONOR BOOKS

Annie and the Old One, by Miska Miles

Headless Cupid, by Zilpha K. Snyder

Incident at Hawks Hill, by Allan W. Eckert

Planet of Junior Brown, by Virginia Hamilton

Tombs of Atuan, by Ursula LeGuin

1973

MEDAL BOOK

Julie of the Wolves, by Jean George

HONOR BOOKS

Frog and Toad Together, by Arnold Lobel

Upstairs Room, by Johanna Reiss

Witches of Worm, by Zilpha K. Snyder

1974

MEDAL BOOK

Slave Dancer, by Paula Fox

HONOR BOOK

Dark Is Rising, by Susan Cooper

1975

MEDAL BOOK

M. C. Higgins, the Great, by Virginia Hamilton

HONOR BOOKS

Figgs & Phantoms, by Ellen Raskin

My Brother Sam Is Dead, by James and Christopher Collier

Perilous Gard, by Elizabeth M. Pope

Phillip Hall Likes Me, I Reckon Maybe, by Bette Greene

1976

MEDAL BOOK

Grey King, by Susan Cooper

HONOR BOOKS

Dragonwings, by Laurence Yep

Hundred Penny Box, by Sharon B. Mathis

1977

MEDAL BOOK

Roll of Thunder, Hear My Cry, Mildred D. Taylor

HONOR BOOKS

Abel's Island, by William Steig

String in the Harp, by Nancy Bond

1938

MEDAL BOOK

Animals of the Bible, il. Dorothy Lathrop

HONOR BOOKS

Four and Twenty Blackbirds, il. Robert Lawson

Seven Simeons, il. Boris Artzybasheff

1939

MEDAL BOOK

Mei Lei, il. Thomas Handforth

HONOR BOOKS

Andy and the Lion, il. James Daughterty

Barkis, il. Clare Newberry

Forest Pool, il. Laura A. Armer

Snow White and the Seven Dwarfs, il. Wanda Gág

Wee Gillis, il. Robert Lawson

1940

MEDAL BOOK

Abraham Lincoln, il. Ingri and Edgar P. D'Aulaire

HONOR BOOKS

Ageless Story, il. Lauren Ford

Cock-a-Doodle Doo, il. Berta and Elmer Hader

Madeline, il. Ludwig Bemelmans

1941

MEDAL BOOK

They Were Strong and Good, il. Robert Lawson

HONOR BOOK

April's Kittens, il. Clare Newberry

1942

MEDAL BOOK

Make Way for Ducklings, il. Robert McCloskey

HONOR BOOKS

American ABC, il. Maud and Miska Petersham

In My Mother's House, il. Velino Herrera

Nothing at All, il Wanda Gág

Paddle-to-the-Sea, il. Holling C. Holling

1943

MEDAL BOOK

Little House, il. Virginia Lee Burton

HONOR BOOKS

Dash and Dart, il. Conrad Buff

Marshmallow, il. Clare Newberry

1944

MEDAL BOOK

Many Moons, il. Louis Slobodkin

HONOR BOOKS

Child's Good Night Book, il. Jean Charlot

Good Luck Horse, il. Plato Chan

Mighty Hunter, il. Berta and Elmer Hader

Pierre Pigeon, il. Arnold E. Bare

Small Rain, il. Elizabeth O. Jones

1945

MEDAL BOOK

Prayer for a Child, il. Elizabeth O. Jones

1945 (cont'd)

HONOR BOOKS

Christmas Anna Angel, il. Kate Seredy

In the Forest, il. Marie H. Ets

Mother Goose, il. Tasha Tudor

Yonie Wondernose, il. Marguerite de Angeli

1946

MEDAL BOOK

Rooster Crows, il. Maud and Miska Petersham

HONOR BOOKS

Little Lost Lamb, il. Leonard Weisgard

My Mother Is the Most Beautiful Woman in the World, il. Ruth C. Gannett

Sing Mother Goose, il. Marjorie Torrey

You Can Write Chinese, il. Kurt Wiese

1947

MEDAL BOOK

Little Island, il. Leonard Weisgard

HONOR BOOKS

Boats on the River, il. Jay H. Barnum

Pedro, the Angel of Olvera Street, il. Leo Politi

Rain Drop Splash, il. Leonard Weisgard

Sing in Praise, il. Majorie Torrey

Timothy Turtle, il. Tony Palazzo

1948

MEDAL BOOK

White Snow, Bright Snow, il. Roger Duvoisin

HONOR BOOKS

Bambino, the Clown, il. Georges Schreiber

McElligot's Pool, il. Dr. Seuss

Roger and the Fox, il. Hildegard Woodward

Song of Robin Hood, il. Virginia Lee Burton

Stone Soup, il. Marcia Brown

1949

MEDAL BOOK

Big Snow, il. Berta and Elmer Hader

HONOR BOOKS

All around the Town, il. Helen Stone

Blueberries for Sal, il. Robert McCloskey

Fish in the Air, il. Kurt Wiese

Juanita, il. Leo Politi

1950

MEDAL BOOK

Song of the Swallows, il. Leo Politi

HONOR BOOKS

America's Ethan Allen, il. Lynd Ward

Bartholomew and the Oobleck, il. Dr. Seuss

Happy Day, il. Marc Simont

Henry—Fisherman, il. Marcia Brown

Wild Birthday Cake, il. Hildegard Woodward

1951

MEDAL BOOK

Egg Tree, il. Katherine Milhous

HONOR BOOKS

Dick Whittington and His Cat, il. Marcia Brown

If I Ran the Zoo, il. Dr. Seuss

Most Wonderful Doll in the World, il. Helen Stone

T-Bone, the Baby Sitter, il. Clare Newberry

Two Reds, il. Nicolas

1952

MEDAL BOOK

Finders Keepers, il. Nicolas

HONOR BOOKS

All Falling Down, il. Margaret B. Graham

Bear Party, il. William Pène du Bois

Feather Mountain, il. Elizabeth Olds

Mr. T. W. Anthony Woo, il. Marie H. Ets

Skipper John's Cook, il. Marcia Brown

1953

MEDAL BOOK

Biggest Bear, il. Lynd Ward

HONOR BOOKS

Ape in a Cape, il. Fritz Eichenberg

Five Little Monkeys, il. Juliet Kepes

One Morning in Maine, il. Robert McCloskey

Puss in Boots, il. Marcia Brown

Storm Book, il. Margaret B. Graham

1954

MEDAL BOOK

Madeline's Rescue, il. Ludwig Bemelmans

HONOR BOOKS

Green Eyes, il. Abe Birnbaum

Journey Cake, Ho!, il. Robert McCloskey

Steadfast Tin Soldier, il. Marcia Brown

Very Special House, il. Maurice Sendak

When Will the World Be Mine?, il. Jean Charlot

1955

MEDAL BOOK

Cinderella, il. Marcia Brown

HONOR BOOKS

Book of Nursery and Mother Goose Rhymes, il. Marguerite de Angeli

Thanksgiving Story, il. Helen Sewell

Wheel on the Chimney, il. Tibor Gergely

1956

MEDAL BOOK

Frog Went a-Courtin', il. Feodor Rojankovsky

HONOR BOOKS

Crow Boy, il. Taro Yashima

Play with Me, il. Marie H. Ets

1957

MEDAL BOOK

Tree Is Nice, il. Marc Simont

HONOR BOOKS

Anatole, il. Paul Galdone

Gillespie and the Guards, il. James Daugherty

Lion, il. William Pène du Bois

Mr. Penny's Race Horse, il. Marie H. Ets

1 Is One, il. Tasha Tudor

1958

MEDAL BOOK

Time of Wonder, il. Robert McCloskey

HONOR BOOKS

Anatole and the Cat, il. Paul Galdone

Fly High, Fly Low, il. Don Freeman

1959

MEDAL BOOK

Chanticleer and the Fox, il. Barbara Cooney

HONOR BOOKS

House That Jack Built, il. Antonio Frasconi

Umbrella, il. Taro Yashima

What Do You Say, Dear?, il. Maurice Sendak

1960

MEDAL BOOK

Nine Days to Christmas, il. Marie H. Ets

HONOR BOOKS

Houses from the Sea, il. Adrienne Adams

Moon Jumpers, il. Maurice Sendak

1961

MEDAL BOOK

Baboushka and the Three Kings, il. Nicholas Sidjakov

HONOR BOOK

Inch by Inch, il. Leo Lionni

1962

MEDAL BOOK

Once a Mouse, il. Marcia Brown

HONOR BOOKS

Day We Saw the Sun Come Up, il. Adrienne Adams

Fox Went Out on a Chilly Night, il. Peter Spier

Little Bear's Visit, il. Maurice Sendak

1963

MEDAL BOOK

Snowy Day, il. Ezra J. Keats

HONOR BOOKS

Mr. Rabbit and the Lovely Present, il. Maurice Sendak

Sun Is a Golden Earring, il. Bernarda Bryson

1964

MEDAL BOOK

Where the Wild Things Are, il. Maurice Sendak

HONOR BOOKS

All in the Morning Early, il. Evaline Ness

Mother Goose and Nursery Rhymes, il. Philip Reed

Swimmy, il. Leo Lionni

1965

MEDAL BOOK

May I Bring a Friend?, il. Beni Montresor

HONOR BOOKS

Pocketful of Cricket, il. Evaline Ness

Rain Makes Applesauce, il. Marvin Bileck

Wave, il. Blair Lent

1966

MEDAL BOOK

Always Room for One More, il. Nonny Hogrogian

HONOR BOOKS

Hide and Seek Fog, il. Roger Duvoisin

Just Me, il. Marie H. Ets

Tom Tit Tot, il. Evaline Ness

1967

MEDAL BOOK

Sam, Bangs and Moonshine, il. Evaline Ness

HONOR BOOK

One Wide River to Cross, il. Ed Emberley

1968

MEDAL BOOK

Drummer Hoff, il. Ed Emberley

HONOR BOOKS

Frederick, il. Leo Lionni
Emperor and the Kite, il. Ed Young
Seashore Story, il. Taro Yashima

1969

MEDAL BOOK

Fool of the World and the Flying Ship, il. Uri Shulevitz

HONOR BOOK

Why the Sun and the Moon Live in the Sky, il. Blair Lent

1970

MEDAL BOOK

Sylvester and the Magic Pebble, il. William Steig

HONOR BOOKS

Alexander and the Wind-Up Mouse, il. Leo Lionni
Goggles, il. Ezra J. Keats
Judge, il. Margot Zemach
Pop Corn & Ma Goodness, il. Robert A. Parker
Thy Friend, Obadiah, il. Brinton Turkle

1971

MEDAL BOOK

Story, a Story, il. Gail Haley

HONOR BOOKS

Angry Moon, il. Blair Lent
Frog and Toad Are Friends, il. Arnold Lobel
In the Night Kitchen, il. Maurice Sendak

1972

MEDAL BOOK

One Fine Day, il. Nonny Hogrogian

HONOR BOOKS

Hildilid's Night, il. Arnold Lobel
If All the Seas Were One, il. Janina Domanska
Moja Means One, il. Tom Feelings

1973

MEDAL BOOK

Funny Little Woman, il. Blair Lent

HONOR BOOKS

Anansi the Spider, il. Gerald McDermott
Hosie's Alphabet, il. Leonard Baskin
Snow-White and the Seven Dwarfs, il. Nancy Burkert
When Clay Sings, il. Tom Bahti

1974

MEDAL BOOK

Duffy and the Devil, il. Margot Zemach

HONOR BOOKS

Cathedral, il. David Macaulay
Three Jovial Huntsmen, il. Susan Jeffers

1975

MEDAL BOOK

Arrow to the Sun, il. Gerald McDermott

HONOR BOOK

Jambo Means Hello, il. Tom Feelings

1976

MEDAL BOOK

Why Mosquitoes Buzz in People's Ears, il. Leo and Diane Dillon

HONOR BOOKS

Desert Is Theirs, il. Peter Parnall

Strega Nona, il. Tomie dePaola

1977

MEDAL BOOK

Ashanti to Zulu: African Traditions, il. Leo and Diane Dillon

HONOR BOOKS

Amazing Bone, il. William Steig

Contest, il. Nonny Hogrogian

Fish for Supper, il. M. B. Goffstein

Golem, il. Beverly McDermott

Hawk, I'm Your Brother, il. Peter Parnall

SUBJECT
BIBLIOGRAPHY

This subject bibliography of primary reference books and resource material used to develop this book follows the format of the text, *i.e.* Awards, Bibliography, Media, Exhibitions, Collections, and Background Reading. These reference books and materials are listed in the category where they were the most helpful. Many of them, of course, did provide various bits of information in the other sections as well.

AWARDS

Children's Books: Awards and Prizes. New York: Children's Book Council, 1977.

BIBLIOGRAPHY

Note: Awardees, their estates, or their representatives were contacted to verify listings. Due to their corrections and additions, individual book entries in the text may be at variance with similar entries listed in the reference books here.

American Library Association. *The National Union Catalog, Pre-1956 Imprints: A Cumulative Author List Representing Library of Congress Printed Cards and Titles Reported by Other American Libraries*. 604 vols. London: Mansell Information/Publishing, 1968-1978.

Book Review Digest: Evaluation of Literature. 73 vols. New York: H. W. Wilson Company, 1905-1978.

Books in Print. 31 vols. New York: R. R. Bowker, 1948-1979.

Cianciolo, Patricia, ed. *Adventuring with Books for Pre-Kindergarten-Grade 8*. Urbana, Illinois: National Council of Teachers of English, 1977.

The Cumulative Book Index: A World List of Books in the English Language, Supplementing the United States Catalog Fourth Edition. 24 vols. New York: H. W. Wilson Company, 1933-1978.

Landau, Robert A., and Nyre, Judith S., eds. *Large Type Books in Print*. New York: R. R. Bowker, 1975.

Landau, Robert A., and Nyre, Judith S., eds. *Large Type Books in Print*. New York: R. R. Bowker, 1976.

Large Type Books in Print. New York: R. R. Bowker, 1978.

Latimer, Louise P. "Illustrators: A Finding List." *Bulletin of Bibliography*, 13 (January, 1927): 20; (May, 1927): 46-48; (September, 1927): 74; (January, 1928): 94-95.

Library of Congress and National Union Catalog Author Lists, 1942-1962; A Master Cumulation: A Cumulative List Representing Entries in the Library of Congress-National Union Catalog Supplements to Catalog of Books Represented by Library of Congress Printed Cards. Vols. 136-152. Detroit: Gale Research Company, 1967-1971.

Mahony, Bertha, and Whitney, Elinor, comps. *Five Years of Children's Books: A Supplement to Realms of Gold*. New York: Doubleday, Doran, and Company, 1936.

Mahony, Bertha, and Whitney, Elinor, comps. *Realms of Gold in Children's Books: The Fifth Edition of "Books for Boys and Girls—A Suggestive Purchase List" Previously Published by The Bookshop for Boys and Girls, Women's Educational and Industrial Union, Boston, Massachusetts*. Garden City, New York: Doubleday, Doran, and Company, 1929.

The National Union Catalog: A Cumulative Author List Representing Library of Congress Printed Cards and Titles Reported by Other American Libraries. 104 vols. Ann Arbor, Michigan: J. W. Edwards, 1973.

The National Union Catalog, 1956-1967: A Cumulative Author List Representing Library of Congress Printed Cards and Titles Reported by Other American Libraries; A New and Augmented Twelve Year Catalog Being a Compilation into One Alphabet the Fourth & Fifth Supplements of the National Union Catalog with a Key to Additional Locations through 1967 and with a Unique Identifying Number Allocated to Each Title. Totowa, New Jersey: Rowman and Littlefield, 1970-1972.

The United States Catalog: Entries under Author, Subject and Title in One Alphabet, with Particulars of Binding, Price, Date, and Publisher. 7 vols. Minneapolis and New York: H. W. Wilson, 1903-1928.

MEDIA

Note: Producers for the nonbook materials listed in the text were contacted to verify their listings. Due to their corrections and additions, individual media entries in the text may be at variance with similar entries listed in the reference books here.

Aros, Andrew A. *A Title Guide to the Talkies: 1964 through 1974 (As Conceived by Richard B. Dimmitt)*. Metuchen, New Jersey: Scarecrow Press, 1977.

Books on Magnetic Tape: A Catalog of Tape Recordings Which Supplement the Talking Book Program. Washington, D.C.: Division for the Blind and Physically Handicapped, Library of Congress, 1962.

Books on Open-Reel Tape. Washington, D.C.: Division for the Blind and Physically Handicapped, Library of Congress, 1971.

Books on Open-Reel Tape. Revised edition. Washington, D.C.: Division for the Blind and Physically Handicapped, Library of Congress, 1973.

Braille Books Provided by the Library of Congress, 1962-1964. New York: American Foundation for the Blind for the Library of Congress, 1964 (?).

Cassette Books. Washington, D.C.: Division for the Blind and Physically Handicapped, Library of Congress, 1972.

Cassette Books. Second edition, Washington, D.C.: Division for the Blind and Physically Handicapped, Library of Congress, 1974.

Cassette Books, 1974-1976. Washington, D.C.: Division for the Blind and Physically Handicapped, Library of Congress, 1977.

Catalog of Braille Books for Juvenile Readers, 1953-1962. Washington, D.C.: Library of Congress, 1962.

Catalog of Talking Books for Juvenile Readers. Washington, D.C.: Library of Congress, 1961.

Catalogs, Films and Other Materials for Projection, 1973. Washington, D.C.: Library of Congress, 1975.

Catalogs, Films and Other Materials for Projection, 1974. Washington, D.C.: Library of Congress, 1975.

Catalogs, Films and Other Materials for Projection, 1975. Washington, D.C.: Library of Congress, 1976.

Copyright Office. *Catalog of Copyright Entries: Cumulative Series, Motion Pictures, 1921-1939*. Washington, D.C.: Library of Congress, 1951.

Copyright Office. *Catalog of Copyright Entries: Cumulative Series, Motion Pictures, Supplements, 1940-1969*. Washington, D.C.: Library of Congress, 1953-1971.

Eisenberg, Philip, and Krasno, Becky. *A Guide to Children's Records: A Complete Guide to Recorded Stories, Songs and Music for Children*. New York: Crown Publishers, 1948.

Esner, A. G. *Filmed Books and Plays. . .Of Books and Plays from Which Films Have Been Made, 1928-1974*. Revised cumulative edition. London: Andre Deutsch, 1975.

For Younger Readers, Braille and Talking Books, 1966-1967: A Catalog of Braille and Recorded Books for Juvenile Readers Provided by the Library of Congress and Announced in Braille Book Review and Talking Book Topics during 1966 and 1967, as Are Available from the Cooperating Regional Libraries. New York: American Foundation for the Blind for the Library of Congress, 1968.

For Younger Readers, Braille and Talking Books, 1968-1971: A Catalog of Braille and Recorded Books for Juvenile Readers Provided by the Library of Congress and Announced in Braille Book Review and Talking Book Topics during 1968 and 1971, as Are Available from the Cooperating Regional Libraries. 2 vols. New York: American Foundation for the Blind for the Library of Congress, 1970-1972.

For Younger Readers, Braille and Talking Books, 1972-1975: A Catalog of Braille and Recorded Books for Juvenile Readers Provided by the Library of Congress and Announced in Braille Book Review and Talking Book Topics during 1972 and 1975, as Are Available from the Cooperating Regional Libraries. Washington, D.C.: Library of Congress, 1976.

Greene, Ellin, and Schoenfeld, Madalynne. *A Multimedia Approach to Children's Literature: A Selective List of Films, Filmstrips and Recordings Based on Children's Books*. Chicago: American Library Association, 1972.

Library of Congress. *Books for the Adult Blind: Including the Talking-Machine Book Activity and Service for the Blind from the Annual Reports, 1937-1938*. Washington, D.C.: Government Printing Office, 1940.

Library of Congress. *Catalog of Press Braille Books Provided by the Library of Congress, 1931-1948*. Washington, D.C.: Government Printing Office, 1949.

Library of Congress. *Catalog of Talking Books for the Blind: Cumulative Supplement, 1938-1948*. Washington, D.C.: Government Printing Office, 1949.

Library of Congress. *Catalog of Talking Books for the Blind: Cumulative Supplement, 1948-1957*. 2 vols. Washington, D.C.: Government Printing Office, 1958.

Library of Congress. *Union Catalog of Hand-Copied Books in Braille*. Washington, D.C.: Government Printing Office, 1949.

Library of Congress. *Union Catalog of Hand-Copied Books in Braille, Revision*. Washington, D.C.: Government Printing Office, 1955.

Library of Congress. *Union Catalog of Hand-Copied Books in Braille, Supplement*. Washington, D.C.: Library of Congress, 1960.

McDaniel, Roderick. *Resources for Learning: A Core Media Collection for Elementary Schools*. New York: R. R. Bowker, 1971.

New York Library Association. *Recordings for Children: A Selection List*. New York: Children's and Young Adults Services Division, 1961.

New York Library Association. *Recordings for Children: A Selection List, Revised*. New York: Children's and Young Adults Services Division, 1964.

Press Braille Books, [1964-1972]: A Catalog of Press Braille Books for Adults Provided by the Library of Congress and Announced in Braille Book Review during [1964 through 1972] and as Available from the Cooperating Libraries. 4 vols. New York: American Foundation for the Blind for the Library of Congress, 1966-1972.

Press Braille Books, [1972-1973]: A Catalog of Press Braille Books for Adults Provided by the Library of Congress and Announced in Braille Book Review during [1972 through 1973] and as Available from the Cooperating Libraries. 2 vols. Washington, D.C.: Division for the Blind and Physically Handicapped, 1974-1976.

Recording for the Blind. *Catalog of Tape Recorded Books—1976*. [Louisville, Kentucky: American Printing House for the Blind, 1976?]

Recording for the Blind. *Catalog of Tape Recorded Books—Supplements, 1977-1978*. 2 vols. [Louisville, Kentucky: American Printing House for the Blind, 1977-1978 (?)]

Rice, Sue, and Ludlum, Barbara. *Films Kids Like: A Catalog of Short Films for Children*. Chicago: American Library Association and the Center for Understanding Media, 1973.

Screen Achievements Records Bulletin. [Hollywood, California?] : Academy of Motion Pictures Arts and Sciences, 1977.

Talking Books, Adult: [1966-1971]. 3 vols. New York: American Foundation for the Blind for the Library of Congress, [1968-1972].

Talking Books, Adult: [1972-1975]. 3 vols. Washington, D.C.: Division for the Blind and Physically Handicapped, Library of Congress, [1974-1976].

Talking Books for Juvenile Readers, 1972-1973: A Catalog of Recorded Books for Younger Readers Provided by the Library of Congress and Announced in Talking Book Topics during 1972 and 1973 as Available from Cooperating Regional and Subregional Libraries. Washington, D.C.: Division for the Blind and Physically Handicapped, Library of Congress, 1974.

Writers Cumulated Bulletin, 1969-1975. [Hollywood, California?] : Academy of Motion Picture Arts and Sciences, 1976 (?).

Zornow, Edith, and Goldstein, Ruth M. *Movies for Kids: A Guide for Parents and Teachers on the Entertainment Film for Children 9 to 13*. New York: Avon Books, 1973.

EXHIBITIONS

Note: Author-illustrators and illustrators in some cases added entries to their listings that may not appear in the following volume and the sources to which it leads readers.

Art Index: A Cumulative and Subject Index to a Selected List of Fine Arts Periodicals and Museum Bulletins. 26 vols. New York: H. W. Wilson, 1933-1977.

COLLECTIONS

Note: Libraries and museums were contacted to verify their holdings. Due to their corrections and additions, the holdings entries in the text may be at variance with similar entries listed in the reference books here.

Ash, Lee, ed. *Subject Collections: A Guide to Special Book Collections and Subject Emphases Reported by University, College, Public and Special Libraries and Museums in the United States and Canada*. Fourth edition revised and enlarged. New York: R. R. Bowker Company, 1974.

Cattell Press, Jacques, ed. *1976-1977 American Library Directory*. Thirteenth edition. New York: R. R. Bowker Company, 1976.

Field, Carolyn W., ed. *Subject Collections in Children's Literature*. Consultants, Virginia Haviland and Elizabeth Nesbitt, for the National Planning Committee for Special Collections, Children's Services Division, American Library Association. New York: R. R. Bowker, 1969.

Hamer, Philip. *Guide to Archives and Manuscripts in the U.S.: Compiled for the National Historical Publications Commission*. New Haven, Connecticut: Yale University Press, 1961.

Modern Language Association. *American Literary Manuscripts: A Checklist of Holdings in Academic, Historical and Public Libraries in the United States*. Austin, Texas: University of Texas Press, 1960.

The National Union Catalog of Manuscript Collections, 1959-1961: Based on Reports from American Repositories of Manuscripts Compiled by the Library of Congress with the Advice of the Advisory Committee on the National Union Catalog of Manuscript Collections under a Grant from The Council of Library Resources, Inc. Ann Arbor, Michigan: J. W. Edwards, 1962.

The National Union Catalog of Manuscript Collections, 1962: Based on Reports from American Repositories of Manuscripts Compiled by the Library of Congress with the Advice of the Advisory Committee on the National Union Catalog of Manuscript Collections under a Grant from The Council of Library Resources, Inc. Hamden, Connecticut: Shoe String Press, 1964.

The National Union Catalog of Manuscript Collections, 1963-1969: Based on Reports from American Repositories of Manuscripts Compiled by the Library of Congress with the Advice of the Advisory Committee on the National Union Catalog of Manuscript Collections under a Grant from The Council of Library Resources, Inc. 6 vols. Washington, D.C.: Library of Congress, 1965-1970.

New York Public Library. *Dictionary Catalog of the Manuscript Division*. Boston: G. K. Hall, 1967.

Official Museum Directory, 1976. Washington, D.C. and Skokie, Illinois: American Association of Museums and National Register Publishing, 1977.

Young, Margaret L., ed. *Directory of Special Libraries and Information Centers*. Detroit: Gale Research, 1977.

BACKGROUND READING

American Federation of the Arts. *Forty Artists under Forty*. New York: The Federation, 1962.

Bader, Barbara. *American Picturebooks from Noah's Ark to The Beast Within*. New York: Macmillan Publishing Company, 1976.

Bair, Frank E., ed. *Biography News: A Compilation of News Stories and Feature Articles from American News Media Covering Personalities of National Interest in All Fields*. 2 vols. Detroit: Gale Research Company, 1974-1975.

Banta, Richard E., comp. *Indiana Authors and Their Books, 1816-1916: Biographical Sketches of Authors Who Published during the First Century of Indiana Statehood, with Lists of Their Books*. Crawfordsville, Indiana: Wabash College, 1949.

Barnes, Walter. *The Children's Poets: Analyses and Appraisals of the Greatest English and American Poets for Children*. Yonkers-on-Hudson, New York: World Book Company, 1932.

Benét, Laura. *Famous English and American Essayists*. New York: Dodd, Mead and Company, 1966.

Benét, Laura. *Famous Poets for Young Readers*. New York: Dodd, Mead and Company, 1964.

Biography Index: A Cumulative Index to Biographical Material in Books and Magazines. 10 vols. New York: H. W. Wilson, 1949-1976.

Bolton, Theodore. *American Book Illustrators: Biographical Checklists of 123 Artists*. New York: R. R. Bowker Company, 1938.

Breit, Harvey. *The Writer Observed*. Cleveland, Ohio: World Publishing Company, 1956.

Burke, W. J., and Howe, Will D. *American Authors and Books, 1640 to the Present Day*. 3rd revised edition. Revised by Irving Weiss and Anne Weiss. New York: Crown Publishers, 1972.

Chandler, Sue P., and Shockley, Ann Allen. *Living Black American Authors: A Biographical Directory*. New York: R. R. Bowker Company, 1973.

Commire, Anne, ed. *Something about the Author: Facts and Pictures about Contemporary Authors and Illustrators of Books for Young People*. 15 vols. Detroit: Gale Research Company, 1971-1978.

Commire, Anne, ed. *Yesterday's Authors of Books for Children: Facts and Pictures about Authors and Illustrators of Books for Young People, from Early Times to 1960*. 2 vols. Detroit: Gale Research Company, 1977-1978.

Contemporary Authors: A Bio-Bibliographical Guide to Current Authors and Their Works. 81 vols. Detroit: Gale Research Company, 1962-1979. This listing also encompasses *Contemporary Authors, Permanent Series* (vols. 1-2), *Contemporary Literary Criticism* (vols. 1-9), as well as the original and revised volumes of *Contemporary Authors*, all published by Gale Research Company.

Cooper, Annie Page. *Authors and Others*. Garden City, New York: Doubleday, Page and Company, 1927.

Cournos, John and Helen. *Famous Modern American Novelists*. New York: Dodd, Mead and Company, 1952.

Coyle, William, ed. *Ohio Authors and Their Books: Biographical Data and Selective Bibliographies for Ohio Authors, Native and Resident, 1796-1950*. Cleveland, Ohio: World Publishing Company, 1962.

Current Biography: Who's News and Why. 39 vols. New York: H. W. Wilson Company, 1970-1978. This listing also incorporates citations from the *Current Biography Yearbook*, published by H. W. Wilson.

Current Biography Cumulated Index, 1940-1970. New York: H. W. Wilson, 1973.

Davis, Arthur P. *From the Dark Tower: Afro-American Writers, 1900-1960*. Washington, D.C.: Howard University Press, 1974.

DeMontreville, Doris, and Crawford, Elizabeth D., eds. *Fourth Book of Junior Authors and Illustrators*. New York: H. W. Wilson Company, 1978.

DeMontreville, Doris, and Hill, Donna, eds. *Third Book of Junior Authors*. New York: H. W. Wilson Company, 1972.

Dissertations Abstracts International. Part A: Humanities and Social Sciences. 40 vols. Ann Arbor, Michigan: Xerox University Microfilms, 1938-1979.

Doyle, Brian. *The Who's Who of Children's Literature*. New York: Schocken Books, 1968.

Dreer, Harry R. *American Literature by American Negroes*. New York: Macmillan Publishing Company, 1950.

Dunbar, Ernest, ed. *Black Expatriots: A Study of American Negroes in Exile*. New York: E. P. Dutton and Company, 1968.

Dykes, Jeff. *Fifty Great Western Illustrators: A Biographical Checklist*. Flagstaff, Arizona: Northland Press, 1975.

The Education Index: A Cumulative Author and Subject Index to a Selected List of Educational Periodicals, Books, and Pamphlets. 29 vols. New York: H. W. Wilson, 1932-1978.

Ellis, Richard. *Book Illustration: A Survey of Its History and Development Shown by the Work of Various Artists Together with Critical Comments*. Kingsport, Tennessee: Kingsport Press, 1952.

Foremost Women in Communications: A Biographical Reference Work on Accomplished Women in Broadcasting, Publishing, Advertising, Public Relations, and Allied Professions. New York: Foremost American Publishing Corporation in association with R. R. Bowker Company, 1970.

Fuller, Muriel, ed. *More Junior Authors*. New York: H. W. Wilson Company, 1963.

Garraty, John, ed. *Dictionary of American Biography: Supplement 4, 1946-1950*. New York: Charles Scribner's Sons, 1974.

Hart, James D. *The Oxford Companion to American Literature*. 4th edition. New York: Oxford University Press, 1967.

Havelice, Patricia Pate. *Index to American Author Biographies*. Metuchen, New Jersey: Scarecrow Press, 1971.

Havelice, Patricia Pate. *Index to Artistic Biography*. Metuchen, New Jersey: Scarecrow Press, 1973.

Havelice, Patricia Pate. *Index to Literary Biography*. Metuchen, New Jersey: Scarecrow Press, 1975.

Hoffman, Miriam, and Samuels, Eva. *Authors and Illustrators of Children's Books: Writings on Their Lives and Works*. New York: R. R. Bowker Company, 1972.

Hopkins, Lee Bennett. *Books Are by People: Interviews with 104 Authors and Illustrators of Books for Young Children*. New York: Citation Press, 1969.

Hopkins, Lee Bennett. *More Books by More People: Interviews with Sixty-five Authors of Books for Children*. New York: Citation Press, 1974.

Index to the Wilson Author Series. New York: H. W. Wilson, 1976.

James, Edward T., ed. *Dictionary of American Biography, Supplement 3, 1941-1945*. New York: Charles Scribner's Sons, 1973.

Johnson, Allen, ed. *Dictionary of American Biography*. Volume 4, new series. New York: Charles Scribner's Sons, 1931.

Johnson, Robert O. *An Index to Profiles in The New Yorker*. Metuchen, New Jersey: Scarecrow Press, 1972.

Kingman, Lee, ed. *Newbery and Caldecott Medal Books, 1956-1965: With Acceptance Papers, Biographies & Related Material Chiefly from The Horn Book Magazine*. Boston: Horn Book, 1965.

Kingman, Lee, ed. *Newbery and Caldecott Medal Books, 1966-1975: With Acceptance Papers, Biographies & Related Material Chiefly from The Horn Book Magazine*. Boston: Horn Book, 1975.

Kingman, Lee; Foster, Joanna; and Lontfot, Ruth Giles; eds. *Illustrators of Children's Books, 1957-1966*. Boston: Horn Book, 1966.

Kingman, Lee; Hogarth, Grace Allen; and Quimby, Harriet; eds. *Illustrators of Children's Books, 1967-1976*. Boston: Horn Book, 1978.

Kirkpatrick, Daniel L., ed. *Twentieth-Century Children's Writers*. New York: St. Martin's Press, 1978.

Klemin, Diana. *The Illustrated Book: Its Art and Craft*. New York: Clarkson N. Potter, 1970.

Kunitz, Stanley J., ed. *Authors Today and Yesterday: A Companion Volume to Living Authors*. New York: H. W. Wilson, 1933.

Kunitz, Stanley J., and Haycraft, Howard, eds. *American Authors, 1600-1900: A Biographical Directory of American Literature*. New York: H. W. Wilson, 1938.

Kunitz, Stanley J., and Haycraft, Howard, eds. *The Junior Book of Authors: An Introduction to the Lives of Writers and Illustrators for Younger Readers from Lewis Carroll and Louisa Alcott to the Present Day*. New York: H. W. Wilson, 1935.

Kunitz, Stanley, and Haycraft, Howard, eds. *The Junior Book of Authors, Second Edition Revised*. New York: H. W. Wilson, 1951.

Kunitz, Stanley, and Haycraft, Howard, eds. *Twentieth Century Authors: A Biographical Dictionary of Modern Literature*. New York: H. W. Wilson, 1942.

Kunitz, Stanley, and Haycraft, Howard, eds. *Twentieth Century Authors: A Biographical Dictionary of Modern Literature, First Supplement*. New York: H. W. Wilson, 1955.

[Kunitz, Stanley J.] Dilly Tante, pseud. *Living Authors: A Book of Biographies*. New York: H. W. Wilson, 1931.

LaBeau, Dennis, and Tarbert, Gary C. *Biographical Dictionaries Master Index, 1975-1976*. Detroit: Gale Research, 1976.

LaBeau, Dennis, and Tarbert, Gary C. *Children's Authors and Illustrators: An Index to Biographical Dictionaries*. Detroit: Gale Research, 1976.

Library Literature: A Supplement to Cannons' Bibliography of Library Economy. 17 vols. New York: H. W. Wilson, 1934-1977.

Mahony, Bertha E., and Whitney, Elinor. *Contemporary Illustrators of Children's Books*. Boston: Bookshop for Boys and Girls, Women's Educational and Industrial Union, 1930.

Maine Writers Research Club. *Maine Writers of Fiction for Juveniles*. Orono, Maine: University of Maine, 1965.

Masters Abstracts. 18 vols. Ann Arbor, Michigan: University Microfilms International, 1962-1979.

Miller, Bertha Mahony, and Field, Elinor Whitney, eds. *Caldecott Medal Books 1938-1957: With the Artist's Acceptance Papers & Related Material Chiefly from The Horn Book Magazine*. Boston: Horn Book, 1957.

Miller, Bertha Mahony, and Field, Elinor Whitney, eds. *Newbery Medal Books 1922-1955: With Acceptance Papers, Biographies & Related Material Chiefly from The Horn Book Magazine*. Boston: Horn Book, 1955.

Miller, Bertha Mahony; Latimer, Louise P.; and Folmsbee, Beulah; eds. *Illustrators of Children's Books, 1744-1945*. Boston: Horn Book, 1945.

Miller, Bertha Mahony; Viguers, Ruth Hill; and Dalphin, Marcia; eds. *Illustrators of Children's Books 1946-1956*. Boston: Horn Book, 1958.

Monson, Diane L., and Peltola, Bette J. *Research in Children's Literature: An Annotated Bibliography*. Newark, Delaware: International Reading Association, 1976.

Montgomery, Elizabeth R. *The Story behind Great Books*. New York: Macbride, 1946.

Montgomery, Elizabeth R. *The Story behind Modern Books*. New York: Dodd, Mead and Company, 1949.

The New York Times Biographical Edition. 15 vols. New York: Arno Press, 1970-1973.

The New York Times Biographical Service. Volume 5. New York: Arno Press, 1975. This title is a continuation of *The New York Times Biographical Edition*, above.

New York Times Obituaries 1858-1968. New York: New York Times, 1970.

Nykoruk, Barbara, ed. *Authors in the News: A Compilation of News Stories and Feature Articles from American Newspapers and Magazines Covering Writers and Other Members of the Communications Media*. 2 vols. Detroit: Gale Research, 1976-1977.

Patterson, Robert et al. *On Our Way: Young Pages from American Biography*. New York: Holiday House, 1952.

Randall, Ada, and Reely, Mary Katharine. *Through Golden Windows: Children's Poets and Storytellers*. Chicago: Albert Whitman and Company, 1934.

Reed, Alma. *Mexican Muralists*. New York: Crown Publishers, 1960.

Richards, Carmen, ed. *Minnesota Writers: A Collection of Autobiographical Stories by Minnesota Prose Writers*. Minneapolis, Minnesota: T. S. Denison and Company, 1961.

Rollins, Charlemae. *Famous American Negro Poets*. New York: Dodd, Mead and Company, 1965.

Rush, John. *Artists of a Certain Line: A Selection of Illustrators for Children's Books*. London: Bodley Head, 1960.

Rush, Theresa Gunnel; Myers, Carol Fairbanks; and Arata, Esther Spring; comps. *Black American Writers Past and Present: A Biographical and Bibliographical Directory*. 2 vols. Metuchen, New Jersey: Scarecrow Press, 1975.

Sarkissian, Adele, ed. *Children's Authors and Illustrators: An Index to Biographical Directories*. Second edition. Detroit: Gale Research, 1978.

Smaridge, Norah. *Famous Author-Illustrators for Young People*. New York: Dodd, Mead and Company, 1973.

Smaridge, Norah. *Famous Literary Teams for Young People*. New York: Dodd, Mead and Company, 1977.

Smaridge, Norah. *Famous Modern Storytellers for Young People*. New York: Dodd, Mead and Company, 1969.

Stoddard, Anne, ed. *Topflight: Famous American Women*. New York: Watson-Guptill, 1946.

Thompson, Donald E., comp. *Indiana Authors and Their Books, 1917-1966: A Continuation of Indiana Authors and Their Books, 1816-1916, and Containing Additional Names from the Earlier Period*. Crawfordsville, Indiana: Wabash College, 1974.

Townsend, John Rowe. *A Sense of Story: Essays on Contemporary Writers for Children*. Philadelphia: J. B. Lippincott Company, 1971.

Wakeman, John, ed. *World Authors 1950-1970: A Companion to Twentieth Century Authors*. New York: H. W. Wilson, 1975.

Ward, Martha E., and Marquardt, Dorothy A. *Authors of Books for Young People, Second Edition*. Metuchen, New Jersey: Scarecrow Press, 1975.

Ward, Martha E., and Marquardt, Dorothy A. *Illustrators of Books for Young People, Second Edition*. Metuchen, New Jersey: Scarecrow Press, 1975.

Warfel, Harry R. *American Novelists of Today*. 1951. Reprint. Westport, Connecticut: Greenwood Press, 1976.

Wintle, Justin, and Fisher, Emma, eds. *The Pied Pipers: Interviews with the Influential Creators of Children's Literature*. New York: Paddington Press, Ltd./Two Continents Publishing Groups, 1974.

Young Wings. *Writing Books for Boys and Girls: A Young Wings Anthology of Essays by Two Hundred Sixteen Authors Who Tell How They Came to Write Their Special Kinds of Books for Young People*. Edited by Helen Ferris. New York: Doubleday and Company, 1952.

Index
TO AUTHORS, ARTISTS, AND WINNING
BOOKS BY SHORT TITLE